social
PROBLEMS

FOURTH EDITION

To B. D. S. and B. W. S.

social

PROBLEMS

FOURTH EDITION

COMMUNITY, POLICY, AND SOCIAL ACTION

ANNA LEON-GUERRERO

Pacific Lutheran University

Los Angeles | London | New Delhi
Singapore | Washington DC

Los Angeles | London | New Delhi
Singapore | Washington DC

FOR INFORMATION:

SAGE Publications, Inc.
2455 Teller Road
Thousand Oaks, California 91320
E-mail: order@sagepub.com

SAGE Publications Ltd.
1 Oliver's Yard
55 City Road
London EC1Y 1SP
United Kingdom

SAGE Publications India Pvt. Ltd.
B 1/I 1 Mohan Cooperative Industrial Area
Mathura Road, New Delhi 110 044
India

SAGE Publications Asia-Pacific Pte. Ltd.
3 Church Street
#10-04 Samsung Hub
Singapore 049483

Acquisitions Editor: David Repetto
Associate Editor: Nathan Davidson
Assistant Editor   Megan Koraly
Editorial Assistant: Lauren Johnson
Production Editor: Jane Haenel
Copy Editor: Melinda Masson
Typesetter: C&M Digitals (P) Ltd.
Proofreader: Kristin Bergstad
Indexer: Terri Corry
Cover Designer: Scott Van Atta
Marketing Manager: Erica DeLuca
Permissions Editor: Karen Ehrmann

Printed in the United States of America

Library of Congress Cataloging-in-Publication Data

Leon-Guerrero, Anna.

Social problems : community, policy, and social action / Anna Leon-Guerrero, Pacific Lutheran University. — Fourth Edition.

pages cm
Includes bibliographical references and index.

ISBN 978-1-4522-0543-4 (pbk. : alk. paper)

1. Social problems—United States. 2. Social problems. 3. Critical thinking. I. Title.

HN59.2.L46 2013
303.3'72—dc23   2012044454

This book is printed on acid-free paper.

SUSTAINABLE FORESTRY INITIATIVE
Certified Chain of Custody
Promoting Sustainable Forestry
www.sfiprogram.org
SFI-01268

SFI label applies to text stock

14 15 16 17 10 9 8 7 6 5 4 3 2

Brief Contents

Detailed Contents

Part IV.   OUR SOCIAL AND PHYSICAL WORLDS

Part V.   INDIVIDUAL ACTION AND SOCIAL CHANGE

Preface

During the 2012 presidential campaign, Americans identified the economy, unemployment, and health care as our most important social problems. The candidates, President Barack Obama and Governor Mitt Romney, offered contrasting perspectives on the causes and solutions of these problems. Voters were asked to consider which candidate could handle these problems best.

Although social problems are an important part of our lives, many of us still do not understand the problems we face. Perhaps you are like my students who have never interacted with a homeless person, never been a victim of a violent crime, or never experienced discrimination. How much do you really know about homelessness, violent crime, or discrimination?

I wrote this text with two goals in mind: to offer a better understanding of social problems and to begin working toward real solutions. In the pages that follow, I present three connections to achieve these goals. The first connection is the one between sociology and the study of social problems. Using your sociological imagination (which you'll learn more about in Chapter 1), you will be able to identify the social and structural forces that determine our social problems. I think you'll discover that this course is interesting, challenging, and sometimes frustrating (sort of like real-life discussions about social problems). After you review these different social problems, you may ask, "What can be done about all this?" The second connection that will be made is between social problems and their solutions. In each chapter, we review selected social policies along with innovative community programs that attempt to address or correct these problems. The final connection is the one that I ask you to make yourself: recognizing the social problems in your community and identifying how you can be part of the solution.

Learning Features of This Text

The three connections are made evident in each chapter and throughout the text through a variety of specific learning features:

- A focus on the basis of social inequalities. Using a sociological perspective, we examine how race and ethnicity, gender, social class, sexual orientation, and age determine our life chances. Chapters 2 through 6 focus specifically on these bases of social inequality and how each contributes to our experience of social problems.

- A focus on the global experience of social problems. Throughout the text, the consequences of social problems throughout the world are highlighted, drawing upon data and research from international scholars and sociologists. In a boxed chapter feature, Taking a World View, specific social problems or responses are examined from a global perspective. We look at Japan's educational tracking system (Chapter 8), Mexico's maquiladoras (Chapter 9), India's all-female international news organization (Chapter 11), and alcoholism in Scotland (Chapter 12).

- A focus on social policy and social action. Each chapter includes a discussion on relevant social policies or programs. In addition, each chapter highlights how individuals or groups have made a difference in their community. The chapters include personal stories, some from professionals in their field, whereas others come from ordinary individuals who accomplish extraordinary things. Several feature college-age activists. For example, in Chapter 8, you'll meet Wendy Kopp, the woman behind the Teach for America program; in Chapter 13, you'll meet Max Kenner, student founder of the Bard Prison Initiative, an educational program for prisoners; and in Chapter 17, you'll read the story of Camila Vallejo, who began her activism while she was a student at the University of Chile. The text concludes with a chapter titled "Social Problems and Social Action" that identifies ways you can become more involved.

- What Does It Mean to Me? and Internet and Community Exercises. Each chapter includes questions or activities that can be completed by small student groups or on your own. Some of the exercises ask you to reflect on the material in the chapter. But many of them require you to collect data and information on what is going on in your own state, city, or campus. These exercises take you out of the classroom, away from the textbook, and into your community!

Highlights of the Fourth Edition

I have made a number of revisions in response to comments and feedback received from the many instructors adopting the earlier editions and from other interested instructors and their students.

- Expanding the sociological perspectives. Four theoretical perspectives (functionalist, conflict, feminist, and interactionist) are presented in each chapter, identifying how each perspective defines the causes and consequences of specific problems. Additional material has been incorporated in Chapter 3 (multiracial and ethnic attrition), Chapter 7 (the changing definition of the family), Chapter 11 (media coverage of female political candidates), Chapter 12 (the influence of the peer subculture and pressure on drug use), Chapter 13 (race, class, and media coverage of crime), and Chapter 16 (the politics of fear). In Chapter 1 I've included a general overview of basic sociological terms and concepts.

- Keeping it current. The focus of this text is unlike most other social problems texts, featuring a strong emphasis on social policy and action. It is necessary with each edition to provide an update on significant social policy decisions and debates. In this edition, the following social policy discussions have been updated: immigration (Chapter 3), same-sex marriage and "Don't Ask, Don't Tell" (Chapter 5), No Child Left Behind (Chapter 8), and an expanded discussion on health care reform, including the

U.S. Supreme Court 2012 ruling on the Affordable Care Act (Chapter 10). The impact of the Great Recession was hard to ignore, with revised discussion on the impact of the economy on the affordability of a college education (Chapters 1 and 8), working poor (Chapter 2), older workers (Chapters 6 and 9), the poor (Chapter 3), and the average American worker (Chapter 9).

- **Data matters.** The chapters focusing on problems, Chapters 2 through 16, have been updated to include U.S. and global data, as well as new U.S. state maps for Chapters 3 through 6. Data are important for understanding the extent of our social problems and recognizing populations vulnerable to them.

I wanted to write a book that captured the experiences that I've shared with students in my own social problems course. I sensed the frustration and futility that many felt by the end of the semester—imagine all those weeks of discussing nothing else but "problems"! I decided that my message about the importance of *understanding social problems* should be complemented with a message on the importance of *taking social action.*

Social action doesn't just happen in Washington, DC, or in your state's capital, and political leaders aren't the only ones engaged in such efforts. Social action takes place on your campus, in your neighborhood, in your town, in whatever you define as your "community."

There were stories to be told by ordinary people—community, church, business, or student leaders—who recognized that they had the power to make a difference in the community. No act is too small to make a difference. Despite the persistence and severity of many social problems, members of our community have not given up. For example, my community was affected by an act of violence Thanksgiving weekend 2009. Four police officers from my hometown of Lakewood, Washington, were gunned down in a local coffee shop. Though the site of horrific violence, the coffee shop was transformed into a makeshift memorial site as individuals and families left flowers, balloons, condolences, and stuffed animals to honor the dead officers. Thirteen days after the shooting, the coffee shop reopened at 8:13 a.m., the exact time of the shootings. The Lakewood police chief was the first in line and behind him were some 150 other customers—fellow officers, family members, friends, and residents—all recognizing the importance of reclaiming the site. The coffee shop and the community continue to thrive today. Stories like this and others inspired me and my students to find our own paths to social action.

I hope that by the time you reach the end of this text, with your newfound sociological imagination, you will find your own path to social action. Wherever it leads you, I wish you all the best.

Instructor Teaching Site

www.sagepub.com/leonguerrero4e

A password-protected instructor teaching site provides one integrated source for all instructor materials, including the following key components for each chapter:

- A test bank offers a diverse set of test questions and answers for each chapter in the book. Multiple-choice, true/false, and short-answer/essay questions for every chapter will aid instructors in assessing students' progress and understanding.
- PowerPoint presentations are designed to assist with lecture and review, highlighting essential content, features, and artwork from the book.
- Lecture notes summarize key concepts on a chapter-by-chapter basis to help with preparation for lectures and class discussions.
- Lively and stimulating ideas for class activities are suggested that can be used in class to reinforce active learning.
- Chapter-specific discussion questions help launch classroom interaction by prompting students to engage with the material and by reinforcing important content.
- Each chapter includes audio links related to important topics and designed to supplement key points within the text. Carefully selected, web-based video links feature relevant interviews, lectures, personal stories, inquiries, and other content for use in independent or classroom-based explorations of key topics.

Student Study Site

www.sagepub.com/leonguerrero4e

An open-access student study site provides a variety of additional resources to build students' understanding of the book content and extend their learning beyond the classroom. Students will have access to the following features for each chapter:

- Mobile-friendly eFlashcards reinforce understanding of key terms and concepts that have been outlined in the chapters.
- Mobile-friendly web quizzes allow for independent assessment of progress made in learning course material.
- Web resources direct students to relevant sites on the Web for further research on important chapter topics.
- Video and audio links feature meaningful content for use in independent or classroom-based exploration of key topics.

Interactive eBook

An *Interactive eBook* version of the text is available to students and provides a contemporary, multimedia-integrated presentation for learning. In addition to a full electronic textbook, students can link directly to video, audio, additional enrichment readings, glossary terms, and other relevant resources, bringing sociology to life in a way that a traditional print text cannot.

Audio

Video

CQ Researcher

Research/Social Impact

SAGE Journal Articles

Reference

CQ Press State Stats Database

STATE STATS

Acknowledgments

Social Problems: Community, Policy, and Social Action represents a deeply personal and professional journey. My heartfelt thanks to Jerry Westby for being the first to recognize and support my vision. Along with Denise Simon, Jerry guided me through the first three editions of this text, sharing my commitment to the message of social action. My work continues to be supported by Dave Repetto, who has helped me imagine how to expand my vision and message.

I am grateful for the kind and consistent production support provided by Laureen Gleason and Jane Haenel, to Melinda Masson for her fine editing, and to Lauren Johnson, Lauren Habib, and Andrea (Dawn) Tawwater for their work on the instructor's manual, ancillary materials, and e-book resources.

The following sociologists served as the first audience and reviewers for this text. Thank you all for your encouragement and for your insightful comments and suggestions, many of which have been incorporated in this fourth edition.

For the fourth edition:

Kathleen Baldwin, *Olympic College*

Angela Jones, *Elon University*

Thomas R. Lake, *SUNY Dutchess Community College*

Minu Mathur, *College of San Mateo*

Johnny Underwood, *Carteret Community College*

For the third edition:

Doug Degher, *Northern Arizona University*

Mark J. Guillette, *Valencia Community College–Osceola Campus*

Eric Jorrey, *Bowling Green State University*

Amanda Jungels, *Georgia State University*

Mary Kniskern, *University of Maryland, Virginia–Maryland Regional College of Veterinary Medicine*

Sandy Martinez, *Central Washington University*

Sophie Nathenson, *The University of Utah*

Bob Parker, *University of Nevada School of Medicine*

Matthew Sargent, *Madison Area Technical College–Downtown*

Athena Smith, *Hillsborough Community College–Dale Mabry Campus*

Annie Tuttle, *The Florida State University College of Law*

Mike Victor, *The University of Texas Science Health Center at Tyler*

For the second edition:

Donna Abrams, *Georgia Highlands College*

Brian C. Aldrich, *Winona State University*

Carl Backman, *Auburn University*

Janet Cosbey, *Eastern Illinois University*

Janine Dewitt-Heffner, *Marymount University*

Ronald Ferguson, *Ridgewater College*

Mark J. Guillette, *Valencia Community College*

Gaetano Guzzo, *Wright State University*

Jason Hendrickson, *State University of New York at Albany*

Judith Hennessy, *Central Washington University*

Ronald Huskin, *Del Mar College*

Richard Jenks, *Indiana University Southeast*

Rohald Meneses, *University of Florida*

Paul Mills, *University of Alabama*

Adam Moskowitz, *Columbus State Community College*

Wendy Ng, *San Jose State University*

Robert Parker, *University of Nevada Las Vegas*

James Roberts, *University of Scranton*

Katherine R. Rowell, *Sinclair Community College*

Rita Sakitt, *Suffolk County Community College*

Frank Salamone, *Iona College*

Jim Sikora, *Illinois Wesleyan College*

For the first edition:

Arfa Aflatooni, *Linn-Benton Community College*

Joanne Ardovini, *Sam Houston State University*

Bernadette Barton, *Morehead State University*

Allison Camelot, *California State University, Fullerton*

Janine Dewitt-Heffner, *Marymount University*

Dan Dexheimer, *University of Florida*

Woody Doane, *University of Hartford*

Joe Dupris, *California State University, Humboldt*

Rachel Einwohner, *Purdue University*

Heather Smith Feldhaus, *Bloomsburg University*

Jim Fenelon, *California State University, San Bernardino*

Bobbie Fields, *Central Piedmont Community College*

Debbie Franzman, *Allan Hancock College*

Marcie Goodman, *University of Utah*

George Gross, *Northern Michigan University*

Mark J. Guillette, *Valencia Community College*

Julia Hall, *Drexel University*

Dan W. Hayden, *University of Southern Indiana*

Chuck Hohm, *San Diego State University*

Leslie Houts, *University of Florida*

James R. Hunter, *Indiana University–Purdue University at Indianapolis*

K. Land, *Duke University*

Nick Larsen, *Chapman University*

Kari Lerum, *Seattle University*

Stephen Light, *SUNY Plattsburgh*

Dennis Loo, *Cal Poly Pomona*

Scott Lukas, *Lake Tahoe Community College*

Christina Myers, *Oklahoma State University*

Paul Roof, *San Juan College*

Kim Saliba, *Portland Community College*

Norma K. Simmons, *Washington State University*

Deborah Sullivan, *Arizona State University*

Mary Texeira, *California State University, San Bernardino*

Linda A. Treiber, *North Carolina State University*

Gailynn White, *Citrus College*

Anthony W. Zumpetta, *West Chester University*

I wish to express my appreciation to my family, friends, and colleagues, who endured my never-ending stories about this project. Mahalo nui loa for supporting my work.

I dedicate this book to the two people who have been with me from the beginning of this journey: to my mentor, Byron D. Steiger, and to my husband, Brian W. Sullivan. From Byron, I learned the importance of loving one's work. Thank you for showing me what an excellent teacher can and should be. From Brian, I learned the value of caring for one's community and the environment. Thank you for all that you do—this book would not have been possible without you.

About the Author

Anna Leon-Guerrero is a professor of sociology at Pacific Lutheran University in Tacoma, Washington. A recipient of the university's Faculty Excellence Award and the K. T. Tang Award for Excellence in Research, she teaches courses on statistics, sociological theory, and social problems. As a social service program evaluator and consultant, she has focused her research on welfare reform, employment strategies for the working poor, and program assessment. She is the coauthor of *Social Statistics for a Diverse Society* and *Essentials of Social Statistics for a Diverse Society* (with Chava Frankfort-Nachmias).

PART I

Social Problems—
Personal Troubles
or Public Issues?

Seeing Problems Sociologically

The sociological imagination reveals the connections between our lives and the social and historical context in which we live.

▼ The 2012 presidential campaign was played out across this country, in cities and towns, in the media, in homes, and in classrooms like yours. President Barack Obama and Governor Mitt Romney promoted their policies on the economy, health care, education, energy, immigration, and foreign relations.

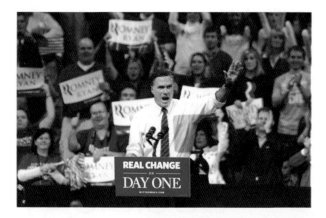

Were you part of this national conversation? What side were you on? How are you connected to the problems and challenges identified by President Obama and Governor Romney?

In the following pages, we examine numerous social problems from different sociological perspectives. Using your sociological imagination, determine your connection to these problems and the final connection among these social problems, your community, and social action.

CHAPTER 1

Sociology and the Study of Social Problems

Financial Assistance

I f I asked everyone in your class what they believe is the most important social problem facing the United States, there would be many different answers: the economy, war, health care, unemployment, homelessness. Most would agree that some or all of these are social problems. But which is the most important, and how would we solve it?

Suppose I asked the same question in a South African college classroom. AIDS is likely to be one of the responses from South African college students. Effective risk reduction strategies, along with new treatments for HIV/AIDS, have saved countless lives in the United States. During the early 1980s, nearly 150,000 Americans were infected with the disease each year, but by the early 1990s, the number of infected cases had dropped to 50,000 per year, where it remains today (Centers for Disease Control and Prevention 2007, 2012). However, Africa remains the epicenter of the pandemic with more than 22.9 million adults and children infected with the disease (refer to Figure 1.1). The prevalence of HIV is predicted to triple during the next decade, especially in Africa, but also in the former USSR, China, and India. The AIDS pandemic has been described as a threat to global stability, a global security concern (Lichtenstein 2004).

Globalization, defined as the process of increasing transborder connectedness (Hytrek and Zentgraf 2007)—whether economically, politically, environmentally, or socially—poses new challenges and opportunities for understanding and solving social problems. We cannot understand the nature of social problems by simply taking a national or local perspective. Taking a global perspective allows us to look at the interrelations between countries and their social problems (Heiner 2002). We are not the only country to experience social problems.

4

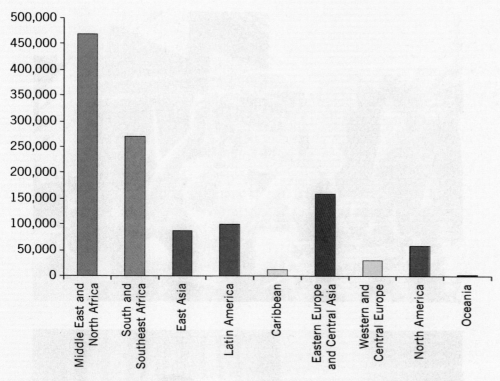

Figure 1.1

Number of HIV
Infections, Regional
Data for 2011
Source: UNAIDS 2011.

Note: The number of HIV infections in Sub-Saharan Africa is 22,900,000.

Knowledge based on research to understand and policies to address social problems here could be applied in other countries, and what other countries have learned based on their social problems could be applied in the United States. Finally, we all need a little help from our neighbors—we can increase our connectedness and goodwill with other countries through implementing solutions collaboratively rather than alone. So what do you think? Is HIV/AIDS in South Africa a problem only for South Africans, or is it also a problem for those living in the United States? Would a college student in South Africa relate to the Occupy movement's message about economic inequality?

Social
Responsibility

This is how we spend much of our public conversation—on the Senate floor, on afternoon talk shows, at work, or in the classroom—arguing, analyzing, and just trying to figure out which problem is most serious and what needs to be done about it. In casual or sometimes heated conversations, we offer opinions about the economy, the wars in Iraq and Afghanistan, a national health care plan, or appropriate policies for the African AIDS pandemic. Often, these explanations are not based on firsthand data collection or on an exhaustive review of the literature. For the most part, they are based on our opinions and life experiences, or they are just good guesses.

What Does It Mean to Me?

What would be at the top of your social problems list? Would your list include AIDS? Why or why not?

 STATE STATS

Photo 1.1a & 1.1b

Social problems have no boundaries, yet some capture our attention more than others. What makes a social problem real to you?

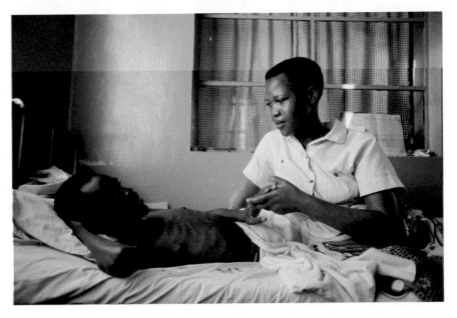

What this text and your course offer is a sociological perspective on social problems. Unlike any other discipline, sociology provides us with a form of self-consciousness, an awareness that our personal experiences are often caused by structural or social forces. **Sociology** is the systematic study of individuals, groups, and social structures. A sociologist examines the relationship between individuals and society, which includes such social institutions as the family, the military, the economy, and education. As a social science, sociology offers an objective and systematic approach to understanding the causes of social problems. From a sociological perspective, problems and their solutions don't just involve individuals; they also have a great deal to do with the social structures in our society. C. Wright Mills (2000) first promoted this perspective in his 1959 essay, "The Promise."

Using Our Sociological Imagination

According to Mills, the sociological imagination can help us distinguish between personal troubles and public issues. The **sociological imagination** links our personal lives and experiences with our social world. Mills ([1959] 2000) describes how personal troubles occur within the "character of the individual and within the range of his immediate relationships with others" (p. 8), whereas public issues are a "public matter: some value cherished by publics is felt to be threatened" (p. 8). As a result, the individual, or those in contact with that individual, can resolve a trouble, but the resolution of an issue requires public debate about what values are being threatened and the source of such a threat.

Let's consider unemployment. One man unemployed is his own personal trouble. Resolving his unemployment involves reviewing his current situation, reassessing his skills, considering his job opportunities, and submitting his résumés or job applications to employers. Once he has a new job, his personal trouble is over. However, what happens when your city or state experiences high levels of unemployment? What happens when there is a nationwide problem of unemployment? This affects not just one person but, rather, thousands or millions. A personal trouble has been transformed into a public issue. This is the case not just because of how many people it affects; something becomes an issue because of the public values it threatens. Unemployment threatens our sense of economic security. It challenges our belief that everyone can work hard to succeed. Unemployment raises questions about society's obligations to help those without a job.

 Unemployment

We can make the personal trouble–public issue connection with regard to another issue, one that you might already be aware of—the increasing cost of college tuition. Brennan Jackson was accepted to the University of California–Berkeley for admission in fall 2009. The university offered him $212 in scholarship aid, but the rest of his tuition and board, estimated at $27,000 for 2009–2010, would have to be borrowed or raised by Brennan and his family (Steinberg 2009a). What can Brennan and his family do? What will they do when Brennan's younger sister is ready for college in several years? Is this a personal trouble facing only the Jackson family? Or is this a public issue?

 Rising College Costs

Though only about a third of students pay the published tuition or sticker price, the cost of tuition has risen at a faster rate than family income or student financial aid. In response to shrinking state support and university endowments, during the 2011–2012 academic year, the average total fees (tuition, room and board) increased more than the rate of inflation, especially at four-year public universities. At a four-year public institution, out-of-state total fees were $29,657 (a 5.2% increase from 2010–2011); at four-year private institutions, the average cost was $38,589 (a 4.4% increase from 2010–2011; College Board 2011).

Although most Americans still believe that a college education is essential for one's success, increasingly they also believe that qualified and motivated students do not have the opportunity to attend college (National Center for Public Policy and Higher Education and Public Agenda 2010). The data support this. Nearly one half of all college-qualified, low- and moderate-income high school graduates are unable to afford college. During the first decade of the twenty-first century, 4.4 million high school graduates will not attend a four-year college, and about 2 million will attend no college at all (Advisory Committee on Student Financial Assistance 2002). In 2007, even after grant aid, low-income families paid or borrowed an amount equivalent to 72% of their family income to cover one year of tuition. In contrast, families with incomes between $54,001 and $80,400 had to finance the equivalent of 27% of their family income for tuition. The percentage was lowest for families with incomes over $115,400 at 14% (Education Trust 2009). The majority of students receive some form of assistance through scholarships, federal grants, or state aid. The average indebtedness for a graduating college senior was $26,600 in 2011 (Institute for College Access & Success 2012). College cost has become a serious social problem because the "barriers that make higher education unaffordable serve to erode our economic well being, our civic values, and our democratic ideals" (Callan and Finney 2002:10).

Due to recent economic and employment downturns, some American families cannot afford the tuition costs for four or five years or even one year. Brennan's father was laid off from his accounting job in a real estate company. Earnings from his mother's part-time job and income from a rental property were enough to support the family, but they were not enough to send Brennan to school. By the May 1 deadline, Brennan had qualified for several merit scholarships and was considering drawing funds from a college savings account of $15,000 set aside by his parents. For more about Brennan, see the "What Does It Mean to Me?" feature below.

As Mills explains, "To be aware of the ideal of social structure and to use it with sensibility is to be capable of tracing such linkages among a great variety of milieus. To be able to do that is to possess the sociological imagination" (Mills [1959] 2000:10–11). The sociological imagination challenges the claim that the problem is "natural" or based on individual failures, instead reminding us how the problem is rooted in society, in our social structures themselves (Irwin 2001). We understand that we cannot resolve unemployment by changing one individual at a time. In the same way, we know that the Jackson family should not be blamed for not being able to support Brennan's education. The sociological imagination emphasizes the structural bases of social problems, making us aware of the economic, political, and social structures that govern employment and unemployment trends and the cost of higher education. Throughout this text, we apply our sociological imagination to the study of social problems. Before we proceed, we need to understand what a social problem is.

College Costs

What Does It Mean to Me?

Brennan was able to attend the University of California–Berkeley, funded in part by a generous supporter. After he was featured in a front-page story in the *New York Times,* Brennan received donations from several anonymous readers. The largest support came from Bill Brandt, an advisory board member of the Institute of Governmental Studies at the University of California–Berkeley. Brandt agreed to provide Brennan $20,000 a year for four years for his education; Brennan was also provided with a part-time job at the institute (Steinberg 2009b). Brennan's story has a happy ending, but what about other students who are still uncertain about how to finance their college education? Brennan's problem is solved, but what about the others? What is the average cost of college in your state?

 STATE STATS

What Is a Social Problem?

The Negative Consequences of Social Problems

 Social Problems

A **social problem** is a social condition or pattern of behavior that has negative consequences for individuals, our social world, or our physical world. A social problem such as unemployment, alcoholism, drug abuse, or HIV/AIDS may negatively affect a person's life and health, along with the well-being of that person's family and friends. Problems can threaten our social institutions, for example, the family (spousal abuse), education (the rising cost of college tuition), or the economy (unemployment and underemployment). Our physical and social worlds can be threatened by problems related to urbanization (lack of affordable housing) and the environment (climate change). You will note from the examples in this paragraph that social problems are inherently social in their causes, consequences, and solutions.

Objective and Subjective Realities of Social Problems

A social problem has objective and subjective realities. A social condition does not have to be personally experienced by every individual to be considered a social problem. The **objective reality** of a social problem comes from acknowledging that a particular social condition does exist. Objective realities of a social problem can be confirmed by collection of data. For example, we know from the Centers for Disease Control and Prevention (2012) that more than 1.2 million Americans are living with HIV/AIDS. You or I do not have to have been infected with HIV to know that the disease is real, with real human and social consequences. We can confirm the realities of HIV/AIDS by observing infected individuals and their families in our own community, at AIDS programs, shelters, or hospitals.

The **subjective reality** of a social problem addresses how a problem becomes defined as a problem. This idea is based on the concept of the **social construction of reality**. Coined by Peter Berger and Thomas Luckmann (1966), the term refers to how our world is a social creation, originating and evolving through our everyday thoughts and actions. Most of the time, we assume and act as though the world is a given, objectively predetermined outside of our existence. However, according to Berger and Luckmann, we also apply subjective meanings to our existence and experience. In other words, our experiences don't just happen to us. Good, bad, positive, or negative—we attach meanings to our reality.

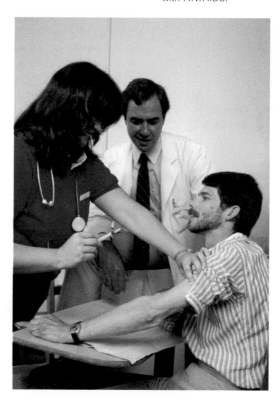

Photo 1.2

The use of antiretroviral therapy has slowed the spread of HIV/AIDS in the United States. The Centers for Disease Control and Prevention (2012) estimates that more than 1 million Americans are living with HIV/AIDS.

From this perspective, social problems are not objectively predetermined. They become real only when they are subjectively defined or perceived as problematic. This perspective is known as **social constructionism**. Recognizing the subjective aspects of social problems allows us to understand how a social condition may be defined as a problem by one segment of society but be completely ignored by another. For example, do you believe AIDS is a social problem? Some may argue that it is a problem only if you are the one infected with the disease or if you are morally corrupt or sexually promiscuous. Actually, some would not consider AIDS a problem at all, considering the medical and public health advances that have successfully reduced the spread of the disease in the United States. Yet others would argue that AIDS still qualifies as a social problem.

Sociologist Denise Loseke (2003) explains, "Conditions might exist, people might be hurt by them, but conditions are not social problems until humans categorize them as troublesome

Social Media Influence

and in need of repair" (p. 14). To frame their work, social constructionists ask the following set of questions:

Social Networks

What do people say or do to convince others that a troublesome condition exists that must be changed? What are the consequences of the typical ways that social problems attract concern? How do our subjective understandings of social problems change the objective characteristics of our world? How do these understandings change how we think about our own lives and the lives of those around us? (Loseke and Best 2003:3–4)

The social constructionist perspective focuses on how a problem becomes defined. In particular, it examines how powerful groups, such as politicians, religious leaders, and the media, can influence our opinions and conceptions of what is a social problem. For example, in an effort to preserve their definition of the "traditional family," conservative political and religious groups encourage laws and practices that discriminate against parents with a gay or lesbian sexual orientation and the families they build. Such groups continue to offer support for the Defense of Marriage Act of 1996, which denies federal recognition of same-sex marriages and gives states the right to refuse to recognize same-sex marriages performed in other states. The act also created a federal definition of marriage: the legal union between one man and one woman as husband and wife. When the act passed, Senator Philip Gramm (R-Texas) explained, "The traditional family has stood for 5,000 years. Are we so wise today that we are ready to reject 5,000 years of recorded history? I don't think so" (CNN 1996). Although conservatives considered the act a victory, opponents expressed concern that the act created a social problem, specifically legislating discrimination against gay and lesbian couples and their families. According to Senator Carol Moseley Braun (D-Ill.), the act was really about "the politics of fear and division and about inciting people in an area which is admittedly controversial" (CNN 1996).

Family and Work Conflict

What Does It Mean to Me?

What are the objective realities of HIV/AIDS in your state? According to the Centers for Disease Control and Prevention (2012), approximately 50,000 new cases of HIV are reported each year. Use the Internet (or local resources) to determine the number of HIV/AIDS cases in your state. What subjective realities of HIV/AIDS can you identify?

 STATE STATS

Taking a World View

A Social Constructionist Approach to AIDS in Africa

Bronwen Lichtenstein (2004) examines AIDS as a socially constructed phenomenon. In the following discussion, she describes how the women of Africa were falsely blamed for the spread of the disease.

  Much of the scientific and public speculation about the origins of the HIV/AIDS epidemic has centered on the African subcontinent. From the

outset, Dr. Robert Gallo (codiscoverer of HIV) stated that he could not conceive of AIDS coming from anywhere else but Africa. The African theory is now widely accepted in the scientific literature, especially after it was linked to a single species of African ape. . . . Gilman (1988) and Fee (1988) have noted that understandings about STI (sexually transmitted infections) and Africa began during colonial times when syphilis was linked with African slavery. They also note that while the Europeans had infected colonized people with STI, blame was attributed to non-Europeans in the racist ideology of the times. Gilman (1988) has argued that such attributions about STI are still very much in line with Western notions that Blacks are inherently different and have a fundamentally different relationship to disease. Blame has also been attributed to women as "natural reservoirs" of such disease, particularly in colonized countries (Kehoe 1992).

The AIDS epidemic in Africa has been defined as heterosexual or Type II in epidemiologic terms (Smallman-Raynor, Cliff, and Haggett 1992). For this reason, and in the tradition of the STI (sexually transmitted infections) epidemics, attributions of blame had again centered on women. Treichler has noted, "African women, whose exotic bodies, sexual practices or who knows what, are seen to be so radically different from those of [other] women that anything could happen in them" (1988a:46). The African "Eve" icon has emerged from this conceptualization as sexually promiscuous and often a prostitute. This iconography is perpetuated in common lore, but also in HIV surveillance that focuses mainly on women as sentinel populations (i.e., pregnant women, female sex workers). This gendered approach has identified the problem of women's greater HIV risk, but the lack of surveillance data for men reinforces the notion of women being the locus of the disease and perpetuates largely unexamined assumptions about heterosexuality being the only mode of transmission in Africa. (Lichtenstein 2004:326)

Lichtenstein (2004) explains that as African women have been cast as the "female, heterosexual equivalent of the gay fast-laner, this focus on female promiscuity has proven a distraction from investigating the broader mechanisms of HIV/AIDS in Africa or men's role in the transmission and thus provided little predictive power for understanding the scope of the epidemic" (p. 326).

Lichtenstein warns,

Further outbreaks of HIV/AIDS in the twenty-first century will depend upon sexual cultures, war, famine, drug routes, and political unrest, as well as access to antiretroviral medicines and treated blood supplies. (Lichtenstein 2004:329)

Nations that have lacked the political will or resources for HIV prevention may face economic and social ruin, particularly in AIDS-ravaged countries in sub-Saharan Africa. The path of HIV transmission will depend on whether these countries perceive HIV/AIDS to be an intractable social problem, like poverty or crime, or whether AIDS as a "special case" will prevail in the interests of humanity. This question will be answered by how much AIDS is perceived as a threat in the twenty-first century and whether the disproportionate suffering of some citizens and countries will continue to be tolerated on a global scale. (Lichtenstein 2004:331)

In signing the Declaration of Commitment drafted by the 2001 United Nations General Assembly on HIV/AIDS, 189 nations unanimously acknowledged that AIDS is among the "greatest development [crises] in human history" (UNAIDS 2006). In 2011, UN member states committed to a goal of universal access to HIV prevention, treatment, care, and support by 2015 (UNAIDS 2011).

Source: Reprinted with permission from Lichtenstein 2004. Copyright © 2005 SAGE Publications.

The History of Social Problems

Problems don't appear overnight; rather, as Malcolm Spector and John Kituse (1987) argue, the identification of a social problem is part of a subjective process. Spector and Kituse identify four stages to the process. Stage 1 is defined as a transformation process: taking a private trouble and transforming it into a public issue. In this stage, an influential

Youth AIDS Coalitions

group, activists, or advocates call attention to and define an issue as a social problem. The first HIV infection cases were documented in the United States in 1979. The disease was originally referred to as the "gay plague" because the first group to be identified with the disease was gay men from San Francisco, Los Angeles, and New York. The association of HIV/AIDS with this specific population led to its first being defined as a sexual epidemic rather than a public health threat. Gay activists and public health officials mobilized to increase awareness and began to change the public's perception of the disease in the early 1980s.

Stage 2 is the legitimization process: formalizing the manner in which the social problems or complaints generated by the problem are handled. For example, an organization or public policy could be created to respond to the condition. An existing organization, such as a federal or state agency, could also be charged with taking care of the situation. In either instance, these organizations begin to legitimize the problem by creating and implementing a formal response. In the early 1980s, HIV/AIDS task forces were created in the Centers for Disease Control and Prevention and the World Health Organization. Similar groups were convened in the United Kingdom, France, and other countries. Although no single organization or country was in charge, all were intent on identifying the disease and finding a cure. Activists looked for public legitimization of the disease from then President Ronald Reagan. But Reagan did not acknowledge AIDS until 1985 when he was asked directly about the disease during a press conference. His first public statement about the disease came in 1987 at the Third International Conference on AIDS. By then nearly 36,000 Americans had been diagnosed with AIDS, and more than 20,000 had died. AIDS advocates blamed Reagan's slow and ineffective response for these deaths and the increasing spread of the disease.

Stage 3 is a conflict stage, when Stage 2 routines are unable to address the problem. During Stage 3, activists, advocates, and victims of the problem experience feelings of distrust and cynicism toward the formal response organizations. Stage 3 activities include readjusting the formal response system: renegotiating procedures, reforming practices, and engaging in administrative or organizational restructuring. Many early public health protocols were revised in response to increased understanding about how HIV/AIDS is spread and treated. For example, patient isolation was common during the first stages of the disease. Teenager Ryan White had to petition for the right to attend public school with his classmates. Ryan and his mother's experiences also shed light on the difficulties faced by low-income, uninsured, or underinsured individuals and families living with HIV/AIDS. After his death in 1990, the U.S. Congress passed the Ryan White CARE Act to provide for the unmet health needs of individuals with HIV/AIDS. The act continues to provide support for nearly 500,000 individuals annually, making it the largest federal government program for those living with the disease.

HIV/AIDS Treatment Act

Finally, Stage 4 begins when groups believe that they can no longer work within the established system. Advocates or activists are faced with two options, to radically change the existing system or to work outside of the system. As an alternative to the government and public health agencies' response to HIV/AIDS, numerous independent advocacy and research groups were formed. Among them, the most critical and vocal voice has come from the AIDS Coalition to Unleash Power (ACT UP). Established in 1987, ACT UP called for direct action to end the epidemic, demanding better access to drugs, increasing AIDS public education, and prohibiting AIDS-related discrimination. Today, ACT UP has widened its focus to advocate on behalf of universal health care and prescription drug pricing controls. ACT UP members joined Occupy movement protestors, asking the government to support health care and services for individuals with HIV.

Understanding the Sociological Perspective

According to Jeanne Ballantine and Keith Roberts (2012), sociologists examine the software and hardware of society. A *society* consists of individuals who live together in a specific geographic area, who interact with each other, and who cooperate for the attainment of common goals. The software is our *culture*. Each society has a culture that serves as a system of guidelines for living. A culture includes *norms* (rules of behavior shared by members of society and rooted in a value system), *values* (shared judgments about what is desirable or undesirable, right or wrong, good or bad), and *beliefs* (ideas about life, the way society works, and where one fits in). The hardware comprises the enduring social structures that bring order to our lives. This includes the positions or *statuses* that we occupy in society (student, athlete, employee, roommate) and the social *groups* to which we belong and identify with (your family, your local place of worship, your workplace). S*ocial institutions* are the most complex hardware. Social institutions, such as the family, religion, or education, are relatively permanent social units of roles, rules, relationships, and organized activities devoted to meet human needs and to direct and control human behavior (Ballantine and Roberts 2012).

The way sociologists conduct sociology and study social problems begins first with their view on how the world works. Based on a **theory**—a set of assumptions and propositions used for explanation, prediction, and understanding—sociologists begin to define the relationship between society and individuals and to describe the causes and consequences of social problems.

Theories vary in their level of analysis, focusing on a **macro** (societal) or a **micro** (individual) level. Theories help inform the direction of sociological research and data analysis. In the following section, we review four theoretical perspectives: functionalist, conflict, feminist, and interactionist. Research methods used by sociologists are summarized in the next section.

Functionalist Perspective

Among the theorists most associated with the functionalist perspective is French sociologist Émile Durkheim. Borrowing from biology, Durkheim likened society to a human body. As the body has essential organs, each with a specific function in the body, he theorized that society has its own organs: institutions such as the family, religion, education, economics, and politics. These organs or social structures have essential and specialized functions. For example, the institution of the family maintains the health and socialization of our young and creates a basic economic unit. The institution of education provides knowledge and skills for women and men to work and live in society. No other institution can do what the family or education does.

Durkheim proposed that the function of society was to civilize or control individual actions. He wrote, "It is civilization that has made man what he is; it is what distinguishes him from the animal: man is man only because he is civilized" (Durkheim [1914] 1973:149). The social order can be threatened during periods of rapid social change, such as industrialization or political upheaval, when social norms and values are likely to be in transition. During this state of normlessness or **anomie**, Durkheim believed, society was particularly prone to social problems. As a result, social problems cannot be solved by changing the individual; rather, the problem has to be solved at the societal level. The entire social structure or the affected part of the social structure needs to be repaired.

The **functionalist perspective**, as its name suggests, examines the functions or consequences of the structure of society. Functionalists use a macro perspective, focusing on how society creates and maintains social order. Social problems are not analyzed in terms of how "bad" they are for society. Rather, a functionalist asks, How does the social problem emerge from society? Does the social problem serve a function?

The systematic study of social problems began with the sociologists at the University of Chicago. Part of what has been called the Chicago School of Sociology, scholars such as Ernest W. Burgess, Homer Hoyt, Robert E. Park, Edward Ullman, and Louis Wirth used their city as an urban laboratory, pursuing field studies of poverty, crime, and drug abuse during the 1920s and 1930s. Through their research, they captured the real experiences of individuals experiencing social problems, noting the positive and negative consequences of urbanization and industrialization (Ritzer 2000). Taking it one step further, sociologists Jane Addams and Charlotte Gilman studied urban life in Chicago and developed programs to assist the poor and lobbied for legislative and political reform (Adams and Sydie 2001).

Diversity as a Dysfunction

According to Robert Merton (1957), social structures can have positive benefits as well as negative consequences, which he called **dysfunctions**. A social problem such as homelessness has a clear set of dysfunctions but can also have positive consequences or functions. One could argue that homelessness is clearly dysfunctional and unpleasant for the women, men, and children who experience it, and for a city or community, homelessness can serve as a public embarrassment. Yet, a functionalist would say that homelessness is beneficial for at least one part of society, or else it would cease to exist. The population of the homeless supports an industry of social service agencies, religious organizations, and community groups and service workers. In addition, the homeless also highlight problems in other parts of our social structure, namely the problems of the lack of a livable wage or affordable housing.

Conflict Perspective

Like functionalism, conflict theories examine the macro level of our society, its structures and institutions. Whereas functionalists argue that society is held together by norms, values, and a common morality, those holding a **conflict perspective** consider how society is held together by power and coercion (Ritzer 2000) for the benefit of those in power. In this view, social problems emerge from the continuing conflict between groups in our society—based on social class, gender, race, or ethnicity—and in the conflict, the dominant groups usually win. There are multiple levels of domination; as Patricia Hill Collins (1990) describes, domination "operates not only by structuring power from the top down but by simultaneously annexing the power as energy of those on the bottom for its own ends" (pp. 227–28).

Conquering AIDS

As a result, this perspective offers no easy solutions to social problems. The system could be completely overhauled, but that is unlikely to happen. We could reform parts of the structure, but those in power would retain their control. The biggest social problem from this perspective is the system itself and the inequality it perpetuates.

The first to make this argument was German philosopher and activist Karl Marx. Conflict, according to Marx, emerged from the economic substructure of capitalism, which defined all other social structures and social relations. He focused on the conflict based on social class, created by the tension between the **proletariat** (workers) and the **bourgeoisie** (owners). Capitalism did more than separate the haves and the have-nots. Unlike Durkheim, who believed that society created a civilized man, Marx argued that a capitalist society created a

Photo 1.3

Individuals come together in public rallies such as this one at the United Nations HIV/AIDS meeting, to voice their concerns about HIV/AIDS policies and funding. These demonstrations galvanize the efforts of advocacy and activist groups, as well as educate the public about HIV/AIDS.

man alienated from his **species being**, from his true self. **Alienation** occurred on multiple levels: Man would become increasingly alienated from his work, the product of his work, other workers, and, finally, his own human potential. For example, a salesperson might be so involved in the process of her work that she doesn't spend quality time with her coworkers, talk with her customers, or stop and appreciate the merchandise. Each sale transaction is the same; all customers and workers are treated alike. The salesperson could not achieve her human potential through this type of mindless unfulfilling labor. According to Marx, workers needed to achieve a **class consciousness**, an awareness of their social position and oppression, so they could unite and overthrow capitalism, replacing it with a more egalitarian socialist and eventually communist structure.

Widening Marx's emphasis on the capitalist class structure, contemporary conflict theorists have argued that conflict emerges from other social bases, such as values, resources, and interests. Mills ([1959] 2000) argued the existence of a "power elite," a small group of political, business, and military leaders who control our society. Ralf Dahrendorf (1959) explained that conflict of interest is inherent in any relationship because those in powerful positions will always seek to maintain their dominance. Lewis Coser (1956) focused on the functional aspects of conflict, arguing that conflict creates and maintains group solidarity by clarifying the positions and boundaries between groups. Conflict theorists may also take a social constructionist approach, examining how powerful political, economic, and social interest groups subjectively define social problems.

Feminist Perspective

Rosemarie Tong (1989) explains that "feminist theory is not one, but many, theories or perspectives and that each feminist theory or perspective attempts to describe women's oppression, to explain its causes and consequences, and to prescribe strategies for women's liberation" (p. 1). By analyzing the situations and lives of women in society, the **feminist perspective** defines gender (and sometimes race or social class) as a source of social inequality, group conflict, and social problems. For feminists, the patriarchal society is the basis of social problems. **Patriarchy** refers to a society in which men dominate women and justify their domination through devaluation; however, the definition of patriarchy has been broadened to include societies in which powerful groups dominate and devalue the powerless (Kaplan 1994).

Internet
Patriarchy

Patricia Madoo Lengermann and Jill Niebrugge-Brantley (2004) explain that feminist theory was established as a new sociological perspective in the 1970s, largely because of the growing presence of women in the discipline and the strength of the women's movement. Feminist theory treats the experiences of women as the starting point in all sociological investigations, seeing the world from the vantage point of women in the social world and seeking to promote a better world for women and for humankind.

Women in Modern
Culture

Although the study of social problems is not the center of feminist theory, throughout its history, feminist theory has been critical of existing social arrangements and has focused on such concepts as social change, power, and social inequality (Madoo Lengermann and Niebrugge-Brantley 2004). Major research in the field has included Jessie Bernard's ([1972] 1982) study of gender inequality in marriage, Collins's (1990) development of Black feminist thought, Dorothy Smith's (1987) sociology from the standpoint of women, and Nancy Chodorow's (1978) psychoanalytic feminism and the reproduction of mothering. Although sociologists in this perspective may adopt a conflict, functionalist, or interactionist perspective, their focus remains on how men and women are situated in society, not just differently but also unequally (Madoo Lengermann and Niebrugge-Brantley 2004).

Interactionist Perspective

An **interactionist** focuses on how we use language, words, and symbols to create and maintain our social reality. This micro level perspective highlights what we take for granted: the expectations, rules, and norms that we learn and practice without even noticing. In our interaction with others, we become the products and creators of our social reality. Through our interaction, social problems are created and defined.

George Herbert Mead provided the foundation of this perspective. Also a member of the Chicago School of Sociology, Mead ([1934] 1962) argued that society consisted of the organized and patterned interactions among individuals. As Mead defined it, the self is a mental and social process, the reflective ability to see others in relation to ourselves and to see ourselves in relation to others. Our interactions are based on language, based on words. The words we use to communicate with are symbols, representations of something else. The symbols have no inherent meaning and require human interpretation. The term **symbolic interactionism** was coined by Herbert Blumer in 1937. Building on Mead's work, Blumer emphasized how the existence of mind, self, and society emerges from interaction and the use and understanding of symbols (Turner 1998).

How does the self emerge from interaction? Consider the roles that you and I play. As a university professor, I am aware of what is expected of me; as university students, you are aware of what it means to be a student. There are no posted guides in the classroom that instruct us where to stand, how to dress, or what to bring into class. Even before we enter the classroom, we know how we are supposed to behave and even our places in the classroom. We act based on our past experiences and based on what we have come to accept as definitions of each role. But we need each other to create this reality; our interaction in the classroom reaffirms each of our roles and the larger educational institution. Imagine what it takes to maintain this reality: consensus not just between a single professor and his or her students but between every professor and every student on campus, on every university campus, ultimately reaffirming the structure of a university classroom and higher education.

Everyday Interactions

So, how do social problems emerge from interaction? First, for social problems such as juvenile delinquency, an interactionist would argue that the problem behavior is learned from others. According to this perspective, no one is born a juvenile delinquent. Like any other role we play, people learn how to become juvenile delinquents. Although the perspective does not answer the question of where or from whom the first delinquent child learned this behavior, it attempts to explain how deviant behavior is learned through interaction with others.

Second, social problems emerge from the definitions themselves. Objective social problems do not exist; they become real only in how they are defined or labeled. A sociologist using this perspective would examine who or what group is defining the problem and who or what is being defined as deviant or a social problem. As we have already seen with the HIV/AIDS epidemic in the United States, the problem became real only when activists and public health workers called attention to the disease. More than any other perspective, interactionists stress **human agency**—the active role of individuals in creating their social environment (Ballantine and Roberts 2012) and in defining and addressing social problems.

Third, the solutions to social problems also emerge from our definitions. Schneider and Ingram (1993) argue that the social construction of target populations influences the distribution of policy benefits or policy burdens. Target populations are groups of individuals experiencing a specific social problem; these groups gain policy attention through their socially constructed identity and political power. The authors identify four categories: advantaged target populations are positively constructed and politically powerful (likely to receive policy benefits), contenders are politically powerful yet negatively constructed (likely to receive policy benefits when public interest is high), dependent target populations have positive social construction but low political power (few policy resources would be allocated to this group), and deviant target populations are both politically weak and negatively constructed (least likely to receive any benefits).

Jean Schroedel and Daniel Jordan (1998) applied the target population model to U.S. Senate voting patterns between 1982 and 1992, examining the allocation of federal funds to four distinct HIV/AIDS groups. As Schneider and Ingram's (1993) theory would predict, the groups receiving the most funding were those in the advantaged category (war veterans and health care workers), followed by contenders (gay and bisexual men and the general population with AIDS), dependents (spouses and the public), and, finally, deviants (IV drug users, criminals, and prisoners).

What Does It Mean to Me?

A summary of these sociological perspectives is presented in Table 1.1. These sociological perspectives are reintroduced in each chapter as we examine a new social problem or set of problems. As you review each perspective, do not attempt to classify one as the definitive explanation. Consider how each perspective focuses on different aspects of society and its social problems. Which perspective(s) best fits with your understanding of society or your understanding of social problems?

Table 1.1

Summary of Sociological Perspectives: A General Approach to Examining Social Problems

	Functionalist	Conflict/Feminist	Interactionist
Level of analysis	Macro	Macro	Micro
Assumptions about society	Order. Society is held together by a set of social institutions, each of which has a specific function in society.	Conflict. Society is held together by power and coercion. Conflict and inequality are inherent in the social structure.	Interaction. Society is created through social interaction.
Questions asked about social problems	How does the problem originate from the social structure? How does the problem reflect changes among social institutions and structures? What are the functions and dysfunctions of the problem?	How does the problem originate from the competition between groups and from the social structure itself? What groups are in competition and why?	How is the problem socially constructed and defined? How is problem behavior learned through interaction? How is the problem labeled by those concerned about it?

The Science of Sociology

Sociology is not commonsense guessing about how the world works. The social sciences rely on "scientific methods to investigate individuals, societies, and social process" and encompass "the knowledge produced by these investigations" (Schutt 2012:9).

HIV Research

Sociological research is divided into two areas: basic and applied. The knowledge we gain through **basic research** expands our understanding of the causes and consequences of a social problem, for example, identifying the predictors of HIV/AIDS or examining the rate of homelessness among AIDS patients. Conversely, **applied research** involves the pursuit of knowledge for program application or policy evaluation (Katzer, Cook, and Crouch 1998). Often, social programs are evaluated for how effective they are in reducing a problem or in creating some desired change. The information gained through applied research can be incorporated into social programs serving HIV/AIDS patients.

All research begins with a theory to help identify the phenomenon we're trying to explain and provide explanations for the social patterns or causal relationships between variables (Frankfort-Nachmias and Leon-Guerrero 2011). **Variables** are a property of people or objects that can take on two or more values. For example, as we try to explain HIV/AIDS, we may have a specific explanation about the relationship between two variables—social class and HIV infection. Social class could be measured according to household or individual income, whereas HIV infection could be measured as a positive test for the HIV antibodies. The relationship between these variables can be stated in a **hypothesis**, a tentative statement about how the variables are related to each other. We could predict that HIV infection would be higher among lower-income men and women. In this hypothesis statement, we've identified a **dependent variable** (the variable to be explained, HIV infection) along with an **independent variable** (the variable expected to account for the cause of the dependent variable, social class). Data, the information we collect, may confirm or refute this hypothesis.

Research methods can include quantitative or qualitative approaches or a combination. Quantitative methods rely on the collection of statistical data. They require the specification of variables and scales collected through surveys, interviews, or questionnaires. Qualitative methods are designed to capture social life as participants experience it. These methods involve field observation, depth interviews, or focus groups. Following are definitions of each specific method.

Survey research: This is data collection based on responses to a series of questions. Surveys can be offered in several formats: a self-administered mailed survey, group surveys, in-person interviews, or telephone surveys. For example, information from HIV/AIDS patients may be collected by a survey sent directly in the mail or by a telephone or in-person interview (e.g., Simoni et al. 2006; Sambisa, Curtis, and Mishra 2010).

Qualitative methods: This category includes data collection conducted in the field, emphasizing the observations about natural behavior as experienced or witnessed by the researcher. Methods include participant observation (a method for gathering data that involves developing a sustained relationship with people while they go about their normal activities), focus groups (unstructured group interviews in which a focus group leader actively encourages discussion among participants on the topics of interest), or intensive (depth) interviewing (open-ended, relatively unstructured questioning in which the interviewer seeks in-depth information on the interviewee's feelings, experiences, and perceptions). Sociologists have used various qualitative methods in HIV/AIDS research—collecting data through participant observation at clinics or support groups and focus groups or depth interviews with patients, health care providers, or key informants (e.g., Chakrapani et al. 2007; Akintola 2010).

Historical and comparative methods: This is research that focuses on one historical period (historical events research) or traces a sequence of events over time (historical process research). Comparative research involves multiple cases or data from more than one time period. For example, researchers have examined the effectiveness of HIV/AIDS treatments over time (e.g., Fumaz et al. 2007) and compared infection rates between men and women (e.g., Ballesteros et al. 2006).

Secondary data analysis: Secondary data analysis usually involves the analysis of previously collected data that are used in a new analysis. Large public survey data sets, such as the U.S. Census, the General Social Survey, the National Election Survey, or the International Social Survey Programme, can be used, as can data collected in experimental studies or with qualitative data sets. For HIV/AIDS research, a secondary data analysis could be based on existing medical records (e.g., Tabi and Vogel 2006) or a routine health survey (e.g., Sambisa et al. 2010). The key to secondary data analysis is that the data were not originally collected by the researcher but were collected by another researcher and for a different purpose.

The Transformation From Problem to Solution

Although Mills identified the relationship between a personal trouble and a public issue more than 50 years ago, less has been said about the transformation of issue to solution. Mills leads us in the right direction by identifying the relationship between public issues and social institutions. By continuing to use our sociological imagination and recognizing the role of larger social, cultural, and structural forces, we can identify appropriate measures to address these social problems.

Tent Cities

Let's consider homelessness. It does not arise from mysterious or special circumstances; rather, it emerges from familiar life experiences. The loss of a job, the illness of a family member, domestic violence, or divorce could make a family more susceptible to homelessness. During this economic recession, foreclosures among renters and homeowners contributed to an increase in the number of homeless. For 2010, there were a record number of foreclosures—3.8 million—highest in Nevada, Arizona, and Florida (Prior 2011).

Among those with HIV/AIDS, more than half will need housing assistance at some point in their lives. Without informal social support, a savings account, or suitable and adequate employment—and with the increasing cost of health care and the lack of affordable housing—a family's economic and emotional resources can quickly be tapped out. What would it take to prevent homelessness in these situations? The answers are not based in each individual or each family; rather, the long-term solutions are structural solutions such as affordable health care, livable wages, and affordable low-income housing.

Modern history reveals that Americans do not like to stand by and do nothing about social problems. Actually, most Americans support efforts to reduce homelessness, improve the quality of education, or find a cure for HIV/AIDS. In some cases, there are no limits to our efforts. Helping our nation's poor has been an administrative priority of many U.S. presidents. President Franklin Roosevelt proposed sweeping social reforms during his New Deal in 1935, and President Lyndon Johnson declared the War on Poverty in 1964. President Bill Clinton offered to "change welfare as we know it" with broad reforms outlined in the Personal Responsibility and Work Opportunity Reconciliation Act of 1996. And in 2003, President George W. Bush supported the reauthorization of the 1996 welfare reform bill. No president or Congress has ever promised to eliminate poverty; instead, each promised only to improve the system serving the poor or to reduce the number of poor in our society.

Solutions require social action—in the form of social policy, advocacy, and innovation—to address problems at their structural or individual levels. **Social policy** is the enactment of a course of action through a formal law or program. Policy making usually begins with identification of a problem that should be addressed; then, specific guidelines are developed regarding what should be done to address the problem. Policy directly changes the social structure, particularly how our government, an organization, or our community responds to a social problem. In addition, policy governs the behavior and interaction of individuals, controlling who has access to benefits and aid (Ellis 2003). According to Jacob Lew, President Barack Obama's budget director, "The [federal] budget is not just a collection of numbers, but an expression of our values and aspirations" (as quoted in Herbert 2011:11).

Social policies are always being enacted. The most recent comprehensive homeless legislation was the Homeless Emergency Assistance and Rapid Transition to Housing (HEARTH) Act of 2009. One of the fundamental features of the act was expanding the federal definition of *homeless* to include persons living in shared housing or in motels due to loss of housing or economic hardship, regardless of their length of stay. These persons would be eligible for rehousing assistance under the new federal definition. In 2009, South Africa's President Jacob Zuma announced sweeping HIV/AIDS policy changes, extending early treatment to HIV-positive pregnant women and individuals with tuberculosis. Such policies were not in place in the previous Mbeki administration. Zuma stated that these new policies mean that "we will be treating significantly larger numbers of HIV positive patients. It means that people will live longer and more fulfilling lives" (Dugger 2009a:A6).

Social advocates use their resources to support, educate, and empower individuals and their communities. Advocates work to improve social services, change social policies, and

Photo 1.4

Lawmakers determine how we choose to respond to a social problem, setting social policy that directly changes our social structure. As a result, social policies govern the behavior and interaction of individuals, controlling who has access to programs and aid.

mobilize individuals. During his first presidential campaign, Barack Obama recalled his work as a community organizer for the Developing Communities Project in Chicago's far South Side. The church-based organization served White, Black, and Latino blue-collar neighborhoods addressing education, public safety, and housing issues. National organizations such as the National Coalition for the Homeless and the National AIDS Housing Coalition or local organizations such as Project H.O.M.E. in Philadelphia provide service, outreach, education, and legal support for the homeless and for homeless AIDS patients.

Social innovation may take the form of a policy, a program, or advocacy that features an untested or unique approach. Innovation usually starts at the community level, but it can grow into national and international programming. Millard and Linda Fuller developed the concept of "partnership housing" in 1965, partnering those in need of adequate shelter with community volunteers to build simple interest-free houses. In 1976, the Fullers' concept became Habitat for Humanity International, a nonprofit, ecumenical Christian housing program responsible for building more than 500,000 houses worldwide. When Millard Fuller was awarded the Presidential Medal of Freedom, the nation's highest civilian honor, President Clinton described Habitat for Humanity as "the most successful continuous community service project in the history of the United States" (Habitat for Humanity 2004).

Making Sociological Connections

In his book *Social Things: An Introduction to the Sociological Life,* Charles Lemert (1997) tells us that sociology is often presented as a thing to be studied. Instead, he argues that sociology is something to be "lived," becoming a way of life. Lemert (1997) writes,

> To use one's sociological imagination, whether to practical or professional end, is to look at the events in one's life, to see them for what they truly are, then to figure out how the structures of the wider world make social things the way they are. No one is a sociologist until she does this the best she can. (P. 105)

We can use our sociological imagination, as Lemert (1997) recommends, but we can also take it a step further. As Marx (1972) maintained, "The philosophers have only interpreted the world, in various ways; the point, however is to change it" (p. 107).

Throughout this text, we explore three connections. The first connection is the one between personal troubles and public issues. Each sociological perspective—functionalist, conflict, feminist, and interactionist—highlights how social problems emerge from our social structure or social interaction. While maintaining its primary focus on problems within the United States, this text also addresses the experience of social problems in other countries and nations. The comparative perspective will enhance your understanding of the social problems we experience here.

Photo 1.5

In 2010, Habitat for Humanity volunteers rebuilt, repaired, and rehabbed more than 2,000 homes in Alabama, Louisiana, Mississippi, and Texas. In this photo, volunteers from the PacifiCare Corporation based in Southern California are building a home for a family whose home was lost during Hurricane Katrina.

The sociological imagination will also help us make a second connection: the one between social problems and social solutions. Mills believed that the most important value of sociology was in its potential to enrich and encourage the lives of all individuals (Lemert 1997). In each chapter, we review selected social policies, advocacy programs, and innovative approaches that attempt to address or solve these problems.

Textbooks on this subject present neat individual chapters on a social problem, reviewing the sociological issues and sometimes providing some suggestions about how it can and should be addressed. This book follows the same outline but takes a closer look at community-based approaches, ultimately identifying how *you* can be part of the solution in your community.

I should warn you that this text will not identify a perfect set of solutions to our social problems. Individual action may be powerless against the social structure. Some individuals or groups will have more power or advantage over others. Solutions, like the problems they address, are embedded within complex interconnected social systems (Fine 2006). Sometimes solutions create other problems. For example, United Nations Children's Fund (UNICEF) Chief of Health Mickey Chopra reports that as countries, such as the United States, have focused their attention and funding on the AIDS epidemic worldwide, deaths due to preventable or treatable diseases (e.g., diarrhea and pneumonia) have increased. Diarrhea kills 1.5 million children a year in developing countries, more than AIDS, malaria, and measles combined (Dugger 2009b). Some solutions fail. A program may have worked, but it might no longer exist because of lack of funding or political and public support. Nevertheless, some policies and programs have been proven effective in helping individuals, families, or groups improve their lives and in reducing or completely eliminating the prevalence of particular problems.

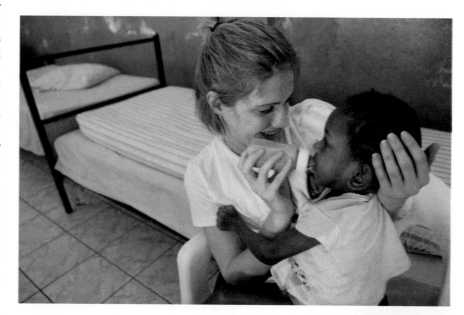

Photo 1.6

Service and volunteer opportunities are available to college and university students in the United States and abroad. The nursing program at Emory University sponsors this service program based in Kingston, Jamaica.

 Social Justice

In communities such as yours and mine, individuals and community groups are taking action against social problems. They are women, men, and children, common citizens and professionals, from different backgrounds and experiences. Whether they are working within the system or working to change the system, these individuals are part of their community's solution to a problem. The goal might be to solve one social problem or several or to create what Joel Feagin (2002) describes as a "new global system that reduces injustice, is democratically accountable to all people, offers a decent standard of living for all, and operates in a sustainable relation to earth's other living systems" (p. 17). As Gary Fine (2006) observes, "Those who care about social problems are obligated to use their best knowledge to increase the store of freedom, justice and equality" (p. 14). In the end, I hope you agree that it is important that we continue to do something about the social problems we experience.

What Does It Mean to Me?

What Feagin (2002) describes has also been referred to as social justice. Though the term is widely used, there is no single definition. Social justice has different meanings and will vary depending on one's ideology, discipline, or experience. One way to think of social justice is to consider what constitutes a "perfect" society and what it takes to make that happen. How would you define social justice? What is your "perfect" society?

Linking Societies

In addition, I ask you to make the final connection to social problems and solutions in your community. For this quarter or semester, instead of focusing only on problems reported in your local newspaper or the morning news program, start paying attention to the solutions offered by professionals, leaders, and advocates. Through the Internet or through local programs and agencies, take this opportunity to investigate what social action is taking place in your community. Regardless of whether you define your "community" as your campus, your residential neighborhood, or the city where your college is located, consider what avenues of change can be taken and whether you can be part of that effort.

I often tell my students that the problem with being a sociologist is that my sociological imagination has no "off" switch. In almost everything I read, see, or do, there is some sociological application, a link between my personal experiences and the broader social experience that I share with everyone else, including you. As you progress through this text and your course, I hope that you will begin to use your own sociological imagination and see connections between problems and their solutions that you never saw before.

Main Points

- Sociology is the systematic study of individuals and social structures. A sociologist examines the relationship between individuals and our society, which includes institutions (the family), organizations (the military), and systems (our economy). As a social science, sociology offers an objective and systematic approach to understanding the causes of social problems.

- The sociological imagination is a way of recognizing the links between our personal lives and experiences and our social world.

- A social problem is a social condition that has negative consequences for individuals, our social world, or the physical world.

- A social problem has objective and subjective realities. The objective reality of a social problem comes from acknowledging that a particular social condition negatively affects human lives. The subjective reality of a social problem addresses how a problem becomes defined as a problem. Social problems are not objectively

predetermined. They become real only when they are subjectively defined or perceived as problematic. This perspective is known as social constructionism.

- Problems don't just appear overnight; rather, as Spector and Kituse (1987) argue, the identification of a social problem is a process.

- Sociologists use four theoretical perspectives: functionalist, conflict, feminist, and interactionist. The functionalist perspective examines the functions or consequences of the structure of society. Functionalists use a macro perspective, focusing on how society creates and maintains social order. A social problem is not analyzed in terms of how "bad" it is for parts of society. Rather, a functionalist asks how the social problem emerges from the society. What function does the social problem serve?

- Conflict, according to Marx, emerged from the economic substructure of capitalism, which defined all other social structures and social relations. Marx focused on the conflict based on social class, created by the tension between the proletariat (workers) and the bourgeoisie (owners). He argued that a capitalist society created a man alienated from his species being, from his true self. Alienation occurred on multiple levels: Man would become increasingly alienated from his work, from the product of his work, from other workers, and, finally, from his own human potential.

■ By analyzing the situations and lives of women in society, feminist theory defines gender (and sometimes race or social class) as a source of social inequality, group conflict, and social problems. For feminists, the patriarchal society is the basis of social problems.

■ An interactionist focuses on how we use language, words, and symbols to create and maintain our social reality. This perspective highlights what we take for granted: the expectations,

rules, and norms that we learn and practice without even noticing. In our interaction with others, we become the products and creators of our social reality. This perspective highlights the role of human agency, the active role of individuals in creating their social environment and how social problems and their solutions are created and defined.

■ Solutions require social action—in the form of social policy, advocacy, and innovation—to address problems at their structural or individual levels. Social policy is the enactment of a course of action through a formal law or program. Social advocates use their resources to support, educate, and empower individuals and their communities. Social innovation may take the form of a policy, a program, or advocacy that features an untested or unique approach. Innovation usually starts at the community level, but it can grow into national and international programming.

On Your Own

Log on to the open-access Student Study Site at www.sagepub.com/leonguerrero4e for these additional learning tools:

■ Interactive quizzes
■ Video clips
■ NPR audio links
■ Handbook articles

■ E-flashcards
■ Journal articles
■ End-of-chapter web exercises
■ Additional web resources and current events

Internet and Community Exercises

1. Review copies of your local newspaper from the past 90 days. Based on the front page or local section, what issues are important for your community (e.g., crime, job layoffs, transportation, pollution)? Examine how the issue is defined and by whom. Is input from community leaders and neighborhood groups being included? Why or why not? Do these include the three elements of a social problem?

2. Social actions or responses are also linked to how we define the problem. If we believe the problem

is structural, we'll find ways to change the structure. If the problem is defined at the individual level, a solution will attempt to change the person. Investigate the programs and resources that are available for the homeless in your community or state. Select three local programs and assess how each defines and responds to the homeless problem in your community.

3. What do you think is the most important social problem? Investigate what federal and state

policies govern or regulate this problem and those it affects. What is the position of the main political parties—Democrats and Republicans—on this problem?

4. What do you think is the most important global social problem? Investigate how the governments of the United States and other nations have responded to this problem. How have citizens responded?

5. Investigate whether there are community groups or organizations that serve the HIV/AIDS population in your city. What activities or programs do they sponsor? How do they provide assistance to those living with HIV/AIDS in your area?

Study Questions

1. How does the sociological imagination help us understand social problems?

2. Select two of the sociological perspectives introduced in this chapter. Compare and contrast how each defines a social problem. What solutions does each perspective offer?

3. Identify the objective and subjective realities of the increasing cost of college.

4. Apply your sociological imagination to the problem of the increasing cost of college. Is this a personal problem only for students who can't afford tuition? Or is the increasing cost of tuition a public issue?

5. Using the social constructionist perspective, analyze how the primary messages in the 2012 presidential campaign were defined by the candidates, political leaders, the media, and public interest groups. In your opinion, what was defined as a social problem?

6. Explain how science and the scientific method help us understand social problems. How is this different from a commonsense understanding of social problems?

7. Select two research methods and explain how each could be used to examine the impact of the rising cost of college on students, their families, and the institution of higher education?

8. What is the relationship among social advocacy, innovation, and policy?

PART II

The Bases
of Inequality

"Like trees in a vast forest, humans come in a variety of sizes, shapes, and colors." Marilyn Loden and Judy Rosener (1991) wrote these words to describe human diversity or what the women call "otherness or those human qualities that are different from our own and outside the groups to which we belong" (p. 18). They created the Diversity Wheel (see Figure II.1) to represent our primary and secondary characteristics.

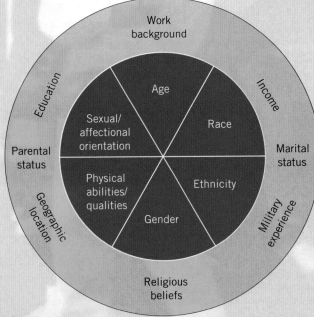

Our primary characteristics are presented in the center of the wheel. These dimensions—age, ethnicity, gender, physical abilities, race, and sexual orientation—serve as our basic self-image and affect our lives from birth. As Loden and Rosener (1991) tell us, "There is no escaping the lifelong impact of these six core elements" (p. 19). Secondary characteristics are less salient than primary characteristics. We can change these characteristics, such as our educational attainment, geographic location, income, marital status, military experience, parental status, religious beliefs, and work experience.

Each characteristic serves as a social boundary, letting us know who should be included in or excluded from our particular social group (Sernau 2001), defining the "otherness" each of us possesses. Sociologists use the term **social stratification** to refer to the ranking of individuals into social strata or groups. We are divided into groups such as women versus men or African Americans versus Asian Americans. Our lives are also transformed because of our group membership. In U.S. society, being different has come to mean that we are unequal.

The differences between social strata become more apparent when we recognize how some individuals are more likely to experience social problems than others are. Attached to each social position are **life chances,** a term Max Weber used to describe the consequences of social stratification, how each social position provides particular access to goods and services such as wealth, food, clothing, shelter, education, and health care.

Figure II.1

Diversity Wheel

Source: From Loden, Marilyn, and Rosener, J. B., Workforce America! Managing Employee Diversity as a Vital Resource. *Copyright © 1991. Reprinted with permission of the McGraw-Hill Companies.*

Sociologists refer to the unequal distribution of resources, services, and positions as **social inequality**. Certain social positions are subject to **prejudice** (a negative attitude based on the attributes of an individual) and to **discrimination** (acts based on prejudiced beliefs against a specific individual or group) not experienced by others. And, sadly, some social positions are also targets of violence.

In the next five chapters, we will explore two basic sociological questions: Why does social inequality exist, and how are we different from one another? We will review sociological theories that attempt to explain and examine the consequences of social inequality. Although the five bases of inequality are discussed in separate chapters, real life happens at the intersection of our social class, racial and ethnic identity, gender, sexual orientation, and age. These bases of inequality simultaneously define and affect us. We need to recognize how each social characteristic (class, race, ethnicity, gender, sexual orientation, or age) shapes the history, experiences, and opportunities of men, women, and children in the United States (Shapiro 2001) and throughout the world. Your life experience may have less to do with your ability or your hard work and more to do with how (well) you are positioned in society. Ultimately, this includes your experience of social problems.

If this is your first sociology course, these chapters will provide you with an overview of several basic sociological concepts. If you have already had a sociology course, welcome back; these chapters should provide a good review.

What Does It Mean to Me?

Based on some of the primary and secondary characteristics identified in the Diversity Wheel, I'd describe myself as a married, college-educated, Asian Pacific Islander, heterosexual female. What social characteristics would you use to describe yourself? Which social characteristics are essential to your identity?

"Invisible" Dividing Lines

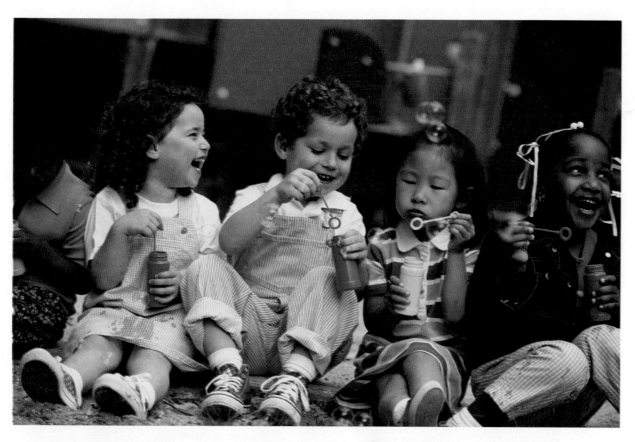

It is difficult to escape from our social differences and the system of stratification that separates us. However, society has attempted to eliminate some of the barriers between groups. In schools and workplaces in particular (where laws have been most stringent), we've had some success in overcoming stratification based on gender, race, and ethnicity.

Americans generally value diversity but remain committed to some dividing lines. For example, many forms of sex-based discrimination and segregation are rigidly enforced by mores, even among the most liberal Americans.

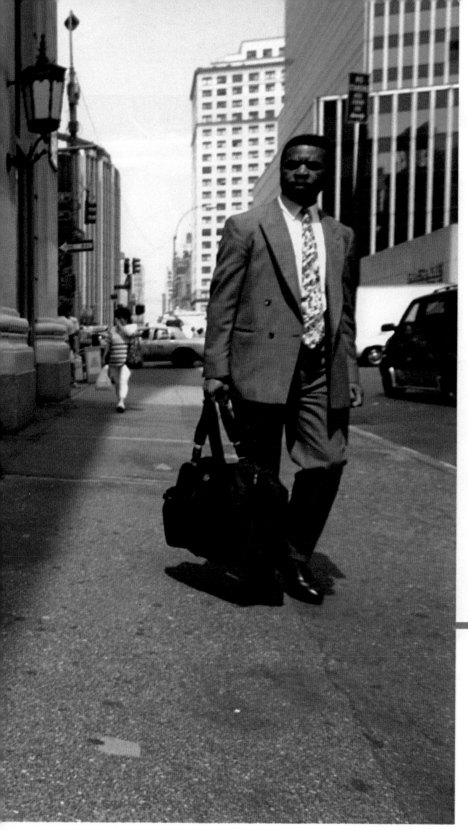

Class distinctions also persist and can be compounded by differences based on ethnicity, race, and gender. About 41.5% of the U.S. poor are non-Hispanic Whites, with African Americans having the highest poverty rate among minority groups.

What "invisible" dividing lines can you think of that people may be taking for granted? What invisible dividing lines exist on your college campus? How are they defined—by race, social class, gender, or something else?

CHAPTER 2

Social Class and Poverty

T he United States is perceived as one of the world's richest countries. Nonetheless, economic inequality is one of the most important and visible of America's social problems (McCall 2002). The Occupy Wall Street movement highlighted wealth and income inequality through its central protest question: Are you a member of the wealthy 1% or part of the remaining 99%? Martin Marger (2002) writes, "Measured in various ways, the gap between rich and poor in the United States is wider than [in] any other society with comparable economic institutions and standards of living" (p. 48). The overall distribution of wages and earnings has become more unequal, and the distance between the wealthy and the poor has widened considerably in recent decades and worsened during the Great Recession of 2007–2009. Since 1970, the residential isolation of both poor and affluent families has increased; that is, high- and low-income families are less likely to live near each other. This income segregation may increase the economic advantages of high-income families and the economic disadvantages of low-income families (Reardon and Bischoff 2011).

Many Americans believe that their economic status is declining or not improving at all and that there is increasing tension between the rich and the poor (Pew Research Center 2008; Morin 2012). Almost 80% of those surveyed by the Pew Research Center (2008) said that it was more difficult over the past five years for middle-class people to maintain their standard of living. About two thirds of the sample agree that the rich are getting richer and the poor are getting poorer. Additionally, two thirds of Americans believe there is a strong or very strong conflict between poor people and rich people (Morin 2012).

 Taxing the Poor

The Great Recession has brought financial havoc to many Americans such as Debra Winchell and Evan Gutierrez. Winchell, an administrative assistant from Latham, New York, was laid off the day after President Barack Obama's 2008 inauguration. She worked for the same employer for

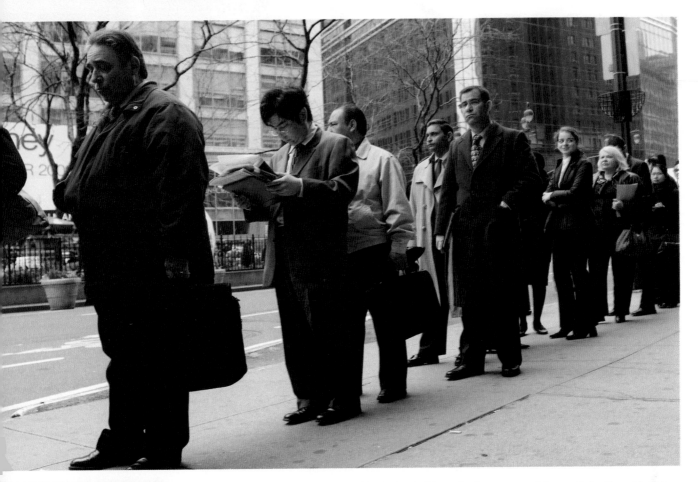

Photo 2.1

People stand in a long line to enter a 2009 New York job fair. As of February 2012, the unemployment rate was 8.3% (U.S. Department of Labor 2012). Unemployment reached a peak of 10.2% in October 2009 (U.S. Department of Labor 2010).

nine years. In two previous layoffs, she was able to find temporary jobs until she found full-time employment. But this time, due to health issues, Winchell needs to find a full-time job with benefits, which has been difficult. Across the country, in Los Angeles, California, Gutierrez, a teacher and administrator, was forced to move to a smaller apartment with his wife and child after losing two jobs. Unable to find employment, he borrowed money from family members and his church to pay the rent. In assessing his situation, Gutierrez says, "We grow up with the impression there's a correlation between effort and the fruits of your labor. To be honest with you, I have very little confidence I'm going to be able to turn this around" (Luo and Thee-Brenan 2009:A26).

The U.S. Census regularly tracks income and wealth. For 2011, the median income was reported at $50,054 (DeNavas-Walt, Proctor, and Smith 2012). Between 2007 and 2010, the median value of real (inflation-adjusted) family income before taxes fell 7.7% (Bricker et al. 2012). The U.S. Census examines income distribution by dividing the U.S. household population into fifths or quintiles. If all U.S. income were equally divided, each quintile would receive one fifth of the total income. However, based on U.S. Census data for 2011, 50% of the total U.S. income was earned by households in the highest quintile or among households making an average of $178,020. The lowest 20% of households (earning an average of $11,239 per year) had 3.2% of the total income (DeNavas-Walt et al. 2012). Inequality first grew between 1973 and 1999, when the top fifth of the distribution began to increase its share of aggregate income, while the bottom four fifths began to lose their share (Jones and Weinberg 2000). A report by the U.S. Congressional Budget Office (2011) revealed that the income for the top 1% increased by 275% from 1979 to 2007. (Refer to Table 2.1.)

What Does It Mean to Me?

Find where your state ranks in terms of median household income. Why do you think it is placed where it is? Which state has the highest median household income?

STATE STATS

Table 2.1

Share of Aggregate Income Received by Each Fifth, 2011

Fifth	Mean Income	Share
Top fifth	$178,020	51.1
Second fifth	$80,080	23.0
Third fifth	$49,842	14.3
Fourth fifth	$29,204	8.4
Lowest fifth	$11,239	3.2

Source: DeNavas-Walt et al. 2012.

Wealth, rather than income, may be more important in determining one's economic inequality. **Wealth** is usually defined as the value of assets (checking and savings accounts, property, vehicles, and stocks) owned by a household (Keister and Moller 2000) at a point in time. Wealth is measured in two ways: gross assets (the total value of the assets someone owns) and net worth (the value of assets owned minus the amount of debt owed; Gilbert 2003). Wealth is more stable within families and across generations than is income, occupation, or education (Conley 1999) and can be used to secure or produce wealth, enhancing one's life chances. Wealth provides access to key social and **cultural capital** (such as a quality of life, social connections, and cultural manners) that can also affect future life outcomes.

Income Inequality

As Melvin Oliver and Thomas Shapiro (1995) explain,

> Wealth is a particularly important indicator of individual and family access to life chances. Wealth is a special form of money not used to purchase milk and shoes and other life necessities. More often it is used to create opportunities, secure a desired stature and standard of living, or pass class status along to one's children. . . . The command over resources that wealth entails is more encompassing than income or education, and closer in meaning and theoretical significance to our traditional notions of economic well-being and access to life chances. (p. 2)

Wealth preserves the division between the wealthy and the nonwealthy, providing an important mechanism for the intergenerational transmission of inequality (Gilbert 2003). Scott Sernau (2001) tells us,

> Wealth begets wealth. . . . It ensures that those near the bottom will be called on to spend almost all of their incomes and that what wealth they might acquire, such as an aging automobile or an aging house in a vulnerable neighborhood, will more likely depreciate than increase in value, and the poor will get nowhere. (p. 69)

Data reveal that wealth is more unequally distributed and more concentrated than income. Since the early 1920s, the top 1% of wealth holders have owned an average of 30% of household wealth. During the late 1980s and 1990s, the top 1% of wealth owners owned

Overcoming Inequality

more than 45% of all net worth and nearly 50% of all financial assets (Keister and Moller 2000; Wolff 2006). From 2007 to 2010, the proportion of families that reported that they had saved money in the previous year fell from 56.4% to 52%. During the same time period, median net worth decreased for all income groups except the top 10% (Bricker et al. 2012).

What Does It Mean to Me?

Consider your own income and wealth status. How would you define your social class based on your own income and wealth? Your family's income and wealth? Which reveals more about your life chances?

STATE STATS

What Does It Mean to Be Poor?

Photo 2.2

The richest U.S. billionaire according to the Forbes 2011 list is Microsoft's Bill Gates, with a fortune estimated at $56 billion. With his wife Melinda, Gates created the Bill and Melinda Gates Foundation, supporting programs and research to reduce inequities in the United States and throughout the world.

The often-cited definition of poverty offered by the World Bank is an income of $1.25 per day. This represents "extreme poverty," the minimal amount necessary for a person to fulfill his or her basic needs. According to the organization (World Bank 2009),

> Poverty is hunger. Poverty is lack of shelter. Poverty is being sick and not being able to see a doctor. Poverty is not being able to go to school and not knowing how to read. Poverty is not having a job, is fear for the future, living one day at a time. Poverty is losing a child to illness brought about by unclean water. Poverty is powerlessness, lack of representation and freedom.

Due to significant improvements in education, gender equality, health care, environmental degradation, and hunger, there has been a decline in both the overall poverty rate and the number of poor according to the World Bank (2012). For 1981, a total of 1.94 billion people (or 52%) in the developing world had consumption levels below $1.25. For 2008, the number had declined to 1.29 billion (or 22%).

Sociologists offer two definitions of poverty, absolute and relative poverty. **Absolute poverty** refers to a lack of basic necessities, such as food, shelter, and income. **Relative poverty** refers to a situation in which some people fail to achieve the average income or lifestyle enjoyed by the rest of society. Our mainstream standard of living defines the "average" American lifestyle. Individuals living in relative poverty may be able to afford basic necessities, but they cannot maintain a standard of living comparable to that of other members of society. Relative poverty emphasizes the inequality of income and the growing gap between the richest and poorest Americans. A definition reflecting the relative nature of income inequality was adopted by the European (EU) Council of Ministers in 1984: "The poor shall be taken to mean persons, families and groups of persons whose resources (material, cultural and societal) are so limited as to exclude them from

Photo 2.3a & 2.3b

Not everyone in our society can attain the dream of owning a home. For more than 600,000 Americans, home is life on the streets, in shelters, and in transitional housing.

the minimum acceptable way of life in the member state in which they live" (European Commission 1985).

The Federal Definitions of Poverty

There are two federal policy measures of poverty: the poverty threshold and the poverty guidelines. These measures are important for statistical purposes and for determining eligibility for social service programs.

The **poverty threshold** is the original federal poverty measure developed by the Social Security Administration and updated each year by the U.S. Census Bureau. The threshold is used to estimate the number of people in poverty. Originally developed by Mollie Orshansky for the Social Security Administration in 1964, the original poverty threshold was based on the economy food plan, the least costly of four nutritionally adequate food plans designed by the U.S. Department of Agriculture (USDA). Based on the 1955 Household Food Consumption Survey, the USDA determined that families of three or more people spent about one third of their after-tax income on food. The poverty threshold was set at three times the cost of the economy food plan.

Photo 2.4

Urban youth are the most vulnerable poor population, barely surviving without shelter, food, and clothing. Cities in developing nations find themselves unable to provide basic services, such as education and health care, to these youth.

The definition of the poverty threshold was revised in 1969 and 1981. Since 1969, annual adjustments in the levels have been based on the consumer price index (CPI) instead of changes in the cost of foods in the economy food plan.

The poverty threshold considers money income before taxes and excludes capital gains and noncash benefits (public housing, Medicaid, and food stamps). The poverty threshold does not apply to people residing in military barracks or institutional group quarters or to unrelated individuals younger than age 15 (foster children). In addition, the definition of the poverty threshold does not vary geographically.

The **poverty guidelines**, issued each year by the U.S. Department of Health and Human Services, are used to determine family or individual eligibility for federal programs such as Head Start, the National School Lunch Program, or the Low Income Home Energy Assistance Program. The poverty guidelines are designated by the year in which they are issued. For example, the guidelines issued in January 2012 are designated as the 2012 poverty guidelines, but the guidelines reflect price changes through the calendar year 2011. There are separate poverty guidelines for Alaska and Hawaii. The current poverty threshold and guidelines are presented in Tables 2.2 and 2.3.

Table 2.2

Poverty Threshold in 2011 by Size of Family and Number of Related Children Under 18 Years (Dollars)

Size of Family Unit	None	1	2	3	4	5	6	7	8+
			Related Children Under 18 Years						
One person under 65	11,702								
65 years or older	10,788								
Two people									
Householder under 65	15,063	15,504							
Householder 65 or older	13,596	15,446							
Three	17,595	18,106	18,123						
Four	23,201	23,581	22,811	22,891					
Five	27,979	28,386	27,517	26,844	26,434				
Six	32,181	32,309	31,643	31,005	30,056	29,494			
Seven	37,029	37,260	36,463	35,907	34,872	33,665	32,340		
Eight	41,414	41,779	41,027	40,368	39,433	38,247	37,011	36,697	
Nine or more	49,818	50,059	49,393	48,835	47,917	46,654	45,512	45,229	43,487

Source: U.S. Census Bureau 2012.

Table 2.3

2012 Federal Poverty Guidelines

Size of Family Unit	48 Contiguous States and District of Columbia	Alaska	Hawaii
1	$11,170	$13,970	$12,860
2	15,130	18,920	17,410
3	19,090	23,870	21,960
4	23,050	28,820	26,510
5	27,010	33,770	31,060
6	30,970	38,720	35,610
7	34,930	43,670	40,160
8	38,890	48,620	44,710
For each additional person, add	3,960	4,950	4,550

Source: U.S. Department of Health and Human Services 2012.

Who Are the Poor?

In 2011, the poverty rate was 15.0%, or 46.2 million, compared with the most recent low poverty rate of 11.3%, or 31.6 million, in 2000 (DeNavas-Walt, Proctor, and Smith 2007; DeNavas-Walt et al. 2012). (See Table 2.4 for a summary of poverty characteristics for 2011 and U.S. Data Map 2.1 for 2011 poverty rates by state.)

Based on 2011 U.S. poverty figures and redefined racial and ethnic categories, Whites (who reported being White and no other race category, along with Whites who reported

 Minority Income

Table 2.4

Selected Poverty Characteristics, 2011 (Numbers in Thousands)

	Number	Poverty Rate (%)
Total	46,247	15.0
Race/Ethnicity		
White alone or in combination	30,849	12.8
White alone, non-Hispanic	19,171	9.8
Black alone or in combination	10,929	27.6
Asian alone or in combination	1,973	12.8
Hispanic (of any race)	13,244	25.3
Age		
Under 18 years of age	16,134	21.9
18 to 64 years	26,492	13.7
65 years or older	3,620	8.7
Inside Metropolitan Areas		
Inside principal cities	20,007	20.0
Outside principal cities	18,195	11.3
Outside Metropolitan Areas	8,045	17.0

Source: DeNavas-Walt et al. 2012.

Note: White alone, Black alone, and Asian alone include respondents who indicated only one race. White alone or in combination, Black alone or in combination, and Asian alone or in combination include respondents who indicated one race or a combination of races.

being White plus another race category) compose the largest group of poor individuals in the United States. About 41.5% of the U.S. poor are non-Hispanic Whites. However, the poverty rate for Whites is the lowest, at 9.9%. Blacks continue to have the highest poverty rate, 27.6%, followed by Hispanics with a rate of 25.3% (DeNavas-Walt et al. 2012). Analysts predict that within a few years, Latinos will have a higher poverty rate than Blacks do. Racial segregation and discrimination have contributed to the high rate of minority poverty in the United States. Minority groups are disadvantaged by their lower levels of education, lower levels of work experience, lower wages, and chronic health problems—all characteristics associated with higher poverty rates (Iceland 2003).

Children and Poverty

According to the National Center for Children in Poverty (2001), children are more likely to live in poverty than Americans in any other age group. Family economic conditions affect the material and social resources available to children. The quality of their education, the neighborhood environment, and exposure to environmental contaminants may reinforce and widen the gaps between poorer and more affluent children and adults (Holzer et al. 2008).

The poverty rate among children is higher in the United States than in most other major Western industrialized nations. In 2009, the United Nations Children's Fund (UNICEF) released its report on child well-being in rich countries, identifying the percentage of children living in relative poverty (in households with income below 50% of the national median income). Romania ranks highest at 25.5%, followed by the United States at 23.1%. UNICEF noted that by its measure more than 15% of 200 million children living in the 35 listed countries are living in relative poverty. (Refer to Figure 2.1 for additional data.)

Single Parenthood

Based on data collected by the U.S. Census, the poverty rate for children peaked in 1993 at 22.5%. In 2011, the poverty rate among children was 21.9% (DeNavas-Walt et al. 2007, 2012). There remains a wide variation in children's poverty rates among states, from 10.8% in New

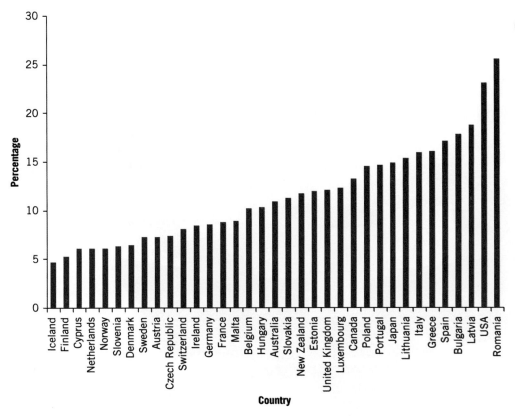

Figure 2.1

The Percentage of Children (Aged 0 to 17) Living in Households With Income Below 50% of the National Median Income, 2009

Source: United Nations Children's Fund 2012.

Hampshire to 31% in Mississippi among children under age 18 (Children's Defense Fund 2011). Rates remain high among specific groups—minority children and children of immigrants. There were more poor Hispanic children than poor Black or poor White children. Almost 60% of all children in poverty lived in single-parent families (Children's Defense Fund 2011).

Families with a female householder and no spouse present were more likely to be poor than were families with a male householder and no spouse present, 31.2% versus 16.1%. In contrast, the poverty rate for married-couple families was 6.2% (DeNavas-Walt et al. 2012). Single-parent families are more vulnerable to poverty because there is only one adult income earner, and female heads of household are disadvantaged even further because women in general make less money than men do.

In their analysis of data from the Luxembourg Income Study, Lee Rainwater and Timothy Smeeding (2003) concluded that American single mothers' children fare worse than the majority of their global counterparts. The poverty rate among U.S. children living in single-mother families is close to 50%; the rate is slightly lower in Germany (48%) and Australia (46%). Countries with poverty rates below 20% include Sweden (7%), Finland (8%), Denmark (11%), Belgium (13%), and Norway (14%). Generous social wage (e.g., unemployment) and social welfare programs reduce the poverty rate in these Nordic countries. Rainwater and Smeeding note that, all combined, U.S. wage and welfare programs are much smaller than similar programs in other countries.

Although the majority of poor women and men live in cities and suburbs within metropolitan areas, poverty was still higher for residents outside metropolitan areas (17.0%) than those inside metropolitan areas (14.6%). Among those living in metropolitan areas, the poverty rate within central cities was 20.0%, higher than the rate in the suburbs, 11.3% (DeNavas-Walt et al. 2012). However, suburban residents experienced a sharp increase in poverty levels, growing from 8% in 2001. The trend has been characterized by demographers as the suburbanization of poverty (Deparle and Tavernise 2011).

 Social Stratification

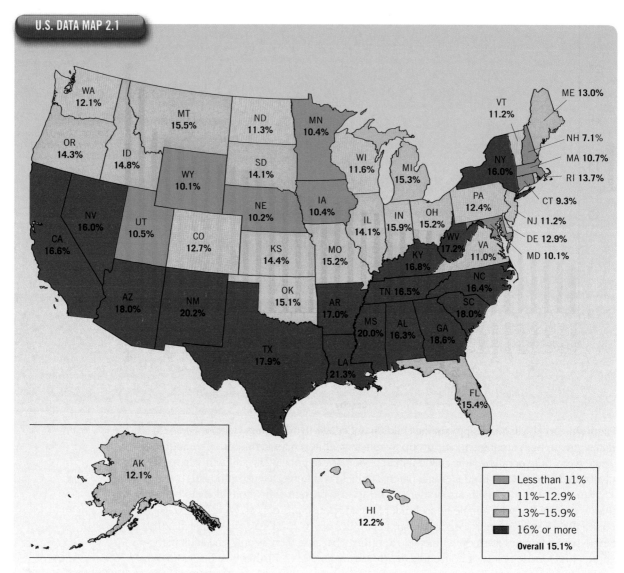

U.S. DATA MAP 2.1

State	Rate
WA	12.1%
OR	14.3%
MT	15.5%
ND	11.3%
MN	10.4%
ME	13.0%
VT	11.2%
NH	7.1%
MA	10.7%
NY	16.0%
RI	13.7%
ID	14.8%
SD	14.1%
WI	11.6%
MI	15.3%
PA	12.4%
CT	9.3%
WY	10.1%
NE	10.2%
IA	10.4%
IL	14.1%
IN	15.9%
OH	15.2%
NJ	11.2%
NV	16.0%
UT	10.5%
CO	12.7%
WV	17.2%
VA	11.0%
DE	12.9%
MD	10.1%
CA	16.6%
KS	14.4%
MO	15.2%
KY	16.8%
NC	16.4%
AZ	18.0%
NM	20.2%
OK	15.1%
AR	17.0%
TN	16.5%
SC	18.0%
MS	20.0%
AL	16.3%
GA	18.6%
TX	17.9%
LA	21.3%
FL	15.4%
AK	12.1%
HI	12.2%

Legend:
- Less than 11%
- 11%–12.9%
- 13%–15.9%
- 16% or more
- **Overall 15.1%**

Percentage of People in Poverty by State, Two-Year Average, 2010–2011

Source: DeNavas-Walt et al. 2012.

Poverty Typologies   The South had the highest poverty rate (16%), followed by the West (15.8%), the Midwest (14%), and the Northeast (13.1%; DeNavas-Walt et al. 2012). The states with the highest two-year average poverty rates in 2011 were Louisiana, New Mexico, and Mississippi. (Refer to U.S. Data Map 2.1.) Poverty rates vary across geographic areas because of differences in person-specific and place-specific characteristics (Levernier, Partridge, and Rickman 2000). A region may have a higher rate of poverty because it contains disproportionately higher shares of demographic groups associated with greater poverty, such as racial/ethnic minority groups, female heads of household, and low-skilled workers. Area poverty is also related to place-specific factors such as the region's economic performance, employment growth, industry structure, and cost of living.

There is an additional category of poverty—the working poor. These are men and women who spent at least 27 weeks working or looking for work, but whose incomes fell below the official poverty level. For 2009, there were 10.4 million working poor (U.S. Bureau of Labor Statistics 2011). Black and Hispanic workers were more likely than White or Asian workers to be working poor. Those with less than a high school diploma are more likely to be classified as working poor than college graduates are. Service occupations accounted for one third of all those classified as working poor (U.S. Bureau of Labor Statistics 2011).

David Brady, Andrew Fullerton, and Jennifer Moren Cross (2010) compared the status of working poor in the United States along with 17 other affluent Western democracies. The rate of working poverty was highest in the United States (14.5% of the population). Belgium had the lowest rate of working poor at 2.23%. The sociologists documented how several demographic characteristics were related to the likelihood of being working poor—individuals from households with one income earner, with more children, or with a young household head with low educational attainment.

Sociological Perspectives on Social Class and Poverty

Why do some prosper while others remain poor? Why does poverty persist in some families, but other families are able to improve their economic situation? In the next section, we will review the four sociological perspectives to understand the bases of class inequality.

Functionalist Perspective

Functionalists assume that not everyone in society can and should be equal. From this perspective, inequality is necessary for the social order. And what is equally important is how each of us recognizes and accepts our status in the social structure. Erving Goffman (1951), an interactionist, offers a functional explanation of social stratification, defining it as a universal characteristic of social life. Goffman argues that as we interact with one another, accepting our status in society and acknowledging the status of others, we provide "harmony" to the social order. But "this kind of harmony requires that the occupant of each status act towards others in a manner which conveys the impression that his conception of himself and of them is the same as their conception of themselves and him" (Goffman 1951:294).

Functionalists contend that some individuals are more important to society because of their function to society. For example, society values the lifesaving work of a medical surgeon more than the retail function of a grocery store cashier. Based on the value of one's work or talent, society rewards individuals at the top of the social structure (surgeons) with more wealth, income, or power than those lower down in the social structure (grocery cashiers). According to this perspective, individuals are sorted according to their abilities or characteristics—their age, strength, intelligence, physical ability, or even sex—to play their particular role for society. Certain individuals are better suited for their positions in society than others. Our social institutions, especially education, sort everyone into their proper places and reward them accordingly. Because not all of us can (or should) become surgeons, the system ensures that only the most talented and qualified become surgeons. In many ways, the functionalist argument reinforces the belief that we are naturally different.

What Does It Mean to Me?

The functionalist perspective is often criticized for its value argument. Does society accurately assess and reward a position for its value, for its function? For example, the average salary for a public elementary school teacher in 2010 was $54,330, whereas the average salary of a National Football League (NFL) player for 2011–2012 was $1.9 million. Before he became a Super Bowl champion in 2007, Indianapolis Colts quarterback Peyton Manning signed a $98 million seven-year deal with his team. How does society determine the value of a professional football player? Of a public school teacher?

STATE STATS

Functionalists observe that poverty is a product of our social structure. Specifically, rapid economic and technological changes eliminated the need for low-skilled labor, creating a population of workers who were unskilled and untrained for this new economy. In many ways, theorists from this perspective expect this disparity among workers, arguing that only the most qualified should fill the important jobs in society and be rewarded for their talent.

Herbert Gans (1971) argued that poverty exists because it is functional for society. Gans explained that the poor uphold the legitimacy of dominant norms. The poor help reinforce cultural ideals of hard work and the notion that anyone can succeed if only people would try (so if you fail, it is your fault). Poverty helps preserve social boundaries. It separates the haves from the have-nots by their economics and according to their educational attainment, marriage, and residence. The poor also provide a low-wage labor pool to do the "dirty work" that no one else wants to do.

Our social welfare system, designed to address the problem of poverty, has been accused of being dysfunctional itself; critics suggest that the welfare bureaucracy is primarily concerned with its own survival. Poverty helps create jobs for the nonpoor, particularly the social welfare system designed to assist the poor. As a result, the social welfare bureaucracy will develop programs and structures that will only ensure its survival and legitimacy. Based on her personal experience working with and for the system, Theresa Funiciello (1993) observed, "Countless middle class people were making money, building careers, becoming powerful and otherwise benefiting from poverty. . . . The poverty industry once again substituted its own interests for that of poor people" (p. xix). We will discuss this further in the next perspective.

Conflict Perspective

Like the functionalist perspective, the conflict perspective argues that inequality is inevitable, but for different reasons. For a functionalist, inequality is necessary because of the different positions and roles needed in society. From a conflict perspective, inequality is systematically created and maintained by those trying to preserve their advantage over the system.

For Karl Marx, one's social class is solely determined by one's position in the economic system: You are either a worker or an owner of the means of production. But social class, according to Weber, is multidimensional. Economic factors include **income**, the money earned for one's work, and **wealth**, the value of one's personal assets such as savings and property. A person's social class is also influenced by **prestige**, the amount of social respect or standing given to an individual based on occupation. We assign higher prestige to occupations that require specialized education or training, that provide some social good to society, or that make more money. A final component of class is **power**. Weber defined power as the ability to achieve one's goals despite the opposition of others. Power is the ability to do whatever you want because no one can stop you.

Power is not limited to individuals. People with similar interests (or with similar income, wealth, and prestige backgrounds) often collaborate to increase their advantage in society. C. Wright Mills ([1959] 2000) argued that the United States is ruled by what he called a **power elite**. According to Mills, this elite group is composed of business, political, and military leaders. This elite group has absolute power because of its ability to withhold resources and prevent others from realizing their interests. Mills identified how the power elite effectively make decisions regarding economic policy and national security—controlling the difference between a boom economy and a bust economy or peace and war abroad (Gilbert 2003). Refer to this chapter's In Focus feature for an in-depth look at the modern power elite.

In Focus

The Power of Political Action Committees

G. William Domhoff (2002) argues that real power is **distributive power**, the power individuals or groups have over other individuals or groups. Power matters when a group has the ability to control strategic resources and opportunities to obtain such resources. Money, land, information, and skills are strategic resources when they are needed by individuals to do what they want to do (Hachen 2001). Domhoff argues that distributive power is limited to an elite group of individuals whose economic, political, and social relationships are closely interrelated. Control over four major social networks—economic, political, military, and religious—can be turned into a strong organizational base for wielding power (Mann 1986).

Political action committees (PACs) have been characterized as extensions of the influence of the power elite. While contributions to a candidate's campaign are limited to $2,500 per election from each individual donor, PACs, or super PACs as they more often referred to, can collect unlimited amounts from individuals and corporations. In 1947, corporations were banned from using their profits to endorse or oppose political candidates; however, in 2010, the U.S. Supreme Court ruled the restriction unconstitutional and allowed corporations the same rights as individuals when it comes to political speech (the donation of money).

Campaign-finance reform activists predicted that the ruling would increase the influence of special interest groups, allowing what has been characterized as a corruption of our democracy or corporate electioneering. Though PACs cannot formally coordinate their activities or communicate exclusively with candidates, PACs are closely aligned with candidates and important sources for campaign money. For example, Sheldon and Miriam Adelson donated $10 million to Winning Our Future, the PAC that supported Newt Gingrich's 2012 presidential campaign. The Adelsons are longtime friends and supporters of Gingrich. Their contribution was described as leveling the political playing field between Gingrich and Governor Mitt Romney in critical primaries in Florida and South Carolina (Confessore 2012). The Adelsons supported Restore Our Future, Romney's PAC.

Another influential political coalition is the group of organizations known as the 527s. These organizations are independent political groups named for a section of the Internal Revenue Service tax code that regulates the financial activities of all political groups. Like PACs, there are no restrictions on contributions to 527s. During the 2004 presidential election, Senator John Kerry was targeted by the 527 Swift Boat Veterans for Truth, falsely attacking his Vietnam service record. The campaign was so memorable that the term *swift boating* has come to refer to an untrue or unfair political attack.

Log on to the Study Site, Chapter 2, at www.sagepub.com/leonguerrero4e for more information.

Michael Harrington (1963) argues, "The real explanation of why the poor are where they are is that they made the mistake of being born to the wrong parents, in the wrong section of the country, in the wrong industry, or in the wrong racial or ethnic group" (p. 21). Inequalities built into our social structure create and perpetuate poverty. As Manning Marable (2000) states, capitalism is fraud. Although it promotes the idea that everyone has a fair and equal chance to succeed, advantages are given to members of particular groups based on their gender, race, or social class.

Conflict theorists assert that poverty exists because those in power want to maintain and expand their base of power and interests, with little left to share with others. Welfare bureaucracies—local, state, and national—represent important interest groups that influence the creation and implementation of welfare policies. A welfare policy reflects the political economy of the community in which it is implemented (Handler and Hasenfeld 1991).

Francis Fox Piven and Richard A. Cloward (1993) state that the principal function of welfare is to allow the capitalist class to maintain control over labor. Welfare policy has been used by the state to stifle protest and to enforce submissive work norms. During periods of economic crisis, the state expands welfare rolls to pacify the poor and reduce the likelihood of serious uprising. However, during economic growth or stability, the state attempts to reduce the number of people on welfare, forcing the poor or dislocated workers back into the expanding labor force. Those who remain on welfare are condemned and stigmatized for their dependence on the system. For example, in 2011, more than 36 states considered drug testing for Temporary Assistance for Needy Families (TANF) recipients (Sulzberger 2011). Opponents of this policy argue that punitive testing policies perpetuate the stereotype that people on public assistance are morally corrupt and more likely to use drugs. It also distracts from the need for and access to drug treatment and prevention. A 2012 assessment of the Florida welfare drug test law revealed that there were no direct savings for the state; contrary to the law's intent, it did not identify many drug users and had no effect on reducing the number of individuals applying for welfare assistance (Alvarez 2012).

 Drug Testing

Feminist Perspective

Feminist scholars define the welfare state as an arena of political struggle. The drive to maintain male dominance and the patriarchal family is assumed to be the principal force shaping the formation, implementation, and outcomes of U.S. welfare policy (Neubeck and Cazenave 2001).

Social welfare scholar Mimi Abramovitz (1996) notes that welfare has historically distinguished between the deserving poor (widows with children) and the undeserving poor (single and divorced mothers). In the 1970s and 1980s, media and politicians created the image of the "Cadillac driving, champagne sipping, penthouse living welfare queens" (Zucchino 1999:13), suggesting that women—specifically, single mothers—were abusing welfare assistance. Women were accused of having more children to avoid work and to increase their welfare benefits. Marriage, hard work, honesty, and abstinence were offered as solutions to their poverty. The negative stereotypes of poor women stigmatized these women and fueled support for punitive social policies (Abramovitz 1996).

As a group, teenage mothers were targeted during welfare reform in the 1990s. They were blamed for everything, as one journalist wrote: "The fact remains: every threat to the fabric of this country—from poverty to crime to homelessness—is connected to out-of-wedlock teen pregnancy" (Alder 1994:41). Even though little empirical evidence supports the link between birthrates and welfare benefits, the government seeks to punish these women, making it difficult for them to obtain and retain public assistance and to gain self-sufficiency.

Fraser (1989) argues that there are two types of welfare programs: masculine programs related to the labor market (social security, unemployment compensation) and feminine programs related to the family or household (Aid to Families with Dependent Children [AFDC], food stamps, and Medicaid). The welfare system is separate and unequal. Fraser believes that masculine programs are rational, generous, and nonintrusive, whereas feminine programs are inadequate, intrusive, and humiliating. The quintessential program for women, AFDC, institutionalized the feminization of poverty by failing to provide adequate support, training, and income to ensure self-sufficiency for women (Gordon 1994). The program operated from 1935 to 1996. As described by Johnnie Tillmon (2002), a welfare recipient and welfare rights organizer,

> The truth is that AFDC is like a super-sexist marriage. You trade in a man for the man. But you can't divorce him if he treats you bad. He can divorce you, of course, cut you off anytime he wants. The man runs everything. In ordinary marriage sex is supposed to be for your husband. On AFDC you're not supposed to have any sex at all. You give [up] control of your own body. . . . You may even have to agree to get your tubes tied so you can never have more children just to avoid being cut off welfare.

Our current welfare system, the Personal Responsibility and Work Opportunity Reconciliation Act (PRWORA), has been criticized for its treatment of women and their families. PRWORA created a pool of disciplined low-wage laborers: women who must take any job that is available or find themselves and their families penalized by the government (Piven 2002). With its emphasis on work as the path to self-sufficiency, PRWORA forces women back to the same low-pay, low-skill jobs that may have led them to their poverty in the first place (Lafer 2002). The new program requirements, as Debra Henderson, Ann Tickamyer, and Barry Tadlock (2005) argue, also deny women the choice to be full-time mothers. Eligibility guidelines force poor women to work, making them choose between the competing roles of good mother and good welfare recipient. The new policies fail to address the real barriers facing women: low job skills and educational attainment, racism and discrimination in the labor market, and the competing demands of work and caring for their children.

Interactionist Perspective

An interactionist would draw attention to how class differences are communicated through symbols, how the meaning of these symbols is constructed or constrained by social forces, and how these symbols reproduce social inequality. Our language reflects the quality of life that is associated with different amounts of economic resources. We distinguish the "very rich" from the "stinking rich" and someone who is "poor" versus "dirt poor" (Rainwater and Smeeding 2003).

Some sociologists have suggested that poverty is based on a **culture of poverty**, a set of norms, values, and beliefs that encourage and perpetuate poverty. In this view, moral deficiencies of individuals or their families lead to a life of poverty. Oscar Lewis (1969), Edward Banfield (1974), and Myron Magnet ([1993] 2000) argue that the poor are socialized differently (e.g., living from moment to moment) and are likely to pass these values on to their children.

Patterns of generational poverty—poor parents have poor children, who in turn become poor adults, and so on—seem to support this theory.

Yet the culture of poverty explanation has been widely criticized. Opponents argue that there is no evidence that the poor have a different set of values and beliefs. This perspective defines poverty as a persistent state; that is, once you are poor, your values prohibit you from ever getting out of poverty. In fact, poverty data reveal that for most individuals and families, continuous spells of poverty are likely to last less than two years (Harris 1993).

 Welfare

Interactionists also focus on the public's perception of welfare and of welfare recipients. Most Americans do not know any welfare recipients personally or have any direct contact with the welfare system. Their views on welfare are likely to be shaped by what they see on television and by what they read in newspapers and magazines (Weaver 2000). As a society, we have developed a sense of the "undeserving poor"; dependent mothers and fathers and nonworking recipients have become powerful negative symbols in society (Norris and Thompson 1995). Program requirements help further stigmatize recipients. For example, though the state of New York stopped requiring fingerprinting for food stamp recipients in 2007, New York City officials continued the practice until 2012. Advocates for the poor and hungry asserted that fingerprinting deterred individuals and families from getting the aid that they needed and that they were eligible for.

Martin Gilens (1999) explains that *welfare* has become a code word for *race*. Race and racism are important in understanding public and political support for antipoverty programs (Lieberman 1998; Neubeck and Cazenave 2001; Quadagno 1994). Gilens states that Americans perceive welfare as a Black phenomenon, believing that Blacks make up 50% of the poor population (compared with an actual 25%). This belief is exacerbated by the notion that Blacks are on welfare not because of blocked opportunities, but largely because of their lack of effort.

 Black Poverty

Gilens (1999) asserts that the news media are primarily responsible for building this image of Black poverty, for the "racialization of poverty." During the War on Poverty in the early 1960s, the media focused on White rural America, but as the civil rights movement began to build in the mid-1960s, the media turned their attention to urban poverty, and the racial character of poverty coverage changed. Between 1965 and 1967, sensationalized portrayals of Black poverty were used to depict the waste, inefficiency, or abuse of the welfare system, whereas positive coverage of poverty was more likely to include pictures and portrayals of Whites. After 1967 and for most of the following three decades, larger proportions of Blacks appeared in news coverage of most poverty topics. "Black faces are unlikely to be found in media stories on the most sympathetic subgroups of the poor, just as they are comparatively absent from media coverage of poverty during times of heightened sympathy for the poor" (Gilens 1999:132). According to Gilens, this exaggerated link between Blacks and poverty is a serious obstacle to public support for antipoverty programs.

What Does It Mean to Me?

Refer to U.S. Data Map 2.1. What percentage of the population in your state is living in poverty? Using our sociological imagination, we begin to recognize the social and institutional conditions that create poverty (see Table 2.5 for a summary). Which of these perspectives best explains why poverty exists in your state?

 STATE STATS

Table 2.5

Summary of Sociological Perspectives: Inequalities Based on Social Class

	Functionalist	Conflict/Feminist	Interactionist
Explanations of social class and poverty	Inequality is inevitable and emerges from the social structure. Poverty serves a social function.	Inequality is systematically maintained by those trying to preserve their class advantage. Class is based on multiple dimensions—income, wealth, prestige, and power. Welfare bureaucracies represent important interest groups that influence the creation and implementation of welfare policies.	Each social class has a specific set of norms, values, and beliefs. Poverty is a learned phenomenon based on a "culture of poverty" that encourages and perpetuates poverty. The public's perception of the welfare system and of welfare recipients is shaped by the media, political groups, and stereotypes.
Questions asked about social class and poverty	What are the functions and dysfunctions of inequality? What portions of society benefit from poverty?	What powerful interest groups determine class inequalities? How do our welfare policies reflect specific political, economic, and social interest groups?	Is poverty learned behavior? How are our perceptions of the poor determined by the media, news reports, and politicians? Has society created two images—the deserving versus the undeserving poor? Are these images accurate?

The Consequences of Poverty

The following section is not an exhaustive list of the consequences of poverty. Remaining chapters will also highlight the relationship between social class and the experience of a specific social problem (such as educational attainment, drug abuse, or access to health care). In addition, given the intersectionality of all the bases of inequality covered in this section of the book, there is a persistent overlap in the experience of social problems as a result of one's class, race, gender, sexual orientation, and age.

Health and Health Care

About 70% of children who live below the poverty line report being in excellent or good health in comparison with 85% of children who live at or above the poverty line. Children below the poverty line have lower rates of immunization and higher rates of activity limitation because of chronic illness than do children who live above the poverty line (Federal Interagency Forum on Child and Family Statistics 2002).

Sociology and Children

The increasing cost of quality health care and prescription drugs is a concern for many elderly. Though Medicare provides health coverage for men and women older than 65 years of age, most elderly still spend their own money for out-of-pocket (OOP) health care expenses, particularly for prescription drugs. In 2003, nearly one third of all elderly spent $100 or more of their own money per month for prescription drugs (Safran et al. 2005). For more on the nation's Medicare program, refer to Chapter 6.

Most of the working poor are not eligible for public assistance medical programs, even though their employers do not provide health insurance (Seccombe and Amey 1995). Most individuals without health insurance coverage make less than $50,000 per year. According to the U.S. Census Bureau, in 2011, 25.4% of households with incomes less than $25,000 and 21.5% of households with incomes between $25,000 and $49,000 did not have health insurance coverage (DeNavas-Walt et al. 2012). As household income increases, so does the likelihood of having health insurance. Only 15.4% and 7.8% of households with incomes between $50,000 and $74,999 and $75,000 or more, respectively, did not have health insurance (DeNavas-Walt et al. 2012). Employment does not guarantee health insurance coverage.

Although the poor are eligible for medical care under Medicaid, Medicaid coverage is not comprehensive, forcing most to seek treatment only in cases of medical emergencies. Having a routine physical or a regular family doctor is rare among poor and low-income families. Until 1997, families were eligible for Medicaid only if they were also receiving government assistance.

In 1997, the State Children's Health Insurance Program was established to help states expand Medicaid coverage, establish a separate child health insurance program, or combine approaches to cover children with family incomes up to 200% of the poverty line or higher. Beginning in 1998, the federal government also provided Transitional Medical Assistance for families leaving welfare for work. The program provides as much as 12 months of coverage when families lose regular Medicaid coverage because of an increase in earnings (leaving welfare for work). Despite these medical provisions, a review of data from 25 states where welfare recipients have left welfare for work indicates that there has been a decline in health coverage among eligible low-income families with children.

Jocelyn Guyer (2000) says that in most states, roughly half of parents in families that left welfare and more than one third of children in those families lose Medicaid coverage. In some states, the problem is severe. In New York, 65% of children lost Medicaid after they left welfare; in Mississippi, 56% of children also lost coverage. Even among families who left welfare for work, fewer than half receive health coverage through their employers. As a result, families are more likely to have unmet medical needs after leaving welfare. Guyer notes that although little is known about why eligible families lose health coverage, some studies reveal that families were unaware of their eligibility for programs such as Medicaid or Transitional Medical Assistance.

Food Insecurity and Hunger

Food Insecurity

About 15% of households, or 17.2 million American families, were food insecure at least some time during 2010 (Coleman-Jensen, Nord, Andrews, and Carlson 2011). Analysts attribute the increase to rising unemployment rates and food prices. **Food insecure** means that these families did not always have access to enough food for all members of the household to enjoy active and healthy lives. Fifty-nine percent of the food insecure households said they participated during the previous month in one or more federal food and nutrition assistance programs—the National School Lunch Program, the Supplemental Nutrition Assistance Program (described below), and the Special Supplemental Nutrition Program for Women, Infants and Children. About 23% obtained food from a food pantry sometime in the year, and 3.8% ate one or more meals at an emergency kitchen. The prevalence of food insecurity is higher for certain groups: single female–headed households with children (35.1%), Black households (25.1%), Hispanic households (26.2%), and households with income below the poverty line (33.8%; Coleman-Jensen et al. 2011).

The USDA provided food assistance through one of 17 public food assistance programs. The U.S. food stamp program, now called the Supplemental Nutrition Assistance Program (SNAP), is the nation's largest nutrition program for low-income individuals and families. During 2008, the program served an average of 40.3 million low-income Americans each month. The average monthly benefit was $134 per person. Food stamps cannot be used to buy nonfood items (personal hygiene supplies, paper products), alcoholic beverages, vitamins and medicines, hot food products, or any food that will be eaten in the store. SNAP was credited with reducing the poverty rate during the recent recession (Center for Budget and Policy Priorities 2012). Counting SNAP benefits as income reduces the number of households in extreme poverty in 2011 from 1.46 million to 800,000. Although SNAP and other USDA programs have been shown to be effective in improving the purchasing power and nutritional status of specific populations, a large segment of low-income Americans are not being adequately served or served at all by these programs (Nicholas-Casebolt and McGrath Morris 2001). In 2009, only 60% of the eligible working poor participated in the program (Center for Budget and Policy Priorities 2012).

For one week in 2007, Governor Theodore R. Kulongoski (D-Ore.) challenged fellow Oregonians to join him and his wife Mary to live on an average Oregon food stamp budget of $21 per week per person or $3 a day. His efforts drew state, national, and global attention to food insecurity in his home state of Oregon, as well as the need for the federal government to preserve the current level of food stamp benefits. A sample of the governor and his wife's dinner items is listed in Table 2.6. Before his challenge week, the governor and his wife spent an average of $51 per week on food, not including his meals while at work or during official functions; during his challenge week, their final food bill was $20.97 per person. Governor Kulongoski reported several challenges he and his wife experienced throughout the week—the demoralizing experience of not having enough to pay for all the food in their cart, having to make tough decisions on the quality and amount of food they could purchase, and experiencing hunger throughout the week as their food supply ran out (Kulongoski 2007). Since Kulongoski's challenge, there have been several food stamp budget challenges sponsored by faith leaders, politicians, or news reporters, highlighting the difficulties of eating a healthy and sustainable diet on the standard food stamp allotments.

As reported by Briefel et al. (2003), food pantries and emergency kitchens play an important role in the nutritional safety net for America's low-income and needy populations. These organizations are part of the Emergency Food Assistance System, a network of private organizations operating with some federal support. Almost one third of pantry client households and two fifths of kitchen client households are at or below 50% of the poverty line. The mean monthly income is $781 for pantry client households and $708 for kitchen client households. Food pantries considered by Briefel et al. were likely to serve families with children (45% of households included children), whereas emergency kitchens were likely to serve men living alone (38%) or single adults living with other adults (18%).

The U.S. Conference of Mayors (2011) reported that emergency food assistance increased by an average of 15.5% in 29 U.S. cities. The increase was attributed to first-time requests for food assistance, most from working families stressed by rising food prices and the recession. Fifty-one percent of individuals requesting emergency food assistance were from families. The U.S. Conference of Mayors attributed the increase primarily to unemployment, poverty, low wages, and high housing costs. In 2011, at least 25% of the people needing emergency food assistance did not receive it.

Table 2.6

The Kulongoskis' Dinner Items for One Week (Food Items for Lunch and Breakfast Not Included)

Meat

1 small chicken	$3.06

Produce

1 can of kidney beans	.49
1 can of corn	.50
1 can of tomatoes	.59
1 can of garbanzo beans	.79
1 carrot	.34
2 onions	.50
2 zucchini	1.10
1 10-lb. bag of potatoes	.99
Lettuce	.99
Cabbage	.85

Pasta

2 cup noodles	.76
3 boxes of macaroni/cheese	1.00
Macaroni	.99

Other

Pie crust	.89
Pesto	1.90
Salad dressing	1.19

Dairy

1 gallon of milk	1.00
1 package of imitation cheese	.99
Eggs	1.09

Source: Yardley 2007.

Poor families are disadvantaged because of their low income and because of their location. They are likely to experience higher food prices than the national average (Kaufman et al. 1997). Suburban supermarkets are likely to have lower food prices and a wider selection of food. Grocery stores in central cities and rural areas, where the poor reside, have higher operating costs and tend to be smaller. In rural areas, food prices are also higher because these markets are likely to be smaller and have lower sales volumes (Kaufman et al. 1997).

Lack of Affordable Housing

In the same way that access to child care, medical care, and transportation has been linked to economic self-sufficiency, research has also established the relationship between having affordable housing and leaving welfare. Welfare reform successes are greater among families with assisted housing than among other low-income families (Sard and Waller 2002). Unfortunately, most families who leave welfare for work do not earn enough to afford decent-quality housing, and because of their employment status, they are not eligible for housing assistance. According to 2006 U.S. Census data, 61% of renter households below the poverty line pay more than half of their income to cover housing costs. These families are on severely limited and strained budgets, forcing them to juggle expenses for food, transportation, child care, or other needs. They are more susceptible to falling behind on housing payments and risking eviction and homelessness (Rice and Sard 2007).

The combination of low earnings and scarce housing assistance results in serious housing problems for the working poor. Nearly three fifths of working-poor renters with children who do not have housing assistance spend more than 50% of their income on housing or live in seriously substandard housing, or both. Among unsubsidized poor renter families with at least full-time year-round minimum-wage earnings, 36% spent more than half their income on housing (Sard and Waller 2002).

According to the National Low Income Housing Coalition (Nelson, Treskon, and Pelletiere 2004), there is no state where a low-income worker can reasonably afford a modest one- or two-bedroom rental unit. More than 50% of low-income renter households paid more than half their income for gross rent expenses (rent plus utilities). In 40 states, workers needed to earn more than two times the minimum wage to afford basic housing. In some states— California, Connecticut, Maryland, Massachusetts, New Jersey, and New York—workers needed to earn three times the minimum wage to afford housing (Clemetson 2003). Federal housing programs only serve about one quarter of the eligible low-income households, and few states invest in low-income housing programs (Sard and Waller 2002).

Although Hurricane Katrina struck advantaged and disadvantaged neighborhoods of New Orleans, Louisiana, the odds of living in a damaged area were greater for Blacks, renters, and the unemployed. Katrina was not an equal opportunity disaster (Dreier 2006). In the Lower Ninth Ward, where many of the homes were destroyed by the breach in the Industrial Canal levee, the neighborhoods were more than 85% Black, more than a third of residents were below the poverty line, and 14% were unemployed before Katrina. Recovery of this neighborhood and others was hampered as these victims had fewer resources to return to and rebuild their lives (Logan 2006). As of April 2010, the Lower Ninth Ward had recovered only 22% (1,061) of the original number of households it had in 2000 (4,820). The total population of the Lower Ninth Ward was 2,842 compared with 14,008 in 2000 (Greater New Orleans Community Data Center 2011). The number of homeless in the New Orleans area is estimated between 4,900 and 6,500, double the amount of homeless pre-Katrina. The city's rate of homelessness is among the highest in the country (City of New Orleans Homeless Services Working Group 2011).

Voices in the Community

Maurice Lim Miller

Maurice Lim Miller is the founder and CEO of the Family Independence Initiative (FII), a nontraditional antipoverty program. FII was launched as a research project by Lim Miller and then Oakland Mayor Jerry Brown in 2001. The program allows low-income families to find their own way to self-sufficiency, establishing their own initiatives and finding success. Instead of telling poor families what to do, FII provides a context in which families "can discover for themselves what's important to them and how they can best achieve those goals" (Burak 2001:27). According to Lim Miller (quoted in Bornstein 2011), "When you come into a community that is vulnerable with professionals with power and preset ideas, it is overpowering to families and it can hold them back. Nobody wants to hear that because we are all good guys. But the focus on need undermines our ability to see their strengths—and their ability to see their own strengths."

The program began with 25 families in three cohorts—8 African American families, 6 Salvadoran refugee families, and 11 Iu Mien families (Bornstein 2011). Family groups were asked to write down their goals (e.g., improving child's grades, starting business, buying a home), with FII promising to pay each family $30 for every success, a maximum of $200 per month. Families need to work on their plans together and report their progress to each other and to FII staff. The program structure builds a social network and social capital among the participating families (Burak 2011). The program is unstructured, but "the families have done well because we give them room to do whatever they feel they need to do to get ahead," says Lim (quoted in Fessler 2012).

Assessment data revealed that among the first group of 25 families, household incomes increased 25% after two years. Even after FII's payments stopped, incomes continued to increase, up to 40% higher than the baseline. Lim Miller also established his program in Hawaii and San Francisco. Client success was documented at these sites, with family incomes increasing by 23% and savings up by 240% (Bornstein 2011).

In 2010, Lim Miller was invited to join President Obama's White House Council for Community Solutions, a group of individuals who have "dedicated their lives and careers to civic engagement and social innovation" (White House 2010).

As of 2012, the program was operating a site in Boston with 152 individuals from 35 households.

Responding to Class Inequalities

U.S. Welfare Policy

Social Security Act

New Deal

Throughout the twentieth century, U.S. welfare policy has been caught between two values: the desire to help those who could not help themselves and the concern that assistance could create dependency (Weil and Feingold 2002). The centerpiece of the social welfare system was established by the passage of the Social Security Act of 1935. The act endorsed a system of assistance programs that would provide for Americans who could not care for themselves: widows, the elderly, the unemployed, and the poor.

Under President Franklin D. Roosevelt's New Deal, assistance was provided in four categories: general relief, work relief, social insurance, and categorical assistance. General relief was given to those who were not able to work; most of the people receiving general relief were single men. Work relief programs gave government jobs to those who were unemployed through programs such as the Civilian Conservation Corps and the Works Progress Administration. Social insurance programs included social security and unemployment compensation. Categorical assistance was given to poor families with dependent children, to the blind, and to the elderly. To serve this group, the original welfare assistance program, Aid to Dependent Children (later renamed AFDC), was created (Cammisa 1998).

Categorical programs became the most controversial, and the social insurance programs were the most popular. It was widely believed that social insurance paid people for working, whereas categorical programs paid people for not working. Shortly after these programs were implemented, officials became concerned that individuals might become dependent on government relief (Cammisa 1998). Even President Roosevelt (quoted in Patterson 1981) expressed his doubts about the system he helped create: "Continued dependence upon relief induces a spiritual and moral disintegration fundamentally destructive to the national fibre. To dole out relief in this way is to administer a narcotic, a subtle destroyer of the human spirit" (p. 60).

The next great expansion of the welfare system occurred in the mid-1960s, when President Lyndon Johnson (1965) declared a War on Poverty and implemented his plan to create a Great Society. Rehabilitation of the poor was the cornerstone of Johnson's policies, and what followed was an explosion of social programs: Head Start, Upward Bound, Neighborhood Youth Corps, Job Corps, public housing, and affirmative action. Although poverty was not completely eliminated, defenders of the Great Society say that these programs alleviated poverty, reduced racial discrimination, reduced the stigma attached to being poor, and helped standardize government assistance to the poor. Conversely, opponents claim that these programs coddled the poor and created a generation that expected entitlements from the government (Cammisa 1998).

War on Poverty

During the more than 50 years when the AFDC program operated, welfare rolls were increasing, and, even worse, recipients were staying on government assistance for longer periods. In a strange irony, welfare, the solution for the problem of poverty, became a problem itself (Norris and Thompson 1995). Between 1986 and 1996, many states began to experiment with welfare reforms. Wisconsin was the first state to implement such a reform with a program that included work requirements, benefit limits, and employment goals.

In 1996, PRWORA was passed with a new focus on helping clients achieve self-sufficiency through employment. PRWORA was a bipartisan welfare reform plan to reduce recipients' dependence on government assistance through strict work requirements and welfare time limits. Replacing AFDC, the new welfare program is called Temporary Assistance for Needy Families (TANF). Instead of treating assistance as an entitlement, as it was under AFDC, TANF declares that government help is temporary and has to be earned. Under TANF, there is a federal lifetime limit of 60 months of assistance, although states may put shorter limits on benefits. PRWORA also gave states primary responsibility for designing their assistance programs and for determining eligibility and benefits. States are penalized for not meeting caseload targets, either reducing the number of welfare cases to below 1995 levels or increasing the percentage of cases involved in work activities.

The Poverty Solution

The act had an immediate effect on the number of poor. When PRWORA became law, the poverty rate was 13.7%; 36.5 million individuals were poor, by the government's definition. A year later, the rate declined to 13.3%, and 35.6 million were poor. Rates declined to their lowest point in 2000, 11.3% or 31.6 million. According to the U.S. Census Bureau, the 2000 poverty rate was the lowest since 1979 (DeNavas-Walt et al. 2007).

PRWORA was reauthorized under the Deficit Reduction Act of 2005. The reauthorization requires states to engage more TANF clients in productive work activities leading to self-sufficiency. The five-year cumulative lifetime limit for TANF recipients remains unchanged. Funding of $150 million per year was also provided for healthy marriage and responsible fatherhood initiatives (U.S. Department of Health and Human Services 2006).

Evaluating Microfinance

Advocates have asked for a reduction in poverty, not just caseloads, as the primary goal of welfare reform. They argue that by removing current limits on education and training, enhancing support services for families, restoring benefits to legal immigrants, and stopping the time clock penalty, TANF could be transformed into an effective poverty-reducing program (Coalition on Human Needs 2003). In addition, advocacy groups have encouraged federal lawmakers to increase funding for the TANF block grants to states, to keep pace with inflation at a minimum. Critics point to the economic fragility of low-income families and identify the need for sufficient health insurance, child care, and transportation assistance to help low-income families during times of crisis.

Others have argued for the importance of restoring support for postsecondary education as a means to promote self-sufficiency. According to the Center for Women Policy Studies (2002), after PRWORA, college enrollment among low-income women declined. Yet studies indicate that former TANF recipients with a college education are more likely to stay employed and less likely to return to welfare. For example, a study among former welfare recipients in Oregon found that only 52% of those with less than a high school diploma were employed after two years. In contrast, 90% of former TANF recipients with a bachelor's degree were still employed. Since 1996, 49 states—Oklahoma and the District of Columbia are exceptions—passed legislation to allow secondary education to count as activity under PRWORA. Georgia is the only state that allows recipients to enroll in graduate programs.

During the 2007–2009 recession there was increased concern that poverty was on the rise, straining the safety net of TANF and other government support programs. A depressed economy challenges everyone, but especially those already poor. According to Austin Nichols (2011), history shows that unemployment and poverty rates continue to rise after a recession ends. The effects of poverty deepen over time as individuals exhaust private resources and temporary benefits. The rate of deep poverty (incomes less than half the poverty level) increased from 6.3% in 2009 to 6.7% in 2010. Nichols (2011) advises, "Federal government initiatives are laudable, but cash-strapped families scarred by the labor market and housing market collapses will need more direct help, temporary or not" (p. 2).

Life After Welfare

A strong economy and increased aid to low-income working families contributed to the immediate decline in welfare caseloads after PRWORA (Besharov 2002). Welfare officials often point to how the first to leave welfare were those with the most employable skills. However, research indicates that the early employment success of welfare reform has diminished as the economy faltered. According to the Urban Institute, 32% of welfare recipients were in paid jobs in 1999, but the number had fallen to 28% by 2002. Employment also declined for those who left welfare, from 50% in 1999 to 42% in 2002 (Zedlewski and Loprest 2003).

Sandra Morgen, Joan Acker, and Jill Weigt (2010) examined the consequences of welfare reform among poor individuals and their families in Oregon from 1998 to 2002. Though more than half to three quarters of the TANF clients they followed were employed when they left the welfare rolls, they were working in low-wage occupations and earning wages so low that almost half had incomes below the official poverty line. Once off of welfare, the majority of families continued to struggle to make ends meet and were forced to make tough decisions—for example, putting off medical care, skipping meals to stretch their food budget, or dealing with their utilities being turned off. Many continued to rely on benefits from Oregon's Adult and Family Services. The sociologists concluded that self-sufficiency was still elusive for many families. "Having to depend on low-wage work leaves millions of families facing a combination of job insecurity, inadequate household income, long hours of work, unsatisfactory child care arrangements, and lack of health insurance, sick leave or retirement benefits" (Morgen et al. 2010:148).

Under PRWORA, adults are limited to five years of federal welfare benefits, although 20 states impose shorter time limits. States are allowed to exempt as much as 20% of their caseloads from time limits and can provide state assistance to families that have used up their federal assistance. The first set of time limits expired on September 30, 2002. By 2008, at least a quarter of a million TANF cases were closed due to reaching the federal time limit. In comparison to other families receiving assistance, families who reach their limit are older, have lower education levels, and are more likely to have a disabled family member (Farrell et al. 2008).

Taking a World View

Child Care in Europe

Child care is not just about fostering a child's development; it also supports parents' employment. Child care is essential to promote employment and reduce welfare use among low-income families. Among the working poor, child care arrangements that are difficult to pay for or difficult to access, that do not cover parents' work hours, or that are unreliable can interfere with parents' employment (Gennetian et al. 2002). In addition, child care policies and funding levels have implications for the development and safety of millions of low-income children and youth (Adams and Rohacek 2002). By 1999, child care represented the largest category of state expenditure of TANF funds after cash assistance. In 2011, federal funding for direct child care services was budgeted at $5 billion (U.S. Department of Health and Human Services 2012b). These funds support child care for low-income parents so they can work or attend training/education activities.

European countries offer comprehensive models of public child care. For example, in Scandinavian countries, there is an integrated system of child care centers and organized family day care serving children from birth till school age and managed by social welfare or educational authorities. Public child care is available to children ages 1 through 12 years. Nearly all employed parents have access to child care with little or no waiting time. In Sweden and Denmark, one third to one half of children under 3 years of age are in some form of full-day, publicly supported day care, along with 72% to 82% of children between the ages of 3 and 5 years (Waldfogel 2001). Children of unemployed parents are not eligible for day care in about 40% of locations (Skolverket/Swedish National Agency for Education 2003). Ken Jaffe, director of the International Child Resource Institute in Sweden, says, "Child care is considered a necessity for the economic and social survival of a country, and there is more universal availability of child care. Every neighborhood has a center" (quoted in Polk 1997).

In France and Belgium, there is a two-phase system of child care. For younger children, full-day child care centers are provided under the authority of the social welfare system. Beginning at age 2 1/2 to 3 years, children are enrolled in full-day preprimary programs within the educational system. Enrollment of younger children in child care is about 30% in Belgium and 24% in France. Nearly 100% of all eligible children are enrolled in preprimary programs (Gornick and Meyers 2002).

Not only are child care services more available to European families, but child care staff are better trained and paid in Europe than they are in the United States. Child care workers and educators in European countries are required to have three to five years of vocational or university training. Funding for these extensive child care programs is provided by local, state, or national governments. Care for very young children is partially funded through parental copayments that are scaled according to family income. Lower-income families generally pay nothing whereas more affluent families pay no more than 10% to 15% of their income toward child care (Gornick and Meyers 2002).

The United States has never embraced a national system for providing, funding, and regulating early childhood education and care. It is estimated that the U.S. government spends between 25% and 30% of the cost of child care for children under the age of 3 years and for children ages 3 to 6. Denmark, Finland, France, Norway, and Sweden pay most of the costs of care, about 68% to 100%. One study found that the United States spends about $600 per year per preschool-age child, whereas France spends about $3,000 and Sweden spends more than $4,500 (Waldfogel 2001).

Though TANF evaluation studies reveal overall increases in employment, income, and earnings of families formerly on welfare, many families remained poor or near poor and struggled to maintain employment (Hennessy 2005) even before the 2007 recession. In their five-year study of TANF recipients in New Jersey, Robert Wood, Quinn Moore, and Anu Rangarajan (2008) found that recipients experienced economic progress and setbacks in the years after entering the program. On average, recipients' employment and income levels increased and poverty levels declined for recipients during the five-year period. However, their average income levels were low, about $20,000 per year, and almost half had incomes below the poverty line. Many recipients exited the labor market or returned to poverty sometime during the five years they were tracked. Most at risk were those without a high school degree, with limited work histories, and with work-limiting health conditions.

An analysis by the National Campaign for Jobs and Income Support (2001) found that leavers have trouble finding employment; lack child care, transportation, nutrition, and health care assistance; and remain concentrated in the low-wage labor market. It appears that individuals and families are cycling in and out of poverty, working when jobs are available but never achieving complete economic independence. Women who have multiple barriers to obtaining and retaining employment will be least likely to achieve economic self-sufficiency. Barriers may include low-level work experiences, less than a high school education, substance dependence, physical health problems, and other barriers such as domestic violence, transportation issues, or child care problems. Critics argue that welfare reform made little impact on the real barriers to self-sufficiency—the need for a livable wage, employment opportunities, education or technical training, child care, health insurance, transportation, and affordable housing—which have only been exacerbated during the recession. Since 2007, facing budget deficits, some states reduced their welfare rolls and benefits and shortened time limits. Eleven states cut their rolls by 10% or more (DeParle 2012).

In 2012, the Obama administration gave states more control over how they administer their TANF program, instituting an experimental program for states to "test alternative and innovative strategies, policies and procedures that are designed to improve employment outcomes for needy families" (U.S. Department of Health and Human Services 2012b).

Changing the Definition—Redefining the Poverty Line

The calculation of the U.S. poverty measure has been described as outdated due to how consumption patterns and the types of family needs have changed. For example, the cost of housing now constitutes a larger proportion of household expenses than it did in the 1960s (Ruggles 1990). Due to the rising costs of goods and services other than food (the primary basis for the current poverty calculation), the poverty measure underestimates the income needed for all household necessities (Christopher 2005).

In 1995, a panel of the National Academy of Sciences (NAS) called for a new poverty measure to include the three basic categories of food, clothing, and shelter (and utilities) and a small amount to cover other needs such as household supplies, child care, personal care, and non–work-related transportation. Because the census measure does not show how taxes, noncash benefits, and work-related child care and medical expenses affect people's well-being, the NAS panel cautioned that the current poverty measure cannot reflect how policy changes in these areas affect the poor. In addition, the measure does not consider how the cost of basic goods (food and shelter) has changed since the 1960s. As we have already discussed, the federal poverty measurement assumes that costs are the same across most of the states, except Hawaii and Alaska. It does not make sense that a family of four in Manhattan, New York, is expected to spend the same amount of money for food, clothing, and shelter as a family of four in Manhattan, Kansas (Bhargava and Kuriansky 2002).

 Poverty Measure

The U.S. Census Bureau has been calculating experimental measures of poverty since 1999. For 2001, in measuring the overall poverty rate, the experimental measures reported higher levels of poverty, especially when accounting for geographic differences in housing costs and for medical out-of-pocket expenses. Although the official rate was 11.7%, experimental measures varied between 12.3% and 12.9%. When looking at the poverty rate for specific groups, the experimental measures tend to present a poverty population that looks more like the total population in terms of its mix of people: the elderly, White non-Hispanic individuals, and Hispanics (Short 2001).

In 2011, the U.S. Census Bureau released the Supplemental Poverty Measure (SPM). Rebecca Blank (2011) explains that the SPM provides an alternative way to look at economic need among the lowest-income families. While adjusting for geographic differences, the measure considers the dollar amount spent on food, clothing, utilities and housing, medical needs, and work-related transportation. The measure also considers household income resources including noncash government benefits. The official poverty statistics, according to Blank, are incomplete when it comes to reporting the effect of the government policy on the poor. Though the SPM will not replace the official measure, it has led to a reexamination of the extent of poverty in the United States. Results showed higher SPM poverty rates than the official measure for most groups. For 2010, according to the official poverty measure, there were 46.6 million people (or 15.2% of the population) living in poverty. With the SPM calculation, the poverty estimate increased to 49.1 million (16%). The distribution of poverty shifts, with higher proportions of poor among adults aged 18–64 years and 65 and older, married-couple families or families with male householders, Whites, Asians, the foreign born, homeowners with mortgages, and those with private health insurance (Short 2011).

Other alternative measures have been introduced. The self-sufficiency standard developed by Diana Pearce defines the amount of income necessary to meet basic needs without public assistance (public housing, food stamps, etc.) or private/informal subsidies (free babysitting by a friend, food provided by churches or local food banks; Family Economic Self-Sufficiency Project 2001). The Self-Sufficiency Standard determines the level of income necessary to raise a family out of welfare into total independence. The standard considers regional variations in cost and takes into account family size and composition (much like the U.S. federal measure) and the age of children in the household. The Economic Policy Institute offers a basic family budget calculator, a more realistic measure of the income required to support a basic standard of living. The budgets are individualized for 600 U.S. communities and for different family types.

 Poverty Metrics

Earned Income Tax Credit

 Welfare Reform

Enacted in 1975, the Earned Income Tax Credit (EITC) program provides federal tax relief for low-income working families, especially those with children. The credit reduces the amount of federal tax owed and usually results in a tax refund for those who qualify. Similar programs are offered in the United Kingdom, Canada, France, and New Zealand. To qualify for the U.S. program, adults must be employed. A single parent with one child who had family income of less than $36,052 (or $40,964 for a married couple with one child) in 2011 could get a credit of as much as $3,094. The EITC can be claimed for children under age 19 or under age 24 if they are still in college.

Expansions of the program in the late 1980s and early 1990s made the credit more generous for families with two or more children. In 1994, a small credit was made available to low-income families without children (Freidman 2000). Receipt of the EITC does not affect receipt of other programs such as food stamp benefits, Medicaid, or housing subsidies. In 2009, the EITC was expanded to low-earning single and married workers without children, noncustodial parents, and parents with adult independent children.

Supporters of the EITC argue that the program strengthens family self-sufficiency, provides families with more disposable income, and encourages work among welfare recipients. The program acts as a short-term safety net during periods of shock to income (e.g., loss of job) or family structure (e.g., divorce) or as a long-term income support for multiple spells of income loss or poverty (Dowd and Horowitz 2011). Families use their credits to cover basic necessities, home repair, vehicle maintenance, or education expenses (Center on Budget and Policy Priorities 2012). Almost half of EITC recipients planned to save all or part of their refund (Smeeding, Ross, and O'Conner 1999). The program is credited with lifting more children out of poverty than any other government program (Llobrera and Zahradnik 2004).

In 2010, 23 states and the District of Columbia offered a state-level earned income credit for residents, usually a percentage of the federal credit. For more information, log on to the Study Site, Chapter 2, at www.sagepub.com/leonguerrero4e.

Main Points

- Absolute poverty refers to a lack of basic necessities, such as food, shelter, and income. Relative poverty refers to a situation where people fail to achieve the average income or lifestyle enjoyed by the rest of society. Relative poverty emphasizes the inequality of income and the growing gap between the richest and poorest Americans.

- The poverty threshold is the original federal poverty measure developed by the Social Security Administration and updated each year by the U.S. Census Bureau. The threshold is used for estimating the number of people in poverty. Poverty guidelines are issued each year by the U.S. Department of Health and Human Services and are used for determining family or individual eligibility for federal programs.

- Whites currently compose the largest group of poor individuals in the United States. However, the poverty rate for non-Hispanic Whites is the lowest, and Blacks continue to have the highest poverty rate, followed by Hispanics.

- Functionalists observe that class inequality is a product of our social structure. Rapid economic and technological changes eliminated the need for low-skilled labor, creating a population of workers who are unskilled and untrained for this new economy. In many ways, theorists from this perspective expect this disparity among workers. Lower wages and poverty are natural consequences of this system of stratification.

- Conflict theorists assert that poverty exists because those in power want to maintain and expand their base of power and interests, with little left to share with others. For Marx, one's social class is solely determined by one's position in the economic system: You are either a worker or an owner of the means of production. According to Weber, however, social class is multidimensional. Economic factors include income, the money earned for one's work, and wealth, the value of one's personal assets such as savings and property. A person's social class is also influenced by prestige, the amount of social respect or standing given to an individual based on occupation. A final component of class is power. Weber defined power as the ability to achieve one's goals despite the opposition of others. Welfare bureaucracies—local, state, and national—represent important interest groups that influence the creation and implementation of welfare policies. Welfare policies reflect the political economy of the community in which they are implemented.

- Feminist scholars argue that the welfare state is an arena of political struggle. The drive to maintain male dominance and the patriarchal family is assumed to be the principal force shaping the formation, implementation, and outcomes of U.S. welfare policy.

- Interactionists attempt to explain how poverty is a learned phenomenon. Some sociologists have suggested that poverty is based on a "culture of poverty" and that moral deficiencies lead to a life of poverty. Opponents argue that there is no evidence that the poor have a different set of values and beliefs. Interactionists also focus on the public's perceptions: Most Americans do not have any direct contact with the welfare system or welfare recipients; thus, their views are likely to be shaped by the media.

■ A new era of social welfare began in 1996 with the Personal Responsibility and Work Opportunity Reconciliation Act. PRWORA was a bipartisan welfare reform plan to reduce recipients' dependence on government assistance through strict work requirements and welfare time limits. The act had an immediate effect on the number of people on welfare. However, although employment has increased among welfare recipients, many recipients have little education or work experience, have limited employment benefits (including health care), and continue to struggle with child care.

■ Food insecurity is defined as insufficient food for all family members to enjoy active and healthy lives for at least some time during the year. The U.S. Department of Agriculture provides food assistance programs, but families often need to rely on private programs (food pantries and soup kitchens) as well. For a variety of reasons, poor families encounter higher food prices and a smaller selection of food than other families. Housing is another problem; the combination of low earnings and scarce housing assistance results in serious housing problems for the working poor.

■ Overwhelming evidence indicates that welfare caseloads have declined since the enactment of PRWORA, perhaps helped by a strong economy and increased aid to low-income working families. However, the early employment success of welfare reform diminished as the economy faltered, and time limits to welfare receipt seem to compound problems. It appears that individuals and families, particularly women and the rural poor, are cycling in and out of poverty, working when jobs are available but never achieving complete economic independence.

On Your Own

Log on to the open-access Student Study Site at www.sagepub.com/leonguerrero4e for these additional learning tools:

- ■ Interactive quizzes
- ■ Video clips
- ■ NPR audio links
- ■ Handbook articles

- ■ E-flashcards
- ■ Journal articles
- ■ End-of-chapter web exercises
- ■ Additional web resources and current events

Internet and Community Exercises

1. Investigate the welfare assistance or TANF program in your state. First, determine the name and administrative agency for the program in your state. Most TANF programs are administered by the Department of Health and Social Services or Department of Human Services. Determine what time limits and work requirement provisions have been legislated in your state. What educational activities can count toward work requirements? Are family support services (parent skill training, housing assistance) provided? What is your state's record on welfare reform? Has welfare reform made a difference for the poor in your state?

2. What is the median income for your state? The median income is the exact point where 50% of all incomes are above and 50% of all incomes are below. Log on to *Study Site Chapter 2* to access the U.S. Census Bureau website.

3. The United Nations *Human Development Report* collects available data on poverty rates,

defined in several ways, including living below $1.25 a day and the percentage of the nation's population that lives below the poverty line. Data are available primarily for lesser-developed nations. Log on to *Study Site Chapter 2* to identify and compare poverty rates for five selected nations.

4. Stanford University established the Center for the Study of Poverty and Inequality in 2006. The center recognizes how universities are obligated to provide leadership on one of the pressing problems of poverty and inequality. The center website includes an inequality quotient quiz. Take a few moments to answer the 20 questions and see how well you understand income inequality in the United States. Log on to *Study Site Chapter 2*.

5. The Roy Rosenzweig Center for History and New Media (CHNM) at George Mason University and the University of New Orleans organized and established the Hurricane Digital Memory Bank (HDMB). HDMB uses electronic media to collect, preserve, and present the stories and reflections from Katrina and Rita survivors, first responders, and relief workers. Click on Collections to access data collected by students and faculty from Mississippi Gulf Coast Community College, the University of New Orleans, Delgado Community College, and McNeese State University.

Study Questions

1. Examine the difference between income and wealth. Which do you think is the better measure of social class?

2. How would you describe a middle-class lifestyle? What are its characteristics—housing, vacations, cars, and lifestyle? Estimate what it takes to lead this middle-class life.

3. Review the different definitions of poverty (from sociologists and according to federal policy). What are the advantages and disadvantages of each?

4. Functionalists assume that not everyone in society can and should be equal. Do you agree with this statement? Why or why not?

5. How would Marx and Weber define your social status, that of Microsoft's Bill Gates, and that of your sociology professor?

6. How has the welfare system (past and present) discriminated against women?

7. The chapter reviews three consequences of poverty—health care, food insecurity, and housing. Which do you think is most serious and why? What other consequences of poverty can you identify?

8. The new welfare legislation, the Personal Responsibility and Work Opportunity Reconciliation Act, became law in 1996. How effective do you think welfare reform has been? Has it changed welfare "as we know it"?

CHAPTER 3

Race and Ethnicity

T
he son of a White woman from Kansas and a Black man from Kenya, Barack Hussein Obama was sworn in as the 44th president of the United States. The ascension of a Black man to the highest office is cause for enormous and justifiable racial pride (Kamiya 2009). Yet, throughout his first campaign and since his 2008 election, much attention has been given to how Obama has handled the subject of race. Though he frequently cited his biracial heritage during the campaign, his message embraced the dream that the nation would transcend the divisiveness of racial politics. In March 2008 he delivered his "More Perfect Union" speech, responding to controversial statements made by his former pastor, Reverend Jeremiah Wright. Obama referred to the complexities of race in America as a stalemate, "a part of our union that we have yet to perfect." He encouraged Americans to look beyond race and skin color to find that "common stake we all have in one another, and let our politics reflect that spirit as well" (Obama 2008).

The United States is a diverse racial and ethnic society. Joe Feagin and Pinar Batur (2004) predict that by the 2050s, the majority of the U.S. population will comprise African, Latino, Asian, Middle Eastern, and Native Americans. Currently, White Americans are a minority in half of the largest 100 U.S. cities and in Hawaii, New Mexico, Texas, and California. Between 2015 and 2040, White Americans are expected to become a statistical minority in many other states. In 2011, about 13% of the U.S. population or 40 million individuals were foreign born (Acosta and de la Cruz 2011).

Adding to the diversity of our population are increasing numbers of immigrants, their migration to the United States and throughout the world spurred on by the global economy. Population mobility since the middle of the twentieth century has been characterized by unprecedented volume, speed, and geographical range (Collin and Lee 2003). At the end of

A More Perfect Union

2005, nearly 200 million people or about 3% of the world's population lived in a country other than their birth country (DeParle 2007). The International Organization for Migration (2003) predicts that by 2030, this figure should increase to 230 million. As Zygmunt Bauman (2000) describes, "The world is on the move" (p. 77). Regionally, Europe has the largest number of international migrants, about 69.8 million (United Nations 2011). North America, including the United States, has the third largest number of migrants, 50 million (refer to Table 3.1).

In this chapter, we explore how one's racial and ethnic status serves as a basis of inequality. Like social class, depending on one's race or ethnicity, one's life chances are altered, and the likelihood of experiencing particular social problems increases. We begin first with understanding how race and ethnicity are defined.

Defining Race and Ethnicity

Post Racial

From a biological perspective, a race can be defined as a group or population that shares a set of genetic characteristics and physical features. The term has been applied broadly to groups with similar physical features (the White race), religion (the Jewish race), or the entire human species (the human race; Marger 2002). However, generations of migration, intermarriage, and adaptations to different physical environments have produced a mixture of races. There is no such thing as a "pure" race.

Social scientists reject the biological notions of race, instead favoring an approach that treats race as a social construct. In *Racial Formation in the United States: From the 1960s to the 1990s,* Michael Omi and Howard Winant (1994) explain how race is a "concept which signifies and symbolizes social conflicts and interests by referring to different types of human

Table 3.1

Regional Distribution of International Migrants, 1960 Versus 2010

	1960		2010	
	Total Immigrants (Millions)	Share of World Immigrants (%)	Total Immigrants (Millions)	Share of World Immigrants (%)
World by region	74.1		213.9	
Africa	9.2	12.4	19.3	9.0
North America	13.6	18.4	50.0	23.4
Latin America and the Caribbean	6.2	8.3	7.5	3.5
Asia	28.5	38.4	61.3	28.7
Europe	14.5	19.6	69.8	32.6
Oceania*	2.1	2.9	6.0	2.8

*Oceania includes Micronesia, Melanesia, Polynesia, Australia, and New Zealand.

Source: United Nations 2009, 2011.

bodies" (p. 54). Instead of thinking of race as something "objective," the authors argued that we can imagine race as an "illusion," a subjective social, political, and cultural construct. According to the authors, "The meaning of race is defined and contested throughout society, in both collective action and personal practice. In the process, racial categories themselves are formed, transformed, destroyed, and reformed" (Omi and Winant 1994:21). Robert Redfield (1958) says it simply: "Race is, so to speak, a human invention" (p. 67).

Race may be a social construction, but that does not make race any less powerful and controlling (Myers 2005). Omi and Winant (1994) argued that although particular stereotypes and meanings can change, "The presence of a system of racial meaning and stereotypes, of racial ideology, seems to be a permanent feature of U.S. culture" (p. 63).

 Race and Ethnic Relations

What Does It Mean to Me?

Former President Jimmy Carter was quoted as saying that racism was fueling a "radical fringe element of demonstrators" against President Obama. He made these comments in 2009 after Representative Joe Wilson shouted "You lie" to Obama during his congressional speech on health care. Do you agree with Carter's statement? What role has race played in President Obama's presidency? Has his racial identity been socially constructed? If yes, then how?

 STATE STATS

Ethnic groups are set off to some degree from other groups by displaying a unique set of cultural traits, such as their language, religion, or diet. Members of an ethnic group perceive themselves as members of an ethnic community, sharing common historical roots and experiences. All of us, to one extent or another, have an ethnic identity. Increasingly the terms *race* and *ethnicity* are presented as a single construct pointing to how both terms are being conflated (Budrys 2003).

Martin Marger (2002) explains how ethnicity serves as a basis of social ranking, ranking a person according to the status of his or her ethnic group. Although class and ethnicity are separate dimensions of stratification, they are closely related: "In virtually all multiethnic societies, people's ethnic classification becomes an important factor in the distribution of societal rewards and hence, their economic and political class positions. The ethnic and class hierarchies are largely parallel and interwoven" (Marger 2002:286).

The federal definition of ethnicity is based on the Office of Management and Budget's 1977 guideline (U.S. Census Bureau 2005), which defines ethnicity in terms of Hispanic/non-Hispanic status, contrary to the conventional social scientific definition as presented in the previous paragraphs. The U.S. Census treats Hispanic origin and race as separate and distinct concepts; as a result, Hispanics may be of any race. As of 2002, Hispanic Americans were the nation's largest ethnic minority group. The U.S. Census Bureau includes in this category women and men who are Mexican, Central and South American, Puerto Rican, Cuban, and other Hispanic.

Photo 3.1

Born in Hawaii to a White American woman and a Black Kenyan student, President Barack Obama was raised by his mother and her parents.

The 2010 ethnic and racial composition of the United States is presented in Table 3.2. For 2010, the majority of respondents, about 97%, indicated only one race. Over the past decade, 2000–2010, the White-alone population had the slowest rate of growth (Humes, Jones, and Ramirez 2011). In 2012, the U.S. Census reported that minority births were the majority—50.4% of children younger than age 1 year were Hispanic, Black, Asian, or of mixed race. Non-Hispanic Whites accounted for 49.6% of all births in a 12-month period (U.S. Census Bureau 2012b). Commenting on the report, demographer William Frey (quoted in Tavernise 2012:A1) said, "This is an important tipping point . . . [a] transformation from a mostly white baby boomer culture to a more globalized multiethnic country that we're becoming."

The U.S. Census distinguishes between native and foreign-born residents. **Native** refers to anyone born in the United States or a U.S. island area such as Puerto Rico or the Northern Mariana Islands or born abroad of a U.S. citizen parent; **foreign born** refers to anyone who is not a U.S. citizen at birth. Elizabeth Grieco (2010) writes, "The foreign born, through their own diverse origins, will contribute to the racial and ethnic diversity of the United States. How they translate their own backgrounds and report their adopted identities have important implications for the nation's racial and ethnic composition." In 2010, among the 40 million foreign born in the United States, most were from Latin America (53.1%, as displayed in Figure 3.1; Acosta and de la Cruz 2011); however, in 2009 Asians became the fastest-growing racial group in the United States, surpassing Hispanics (Taylor 2012). The shift in the number-one ranking from Hispanic to Asian immigrants is mostly due to the sharp decline in Hispanic immigration because of the Great Recession and the overall state of the U.S. economy, immigration politics, and increased border and deportation enforcement (Semple 2012).

Refugees are defined by the Immigration and Nationality Act of 1980 as "aliens outside the United States who are unable or unwilling to return to his/her country of origin for persecution or fear of persecution on account of race, religion, nationality, membership in a particular social group, or political opinion." Data on the number of admitted refugees are collected annually by the U.S. Department of State. In 2010, 73,293 persons were admitted as refugees. Almost 65% of all admitted refugees were from three countries: Burma (22.8%), Iraq

Table 3.2

Race and Hispanic Origin, United States, 2010 (Numbers in Thousands)

	Total	Percentage
One Race		
White	223,553	72.4
Black or African American	38,929	12.6
American Indian and Alaska Native	2,932	0.9
Asian	14,674	4.8
Native Hawaiian and Other Pacific Islander	540	0.2
Some other race	19,107	6.2
Two or More Races	9,009	2.9
Hispanic or Latino (of any race)	50,477	16.3

Source: Humes, Jones, and Ramirez 2011.

(24.6%), and Bhutan (16.9%). The majority of admitted refugees were less than 25 years of age (51%), male (52%), and single (54.7%; Martin 2011).

Tracy Ore (2003) acknowledges that externally created labels for some groups are not always accepted by those viewed as belonging to a particular group. For example, those of Latin American descent may not consider themselves to be "Hispanic." In this text, I've adopted Ore's practice regarding which racial and ethnic terms are used. In my own material, I use *Latino* to refer to those of Latin American descent, and *Black* and *African American* interchangeably. However, original terms used by authors or researchers (e.g., *Hispanic* as used by the U.S. Census Bureau) are not altered.

Patterns of Racial and Ethnic Integration

Sociologists explain that ethnocentrism is the belief that one's own group values and behaviors are right and even better than all others. Feeling positive about one's group is important for group solidarity and loyalty. However, it can lead groups and individuals to believe that certain racial or ethnic groups are inferior and that discriminatory practices against them are justified. This is called racism.

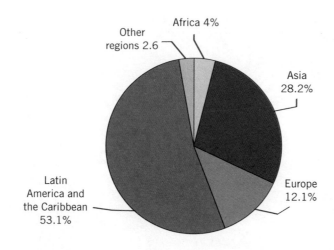

Figure 3.1

U.S. Foreign Born by World Region of Birth, 2010

Source: Acosta and de la Cruz 2011.

What Does It Mean to Me?

You may not be able to tell from my last name (Leon-Guerrero), but I consider my ethnic identity to be Japanese. I am Japanese not only because of my middle name (Yuri) and because of my Japanese mother, but also because of the Japanese traditions that I practice, the Japanese words that I use, and even the Japanese foods that I like to eat. Do you have an ethnic identity? If you do, how do you maintain it?

Though not all inequality can be attributed to racism, our nation's history reveals how particular groups have been singled out and subject to unfair treatment. Certain groups have been subject to individual discrimination and institutional discrimination. **Individual discrimination** includes actions against minority members by individuals. Actions may range from avoiding contact with minority group members to physical or verbal attacks against minority group members. **Institutional discrimination** is practiced by the government, social institutions, and organizations. Institutional discrimination may include segregation, exclusion, or expulsion.

Segregation refers to the physical and social separation of ethnic or racial groups. Although we consider explicit segregation to be illegal and a thing of the past, ethnic and racial segregation still occurs in neighborhoods, schools, and personal relationships. According to Debra Van Ausdale and Joe Feagin (2001),

> Racial discrimination and segregation are still central organizing factors in contemporary U.S. society. For the most part, Whites and Blacks do not live in the same neighborhoods, attend the same schools at all educational levels, enter into close friendships or other intimate relationships with one another, or share comparable opinions on a wide variety of political matters. The same is true, though sometimes to a lesser extent, for Whites and other Americans of color, such as most Latino, Native and Asian American groups. Despite progress since the 1960s, U.S. society remains intensely segregated across color lines. Generally speaking, Whites and people of color do not occupy the same social space or social status. (p. 29)

Racial Profiling

Photo 3.2

In 2006, a "Day Without an Immigrant" rally was organized by pro-immigrant organizations supporting immigrant-friendly legislation. North America ranks second in the number of international migrants (50 million). Asia has the largest number of migrants, about 56 million.

Exclusion refers to the practice of prohibiting or restricting the entry or participation of groups in society. In March 1882, U.S. Congressman Edward K. Valentine declared, "The [immigration] gate must be closed" (Gyory 1998:238). That year, Valentine, along with other congressional leaders, approved the Chinese Exclusion Act. From 1882 to 1943, the United States prohibited Chinese immigration because of concerns that Chinese laborers would compete with American workers. Through the 1940s, immigration was defined as a hindrance rather than a benefit to the United States.

Finally, **expulsion** is the removal of a group by direct force or intimidation. Native Americans in the United States were forcibly removed from their homelands by early settlers and the federal government before and after the American Revolutionary War. During the 1830s, members of the Cherokee and other nations were forcibly relocated to government-designated Indian territory (present-day Oklahoma). Their journey is known as the Trail of Tears, where thousands died along the way. In 2006, journalist Eliot Jaspin documented the extent of racial expulsion that occurred in towns from Central Texas through Georgia. After the Civil War through the 1920s, White residents expelled nearly all Black persons from their communities, usually using direct physical force. Thirteen countywide expulsions were documented in eight states between 1864 and 1923 in which 4,000 Blacks were driven out of their communities.

What Does It Mean to Me?

The DREAM Act, also known as the Development, Relief, and Education for Alien Minors Act, was considered by the U.S. Congress in 2010–2011. If passed, the DREAM Act would enact two major changes in the current law: (1) Certain immigrant students who have grown up in the United States would be permitted to apply for temporary legal status and to eventually obtain permanent legal status and qualify for U.S. citizenship if they go to college or serve in the U.S. military, and (2) the federal provision that penalizes states that provide in-state tuition without regard to immigration status would be eliminated. Twelve states passed laws that permit anyone, including undocumented immigrants, who attended and graduated from high school in the state to pay the in-state tuition rate at public colleges and universities. For allowing this, these states are penalized. Should these young immigrants be eligible for legal residency and in-state tuition? Why or why not?

In Focus

Japanese American Internment Camps

Asian Americans are often characterized as the "model minority," which focuses on their socioeconomic achievement. Native-born Asian Americans as a group have achieved educations, occupations, and income levels that are the same as or better than those of White Americans. Yet, social scientists observe how this image of success ignores Asian Americans' history and experience of discrimination in the United States. Part of their history is the internment of Japanese Americans between 1942 and 1945.

In August 1941, U.S. Representative John Dingell (D-Mich.) wrote to President Franklin D. Roosevelt, suggesting that 10,000 Hawaiian Japanese be incarcerated to ensure "good behavior" by Japan. Roosevelt did

(Continued)

(Continued)

not act on Dingell's suggestion. But two months later, when Japan attacked Pearl Harbor in December 1941, Roosevelt signed Executive Order 9066, which allowed the Secretary of War to "prescribe military areas from which any or all persons may be excluded." Though no single ethnic group was identified, the order targeted Japanese Americans, most residing in the western states. War Department officials argued that Japanese Americans could not be trusted to serve in the Pacific theater because it was difficult to separate "the sheep from the goats" (Asahina 2006:19).

Photo 3.3

From 1941 to 1945, about 120,000 Japanese Americans were relocated to internment camps. Like the Mochida family, most were instructed to pack their belongings in a single suitcase. The camps were closed at the end of World War II.

Scholars and historians have identified racism as the root explanation for Roosevelt's executive order and for the lack of public outcry against the action. Cheryl Greenberg (1995) explains how anti-Asian prejudice predated Pearl Harbor, evidenced by immigration and citizenship restrictions, prohibition in several western states against property ownership or practicing certain trades, employment discrimination, and residential segregation. That there were no similar wartime incarceration programs for German or Italian Americans suggests that Japanese Americans were singled out based on racist decisions.

For the next four years, 120,000 Japanese Americans were relocated to several sites—undeveloped federal reclamation projects (Tule Lake, Minidoka, and Heart Mountain), land meant for subsistence homesteads (Rohwer and Jerome), Indian reservations (Poston and Gila River), and unused public city or county land (Manzanar and Topaz). Men, women, and children were given short notice to pack all their personal items in a single suitcase. It is estimated that as a group, they left behind about $200 million worth of real, personal, and commercial property (about $6.4 billion in current dollars; Asahina 2006).

On February 1, 1942, Roosevelt authorized the formation of a regimental combat team made up of Japanese American volunteers. The 442nd Regimental Combat Team would become the most decorated unit in World

War II history for its size and length of service. In less than two years, the 442nd participated in seven major campaigns in Italy and France, received seven Presidential Distinguished Unit Citations, and was awarded 18,142 individual decorations. Approximately 22,500 Japanese Americans served in the U.S. Army during World War II in the 442nd, the 100th Infantry Battalion, and the 1399th Engineer Construction Battalion (Asahina 2006).

At the end of World War II, the internment camps began to shut down. Japanese Americans were instructed to return home, but the reality was that they had no homes to return to. Most were poor and homeless.

In 1948, President Harry Truman signed the Japanese American Evacuation Claims Act, to compensate Japanese Americans for certain economic losses attributable to their forced evacuation. President Gerald Ford finally rescinded Executive Order 9066 (the original order that led to their internment) in 1976. In 1988, President Ronald Reagan signed a presidential apology to those interned. Reagan also signed HR 442 into law, providing for individual payments of $20,000 to each surviving internee and a $1.25 billion education fund, among other provisions. Bruce Ackerman (2004) observes, "It took almost half a century before the Japanese-American victims of war time concentration camps gained financial compensation, and then only by a Special Act of Congress that awarded incredibly tiny sums" (p. 1063).

In 2006, President George W. Bush signed a law providing federal funding to restore and preserve 10 internment camps for education and to serve as a memorial. U.S. Representative Doris Matsui (D-Calif.), who was born in the Poston, Arizona, camp, said at the law's signing, "Preserving these internment sites is a solemn task we all bear. Those who come after us will have a physical reminder of what they will never allow to happen again."

Sociological Perspectives on Inequalities Based on Race and Ethnicity

Functionalist Perspective

Theorists from this perspective believe that the differences between racial and ethnic groups are largely cultural. The solution is **assimilation**, a process where minority group members become part of the dominant group, losing their original distinct group identity. This process is consistent with America's image as the "melting pot." Milton Gordon (1964) presents a seven-stage assimilation model that begins first with cultural assimilation (change of cultural patterns, e.g., learning the English language), followed by structural assimilation (interaction with members of the dominant group), marital assimilation (intermarriage), identification assimilation (developing a sense of national identity, e.g., identifying as an American, rather than as an Asian American), attitude receptional assimilation (absence of prejudiced thoughts among dominant and minority group members), behavioral receptional assimilation (absence of discrimination, e.g., lower wages for minorities would not exist), and finally civic assimilation (absence of value and power conflicts).

Assimilation is said to allow a society to maintain its equilibrium (a goal of the functionalist perspective) if all members of society, regardless of their racial or ethnic identity, adopt one dominant culture. This is often characterized as a voluntary process. Critics argue that this perspective assumes that social integration is a shared goal and that members of the minority group are willing to assume the dominant group's identity and culture, assuming that the dominant culture is the one and only preferred culture (Myers 2005). The perspective also assumes that assimilation is the same experience for all ethnic groups, ignoring the historical legacy of slavery and racial discrimination in our society.

Assimilation is not the only means to achieve racial-ethnic stability. Other countries maintain **pluralism**, where each ethnic or racial group maintains its own culture (cultural pluralism) or a separate set of social structures and institutions (structural pluralism). Cultural pluralism is also referred to as multiculturalism. Switzerland, which has a number of different nationalities and religions, is an example of a pluralistic society. The country, also referred to as the Swiss Confederation, has four official languages: German, French, Italian, and Romansh. Relationships between each ethnic group are described for the most part as harmonious because each of the ethnically diverse parts joined the confederation voluntarily seeking protection (Farley 2005). In his examination of pluralism in the United States, Min Zhou (2004) notes, "As America becomes increasingly multiethnic, and as ethnic Americans become integral in our society, it becomes more and more evident that there is no contradiction between an ethnic identity and an American identity" (p. 153).

Conflict Perspective

Du Bois's Policy

According to sociologist W. E. B. Du Bois (1996), perhaps it is wrong "to speak of race at all as a concept, rather than as a group of contradictory forces, facts and tendencies" (p. 532). The problem of the twentieth century, wrote Du Bois, is "the color line."

Conflict theorists focus on how the dynamics of racial and ethnic relations divide groups while maintaining a dominant group. The dominant group may be defined according to racial or ethnic categories, but it can also be defined according to social class. Instead of relationships based on consensus (or assimilation), relationships are based on power, force, and coercion. Ethnocentrism and racism maintain the status quo by dividing individuals along racial and ethnic lines (Myers 2005).

Drawing upon Marx's class analysis, Du Bois was one of the first theorists to observe the connection between racism and capitalist-class oppression in the United States and throughout the world. He noted the link between racist ideas and actions to maintain a Eurocentric system of domination (Feagin and Batur 2004). Du Bois (1996) wrote,

The Color Line

Throughout the world today organized groups of men by monopoly of economic and physical power, legal enactment and intellectual training are limiting with great determination and unflagging zeal the development of other groups; and that the concentration particularly on economic power today puts the majority of mankind into a slavery to the rest. (p. 532)

Marxist theorists argue that immigrants constitute a reserve army of workers, members of the working class performing jobs that native workers no longer perform. Michael Samers (2003) suggests that immigrants are a "quantitatively and qualitatively flexible labour force for capitalists which divides and weakens working class organization and drives down the value of labour power" (p. 557). Capitalist businesses profit from migrant workers because they are cheap and flexible—easily hired during times of economic growth and easily fired during economic recessions.

Though most theorists from this perspective see conflict as emanating from one dominant group, conflict may also be mutual. Edna Bonacich (1972) offers a theory of ethnic antagonism, encompassing all levels of mutual intergroup conflict. She argues that this ethnic antagonism emerges from a labor market split along ethnic and class lines. To be split, the labor market must include at least two groups of workers whose price of labor differs for the same work. Conflict develops between three classes: businesses or employers, higher paid labor, and cheaper labor. Bonacich explains that as businesses attempt to maintain a cheap workforce (not caring about who does the work as long as it gets done), higher-paid workers attempt to maintain their prime labor position (resisting the threat of lower-wage laborers), and cheaper laborers attempt to advance their position (threatening higher-paid workers). Higher-paid workers may use exclusionary practices (attempting to prevent the importation of cheaper nonnative labor) or caste arrangements (excluding some groups from certain types of work) to maintain their advantage in the labor market. According to Bonacich, the presence of a cheaper labor group threatens the jobs of higher-paid workers and the standard for wages in all jobs. Under these conditions, laborers remain in conflict with each other, and the interests of capitalist business owners are maintained.

Feminist Perspective

Honor Killings

Feminist theory has attempted to account for and focus on the experiences of women and other marginalized groups in society. Feminist theory intersects with multiculturalism through the analysis of multiple systems of oppression, not just gender, but including categories of race, class, sexual orientation, nation of origin, language, culture, and ethnicity. Emerging from this is Patricia Hill Collins's (2000) Black feminist theory. Black feminists identify the value of a theoretical perspective that addresses the simultaneity of race, class, and gender oppression.

Black feminist scholars note the misguided application of traditional feminist perspectives of "the family," "patriarchy," and "reproduction" to understand the experience of Black women's lives. Black women do not lead parallel lives, but rather lead different lives. British scholar Hazel Carby (1985) argues that because Black women are subject to simultaneous oppression based on class, race, and patriarchy, the application of traditional (White) feminist perspectives is not appropriate and is actually misleading in attempts to comprehend the true experience of Black women. She argues that White feminist theory has to recognize that "White women stand in a power relation as oppressors of Black women" (Carby 1985:390).

As an example, Carby (1985) analyzes an article on women in Third World manufacturing. Carby highlights how the photographs accompanying the article are of "anonymous Black women." She observes, "This anonymity and the tendency to generalize into meaninglessness, the oppression of an amorphous category called 'Third World Women,' are symptomatic of the ways in which the specificity of our experiences and oppression are subsumed under inapplicable concepts and theories" (Carby 1985:394).

Interactionist Perspective

Social Construct

Sociologists believe that race is a social construct. We learn about racial and ethnic categories of White, Black, Latino, Asian, Native American, and immigrant through our social interaction. The meaning and values for these and other categories are provided by our social institutions, families, and friends (Ore 2003). As much as I and other social scientists inform our students about the unsubstantiated use of the term *race,* for most students, race is real. The term is loaded with social, cultural, and political baggage, making deconstructing it difficult to accomplish.

Social scientists have noted how people are raced, how race itself is not a category but a practice. Howard McGary (1999) defines the practice as "a commonly accepted course of action that may be over time habitual in nature; a course of action that specifies certain forms of behavior as permissible and others impermissible, with rewards and penalties assigned accordingly" (p. 83). In this way, racial categories and identities serve as intersections of social beliefs, perceptions, and activities that are reinforced by enduring systems of rewards and penalties (Shuford 2001).

Individuals are attempting to redefine racial boundaries by proposing the creation and acknowledgment of a new racial category—**multiracial**—or mixed race. This is different from other ethnic movements that work within the existing racial frameworks. For example, Latinos may challenge the meaning and use of the Census category Hispanic, but they are not trying to create a new racial identity (DaCosta 2007). Members of the multicultural movement advocate for the formal acceptance of the multiracial category on U.S. Census and other governmental forms and have also worked on broader issues of racial and social justice (Bernstein and De la Cruz 2009).

Scholars have also observed the phenomenon of **ethnic attrition**, individuals choosing not to self-identify as a member of a particular ethnic group. Brian Duncan and Stephen Trejo (2011) found that about 30% of third-generation Mexican youth in their study failed to identify as Mexican, choosing instead to identify as White. These youth were more likely to have parents with higher levels of educational attainment and have more years of schooling themselves than youth who identified as Mexican. Scholars of race in Latin America have also confirmed patterns of intergenerational Whitening. Highly educated non-White Brazilians were found to be more likely to label their children White than less-educated non-White Brazilians (Schwartzman 2007).

A summary of all theoretical perspectives is provided in Table 3.3.

What Does It Mean to Me?

There were 12 racial categories listed in the 1920 U.S. Census. The categories included four variations of White, Negro, Mulatto, Indian, Chinese, Japanese, Native, Foreign-born, and "All other." The number of racial categories was reduced to 8 in the 1960 Census and expanded again to 31 racial categories in the 2000 and 2010 Census. Based on the current definition, how would you identify your racial identity? From your perspective, are any racial categories missing from the list?

The Consequences of Racial and Ethnic Inequalities

Income and Wealth

"Race is so associated with class in the United States that it might not be direct discrimination, but it still matters indirectly," says sociologist Dalton Conley (Ohlemacher 2006:A6). Data reported by the U.S. Census reveal that Black households had the lowest median income in 2011, $32,229, 58% of the median income for non-Hispanic White households, $55,412. The median income for Hispanic households was $38,624, 70% of the median for non-Hispanic White households. Asian households had the highest median income, $65,129, 117% of the median for non-Hispanic White households (DeNavas-Walt, Proctor, and Smith 2012).

Because of years of discrimination, low educational attainment, high unemployment, or underemployment, African Americans have not been able to achieve the same earnings or level of wealth as White Americans have. Studies indicate that for every dollar earned by White households, Black households earned 62 cents (Oliver and Shapiro 1995). Blacks have between

Table 3.3

Summary of Sociological Perspectives: Inequalities Based on Race and Ethnicity

	Functionalist	Conflict/Feminist	Interactionist
Explanations of racial and ethnic inequality	Assimilation into a dominant culture preserves the stability of society. Ethnic pluralism may also achieve stability.	Inequality is systematically maintained by those trying to preserve their advantaged positions. Class divisions overlap with racial and ethnic divisions. Feminist scholars advocate for a theoretical perspective that simultaneously considers the intersection of race, class, and gender.	Race is a social construct. Racial and ethnic categories are also linked with positions of privilege or marginalization.
Questions asked about racial and ethnic inequality	How can minority groups be assimilated into mainstream society? Can cultural and structural pluralism be maintained?	What powerful interest groups determine racial and ethnic inequalities? How are these structures maintained?	How do we learn about race and ethnicity? How are some groups more privileged than others? How do our perceptions and beliefs perpetuate racial and ethnic inequalities?

$8 and $19 of wealth for every $100 possessed by Whites. Whites have nearly 12 times as much median net worth as Blacks, $43,000 compared with $3,700 (Oliver and Shapiro 1995).

One measure of wealth is home ownership. Home ownership is one of the primary means to accumulate wealth (Williams, Nesiba, and McConnell 2005). It enables families to finance college and invest in their future. Historically, home ownership grew among White middle-class families after World War II, when veterans had access to government and credit programs making home ownership more affordable. However, Blacks and other minority groups have been denied similar access because of structural barriers such as discrimination, low income, and lack of credit access. Feagin (1999) identifies how inequality in home owner-ship has contributed to inequality in other aspects of American life. Specifically, Blacks have been disadvantaged because of their lack of home ownership, particularly in their inability to provide their children with "the kind of education or other cultural advantages necessary for their children to compete equally or fairly with Whites" (Feagin 1999:86).

In 2004, U.S. home ownership reached a record high of 69.2% with nearly 73.4 million Americans owning their own homes. However, racial gaps in home ownership persist. In 2011, 73.8% of White households owned their own homes, compared with 44.9% of Black and 46.9% of Hispanic households (U.S. Census Bureau 2012a).

Education

The U.S. Supreme Court's 1954 decision in *Brown v. Board of Education* ruled that racial segregation in public schools was illegal. Reaction to the ruling was mixed, with a strong response from the South. A major confrontation occurred in Arkansas, when Governor Orval

Brown v. Board of Education

Photo 3.4

Interactionists examine the privilege bestowed on one group vis-à-vis another. For example, why do we accept White women adopting children of color, but not women of color adopting White children? Angelina Jolie has adopted three children of color. Pictured here, with Jolie and Brad Pitt, are daughter Zahara from Ethiopia and son Maddox from Cambodia. A second son, named Pax, was adopted from Vietnam in 2007.

Education and Housing

Faubus used the state's National Guard to block the admission of nine Black students into Little Rock Central High School. The students persisted and successfully gained entry into the school the next day with 1,000 U.S. Army paratroopers at their side. The Little Rock incident has been identified as a catalyst for school integration throughout the South. Despite resistance to the Court's ruling, legally segregated education had disappeared by the mid-1970s.

However, a different type of segregation persists, called de facto segregation. **De facto segregation** refers to a subtler process of segregation that is the result of other processes, such as housing segregation, rather than because of an official policy (Farley 2005). Here, we clearly see the intersection of race and class. Schools have become economically segregated, with children of middle- and upper-class families attending predominantly White suburban schools and the children of poorer parents attending racially mixed urban schools (Gagné and Tewksbury 2003). Researchers, teachers, and policy makers have all observed a great disparity in the quality of education students receive in the United States (for more on social problems related to education, turn to Chapter 8). Educational systems reinforce patterns of social class inequality and, along with it, racial inequality (Farley 2005).

Latinos have the lowest educational achievement rates—for high school and college degrees—compared with all other major racial and ethnic groups in the United States (refer to Table 3.4.). Richard Fry (2004) explains that although more than 300,000 young Hispanics will graduate from high school each year, fewer than 60,000 will complete a bachelor's degree. Data indicate that about half of young Latinos who enroll in college are at least minimally prepared academically to succeed in a four-year college. Even among the best-prepared Latino students, only 57% finish a bachelor's degree compared with 81% of their White counterparts. Hispanic undergraduates disproportionately enroll in "open-door" institutions that have lower degree completion rates (Fry 2004).

Much of the research on the achievement gap between Latinos and White students has focused on the characteristics of the students (family income, parents' level of education). However, according to the Pew Hispanic Center (Fry 2005), we need to also consider the social context of Hispanic students' learning, noting how educators and policy makers have more influence over the characteristics of their schools than over the characteristics of students.

Based on their state and national assessment of the basic characteristics of public high schools for Hispanic and other students, the Pew Hispanic Center found that Latinos were more likely than Whites or Blacks to attend the largest public high schools (enrollment of

Table 3.4

Educational Attainment by Race and Ethnicity (Percentages Reported), 2009

	Less Than 9th Grade	9th to 12th Grade	High School Graduate	Some College	College Graduate
Hispanic	23.5	15.5	26.0	22.2	12.7
Native born	8.9	13.5	29.2	31.9	16.6
Foreign born	34.6	17.1	23.7	14.9	9.7
White alone	3.0	6.6	29.3	30.0	31.1
Black alone	5.4	13.0	31.6	32.3	17.7
Asian alone	8.6	6.0	16.0	19.6	49.9
Other, not Hispanic	5.0	9.6	27.6	35.3	22.6
All	6.3	8.5	28.5	28.9	27.9

Source: Pew Hispanic Center 2011.

at least 1,838 students). More than 56% of Hispanics attend large schools, compared with 32% of Blacks and 26% of Whites. Schools with larger enrollments are associated with lower student achievement and higher dropout rates. In addition, the center reported that Hispanics are more likely to be in high schools with lower instructional resources, which includes higher student-to-teacher ratios associated with lower academic performance. Nearly 37% of Hispanics are educated in public high schools with a student-teacher ratio greater than 22 to 1, compared with 14% of Blacks and 13% of White students (Fry 2005).

In June 2007, the U.S. Supreme Court, voting 5 to 4, invalidated the use of race to assign students to public schools, even if the goal was to achieve racial integration of a district's schools. The ruling addressed public school practices in Seattle, Washington (where 41% of all public school students are White), and Louisville, Kentucky (where two thirds of all public school students are White). Legal experts and educators were divided about whether the ruling affirmed or betrayed *Brown v. Board of Education.* Though he voted with the majority, Justice Anthony M. Kennedy said in a separate statement that achieving racial diversity and addressing the problem of de facto segregation were issues that school districts could constitutionally pursue as long as the programs were "sufficiently 'narrowly tailored'" (Greenhouse 2007:A1). It is unclear how the ruling will affect integration strategies adopted in school systems across the country.

Health

"Although race may be a social construct, it produces profound biological manifestations through stress, decreased services, decreased medications, and decreased hospital procedures" (Gabard and Cooper 1998:346). Racial disparities in access to health care and outcomes are pervasive, according to Sara Rosenbaum and Joel Teitelbaum (2004). The issue is twofold—access to health care and the quality of care received once in the system. First, the researchers point to this nation's approach to health insurance as a system that "significantly discriminates against racial and ethnic minorities" (Rosenbaum and Teitelbaum 2004:138). Data reveal how in a voluntary, employment-based health care system, racial and ethnic minority group members are more likely to be uninsured or publicly insured. In 2011, White non-Hispanics had the lowest uninsured rate (11.1%), compared with Blacks (19.5%), Asians (16.8%), and Hispanics (30.1%; DeNavas-Walt et al. 2012). These disparities continue into old age—among those 65 years or older, non-Latino White seniors are more likely to have a private or employer-based supplemental health policy in addition to their Medicare coverage, whereas minority seniors are six to seven times more likely to have Medicaid (public assistance) in addition to Medicare.

Second, the researchers observe that even after minority patients enter a particular facility, they are less likely to receive the level of care provided to nonminority patients for the same condition regardless of their insurance status. For example, Latino and African American patients with public insurance do not receive coronary artery bypass surgery at rates comparable to those of White, publicly insured patients. African American patients are also less likely to receive treatment for early-stage lung cancer and as a result have a lower five-year survival rate. Medicaid-insured African American and Latino children use less primary care (depending usually on emergency treatment), experience higher rates of hospitalization, and die at significantly higher rates than do White children. Though the U.S. government has invested in community-based primary health centers and programs to address these health care gaps, Rosenbaum and Teitelbaum (2004) conclude that these programs can hardly overcome the immense and inaccessible system of specialized and extended health services.

Desegregation and Cognition

W. Michael Byrd and Linda Clayton (2002) assert that the health crisis among African Americans and poor populations is fueled by a medical-social culture laden with ideological, intellectual and scientific, and discriminatory race and class problems. They believe that America's health system is predicated on the belief that the poor and "unworthy" of our society do not deserve decent health. Consequently, health professionals, as well as research and educational systems, engage in what they describe as "self serving and elite behavior" that marginalizes and ignores the problems of health care for minority and disadvantaged groups. They caution that our

> failure to address, and eventually resolve, these race- and class-based health policy, structural, medical-social and cultural problems plaguing the American health care system could potentially undermine any possibility of a level playing field in health and health care for African American and other poor populations—eroding at the front end the very foundations of American democracy. (Byrd and Clayton 2002:572–73)

U.S. Immigration: Past and Present

Approaches to Immigration

Most U.S. families have an immigration history, whether it is based upon stories of relatives as long as four generations ago or as recent as the current generation. Immigration involves leaving one's country of origin to move to another. Though immigration has always been a part of U.S. history, the recent wave of immigration, particularly in the end of the 20th century and the beginning of the 21st, has led to the observation that we are in the "age of migration" (Castles and Miller 1998).

Immigration Regulation

The regulation of immigration became a federal responsibility in 1875, and the Immigration Service was established in 1891. Before this, all immigrants were allowed to enter and become permanent residents. The Great Wave of immigration occurred from 1900 to 1920, when nearly 24 million immigrants, mostly European, arrived in the United States. Congress passed a national immigrant quota system in 1921, limiting the number of immigrants by national groups based on their representation in U.S. Census figures. The quota system, along with the Depression and World War II, slowed the flow of immigrants for several decades.

In 1965, Congress replaced the national quota system with a preference system designed to reunite immigrant families and attract skilled immigrants. Most of the immigrants who arrived after 1970 were from Latin America and Asia. Legislative reforms continued through the 1990s, targeting amnesty policies for illegal aliens (Center for Immigration Studies 2009). Despite the events of September 11, 2001, and a recent federal crackdown on illegal immigration, the United States still has the most open immigration policy in the world.

Most immigrants are motivated by the global economics of immigration—men and women will move from low-wage to high-wage countries in search of better incomes and standards of living. **Labor migration**, the movement from one country to another for employment, has been a part of U.S. history, beginning with Chinese male workers brought to build railroads in the 1800s. These men never brought their families or had any intention of staying after their work was completed.

Sociology of Migration

In their analysis of current migration trends, Gary Hytrek and Kristine Zentgraf (2007) note how an increasing number of highly skilled laborers are moving from less developed areas around the world to the United States and Europe. These migrants are more likely to return to their place of birth or move on to a third country. Migration tends to occur between geographically proximate countries—Turkish and North African migration to Western Europe and Mexican and Central American migration to the United States.

In 2010, there were 40 million foreign-born individuals in the United States. This is the highest number of foreign born ever recorded in U.S. history. Our immigrant population is concentrated in five states. California, New York, Texas, Florida, and New Jersey account for 65% of the immigrant population (refer to U.S. Data Map 3.1). Steven Camarota (2007), reporting for the Center for Immigration Studies, notes that one of the striking patterns of recent immigration is the lack of diversity among immigrants themselves. Immigrants from Mexico and South and East Asia account for the majority of the foreign-born population (refer to Table 3.5).

The United Nations uses the analogy of multiple doors of a house to describe the different ways migrants enter a country. Migrants can enter a house through the front door (as permanent settlers), the side door (temporary visitors and workers), or the back door (irregular or illegal migrants). Back-door migrants have been the recent focus of political and economic debate.

Table 3.5

Country of Birth for Foreign-Born Population in the United States, 2010 (in Thousands)

Country	Number	Percentage
Mexico	11,747	29
Central America	2,989	7
Caribbean	3,749	9
South America	2,740	7
South and East Asia	9,985	25
Middle East	1,384	3
Europe and Canada	5,798	15
Africa and Oceania	1,501	4
Other	37	0.001

Source: Passel and Cohn 2012.

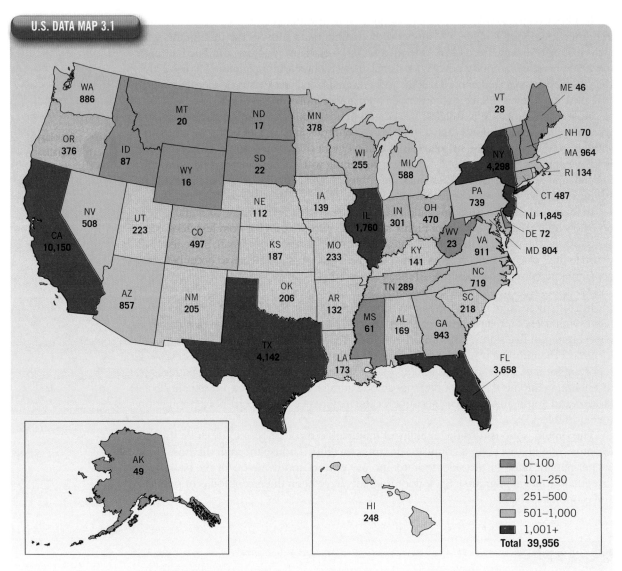

U.S. DATA MAP 3.1

	0–100
	101–250
	251–500
	501–1,000
	1,001+
Total	**39,956**

Foreign-Born Population by State, 2010 (in Thousands)

Source: Walters and Trevelyan 2011.

The number of unauthorized or illegal immigrants peaked at 12 million in 2007. As of 2010, the number declined to 11.2 million (Passel and Cohn 2012). The majority of legal or illegal immigrants in the United States are from Mexico. The number of unauthorized Mexican immigrants has been declining since 2007. According to Jeffrey Passel, D'Vera Cohn, and Ana Gonzalez-Barrera (2012), as of 2011 there were 6.1 million unauthorized Mexican immigrants in the United States, compared with a peak of 7 million in 2007. Their emigration decline was attributed to the Great Recession, declining job opportunities in the housing and construction industry, increasing border enforcement, a rise in deportations, and increasing dangers associated with border crossings.

In 2006 and 2007, the George W. Bush administration proposed comprehensive immigration reforms (CIR). Illegal immigration became a primary concern for Americans, responding to the threat of terrorism and increasing competition in a struggling economy. While acknowledging the country's immigration heritage, the administration proposed strengthening security at our southern border with Mexico and establishing a temporary worker program without the benefit of amnesty. The plan was criticized for creating a class of workers who would never become fully integrated in U.S. society and for focusing specifically on Mexican workers, ignoring all other immigrant groups.

Illegal Immigration

In 2009, Homeland Security Secretary Janet Napolitano laid out the Obama administration's CIR proposal. Similar to the Bush plan, Obama officials promoted the need for tougher enforcement laws against illegal immigrants and employers who hire them, a streamlined system for legal immigration, and a system for illegal immigrants to earn legal status (Preston 2009). However, the administration's continuing focus on punitive enforcement strategies has been criticized for failing to encourage and promote assimilation among immigrants and their children. Nationwide polls show broad support for tougher border and workplace enforcement, while also establishing an opportunity for citizenship.

After the U.S. Congress was unable to pass a bipartisan immigration bill, the states took matters into their own hands, debating similar immigration issues in their own state legislatures (Preston 2007). Between 2005 and 2011, more than 8,000 bills related to immigration were introduced throughout the country, and approximately 1,700 were signed into law (National Conference of State Legislatures 2011). These laws addressed a range of immigration issues—the use of unauthorized illegal workers, the use of false identification (e.g., Social Security), and the extension of education and health care benefits to legal immigrants. Arizona legislators passed SB 1070, the toughest immigration bill in 2010, requiring local law enforcement agencies and officers to demand proof of citizenship from suspected illegal immigrants. Failure to carry proper documentation, even if one is a legal immigrant, is defined as a misdemeanor. In 2011, 31 states introduced legislation replicating all or part of SB 1070. Voters in five states—Alabama, Georgia, Indiana, South Carolina, and Utah—successfully passed immigration laws modeled after SB 1070. In 2012, the Supreme Court upheld part of Arizona's law, permitting the "show me your papers" provision, while ruling that the state could not pursue policies that undermined or conflicted with federal law, for example making it a crime under state law for immigrants to fail to register under a federal law, making it a state crime for illegal immigrants to work, and allowing police to arrest individuals without warrants (Liptak 2012a). The decision will affect similar laws in the five other states. Civil rights groups and immigration advocates expressed concern that the justices' decision would encourage racial profiling. The Court suggested that it would be open to hearing new challenges based on any adverse impact its ruling might have on the civil rights of Arizona residents (Preston 2012a).

Arizona's Immigration Law

The Immigrant Experience

While most immigrants come to the United States to pursue the promise of the freedom of choice, education, economic opportunity, and a better quality of life, their lives are often filled with challenges and problems.

Hispanic America

The post-2000 wave of immigrants included men and women with lower educational attainment—34% have less than a high school education. Considering the population of illegal immigrants, the foreign-born population as a whole is much less educated than the native-born population. Camarota (2007) observes that these individuals' lower educational attainment has "enormous implications" for their economic and social integration. A larger proportion of immigrants than those who are native born have low incomes, lack health insurance, and rely on social assistance programs.

Data from the U.S. Census Current Population Survey reveals that 15.2% of immigrants lived in poverty in 2006. One in six persons living in poverty was an immigrant. The higher incidence of poverty among immigrants as a group has increased the overall size of the population living in poverty. The lack of health insurance is also a significant problem for immigrants—33.8% of foreign-born individuals lack insurance compared with 13% of natives. Illegal immigrants are not eligible for Medicare, and legal immigrants must wait five years to qualify for the program. Camarota (2007) notes that immigrants' low rate of health insurance is associated with a lower level of education and their employment. Unskilled immigrants are likely to work at jobs that do not offer health insurance, or they are unable to purchase insurance on their own.

Immigrant labor is concentrated in construction, cleaning and maintenance, production, and farming occupations. Illegal immigrants are employed in similar areas: construction, building cleaning and maintenance, food preparation and service, transportation and moving, and agriculture. There are an estimated 8 million illegal immigrants in the labor force (Passel and Cohn 2012). Foreign-born workers are especially susceptible to abuse, stress, and unsafe working conditions due to their overrepresentation in dangerous industries, combined with their undocumented worker status, lack of training, and lack of English literacy (Migrant Clinicians Network 2009). As reported by the U.S. Bureau of Labor Statistics (2010), in 2009, Hispanics accounted for the largest proportion (40%) of foreign-born workers who died on the job. A total of 740 foreign-born workers died of fatal work injuries in 2009.

With the exception of the agricultural sector, the majority of workers in occupations where immigrants are concentrated are native-born workers (Camarota and Jensenius 2009). Yet, no single occupation is composed entirely of immigrant labor (Camarota 2009). Immigration has been found to have a negative effect on the wages of native-born Americans primarily in low-paying, low-skilled occupations, reducing wages by an estimated 4% to 7% (Camarota 2009). As Camarota (2007) observes, "A central question for immigration policy is whether we should allow in so many people with little education—increasing job competition for the poorest American workers and the population needing assistance" (p. 39).

Carola Suárez-Orozco et al. (2011) report that there are an estimated 5.5 million children and adolescents living with illegal immigrant parents. Suárez-Orozco and her colleagues documented how the children of illegal immigrant parents lack access to quality educational (child care, preschool, school, and higher education) and employment opportunities. Despite having the same level of commitment to their children's education as authorized legal parents, illegal parents have fewer resources and skills (low social and educational capital) to help their children realize their educational goals. In addition, illegal parents' fear of deportation leads to lower levels of engagement with teachers or schools. They conclude, "For millions of children and youth growing up in unauthorized families, the American Dream and the promise of a better tomorrow have become an elusive mirage" (Suárez-Orozco et al. 2011:462).

As it has increased its immigration enforcement (including detainment and deportation), the Department of Homeland Security has been criticized for targeting immigrants with minor offenses, sometimes breaking up families in the process. Human Rights

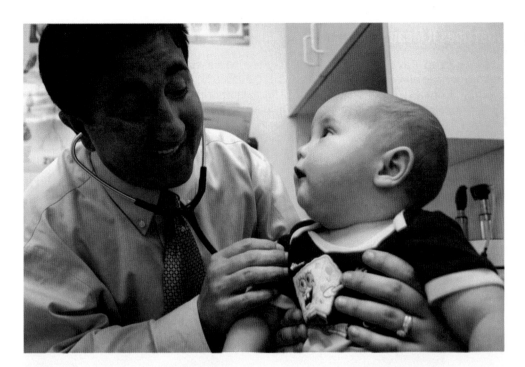

Photo 3.5

Not all high-immigrant occupations are lower skilled and lower wage. For example, 44% of medical scientists are immigrants, as are 27% of physicians (Camarota and Zeigler 2009).

Watch (2009) reported that since stricter deportation laws were passed in 1996, most immigrants have been deported for minor offenses (such as marijuana possession or traffic offenses). The new laws disallowed judges to consider in deportation cases non-citizens' ties to the United States, including family, business or property ownership, and service in the U.S. armed forces. Among legal immigrants who were deported, over 70% had been convicted for nonviolent crimes. Many lived in the United States for years and were separated from family members. Researchers from the Urban Institute documented short- and long-term effects on children with deported or detained parents. These children experienced financial, food, and housing hardships in addition to behavioral changes such as changes in eating and sleeping habits and higher degrees of fear and anxiety (Chaudry et al. 2010).

The Obama administration promised a more compassionate approach to enforcement that would focus on felony criminal offenders. In 2011, 396,906 immigrants were deported—the largest number in the history of Immigration and Customs Enforcement. Fifty-five percent were convicted of felonies or misdemeanors (U.S. Immigration and Customs Enforcement 2011).

In 2012, through executive action, the Obama administration blocked the deportation of more than 800,000 migrants who came to the United States before age 16 (Preston and Cushman 2012; White House 2012). The stopgap measure allows those who have lived in the United States for at least five years and are currently enrolled in school, high school graduates, or military veterans in good standing to work legally and to obtain driver's licenses. An immigrant convicted of a felony, a serious misdemeanor, or three less serious misdemeanors would not be eligible. The Pew Hispanic Center estimated that as many as 1.4 million immigrants would be eligible for this measure (Preston and Cushman 2012), most of them (about 460,000) living in California (Preston 2012b).

What Does It Mean to Me?

Immigration is part of a complex interdependent system, where native-born Americans depend on immigrants for their labor and immigrants depend on the economic opportunities that are available in our society. How does your state rank in terms of the number of immigrants (refer to U.S. Data Map 3.1)? Is immigration a problem in your state? Who is affected and how? Is the 2010 Arizona law an effective solution to the problem of immigration?

STATE STATS

Photo 3.6

This sign near San Ysidro, California, warns motorists to look out for immigrants crossing the Interstate 5 highway. According to the U.S. Border Patrol, 1,954 people died crossing the U.S.-Mexico border illegally between 1998 and 2004. The leading causes of death were heat stroke, dehydration, and hypothermia; others also die in car accidents or by other accidental causes.

Taking a World View

Global Immigration

The United States is not the only country grappling with the issue of immigration. Great Britain, Greece, France, Germany, Australia, and other countries have seen an increase in pro- and anti-immigration protests, as well as increased hate crime acts against immigrants in recent years.

Migration has been elevated to a top international policy concern (Düvell 2005) largely because of the threat of terrorism and the challenge of global politics. Migrants now depart from and arrive in almost every country in the world. During the past 30 years, the proportion of foreign-born residents living in developed countries has generally increased, whereas the proportion has remained stable or decreased in developing countries. Migrant labor has been used at both ends of the labor market—low-wage/manual labor to high-wage/knowledge-based labor. Though globalization has created wealth, lifting many out of poverty, it still has not narrowed the gap between the rich and the poor (Global Commission on Immigration 2005).

Consider France's immigration situation. One in every four French citizens has a non-French parent or grandparent (Silverman 1992). About 25% of France's immigrant population comprises men and women of color from

North Africa or sub-Saharan Africa. The French government estimates there are more than 400,000 illegal immigrants in France (Sayare 2009). During fall 2005, France experienced its worst civil unrest in decades. North African rioters targeted schools, hospitals, and cars, prompting authorities to declare a state of emergency and impose curfews. The unrest broke out following the deaths of two young North African men who were electrocuted when they hid from police in an electricity substation in a Paris suburb.

The riots were characterized as France's Katrina, exposing poverty and discrimination experienced by African French. Godoy (2002) reports that an invisible ceiling exists in France's social and economic life that prohibits the job mobility of qualified individuals. Discrimination in housing, employment, and education is commonplace for France's immigrants. Many bars and clubs remain closed to African French. As the rioting subsided, Prime Minister Dominique de Villepin acknowledged in his remarks to the French National Assembly that the violence was the result of France's failure to provide hope to thousands of young immigrants. Sweeping social and economic reforms were implemented after the riots.

The riots in France were not the only race-related riots. Immigrant attacks also occurred in Italy during 2008–2010. There are 4 million legal immigrants and estimates of more illegal immigrants residing in the country. Flavio Di Giacomo, a spokesman for the International Organization for Migration, described how immigrant workers live in semislavery. The riots, according to Di Giacomo, revealed how "many Italian economic realities are based on the exploitation of low-cost foreign labor, living in subhuman conditions, without human rights" (Donadio 2010a:A7). The African laborers were paid under the table, about $30 a day for picking fruit (Donadio 2010b). Asian and African immigrants in Greece have been the targets of violence and physical attacks since 2010. The violence was fueled by public discontent over the economy and concern over job losses and demonization of immigrants in the press and in the political arena. From a social constructionist's perspective, immigrants were portrayed as the source of Greece's economic woes, defining them as a social problem and threat.

Globalization has intensified the need to coordinate and harmonize government policies. Migration flows are regarded as a threat to national and global stability, with some calling for an international migration policy (Düvell 2005). The United States, Canada, Great Britain, France, Germany, Belgium, Italy, Spain, and Japan have increased policy coordination regarding immigration, refugee admissions, and programs to integrate foreigners and their family members already present in each country (Lee 2006).

Photo 3.7

In October 2005, violence broke out between North African immigrant youths and French security forces in a Paris suburb. Hundreds rioted for days, responding to the deaths of two teens accidentally electrocuted while fleeing police. In 2007, the deaths of two additional teens, sons of African immigrants, renewed violent protests throughout France.

Responding to Racial and Ethnic Inequalities

Encouraging Diversity and Multiculturalism

Accelerated global migration and a resurgence of racial/ethnic conflicts characterized the close of the twentieth century (Wittig and Grant-Thompson 1998) and certainly the beginning of the twenty-first. In an effort to reduce racial/ethnic conflict and to encourage multiculturalism, researchers, educators, political and community leaders, and community members have implemented programs targeting racism and prejudice. Acknowledging that both are complex phenomena with individual, cultural, and structural components, these strategies attempt to address some or most of the components.

 White Privilege

Kathleen Korgen, J. Mahon, and Gabe Wang (2003) believe that colleges and universities have the potential to counter the effects of segregated neighborhoods and socialization in primary and secondary schools. Interaction among races thrust together on a college campus provides a unique opportunity for individuals to experience and discuss the aspects of racial/ethnic diversity in their lives, some for the first time (Odell, Korgen, and Wang 2005). Increased interaction with members of different groups should allow individuals an opportunity to learn from others, reducing hostility and prejudice (Shook and Fazio 2008). Gordon Allport (1954) argues that intergroup contact can have a positive effect in reducing interracial prejudice and increasing tolerance if four conditions are met: (1) There is cooperative interdependence among the groups, (2) the groups share a common goal, (3) the groups are of equal status during contact, and (4) the groups have the support of authority figures.

Increasing numbers of colleges and universities are instituting course requirements that encourage students to examine diversity in the United States and globally. The Association of American Colleges and Universities (2000) reported that 62% of schools have a diversity course requirement or were in the process of developing one. This is quite an increase from 1990, when only 15% of colleges and universities had such a requirement. Research is emerging on the effectiveness of diversity programming on college and university campuses. In one such study, D. A. Grinde (2001) found that more than 85% of University of Vermont students believed that diversity courses strengthened their understanding and appreciation of cultural diversity.

 Reducing Prejudice

Educational programs are used most often to promote diversity in public and private workplaces. These programs attempt to eliminate incorrect stereotypes and unfounded prejudices by providing new information to participants (Farley 2005). Diversity training is thought to make managers aware of how their biases affect their actions in the workplace (Kalev, Dobbin, and Kelly 2006). Research indicates that such programs are effective when people are not made to feel defensive over past behavior but are participating in a learning process of new (vs. old) ideas. This has also been found to be effective in diversity simulation and experiential exercises (i.e., role-playing; Farley 2005). These programs are designed to familiarize employees with antidiscrimination laws, to suggest behavioral changes that could address bias, and to increase cultural awareness and cross-cultural communication among employees (Bendick, Egan, and Lofhjelm 1998).

Business leaders are motivated to address diversity on principle and because they recognize how their company's productivity and success depend on it (Galagan 1993). General diversity and management programs have been established in companies such as Aetna, Ernst & Young, General Mills, and Hewlett-Packard. All programs note the importance of creating an "inclusive" workforce and work environment. In addition to diversity training or sensitivity programs, businesses have successfully implemented diversity management programs, targeting the development and advancement of women and people of color in their organizations.

AT&T is an example of a corporation that has attempted to address diversity in its organization and the communities it serves. AT&T supports the Hispanic/Latino Employee Association of AT&T (HACEMOS), a volunteer employee group that develops educational and community programs. Similar employee resource groups have also been established at Microsoft and Johnson & Johnson. AT&T San Diego has been a partner in community events and programming, including San Diego's Latino Film Festival, Fiestas Patrias, and World Soccer parties. The San Diego HACEMOS chapter, along with other city chapters (Los Angeles and Dallas), offers Internet services and training for low-income and non-English-speaking communities.

Voices in the Community

Rosa Parks

Rosa Parks

Most would mark the beginning of the U.S. civil rights movement as December 1, 1955. On that day, a Black seamstress in Montgomery, Alabama, refused to give up her seat on the bus to a White person. Rosa Parks explains,

> People always say that I didn't give up my seat because I was tired, but that isn't true. I was not tired physically, or no more tired than I usually was at the end of a working day. I was not old, although some people have an image of me as being old then. I was forty-two. No, the only tired I was, was tired of giving in. (Academy of Achievement 2005)

For her actions, Parks was arrested and fined for violating a city ordinance, thrusting her in the middle of America's civil rights movement.

The bus incident led to the formation of the Montgomery Improvement Association, with a young Martin Luther King Jr. elected as its leader. The association promoted its first nonviolent protest, boycotting the city-owned bus company. The boycott lasted 381 days, ending in November 1956, when the U.S. Supreme Court struck down the Montgomery ordinance under which Parks had been fined, outlawing racial segregation on public transportation.

When asked about the historical bus boycott, Parks remembers,

> As I look back on those days, it's just like a dream. The only thing that bothered me was that we waited so long to make this protest and to let it be known wherever we go that all of us should be free and equal and have all opportunities that others should have. (Academy of Achievement 2005)

Parks remained active in the civil rights movement until her death in 2005. In 1957, she and her husband, Raymond, moved to Detroit, Michigan. Parks worked for U.S. Congressman John Conyers. President Bill Clinton honored Parks with the Presidential Medal of Freedom in 1996. Upon her death in 2005, her body was laid in state in the Capitol rotunda, the first woman to be so honored.

Parks was asked what advice she would give a young person who wants to make a difference. She replied,

> The advice I would give any young person is, first of all, to rid themselves of prejudice against other people and to be concerned about what they can do to help others. And of course, to get a good education, and take advantage of the opportunities that they have. In fact, there are more opportunities today than when I was young. And whatever they do, to think positively and be concerned about other people, to think in terms of them being able to not succumb to many of the temptations, especially the use of drugs and substances that will destroy the physical health, as well as mental health. (Academy of Achievement 2005)

Affirmative Action

Discrimination

Since its inception nearly 50 years ago, affirmative action has been a "contentious issue on national, state, and local levels" (Yee 2001:135). Affirmative action is a policy that has attempted to improve minority access to occupational and educational opportunities (Woodhouse 2002). No federal initiatives enforced affirmative action until 1961, when President John Kennedy signed Executive Order 10925. The order created the Committee on Equal Employment Opportunity and forbade employers with federal contracts from discriminating on the basis of race, color, national origin, or religion in their hiring practices. In 1964, President Lyndon Johnson signed into law the Civil Rights Act, which prohibits discrimination based on race, color, religion, or national origin by private employers, agencies, and educational institutions receiving federal funds (Swink 2003).

In June 1965, during a graduation speech at Howard University, President Johnson spoke for the first time about the importance of providing opportunities to minority groups, an important objective of affirmative action. According to Johnson (1965),

> You do not take a person who, for years, has been hobbled by chains and liberate him, bring him to the starting line of a race and then say, "You are free to compete with all others" and still justly believe you have been completely fair. Thus it is not enough just to open the gates of opportunity. All our citizens must have the ability to walk through those gates. This is the next and the more profound stage of the battle for civil rights. We seek not just freedom but opportunity. (p. 366)

Employment

In September 1965, President Johnson signed Executive Order 11246, which required government contractors to "take affirmative action" toward prospective minority employees in all aspects of hiring and employment. Contractors are required to take specific proactive measures to ensure equality in hiring without regard to race, religion, and national origin. The order also established the Equal Employment Opportunity Commission (EEOC), charged with enforcing and monitoring compliance among federal contractors. In 1967, President Johnson amended the order to include discrimination based on gender (Swink 2003). In 1969, President Richard Nixon initiated the Philadelphia Plan, which required federal contractors to develop affirmative action plans by setting minimum levels of minority participation on federal construction projects in Philadelphia and three other cities (Idelson 1995). This was the first order that endorsed the use of specific goals for desegregating the workplace (Kotlowski

1998), but it did not include fixed quotas (Woodhouse 2002). In 1970, the order was extended to all federal contractors (Idelson 1995).

According to Dawn Swink (2003), "While the initial efforts of affirmative action were directed primarily at federal government employment and private industry, affirmative action gradually extended into other areas, including admissions programs in higher education" (pp. 214–15). State and local governments followed the lead of the federal government and took formal steps to encourage employers to diversify their workforces.

Opponents of affirmative action believe that such policies encourage preferential treatment for minorities (Woodhouse 2002), giving women and ethnic minorities an unfair advantage over White males (Yee 2001). Affirmative action, say its critics, promotes "reverse discrimination," the hiring of unqualified minorities and women at the expense of qualified White males. Some believe affirmative action has not worked and ultimately results in the stigmatization of those who benefit from the policies (Heilman, Block, and Stahatos 1997; Herring and Collins 1995).

Proponents argue that only through affirmative action policies can we address the historical societal discrimination that minorities experienced in the past (Kaplan and Lee 1995). Although these policies have not created true equality, there have been important accomplishments (Tsang and Dietz 2001). As a result of affirmative action, women and people of color have gained increased access to forms of public employment and education that were once closed to them (Yee 2001). Yet, research indicates that ethnic minorities and women do not have an unfair advantage over White men. Women and ethnic minorities are not receiving equal compensation compared with White males with similar education and background (Tsang and Dietz 2001).

G. L. A. Harris (2009) explains that although the record on affirmation action is mixed, there is evidence that without the policy and the use of gender, race, and/or other ethnicity as part of the employment hiring process, the employment status of women and underrepresented minorities would be worse. Affirmative action has been the "only comprehensive set of policies that has given women and people of color opportunities for better paying jobs and access to higher education that did not exist before" (Yee 2001:137). There is also evidence of how White employees benefit from the inclusion of these groups in the workplace; for example, companies with more than 100 employees with affirmation action programs have higher earnings for Whites, women, and minority employee groups (Pincus 2003).

Shawn Woodhouse (1999, 2002) argues that the differences in individual perceptions of affirmative action policy may be related to the differences of racial group histories and socialization experiences. She writes,

> Based upon these rationalizations, it is implicit that individuals interpret affirmative action through an ethnic specific lens. In other words, most individuals will assess their group condition when considering contentious legislation such as affirmative action because after all, a group's history impacts its view of American society. (Woodhouse 2002:158)

Education

Based on Title VI of the 1964 Civil Rights Act, affirmative action policies have been applied to student recruitment, admissions, and financial aid programs. Title VI permits the consideration of race, national origin, sex, or disability to provide opportunities to a class of disqualified people, such as minorities and women, who have been denied educational opportunities. Affirmative action policies have been supported as remedies for past discrimination and as means to encourage diversity in higher education. Affirmative action practices were affirmed in the 1978 Supreme Court decision in the *Regents of the University of*

California v. Bakke, suggesting that race-sensitive policies were necessary to create diverse campus environments (American Council on Education and American Association of University Professors 2000; Springer 2005).

Although affirmative action has been practiced since the *Bakke* decision, it has recently become vulnerable, particularly to challenges of the diversity argument in the Supreme Court's decision. The first challenge occurred in one of our most diverse states, California. In 1995, the California Board of Regents banned the use of affirmative action guidelines in admissions. In 1996, California voters followed and passed Proposition 209, the California Civil Rights Initiative, which effectively dismantled the state's affirmative action programs in education and employment. Also in 1996, a federal appeals court ruling struck down affirmative action in Texas. In the *Hopwood v. Texas* decision, the ruling referred to affirmative action policies as a form of discrimination against White students. State of Washington voters passed an initiative in 1998 that banned the use of race-conscious affirmative action in schools. In 1999, Florida Governor Jeb Bush banned the use of affirmative action in admission to his state's schools.

The *Hopwood* ruling led to a decline in the number of minority students enrolling in Texas A&M and the University of Texas (Yardley 2002). California's state universities experienced a similar drop in minority student applications and enrollment after the *Bakke* decision and the California Civil Rights Initiative. In response, states have instituted other practices with the goal of increasing minority student recruitment. For example, California and Texas have initiated percentage solutions. In Texas, the top 10% of all graduating seniors are automatically admitted into the University of Texas system. (In 2009, the Texas Legislature voted to put limits on the program, setting enrollment caps on the number of students let in under the rule at 75% of the entering class.) California initiated a similar plan, covering only the top 4% of students, and Florida implemented the One Florida Initiative, allowing the top 20% of graduating high school seniors into the state's public colleges and universities. The University of Georgia increased its recruitment efforts among minority students, hoping to enlarge the pool of applications from minorities (Schemo 2001).

For more than a decade, the University of Michigan's affirmation action program has been disputed. In 2000, a federal judge upheld the University of Michigan's program, ruling that "a racially and ethnically diverse student body produces significant educational benefits such that diversity, in the context of higher education, constitutes a compelling governmental interest" (Wilgoren 2000:A32). In 2003, the case was considered by the U.S. Supreme Court, and in a 5 to 4 vote, the Court upheld the University of Michigan's consideration of race for admission into its law school. Writing for the majority, Justice Sandra Day O'Connor stated, "In order to cultivate a set of leaders with legitimacy in the eyes of the citizenry, it is necessary that the path to leadership be visibly open to talented and qualified individuals of every race and ethnicity" (Greenhouse 2003:A1). In a separate decision, the U.S. Supreme Court voted 6 to 1, invalidating the university's affirmative action program for admission into its undergraduate program. Unlike the law school program, the undergraduate program used a point system based on race. Twenty points on a scale of 150 were awarded for membership in an underrepresented minority group; 100 points were necessary to gain admission into the university (Greenhouse 2003).

In November 2006, Michigan voters approved Proposal 2, a state law banning consideration of race or gender in public university admissions or government hiring or contracting. After asking the courts if it could delay complying with the new law until its current admission process had been completed, the University of Michigan announced in January 2007 that it would comply with the law and stop considering race or gender in its admissions decisions. In 2011, a federal appeals court struck down Michigan's 2006 ban. The decision was thrown out a few months later.

In 2012, the U.S. Supreme Court heard arguments in the latest challenge of race-conscious admission practices, *Fisher v. University of Texas* (Liptak 2012b). Abigail Fisher, a White student, was denied admission to the University of Texas at Austin. She was ineligible for the state's top 10% pool and was eventually considered with a pool of other students under admission standards that included race among other factors. She filed suit against the university, claiming that she was denied admission due to her race. The court's decision is expected in 2013.

Main Points

- From a biological perspective, a **race** can be defined as a group or population that shares a set of genetic characteristics and physical features. Social scientists reject the biological notion of race, instead treating race as a social construct.

- Ethnic groups are set off to some degree from other groups by displaying a unique set of cultural traits, such as their language, religion, or diet. Members of an ethnic group perceive themselves as members of an ethnic community, sharing common historical roots and experiences.

- Sociologists explain that **ethnocentrism** is the belief that the values and behaviors of one's own group are right and actually better than all others. Although feeling positive about one's group is important for group solidarity and loyalty, it can lead groups to believe that certain racial or ethnic groups are inferior and that discriminatory practices against them are justified. This is called **racism.**

- Certain ethnic/racial groups have been subject to institutional discrimination, discrimination practiced by the government, social institutions, and organizations. Institutional discrimination may include segregation, exclusion, or expulsion.

- Segregation refers to the physical and social separation of ethnic or racial groups. **Exclusion** refers to the practice of prohibiting or restricting the entry or participation of groups in society. Expulsion is the removal of a group by using direct force or intimidation.

- The impact of race and social class has been documented in studies regarding income attainment and mobility, educational attainment, and health and medical care. In all three areas, racial and ethnic minorities are disadvantaged.

- Migration has been identified as a global issue, partly because of its impact on the global economy and terrorism. Globalization has intensified the need to coordinate and harmonize government policies worldwide.

- Multiculturalism is promoted in schools and businesses through educational programming. Most U.S. colleges and universities require a diversity course as a general requirement.

- Affirmative action is a policy that has attempted to improve minority access to occupational and educational opportunities. Since its inception, it has been a controversial issue on federal, state, and local levels.

On Your Own

Log on to the open-access Student Study Site at www.sagepub.com/leonguerrero4e for these additional learning tools:

- Interactive quizzes
- Video clips
- NPR audio links
- Handbook articles

- E-flashcards
- Journal articles
- End-of-chapter web exercises
- Additional web resources and current events

Internet and Community Exercises

1. In what ways does your college encourage or celebrate racial and ethnic diversity (among its students, faculty, and staff)? Consider specific college-sponsored clubs, activities, or events that highlight diversity on your campus.

2. To learn more about the internment of Japanese Americans during World War II, visit the websites for the Manzanar War Relocation Center and internment camps located in Tule Lake, California, and Topaz, Utah. These websites feature virtual tours, photographs, and testimony from those interned. Log on to *Study Site Chapter 3* for links.

3. Identify the largest private employer in your city or state. Investigate through the Internet or direct contact whether a diversity program or development office is in place. What are the diversity goals of this business, and how does it implement these goals (what specific program practices are in place)?

4. The International Organization for Migration, established in 1951, is an intergovernmental organization working with 146 member states to promote and support humane and effective migration management. The organization also conducts immigration research worldwide. Its website includes a global map, noting migration problems affecting a selected nation. Log on to *Study Site Chapter 3* for links.

5. Interview a student who is an immigrant. Ask the student about his or her migration experience and educational path to your college or university. Does the student's experience confirm a pattern of assimilation, pluralism, or transnationalism?

6. Does your college have a diversity requirement? If you have completed the course, do you believe the learning experience changed your diversity beliefs and values? Why or why not?

Study Questions

1. How are race and ethnicity socially constructed? Why do you think racial distinctions persist?

2. Distinguish between assimilation and pluralism (or multiculturalism). What are the advantages and disadvantages of each? Which model best describes racial and ethnic relations in the United States?

3. The term **transnational** has been used to describe the immigrants who "maintain familial, economic, cultural, and political ties across international borders, in effect making the home and host society a single arena for social action" (Foner 2000:170). In effect, transnationals have two homes. Is this functional for society? Is it functional for the life of an immigrant?

4. The interactionist perspective argues that certain races or ethnicities are bestowed power and privilege not given to other groups. Do you agree with this statement? What examples of privilege can you think of, and what are their consequences?

5. Identify and explain the two types of racial disparities in health care.

6. What are the consequences of a less-educated, lower-skilled immigrant population? How is this associated with employment, economic inequality, and health care access?

7. Which sociological perspective best explains the problem of immigration in our society? Explain.

8. Explain how having contact and interaction with other racial or ethnic groups (at school or at work) reduces interracial prejudice.

CHAPTER 4

Gender

I n 2012 an all-male panel testified on Capitol Hill on the Blunt Amendment, a proposed federal policy exception that would have allowed religious groups and employers to opt out of providing any kind of health care service, including contraception, for religious reasons. The photo of the panel was widely distributed in the media, often accompanied by the headline "What is wrong with this picture?" The exclusion of a female voice on a panel on contraception stirred up a firestorm. Two female House representatives walked out of the hearing. House representatives followed with their own hearing featuring one female witness, Georgetown student Sandra Fluke, who had been turned away from the original hearing. Democrats argued that Republicans were turning back the clock on women's rights (Pear 2012).

 Women and Politics

There is no society where men and women perform identical functions, nor are they ranked or treated equally. Regardless of their level of technological development or complexity of their social structure, all societies have some form of gender inequality (Marger 2008). Some may argue that there are fundamental differences between males and females based on fixed physiological differences or our **sex**. Yes, there are biological differences—our sexual organs, our hormones, and other physiological aspects—that are relatively fixed at birth (Marger 2008), but more than that makes us unequal.

Sociologists focus on the differences determined by our society and our culture, our **gender**. Although we are born male and female, we must understand and learn masculine or feminine behaviors. Gender legitimates certain activities and ways of thinking over others; it grants privilege to one group over another (Tickner 2002). **Sexism** refers to prejudice or discrimination based solely on someone's sex or gender. Although sexism has come to refer to negative beliefs and actions directed toward women, men can also be subject to sexism.

 Media and Constructs of Masculinity

Social scientists believe that gender differences are not caused by biological differences; rather, they are a product of socialization, prejudice, discrimination, and other forms of social

97

Photo 4.1

Representative Nancy Pelosi (D-Calif.) was elected Speaker of the House in 2007, the first woman to fill this role in the history of the U.S. Congress.

control (Bem 1993). For example, religious ideologies can define and regulate gender differences. According to Islamic tradition, women are relegated to home and family life, while men dominate everything outside of the home. A strong patriarchal system is enforced among Mormon Fundamentalists in the United States.

Consider the history of women in the U.S. Senate. There is nothing automatic at birth that makes men more suited to become senators than women. The first woman senator was Rebecca Latimer Felton, sworn into office on November 21, 1922. The Georgia senator was appointed to fill a vacancy and served for only one day. In the early 1990s, there were only two women senators. In 1992, Patty Murray, from my home state of Washington, was the first elected woman senator to have young children at home during her term in office (Stolberg 2003). A record number of 20 women were elected to serve in the 2013 U.S. Senate.

On January 4, 2007, U.S. Representative Nancy Pelosi (D-Calif.) was elected Speaker of the House, the first woman to fill this role in the history of the House of Representatives. Pelosi was second in line for the succession of the presidency, after the vice president. On the day of her induction, Pelosi not only noted how her election was an important victory for her party but also acknowledged the importance of her election for women. She said, "For our daughters and granddaughters, today we have broken the marble ceiling. For our daughters and our granddaughters now, the sky is the limit" (Pelosi 2007). Yet a few months later, as Pelosi celebrated Women's History Month, she is quoted as saying,

> Women want what men want: an equal opportunity to succeed, a safe and prosperous America, good paying jobs, better access to health care, and the best possible education for our children. . . . Yet in terms of policies to assist women, we are lagging behind. Paychecks for women have dropped three years in [a] row by almost $1,000. On average, working women earn only 77 cents for every dollar working men earn, and over the last five years, the number of women living in poverty has grown by almost 3 million. (Pelosi 2007)

Despite the record number of women serving in Congress, the United States is behind other countries in female representation in a national parliament or congress. Refer to Table 4.1 for more information.

What Does It Mean to Me?

In 2011, the U.S. Coast Guard Academy named Rear Admiral Sandra Stosz its first female superintendent. She is the first woman to lead a U.S. service academy. Examine the academic leadership in your university. How many top positions are held by men? By women? Is leadership gendered at your university?

 STATE STATS

Table 4.1

Top 10 Countries With the Highest Percentage of Seats in National Parliaments Held by Women, as of February 2013

Country	Percentage of Women	Country	Percentage of Women
Rwanda	56.3	Senegal	42.7
Andorra	50.0	Finland	42.5
Cuba	45.2	South Africa	42.3
Sweden	44.7	Nicaragua	40.2
Seychelles	43.8	Iceland	39.7

Source: Inter-Parliamentary Union 2013.

Note: In the list compiled by the Inter-Parliamentary Union (2013), the United States ranks 77th with 17.8% of seats held by women.

Sociological Perspectives on Gender Inequality

Functionalist Perspective

Functionalists argue that gender inequality is inevitable because of the **gendered division of labor** in the household. According to Émile Durkheim, social evolution led to the exaggeration of sex differences in personalities and abilities. In the most basic of social institutions, the family, it became necessary for men and women to establish role differentiation as well as functional interdependence. In other words, men and women would have complementary but different roles in the household.

Durkheim (2007) wrote of the biological differences between men and women, claiming that women had smaller brain capacity than males: "Woman retired from warfare and public affairs and consecrated her entire life to her family" (p. 43). As a result, women led completely different lives than men. This division of labor applied both in and out of the home—women were charged with familial roles, taking care of their children and their home, while men were charged with public work roles, assuming their primary role as family breadwinner. Although this division of labor may have been practical in preindustrial society, these roles remain gender specific in modern society (Marger 2008). Though women have transitioned from a housekeeper role to a dual role of earner and caregiver, men's involvement in domestic work remains low.

The principle that women and men are suited for different roles extends to the workplace. Women dominate service and caring professions (e.g., teaching, health care, sales, and administrative support), while men are overrepresented in instrumental work (e.g., construction, heavy labor, and mechanics). Even in the same professions, men and women are on different professional tracks. Among medical students, women choose primary care specialties, while a higher percentage of men choose surgical specialties. Women place a greater emphasis on the physician–patient relationship than men (McFarland and Rhoades 1998). For more

Gender Roles in the Workplace

on occupational segregation, refer to the section of this chapter titled "The Consequences of Gender Inequality."

This gendered division of labor and gender roles is held as the standard for society. Gender inequality is defined not as a product of differential power but, rather, as a functional necessity (Marger 2008). Women who assert their rights for social and economic equality are seen as attacking the structure of society (Bonvillian 2006). Theorists from this perspective note that as increasing numbers of women have entered the workforce, the number of divorces and the frequency of nonmarital childbearing have also increased. They suggest that children are more likely to suffer from divorce, more likely to become delinquent without adequate parental supervision, and more likely to be disadvantaged economically and socially if born to a single mother (Bonvillian 2006; Farley 2005). From this perspective, a change in gender roles (among women in particular) undermines the stability of the family (Farley 2005) and, ultimately, society.

Conflict and Feminist Perspectives

Benevolent Sexism

Gender inequality exists because it benefits a group in power and with power to shape society—men. Theorists from both perspectives argue that women will remain in their subordinate position as long as men maintain their social, economic, and cultural advantage in society. A system where men are dominant over women is referred to as a patriarchy, as defined earlier in Chapter 1.

Women's subordinate position in society is linked to their relationship to the means of production. As the next section of this chapter describes, compared with women, men are rewarded in our capitalist economy with higher wages, more prestige, and greater authority in the workplace (Bonvillian 2006). At home, men are treated with deference by their wives and children.

Bonvillian (2006) explains the interrelationship between patriarchal social relations and capitalist economies. As capitalistic economies developed, they incorporated preexisting patriarchal relations. Capitalism benefits from women's subordinate position at home. Women are willing to work in different types of jobs and for different wages than men because they define themselves according to their familial relationships as supporters rather than as breadwinners.

Capitalism also takes advantage of men's adherence to patriarchal values, subordinating men to their employers just as patriarchal relations subordinate women to men. Men are duty bound to their jobs because of a sense of self-worth and obligation tied to their ability to provide for their families (Bonvillian 2006). As men are limited to their prescribed positions in the economy and production, their inner emotional states are devalued in society. According to Böhnisch (2003), this limits the development of their full human potential (much like Marx cautioned), also contributing to a range of male problems (e.g., health and chronic illnesses, risk taking, and violence).

Photo 4.2

Georgetown law student Sandra Fluke testified on women's health and contraceptive coverage before the House Democratic Steering and Policy Committee in 2012.

Early feminist scholars treated gender as an individual attribute, as a property of individuals or as part of the role that was acquired through socialization. However, contemporary feminist theorists define gender as a system of social practices that creates and maintains gender distinctions and inequalities (Ridgeway and Smith-Lovin 1999). Gender is referred to as a process, where gender is continually produced and reproduced. Not only is this an individual characteristic, but also it exists within patterns of social interaction and social institutions (Wharton 2004).

Gender inequality is a product of a complex set of social forces: "These may include the actions of individuals, but they are also found in expectations that guide social interaction, the composition of social groups, and the structures and practices of the institutions" (Wharton 2004:157). Sexism may be an individual act, but it can also become institutionalized in our organizations or through laws and common practices.

True gender equality is possible only if women are able to assume positions of power in the economy and political system (Marger 2008) and redefine the structures and practices that oppress them. Though gender issues have been defined primarily as women's issues, the call for integrating men's issues into the discussion of gender inequality has become louder (Scambor and Scambor 2008). Structural inequalities between men and women don't just discriminate against women. From this perspective, tackling gender inequality means to question gendered structures at various levels (labor, child care, socialization, family) and to address the experience of men and women equally.

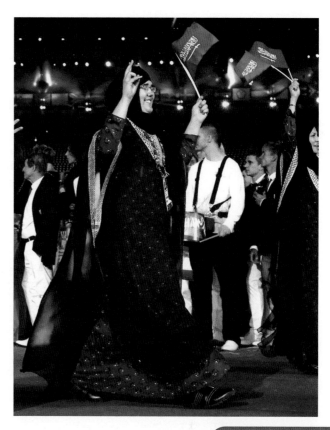

Photo 4.3

In 2011, King Abdullah of Saudi Arabia granted women the right to vote and to run for office in municipal elections. In January 2012, the Saudi Ministry of Labor began enforcing a royal decree that allowed female sales personnel in shops selling garments and goods (such as lingerie and cosmetics) that are only for women. Before the decree, women were not allowed in the public workforce. For the 2012 Summer Olympic Games, the Saudi Olympic Committee agreed to send its first female athletes, one in track and field and the other in judo (pictured here, Wojdan Ali Seraj Abdulrahim Shahrkhani). During the opening ceremonies, the female athletes walked behind the male athletes, not alongside them.

Interactionist Perspective

As interactionists explain, many social values and meanings are expressed in our language. Language, write Stephanie Wildman and Adrienne Davis (2000), "contributes to the invisibility and regeneration of privilege" (p. 50). These scholars argue that we need to sort individuals into categories such as race and gender. Upon hearing that someone has a new baby, why is it important to ask if it's a girl or a boy? This type of social categorization is important because it sets into motion the production of gender difference and inequality. Norms, values, and beliefs about the differences between boys and girls and men and women are reinforced through the gender socialization process. We won't know how to relate to this child without knowing its gender, and children won't understand what it means to be male or female in our society unless they are socialized accordingly. People respond to others based on what they believe is expected of them and assume that others will do the same (Wharton 2004).

Wildman and Davis note that characteristics of those who are privileged become societal norms—the standard of what is good, correct, and normal versus bad, incorrect, and aberrant. In terms of gender, men are privileged and serve as the standard. Wildman and Davis (2000) refer to Catharine MacKinnon's observation that among many things, "men's physiology defines most sports, their health needs largely define insurance coverage . . . their perspectives and concerns define quality in scholarship, their experiences and obsessions define merit, . . . their image defines god, and their genitals define sex" (p. 54).

Gender Biased Nouns

Male privilege defines many aspects of American culture from a distinctly male point of view. For example, the use of *he* is accepted as an all-inclusive pronoun, but a generic *she* is not permitted; some actually get upset if you try to use it (if you have any doubt, try referring to God as *she*). The response, according to Wildman and Davis, is not about incorrect grammar; rather, it is about challenging the system of male privilege.

A summary of the sociological perspectives is presented in Table 4.2.

Table 4.2

Summary of Sociological Perspectives: Inequalities Based on Gender

	Functionalist	Conflict/Feminist	Interactionist
Explanations of gender inequality	Gender inequality is a functional necessity. A gendered division of labor and gender roles is needed to ensure the stability of society.	Women will remain in their subordinate position as long as men maintain their social, economic, and cultural advantage. Conflict theorists identify how women's subordinate position is linked to their relationship to the means of production. Feminist theorists refer to gender as a process, a system of social practices that creates and maintains gender distinctions and inequalities.	Social values and meanings are expressed in our language. Our language reflects the privileged position granted to men.
Questions asked about gender inequality	What societal values are supported by our (traditional) gender roles? Can gender roles be changed without jeopardizing the stability of society?	How is gender inequality created and maintained? How can the gender inequality structures and practices be altered? Can they be eliminated?	How does our use of language identify the privileged position of men in society? Can language be changed to reflect gender equality?

What Does It Mean to Me?

The Disney Channel's Doc McStuffins features an African American girl in pigtails who runs a home clinic for her stuffed animals and dolls. Her mom is a doctor, and her dad stays at home. Doc McStuffins has been praised for being a positive and inspirational role model for African American girls. According to the American Medical Association, in 2012, there were 18,533 Black female physicians, 2% of all U.S. doctors (Elber 2012). What role do the media play in shaping gender identity? In shaping occupational choices for boys and girls?

The Consequences of Gender Inequality

Gender inequality is a persistent feature of all modern societies. In this section, we will review the consequences of inequality in the following areas: employment, income, and education. Additional discussions on gender inequality are presented in Chapter 8, "Education," and Chapter 9, "Work and the Economy."

Occupational Sex Segregation

Sex segregation in the workplace remains a historical and contemporary fact. Despite educational and occupational gains made by women, women continue to dominate traditionally female occupations, which is referred to as **occupational sex segregation**. These occupations include secretaries (96.1% are women), child care workers (94.7%), receptionists (92.7%), and teacher assistants (92.4%) (U.S. Department of Labor, Women's Bureau 2010). (Twenty women senators out of 100 U.S. senators constitute 20%. In contrast, Iraq's temporary constitution adopted in 2004 required 25% of national assembly seats to be filled by women. Yet equal rights for Iraqi women regarding marriage and inheritance were not guaranteed by the constitution.) For the top 10 leading occupations of employed U.S. women, refer to Table 4.3.

 Working Dads

Social scientists examine two types of sex segregation in the workplace—horizontal and vertical. **Horizontal segregation** represents the separation of women into nonmanual labor and men into manual labor sectors. **Vertical segregation** identifies the elevation of men into the best-paid and most desirable occupations in nonmanual and manual labor sectors, whereas women remain in lower-paid positions with no job mobility.

Maria Charles and David Grusky (2004) identify several social factors that promote and reproduce horizontal segregation. Employer and institutional discrimination help maintain the separation of women and men in the workplace, for example, by excluding women

Table 4.3

10 Leading Occupations of Women, 2010

Occupation	Women (%)	Median Weekly Earnings
Secretaries and administrative assistants	96.1	$657
Child care workers	94.7	398
Receptionists and information clerks	92.7	529
Teacher assistants	92.4	485
Registered nurses	91.1	1,039
Bookkeeping, accounting, and auditing clerks	90.9	628
Maids and housekeeping cleaners	89.0	376
Nursing, psychiatric, and home health aides	88.2	427
Personal and home care aides	86.1	405
Office clerks, general	84.2	597

Source: U.S. Department of Labor, Women's Bureau 2010.

intentionally or unintentionally from physically strenuous jobs. The process of child socialization encourages girls and boys to internalize sex-typed expectations of others, which in turn shapes their occupational aspirations and preferences. Sociologists have examined how girls and boys are subject to differential gender socialization from birth. Traditional gender role stereotypes are reinforced through the family, school, peers, and the media with images of what is appropriate behavior for girls and boys. This includes defining appropriate occupations for women versus men.

Internalization of sex-typed expectations also leads workers to believe that if they transgress norms about gender-appropriate labor, they are subject to sanctions (from disapproval from their parents to harassment from fellow workers). Years of horizontal segregation have given the advantage to men who have a disproportionate number of peers and network ties into the manual sector.

Vertical segregation is based on deeply rooted and widely shared cultural beliefs that men are more competent than women and are better suited than women for positions of power. According to Charles and Grusky (2004), vertical segregation is reproduced because it is consistent with the value of "male primacy." In her analysis of vertical segregation among men and women on Wall Street, Louise Marie Roth (2006) discovered how the gendered division of labor in the family spilled over into the workplace. Wall Street's workaholic culture assumes that the ideal employee has no external (family) obligations, setting work as the primary priority. Since child care is defined as women's responsibility, Wall Street women were routinely penalized for having families—women were expected to quit once they had children and were often treated differently after the birth of children. On the other hand, male Wall Street professionals were perceived as more committed and stable when they were married and had children. Roth concludes that males with traditional stay-at-home wives were able to maintain their ideal employee role.

Occupational sex segregation is a worldwide phenomenon. Many studies have examined segregation cross-nationally and have found that though it is a feature of all industrial societies, the degree to which it exists varies. In her analysis of vertical and horizontal segregation in 10 countries including the United States, Charles (2003) found that women were underrepresented in the manual sector and that within the manual and nonmanual sectors, women's occupations were of lower average status. She reports the highest levels of horizontal segregation in Sweden and France, where women are about 30 times more likely to work in white-collar than in blue-collar sectors. The likelihood is lower in the United States—women are 14 times more likely to work in white-collar sectors. The highest level of vertical segregation was found in France and in the United Kingdom. Vertical segregation for the United States was third lowest among the 10 countries Charles examined. The countries with the lowest levels of horizontal and vertical segregation were Portugal and Italy, which Charles attributed to the countries' development of two main occupational groups—professionals and craft-operations workers.

Jane Elliot's (2005) research revealed that there was greater occupational segregation between men and women and between full-time and part-time working women in the United Kingdom than in the United States. She characterizes employed women in the United Kingdom as having a "returner" pattern of labor participation (periodic employment vs. continual employment as in the United States) and notes that U.K. women are primarily concentrated

Greatness of Girls

Photo 4.4

The U.S. labor force continues to be segregated along gender lines. Although a small percentage of women, 25% or less, are employed in traditionally male blue-collar occupations (such as construction, truck driving, and manufacturing), women continue to dominate administrative (clerical) and service occupations, constituting more than 80% of employees in these occupations (U.S. Department of Labor, Women's Bureau 2009).

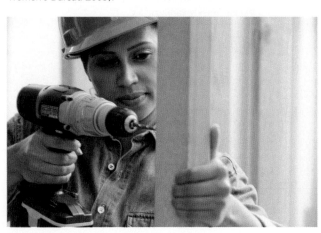

in occupational groups that rely on part-time labor. U.K. labor laws encourage the hiring of part-time employees versus full-time employees, which encourages women's employment patterns. Elliot suggests that U.K. women may be less attached to their employment than U.S. women are because national health services are available regardless of employment. In the United States, one's employer usually provides health insurance.

Income Inequality

According to the National Committee on Pay Equity (2011), in 2010, for every dollar earned by a man, a woman made 77 cents (refer to Table 4.4 for wage gap data from 1960 to 2010). U.S. Data Map 4.1 reports the wage gap between women and men by state. Another way to measure the earning difference is to examine wage ratios, comparing the annual earnings of women and women who work full-time all year—what is the difference in men's and women's lifetime earnings? Stephen Rose and Heidi Hartmann (2004) examined data for 1983 to 1998 and concluded that women workers in their prime earning years make 38% of what men make. During the 15-year period, an average prime-age working woman earned only $273,592 compared with $722,693 earned by the average working man (in 1999 dollars). (For information regarding the gap between college men and women graduates, turn to this chapter's In Focus feature.)

Why do men earn more? Social scientists have attempted to answer the question, offering different explanations for the earning gap. Some have emphasized the role of **human capital**, the skills workers acquire through education and work experience. **Human capital theory** suggests that women earn less than men do because of differences in the kind and amount of human capital they acquire (Wharton 2004). Because their labor force participation is assumed to be interrupted by marriage and child-rearing responsibilities, most women will invest less in their job-related human capital or will choose occupations that provide flexible hours or lesser penalties after reentry (e.g., teaching). In the United States, women do have less continuous work experience than men do; their labor is interrupted by childbirth and child rearing. Yet, research indicates that even among women with continuous work experience, their earnings are less than men's (England 2001).

Another explanation offered by social scientists focuses on the **devaluation of women's work**. A higher societal value is placed on men than on women, and this is reproduced within the workplace. The relative worth of men's and women's economic activities is

Gender Inequality

Equity & Gender

Salary Gap

| Table 4.4 |

Gender Wage Gap, 1960–2010

Year	Women's Earnings	Men's Earnings	Women's Earnings as a Percentage of Men's Earnings (%)
1960	$16,144	$26,608	60.7
1970	20,567	34,642	59.4
1980	22,279	37,033	60.2
1990	25,451	35,538	71.6
2000	27,355	37,339	73.3
2005	31,858	41,386	77.0
2010	36,931	47,715	77.4

Source: National Committee on Pay Equity 2011.

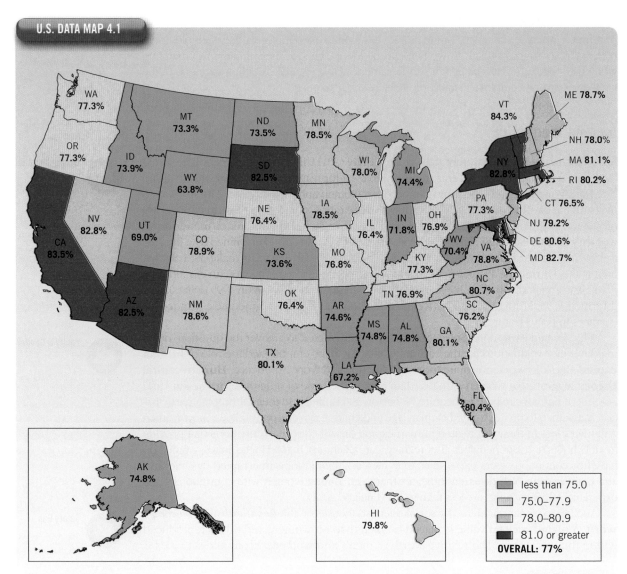

U.S. DATA MAP 4.1

		less than 75.0
		75.0–77.9
		78.0–80.9
		81.0 or greater

OVERALL: 77%

Gender Wage Gap by State, 2010, Ratio of Median Earnings for Women and Men Working Full-Time, Year-Round

Source: National Women's Law Center 2010.

assessed within this value system, with men and masculine activities valued more highly than women and feminine activities (Wharton 2004). Still, as Table 4.5 reveals, even in identical occupations, women earn less than men.

Women in the Workplace

In 2007, the Supreme Court limited workers' ability to challenge wage discrimination in court. The Supreme Court ruled that employees could not challenge ongoing compensation discrimination if the employer's original discriminatory act or decision occurred more than 180 days earlier. Prior to this decision, each discriminatory paycheck was treated as a separate discriminatory act and reset that 180-day clock to file a claim. In the original case, Lilly Ledbetter, an area manager at Goodyear Tire and Rubber Company, charged that she was paid less than her 15 male counterparts. Ledbetter was paid $3,727 per month, and the

Table 4.5

20 Occupations With the Highest Median Earnings by Sex, 2008

Men's Occupations	Median (Dollars)	Women's Occupations	Median (Dollars)
Physicians and surgeons	185,490	Engineering managers	118,170
Dentists	150,690	Physicians and surgeons	112,690
Lawyers	126,650	Pharmacists	101,610
Chief executives	122,770	Dentists	101,510
Engineering managers	112,630	Actuaries	99,110
Pharmacists	111,500	Lawyers	93,320
Judges, magistrates, and other judicial workers	111,270	Chief executives	91,460
Actuaries	109,360	Computer and information systems managers	82,540
Natural sciences managers	107,750	Optometrists	81,630
Economists	105,050	Computer software engineers	77,070
Petroleum engineers	103,440	Electrical and electronics engineers	77,060
Podiatrists	102,430	Chemical engineers	76,550
Optometrists	101,270	Engineers, all others	75,370
Astronomers and physicists	98,360	Aerospace engineers	74,580
Computer and information systems managers	95,400	Veterinarians	71,850
Air traffic controllers and airfield operations specialists	95,350	Physician assistants	71,830
		Statisticians	70,520
Financial analysts	95,190	Computer programmers	68,920
Veterinarians	93,670	Computer hardware engineers	68,400
Aerospace engineers	92,650	Judges, magistrates, and other judicial workers	68,150
Personal financial advisers	92,350		

Source: Adapted from Day and Rosenthal 2009.

Note: Twelve occupations appear on both lists, and in all cases except engineering managers, women make less than men in the same occupation.

lowest paid male manager received $4,286 per month. Though a jury awarded Ledbetter $3.3 million in damages, the Court of Appeals reversed the verdict, stating that her case was filed too late.

The Lilly Ledbetter Fair Pay Act was signed into law by President Barack Obama in January 2009. The act reinstated the prior law that allowed pay discrimination claims on the basis of sex, race, national origin, age, religion, and disability to accrue whenever an employee received a discriminatory paycheck. At the signing of the bill, Ledbetter acknowledged that she would not receive any money as a result of the law named after her. "Goodyear will never have to pay me what it cheated me out of. . . . But with the president's signature today I have an even richer reward" (quoted in Stolberg 2009).

What Does It Mean to Me?

Where does your state rank in the gender wage gap? Refer to U.S. Data Map 4.1. In your opinion, which theories offer the best explanation for why the gender wage gap still exists?

 STATE STATS

Photo 4.5

At the signing of the Lilly Ledbetter Fair Pay Act of 2009, President Obama stated that the issue of fair pay isn't just a women's issue. According to Obama, the bill ensures that all Americans are able to make a living and provide for their families. The law's namesake was at the president's side at the signing of the act (she is shown standing behind him, just to his right, in this photo).

College Admissions

Educational Attainment

In the fall of 2009, nearly 10 million women and 7.6 million men enrolled in undergraduate programs. In postbaccalaureate programs, there were 1.7 million females and 1.2 million males (U.S. Department of Education 2011). According to the American Council on Education (ACE), women now represent a 57% majority in higher education (college or university) enrollment (King 2006). In all measures—percentage of high school graduates completing college preparatory curriculum, percentage of high school graduates immediately enrolling in college, and total higher education enrollment—women rank higher than men.

The share of conferred degrees has also increased for minority women and men. Refer to Figure 4.1 for the percentage distribution of conferred bachelor's degrees by gender and race. Does this mean that fewer White men are earning bachelor's degrees than women or minority students? ACE reports that this is not the case:

> The number of white men earning bachelor's degrees has been essentially flat during this period [1996–2004], while the number of white women, and men and women of color earning bachelor's degrees has grown. So, the story has been one of increasing attainment for these groups, but no less attainment by white men. (King 2006:17)

The report notes that there is still some gender segregation by major. Men constitute most majors in theology (77%), masters of business administration (MBAs; 59%), noneducation doctorates (55%), law majors (54%), and masters of science programs (52%). Women are overrepresented in education programs (80% at the master's level and 64% at the doctoral level) but have increased their enrollment in medicine (51%) and other health science professional programs (53%).

ACE attributes the increasing enrollment and degree attainment figures for women to the rising share of young women taking college preparatory courses during the 1990s and 2000s. Yet ACE concludes that there is "no consensus on the causes of the gender gap and little

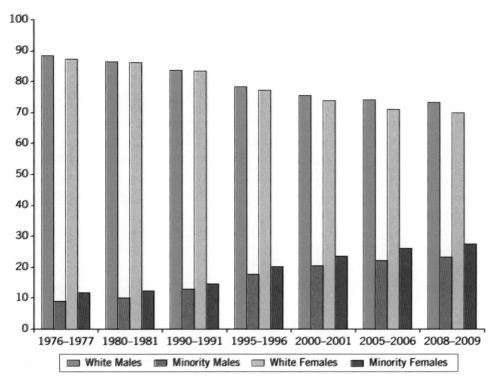

Figure 4.1

Percentage Distribution of Bachelor's Degrees Conferred by Gender and Race and Ethnicity, Selected Years 1976–1977 to 2008–2009

Source: National Center for Education Statistics 2010.

comprehensive empirical research upon which to base firm conclusions" (King 2006:20). That other industrialized countries are experiencing similar educational gains for women suggests that this phenomenon is not just an American one.

In Focus

The Pay Gap Between College-Educated Men and Women

In 2010, women working full-time still earned just 77% of what men earned. In separate analyses of data from the U.S. Department of Labor and the U.S. Department of Education, the Economic Policy Institute (a nonprofit nonpartisan think tank) and the American Association of University Women (AAUW) Educational Foundation revealed surprising earning disparities between men and women college graduates. Though the wages of college-educated women grew rapidly since 1979, a female college graduate still earned $6.76 less per hour (or 24% less) than a male college graduate in 2005 (Mishel, Bernstein, and Allegretto 2007). One year out of college, women working full-time earn only 80% as much as their male peers. Ten years after graduation, women's earnings drop to 69% of men's. Despite controlling for hours of work, occupational type, and family status, college-educated women still earn less than college-educated men (Dey and Hill 2007).

A 2012 report by the U.S. Census Bureau also documented the persistent wage gap between college-educated men and women (refer to Table 4.6). Women earned less per month than men at every degree level and in all fields of training. Stephanie Ewert (2012) highlighted the progress made by women in the natural sciences. In this field men's and women's median monthly earnings did not significantly differ at the bachelor's degree levels (and associate's degree, not shown here), but women still earned significantly less than men at the advanced degree level.

(Continued)

(Continued)

Table 4.6

Median Monthly Earnings by Educational Attainment, Sex, and Field of Training Among the Population Aged 18 and Older, 2009

	Median Earnings	
	Men	Women
Bachelor's Degree	5,117	3,750*
Business	5,000	4,000*
Computers	5,833	4,900
Engineering	6,250	(B)
Liberal Arts	4,600	3,599*
Social Science	4,314	3,417
Natural Science	4,583	4,200
Education	3,984	3,333*
Other	5,000	4,000*
Advanced Degree	6,667	5,000*
Business	7,250	5,833*
Computers	8,333	(B)
Engineering	7,794	(B)
Liberal Arts	5,000	4,500
Social Science	7,416	5,400*
Natural Science	8,334	5,724*
Education	5,167	4,642*
Other	6,250	5,000*

Source: Ewert 2012.

*Notes: (B) denotes base < 200,000; * significant difference at the .10 level.*

Responding to Gender Inequalities

Feminist Movements and Social Policies

Historians mark the beginning of the feminist movement in the United States and throughout the world in the nineteenth century. The U.S. feminist movement began in 1848 with the first Women's Rights Convention. A group of women, lead by Elizabeth Cady Stanton and Lucretia Mott, adopted a declaration of sentiments demanding, among other things, women's right to vote. During the same time, the women's suffrage movement began in Great Britain, with increasing demands for women's political and economic equality. The Nineteenth Amendment in 1920 affirmed for U.S. women the right to vote. In Great Britain, women were given the right to vote in 1918.

The feminist movement has been defined in "waves," the first beginning in the nineteenth century, followed by the second one during the twentieth century. Politically, the second wave focused on expanding legal rights for women. During this period, Title VII of the Civil Rights Act of 1964 was passed prohibiting sexual harassment in the workplace and providing equal workplace opportunities for women and minorities (refer to Chapter 3, "Race and Ethnicity," for a discussion on affirmative action in employment and education), and Title IX of the Education Amendments was passed in 1972 (refer to the next section). Still, the movement was unsuccessful in passing the Twenty-Seventh Amendment to the U.S. Constitution, the Equal Rights Amendment (ERA), which proposed, "Equality of rights under law shall not be denied or abridged by the United States, or by any state, on account of sex." Though passed by the U.S. Congress in 1972, it was not ratified by the required 38 states to become a constitutional amendment. In 1977, Indiana became the 35th state, the last state, to ratify the amendment. ERA ratification bills have been introduced in remaining states without any success.

Workplace Discrimination

Domestic Violence

Taking a World View

Violence Against Women

Femicide, sexual violence, sexual harassment, sex trafficking, and other forms of violence against women were recently documented in the UN Secretary-General's 2006 report on violence against women. "Punished for being female" is how Herbert (2006) described the findings of the UN report.

Based on surveys on violence against women conducted in 71 countries, the report revealed that a significant proportion of women suffer physical, sexual, or psychological abuse, with the most common form of abuse being physical violence inflicted by an intimate partner. The United Nations stated that at least one in three women is subjected to intimate partner violence in her lifetime.

The systematic killing of women, **femicide**, is different from the murder of men and often involves sexual violence. The UN report indicates that between 40% and 70% of women murder victims are killed by husbands or boyfriends in Australia, Canada, Israel, South Africa, and the United States. One woman is reportedly killed by an intimate partner every six days in Colombia.

Female infanticide, prenatal sex selection, and the neglect of girls are widespread in South and East Asia, North Africa, and the Middle East. The United Nations estimates that more than 130 million girls have experienced or are dealing with the consequences of female genital mutilation.

The report attributes violence against women to historically unequal power relations between men and women and pervasive discrimination against women. Violence, said the United Nations, "is one of the key means through which male control over women's agency and sexuality are maintained" (United Nations 2006a:1). The report makes clear that violence is not confined to one nation, culture, or region; however, a woman's personal experience of violence is likely to be shaped by her ethnicity, class, age, sexual orientation, disability, nationality, and/or religion.

The study identifies the short- and long-term effects of violence against women. Women are more likely to suffer from physical, mental, chronic health, and reproductive health problems. Depression is a common response to sexual and physical violence. Violence against women may stop them from fulfilling their potential, restrict their economic activity and growth, and undermine their personal development. The costs of violence against women are both direct (services to treat and support women and their children and to bring their perpetrators to justice) and indirect (loss of productivity, as well as human suffering). The United Nations concluded by saying that violence against women "can only be eliminated, therefore, by addressing discrimination, promoting women's inequality and empowerment, and ensuring that women's human rights are fulfilled" (United Nations 2006b:1).

Source: United Nations 2006a, 2006b.

The third wave of feminism began in the 1990s. Though second-wave feminists are credited with achieving greater gender equality, they are criticized for assuming the universalization of the White woman's experience and for focusing exclusively on oppression based solely on sex. The third wave of feminism attempts to address multiple sources of oppression—acknowledging oppression based on race and ethnicity, social class, and sexual orientation in addition to sex. Instead of focusing on gender equality within one country or nation, the focus has also expanded to a goal of global equality. Some even distance themselves from the use of the term *feminist*, believing the term is too confining or negative.

A fourth wave of feminism has been noted in scholarly and popular literature. The wave is defined in various ways. Brazilian sociologists Solange Simões and Marlise Matos (2009) define the term as a process of gendered democratic institutionalization and policy making, which includes a "revitalization of a classic feminist rights agenda under the influence of transnational feminism and the globalization of local women's agendas" (p. 95). The fourth wave synthesizes the second wave's emphasis on equality and the third wave's focus on global inequality. Fourth-wave feminism has also been described as a movement without one cohesive cause, leader, or platform. Younger women, for whom equality and rights were always granted, seek new ways to remain politically and socially engaged (e.g., the Internet).

The European Union, since the late 1990s, has embraced **gender mainstreaming** as its main strategy to address inequalities between men and women. It is defined as the integration of the gender perspective into every stage of the policy process (design, implementation, monitoring, and evaluation). Before this, gender equality policies focused primarily on the experience of women. In contrast, gender mainstreaming explicitly addresses the experiences of men, such as parental leave as a jurisdictional claim for men or labor policies for men in female-dominated occupations (e.g., nursing) (Scambor and Scambor 2008). Sweden has been described as a pioneer in developing policies for men's involvement in child care. Paternity leave campaigns of 2002 to 2006 not only featured a positive image of fatherhood but also defined parenthood as a long-term commitment, an equal responsibility for women and men.

Title IX

Among the achievements of the second wave of feminism was the passage of Title IX of the Education Amendments of 1972. Title IX of the Education Amendments prohibits the exclusion of any person from participation in an educational program or the denial of benefits based on one's sex (Woodhouse 2002). The preamble to Title IX states, "No person in the United States shall, on the basis of sex, be excluded from participation in, be denied the benefits of, or be subject to discrimination under any educational programs or activity receiving federal financial assistance." In particular, the law requires that members of both sexes have equal opportunities to participate in sports and enjoy the benefits of competitive athletics (National Women's Law Center 2002b). In this chapter's Voices in the Community, Bernice Sandler explains how she became part of the Title IX legislation.

 Gender and Sports

According to Title IX, schools receiving federal aid are required to offer women and men equal opportunities to participate in athletics. This can be done in one of three ways: Schools demonstrate that the percentage of men and women athletes is about the same as the percentage of men and women students enrolled (also referred to as the "proportionality rule"), or the school has a history and a continuing practice of expanding opportunities for women students, or the school is fully and effectively meeting its women students' interests and abilities to participate in sports. In addition, schools must equitably allocate athletic scholarships. The overall share of financial aid going to women athletes should be the same as the percentage of women athletes participating in their athletic program. Finally, schools must treat men and women equally in all aspects of sports programming. This

The first time the Olympic Games included men's basketball as a medal sport was in 1936. Women's basketball became a medal sport 40 years later, in 1976. A women's senior national team (like members of the team pictured in this photo) regularly competes in national and international competitions in addition to the Olympic Games.

 Pro Sports

requirement applies to supplies and equipment, the scheduling of games and practices, financial support for travel, and the assignment and compensation of coaches (National Women's Law Center 2002a).

The law has been widely credited with increasing women's participation in high school and collegiate sports and for women's achievement in education. For instance, in the 1971–1972 season, 294,015 girls participated in high school athletics (comprising 7% of all high school athletes); by 2006, the number had grown to nearly 3 million (41% of all high school athletes). In 1971–1972, 29,977 females participated in collegiate athletics (15% of all college athletes); by 2005, the number had grown to 166,728 (43% of all college athletes) (National Coalition for Women and Girls in Education 2008). The representation of women in athletic leadership has also increased. In 2008, almost 15,000 women were employed in intercollegiate athletics, as athletic directors, coaches, or trainers. One out of five athletic directors is a woman, the highest representation since the mid-1970s (Acosta and Carpenter 2009). Regarding college enrollment, in 1973, 41% of women high school graduates were enrolled in college; in 2010 the percentage increased to 74% (U.S. Department of Labor, Bureau of Labor Statistics 2011).

After more than 35 years, the controversy regarding Title IX continues. Many blame Title IX for the demise of some 400 collegiate men's programs. To achieve proportionality between the number of men and women athletes, schools have reduced the number of men athletes in minor sports programs such as wrestling, gymnastics, golf, and tennis (Garber 2002). In 2002, the National Wrestling Coaches Association filed a lawsuit against the U.S. Department of Education, claiming that by enforcing Title IX, the department was practicing sex discrimination against men. In June 2003, a federal judge threw out the lawsuit, ruling that the coaches did not have standing to bring the lawsuit.

Social Structure

Evidence also indicates that not all colleges and universities are complying with the law. Although women in Division I colleges represent more than half the student body, women's sports receive only 42% of athletic scholarships, 31% of recruiting funds, and 28% of operating budgets (National Women's Law Center 2012). Most surveyed Americans, about 70%, think Title IX should be strengthened or left alone (Brady 2003).

Voices in the Community

Bernice R. Sandler

In this feature, Bernice Sandler (1997), the woman behind Title IX, explains how she was transformed into a voice of change.

The year was 1969. I had been teaching part-time at the University of Maryland for several years during the time that I worked on my doctorate and shortly after I finished it. There were seven openings in the department, and I had just asked a fellow faculty member and friend why I was not considered for any of the openings. My qualifications were excellent. "But let's face it," he said. "You come on too strong for a woman." I had no idea that this rejection would not only change my life but would ultimately change the lives of millions of women and girls because it triggered a series of events that would lead to the passage of Title IX.

Although sex discrimination was illegal in certain circumstances, I quickly discovered that none of the laws prohibiting discrimination covered sex discrimination in education. I turned to the civil rights movement to see what African Americans had done to break down segregated school systems and employment discrimination, with the hope of learning what might be applicable to women's issues. I discovered a presidential executive order prohibiting federal contractors from discrimination in employment on the basis of race, color, religion, and national origin that had been amended by President Johnson, effective October 13, 1968, to include discrimination based on sex. This discovery meant that there was a legal route to combat sex discrimination on campuses that held federal contracts.

The director of the Office of Federal Contract Compliance Programs at the Department of Labor, Vincent Macaluso, had been waiting for someone to use the executive order in regard to sex discrimination. Together we planned the first complaint against universities and colleges, and the strategies to bring about enforcement of the executive order.

Two months later under the auspices of the Women's Equity Action League (WEAL), I began what quickly became a national campaign to end discrimination in education and eventually culminated in the passage of Title IX. On January 31, 1970, WEAL filed a historic class action complaint against all universities and colleges in the country with specific charges against the University of Maryland. During the next two years, I filed charges against approximately 250 institutions. Another 100 or so were filed by other individuals and organizations such as the National Organization for Women (NOW); in tandem with these administrative charges, we began a massive letter-writing campaign to members of Congress.

Rep. Edith Green (D-Ore.), chair of the subcommittee that dealt with higher education, agreed to hold congressional hearings in June and July 1970 on education and employment of women. It was a time when there were virtually no books and only a few articles that addressed the issue of discrimination against women in education. There was little research or data, and barely a handful of unnoticed women's studies courses. There were no campus commissions on the status of women and only a few institutions had even begun to examine the status of women on their campus.

In the spring of 1972, two years after the hearings, a portion of Rep. Green's original bill became law when Title VII of the Civil Rights Act was amended by Congress to cover all employees in educational institutions. Initially, Rep. Green had also sought to amend Title VI of the Civil Rights Act to include sex discrimination. However, at the urging of African American leaders and others, who were worried that opening Title VI for amendment could weaken its coverage, she proposed a separate and new title, which became Title IX.

On June 23, 1972, Title IX of the Education Amendments of 1972 was passed by Congress, and on July 1 it was signed into law by President Richard Nixon.

The words "too strong for a woman" turned me into a feminist. At that time, I had no legal, political, or organizing experience. I was also extraordinarily naïve; I believed that if we passed Title IX, it would only take a year or two for the all the inequalities based on sex to be eliminated. Eventually, I realized that the women's movement was trying not simply to pass a piece of legislation, but to alter strongly embedded gender patterns of behavior and belief. To change all that would take masses of strong women and more than my lifetime to accomplish.

Source: Sandler 1997. Adapted with permission from Bernice Resnick Sandler, Senior Scholar, Women's Research and Education Institute, Washington, DC. E-mail: sandler@bernicesandler.com; website: www.bernicesandler.com.

What Does It Mean to Me?

Investigate how Title IX is administered in your college or university. How many men and women athletes are at your university? How many programs exist for each? Have any programs been cut as a result of Title IX requirements? Interview coaches, athletes, and administrators on their view of Title IX: Has it made a difference for students and athletes at your school?

Main Points

- All societies have some form of gender inequality. Whereas sex refers to our biological differences (those set at birth), gender refers to our masculine and feminine behaviors (those set by our society or culture). Gender legitimates certain activities and ways of thinking over others; it grants privilege to one group over another.
- Sexism refers to prejudice or discrimination based solely on someone's sex. Sexism may be an individual act, but it can also become institutionalized in our organizations or through laws and common practices.
- According to functionalists, our gendered division of labor and gender roles is the standard for society. Gender inequality is defined not as a product of differential power but, rather, as a functional necessity. Women who assert their rights for social and economic equality are seen as attacking the structure of American society.
- Gender inequality exists because it benefits a group in power and with power to shape society:

men. Theorists from both conflict and feminist perspectives argue that women will remain in their subordinate position as long as men maintain their social, economic, and cultural advantage in society. A system where men are dominant over women is referred to as a patriarchy. From a conflict perspective, women's subordinate position in society is linked to their relationship to the means of production. Contemporary feminist theorists refer to gender as a process, a system of social practices that creates and maintains gender distinctions and inequalities.

- From an interactionist's perspective, social values and meanings are expressed in our language. Language defines and maintains privilege in society; regarding gender, men are privileged and set many standards.

- Despite educational and occupational gains made by women, women continue to dominate traditionally female occupations, a situation referred to as occupational sex segregation. Social scientists identify two types of sex segregation in the workplace—horizontal and vertical. Horizontal segregation represents the separation of women into nonmanual labor and men into manual labor sectors. Vertical segregation identifies the situation in which men are elevated into the best-paid and most desirable occupations in nonmanual and manual labor sectors whereas women remain in lower-paid positions with no job mobility.

- Social scientists have attempted to explain the earning gap between men and women. Human capital theory suggests that women earn less than men do because of differences in the kind and amount of human capital they acquire. Another explanation offered by social scientists focuses on the devaluation of women's work.

- For many educational measures, including the percentage of high school graduates completing college preparatory curriculum, the percentage of high school graduates immediately enrolling in college, and the total higher education enrollment, women exceed men.

- The feminist movement has been defined in waves. The first began in the nineteenth century, with women's suffrage as its primary goal. The second wave began in the twentieth century with increased political focus on ensuring legal rights for women. The third wave of feminism began in the 1990s, attempting to address multiple sources of oppression—acknowledging oppression based on race and ethnicity, social class, sexual orientation, and sex. The emerging fourth wave synthesizes the second wave's emphasis on equality and the third wave's focus on global inequality. Fourth-wave feminism has also been described as a movement without one cohesive cause, leader, or platform.

- Title IX of the Education Amendments of 1972 prohibits the exclusion of any person from participation in an educational program or the denial of benefits based on that person's sex. As one of the provisions of Title IX, schools are required to offer women and men equal opportunities to participate in athletics. The law has been widely credited with increasing women's participation in high school and collegiate sports and for supporting women's achievement in education. However, some feel Title IX has been harmful to collegiate men's programs.

On Your Own

Log on to the open-access Student Study Site at www.sagepub.com/leonguerrero4e for these additional learning tools:

- Interactive quizzes
- Video clips
- NPR audio links
- Handbook articles

- E-flashcards
- Journal articles
- End-of-chapter web exercises
- Additional web resources and current events

Internet and Community Exercises

1. Several policy and advocacy organizations focus on the earnings gap between men and women. The National Committee on Pay Equity (established in 1979) provides a state ranking of pay equity on its website. The committee also provides information on what you can do to promote pay equity in your state. The Institute for Women's Policy Research supports research on women's economic status. To learn more, log on to *Study Site Chapter 4*.

2. The Center for American Women and Politics (CAWP) at Rutgers University was founded in 1971. CAWP provides informational materials on women in federal and state political offices, convenes national forums for women public officials, and organizes educational programs to prepare young women for public leadership. To find out the history of female public officials in your state, go to the center's website (log on to *Study Site Chapter 4*). The site also provides current fact sheets about women in the U.S. Senate and House of Representatives. The site also provides links to other political women's groups such as Emily's List ("Early Money Is Like Yeast"), a political organization for pro-choice Democratic women, and the National Federation of Republican Women, a political organization for women in the Republican Party.

3. The UN Development Programme created a gender inequality index in three dimensions—reproductive health, empowerment, and labor market. Review the scores on the UN website (log on to *Study Site Chapter 4*) and identify the top five and bottom five nations on the list.

Study Questions

1. What is the difference between sex and gender? How is gender socially constructed?

2. Define sexism. Identify one example of institutional sexism.

3. Examine occupational segregation from the functionalist and conflict perspectives.

4. From an interactionist perspective, Wildman and Davis (2000) offer several examples of how our language privileges men over women. Can you identify cases of female privilege over men?

5. The gender role socialization process reinforces our beliefs about the differences between men and women. Is it possible to raise boys and girls the same way, to be gender neutral in the socialization process? Why or why not?

6. How do sociologists explain the wage gap between men and women? Do you think it is possible to reduce or eliminate the gap?

7. Explain the importance of the four waves of feminism.

8. We take special note of female firsts—the first woman secretary of state (Madeleine Albright), the first woman Speaker of the House (Nancy Pelosi), the first women presidents of Princeton University (Shirley M. Caldwell Tilghman) and Harvard University (Drew Gilpin Faust), and the first woman to receive an Academy Award for directing (Kathryn Bigelow). All of these events occurred during the late twentieth and early twenty-first centuries, two centuries after the beginning of the feminist movement. In your opinion, has the feminist movement been successful? What remains to be achieved? Would you describe yourself as a feminist? Why or why not?

CHAPTER 5

Sexual
Orientation

Uganda's Anti-Homosexual Bill

In an announcement that led to worldwide condemnation, lawmakers in Uganda considered adopting an antihomosexuality law in 2009, proposing the death penalty for certain homosexual acts (e.g., with a minor, if the perpetrator is HIV positive, or for serial offenders) (Gettleman 2010). David Kato was one of the leading voices against the legislation. Despite threats of violence and harm, Kato, an openly gay man, maintained, "If we keep on hiding, they will say we are not here." Kato cofounded the advocacy group Sexual Minorities Uganda (SMUG). In 2011, Kato was murdered several weeks after winning a court decision over a Ugandan tabloid that called for the killing of homosexuals. The antihomosexuality law was reintroduced in 2012, excluding the death penalty clause. Currently, homosexuality in Uganda is punishable by incarceration for up to 14 years.

One's sexual orientation serves as a basis of inequality. **Sexual orientation** is defined as the classification of individuals according to their preference for emotional-sexual relationships and lifestyle with persons of the same sex (**homosexuality**) or persons of the opposite sex (**heterosexuality**). **Bisexuality** refers to emotional and sexual attractions to persons of either sex. The term **transgendered** does not refer to a specific sexual orientation; rather, it refers to individuals whose gender identity is different from the one assigned to them at birth. The term **LGBT** is often used to refer to lesbians, gays, bisexuals, and transgendered individuals as a group.

There is no definitive study on the number of individuals who identify as homosexual or bisexual. The study that is most often cited was conducted in 1994 by Robert Michael and his colleagues. Based on a random survey of 3,432 U.S. adults ages 18 to 59 years, Michael et al. found that 2.8% of men and 1.4% of women thought of themselves as homosexual or bisexual. About 5% of surveyed men and 4% of women said they had had sex with someone of the same gender after they turned 18. About 6% of men and 4% of women reported that they were sexually attracted to someone of the same gender.

Based on the U.S. Census 2000 and election voter polls, David Smith and Gary Gates (2001) estimated the gay and lesbian population at 5%, or more than 10 million men and women. A total of 601,209 gay and lesbian families were reported by the 2000 U.S. Census. When the Gallup Organization conducted a national survey of more than 120,000 Americans in 2012, 3.4% of respondents identified as lesbian, gay, bisexual, or transgendered (Gates and Newport 2012).

Gay rights have progressed in the United States and globally. In 1996, South Africa became the first country to establish a constitutional ban against discrimination based on sexual orientation. In 2000, Vermont was the first U.S. state to recognize civil unions between same-sex partners; in 2004, Massachusetts was the first state to legalize same-sex marriage. Though national polls indicate increased support of gay and lesbian individuals, as a group they are still not immune to the experience of social problems. Based on their sexual orientation, gay and lesbian individuals continue to experience prejudice and discrimination regarding equal protection under family law and equal opportunities in the workplace.

Repeal of Don't Ask Don't Tell

Sociological Perspectives on Sexual Orientation and Inequality

Our understanding of sexual orientation is based upon research from biology, psychology, and sociology. Each examines the causes and consequences of sexual orientation from its unique and sometimes controversial point of view.

Researchers exploring the biological basis of sexual orientation have considered two theoretical approaches. The first is neurohormonal theory, arguing that homosexuality is caused by atypical sex hormone levels in utero. Human studies have suggested that specific centers in the brain are related to sexual orientation and sexual behavior. The second approach is based upon behavioral genetics, identifying the source and magnitude of genetic influences on sexual orientation. This line of research was first motivated by the idea that gay men are genetically female, a hypothesis that was eventually discredited.

Confirmation of the genetic link to sexual orientation has been found through comparative studies of identical twins (twins who have nearly identical genetic makeup) and fraternal twins (twins who share some similar genetic makeup). Bailey and Pillard (1991) and Bailey and Bell (1993) found it more likely that identical twins are both gay (if one is gay) than is the case for fraternal twins. In their assessment of biological research on sexual orientation, Brian Mustanski, Meredith Chivers, and Michael Bailey (2002) conclude that sexual orientation is influenced by biological factors to some degree. They say that the questions that remain to be answered are how and when these biological factors act and to what degree these factors influence sexual orientation in women and men.

Early psychological studies treated homosexuality as a pathology, as a mental illness. This perspective was not universal among psychologists. Havelock Ellis argued that homosexuality was inborn, and therefore it could not be considered a disease (Robinson 1976). Sigmund Freud believed that all humans were innately bisexual and that homosexuality and

Photo 5.1

David Kato, an advocacy leader for Sexual Minorities Uganda, was murdered in 2011. He was considered a founding father of Uganda's gay rights movement.

Gay Lifestyle

heterosexuality were the result of social and personal experiences. Both agreed that homosexuality was not an illness.

However, homosexuality was explicitly defined as a mental illness by the American Psychiatric Association in its *Diagnostic and Statistical Manual of Mental Disorders* until 1973; a diagnosis for ego-dystonic homosexuality was introduced in 1980 but removed entirely in 1986. The World Health Organization removed a similar classification from its *International Classification of Diseases and Related Health Problems* in 1992. The declassification of homosexuality as a mental illness was in response to empirical research but also to more favorable cultural and social norms pertaining to homosexuality.

LGBT in Higher Education

Shifting away from homosexuality as an illness, psychologists currently examine the impact of a homosexual identity. Rates of mental health problems (e.g., depression, anxiety, substance abuse, and suicidality) are higher among homosexual men and women due in part to the social discrimination and cultural stigmatization they experience. Researchers in this field also examine the causes of attitudes toward homosexuality, particularly homophobia. A socially determined prejudice, **homophobia** is an irrational fear or intolerance of homosexuals (Lehne 1995). Homophobia is particularly directed at gay men.

In contrast to these biological and psychological perspectives, the sociological perspective examines the social and structural factors that affect sexual orientation.

Functionalist Perspective

Theorists in this perspective examine how society maintains our social order. Émile Durkheim argued that our social order depended on how well society could control individual behavior. Our most basic human behavior—our sexuality—is controlled by society's norms and values. Functionalists identify how society upholds heterosexuality and a marital union between a man and a woman as ideal normative behavior. This is also referred to as institutionalized heterosexuality, the set of ideas, institutions, and relationships that define the heterosexual family as the societal norm (Lind 2004).

Our legal, political, and social structures work in harmony to support these ideals (the conflict perspective of this is presented in the next section). The 1996 Defense of Marriage Act (DOMA) denies federal recognition of same-sex unions, defining marriage as a legal union only between a man and a woman. This legislation serves as a declaration about how the heterosexual family is valued and how all other family forms are not. Society grants legitimate kinship and familial obligations only through the heterosexual family. Consequently, society defines all other forms of sexuality and families that do not fit this ideal image as problematic. These forms are considered deviant or unnatural because they do not fit society's ideal.

Nonetheless, during the past decades, the gay rights movement has effectively influenced family rights, employment, and discrimination policies throughout the world. The movement has been successful largely because of its ability to affect institutional (macro) level changes—the focus of the functionalist perspective.

Conflict and Feminist Perspectives

Gore Vidal (1988) observed the following:

> In order for a ruling class to rule, there must be arbitrary prohibitions. Of all prohibitions, sexual taboo is the most useful because sex involves everyone. . . . We have allowed our governors to divide the population into two teams. One team is good, godly, straight; the other is evil, sick and vicious.

Vidal's statement addresses the focus of both these perspectives, how conflict in our society is based on sexual orientation, with heterosexuals given the advantage. This reaffirmation of heterosexuality as the moral standard is the basis of the culture wars, the struggle over creating and regulating codes of personal, social, and sexual behavior for every American. Contemporary culture wars have also concerned issues of race, ethnicity, and immigration, but the majority of culture wars revolve around issues of sexuality and gender (Bronski 1998).

Sociologists recognize that heterosexuals are granted a privileged place in our society. **Heterosexism** assumes that heterosexuality is the norm, encouraging discrimination in favor of heterosexuals and against homosexuals. Heterosexual privilege is defined as the set of privileges or advantages granted to some people because of their heterosexuality. For example, married couples receive more than 1,000 government benefits, including the right to sue based on wrongful death of a partner, access to employment-based health benefits, the ability to make medical decisions on behalf of a partner (Feigenbaum 2007), and access to social security and survivor pension benefits.

 Queer Theory

From a conflict perspective, Amy Lind (2004) identifies how the DOMA helped institutionalize heterosexism because it blocks future proactive and protective legislation for gays and lesbians. She focuses specifically on heterosexual biases in social welfare policy, identifying its impact in three ways: through policies that explicitly target LGBT individuals as abnormal or deviant, through federal definitions that assume that all families are heterosexual, and through policies that overlook LGBT poverty and social needs because of stereotypes about affluence among LGBT families.

Evidence of the first type of heterosexual bias can be found in federal legislation such as the DOMA and policy initiatives such as the healthy marriage promotion and fatherhood programs promoted by President George W. Bush. Current legislation funds abstinence only through marriage education programs in schools. Lind (2004) explains that gay, lesbian, and bisexual adolescents have no access to sexual education that pertains to their sexual experience. In an effort to preserve the traditional heterosexual family, these programs deny LGBT people their rights and needs.

 LGBT Discrimination

The second type of heterosexual bias concerns how the U.S. Census defines the family and household. Lind (2004:28) refers to the 2003 definitions used by the U.S. Census. Family is defined as "a group of two or more (one of whom is the householder) related by birth, marriage, or adoption and residing together." A household "consists of all people who occupy a housing unit" and is distinguished by family versus nonfamily households. Family households are defined as "a household maintained by a householder who is in a family (as defined above) and includes any unrelated people who may be residing there," whereas a nonfamily household is "a householder living alone or where the householder shares a home exclusively with people to whom he/she is not related." Lind argues that these definitions privilege marital unions over domestic partnerships and the status of heterosexual families over other types of families. Beginning with the 2010 Census, same-sex couples can select between two options to indicate their relationship status: "husband and wife" and "unmarried partners."

What Does It Mean to Me?

Find which state, in the 2010 Census report about same-sex partnerships, has the lowest number of total same-sex unmarried partnerships. Which state has the highest number? How does your state compare?

Finally, the third type of heterosexual bias is based on stereotypes of lesbian, gay, and bisexual (LGB) individuals and families as affluent, despite evidence that LGB families are as economically diverse and stratified as heterosexual families. Lesbians, gays, and bisexuals remain invisible in poverty studies or policies because they are assumed to be childless, have fewer family responsibilities, and thus have higher overall incomes than heterosexual households. The Movement Advancement Project, the Family Equality Council, and the Center for American Progress (2012) report that contrary to the stereotype, children raised by same-sex couples are twice as likely to live in poverty than children raised by heterosexual couples. With the exception of HIV/AIDS, it is assumed that LGB individuals do not need any economic, social, or health-related services.

From a feminist perspective, the question about gay marriage rights is bound to the ongoing critique of marriage as an institution (Bevacqua 2004). Scholars have argued that lesbian and gay marriages will positively disrupt the gendered definitions of marriage and the assumption that marriage is a prescribed hierarchy (Hunter 1995). However, just as feminists have criticized traditional marriage as an oppressive and dominating institution against women, feminists have also supported sexual freedom. Supporting gay marriages would mean that feminists would be supporting the very institution that perpetuates women's inequality.

Ann Ferguson (2007) explains that there are two main sides of the feminist argument: radical feminists who reject marriage outright on the basis of marriage as an oppressive institution versus liberal reform feminists who support the choice to marry on the understanding that men and women (or same-sex couples) can conduct their marriages in nontraditional ways. While she does not oppose long-term relationships or partnerships, radical feminist Claudia Card (1996) objects to the origins and consequences of marriage. Marriage, according to Card, has its roots not in love but in property and power, which may include the power of men over women and children. Ultimately the state, an authority external to the relationship, legitimates marriage and its subsequent benefits (i.e., federal, state, and legal benefits extended to heterosexual couples). Card states that since the institution of marriage is flawed in its origin and practice, gays and lesbians should focus their efforts on other institutional changes, such as a national health care policy that provides everyone with health coverage and access. On the other hand, Ferguson (2007) supports the liberal reform side, arguing, "We should not simply reject marriage and hope it withers away, but instead should attempt to reform it as a better way to achieve these feminist goals [equality, freedom, and care]" (p. 52). On the topic of gay marriage, however, she concludes that some gay persons should not marry, not because it is a risky institution for women, but because the right to form one's family should not be tied to one's marital status. "We should defend gay marriage as the formal right to access a basic citizen right" (Ferguson 2007:54).

What Does It Mean to Me?

Though same-sex couples would not have the same legal protection under civil unions or domestic partnerships as they would under marital law, these unions continue to be promoted by politicians and social leaders as viable alternatives to marriage. What do you think? Should civil unions or domestic partnerships be advocated as acceptable alternatives to marriage for same-sex couples? Why or why not?

Interactionist Perspective

In our society, no one gets "outed" for being straight. There is little controversy in identifying someone as heterosexual. Socially, culturally, and legally, the heterosexual lifestyle is promoted and praised. Although homosexuality has existed in most societies, it has usually been attached to a negative label—*abnormal, sinful,* or *inappropriate.* A homosexual identity also becomes a **master status**, an identity that determines how others view individuals and how individuals view themselves.

Interactionists examine how sexual orientation is constructed within a social context. We tend to think of heterosexuality as unchanging and universal; however, Jonathan Katz (2003) explains how the term is a social invention that "designates a word and concept, a norm and role, an individual and group identity, a behavior and a feeling, and a peculiar sexual-political institution particular to the late nineteenth and twentieth centuries" (p. 145). Though heterosexuality existed before it was actually named in the early nineteenth century, "The titling and envisioning of heterosexuality did play an important role in consolidating the construction of the heterosexual's social existence" (Katz 2003:145). He argues that acknowledging heterosexuality as a social invention—time bound and culturally specific—challenges the power of the heterosexual ideal.

Interactionists also examine the process of how individuals identify themselves as homosexual, what scholars describe as part of the development of a gay identity. Coming out (being gay and disclosing it to others) has come to symbolize the pursuit of individual rights and self-identification (Chou 2001). Coming out implies not just the disclosure of a gay identity but also the individual's positive attitude toward and commitment to that identity (Dubé 2000). The disclosure of a gay identity merges a private sexual identity with a public social identity (Cass 1979). To come out successfully, a gay individual needs social and institutional support, in the form of support from family and friends, legal protection from discrimination and violence, cultural acceptance, financial equality, and access to health services (D'Augelli 1998).

The process of coming out to family members is particularly stressful for LGB youth. Fear of parental reactions has been identified as a major reason that LGB youth do not come out to their families (D'Augelli, Hershberger, and Pilkington 1998). Following disclosure, youth report verbal abuse and even physical attacks by family members. Youth who lived with their families and disclosed their sexual orientation were victimized by their families more often than were youth who had not disclosed their orientation (D'Augelli et al. 1998).

To avoid negative response from others, young lesbians and gay men hide their sexual orientation from family and friends (Rivers and Carragher 2003). Gay and lesbian youth may use one or more of the following concealment strategies: inhibiting behaviors and interests associated with homosexuality, limiting exposure to the opposite sex, avoiding exposure to information about homosexuality, assuming antigay positions, establishing heterosexual relationships, and avoiding homoerotic feelings through substance abuse (Radkowsky and Siegel 1997). Research is inconclusive about how effective such concealment strategies are in reducing anxiety among lesbian and gay youth.

A summary of sociological theories regarding sexual orientation and inequality is presented in Table 5.1.

Table 5.1

Summary of Sociological Perspectives: Inequalities Based on Sexual Orientation

	Functionalist	Conflict/Feminist	Interactionist
Explanations of sexual orientation and inequality	The heterosexual family is the way in which society identifies legitimate kinship and familial obligations. Society defines all other forms of sexuality and families that do not fit this ideal image as problematic in society.	Inequality is based on one's sexual orientation. Heterosexuality is privileged in our society. Debate about same-sex marriage is bound to the feminist critique about the oppressive nature of marriage.	Sexual orientation is a social construct—time bound and culturally specific. The development of a gay identity also depends on the support and reactions of others.
Questions asked about sexual orientation and inequality	How do our social structures endorse the heterosexual family? Is it possible to change the structures, to allow inclusiveness of other family forms and other sexual orientations?	In what ways do our social structures maintain heterosexism? What other forms of oppression exist for the LGBT community? Will same-sex marriage challenge the gendered definitions of marriage?	Who or what shapes our definitions of sexual orientation? How are LGBT individuals affected by inaccurate stereotypes or labels? How can negative stereotypes or labels be changed? What social support is necessary for someone to develop a positive gay identity?

Sexual Orientation and Inequality

U.S. Legislation on Homosexuality

Queer Studies

Bisexual or homosexual men, women, and their families are subject to social inequalities through practices of discrimination and prejudice, many of them surprisingly institutionalized in formal law.

Sodomy laws criminalize oral and anal sex between two adults. Although the laws may apply to homosexuals and heterosexuals, sodomy laws are more vigorously applied against same-sex partners. Thirteen U.S. states still had state sodomy laws in 2003 (in 1960, sodomy was outlawed in every state).

In 1998, John Lawrence and Tyron Garner were fined $200 and spent a night in jail for violating a Texas statute that prohibits "deviate sexual intercourse" between two people of the same sex. The Texas statute does not apply to heterosexual couples. Their case was heard before the U.S. Supreme Court in March 2003. Attorneys for Lawrence and Garner argued that the Texas law was an invasion of their privacy and violated the equal protection clause of the Fourteenth Amendment because the law unfairly targets same-sex couples. Attorneys for the state argued that Texas has the right to set moral standards for its residents. In June 2003, the Court voted 6 to 3 to overrule the Texas law and all other remaining sodomy laws. Writing for the decision, Justice Anthony Kennedy said, "The state cannot demean their [homosexuals'] existence or control their destiny by making their private sexual conduct a crime" (Greenhouse 2003:A17). According to Kevin Cathcart, executive director of Lambda Legal (2003), "This ruling starts an entirely new chapter in our fight for equality for lesbian, gay, bisexual, and transgendered people."

In 2009, the U.S. Congress passed legislation to grant gay individuals protection under hate-crime laws. The legislation was in response to the brutal deaths of James Byrd Jr., an African American who was dragged to death in Texas, and Matthew Shepard, a gay college student who was beaten and left to die in Wyoming. The federal hate-crime law, enacted in 1968, had been limited to crimes based on race, color, religion, and national origin. Though supported by civil rights and law enforcement groups, some conservative and religious groups opposed the legislation, saying that the bill would create special classes of federally protected crime victims. The 2009 legislation also extended protections for disabled individuals. At the signing of the bill, President Barack Obama promised that people would be protected from violence based on "what they look like, who they love, how they pray or who they are" (Feller 2009).

Matthew Shepard

The Rights and Recognition of Same-Sex Couples

The DOMA permits states to ban all recognition of same-sex marriages, and now more than 41 states have such bans in place. According to the law, the federal government will not accept marriage licenses granted to same-sex couples, regardless of whether a state provides equal license privileges to all types of partnerships. The DOMA denies these couples the same federal benefits that are available to or required for married opposite-sex couples. Gay and lesbian families are denied common legal protections that nongay families take for granted such as adoption, custody, guardianship, social security, and inheritance.

In June 2002, however, President George W. Bush signed into law the Mychal Judge Act, which allows federal death benefits to be paid to the same-sex partners of firefighters and police officers who die in the line of duty (Bumiller 2002). The bill was named after the Reverend Mychal Judge, the New York City Fire Department chaplain who died in the collapse of the World Trade Center. Although White House officials say that President Bush did not consider the bill a gay issue, gay rights organizations considered its signing a milestone for gays (Bumiller 2002).

In 2006, the federal Pension Protection Act became law, containing two key provisions that extend financial protections to same-sex couples and Americans who leave their retirement savings to nonspouse beneficiaries. Under the new law, an individual's retirement plan benefit can be transferred to a domestic partner or other nonspouse beneficiary. The second provision allows gay couples and others with nonspouse beneficiaries to draw on their retirement funds in the case of a medical or financial emergency.

In 2010, President Barack Obama instructed the secretary of the Department of Health and Human Services to draft rules requiring hospitals that receive Medicare and Medicaid payments (which includes most of the nation's medical facilities) to grant all patients the right to say who has visitation rights and who can help make medical decisions. These new rules would allow full recognition of advanced health directives among gay and lesbian couples.

Reacting to what he called the "divisiveness" of President George W. Bush's 2004 State of the Union address on the issue of gay marriage, San Francisco Mayor Gavin Newsom secretly

Photo 5.2

In 2004, Del Martin (left) and Phyllis Lyon were the first legally married, same-sex couple in California, after San Francisco Mayor Gavin Newsom (center) allowed marriage licenses to be issued to same-sex couples. Within a few months, their marriage license, along with several thousand other licenses, was declared invalid. They were married again in 2008, after the California Supreme Court ruled that same-sex marriage was legal.

 Marriage

began planning to marry gay and lesbian couples and convinced longtime lesbian rights activists Del Martin, 83, and Phyllis Lyon, 79, to be the first to get married (Quittner 2004). Said Newsom, "We wanted to put a human face on this, and Phyllis and Del were critical. . . . To deny them the same protections as married couples would be to deny them as human beings, not as theory" (Quittner 2004). Between February 12 and March 10, 2004, more than 4,000 same-sex marriage licenses were issued in San Francisco. Although the majority of the couples were from California, couples from 45 other states and eight countries also applied for marriage licenses in the city (Leff 2004).

The California Supreme Court ordered San Francisco to stop issuing same-sex marriage licenses on March 11, 2004. In August 2004, the California Supreme Court ruled that Mayor Newsom did not have the authority to issue marriage licenses to same-sex couples and declared the marriage licenses invalid. At the time of the decision, Phyllis Lyon said, "It is a terrible blow to have the rights and protections of marriage taken away from us. At our age, we do not have the luxury of time" (Lambda Legal 2004).

In response to the same-sex marriages in California, President Bush endorsed a constitutional amendment that would restrict marriage to two people of opposite sexes but left open the possibility that states could allow civil unions in same-sex relationships. However, in July 2004, the U.S. Senate failed to pass a constitutional amendment that would have declared marriage a union only between a man and a woman.

The author of the DOMA legislation, Representative Bob Barr (R-Ga.), publicly expressed his concern about the effectiveness of the law and sided with President Obama's calls to repeal the law. Explaining how the DOMA's language reflects one-way federalism—protecting only those states that don't want to accept a same-sex marriage granted by another state—he agreed that the DOMA should be repealed. Barr (2009) wrote, "I believe we need to reduce federal power over the lives of citizenry and over the prerogatives of the states. It truly is time to get the federal government out of the marriage business. In law and policy, such decisions should be left to the people themselves" (p. B5). In 2011, President Obama directed the U.S. Justice Department to stop defending the DOMA in court after concluding that the law was unconstitutional (Savage and Stolberg 2011). In 2012, President Obama expressed his support for marriage of same-sex couples. Governor Mitt Romney, the 2012 Republican presidential nominee, continued to advocate for marriage as a relationship between one man and one woman.

For more on same-sex marriage legislation, refer to the discussion on family legislation in the last section of this chapter.

What Does It Mean to Me?

A public opinion survey conducted by the Gallup Organization in 2010 revealed the highest level of support for gay rights during the past three decades. The Gallup Organization reported that the majority of surveyed Americans believe that homosexuals should be able to legally adopt children (54%) and have health insurance and other employee benefits (67%) and inheritance rights (73%) for gay and lesbian domestic partners. In 2011, Frank Newport (2011) reported that, for the first time, the majority of Americans (53%) believe same-sex marriage should be legally recognized, with the same rights as traditional marriages. Pollsters noted that there has been a shift in support for homosexual rights, especially among young adults. What is your opinion on the rights of same-sex couples? Who or what has influenced your beliefs?

Employment

 Workplace Performance

 Career Development

The need to "manage a disreputable sexual identity at the workplace" has been called the most persistent problem facing lesbians and gay men (Schneider 1986:464). Between 16% and 46% of gays, lesbians, and bisexuals have experienced discrimination based on sexual orientation (Katz and LaVan 2004). Title VII of the Civil Rights Act prohibits discrimination because of sex. Sex has been interpreted to mean gender, which means that protection for homosexuals based on sexual orientation is not covered.

M. V. Badgett and Mary King (1997) note that, unlike discrimination based on easily observable characteristics such as skin color or gender, discrimination against gays and lesbians must be based on knowledge or suspicion of someone's sexual orientation. Lesbians and gay men who reveal their sexual orientation risk loss of income and lower chances at career advancement. A review of existing studies on workplace discrimination reveals that somewhere between one quarter and two thirds of LGB people report losing their jobs or missing promotions because of their sexual orientation. In addition, studies that compared gay and heterosexual workers with similar backgrounds and qualifications found that gay workers earn less than heterosexual workers (Badgett 1997).

 Photo 5.3

Brittany Geldert was one of the student plaintiffs in the federal gender and sexual orientation harassment lawsuits against Minnesota's Anoka-Hennepin School District. Geldert and other students challenged the school district's Sexual Orientation Curriculum Policy that prohibited staffers from offering their support to LGBT students or acknowledging the existence of LGBT people. The Anoka-Hennepin School Board agreed to end the policy and strengthen the district's efforts to prevent sex-based harassment.

Gay-Friendly High Schools

Protections against public and private workplace discrimination because of one's sexual orientation exist in 21 states, the District of Columbia, and several hundred U.S. cities and counties. Eighty-eight percent of all Fortune 500 companies have antidiscrimination policies that include sexual orientation, and 57% have policies that include gender identity (Human Rights Campaign 2013). Currently there is no federal law that protects LGBT individuals from employment discrimination. In 2009, the Employment Non-Discrimination Act (ENDA) was introduced in the U.S. Congress. If passed, the act would provide basic protections against workplace discrimination on the basis of sexual orientation or gender identity.

In Focus

Gay-Friendly Campuses

"What campuses do you consider to be LGBT-friendly?" This question was posed by the editors of the *Advocate College Guide for LGBT Students*. During 2006, the editors collected nominations from current LGBT college students and collected additional information based on interviews from students and faculty or staff members from the nominated schools.

The editors based their 100 final selections on 10 criteria, as reported in the guide. According to editor Bruce Steele, the editors intended to assess "the effort that's being put forth by the colleges themselves to make their LGBT students comfortable" (Rosenbloom 2006:S2). Their 10 criteria included the following:

1. Active LGBT student organization(s) on campus. Prospective LGBT students are looking for a sense of community with their peers and organizations that can offer social, educational, and leadership opportunities on campus.

2. Out LGBT students. Prospective students look for other LGBT students to be visible and active in academic and campus life settings.

3. Out LGBT faculty and staff. LGBT faculty and staff can serve as advisers and visible role models for LGBT students.

4. LGBT-inclusive policies. Supportive campuses should have policies that include "sexual orientation" in their discrimination policy or have policies supporting same-sex domestic partner benefits.

5. Visible signs of pride. The prominent presence of rainbow flags and pink triangles can create a sense of openness, safety, and inclusion.

6. Out LGBT allies from the top down. Support from college administrators and alumni is essential to LGBT students.

7. LGBT-inclusive housing and gender-neutral bathrooms. Campuses may have options for LGBT-themed housing to foster a living and learning atmosphere for students.

8. Established LGBT campus center. What committed campus resources are available for LGBT students and organizations?

9. LGBT/Queer Studies academic major or minor. Students are looking for classes where they can learn about LGBT identity, politics, and history.

10. Liberal attitude and vibrant LGBT social scene. LGBT students want to be accepted fully. Students may want to live on a campus or in a city that offers queer entertainment.

The guide includes a list of top-20 U.S. campuses, described as "pioneering LGBT leaders in higher education":

American University	University of California–Berkeley
Duke University	University of California–Los Angeles
Indiana University	University of California–Santa Cruz
New York University	University of Massachusetts–Amherst
Oberlin College	University of Michigan
The Ohio State University	University of Minnesota–Twin Cities
Pennsylvania State University	University of Oregon
Princeton University	University of Pennsylvania
Stanford University	University of Puget Sound
Tufts University	University of Southern California

Source: Windmeyer 2006.

What Does It Mean to Me?

Lambda Legal is a national organization committed to achieving full recognition of the civil rights of lesbians, gay men, the transgendered, and people with HIV/AIDS. The organization identifies each state that prohibits sexual orientation discrimination in employment. Investigate your state's discrimination laws by logging on to Lambda Legal's website. If your state does include such laws, a brief summary of the legislation is included.

Responding to Sexual Orientation Inequalities

Family Legislation

In 2003, the Massachusetts Supreme Judicial Court ruled that same-sex and opposite-sex couples must be given equal civil rights under the state's constitution. The ruling would allow same-sex couples in Massachusetts to obtain a civil marriage license, to make health and financial decisions for each other, to file joint state tax returns, and to receive other protections under state law. In early 2004, the court reaffirmed its decision, adding that only full marriage rights for gay couples, not just civil unions, would conform to the state's constitution. In May 2004, Massachusetts became the first state in the nation to let same-sex couples marry. In 2009, Massachusetts became the first state to sue the U.S. government over the DOMA, arguing that the law discriminates and deprives gay couples in their state from certain federal spousal benefits. As of November 2012, in addition to Massachusetts, eight states—Connecticut, Iowa, Maine, Maryland, New Hampshire, New York, Vermont, and Washington—and the District of Columbia have legalized gay marriage. Refer to U.S. Data Map 5.1 for marriage equality and other relationship recognition laws.

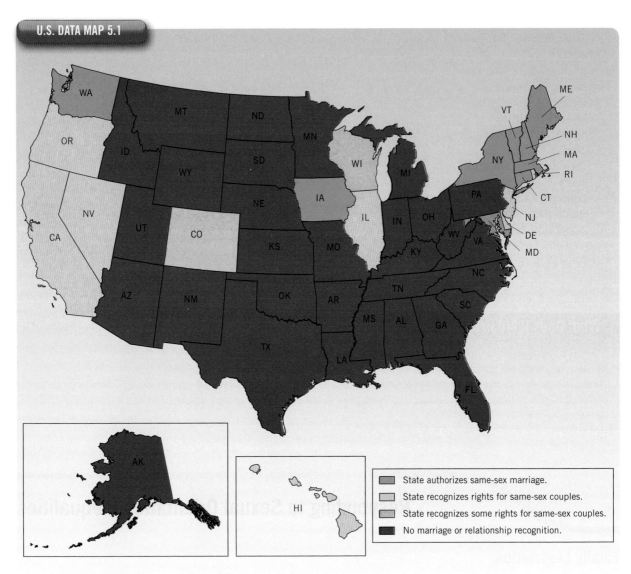

U.S. DATA MAP 5.1

State authorizes same-sex marriage.
State recognizes rights for same-sex couples.
State recognizes some rights for same-sex couples.
No marriage or relationship recognition.

Same-Sex Marriage and Relationship Recognition Laws by State, 2012

Source: Human Rights Campaign 2012.

Proposition 8

The battle over the legal status of same-sex marriage in California continued after Phyllis Lyon and Del Martin's 2004 historic ceremony. In May 2008, the California Supreme Court overturned the state's ban on same-sex marriage. The justices, in a 4 to 3 vote, declared that the fundamental "right to marry" extends equally to same-sex couples under the state constitution. Lyon and Martin were legally wed in June 2008 by Mayor Newsom. Yet, on November 4 of the same year, 52% of California voters approved Proposition 8, a measure that restricted the definition of marriage to opposite-sex couples. The proposition did not affect domestic partnerships. The California Supreme Court upheld the proposition's passage but also ruled that the 18,000 same-sex marriages that took place before the November vote would remain legal. In 2012, a federal appeals court panel overturned Proposition 8 claiming that the voter-approved measure violated the constitutional rights of gay men and women.

Data on same-sex marriages were first released by the U.S. Census Bureau in 2009. Previously the bureau argued that the DOMA prevented the federal government from recognizing these marriages, and as a result, it would not include them in any census reporting. Same-sex marriages, unions, and partnerships were counted for the first time in the 2010 Census. The 2010 U.S. Census estimated 131,729 same-sex married couple households and 514,735 same-sex unmarried partner households (O'Connell and Feliz 2011). The cities with the highest rates of same-sex couples were Provincetown, Massachusetts; Wilton Manors, Florida; and Palm Springs, California (Tavernise 2011). It is estimated that 2 million children are being raised in LGBT families (Movement Advancement Project et al. 2012).

U.S. Surveys

Voices in the Community

Dan Savage

Dan Savage

After hearing the news of the suicide of Billy Lucas, a 15-year-old gay teen, who reportedly endured bullying at school, Dan Savage and his husband, Terry Miller, posted a video about their lives—their family, their friends, and experiences they say they would have missed if they had killed themselves when they were bullied as teens.

Explaining how gay teenagers do not have access to positive gay role models, information, or resources, Savage wrote, "I wish I could have talked to this kid for five minutes. I wish I could have told Billy that it gets better. I wish I could have told him that, however bad things were, however isolated and alone he was, it gets better" (Savage 2010). Savage invited others to tell gay, lesbian, bisexual, or transgendered teens how "it gets better" and submit their video to his YouTube channel. Savage (quoted in Chen 2012) explains, "The goal is to build and maintain these videos and all the support in them for LGBT kids who are growing up right now: 13-, 14-, and 15-year-olds; people who are nine years old right now but who will see these videos in five to six years. We want to make sure that videos are still being made and that LGBT kids know how to find these videos, how to find us."

As described on its website, the It Gets Better Project has become a worldwide movement, with more than 30,000 personal videos with the reminder for LGBT teens that they are not alone and that it will get better. Celebrities, politicians, professional athletes, and activists have posted their submissions.

Visit the website at www.itgetsbetter.org.

Denmark was the first European country to recognize same-sex unions, in 1989. Civil unions or gay marriages or partnerships are legal in Belgium (since 2003), France (2000), Germany (2001), the Netherlands (2001), and Spain and Canada (2005). In 2006, South Africa passed its Civil Union Act, extending the legal rights of marriage to same-sex unions. The act is based on South Africa's constitution, which was the first in the world to prohibit discrimination based on sexual orientation. Marriages legal in these countries may not be recognized by other countries. (Refer to Table 5.2 for a complete list of same-sex marriage and partnership recognition throughout the world.)

The laws governing the rights and responsibilities of gay parents vary from state to state. Every state allows an individual to petition to adopt a child. (Until 2010, Florida was the only state that explicitly forbade adoption by unmarried gay, lesbian, or bisexual individuals. First enacted in 1977, the Florida law was ruled unconstitutional by a state court

Table 5.2

Countries Where Same-Sex Marriage Is Legal Nationwide, as of February 2012

Country	Year First Recognized
The Netherlands	2001
Belgium	2003
Canada	2005
Spain	2005
South Africa	2006
Norway	2008
Sweden	2009
Argentina	2010
Iceland	2010
Portugal	2010

Note: Countries that offer most or all spousal rights to same-sex couples, but stop short of marriage, include the following: Denmark, Finland, Germany, Italy, and the United Kingdom.

Countries that offer some spousal rights to same-sex couples include the following: Brazil, Croatia, France, Hungary, Israel, New Zealand, and Switzerland.

of appeals.) As of 2012, 30 states do not have laws that allow same-sex parents to adopt; 6 states restrict or ban these adoptions (Movement Advancement Project et al. 2012).

Academic research has consistently indicated that gay parents and their children do not differ significantly from heterosexual parents and their children (McLeod and Crawford 1998). There is little or no evidence that the children of gay or lesbian parents are disadvantaged in any important way in comparison with children of heterosexual parents (Patterson and Redding 1996). For their 2001 research, Judith Stacey and Timothy Biblarz examined the findings of 21 studies that explored how parental sexual orientation affected children. Based on the evidence, they concluded that there are no significant differences between children of lesbian mothers and children of heterosexual mothers in measures of social and psychological adjustment, such as self-esteem, anxiety, and depression. Across studies, there was no relationship between parental sexual orientation and measures of children's cognitive ability. Also, levels of closeness and the quality of parent-child relationships did not vary significantly by parental sexual orientation. Stacey and Biblarz (2001) concluded,

> We propose that homophobia and discrimination are the chief reasons why parental sexual orientation matters at all. Because lesbigay parents do not enjoy the same rights, respect and recognition as heterosexual parents, their children contend with the burdens of vicarious sexual stigma. (p. 177)

In their 2012 report, the Movement Advancement Project et al. document how difficult it was for same-sex couples to establish legal ties to each other and to their children. Due to outdated state family laws that do not recognize or support contemporary family structures, children living in LGBT families are more likely to have legal ties to only one parent than children living with heterosexual married parents. As a result, LGBT families bear a variety of financial, legal, and emotional costs. For example, only one parent may have the authority to make routine or emergency decisions for the child, or the child may not be eligible to receive medical coverage through the employer of the nonbiological or nonlegal parent. If the biological or legal parent were to die, the child would be placed with a distant relative or in foster care instead of being placed with the nonlegal parent. The report concludes with recommendations for legislative solutions focusing on the best interests of the children, establishing legal ties to both parents, and eliminating the potential for bias and discrimination against LGBT families.

Military Service

During his first presidential campaign, Bill Clinton promised to extend full civil rights to gays and lesbians, including those in military service (Belkin 2003). The military policy at that time banned gay and lesbian individuals from the armed forces, stating that homosexuality was incompatible with military service. (For information on gay military service in other countries, refer to this chapter's Taking a World View feature.) In 1993, President Clinton suspended the policy, and the National Defense Authorization Act became law.

Part of the law is the infamous "Don't Ask, Don't Tell" (DADT) policy, a political compromise criticized since its inception. According to the policy, known homosexuals were not allowed to serve in the U.S. military, but the military was banned from asking enlistees questions about their sexual orientation. In addition, significant restrictions were placed on commanders wanting to investigate whether a soldier was gay (the complete policy is actually "Don't Ask, Don't Tell, Don't Pursue, Don't Harass"). Service members who disclosed that they were homosexual were still subject to military discharge. Between its inception and the end of 2009, more than 13,000 service members were discharged (Servicemembers Legal Defense Network 2007). It is not known how many gay and lesbian service members did not reenlist because of the policy without revealing their homosexuality.

 Recruitment Policy

In 2007, John Shalikashvili, retired Army general and former chairman of the Joint Chiefs of Staff, declared his support for the repeal of the DADT policy. Shalikashvili (2007) described how his conversations with gay soldiers and marines, some with Iraq combat experience, "showed me how much the military has changed, and that gays and lesbians can be accepted by their peers" (p. A19). He also cited evidence from a recent poll of 500 service members returning from service in Afghanistan and Iraq, indicating that 75% of those surveyed were comfortable interacting with gay people. In the same year, the Pentagon revealed that 58 Arabic-language experts were discharged from military service since the inception of the policy because they were gay. U.S. House representatives were critical of the Pentagon, believing that the policy and its actions were homophobic rather than focused on the country's national security needs.

President Obama delivered on his campaign pledge to end DADT. A congressional bill to repeal DADT was enacted in December 2010. In 2011, a ruling from a federal appeals court barred further enforcement of DADT. DADT ended on September 20, 2011. However, gay soldiers are not able to use certain benefits (e.g., health insurance) for their partners that are provided to married heterosexual soldiers. In their assessment of the repeal of DADT, Aaron Belkin and his colleagues (2012) concluded that the repeal "has had no overall negative impact on military readiness or its component dimensions, including cohesion, recruitment, retention, assaults, harassment, or morale. . . . [G]reater openness and honesty resulting from the repeal seem to have promoted increased understanding, respect and acceptance" (p. 4). It is estimated that gay, lesbian, and bisexual service members make up at least 2% of the U.S. military's active duty and reserve forces (Bumiller 2012).

Taking a World View

Gay Military Service Policies

In addition to the United States, the NATO (North Atlantic Treaty Organization) and non-NATO countries whose militaries have lifted their bans on gay military service are Australia, Austria, Belgium, Canada, the Czech Republic, Denmark, Estonia, Finland, France, Germany, Greece, Hungary, Ireland, Israel, Italy, Lithuania, Luxembourg, the Netherlands, New Zealand, Norway, Poland, Portugal, Slovenia, South Africa, Spain, Sweden, Switzerland, and the United Kingdom (Belkin 2003). Turkey is the only NATO country that does not permit gays and lesbians to serve openly in the military.

Aaron Belkin (2003) examined the early experiences of four countries that lifted their bans on homosexual military personnel. In each country—Australia, Canada, Israel, and Great Britain—the bans were lifted in opposition from the military services.

Belkin explains that each country lifted its ban for different reasons. In Canada, the ban was lifted in 1992, after federal courts ruled that the military policy violated the Canadian Charter of Rights and Freedoms. The ban was also lifted in 1992 in Australia, when Prime Minister Paul Keating argued that the ban was not consistent with his country's integration of several international human rights conventions into its domestic laws and codes. Israel's military ban was lifted in 1993 after public response to Knesset hearings on the matter. In 1999, the European Court of Human Rights ruled that Great Britain's gay ban violated the right to privacy guaranteed in the European Convention on Human Rights.

All military personnel, academics, veterans, politicians, and nongovernmental observers interviewed for his research did not believe that lifting the gay bans undermined "military performance, readiness, or cohesion, lead [*sic*] to increased difficulties in recruiting or retention or increased the rate of HIV infection among the troops" (Belkin 2003:110). Grim predictions and anxiety about how military personnel would refuse to work with or share showers, undress, or sleep in the same room with gay soldiers were not substantiated in these countries. Many interviewed described the policy change as a "nonevent" or "not that big a deal for us" and said that the change was "accepted in 'true military tradition'" (Belkin 2003:110–11).

Interviewed military leaders stressed how all soldiers were held to the same standard of professional conduct regardless of sexual orientation or personal beliefs about homosexuality. Belkin (2003) states that none of the four militaries attempted to force military personnel to accept homosexuality. Data from the four countries confirm that soldiers refrained from the abuse and harassment of homosexual military personnel, though gay bashing and sexual harassment cases were documented in two of the countries (Australia and Israel).

During the war with Iraq, before the repeal of "Don't Ask, Don't Tell," U.S. forces served side by side with allied forces from nine countries that allowed gays and lesbians to serve openly. In some cases, these forces worked together in integrated units (Servicemembers Legal Defense Network 2007).

Photo 5.4

In 2012, the U.S. Department of Defense allowed gay soldiers to march in their uniforms in a gay pride parade for the first time in U.S. history.

Main Points

- One's sexual orientation serves as a basis of inequality. Sexual orientation is defined as the classification of individuals according to their preference for emotional-sexual relationships and lifestyle with persons of the same sex (homosexuality) or persons of the opposite sex (heterosexuality). Bisexuality refers to emotional and sexual attractions to persons of either sex. The term *transgendered* does not refer to a specific sexual orientation; rather, it refers to individuals whose gender identity is different from the one assigned to them at birth. The term *LGBT* is often used to refer to lesbians, gays, bisexuals, and transgendered individuals as a group.

- There is no definitive study on the number of individuals who identify themselves as homosexual or bisexual.

- Functionalists identify how society upholds heterosexuality and a marital union between a man and a woman as ideal normative behavior. This is also referred to as institutionalized heterosexuality, the set of ideas, institutions, and relationships that define the heterosexual family as the societal norm.

- Sociologists recognize that heterosexuals are granted a privileged place in our society. Heterosexism assumes that heterosexuality is the norm, encouraging discrimination in favor of heterosexuals and against homosexuals. Heterosexual privilege is defined as the set of privileges or advantages granted to some people because of their heterosexuality.

- From a feminist perspective, scholars have argued that lesbian and gay marriages will positively disrupt the gendered definitions of marriage. However, just as feminists have criticized traditional marriage as an oppressive and dominating institution against women, feminists have also supported sexual freedom. Supporting gay marriages would mean that feminists would be supporting the very institution that perpetuates women's inequality.

- Although homosexuality has existed in most societies, it has usually been attached to a negative label—abnormal, sinful, or inappropriate. A socially determined prejudice, homophobia, is an irrational fear or intolerance of homosexuals. Interactionists examine how sexual orientation is constructed within a social context. The development of a gay identity has familial, social, legal, financial, religious, and health implications.

- Bisexual or homosexual men and women and their families are subject to social inequalities through practices of discrimination and prejudice, many of them surprisingly institutionalized in formal law.

- Gay and lesbian couples are denied the same legal and social support given heterosexual couples. Their families are denied common legal protections that nongay families take for granted such as adoption, custody, guardianship, social security, and inheritance.

- Between 16% and 46% of gays, lesbians, or bisexuals have experienced discrimination based on sexual orientation. Under current federal law, discrimination based on sexual orientation is not prohibited.

On Your Own

Log on to the open-access Student Study Site at www.sagepub.com/leonguerrero4e for these additional learning tools:

- Interactive quizzes
- Video clips
- NPR audio links
- Handbook articles

- E-flashcards
- Journal articles
- End-of-chapter web exercises
- Additional web resources and current events

Internet and Community Exercises

1. The Human Rights Campaign, founded in 1980, is the largest national lesbian, gay, bisexual, and transgender advocacy organization in the United States. On its website, the organization posts information on specific LGBT laws and legislation. Go to *Study Site Chapter 5* to learn about LGBT legislation in your state.

2. Does your campus have an LGBT organization? If it does, interview an administrator or a student member to learn more about the organization. In what ways do the organization and your school's administration support LGBT students? If your campus does not have an LGBT organization, why doesn't it?

3. GLSEN, or the Gay, Lesbian and Straight Education Network, is the leading national education organization focused on ensuring safe schools for all students. The network focuses on educating teachers, students, and parents about how to reduce anti-LGBT name-calling, bullying, and harassment. GLSEN published the 2011 National School Climate Survey (see *Study Site Chapter 5*), an analysis of experiences of LGBT students and the benefits of safe school laws and policies. Go to this chapter's *Study Site Community and Policy Guides* to access information on your state's safe school policies.

Study Questions

1. Compare and contrast the biological, psychological, and sociological perspectives on sexual orientation.
2. Examine how heterosexuality is privileged in society.
3. How, from a sociological perspective, is our sexuality defined/controlled by our norms, values, and language?
4. Explain the role of power and privilege in understanding sexual orientation.
5. How has the military policy of "Don't Ask, Don't Tell" affected military service by gays and lesbians?
6. Explain how gays and lesbians are discriminated against in the workplace and in the military.

CHAPTER 6

Age and Aging

More than 500 retired scientists and researchers volunteered as first responders to the nuclear plant accident at the Fukushima Daiichi power plant in 2011. The Skilled Veterans Corps volunteers ranged in age from 60 to 78 years. According to Yasuteru Yamada, a retired physicist, "Young workers who may reproduce a younger generation and are themselves more susceptible to the effects of radiation should not be engaged in such work. This job is a call for senior citizens like me" (as quoted in Glionna 2011a). The story of Yamada and his colleagues was characterized as "a lesson about growing old gracefully, about demonstrating the sheer willfulness in an aging body" (Glionna 2011b). Yamada maintains that he is nobody's hero. Despite their expertise and their willingness to help, the volunteers were not permitted to assist with the cleanup.

Age is both a biological and a social classification (McConatha et al. 2003). There are social dictates regarding age—socially and culturally defined expectations about the meaning of age, our understanding of it, and our responses to it (Calasanti and Slevin 2001). We make a fuss over the 77-year-old Ironman triathlete or the 13-year-old college student because they are unexpected or deemed unusual for people of their age. Age distinguishes acceptable behavior for different social groups. Voting, the legal consumption of alcohol, military enlistment, and the ability to hold certain elected offices (you can't be president of the United States until you are at least 35 years old) are examples of formal age norms. Informal age norms also demonstrate how a society defines what is considered appropriate by age (Calasanti and Slevin 2001).

 Mothers and Age

Sociologists examine age and the process of aging through a **life course perspective**. This perspective examines the entire course of human life from childhood, adolescence, and adulthood to old age. The life course perspective tends to view "stages of life" as social

Photo 6.1

Age is both a biological and a social classification. Active seniors, such as Carol Johnston pictured in this photo, expand our beliefs and expectations of elderly behavior and roles. As of December 2007, Johnston held the world record for pole-vaulting, 2.24 meters for his age group (85 years).

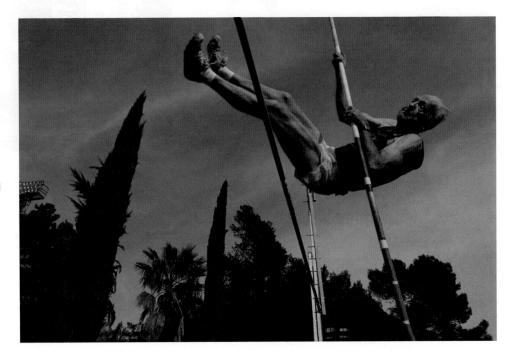

constructions that reflect the broader structural conditions of society (Moody 2006). Aging occurs within a social context: One's social class, education, occupation, gender, and race will determine how one experiences adolescence or old age. However, there is also room for individuals to make their own choices in interpreting or embracing age-related roles (Moody 2006). **Gerontology** is the specific study of aging and the elderly, the primary focus of this chapter.

Our Aging World

Much has been written about the graying or aging of America, a change in our demographic structure referred to as **population aging** (Clark et al. 2004). One way to confirm population aging is to look at the median age of the U.S. population. (The median age is the age where half the population is older and the other half is younger.) The median age was 17 years in 1820 and 23 years in 1900, and by 2000, it increased to 35 years. By 2030, the median age is predicted to increase to 42 years.

Demography is the study of the size, composition, and distribution of populations, and demographers have identified several reasons for population aging. First, population aging is caused by a decline in birth rates (Moody 2006). With a smaller number of children, the average age of the population increases. In 1900, America was a relatively young population, with children and teenagers making up 40% of the population. But by 1990, the proportion of youth dropped to 24%. In U.S. Data Map 6.1, the percentage of adults aged 65 years or older is presented for each state. Overall, the percentage of elderly for the United States is 13.0%. The state with the lowest percentage of elderly is Alaska (7.7%); the state with the highest percentage is Florida (17.3%).

Population aging can also occur because of improvements in life expectancy as a result of medical and technological advances (Moody 2006), improved access to health care, healthier lifestyles, and better health before 65 years of age (National Center for Health Statistics 2009). As people live longer, the average age of the population increases. In 1900, life expectancy at birth was 47 years; according to the Centers for Disease Control and Prevention, the life expectancy for a child born in 2010 is 78.7 years (National Center for Health Statistics 2009; Murphy, Xu, and Kochanek 2012).

Longer life expectancy has also made it necessary to redefine what it means to be old or elderly. Gerontology scholars and researchers now make the distinction between the young-old (aged 65 to 75), the old-old (aged 75 to 84), and the oldest-old (aged 85 or older;

 Aging Society

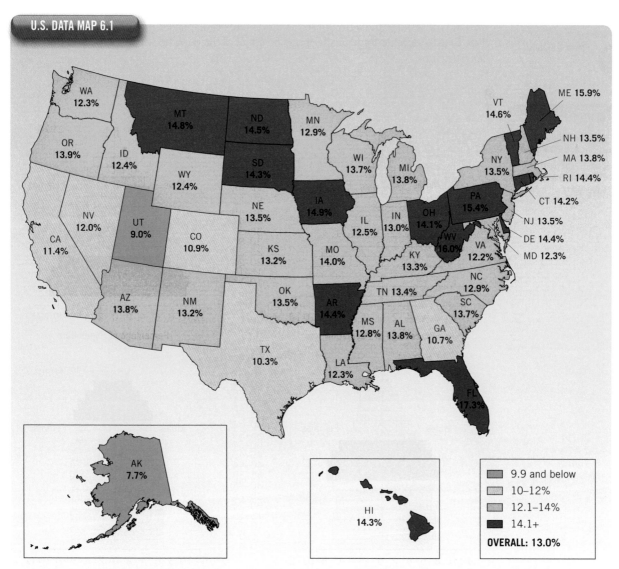

U.S. DATA MAP 6.1

WA 12.3%
MT 14.8%
ND 14.5%
MN 12.9%
VT 14.6%
ME 15.9%
OR 13.9%
ID 12.4%
SD 14.3%
WI 13.7%
MI 13.8%
NH 13.5%
NY 13.5%
MA 13.8%
WY 12.4%
IA 14.9%
PA 15.4%
RI 14.4%
NV 12.0%
UT 9.0%
NE 13.5%
IL 12.5%
IN 13.0%
OH 14.1%
CT 14.2%
CA 11.4%
CO 10.9%
KS 13.2%
MO 14.0%
WV 16.0%
VA 12.2%
KY 13.3%
NJ 13.5%
DE 14.4%
MD 12.3%
AZ 13.8%
NM 13.2%
OK 13.5%
AR 14.4%
TN 13.4%
NC 12.9%
SC 13.7%
TX 10.3%
MS 12.8%
AL 13.8%
GA 10.7%
LA 12.3%
FL 17.3%
AK 7.7%
HI 14.3%

Legend:
- 9.9 and below
- 10–12%
- 12.1–14%
- 14.1+
- **OVERALL: 13.0%**

Persons Aged 65 Years or Older, Percent of Population, 2010

Source: U.S. Census Bureau 2012a.

Moody 2006). Unless noted otherwise, the use of the term *elderly* in this chapter will refer to those aged 65 years or older.

Finally, the process of population aging can be influenced because of birth cohorts (Moody 2006). A cohort is a group of people born during a particular period who experience common life events during the same historical period. For example, the Depression of the 1930s produced a small birth cohort that had a minimal impact on the average age of the population. However, the baby boom cohort after World War II is a very large cohort, and its middle-age baby boomers will contribute to the aging of the U.S. population. When Kathleen Casey-Kirschling, our nation's first baby boomer, born January 1, 1946, applied for her social security benefits in 2007, Social Security Commissioner Michael Astrue said it signaled "America's silver tsunami" (Ohlemacher 2007:A1). An estimated 10,000 people a day will become eligible for social security benefits during the next two decades (Ohlemacher 2007). Graphically, the aging of the United States is displayed in Figure 6.1. Data from the U.S. Census Bureau dramatically show the effect of the baby boom generation on the overall age structure.

 Power & Culture

Figure 6.1

The Dramatic Aging of America, 1900–2030

Source: U.S. Census Bureau. Adapted from Himes 2001.

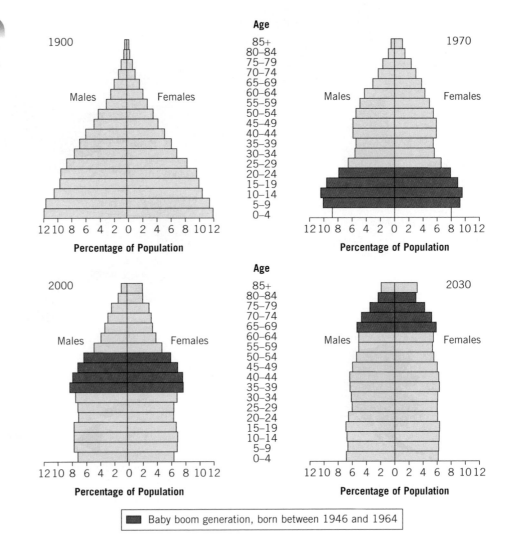

Baby boom generation, born between 1946 and 1964

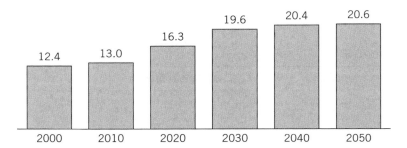

Figure 6.2

Percentage Aged 65 or Older of the Total U.S. Population: 2000–2050, Projected

Source: He et al. 2005.

Note: The reference population for these data is the resident population.

Demographers predict that the number of Americans aged 65 years or older will increase over several decades (refer to Figure 6.2). To provide a context for aging in the United States, it is helpful to examine trends in the rest of the world (He et al. 2005). Populations are aging in all countries, though the level and pace vary by geographic region. Fertility decline, improved health and longevity, and increasing urbanization have contributed to the unprecedented growth of older populations throughout the world. In 2008, 506 million people (7%) in the world were 65 years old or older; by 2040, the number is projected to increase to 1.3 billion (14% of the total). For the first time, people aged 65 or over are expected to outnumber children under age 5 by 2020.

Table 6.1 reports the percentage of elderly by age in the population from 2008 and projected through 2020 and 2040. By 2040, Eastern and Western Europe will have the highest percentage of elderly; that year, nearly a quarter of Europeans are likely to be at least 65 years of age. Northern America and Oceania will continue to have a high percentage of elderly, at or near 20% by 2040. Rates for Northern Africa, Asia, and Latin America and the Caribbean are predicted to more than double. However, percentages remain lower in Sub-Saharan Africa due to continued high fertility rates, along with the deadly consequences of HIV/AIDS (Kinsella and He 2009).

Gerontologist Harry Moody (2006) warns, "Population aging is a long-range trend that will characterize our society as we continue into the 21st century. It is a force we all will cope with for the rest of our lives" (p. xxiii). Population aging means an increase in the number or proportion of elderly and signals the need for changes in health care, employment status, living arrangements, and social welfare for the elderly and the rest of society.

The aging of U.S. society is likely to transform state, regional, city, and suburban populations. A 2007 Brookings Institution report (Frey 2007) predicts the emergence of two major senior populations, each with a set of specific needs and geographic impacts. "Yuppie senior" affluent populations are expected to emerge in the South and West (in cities such as Las Vegas, Denver, Dallas, and Atlanta), increasing their demands for new types of community cultural amenities. Their affluence will continue to support and encourage the economic and civic growth of their geographic areas. Conversely, cities in the Northeast and Midwest are

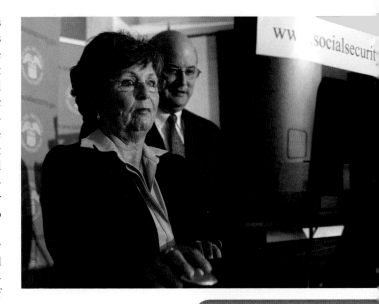

Photo 6.2

On October 15, 2007, Kathleen Casey-Kirschling signaled the beginning of the senior boom in the United States. Casey-Kirschling is pictured here with Michael Astrue, Commissioner of the Social Security Administration, on the day she filed for her Social Security benefits. Approximately 10,000 people a day will become eligible for Social Security benefits during the next two decades.

A Roadmap to End Aging

Table 6.1

Percentage Elderly by Age: 2008 to 2040

Region	65 Years or Older	75 Years or Older	80 Years or Older
Northern Africa			
2008	4.9	1.6	0.7
2020	6.7	2.2	1.1
2040	12.8	5.0	2.5
Sub-Saharan Africa			
2008	3.0	0.9	0.3
2020	3.3	1.0	0.4
2040	4.2	1.4	0.6
Asia (excluding Near East)			
2008	6.8	2.4	1.1
2020	9.3	3.3	1.7
2040	16.2	6.8	3.7
Near East			
2008	4.6	1.7	0.8
2020	5.7	2.0	1.1
2040	9.9	3.8	2.0
Eastern Europe			
2008	14.5	6.0	3.0
2020	17.3	6.9	4.3
2040	24.4	12.6	7.8
Western Europe			
2008	17.8	8.5	4.9
2020	20.9	10.1	6.2
2040	28.1	15.0	9.3
Latin America/Caribbean			
2008	6.5	2.5	1.2
2020	8.8	3.3	1.8
2040	15.3	6.6	3.7
North America			
2008	12.8	6.2	3.8
2020	16.5	6.9	4.0
2040	20.8	11.6	7.3
Oceania			
2008	10.8	4.9	2.9
2020	13.7	5.7	3.3
2040	18.5	9.1	5.5

Source: Kinsella and He 2009.

predicted to have a disproportionately higher population of "mature seniors"—less financially stable or physically able than yuppie seniors. Mature seniors are likely to require more social and public support programs, along with affordable private and institutional housing and accessible health care providers (Frey 2007).

What Does It Mean to Me?

The younger population in the United States has become more ethnically diverse. According to Frey (2011), minorities now comprise at least 40% of infants in more than half of all states. Minority infants represent the majority of births in 14 states led by California and New Mexico. On the other hand, minorities make up only 15% of those aged 85 years or older. What is the impact of this race-generational divide for communities? What are some of the policy and budgetary implications of this divide? How is the demographic profile changing in your community?

 STATE STATS

Taking a World View

Aging in China

The growth of the older population in China is expected to accelerate in the next 50 years, surpassing the aging population in many Western European countries and the United States. Charles Kincannon, Wan He, and Loraine West (2005) report that more than a half-century ago, 1 in 25 Chinese people was aged 65 years or older, but by the beginning of the twenty-first century, 1 in every 14 Chinese was an older person.

According to population projections by the U.S. Census Bureau's International Programs center, China's older population will quadruple. Given China's total population of over 1.2 billion in 2000, this accelerated aging process will involve huge numbers of people. By 2050, it is projected that there will be 349.0 million people 65 years old or older in China, almost one-fourth more than the total population of the United States in 2000 (Kincannon et al. 2005:245). (In contrast, the 2050 projection for the number of elderly in the United States is 33.7 million.)

Elderly Chinese rely on a variety of sources for financial support. In 2000, just over half of the Chinese men aged 65 years or over who were no longer working relied primarily on their family for financial support, while 4 in 10 received primary support from a retirement pension. Older women were far more likely to be dependent on their families for support—82%—and much less likely to rely on a retirement pension—13% (Kincannon et al. 2005:250).

Reliance on family support is greatest among the oldest-old Chinese population, largely because they are not eligible to receive benefits under China's pension system (first established in the 1950s and limited to those with at least 20 years of employment) or, if they do qualify, because pension benefits are insufficient to use as the primary source of financial support. The researchers predict that as China expands its system of social insurance programs, reliance on family support is likely to decline.

Employment continues to serve as a source of support for China's elderly; in fact, the employed percentage of the older population in China is higher than that in the United States. According to the U.S. Census 2000, 18% of men and 9% of women aged 65 years or older were employed in the United States, whereas China's census data for 2000 reveal that nearly 34% and 17% of similarly aged men and women were employed in China. More than 90% of employed Chinese elderly were engaged in agriculture; in China's urban areas, the employment rates of the older population were slightly below those in the United States (Kincannon et al. 2005).

The progressive aging of its older population is a serious issue for China. Better medical care and health conditions in China have led to longer lives for older people in the country. The result, as Kincannon et al. (2005) observe, is that,

> over time, a nation's older population may grow older on average as a larger proportion survives to 80 years and beyond (the oldest old). The oldest old and the young old have very different economic, demographic, and health statuses, thus they also have very different needs for health services, old-age care, residential arrangements, or assistance with the requirements of daily life. The oldest old are more likely to be widowed (especially the oldest-old women), to be frail or sick, and to be unemployed and lack financial resources. Their needs may put tremendous pressures on their families as well as on society. The oldest old, therefore, are a group within the older population that warrants special attention. (p. 245)

Sociological Perspectives on Age, Aging, and Inequality

Functionalist Perspective

Healthy Lifestyles

Age helps maintain the stability of society by providing a set of roles and expectations for each particular age group or for a particular life stage. These roles are reinforced by our major social institutions—education, the economy, and family. We assume that children, 18 years old or younger, should be in school. After high school graduation, young adults have the choice of entering the workforce or continuing their education (where their student role continues), whereas adulthood is a time set aside to build one's career and to begin a family. Retirement is another important age-related stage, with societal roles and expectations for a retired person.

What Does It Mean to Me?

The term **boomerangers** refers to young adults who leave home for college but return after graduation because of economic constraints or personal choice. Surveys of recent college graduates conducted in the early 2000s noted that nearly half of those surveyed expected to live with their families for some period. According to a 2009 Pew Research Center survey, 10% of adults younger than 35 years old moved back in with their parents due to the recession (Wang and Morin 2009). Is boomeranging a viable transitional stage for recent college graduates? For yourself?

Sociology of Aging

Consider how each age group has its own function or role—the young attend school preparing for their adult lives, adults are employed and building their lives, and the elderly retire. **Disengagement theory** defines aging as a natural process of withdrawal from active participation in social life. Older people disengage from society (from their work and certain parts of their lives), and in turn, society disengages from them (Turner 1996). The theory contends that people enter and exit a set of roles throughout their lives. These transitions are natural and functional for society (Mabry and Bengston 2005; Moody 2006).

Retirement Costs

This process is portrayed as orderly, timely, and necessary for the well-being of the entire society. For example, in the workplace, older workers must relinquish their jobs to make room for younger workers in the labor market. This process is socially supported through retirement plans, pensions, and Medicare (Mabry and Bengston 2005). Disengagement is portrayed as positive for the elderly because it enables them to participate in activities and a lifestyle that earlier would not have been possible (they may become more fully engaged in community, family, or leisure activities). The final form of disengagement is death.

However, this perspective fails to acknowledge how vulnerable and powerless adults are in their older years. Is this disengagement natural or forced by society? The next perspective answers this question.

Conflict Perspective

The **modernization theory of aging** suggests that the role and status of the elderly declines with industrialization. Specifically, their power, wealth, and prestige are linked with

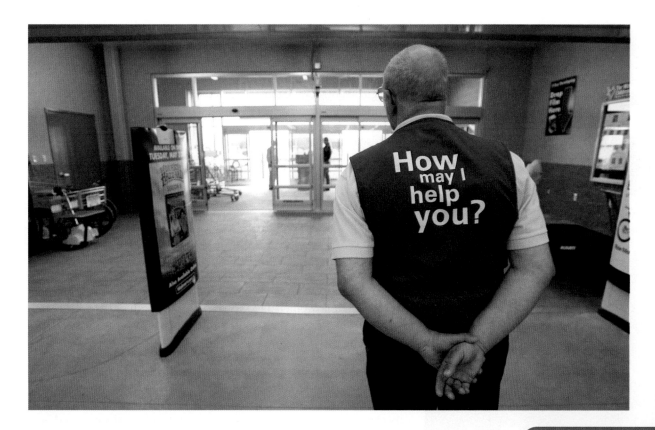

their labor contribution or relationship to the means of production. In hunting and gathering societies, the elderly had a low status because they were unable to contribute to the primary means of production. However, their status increased during the time of stable agricultural societies, when older people controlled land ownership. In modern industrial society, life experience is surpassed by technological expertise; thus, the status of the elderly declines.

From a conflict perspective, the two groups at odds with one another are the young and the old. As Donald Cowgill (1974) explains, society systematically advantages the young, supported by what he calls the "cult of youth"—a value system that glorifies youth "as a symbol of beauty, vigor and progress and discriminates in favor of youth in employment and in the allocation of community resources" (pp. 15–16).

Cowgill (1974) identifies how four aspects of modernization lower the status of older people. The first is health technology. Modern health advances improve the population's overall health and longevity. This creates an older and healthier workforce, willing and able to stay in the labor force a bit longer: "As the lives of workers are prolonged, death no longer creates openings in the labor force as it once did" (Cowgill 1974:12). Society then creates a new opening through retirement, forcing people out of their most valued and senior roles in the labor force. Elderly workers are reduced to retirement status with less income and influence.

The next two aspects, education and economic technology, are related to one another. In a modern society, the young have more opportunities to acquire education and training. The status of younger members of society is elevated because they become more literate than their parents. Society relies on their increased literacy in the workplace, creating new information- and technology-based occupations. The people most qualified for these positions are the younger, more literate workers. Older workers perform more traditional jobs, some that are less valued or that eventually become obsolete.

Photo 6.3

The modernization theory of aging suggests that the declining status of the elderly is associated with their decreasing economic and labor contribution. What status do we attribute to the position of store greeter? High or low?

 Aging Workforce

The final aspect is urbanization. A modern society is more urban, characterized by increased social mobility and migration. Cowgill (1974) argues that the young migrate more than the old do. The migration produces a physical and emotional separation between a child and the family of origin, tearing down the bonds of the extended family. Yet it also promotes the cultural image of the young moving to something better, while the old are left behind.

Researchers have challenged the assumption that modernization and economic conditions automatically lead to the status decline of the elderly. Sociologists and anthropologists have documented how the status of older persons varies by race and ethnicity, gender, culture, and social class. Among Hispanics and Asians, where multigenerational households are common, the elderly are respected and honored.

Feminist Perspective

Women constitute the majority in the U.S. older population. In 2010, there were 23 million women aged 65 years or older compared with 17 million men (U.S. Census Bureau 2012b). The standards of our culture create more problems for women than for men as they transition into their middle and later years. Women seem more vulnerable to societal pressure to retain their youth and, consequently, face more questions about their self-worth, which may lead to serious problems ranging from low self-esteem to depression (Saucier 2004). Questions about self-worth and value are also raised in the workplace, where researchers have documented how women experience greater age discrimination during all ages than do men (Duncan and Loretto 2004).

Susan Sontag (1979) notes how society is much more permissive about aging in men. She writes about the **double standard of aging**—men are judged in our culture according to what they can do (their competence, power, and control), but women are judged according to their appearance and beauty. Women's identity is more closely associated with their physical appearance than is the identity of men. As a result, society considers men "distinguished" in their old age, but women must disguise the fact that they are aging. Sontag argues that because women are unable to maintain their youthful looks as they age, they are pressured to defend themselves against aging at all costs.

Feminist scholars argue that the cosmetic industry focuses on a male and youth standard. Though cosmetic products are advertised for women's use (ever notice that there are no male cosmetic counters at your department store?), feminists assert that the industry is responding to the male-defined standard of female beauty. In addition, the industry is responding to the image of unattainable youthful beauty upheld by society (Calasanti, Slevin, and King 2006). When she interviewed women aged 61 to 92, Laura Hurd Clarke (2000) discovered that while older women say that their overall health is more important to them than physical attractiveness, they still exhibit an internalization of ageist beauty norms. As Sontag (quoted in Freedman 1986:200) says, "Women are trained to want to continue looking like girls forever."

This perspective also examines how ageism and sexism are reflected in the media. Though older adults are underrepresented in U.S. film, television programs, and advertisements in comparison with younger adults, older women are less likely to be featured than

Photo 6.4

This fashion model promotes a particular image of beauty and of the ideal body shape. How does this image influence the self-image of young girls, adult women, and older women? Are alternative images of beauty promoted in fashion? In the media?

The Graying Planet

Unemployment

older men (Peterson and Ross 1997; Sanders 2002). When older women are portrayed, their characters represent negative stereotypes and are often shown as less successful compared with older men. Similar patterns were also documented in German media (Kessler, Rakoczy, and Staudinger 2004).

Eve Ensler

Interactionist Perspective

Interactionists reveal how our age-related roles are socially defined and expected. Age is tied to a system of matching people and roles (Hagestad and Uhlenberg 2005). What does it mean to be middle aged? Middle age is not just measured according to years, but is also associated with a set of role expectations. We share a definition of what it means to be middle aged, and there is an expectation that we need to assume a particular role once we are middle aged.

What Does It Mean to Me?

Who or what defines aging in our society? How are these definitions perpetuated, and how can they be altered?

These role expectations stigmatize particular age groups. **Stigma**, coined by Erving Goffman ([1963] 1986), is defined as a discrediting attribute. Older adults are discredited in society, stereotyped as less capable, fragile, weak, and frail. **Ageism** or the stereotyping of (or discrimination against) older adults can damage the self-concepts of the elderly (Miller, Leyell, and Mazachek 2004) and represents a self-perpetuating cycle of fears that old and younger adults have toward aging in general, disability, death, competition for resources, and the perceived inferiority of particular individuals (Yang and Levkoff 2005). These images may increase social isolation, dependency, and elderly abuse and may become a self-fulfilling prophecy for others (Thornton 2002). However, researchers have found that older adults from cultures with more positive attitudes toward aging than mainstream society may be able to avoid exposure to or internalization of the negative stereotypes of old age (Levy and Langer 1994).

Interactionists examine how the problems associated with aging have been defined and by whom. Society relies on trained experts such as gerontologists, physicians, nurses, and social workers to identify and respond to the problems of aging. Yet research indicates that this group of professionals is just as likely to be prejudiced against older people as other groups are. A. J. Levenson (1981) argues, "Medical students' attitudes have reflected a prejudice against older persons surpassed only by their racial prejudice" (p. 61). He points to medical schools as part of the problem, putting little value on geriatrics as a specialty. Doctors often think that because aging cannot be stopped, illnesses associated with old age are not that important.

The medical industry has not ignored aging completely. Though controversial, the medical and cosmetic industries actively promote antiaging vitamins, hormones, surgeries, and pharmaceutical drugs, encouraging wellness to patients and clients while sending a message that they can "beat back old age" (Wilson 2007:BU1). Americans spend nearly $50 billion per year in antiaging vitamins, treatments, hormones, and pharmaceutical drugs (Wilson 2007). Are we responding to a genuine problem or one carefully manufactured by the medical and cosmetic industries?

A summary of all sociological perspectives is presented in Table 6.2.

Table 6.2

Summary of Sociological Perspectives: Inequalities Based on Age and Aging

	Functional	Conflict/Feminist	Interactionist
Explanations of age and inequality	As we age, we enter and exit age-specific roles and statuses. Each status helps maintain social stability. Elderly disengagement is a normal and necessary process.	Inequality is based on one's relationship to the labor force—with the elderly having the least amount of power in society. Women are disadvantaged in the aging process more than men are.	Our age-related roles are socially defined and expected.
Questions asked about age and inequality	How do our age-related roles and statuses contribute to the stability of society? Is there a way to successfully disengage the elderly from society?	How does modernization contribute to lowering the status of the elderly? What can be done to improve the status of the elderly? How and why does society have two standards for aging—one for men, the other for women? What can be done to reduce the negative impact of the aging standard for women?	How do we learn our age-related roles? In what ways do our perceptions and beliefs perpetuate ageism?

The Consequences of Age Inequality

Ageism

Ageism is defined by Robert Butler (1969) as the "systematic stereotyping of and discrimination against people because they are old, just as racism and sexism accomplish this with skin color and gender" (p. 243). Todd Nelson (2005) described ageism as "prejudice against our feared self." He suggests that age prejudice is one of the most socially condoned and institutionalized forms of prejudice. For example, a standard message in birthday greeting cards is how unfortunate one is to be a year older. In 2012, researcher Ye Luo and his colleagues reported that 63% of older adults reported at least one type of everyday discrimination (e.g., being treated with less courtesy, receiving poorer service, being threatened or harassed). Among older adults, Blacks; separated, widowed, or divorced individuals; and those with lower household assets have higher levels of discrimination than Whites, married individuals, and those with more assets (Luo et al. 2012).

Ageism marks a sharp distinction between "us" and "them." William Bytheway (1995) explains it this way: "The issues of these pronouns creates a conceptual map on which groups of people are variously included and excluded. In particular, the old who are discriminated against occupy a different territory on these us/them maps from 'us'" (p. 117).

Older adults tend to be marginalized, institutionalized, and stripped of their responsibility, dignity, and power (Nelson 2002). Dependency is one of the most negative attributes of being identified as "old" in our society (Calasanti and Slevin 2001). Stereotypes about the capacities, activities, and interests of older people reinforce the view that they are incapable of caring for themselves (Pampel 1998). Older adults are not generally disliked, but they are likely to be victims of paternalistic prejudice, which stereotypes them as likable but incompetent (Packer and Chasteen 2006). There is widespread acceptance of negative stereotypes about the elderly regarding their intellectual decline, conservatism, sexual decline, and lack of productivity (Levin and Levin 1980).

In a comparative study of young adults in the United States and Germany, German young adults tended to view aging more negatively than did Americans in the sample (McConatha et al. 2003). Germans were more likely to be pessimistic about the likelihood of finding contentment in old age and did not expect to feel good about life when they were older. The study attributed the differences in aging attitudes to Germany's more prevalent negative stereotypes of older people, a response to the increasing costs of providing extension pension and health benefits to the elderly in Germany. On the other hand, in the United States, effective political advocacy groups, increasingly healthy and influential older adults, and educational aging programs may account for a reduction of ageism. The study also revealed that American and German women were more concerned about age-related physical changes than were men.

What Does It Mean to Me?

Jasim McConatha and her colleagues (2003) asked young adult Germans and Americans what age they consider as "old." The average age that Germans reported was 64 years for men and 60 for women; the U.S. sample reported younger ages—53 years for men and 48 for women. What age do you consider as old? What expectations do you have about growing older?

 STATE STATS

Age and Social Class

The most economically vulnerable in our society are very young or old. As discussed in Chapter 2, the rate of child poverty in the United States is one of the highest among Western industrialized countries. According to the U.S. Census, the poverty rate for children was 21.9%, or 16.1 million, in 2011 (DeNavas-Walt, Proctor, and Smith 2012). For a more extensive discussion on children and poverty, refer to Chapter 2, "Social Class and Poverty."

Though most of us envision a retirement filled with leisure activities, travel, and good living, there is another possibility—that one's retirement will be a time of serious economic hardship. In 2011, 3.6 million elderly (or 8.7%) were living in poverty in the United States. Retirement represents a precipitous income drop for most elderly (De-Navas-Walt et al. 2012). The median income by age of householder was highest, at $63,861, for those aged 45 to 54 years for 2003 (De-Navas-Walt et al. 2012). Median income begins to decline with the next age group, those aged 55 to 64, to $55,937. Finally, for those aged 65 or older, the reported median income was $33,118 (De-Navas-Walt et al. 2012). For 2009, poor older adults relied on social security benefits more than higher-income older adults. Social security accounted for 71.9% of the cash income of the poor compared to only 28.8% for older adults not poor or not near poor (Issa and Zedlewski 2011) (refer to Figure 6.3).

The economic recession has depleted the incomes and savings of many older workers, leading some to admit that they are unable or afraid to retire. For example, 58-year-old Barbara Petrucci, a hospital employee from Atlanta, Georgia, set aside her dreams for an early retirement. After family savings were depleted by the declining stock market, Petrucci admits that retirement is "an elusive dream" (Rampell and Saltmarsh 2009).

As we have discussed in the earlier chapters of this section, the inequalities based on race/ethnicity and gender will also determine one's economic status. Poverty rates among

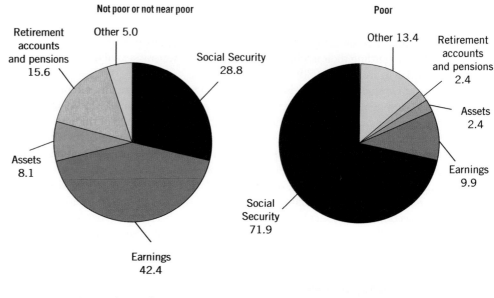

Figure 6.3

Shares of Family Cash Income for Older Adults by Poverty Status, Percentages Reported, 2009

Source: Issa and Zedlewski 2011.

Not poor or not near poor

Poor

Other 5.0

Retirement accounts and pensions 15.6

Social Security 28.8

Assets 8.1

Earnings 42.4

Other 13.4

Retirement accounts and pensions 2.4

Assets 2.4

Earnings 9.9

Social Security 71.9

Average income $69,335

Average income $7,783

the elderly vary by race/ethnicity and gender. Older women have higher rates of poverty than older men do, 10.7% versus 6.6% (Issa and Zedlewski 2011). Women are especially susceptible to economic insecurity because of a number of factors. Women have longer life expectancies and are more likely to be widowed and live alone in old age. Because of gender differences in employment and salaries, women are likely to have less retirement income than men do. During 1999, women aged 65 or older received, on average, $8,000 annually as pension income, whereas men received $14,000 annually (He et al. 2005). Non-Hispanic Whites have lower poverty rates than other reported racial groups. Blacks have the highest rate (19.3%), followed by Latinos (19.0%) and Whites (7.4%) (Rhee 2012).

In the European Union (EU25), about one in six elderly persons is at risk for living in poverty. In 14 of all EU25 countries, the elderly populations are at higher risk of being poor compared with working-age populations. The risk of poverty is highest in Cyprus, Ireland, and Slovenia. Rates are lowest among the elderly residing in the Czech Republic, Slovakia, Lithuania, Latvia, the Netherlands, and Luxembourg (Zaidi 2006).

Health and Medical Care

Aging Costs

Much as they are more economically vulnerable, the young and the old experience the highest health risks among all age groups. We think of death as something that happens in one's old age; yet the age group with the highest risk of mortality is newborns and infants within their first year of life. For 2009, the infant mortality rate was 6.39 deaths per 1,000 births (Murphy et al. 2012). The three leading causes of death among infants are congenital birth defects, low birth weight, and sudden infant death syndrome. Among the elderly, the majority of deaths are caused by heart disease, cancer, and stroke. The elderly also experience chronic conditions such as hypertension (high blood pressure) and heart disease that may contribute to fatal disorders. The elderly are more likely to experience chronic illnesses than younger age groups do, 46% versus 12% (Moody 2006).

Geriatrics is a medical specialty that focuses on diseases of the elderly; some are chronic, not all are life threatening, and others will eventually lead to death. The most prevalent chronic disease of the elderly is arthritis, inflammation of the joints and a leading cause of disability in the United States. Other geriatric diseases include osteoporosis (deterioration of bone tissue, prevalent among women), Parkinson's disease (a degenerative neurological disorder), and dementia and Alzheimer's disease (progressive loss of mental abilities and functions). For the last set of diseases, it should be noted that most older adults experience no mental impairment at all (Moody 2006). (A discussion of caregiving and elder abuse is presented in Chapter 7, "Families.")

The Aging Experience

American elderly, who constitute 13% of our population, consume more than 35% of total health expenditures—more than four times what is spent on younger people (Moody 2006). The United States spends about 17.4% of its gross domestic product (GDP) on health care—the largest expenditure in this category among industrialized countries. During 2010, total health care spending reached $2.6 trillion, with an average of $8,086 spent per person (Centers for Medicare and Medicaid Services 2012).

According to the Centers for Disease Control and Prevention (Robinson 2007), older women face distinctly different challenges to maintain their health compared with older men. The financing and availability of health care is particularly important for older women. Because women make up a higher proportion of the older and frailer population, are less likely to have a spouse to assist them, and need more help with personal care and routine needs, older women use more health care and long-term care services than men do. Most older adults are covered by Medicare, but because older women rely on long-term care (not covered under Medicare), they make higher out-of-pocket payments or rely on Medicaid more often than older men do. Women rely on informal (unpaid) caregivers (adult children, family members, or friends), community-based services (senior centers and convenient transportation), and formal (paid) care services (home health care and nursing home care).

Ageism in the Workplace

Age Stereotypes

In some businesses, age discrimination has an acronym, TFO, "too f___ing old" (Fisher 2004:46). Although much attention has been given to the marginalization of Black, Latino, or female workers, members of another labor force group—older workers—have experienced their own set of unique problems. In 2011, 22.1 million Americans aged 55 to 64 years were employed (U.S. Census Bureau 2011).

Helen Dennis and Kathryn Thomas (2007) document how ageism continues to affect the hiring and promotion of older workers and workplace attitudes toward them. For example, most interview research indicates that older job interviewees whose qualifications are equal to those of younger candidates are less likely to be hired. Ageism restricts job opportunities for mature workers, as they are not offered the same promotion opportunities, training, or compensation as younger workers. Managers have mixed perceptions about older workers. Although older workers are valued for their work habits, skills, and performance, negative perceptions also exist. Older workers are perceived as inflexible, unwilling to adapt to technology, and more expensive (due to health insurance costs) when compared with younger workers.

Elderly Inmates

In the United States, older workers are protected under the Age Discrimination in Employment Act of 1967. The act prohibits employers from discriminating based on age against people 40 to 64 years old. However, in 2008 the U.S. Supreme Court created a tougher burden of proof for plaintiffs in age bias cases. An employee would have to prove that age was the decisive factor (as opposed to a motivating factor) in an adverse employment decision. All EU countries have legislation banning age discrimination in employment, though in the United Kingdom 65 years old is considered the default mandatory retirement age.

In their analysis of the effectiveness of similar age discrimination policies in New Zealand, Geoffrey Wood, Mark Harcourt, and Sondra Harcourt (2004) reported widespread noncompliance among employers. Two New Zealand laws, the New Zealand Human Rights Act of 1993 and the New Zealand Employment Relations Act of 2000, prohibit age discrimination in the workplace. Yet based on job applications from New Zealand businesses, the researchers found that 56% of job applications asked one or more unlawful questions about the applicant's age. Wood et al. characterize New Zealand's labor force composition as skewed toward younger workers. Part of the reason is functional (younger workers are cheaper in terms of salaries and pension investments), yet the researchers note that discriminatory managerial practices are so embedded in social and economic structures that they are not easily changed with legislation.

Responding to Age Inequalities

Social security and Medicare are social insurance programs designed to protect citizens against a specific set of risks. In the case of social security, the risk is that one might have insufficient resources at retirement and that one's resources might not last one's lifetime. How much health care will we need, and for how long are the risks addressed by Medicare? Both are proven, effective antipoverty programs, supporting elderly financial independence and enabling the elderly to live better and healthier lives (Feder and Friedland 2005). Since their inception, however, both programs have been the subjects of much debate.

Social Security

Social Security Funds

Social security was first enacted with the Social Security Act of 1935. A year before, President Franklin D. Roosevelt convened an executive committee to examine economic insecurity, responding to the nation's Great Depression. The committee's recommendation was to create a program to address the long-range problem of economic security for the aged and poor, focusing not on providing social assistance (such as welfare assistance) but, rather, on a social insurance plan against an uncertain future (Social Security and Medicare Boards of Trustees 2007). We tend to think of social security only as the monthly payments one receives after retiring, but the program also supports unemployment insurance, aid to dependent children, and state grants to provide medical care.

Demographic shifts have led to new ways to think about aging and economic security throughout the globe. The current public pension system in the United States and in most of Europe is a pay-as-you-go system—current workers support current beneficiaries of the program (Curl and Hokenstad 2006), or today's workers pay for today's retirees (Moody 2006). Angela Curl and M. C. Hokenstad (2006) compared the U.S. social security system with public pension systems in Sweden and Canada. In Sweden, pensions are based on average life expectancy at the time of retirement. Workers can retire anytime after 61 years of age, but the later they retire, the higher their payments will be. Because of the availability of part-time jobs and the flexible work environment, the program allows Swedes to draw a partial pension for partial retirement. The elderly can mix their employment income with their pension funds. The system is funded by an 18.5% payroll tax (the United States collects 12.4%). Unlike the U.S. system, Sweden's system is partially privatized. Individuals can invest the money from their pension account, or the government invests on their behalf.

The Canadian public pension system is described as combining "income protection for older adults with policies that promote flexibility" (Curl and Hokenstad 2006:95). The Canadian system has three parts: the Old Age Security program, the Canada Pension Plan, and private pensions and savings. The minimum age of eligibility for early retirement benefits is 60 years. Canada collects a 9.9% payroll tax to support the program. As in the United States, both Canada and Sweden have residency requirements (requiring that persons must have lived for a certain number of years in the country) and a universal guaranteed monthly minimum benefit. The researchers praised both countries for promoting flexibility in retirement through gradual or partial retirement programs.

In the United States, policy analysts have long warned about the danger of having few workers paying for the benefits for a growing number of retirees. At the time the social security system was established, the elderly constituted 5% of the population (Moody 2006), and the average life expectancy was about 50 years of age (Curl and Hokenstad 2006). The proportion of the elderly in 2000 grew to 12%, and is projected to increase to 21% by 2050 (He et al. 2005). For 2011, the U.S. Social Security Administration paid benefits of $727 billion to nearly 55 million beneficiaries.

The Social Security and Medicare Boards of Trustees (2007), a nonpartisan panel responsible for reporting on the financial status of the Social Security Trust Funds, projects that tax revenues will fall below actual program costs in 2017. This is the year when the program will spend more than it receives through payroll deductions. The trustees predict that the trust funds will be exhausted in 2041 (OASDI Trustees 2007). Any worker born after 1975 will reach full retirement age after the trust fund is depleted. At the release of their 2007 report, the Social Security and Medicare Boards of Trustees warned, "The longer we wait to address these

Photo 6.5

President George W. Bush praises the U.S. Congress for passing the Medicare Reform Law of 2003. Ensuring Medicare's financial stability while meeting the health care needs of an aging population is a political and economic challenge.

challenges, the more limited will be the options available, the greater will be the required adjustments, and the more severe the potential detrimental economic impact on our nation."

Medicare

 Medicare

The nation's largest health insurance program, Medicare, covers about 43 million elderly or disabled Americans. Medicare has two parts: Part A (hospital insurance) helps pay for care received as an inpatient in critical access hospitals or skilled nursing facilities, as well as some home health care; Part B (physician and outpatient coverage) pays for medically necessary services and supplies that are not covered under Part A. Each part is financed under a different structure. Part A is offered as an automatic premium because most recipients (or their spouses) paid Medicare taxes while they were working. Part A is financed through a payroll tax paid equally by employers and workers. Three-fourths of the financing for Medicare Part B is received from general tax revenues, and the remaining quarter is financed directly through paid premiums, $99.90 (for those with individual incomes of $85,000 or less) or $139.90 or higher (for those with individual incomes higher than $85,000) in 2012.

Since the program's inception, some have been concerned that Medicare spending, especially for Part A, will outpace its revenue sources (Moon 1999). Medicare has been referred to as a pay-as-you-go system; every payroll tax dollar that is contributed into the fund is immediately spent by those currently enrolled (Goodman 1998). Because of increases in health care costs, per capita expenditures for Medicare will increase from $5,943 in 1998 to $10,235 in 2025 (Moon 1999). Out-of-pocket expenses are also expected to increase, from $2,508 per beneficiary in 1998 to $4,855 in 2025. One additional projection casts more doubt on the stability of the system. The number of elderly beneficiaries is expected to continually increase. By 2025, the number of eligible elderly is projected to reach 69.3 million, about 21% of the U.S. population (Moon 1999).

Political rhetoric continues to swirl around how to preserve the system while trying to expand its services to an ever-increasing population of elderly. In 2003, the U.S. Congress passed the Medicare reform law, which included a prescription drug benefit for the first time in the program's history. The bill provides for a prescription drug benefit for older and disabled Americans, offered and managed by private insurers and health plans under contract with the federal government. Critics attacked the plan for its coverage gap, arguing that the bill failed to provide seniors with substantial relief for the cost of prescription drugs. Seniors with low incomes will qualify for extra assistance under the bill. The cost of the bill is estimated at more than $900 billion over 10 years. Analysts predict that the reform bill will have little effect on slowing down the increasing costs of prescription drugs and medical services for the elderly.

The traditional nursing home care model is no longer considered financially viable or medically justified. There has been an increase in the utilization of older adult managed care at home, at day care centers, and in visits to specialists (Berger 2012). Similar programs have been adopted in Canada, like the Comprehensive Home Option for Integrated Care of the Elderly (CHOICE). CHOICE has been credited with keeping elderly men and women healthier longer and out of long-term care homes because medical workers are able to more closely monitor their patients' health (Howell 2011). Medicare and other medical service organizations have encouraged the use of older volunteers as health coaches, advocates, and aides to help individuals and families navigate through the health care system. For example, the Rose Community Foundation in Denver trains older adults as community health workers (Pope 2012).

For more on increasing medical costs and alternative models of care, refer to Chapter 10, "Health and Medicine."

In Focus

The Political Influence of Young and Older Voters

The enactment of social security, Medicare, and other old-age–related policies has created a political constituency of older beneficiaries (Campbell 2003) and, along with it, the perception of political might. A form of ageism, the stereotype of "greedy" older voters willing to put their needs (social security and Medicare) ahead of the needs of other age groups is accepted in many social, political, and media circles (Street and Crossman 2006).

Robert Binstock (2005, 2006) reveals some truths and myths about this perception of senior power. He explains that the senior political power model builds on the fact that older people represent a significant proportion of the electorate. Age is associated with voter registration and actual voting, which is also related to the length of residence in one's home, along with one's level of knowledge about political and social issues. Older persons are likely to have resided in their homes longer than have younger persons, and older people tend to be more knowledgeable about politics and news issues than younger people are. Studies indicate that older persons' high level of interest in politics does not decline even as they reach advanced old age.

In addition to their higher rates of voting participation, the elderly have higher rates of participation in other political areas. Elderly make campaign contributions at higher rates than do younger people—about 28% of all contributions to the 2000 presidential campaign. Older voters are twice as likely to contact their state and federal representatives about issues that matter to them as younger voters are. Doris Haddock's story as a successful grassroots lobbyist is highlighted in this chapter's Voices in the Community feature.

So, what impact does the voting participation by elderly Americans have on elections? One noticeable impact is on how it shapes candidate behavior—candidates actively court the senior vote. Recent presidential candidates have made key appearances at senior centers or promoted their proposals on social security and Medicare to selected senior audiences. But Binstock (2006) argues that the senior vote does not have a "distinctive impact on the outcome of elections" (p. 26). He explains that older Americans do not vote cohesively or as a bloc. Their votes are as diverse as those of any other age group, divided along partisan lines, class, gender, and race. Age is just one characteristic among many that influence voting patterns.

For example, in the 2004 presidential election, the 65-or-older votes were distributed in approximately the same proportions—52% for President George W. Bush and 47% for Senator John Kerry—as were the votes of the general electorate—51% for Bush and 48% for Kerry. In the 2012 presidential election, older voters went against the popular vote—56% supported Governor Romney versus 44% who supported President Obama.

Photo 6.6

Recent protests across the Arab world were led by young adults. Sixty-three percent of the population in the Arab countries is under 30 years of age. In the United States, 41% of the population is under 30 years of age (Slackman 2011).

(Continued)

(Continued)

According to Scott Keeter, Juliana Horowitz, and Alec Tyson (2008), young voters have emerged as a key voting block for the Democratic Party. Since 2004, the majority of those under the age of 30 years have voted for a Democratic candidate in the general election. In 2008, 66% of voters 18 to 29 years of age voted for Barack Obama compared to 53% of all voters. This is the largest measured difference since exit polling began in 1972. Young voters are more ethnically and racially diverse and are less likely to be affiliated with a religious tradition than voters age 30 years or older. Additionally, voters 18 to 29 years of age expressed liberal views on the role of government (to solve problems) and were more likely to disapprove of the Iraq war than older voters. Though younger voters were less likely to contribute money to a campaign, the 18- to 29-year-old voter group had a rate of campaign event participation in battleground states higher than that of any other age group (Keeter et al. 2008). In 2012, President Obama received 60% of the youth vote in his campaign for reelection (Center for Information and Research on Civic Learning and Engagement 2012).

Voices in the Community

Doris Haddock

Granny D. Haddock

Eight years ago, Doris Haddock, known affectionately as "Granny D," embarked on a remarkable journey. She was 89 years old. Despite an arthritic back, she walked—and skied—all the way across America, holding tight to her trademark straw hat while spreading the word about the need for federal campaign finance reform.

Granny D weighed less than 45 kilograms back then. She's even tinier now. A self-described "class clown" growing up, she studied elocution in college. But her only speeches at first were to clerks in the shoe-company office that she ran. Doris Haddock soon had her say, though. She and her husband, Jim, shared a passion for social justice, and for decades, they championed many causes together until Jim's death in 1993.

One day five years later, Granny D's eyes fastened on a lone paragraph in a newspaper article about two U.S. congressmen who had slipped $50 million into an appropriations measure late one night. The money was a subsidy for a tobacco company.

Furious, Granny D picked up the phone and called the advocacy group Common Cause. "I said, 'But that's corruption!' They said, 'Of course it's corruption. You cannot run (for Congress) today without being a multi-millionaire; or you take illegal money from corporations or special interests.' I wasn't even conscious of this. I said, 'I'm old, I'm tired. What can I do?' And they said, 'Try to get the McCain-Feingold Bill passed.' So I said, 'OK'".

McCain-Feingold was a bipartisan measure pending in Congress to eliminate unregulated donations, or "soft money," from federal election campaigns. But Haddock wondered how one person could help make the bill the law of the land.

She talked the matter over with her friends in a local discussion group that calls itself the "Tuesday Morning Academy." Before long, they were contacting friends, who were contacting THEIR friends all across America, getting signatures on petitions in support of campaign finance reform.

Granny D says those petitions were sent to the senators. "And within a couple of months, we got letters back saying, 'Dear Little Old Ladies. Don't worry yourselves. We are going to pass the McCain-Feingold Bill.' Two months later, they didn't pass it. I went into deep depression. All the ladies who had been helping me left, and I was stuck with egg on my face."

Soon afterward, Granny D and her son happened to drive past an old man who was walking down a road, carrying a peace sign. "What if I did that?" she asked her son. "My son said, 'You have to have a reason.' I said, 'Oh, I have a reason.' He said, 'Oh, my God. Campaign finance reform.' And I said, 'Yes!' He said, 'You don't have any money. How are you going to do it? You live on Social Security.' I said, 'I'll go as a pilgrim. I'll walk until given shelter, fast until given food.'"

And that's exactly what she did for 14 straight months, from Pasadena, California, to Washington, D.C. Along the way, she relied on strangers for food and a place to lay her head at night. "Granny's Angels," she called them. Trudging along, she had no idea whether her journey would make any difference. "I'm walking for future generations," she told herself. "For my 16 great-grandchildren."

However, she says, "As I progressed, I became a circus. People were lining up on either side of the road, waiting for me. Or they were telling people ahead, 'She's coming! She's coming!'"

Granny D reached the nation's capital after skiing through the snow on the towpath of an old canal that reaches the city from the Maryland mountains. Only three people greeted her at her last stop, at Arlington National Cemetery.

But then a Metro subway train pulled up to the cemetery station. "And suddenly the cars stopped, and people poured out. And the next one came, and they poured out. So I had 2,300 people walking with me. And when we got near, quite a few of the senators and House members walked with me, too. It was grand! And we went down K Street, because that's where the lobbyists are. And girls in these great, high buildings put out signs saying, 'Go Granny, Go!' I was in tears to think that people cared."

That was in early 2000. The McCain-Feingold bill passed the Senate and the House, and was signed into law by President Bush two years later.

Granny D went back to New Hampshire, but not to a rocking chair. She spoke at several rallies, and, in 2005, delivered the graduation address at Hampshire College in Amherst, Massachusetts. Showing the effects of emphysema brought on by 50 years of smoking, she told the audience that she had recently been jailed for reading from the U.S. Constitution in the rotunda of the Capitol Building in Washington.

"As I thought that did violence to my free-speech rights under the Constitution, I went back and read from the [constitutional amendments called the] Bill of Rights," she told the graduates. "That landed me in jail, too. I felt freer in that jail, because I had spoken out as a free person, than I have ever felt in the open air. Be involved! Get involved! Stay involved!"

Haddock died in March 2010. She was 100 years old.

Source: Quoted material is from Landphair 2007.

Main Points

- Age is both a biological and a social classification. We have socially and culturally defined expectations about the meaning of age, our understanding of it, and our responses to it. Age distinguishes acceptable behavior for different social groups.
- Sociologists examine age and the process of aging through a life course perspective. This perspective examines the entire course of human life from childhood, adolescence, and adulthood to old age. Gerontology is the specific study of aging and the elderly, which is the primary focus of this chapter.
- Demography is the study of the changes and trends in a population, and demographers have identified several reasons for population aging.

First, population aging is caused by a decline in birth rates. Second, population aging can also occur because of an improvement in life expectancy as a result of medical and technological advances. Finally, the process of population aging can be influenced by characteristics of birth cohorts.

- Populations are aging in all countries, though the level and pace vary by geographic region.

- Functionalists rely on disengagement theory to explain aging as a natural process of withdrawal from active participation in social life. The theory contends that people enter and exit a set of roles throughout their lives. Conflict theorists offer the modernization theory of aging to explain how the role and status of the elderly decline with industrialization. The power, wealth, and prestige of the elderly are linked with their labor contribution or their relationship to the means of production. According to the feminist perspective, the standards of our culture create more problems for women than for men as they transition into their middle and later years. Women are more vulnerable to societal pressure to retain their youth. Interactionists reveal how our age-related roles are socially defined and expected. Age is tied to a system of matching people and roles, some stigmatized.

- Age also serves as a basis for prejudice or discrimination. Ageism is defined by Robert Butler (1969) as the "systematic stereotyping of and discrimination against people because they are old, just as racism and sexism accomplish this with skin color and gender" (p. 243). Age distinguishes acceptable behavior for different social groups. Research suggests that ageist attitudes may affect a physician's therapeutic decisions toward older patients.

- Social security and Medicare are U.S. social insurance programs designed to protect citizens against a specific set of risks. Both have proven to be effective antipoverty programs for older Americans, supporting financial independence and enabling the elderly to live better and healthier lives. Since their inception, however, both programs have also been the subject of debate.

On Your Own

Log on to the open-access Student Study Site at www.sagepub.com/leonguerrero4e for these additional learning tools:

- Interactive quizzes
- Video clips
- NPR audio links
- Handbook articles

- E-flashcards
- Journal articles
- End-of-chapter web exercises
- Additional web resources and current events

Internet and Community Exercises

1. The Gray Panthers, organized in 1970 by Maggie Kuhn and five of her friends, is a national advocacy organization for older and retired adults. The Gray Panthers' first goal was to combat ageism, but the group has also taken a stand on other important social issues: economic justice, medical care, education, and peace. Recent efforts have been directed toward policies ensuring affordable prescription drugs for seniors, children, cancer patients, and HIV patients. The Gray Panthers have more than 50 local chapters. To see if there is a chapter in your state, log on to *Study Site Chapter 6*. Contact the chapter for information about what activities are supported in your area.

2. The National Institute on Aging (NIA), part of the National Institutes of Health, leads the country's

scientific effort to understand the nature of aging and to extend the healthy, active years of life for Americans. Formed in 1974, the NIA provides leadership in aging research, training, health information dissemination, and other programs relevant to aging and older people. Its website includes resource materials on healthy aging, caregiving, medications, dietary supplements, and diseases. Log on to *Study Site Chapter 6* for links to the NIA resource page.

3. The private, not-for-profit Alliance for Aging Research is the nation's leading citizen advocacy organization for improving the health and independence of older Americans. Founded in 1986, the goal of the Alliance for Aging Research is to promote medical and behavioral research into the aging process. The organization also serves as an advocate of consumer health education and public policy. On its website, the Alliance for Aging

Research includes surveys and quizzes pertaining to healthy aging, such as heart disease, general aging, and cognition. Log on to *Study Site Chapter 6* to test your knowledge in these areas.

4. Gay seniors are more likely to live alone, are four times less likely to have adult children to care for them, and remain fearful of discrimination from health care and social service workers (Crary 2008). Services and Advocacy for Gay, Lesbian, Bisexual, and Transgender Elders (SAGE) is a nonprofit organization based in New York City. The program focuses on the specific needs of lesbian, gay, bisexual, and transgendered (LGBT) elders, including establishing a network of caregiving services, support groups for seniors with HIV, and home visiting programs. Log on to *Study Site Chapter 6* for links to SAGE's services and programs. Are similar programs available in your community?

Study Questions

1. How do social norms—formal or informal—shape our definition of age?
2. Identify the societal consequences of population aging.
3. Disengagement theory defines aging as a natural process of withdrawal from active social participation. Do you think this disengagement is a natural process or brought on by social factors? Explain.
4. From an interactionist's perspective, how can we improve the status of the elderly?
5. In what ways are elderly women disadvantaged in society in comparison with elderly men?
6. Compare and contrast the U.S. social security system with the pension systems in Sweden and Canada.

PART III

Our Social Institutions

É mile Durkheim first described the importance of social institutions in society. He likened them to organs in a human body. Each organ does one specific thing—a heart is responsible for our circulatory system, a brain is the key to our nervous system, and a pair of lungs regulates our respiratory system. If something happens to the heart, its functions cannot be assumed by other organs, and as a result, the body as a whole becomes compromised.

Social institutions are defined as a stable set of statuses, roles, groups, and organizations that provides a foundation for addressing fundamental societal needs (Newman 2006). For our discussion, we focus on five institutions—family, education, work and the economy, health and medicine, and the media—each with a specific role in society. In the chapters that follow, we review the importance of each institution but also highlight the social problems affecting it. The bases of inequality we reviewed in Part II are intricately related to the social problems based in each institution. Each chapter concludes with a discussion about the policies and community efforts that are being made to address these social problems.

What Is a Family?

◀ We have all grown up with an understanding of what a family is. If asked to describe a "typical" family, most Americans would first think of something like the nuclear family shown in this image: a woman and a man and their children.

▲ And yet, our description could be broader, encompassing grandparents, aunts, uncles, and cousins—in other words, an extended family.

What is it about the two groups of people shown in these images that makes them seem like a "family"?

Now think about your own experience: the family you grew up in and the family you are a part of now. Is your family consistent with the previous images? Does your own family fit the traditional definition of "family"? Or does your family more closely resemble these other images?

▲ The social reality of what a family is has changed considerably in the past few decades. But our social definition of what constitutes a "typical" family is changing more slowly.

What social problems might be caused by the conflict between our mythology—the notion that most families are "traditional" families—and the reality of the growing diversity in family form?

CHAPTER 7

Families

D o you recall the first "crew" you ever hung out with? You know the one—all of its members know each other, speak the same language, laugh at the same jokes, dress alike, and maybe even look alike. Sound familiar? These are the people with whom you slept, ate, and lived in your own home: your family.

You may not always think of it this way, but your family is part of the larger social institution of "the family." Consider for a moment that your family was among the 117 million family groups counted by the U.S. Census in 2010 (U.S. Census Bureau 2012a). What does your family have in common with the other family groups? Your first response might be that your family has nothing in common with the others. No other family has the unique arrangement or history of individuals related through blood or by choice. From this position, any problem experienced by your family, such as a divorce, would be defined as a personal trouble. A divorce is a private family matter kept among immediate family members. It would be none of anyone else's business.

If we use our sociological imagination, however, we can uncover the links between our personal family experiences and our social world. Divorce is not just a family matter but also a public issue. Looking at the recent divorce rate of 3.4 divorces per 1,000 people, divorce occurs not in just one household but in millions of U.S. households. It affects the economic and social well-being of millions of women, men, and children. Divorce challenges the fundamental values of home and love and the value of the family itself. Divorce could be everyone's business.

In this chapter, our goal is to explore this private, yet public, world of the family. For our discussion, we define the family as a construct of meaning and relationships both emotional and economic. The **family** is a social unit based on kinship relations—relations based on blood, and those created by choice, marriage, partnership, or adoption. A **household** is defined as an economic and residential unit. These definitions allow for the diversity of families that we discuss in this chapter, while not presenting one configuration as the standard. As you'll see, the family as we think we know it may not exist at all.

What Does It Mean to Me?

In January 2007, two abducted boys were discovered in St. Louis, Missouri. Michael Devlin was charged with the felony kidnapping of the boys. The older boy, Shawn Hornbeck, lived with Devlin for more than four years in the apartment complex where he, along with William Ownby, was finally discovered. Neighbors reported that they assumed Hornbeck and Devlin were family and had no reason to interfere, despite occasionally hearing violent noises coming from their apartment. This incident highlights how family life is considered private by society and how, in this case, a child kidnapper went unsuspected for many years. What would you have done if you were a neighbor? Should problems in the family be considered private troubles or public issues?

Myths of the Family

Family Sociology

The **nuclear family**—two parents and their biological children living together—is exalted as the ideal family. Yet, families are much more diverse than this. First, the percentage of families composed of married couples with children declined from 40.3% in 1970 to 21% in 2010 (U.S. Census Bureau 2012a). Take note—the traditional family form, married with children, is less than a quarter of all U.S. households. The largest family form is married couples without children (29%).

Public attitudes are shifting away from traditional ideals of marriage and childbearing in Western industrialized societies such as the United States, Austria, (West) Germany, Great Britain, Ireland, and the Netherlands. Zoya Gubernskaya (2010) found that female, never married, better educated, employed, and secularized individuals had less-traditional views about marriage and children. Support for the statement that "people who want children ought to get married" declined in these countries from 1988 to 2002. Gubernskaya attributes the increasing nontraditionalism to a rise in secularization, a shift toward individualism, and an increasing focus on education and employment achievement that are at odds with traditional family formation.

Second, the only increase in family groups during the period came in the category of "other family households." Other family households include families with other relatives residing, what we also refer to as **extended families**. When President Obama moved into 1600 Pennsylvania Avenue, much attention was paid to the fact that his mother-in-law, Marian Robinson, would also be a resident. The last time a mother-in-law was a full-time White House resident was during Harry Truman's presidency. Other family households made up 17% of all U.S. households, increasing from 10.6% in 1970. Included in this category are 10 million single-parent families, 8 million headed by mothers and 2 million headed by fathers. Finally, there has been an increase in the percentage of nonfamily households (refer to Table 7.1).

Single Parents

Female Single Parents

In 2007, U.S. Census data revealed that for the first time, more American women were living without a husband than with one. Based on 2005 data, 51% of women were living without a spouse, an increase from 35% in 1950 and 49% in 2000. In contrast, 47% of men reported living without a spouse in 2005. The pattern varies by race, with 30% of Black women, 49% of Hispanic women, 55% of non-Hispanic White women, and 60% of Asian women reporting that they were living with a spouse. Analysts reported that several factors contributed to the increase in the number of single women: late marriage for women, women living longer as widows or after a divorce, and women being more likely than men to delay remarriage (Roberts 2007).

Table 7.1

Households by Type: 1970 and 2010 (Percentage)

	1970	2010
Total number of households	63 million	117 million
Nonfamily households		
Men living alone	5.6	15.5
Women living alone	11.5	17.4
Family households		
Married couples with children	40.3	20.9
Married couples without children	30.3	28.8
Other family households	10.6	17.4

Source: Kreider and Elliot 2009, Figure 1; U.S. Census Bureau 2012a.

Note: Columns may not add to 100% due to rounding.

Photo 7.1

Shawn Hornbeck is embraced by his mother Pam Akers during a press conference. Missing since October 2002, Hornbeck was found in 2007 living with another boy and their abductor, Michael Devlin, in St. Louis, Missouri. Devlin was sentenced to multiple life terms for his crimes.

In addition to the false image of the nuclear family, we also embrace other myths about the family. We tend to believe that the families of the past were better and happier than modern families are. We believe that families should be safe havens, protecting their members from harm and danger. And a final myth relates to the topic of this book: We also assume that the family and its failings lead to many of our social problems.

There is a persistent belief that nontraditional families, such as divorced, fatherless, or working-mother families, threaten and erode the integrity of the family as an institution. These "pathological" family forms are blamed for drug abuse, delinquency, illiteracy, and crime. As a group, female-headed households were condemned in the Personal Responsibility and Work Opportunity Reconciliation Act of 1996, also known as the Welfare Reform Act, for their dependency on the public welfare system.

Sociological Perspectives on the Family

Functionalist Perspective

From a functionalist perspective, the family serves many important functions in society. Some functionalists claim that the family is the most vital social institution. The family serves as a child's primary group, the first group membership we claim. We inherit not only the color of our hair or eyes but also our family's social position. The family confers social status and class. The family helps define who we are and how we find our place in society. And, without the family, who would provide for the essential needs of the child: affection, socialization, economic support, and protection?

Social problems emerge as the family struggles to adapt to a modern society. Functionalists have noted how many of the family's original functions have been taken over by organized religion, education, work, and the government in modern society (Lenski and Lenski 1987), but still, the family is expected to provide its remaining functions of raising children and providing affection and companionship for its members (Popenoe 1993). From a functionalist perspective, the family is inextricably linked to the rest of society. The family does not work alone; rather, it functions in concert with the other institutions. Changes in other institutions, such as the economy, politics, or law, contribute to changes and problems in the family.

Consider the education of children. Before the establishment of mandatory public school systems, the family educated its own children. As a formal system, education has become its own institution, taking primary responsibility for educating and socializing everyone's children. Functionalists examine how the institutions of the family and education effectively work together. To what extent should parents participate in their children's education, and to what extent is the educational system responsible for raising our children?

Because of this perspective's emphasis on the family and its social and emotional functions, when the family fails—as in the case of divorce or domestic violence—functionalists take these problems seriously. These problems afflict the family and, according to functionalists, can lead to additional problems in the society, such as crime, poverty, or delinquency.

Conflict and Feminist Perspectives

For the conflict theorist, the family is a system of inequality where conflict is normal. Conflict can derive from economic or power inequalities between spouses or family members. From a feminist perspective, inequality emerges from the patriarchal family system, where men control decision making in the family. The persistent social ideals that view the woman as homemaker and the man as breadwinner are problematic from both perspectives. Men's social and economic status increases as their work outside of the home is more visible and rewarded, whereas women's work inside the home remains invisible and uncompensated.

Work/Family Conflict

The family structure, as our society has come to define it, upholds a system of male social and economic domination. Theorist Friedrich Engels argued that the family was the chief source of female enslavement. Within the family, Engels believed the husband represented the bourgeois, whereas his wife represented the proletariat (Engels 1902). Among the middle class, where property is the primary consideration, marriage was a respectable form of prostitution. Just as members of the proletariat were oppressed in the economy, women were oppressed at home. Freedom for women, wrote Engels, would come with their economic independence and participation in the workplace (activities based outside of the home).

Feminist theory also examines power within the family. According to this perspective, men can maintain their position of power in the family through violence or the threat of violence against women. Feminists argue that domestic violence cannot be solely explained by men's individual attitudes and behavior. Rather, violence against women is linked to larger social structures of male dominance, such as political, economic, and other social institutions like the family. Theorists have encouraged the integration of feminist analyses of gender and power to better comprehend the mechanisms leading to violence, arguing that to stop such violence, structures of gender inequality must change (Brownmiller 1975).

Feminist theorists have also acknowledged how the cultural differences of domestic violence have not been fully recognized. According to Tricia Bent-Goodley (2005), "Research has largely focused on White and poor women, despite the fact that domestic violence crosses race, ethnicity, socioeconomic status, religion and sexual orientation" (p. 197). She notes that this narrow research focus has encouraged the perception that women of color, middle- and upper-class women, and women in same sex-relationships do not experience domestic violence, despite evidence to the contrary. And though data indicate that disabled women experience a greater risk of abuse and violence in comparison with the general population, studies on the nature of the oppression and consequences of domestic abuse against women with disabilities still remain largely ignored (Mays 2006).

Families are also subject to powerful economic and political interest groups that control family social programs and policies. Conflict arises when the needs of particular family forms are promoted while others are ignored. For example, formal law and social policies recognize heterosexual marriages, but homosexual marriages and families are largely ignored. To resolve social problems in the family, both perspectives suggest the need for structural change.

Interactionist Perspective

Through social interaction, we create and maintain our definition of a family. As we do this, it affects our larger social definition of what everyone's family should be like and how we envision the family that we create for ourselves.

Within our own families, our interaction through words, symbols, and meanings defines our expectation of what the family should be like. How many children are in the family? Who does the house cleaning? Who gets to carve the holiday turkey? What does it mean to be a wife, a husband, a partner? As a family, we collectively create and maintain a family definition on which members agree. Problems arise when there is conflict about how the family is defined. A couple starting their own family must negotiate their own way of doing things. Two partners may carry definitions and expectations from their families of origin, but together, they create a new family reality.

Problems may also occur when partners' expectations of family or marriage do not match their real lives. In our culture, romantic love is idealized, misleading individuals to believe that they are destined for a fulfilling emotional partnership with one perfect mate. After the realities of life set in, including the first fight, the notion of romantic love is shattered. Couples recognize that it may take more than romantic love to make a relationship work.

Conflict also arises when a family arrangement is different from societal norms and expectations. Blended families, gay or lesbian families, or single-parent families become social problems based only on how they deviate from the definition of a "normal" family. Society assigns meaning to particular family groups or relations. More than half a century ago, when a child was born to unmarried parents, it was assumed that the child was unwanted and that the child's future would be less than promising. There was a major social stigma with being referred to as a bastard child. But because currently one in three births involves parents who are not legally married, and most births are wanted or planned, the use of the term *bastard* has disappeared as has the stigma attached to such a birth (Rutter and Tienda 2005).

But definitions vary by culture. In South Korea, there is still a strong negative stigma regarding unwed motherhood. In 2007, 2% of all births in South Korea were to unmarried women, compared with 40% of all U.S. births. The Korean discussion on unmarried motherhood has focused on how to eradicate the "evil" of unmarried motherhood as it threatens the patriarchal social structure (Kim and Davis 2003). Journalist Choe Sang-Hun (2009) reports how "social pressure drives thousands of unmarried women to choose between abortion, which is illegal but rampant, and adoption, which is considered socially shameful but is encouraged by the government" (p. A6). Unmarried women who decide to raise a child risk a life of poverty and disgrace, even being ostracized by family members. Lee Mee-Kyong, whose family disowned her after the birth of her son, says, "Once you become an unwed mom, you're branded as immoral and a failure. You fall to the bottom rung of society" (as quoted in Sang-Hun 2009:A6).

Putting all our separate definitions of the family together, we create a portrait of what the family should be like. But as political and religious forces uphold and encourage a heteronormative conception of the nuclear family as the norm, by default, other family forms are considered deviant or against some set of moral codes. Other family forms are considered lesser families or not families at all (Smith 1993).

Sociologists Brian Powell, Catherine Bolzendahl, Claudia Geist, and Lara Carr Steelman (2010) reported how our definition of the family was expanding. In the 2003 Constructing the Family Survey, respondents were asked about which living arrangements constituted a family. Each survey respondent indicated that an arrangement with a husband, a wife, and children constituted a family. However, the majority also defined the following as a family: single mothers (94%) or single fathers (94.2%) with children and a married couple with no children (93.1%). According to the researchers, "The most-agreed-upon family forms tend to rely on at least one of two prerequisites: the presence in the home of a child, and a legal heterosexual relationship—or, more precisely, a relationship that is not a same-sex relationship or a cohabitating heterosexual one" (Powell et al. 2010:20). There was less agreement that an unmarried cohabitating couple with children could be defined as a family (78.7%). For arrangements with same-sex couples, couples with children were more likely to be defined as a family than couples without children (e.g., 55% of the sample defined two women with children as a family compared with 26.8% who defined two women with no children as a family) (Powell et al. 2010).

Refer to Table 7.2 for a summary of all sociological perspectives on the family.

Sociology of Love

Traditional Families

What Does It Mean to Me?

In 2012, it was reported that more than half of births to American women under 30 years old occur outside of marriage. The fastest growth in nonmarital births is among White women in their 20s with some college education. Women with college degrees are still more likely to marry before having children (DeParle and Tavernise 2012). Is there a social stigma related to nonmarital birth? Why is there an increasing number of nonmarital births?

 STATE STATS

Table 7.2

Summary of Sociological Perspectives: The Family

	Functional	Conflict/Feminist	Interactionist
Explanation of the family and its social problems	Functionalists examine how the family interacts with other social institutions. Functionalists believe that social problems emerge as the family struggles to adapt to a modern society. Functionalists also examine the manifest and latent functions of the family.	Problems emerge from conflict inherent in the family structure. Conflict can derive from economic or power inequalities between family members. From a feminist perspective, the family is a patriarchal system, where men dominate social and economic spheres.	An interactionist focuses on the social meaning and expectations of the "family." Interactionists will also focus on how family members define their own families.
Questions asked about the family	What functions does the family serve? How is the family affected by other social institutions? How does the problem reflect changes between the family and other social institutions?	What is the basis of conflict within the family? How does conflict affect family members and their relationships?	How do we define the "family"? What social forces influence our definition of the family? What are the consequences of these definitions?

Problems in the Family

Divorce

If you do an Internet search on divorce, you might be surprised at your search results. In addition to divorce facts and access to support groups, you'll also find handy guides to complete your own divorce paperwork. Looking to save time, money, and pain? Please try our services. Looking for a divorce lawyer? Why not search for one online? And if you'd like to send a divorce greeting card that says, "Happy to be without you," you can find one of those online, too.

Divorce was a rare occurrence until the 1970s. In the 1950s and 1960s, the divorce rate was about 2.2 to 2.6 per 1,000 individuals (U.S. Census Bureau 1999). With the introduction of no-fault divorce laws in the 1970s, the divorce rate began to climb, reaching a high of 5.3 in 1979 and 1981 (U.S. Census Bureau 1999). The increase in divorce rates has been attributed to other factors: the increasing economic independence of women, the transition from extended to nuclear family forms, and the increasing geographic and occupational mobility of families. Furthermore, as our societal and cultural norms about divorce have changed, the stigma attached to divorce has decreased.

In recent years, the divorce rate has remained stable around 4.0 divorces per 1,000 individuals in the total U.S. population. The rate was 4.2 in 2000, declining to 3.4 in 2009 (Centers for Disease Control and Prevention 2002, 2010). The U.S. marital rate declined for the same period: 8.7 for 2000 to 6.8 for 2009 (Centers for Disease Control and Prevention 2002, 2010). When compared with European Union (EU) countries, the United States has the higher divorce rate. In 2008, the estimated divorce rate for the EU was 2.0 per 1,000 (Eurostat 2009). EU marital rates were also lower for 2008, at 4.87 per 1,000 (Eurostat 2009).

Recent census data on divorce indicate that certain groups are more susceptible to divorce than others. Based on 2001 Census data, Rose Kreider (2005) reported that although one in five U.S. adults has been divorced, the percentage of those having been divorced was highest among men and women 50 to 59 years of age (41% and 39%, respectively). The majority of separated and divorced men and women were between 25 and 44 years of age. The median age of divorce from first marriage was 29.4 years for women and 31.4 years for men. Divorce rates are higher among couples married before 20 years of age, living at 200% of the poverty level, with a high school degree or some college, or working full-time (Kreider and Fields 2002).

Sociologists have paid particular attention to immediate and long-term effects of divorce on children. In general, the research indicates that children with divorced parents have moderately poorer life and educational outcomes (emotional well-being, academic achievement, labor force participation, divorce, and teenage childbearing) than do children living with both parents (Amato and Keith 1991). For example, boys living with a divorced mother are four times more likely to display severe delinquency or to engage in early sexual intercourse than are those living in two-parent households (Simons 1996). Some of these effects carry into adolescence and young adulthood (Amato and Keith 1991; Cherlin, Kiernan, and Chase-Lansdale 1995), with more negative outcomes for adult females than for adult males, such as a greater incidence of relationship conflict or difficulty with intimate relationships.

Conversely, research also suggests that marital separation is beneficial to the well-being of children (Videon 2002). Favorable outcomes have included increased maturity, enhanced self-esteem, and increased empathy among children from divorced families (Brooks Conway, Christensen, and Herlihy 2003). Parental divorce may shift children from traditional sex-role beliefs and behavior toward more androgynous attitudes and behavior (MacKinnon, Stoneman, and Brody 1984). Parent-child relations are important influences on children's well-being, even mediating the effects of marital dissolution (Videon 2002). Divorce is less disruptive if both parents maintain a positive relationship with the child, if parental conflict decreases after separation or divorce, and if the level of socioeconomic resources for the child is not reduced (Amato and Keith 1991).

Research consistently indicates that although men experience minimal economic declines after divorce, most women experience a substantial decline in household income and increased dependence on social welfare (Smock 1994). Data from the 2001 U.S. Census show that although only 15% of recently divorced men lived in households where they (or someone they lived with) received noncash public assistance, more than twice as many recently divorced women (or someone they lived with) received noncash public assistance (34%; Kreider 2005). As first reported in Chapter 2, the poverty rate among female-headed households (no male present) is 31.2% compared with 16.1% among male-headed households (no female present).

In his analysis of 14 countries in the EU, Wilfred Uunk (2004) documented a 24% decline in women's median household income after divorce, comparable, he says, to the income change experienced by U.S. women after divorce. His research revealed how median income declines were lower among divorced women from southern European countries (Greece, Italy, Spain, and Portugal) and Scandinavian countries (Demark and Finland), but higher among women from Austria, France, Luxembourg, and the United Kingdom.

Taking a World View

The Family in Sweden

Family sociologist David Popenoe (2006) writes,

> Many Americans have long had a ready answer to America's family problems: We should be more like Scandinavia. Whether the issues are work-family, teen sex, child poverty, or marital breakup, a range of Scandinavian family and welfare policies is commonly put forth with the assertion that, if only these could be instituted in America, family life in our nation would be improved significantly. (p. 68)

Focusing on Sweden, Scandinavia's largest country, Popenoe argues that there are fundamental differences in the family experience in Sweden and the United States. He concludes that it would be a mistake to think that what works in Sweden could be successfully transferred to the United States.

First, he reminds us that the population of the Scandinavian countries is smaller and more homogeneous than that of the United States. The population of Sweden is 9.4 million, compared with the U.S. population of 313 million.

Second, the marital rate in Sweden is one of the lowest in the world. The number of marriages per 1,000 unmarried women in 2002 was 43.4 in the United States compared with 17.5 in Sweden. Popenoe observes that if this rate holds, only about 60% of Swedish women today will ever marry (compared with more than 85% in the United States). This is a recent demographic shift—in the 1950s, the marital rate was 95% for the United States and 91% for Sweden.

Popenoe attributes Sweden's low marital rate to the country's weak religious structure, a dominant left-wing ideology, and a government that has removed all state benefits for marriage. A secular country, Sweden has no religious pressure to maintain the image and sanctity of marriage.

There are no religious or cultural stigmas against cohabiting couples. Popenoe writes that the political left wing in Europe has taken an "antagonistic" stance against strong families—based on feminist concerns about patriarchy, an antipathy toward a bourgeois institution linked to privilege, and the belief that families are an impediment to full equality. All government benefits are given to individuals regardless of their marital or cohabiting status. There are no spousal health care benefits in Sweden as there are in the United States, and individuals are taxed (there is no joint income tax).

As a result, Sweden has a higher rate of nonmarital cohabitation than other Western countries. Popenoe reports that nearly all Swedish couples live together before marriage, compared with two thirds of U.S. couples. Many Swedish couples don't marry even after children are born. The nonmarital birthrate is higher in Sweden than in the United States, 56% versus 35%. However, most nonmarital births in Sweden, about 90%, are to biological parents living together. In the United States, 60% of nonmarital births occur with single, noncohabiting mothers.

Finally, Sweden's divorce rate is lower than the divorce rate in the United States. Popenoe attributes the higher U.S. rate to our ethnic, racial, and religious heterogeneity and higher residential mobility. In addition, Americans marry at a younger age (another risk factor)—25 years of age for women and 27 years of age for men. In Sweden, the age at first marriage is 31 for women and 33 for men. All Swedish married couples with children 16 years of age or younger, if they want a divorce, need to go through a mandatory six-month waiting period before the divorce is declared final.

Source: Popenoe 2006.

Cohabitation

Decline in economic well-being also occurs among women from previously cohabiting couples (Avellar and Smock 2005). Cohabiting couples have more precarious financial circumstances, experiencing lower personal and household incomes than married couples. After the dissolution of a relationship, the level of household income for cohabiting men declines 10%, but it declines 33% for cohabiting women. After the dissolution of a cohabiting relationship, women have a higher level of poverty than men, 30% versus 20%. Hispanic and African American women are more vulnerable than White women in experiencing economic decline. Cohabiting relationships may also include children affected by the same economic decline. These children are even more vulnerable because cohabiting mothers have less access to their former partners' income than divorced mothers do.

Violence and Neglect in the Family

Intimate Partner Violence

One of the myths mentioned at the beginning of this chapter is that the family provides a safe place for its members. This myth ignores the incidence of violence and abuse in families. Family violence is unique because the aggressor and the victim(s) are part of the same relational unit, with emotional bonds, attachments, and particular power dynamics (Breines and Gordon 1983).

Domestic Violence

In the United States, nearly 25% of surveyed women and 8% of surveyed men reported that they had been raped or physically assaulted by a current or former intimate partner in their lifetime. Based on these estimates, approximately 1.5 million women and 835,000 men are raped or physically assaulted by an intimate partner annually in the United States (Tjaden and Thoennes 2000). (Refer to Table 7.3 for Bureau of Justice Statistics data from 2001 to 2005.) In 2010, 669,850 violent crimes were committed by an intimate partner: a current or former spouse, boyfriend, or girlfriend. In about 80% of these crimes, the victims were women (Truman 2011). Data confirm that violence by an intimate partner is a common experience worldwide. A review of more than 50 population-based studies in 35 countries revealed that between 10% and 52% of women reported that they had been physically abused by an intimate partner at some point in their lives (Garcia-Moreno et al. 2006).

Violence Against Women

Research has consistently linked specific social factors to family violence: low socioeconomic status, social and structural stress, and social isolation (Gelles and Maynard 1987). Feminist researchers argue that domestic violence is rooted in gender and represents men's attempts to maintain dominance and control over women (Anderson 1997). Comparative data reveal how the severity and pattern of violence against women is higher in countries with high societal violence and low empowerment of women (Garcia-Moreno et al. 2006).

Studies have also documented how domestic violence is a significant predictor in maternal parenting behavior. Intimate partner violence involving a female victim often occurs in a household where a child is present (refer to Figure 7.1). According to Alytia Levendosky and Sandra Graham-Bermann (2000), psychological abuse, rather than physical abuse, is more likely to negatively affect a mother's parenting, which in turn is related to children's behaviors. The researchers report that a mother's experience with psychological abuse was significantly related to a child's antisocial behavior. Children in middle childhood begin to identify with the aggressor and act in emotionally aggressive ways toward their mothers. Yet, female victims identify positive and negative impacts on their parenting because of domestic violence (Levendosky, Lynch, and Graham-Bermann 2000). Battered women report that their emotional feelings or concerns make parenting difficult, noting the reduced amount of quality time or emotional energy they can devote to their children. But these women also report that they had increased empathy and caring toward their children. Researchers suggest that battered women were actively working to protect their children from the effects of violence in their household.

Table 7.3

Victim-Offender Relationship in Nonfatal Violent Victimization, by Gender of Victim, 2001–2005

Victim/Offender Relationship	Female		Male	
	Rate	Percentage	Rate	Percentage
Intimates	4.2	21.5	0.9	3.6
Other relatives	1.7	8.9	1.2	4.6
Friends/acquaintances	7.0	36.2	8.6	34.3
Strangers	6.5	33.4	14.4	57.4

Average Annual Rate per 1,000 Age 12 or Older

Source: Bureau of Justice Statistics 2012.

a. Female Victim Households

b. Male Victim Households

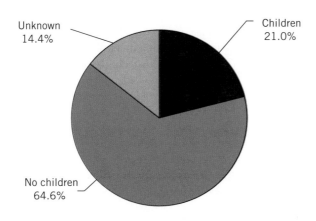

Figure 7.1

Percentage of Households Experiencing Nonfatal Intimate Partner Violence Where Children Under Age 12 Resided, by Gender of Victim, 2001–2005

Source: Bureau of Justice Statistics 2012.

Child Abuse and Neglect

Some children are subject to abuse and neglect in their families. The immediate emotional and behavioral effects of abuse and neglect—isolation, fear, low academic achievement, delinquency—may lead to lifelong consequences, including low self-esteem, depression, criminal behavior, and adult abusive behavior (Child Welfare Information Gateway 2006). In 2010, 754,000 children were victims of maltreatment. Most child victims, about 78%, suffered from neglect. The highest rates of victimization (per 1,000 children) were among ethnic minorities: African Americans (14.6%), American Indians or Alaska Natives (11.0%), and children of multiple races (12.7%). Tragically, about 1,560 children died as a result of abuse or neglect in 2010 (U.S. Department of Health and Human Services, Administration for Children and Families, Administration on Children, Youth and Families, Children's Bureau 2011).

Multiple factors related to the child, the parent or caregiver, the family structure, and the environment have been identified as contributing to child maltreatment. Though children are not responsible for being victims of maltreatment, certain factors make some children more vulnerable than others. For example, children with physical, cognitive, and emotional disabilities are at higher risk for maltreatment than other children. Infants and young children are vulnerable to particular forms of maltreatment, such as shaken baby syndrome. Teenagers are at greater risk for sexual abuse. Evidence indicates that abusing parents were victims of abuse and neglect themselves as children. Marital conflict, domestic violence, single parenthood, unemployment, and financial stress may increase the likelihood of maltreatment (Goldman et al. 2003). Poverty is consistently identified as a risk factor for child abuse. It is not clear whether the relationship exists because of the stresses associated with poverty or if reporting is higher because of the constant scrutiny of poor families by social agencies. Poor health care, lack of social and familial support, and fragmented social services have been linked with both poverty and child abuse (Bethea 1999).

While physical, sexual, and emotional abuses are often identified, cases of neglect often go unnoticed. **Neglect** is characterized by a failure to provide for a child's basic needs, and it can be physical (inflicting physical injury), educational (failure to enroll a school-age child in school, allowing chronic truancy), or emotional (spousal abuse in the child's presence, permission for drug or alcohol use by the child, inattention to a child's needs for affection) in nature (Child Welfare Information Gateway 2007).

Elder Abuse and Neglect

Elder Abuse

The elderly are also victims of abuse, usually when in the care of their older children and their families. Elder abuse can also occur within a nursing home or hospital setting. Federal definitions of elder abuse, neglect, and exploitation first appeared in the 1987 Amendments to the Older Americans Act (National Center on Elder Abuse 2002a). Elder abuse can consist of physical, sexual, or psychological abuse, neglect or abandonment, or financial exploitation. Domestic elder abuse refers to any form of maltreatment of an older person by someone who has a special relationship with the elder (a spouse, child, friend, or caregiver); institutional elder abuse refers to forms of abuse that occur in residential facilities for older people.

The number of U.S. adults aged 60 years or older is projected to increase from 35 million in 2000 to more than 72 million by 2030 (He et al. 2005). As the population ages, there will be an increased need for long-term care of the elderly, with spouses and adult children assuming the role of caretaker. An estimated 15 million individuals provide informal care to relatives and friends (Navaie-Waliser et al. 2002). Although caregiving can positively affect the physical and psychological well-being of the care recipients, the added burden of elder care may strain the family's and the caregiver's emotional and financial resources.

There were 465,747 reports of elder abuse in domestic settings in 2004 (National Center on Elder Abuse 2006). Men and women 80 years old or older were at higher risk for abuse or maltreatment. The majority of reported victims were women (65.7%). Among incidents with a known perpetrator, most alleged perpetrators were female and related to the victim (33% adult children). Elder abuse, particularly with family perpetrators, has been attributed to social isolation, personal problems such as mental illness or abuse of alcohol or drugs, and domestic violence (spouses make up a large percentage of elder abusers) (National Center on Elder Abuse 2002a). A major risk factor is dependency: Abusers tend to be more dependent on the elderly person for housing, money, and transportation than are relatives who do not abuse (Lang 1993).

Teen Pregnancies and Newborn Abandonment

The U.S. teen birthrate is the highest in the developed world. The birthrate for teenagers (aged 15–19 years) declined from 1991 through 2008, falling from 62 live births per 1,000 teenagers in 1990 to 41.5 in 2008 (Martin et al. 2010). Despite the overall decline, birthrates for Black (62.8) and Hispanic (77.5) teens remain higher than for any other ethnic/racial group. The lowest rate was reported for Asian or Pacific Islander teens at 16.2 live births per 1,000 women (Martin et al. 2010). The U.S. teen birthrate has been attributed to a range of factors, from inadequate sexuality education to declining morals (Somers and Fahlman 2001). Research suggests that earlier or more frequent sexual activity among U.S. teens is not the cause of the higher birthrates; rather, sexually active American teens are less likely

Photo 7.2

As the U.S. population ages, there will be an increased need for elder long-term care. Senior men and women have the option of living alone, with spouses or adult children as caretakers, or in residential care facilities (pictured here).

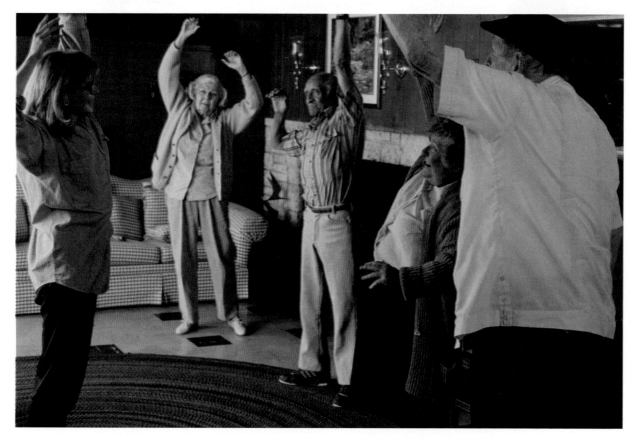

to use contraceptives than are their European peers (Card 1999; Kirby 2007). Refer to U.S. Data Map 7.1 for birthrates for teenagers by state.

Heather Weaver, Gary Smith, and Susan Kippax (2005) noted that the number of births per 1,000 U.S. adolescents between the ages of 15 and 17 years is 8.5 times greater than in the Netherlands, 5.5 times greater than in France, and 3 times greater than in Australia. In contrast, the rate of contraceptive use at first intercourse was highest among Dutch (85%) and Australian (90% for males and 95% for females) teens, followed by French (74% and 77%) and U.S. (a minimum of 65%) youth. School-based sex education programs are mandatory in the Netherlands, France, and Australia. There are no federal laws in the United States that require sexual health education in schools.

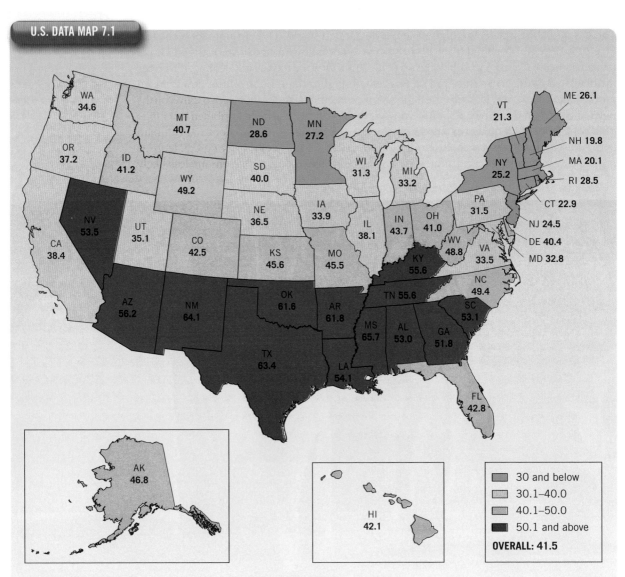

U.S. DATA MAP 7.1

Live Births per 1,000 Teenagers Aged 15–19 Years, by State, 2008

Source: Martin et al. 2010.

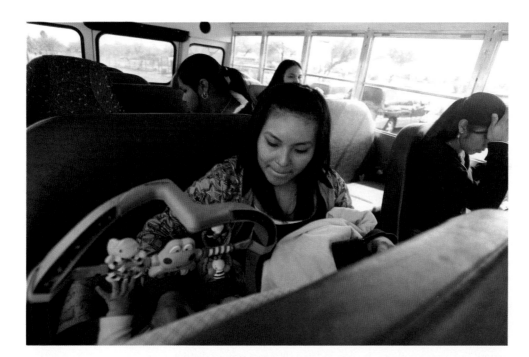

In Focus

Teen Parenting and Education

Pregnant teens or teen parents were routinely expelled from school until Title IX prohibited public schools from discriminating against them. High school graduation rates and college enrollment are lower for teen mothers than for those bearing children later in life, though some longitudinal research reveals that most teen mothers do gain a high school diploma and are employed in stable jobs (Furstenberg, Brooks-Gunn, and Morgan 1987). Frank F. Furstenberg et al. (1987) found that teen mothers with the best life outcomes are those who had higher educational aspirations and better-educated and financially stable families.

In her longitudinal study, Lee SmithBattle (2007) examined the impact of parenting on 19 teen mothers' educational goals and school progress. Contrary to popular belief, she observed the teens' renewed commitment to their education. However, based on the accounts of the teen mothers, she discovered that "schools exacerbated their difficulties by failing to provide educational options or by enforcing policies that disregard their complex realities" (SmithBattle 2007:366). She writes,

> In addition to work demands, family responsibilities, and transportation difficulties, school policies and practices created additional barriers that undermined teens' aspirations and hindered their school progress . . . continuing or remaining in school was complicated by cumbersome enrollment processes, stringent attendance policies, lack of educational options, and bureaucratic mismanagement.
>
> Kate's schooling was interrupted for a full year as a result of enrollment difficulties and limited-schooling options. When morning sickness led to many school absences early in her pregnancy, she was referred to the pregnancy school in her urban district. Because home tutoring was not offered as an option, she was forced to withdraw when enrolling in the pregnancy school proved insurmountable. . . .

(Continued)

(Continued)

Kate's mother added that "we just gave up" when Kate's home school failed to transfer her transcript to the pregnancy school in a timely manner. Jenna was also referred to the pregnancy program but refused to be transferred because of its poor academic reputation. She dropped out near the end of her pregnancy for a full year because homeschooling was not offered. As she said, "When I was 7 or 8 months pregnant, I stopped going to school. When the new semester started, I withdrew, because after the baby, I would have had to wait a certain amount of weeks to go back and then I'd end up failing. So it was no use." . . .

[A] cascade of negative events, including inflexible school policies and disciplinary practices, landed Dawn, a suburban student, in educational limbo. After being homeschooled for several months, she returned to her senior year expecting to graduate with her class. She was eventually notified that she would not graduate because she had not completed assignments for one course, presumably because the teacher of that course had not relayed them to her homeschooling teacher. Deeply disappointed, Dawn resolved to return to school the following fall and take the few credits she needed to graduate. At the beginning of the fall semester, Dawn was driving her son to day care, going on to school, and leaving midmorning for work. Her plan to graduate at the end of the fall semester crumbled when the school principal revoked her parking privileges for a declining grade point average after a car accident led to the lack of transportation and several absences. Without a parking pass, Dawn could not drive her son to day care or go to work after school. She was thoroughly discouraged and lacked the skills and family support to appeal to the school board. Her student status was further complicated when she was kicked out of her home and moved in with her grandmother who resided in a different school district.

"I'm tryin' to get into a school here in the city. But they're tellin' me that I have to go two semesters in order to graduate from this new school, when I only would have had to go one semester to graduate from my school. It's just a mess . . . I actually want to go to school and they won't let me because of something stupid."

At her last interview, she was considering reenrolling in her suburban school so that she could complete the few credits she needed to graduate. Her plans seemed unrealistic because of the lengthy driving time involved (at least 30 to 40 minutes one way) and the complex scheduling that would be required with day care and an employer. (SmithBattle 2007:360–63)

SmithBattle (2007) concludes,

The gap between teen mothers' aspirations and the support to achieve them suggests that educators and other professionals are missing a critical opportunity to promote teen mothers' school-progress and their long-term educational attainment and success. Schools that cultivate teen mothers' educational ambitions may ultimately contribute to positive chain reactions and the reduction of teen mothers' prior adversity. (p. 369)

Source: Reprinted with permission from SmithBattle 2007.

Teen mothers, in comparison with their childless peers, are likely to be poorer and less educated, less likely to be married, and more likely to come from families with lower incomes (Hoffman 1998). Their children often lag behind in standards of early development (Hoffman 1998); are less likely to receive proper nutrition, health care, and cognitive stimulation (Annie E. Casey Foundation 1998); and are at greater risk of social behavioral problems and lower intellectual and academic achievement (Hoffman 2006). Early childbearing also affects teen fathers. Teen fathers are more likely to engage in delinquent behaviors such as alcohol abuse or drug dealing. In addition, they complete fewer years of school and earn less per year (Annie E. Casey Foundation 1998).

Significant public costs are also associated with adolescent childbearing. For 2004, the estimated annual cost to taxpayers of births to young mothers was $9 billion, taking into consideration lost tax revenue, public assistance, health care for children, child welfare, and the criminal justice system (Hoffman 2006). Costs related to births to women 17 years old or younger were higher per birth than for those 18 to 19 years of age.

Although teenage childbirth has always been considered a social problem, another phenomenon has captured the public's attention. Reports of abandoned babies found in trash bins, restrooms, parks, and public buildings have become more frequent since the late 1990s. The first case that caught national attention was "Prom Mom" Melissa Drexler. While attending her senior prom in 1997, Drexler gave birth to a full-term baby boy in a bathroom stall. She wrapped her baby in several plastic bags, left him in a garbage can, and returned to her prom. She pleaded guilty to manslaughter. There is no comprehensive national reporting system for abandoned babies.

The Problems of Time and Money

In a survey conducted by the Radcliffe Public Policy Center (2000), 79% of respondents reported that having a work schedule that enabled them to spend time with their family was a top priority. Nearly everyone reported feeling pressed for time in their lives, wanting to spend more time with their families, have more flexible work options, and even just have more time to sleep (Radcliffe Public Policy Center 2000).

Families with children must determine how best to provide financial support, while making sure their children have parental time. Suzanne Bianchi, John Robinson, and Melissa Milkie (2006) reported that in about 30% of families with children, both parents work full-time. Compared with their counterparts in other countries, a higher percentage of American dual-worker couples work long weeks (80 or more hours combined), leaving less family time during the week. Mothers still spend more time with children, an average of 13 hours per week compared with 7 hours per week for fathers. Mothers do most of the routine care (custodial daily care) of children, whereas fathers spend their time with children doing interactive activities (enrichment activities such as talking or reading to them) (Bianchi et al. 2006).

According to Lillian Rubin (1995), economic realities make it especially difficult for working-class parents to maintain their juggling act. In her book *Families on the Fault Line,* Rubin documented how structural changes in the economy undermine the quality of life among working-class families. This is a functional argument: Because the family is part of our larger social system, what happens at an economic level will inevitably affect the family. The reality of long workdays and workweeks does take its toll on families: The loss of intimacy between couples, the lack of time for couples and their children, tense renegotiations over household work, and juggling child care arrangements are just some of the issues that working families face.

 Work/Home Balance

Rubin's study shed some light on the condition of working-class families, but often overlooked is the plight of lower-income families—too rich to be classified as living in poverty, but still too poor to be working class. In their two-year study, Lisa Dodson, Tiffany Manuel, and Ellen Bravo (2002) studied lower-income families in Milwaukee, Wisconsin; Denver, Colorado; and Boston, Massachusetts. The researchers concluded that lower-income families deal with basic problems on a daily basis: managing the safety, health, and

Photo 7.4

An estimated 1.2 million children live with military families, and approximately 700,000 have at least one parent deployed (Johnson et al. 2007).

 Military Families

education of their children while staying employed. Lower-income parents are not "bad" parents; it's just that their parenting may require more time and resources than they have. Among low-income families, there is a higher prevalence of children with chronic health issues or special learning needs; at least two thirds of the families in the Dodson et al. study reported having a child with special needs. These children require much more time and patience from their parents, sometimes jeopardizing parents' ability to maintain employment and earnings. To support lower-income parents, the authors recommend comprehensive and flexible child care, along with workplace flexibility (taking time off work, adjusting their work schedule) (Dodson et al. 2002).

The Iraq and Afghanistan wars have heightened our awareness of the difficulties associated with families separated by war. An estimated 1.2 million children live with military families, and approximately 700,000 of them have at least one parent deployed (Johnson et al. 2007). Research on the adjustment of children and adolescents of deployed military personnel indicates that the separation experience is stressful. Parental deployment has been linked with several negative youth outcomes, including depression (Jensen, Martin, and Watanabe 1996), behavioral problems (Levai et al. 1994), and poor academic performance (Hiew 1992). Boys suffer more effects of disruption than girls (Johnson et al. 2007). More than 100,000 female soldiers who have served in the Iraq and Afghanistan wars were mothers. As reported by Lizette Alvarez (2009), the majority of deployed women are primary caregivers, and a third are single mothers like Army Specialist Jaymie Holschlag. While she was deployed in Iraq, Holschlag's 10-year-old son and 4-year-old daughter lived with their grandparents. Concerned about the effects of her deployment on herself and her children, Holschlag requested a transfer when she returned home.

Community, Policy, and Social Action

Family and Medical Leave Act of 1993

The Family and Medical Leave Act (FMLA) of 1993 was envisioned as a way to help employees balance the demands of the workplace with the needs of their families. The act provides employees with as many as 12 weeks of unpaid, job-protected leave per year. It also provides for group health benefits during the employee's leave. The FMLA applies to all public agencies and all private employers with 50 or more workers. To be eligible, employees must work at least 1,250 hours per year. In 2008, the FMLA was expanded to include families of wounded military personnel.

As of 2012, 11 states and the District of Columbia have enacted their own family and medical leave laws, extending the coverage provided by the FMLA or extending coverage to those not eligible under FMLA guidelines. In 2004, California became the first state to enact a law that provides paid family care leave. The California Family Rights Act allows employees to take a paid leave to care for a child, spouse, parent, or domestic partner who has a serious health condition or to bond with a new child. Employees who take such leave can receive 55% of their pay up to $780 per week for a maximum of six weeks. The California law applies to all employers, not just those with 50 or more employees (U.S. Department of Labor 2007).

Although there is strong support for the FMLA and its stated goals, the act has also been criticized since its enactment. Almost 50% of workers are not covered by the FMLA because they work for private employers not covered under the law or small businesses employing fewer than 50 people. Though it has been used an estimated 100 million times, nearly two thirds of eligible workers have not taken advantage of the FMLA because they can't afford the lost wages (National Partnership for Women and Families 2009).

Based on their analysis of public policies for working families in more than 170 countries, Jody Heymann, Alison Earle, and Jeffrey Hayes (2007) concluded that U.S. policies lag behind all high-income countries, as well as most middle- and low-income countries in their study. The United States does not offer paid leave for mothers in any segment of the workforce. Only three other nations have no paid leave—Liberia, Papua New Guinea, and Swaziland; 169 countries offer guaranteed leave with income to women. Sixty-six countries offer fathers paid paternity leave or the right to paid parental leave; the United States offers neither.

Community Responses to Domestic Violence and Neglect

Responses to domestic violence can be characterized as having a distinct community approach. In the area of child abuse, the U.S. Office of Juvenile Justice and Delinquency Prevention established community-based children's advocacy centers to provide coordinated support for victims in the investigation, treatment, prosecution, and prevention of child abuse in all 50 states. Programs at each center are uniquely designed by community professionals and volunteers to best meet their community's needs. One such center is Project Harmony, based in Omaha, Nebraska. Project Harmony provides medical exams, assessment, and referrals. Project Harmony serves children who are victims of abuse and their nonabusing family members. By placing project staff and representatives from child protective services and law enforcement in the same facility, Project Harmony attempts to improve communication and coordination between all professionals involved in a child's case. Refer to this chapter's Voices in the Community feature to learn more about a rural support program based in Vermont.

Since its inception in 1995, the Violence Against Women Office (VAW) has handled the U.S. Department of Justice's legal and policy issues regarding violence against women. The office offers a series of program and policy technical papers for individuals, leaders, and communities to support their efforts to end violence against women. These papers highlight some of the best program models and practices and were produced by the Promising Practices Initiative of the STOP Violence Against Women Grants Technical Assistance Project (Little, Malefyt, and Walker 1998). Two featured programs are the following:

- The Minnesota Domestic Abuse Intervention Project (DAIP) was developed in 1980 and serves as a national and international program model. It was the first program of its kind to coordinate the intervention activities of each criminal justice agency in one city. The goals of the program include victim safety, offender accountability, and changes in the climate of tolerance toward violence in the Duluth community. The program also offers a men's nonviolence education program, a national training and technical assistance program, and a victim advocacy program for Native Americans through the Mending the Sacred Hoop project.
- The Women's Center and Shelter (WC&S) of Greater Pittsburgh was founded in 1974. WC&S coordinates its program efforts with the medical community, criminal justice agencies, and other organizations. The programs focus on the ability of women to take control of their own lives. WC&S provides comprehensive victim services, which include parenting education and legal and medical advocacy. WC&S has also created a school-based curriculum called Hands Are Not for Hurting. The curriculum uses age-appropriate lessons that encourage nonviolent conflict resolution and teach youth that they are responsible for the choices they make.

The National Center on Elder Abuse (NCEA) believes that community education and outreach are important in combating the problem of elder abuse and neglect. The NCEA supports community "sentinel" programs, which train and educate professionals and volunteers to identify and refer potential victims of abuse, neglect, or exploitation. In 1999, the NCEA established partnerships with the Humane Society of the United States (HSUS), Meals on Wheels Association of America (MOWAA), and the National Association of Retired and Senior Volunteer Program Directors. These organizations were selected because of their unique access to isolated elders in their homes. The NCEA funded six coalition projects in Arizona, California, New York, North Carolina, and Utah. The program trained more than 1,000 professionals and volunteers to serve as sentinels; as a result, there was an increase in the number of abuse referrals in communities where sentinels were used. Administrators also noticed an increase in the level of satisfaction among volunteers, who as a result of the project were able to assist individuals who they believed might be victims or potential victims (National Center on Elder Abuse 2002b).

Voices in the Community

Wynona Ward

Wynona Ward

Wynona Ward thought she left her violent childhood behind her. But in 1991, when her sisters called to inform her that their brother Richard had raped a child in the family, she was not surprised. The child was also raped by her grandfather—Ward's father—years earlier. She describes Richard as "living up to his father's expectations. He was expected to grow up to be a child abuser" (quoted in Jetter 2000). Ward, her mother, and her siblings were subjected to years of sexual and physical abuse by her father. She and other family members supported the victim during her brother's trial and subsequent incarceration. The experience motivated Ward to enroll in law school, and after graduating from Vermont Law School, Ward established Have Justice—Will Travel, a mobile law office serving battered women in Vermont.

Driving more than 30,000 miles a year, Ward is able to reach victims who otherwise would not have access to legal or social services. With her mobile office (her truck is equipped with a radio, scanner, computer, and printer), Ward brings support and hope to women who have none. The group also provides transportation to and from court hearings and free legal representation. Ward says, "[We] work with these women so they can become strong and independent and self-reliant and be able to support themselves and their children" (as quoted in Brown 2010).

Since 1998, Have Justice—Will Travel has assisted 10,000 victims with legal and social services. From its humble start from Ward's kitchen table, the program has expanded to four locations with the assistance of staff and student volunteers from Ward's alma mater, Dartmouth College, and other local colleges. Ward divides her time on the road working with clients and writing grant proposals to support the program. Growing her program to serve more women and their families continues to be her goal. "Everyday [*sic*] in this country, we have more and more women that are working in social services, more women that are entering the legal field, more people that can have empathy for victims. . . . Different donors have asked me, 'well, how are you going to expand Have Justice?' There's only one Wynona. But I say to them, 'no, you're wrong. There are many Wynonas out there'" (Ward 2002).

Teen Pregnancy and Infant Abandonment

As noted earlier, there are no U.S. federal laws that require sexual health education in schools. Instead, sexual health education has been defined as the responsibility of social and health service programmers. In the 1980s, these programmers defined prevention as an effective way to address the problems of teen pregnancy and parenthood (Card 1999). In the 1990s, several new prevention approaches emerged, particularly after the passage of the Welfare Reform Act of 1996. Under Section 905 of the act, the U.S. Department of Health and Human Services (HHS) was mandated to ensure that at least 25% of all U.S. communities had teen pregnancy prevention programs in place. Most states identified target goals related to teen birthrates. For example, New Hampshire's goal was to reduce the nonmarital teen rate to 21.0 births per 1,000 teens by 2005; in North Dakota, the goal is to reduce its teen birthrate by 2% per year.

 Teen Pregnancies

Along with funding national educational programs such as the Girl Neighborhood Power: Building Bright Futures for Success program, HHS also funded comprehensive statewide and community-wide initiatives through the Abstinence Only Education Program and the Adolescent Family Life Program (administered through the Office of Population Affairs). An example of this approach is School-Linked Reproductive Health Services (The Self Center), a school-neighborhood clinic partnership in Baltimore, Maryland. The program offers education, counseling, and reproductive services to teens. Students at participating schools reported reduced levels of sexual activity, and among those already sexually active, there was more effective contraceptive use. Also reported was a delay in the onset of sexual activity among abstinent youth (Card 1999).

Curriculum-based sexual health education programs are categorized into two groups (Kirby 2007). The most prominent form, abstinence-only programs, promotes abstinence from sex and not condom or other contraceptive use. Comprehensive programs promote abstinence along with condom and other contraceptive use. Programming in both groups may vary. For example, some abstinence programs emphasize abstinence until marriage, while others do not. Some comprehensive programs only feature an educational component, while others include contraceptive services.

In his review of abstinence-only program evaluations, Douglas Kirby (2007) noted that only a small number of abstinence programs have been evaluated. He concluded, based on the limited research, that there was little evidence to suggest that any particular abstinence program delays the initiation of sex. Kirby found that comprehensive programs were more likely to have a positive impact on teen sexual behavior—at least 40% of the programs resulted in increased condom and contraceptive use. Researchers also documented increased abstinence, reduced number of sexual partners, and delayed initiation of sex among students participating in comprehensive programs.

In response to newborn and infant abandonment, all states have passed laws since 1999 that offer safe and confidential means to relinquish unwanted newborns without the threat of prosecution for child abandonment. State laws vary according to child's age (72 hours to 1 year old) and the personnel or places authorized to accept the infant (hospital personnel, emergency rooms, church, and police).

It is unclear how effective these safe-surrender or safe-haven laws have been in reducing infant abandonment or death. New Jersey, home of the first infant abandonment case that gained national attention, passed a safe-haven law in August 2000, modeled after Texas 1999 legislation. Between August 2000 and November 2003, New Jersey officials assisted 17 babies. These children were adopted, placed in foster care, or returned to their mothers (New Jersey Safe Haven Protection Act 2007). In 2006, however, six dead newborns were found abandoned in New York, despite the state's safe-haven laws. Critics argue that the state's safe-haven laws were poorly advertised, with most residents not knowing about the laws' provisions. In Illinois, a discussion of the safe-haven law is included in the high school health curriculum, possibly ensuring more awareness among high-risk youth (Buckley 2007).

In 2007, a mother abandoned her 3-month-old baby boy at a neonatal clinic in Rome, Italy. She was the first to use Casilino Polyclinic's modern foundling wheel. The original foundling wheel, used in the Middle Ages, was a revolving wooden barrel built into the church's exterior wall; the mother could deposit her baby and turn the wheel, and the baby would be safely protected inside the church. The Rome clinic uses a small modern structure equipped with a heated cradle and a respirator. Also available at other Italian hospitals and churches, these structures are equipped with an alarm to alert medical or church staff when a child is deposited. Foundling wheels or designated drop-off locations for unwanted newborns are used in other countries such as Germany, Switzerland, and the Czech Republic (Povoledo 2007).

What Does It Mean to Me?

Investigate your state's safe-haven law. What are the features of the law? What protections does it offer the mother? How many children have been protected under the law? How well do you think the law has been promoted?

Supporting Different Family Forms

According to sociologist David Popenoe (1993), there has been a serious decline in the structure and function of the family since the 1960s. Families are not meeting society's needs as they once did and have lost most of their "functions, social power and authority over their members" (Popenoe 1993:527–28). He attributes the weakening of family function to high divorce rates, declining family size, and the growing absence of fathers and mothers in their children's lives. Data reviewed at the beginning of this chapter—the declining percentage of nuclear families, along with the increase in single-parent families and nonfamily households—lend support to his observation.

But critics of Popenoe's position argue that the family in decline hypothesis relies too heavily on the definition of family in its nuclear form (Bengston 2001). Sociologist Judith Stacey (1996) agrees that the "family" as defined by a nuclear form of mom, dad, and children is in decline. This family system has been replaced by what Stacey calls a postmodern family condition, one characterized by diverse family patterns and forms, where no single family form is dominant. There have been significant changes in the traditional family's structure and functions (Bengston 2001); modern families are best characterized by their diversity (Hanson and Lynch 1992).

Big Love

The proportion of nuclear families is decreasing and being replaced with family structures that include single-parent, blended, adoptive, foster, grandparent, and same-sex partner households (Copeland and White 1991). The increasing diversity of American families requires that we broaden our research and policy agendas beyond traditional family forms (Demo 1992). Perhaps one solution to the "problem" of families is to appreciate and embrace other family forms. Let's examine two family forms: cohabitation and grandparents as primary caregivers to grandchildren.

Cohabitation

Larry Bumpass (1998) argues that the increase in cohabitation reflects and reinforces the declining significance of marriage as a life course marker in our society. He reports that almost half of the young adults in the United States have lived in a cohabiting union at some point in their lives, a trend reflected in most Western societies. **Cohabiting** is defined as sexual partners not married to each other but residing in the same household.

The Sanctity of Marriage

There were nearly 7.5 million cohabiting (opposite sex) couples in 2010 (Kreider 2010). A quarter of unmarried women aged 25 to 39 are currently living with a partner, and an additional quarter have lived with a partner sometime in the past. More than 60% of cohabiting couple households contain children (National Marriage Project 2011). According to the National Marriage Project (2009), cohabitation is more likely to occur among those of lower educational and income levels and among those who are less religious than their peers and who experienced parental divorce or high levels of marital discord during childhood. Barbara Dafoe Whitehead and David Popenoe (2005) report that more than half of all marriages are preceded with a period of living together, compared with virtually none more than 50 years ago.

Data on the proportion of households cohabiting for selected countries are presented in Table 7.4. In 11 European countries, cohabiting partners have the possibility of entering a civil union (via registration) other than marriage. In other countries, cohabiting couples who have not registered their union, but have lived together for a specific period of time, are considered to have the same legal rights and obligations as married couples or partners who have formalized their relationships. For example, in Australia and New Zealand, couples living together for a specific period of time are legally considered to be in a partnership with status equal to marriage (Organisation for Economic Co-operation and Development 2009).

Traditional Marriage

Researchers increasingly acknowledge that not all cohabitations will eventually lead to marriage and may instead serve as alternative forms of marriage (Manning and Smock 2002). The pattern is particularly true for Black, Hispanic, and mainland Puerto Rican women compared with White women (Bumpass and Lu 2000). Cohabitation rates have increased among

Table 7.4

Percentage of Cohabiting Households, for Various Years Since 2000

Country	Percentage of Population of Both Sexes
Australia	8.9
Austria	6.5
Belgium	6.4
Bulgaria	4.2
Canada	8.9
Czech Republic	2.9
Denmark	11.5
Estonia	11.8
Finland	11.8
France	14.4
Germany	5.3
Greece	1.7
Hungary	6.3
Ireland	5.9
Italy	2.0
Japan	2.0
Latvia	5.5
Lithuania	4.1
Luxembourg	14.0
Malta	2.1
Netherlands	9.3
New Zealand	9.3
Norway	10.7
Poland	1.3
Portugal	4.1
Romania	4.3
Slovenia	5.4
Spain	3.3
Switzerland	5.9
Turkey	0.2
United Kingdom	8.7
United States	5.5

Source: Organisation for Economic Co-operation and Development 2010.

Black and White adults, with higher increases observed among Whites. Larry Bumpass and Hsien-Hen Lu (2000) report that for women aged 19 to 44 years, 59% of high school dropouts have cohabited compared with 37% of high school graduates.

Dafoe Whitehead and Popenoe (2005) cite a study that concluded that premarital cohabitation, when limited to a woman's future husband, was not associated with an elevated risk of divorce. Conversely, they observe, "No evidence has yet been found that those who cohabit before marriage have stronger marriages than those who do not." For data collected in 2002, the probability of a woman's marriage lasting 10 years if she had cohabitated before marriage was lower than the probability of a woman's marriage lasting the same amount of time if she did not cohabit before marriage, 61% versus 66% (Goodwin, Mosher, and Chandra 2010). However, the difference between the two groups is not significant. If a couple were engaged when they began cohabiting, the probability that the woman's marriage would survive 10 years was similar (65%) to the probability for couples who did not cohabit at all (66%) (Goodwin et al. 2010).

The increase of cohabitation has coincided with the increase in unmarried childbearing—currently about 40% of all cohabiting households contain children (Dafoe Whitehead and Popenoe 2005). Though data indicate that about two fifths of all children will live with their mother and a cohabiting partner and about a third of the time children spend with unmarried mothers is spent in a cohabiting relationship, family scholars acknowledge that more needs to be known about the impact of cohabitation on the family experiences and life outcomes of these children (Bumpass and Lu 2000).

What Does It Mean to Me?

Does cohabitation threaten the institution of marriage? How does it redefine our understanding of the "family"?

 STATE STATS

Grandparents as Parents

Fifty-nine-year-old Pat and Ken Owens of Lewistown, Maryland, are the primary caretakers of their grandchildren, Michael and Brandi (Armas 2002). Michael and Brandi are among 5.4 million children living in households where the grandparent is the primary householder (U.S. Census Bureau 2012b), an increase from 2.2 million grandchildren in 1970 (Casper and Bryson 1998). Approximately 918,000 grandchildren live in a grandparent household where a parent is not present. According to the 2010 U.S. Census, White children were more likely than children of other ethnic/racial groups to live in a grandparent's household with or without a parent present (U.S. Census Bureau 2012b).

Grandparents may assume caretaking responsibilities when parents are unable to live with or care for their children because of death, illness, divorce, incarceration, substance abuse, or child abuse or neglect. Pat and Ken Owens have not heard from Michael and Brandi's mother in the past two years and only recently began receiving financial support from Michael's father. The alternative for their grandchildren would have been foster care, something that Pat Owens did not want to happen: "I don't want to make it sound like it's easy because there are some tough, tense times. But I'm very proud of the fact that all the grandchildren still play together and go to school together" (Armas 2002:A6).

Research identifies how grandparents who care for their grandchildren are at high risk for emotional and physical distress. This distress is related to a deficit of social resources, such as marital status, social support, economic resources, and the demands of the caregiving role itself. Grandparent caregivers are more likely to experience depression and suffer from fair to poor physical health and activity limitations than are grandparents in more traditional roles (Chase Goodman and Silverstein 2006). Counseling and the use of school programs (tutoring and special education) provide grandparents with some stress and depression relief (Trail Ross and Aday 2006). Despite the negative consequences, grandparents also report the satisfaction and rewards related to caring for their grandchildren.

The sudden responsibility for children leaves many grandparents on fixed incomes with unexpected financial burdens. In one study, children living in a grandparent's household without a parent present were twice as likely to be living below the poverty level as were children living with both grandparents and a parent. In addition, children who lived with just their grandparents were also at risk of not being covered by health insurance (Fields 2003). If eligible, grandparents can get assistance through HHS Temporary Assistance for Needy Families (TANF). Some states, such as Illinois, Pennsylvania, and Wisconsin, offer guardianship or kinship care subsidy programs for grandparents.

Emotional and social support is available for grandparent-headed households. Local grandparent support groups are listed by organizations such as AARP, Generations United, and GrandsPlace. These organizations also provide fact sheets, community links, and suggestions for clothing and school supplies, recipes, and travel and activity guides for grandparents and their grandchildren. AARP (2002) recognized several model support programs such as the Kinship Support Network in San Francisco, California; Project Healthy Grandparents in Atlanta, Georgia; and Grandma's Kids Kinship Support Program in Philadelphia, Pennsylvania.

Photo 7.5

The U.S. Census reports that 5.4 million children reside in households where the grandparent is the primary householder. About 900,000 children live with their grandparents alone, with neither parent present.

Main Points

- The family is defined as a construct of meaning and relationships both emotional and economic. The family is a social unit based on kinship relations—relations based on blood and those created by choice, marriage, partnership, or adoption.

- A household is defined as an economic and residential unit.
- From a functionalist perspective, social problems emerge as the family struggles to adapt to a modern society. Functionalists have noted

how many of the original family functions have been taken over by organized religion, education, work, and the government in modern society, but still, the family is expected to provide its remaining functions of raising children and providing affection and companionship for its members.

■ For the conflict theorist, the family is a system of inequality where conflict is normal. Conflict can derive from economic or power inequalities between spouses or family members. From a feminist perspective, inequality emerges from the patriarchal family system, where men control decision making in the family.

■ According to an interactionist, through social interaction, we create and maintain our definition of a family. As we do this, it affects our larger social definition of what everyone's family should be like and the kind of family that we create for ourselves.

■ In this chapter, we reviewed several problems based on the family:

– *Divorce.* The U.S. divorce rate has remained stable between 3 and 4 divorces per 1,000 individuals in the total U.S. population. Census data on divorce indicate that certain groups are more susceptible to divorce than others. Research indicates both positive and negative consequences of divorce.

– *Domestic violence.* Research has consistently linked the following social factors to family violence: low socioeconomic status, social and structural stress, and social isolation. Feminist researchers argue that domestic violence is rooted in gender and represents men's attempts to maintain dominance and control over women.

– *Child abuse and neglect.* Neglect is characterized by a failure to provide for a child's basic needs. It can be physical, educational, or emotional in nature. Responses to domestic violence can be characterized as having a distinct community approach. In the area of child abuse, the U.S. Office of Juvenile Justice and Delinquency Prevention established community-based children's advocacy centers to provide coordinated support for victims in the investigation, treatment, prosecution, and prevention of child abuse.

– *Elder abuse and neglect.* Elder abuse can occur for elders in the care of their older children and their families or within a nursing home or hospital setting. Domestic elder abuse refers to any form of maltreatment of an older person by someone who has a special relationship with the elder (a spouse, child, friend, or caregiver); institutional elder abuse refers to forms of abuse that occur in residential facilities for older people. The National Center on Elder Abuse (NCEA) believes that community education and outreach are important in combating the problem of elder abuse and neglect. The NCEA supports community "sentinel" programs, which train and educate professionals.

– *Teen pregnancy.* The United States has the highest teen birthrate in the developed world. Teen pregnancy has been attributed to the lack of sex education in school, low morals, and low contraception use among teens.

– *The problems of time and money.* Economic realities make it especially difficult for working-class parents to maintain their juggling act. The Family and Medical Leave Act (FMLA) of 1993 was envisioned as a way to help employees balance the demands of the workplace with the needs of their families. Although there is strong support for the FMLA, the act has also been criticized since its enactment.

■ The proportion of nuclear families is decreasing, and these families are being replaced with family structures that include single-parent, blended, adoptive, foster, grandparent, and same-sex partner households. The increasing diversity of American families requires that we broaden our research and policy agendas beyond traditional family forms. Perhaps one solution to the "problem" of families is to appreciate and embrace other family forms.

On Your Own

Log on to the open-access Student Study Site at www.sagepub.com/leonguerrero4e for these additional learning tools:

- Interactive quizzes
- Video clips
- NPR audio links
- Handbook articles

- E-flashcards
- Journal articles
- End-of-chapter web exercises
- Additional web resources and current events

Internet and Community Exercises

1. Interview a student who is also a parent. The student can be from your social problems class or any of your other classes. What challenges do student-parents face? How are their challenges different from those of students who are not parents? Does your school support programs or services for parents? Check with your professor about campus policies regarding research involving human subjects.

2. Contact two domestic violence shelters in your community. What is the mission of each organization? Do different shelters serve different groups? If so, how are services tailored to various groups? Does each program promote violence prevention? Domestic shelters often support student internships for a quarter or semester. If you're interested in learning more about a shelter, ask about its internship program.

3. Identify your school's family-friendly policies. Does your school provide child care on-site? Has your school provided leaves under the Family and Medical Leave Act? You may have to contact the human resources department in your school for more information.

4. Investigate your state's safe-haven law for abandoned babies. Have there been any recent cases of abandonment?

Study Questions

1. Compare and contrast the myths and realities of the American family.

2. Even though the nuclear family is not the statistical majority in our society, its image as the "perfect" family persists. Why do you think this is the case? How could the "perfect" family be redefined?

3. How does capitalism influence family structure and relationships? Do you agree with this perspective? Why or why not?

4. How does society's definition of the "family" lead to social problems, prejudice, and discrimination?

5. Identify the effects of divorce on children and adults.

6. What is the relationship between teen parenthood and educational attainment? What can be done to support academic success of teen parents?

7. Explain the difference between abstinence-only and comprehensive sexual health education programs.

8. Compare the United States with other countries on the following family demographics (as reported in this chapter): marriage, divorce, teen pregnancy, and cohabitation.

CHAPTER 8

Education

E ducation is assumed to be the great equalizer in our society. There are inspirational stories of women and men who, after a tough childhood or adulthood, complete their education, become successful members of society, and are held as role models. Education is presented as an essential part of their success, serving as a cure for personal or situational shortcomings. If you are poor, education can make you rich. If your childhood was less than perfect, a college degree can make up for it. On the occasion of launching the Head Start program in 1965, President Lyndon Johnson is quoted as saying, "If it weren't for education, I'd still be looking at the southern end of a northbound mule" (Zigler and Muenchow 1992).

Yet along with these images of success, we are bombarded with images of failure. Media coverage and political rhetoric highlight problems with our educational system, particularly with our public schools. In recent state and national political campaigns, the quality of teaching and the preparation of teachers were scrutinized, and school districts with low scores on standardized exams were criticized. U.S. students are said to be falling behind the accelerated pace of higher education internationally. Though the United States still ranks among the top nations in the educational attainment of older adults 35 to 64 years of age (percentage holding an associate's degree or higher), it ranks 15th in the number of certificates and degrees awarded per 100 students enrolled (Callan 2008). In 2008, more than 50% of Canadian, Japanese, and Korean 25- to 34-year-olds earned a college degree, compared with 39% of Americans 25 to 34 years old (refer to Figure 8.1; Callan 2008). The U.S. ranking has declined since 2003. In 2006, a panel of education, labor, and public policy experts, including two former education secretaries, warned that if the United States does not keep pace with the educational gains made in other countries, our standard of living will be seriously compromised. During his first year in office, President Barack Obama set a goal for the United States to have the highest proportion of college students in the world.

Race and College Graduation

Figure 8.1

Percentage of Adults
With an Associate
Degree or Higher, by
Age, Top 10 Countries,
2003, 2005, and 2008

*Source: Callan 2006,
2008.*

a. Older Adults (Ages 35 to 64), 2003

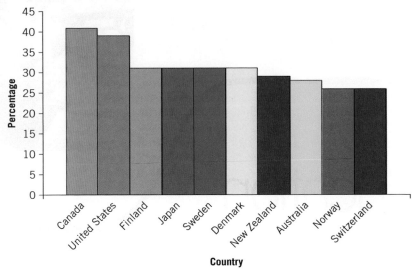

b. Older Adults (Ages 35 to 64), 2005

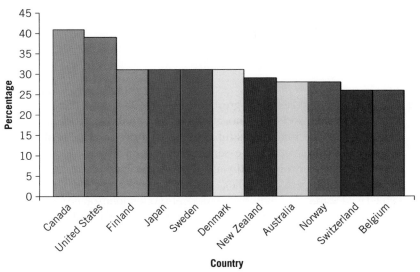

c. Older Adults (Ages 35 to 64), 2008

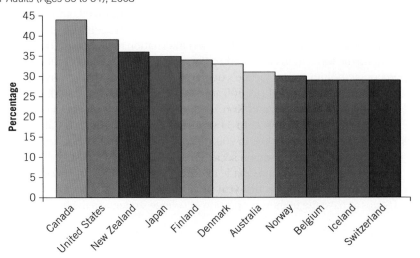

d. Younger Adults (Ages 25 to 34), 2003

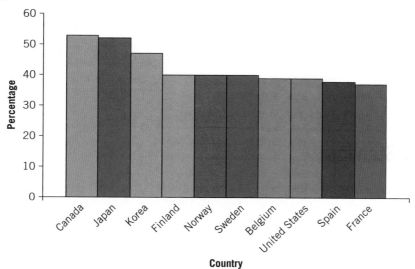

e. Younger Adults (Ages 25 to 34), 2005

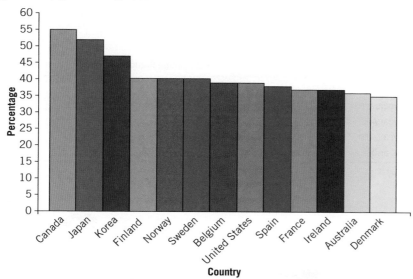

f. Younger Adults (Ages 25 to 34), 2008

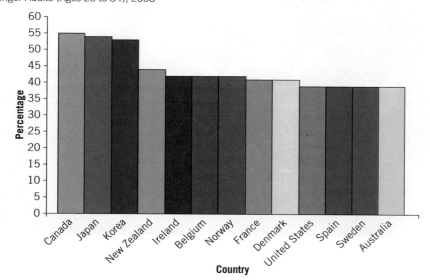

So which is it: Is education a key to individual success or an institutional failure? In this chapter, we'll first examine this question by reviewing our educational system from different sociological perspectives. Then we'll explore current social problems in education, along with policy and program responses.

The New Educational Standard

We tend to define a high school degree as the educational standard of the past, now replaced with a bachelor's degree. Actually, data from the U.S. Census Bureau confirm that the United States has an increasingly more educated population (see Table 8.1 and U.S. Data Map 8.1).

Table 8.1

Educational Attainment of the Population, 25 Years and Older, 2009

Characteristics	High School Graduate or More	Bachelor's Degree or More
Population age 25 years and over	85.3	27.9
25–34 years old	87.0	30.9
35–44 years old	87.2	30.9
45–64 years old	87.7	28.6
65 years and over	76.5	20.2

Source: Ryan and Siebens 2012.

Photo 8.1

According to the U.S. Census Bureau (Ryan and Siebens 2012), in 2009, 85.3% of adults (25 years and older) completed at least a high school degree. More than 27% of all adults had attained at least a bachelor's degree.

U.S. DATA MAP 8.1

WA 31%
MT 27.4%
ND 25.8%
MN 31.5%
ME 26.9%
VT 33.1%
NH 32%
OR 29.2%
ID 23.9%
WY 23.8%
SD 25.1%
WI 25.7%
MI 24.6%
NY 32.4%
MA 38.2%
RI 30.5%
PA 26.4%
CT 35.6%
NV 21.8%
UT 28.5%
NE 27.4%
IA 25.1%
IL 30.6%
IN 22.5%
OH 24.1%
NJ 34.5%
CA 29.9%
CO 35.9%
KS 29.5%
MO 25.2%
KY 21%
WV 17.3%
VA 34%
DE 28.7%
MD 35.7%
AZ 25.8%
NM 25.3%
OK 22.7%
AR 18.9%
TN 23%
NC 26.5%
SC 24.3%
TX 25.5%
MS 19.6%
AL 22%
GA 27.5%
LA 21.4%
FL 25.3%

AK 26.5%

HI 29.6%

Legend:
- 24.9% or fewer
- 25.0–29.9%
- 30.0–35.9%
- 36.0% or greater
- **Overall 27.9%**

Percentage of Adult Population 25 Years and Older With Bachelor's Degree or More by State, 2009

Source: Ryan and Siebens 2012.

For 2009, the U.S. Census Bureau (Ryan and Siebens 2012) reported that 85.3% of adults (25 years and older) completed at least a high school degree, and more than 27% of all adults had attained at least a bachelor's degree. Younger Americans are more educated than are older Americans. Based on the data presented in Table 8.1, 76.5% of all Americans age 65 years or older attained a high school degree or more compared with 87% of those 25 to 34 years old. The percentage attaining a bachelor's degree has also increased, from 20.2% of Americans age 65 years or older to 30.9% of Americans 25 to 34 and 35 to 44 years of age (the highest among all age groups reported) (Ryan and Siebens 2012). As indicated in U.S. Data Map 8.1, populations in the Northeast had the highest proportions with a bachelor's degree or higher. The state with the highest proportion was Massachusetts (38.2%). West Virginia had the lowest proportion (17.3%). Educational attainment level of adults will continue to rise as younger, more-educated age groups replace older, less-educated ones.

Value of Higher Education

What Does It Mean to Me?

Compare the educational attainment of three generations of your family: yourself, your parents, and your grandparents. Does your family reflect the same educational attainment pattern as the census data indicate? Are younger generations more educated than older generations in your family? Why or why not?

 STATE STATS

Sociological Perspectives on Education

Functionalist Perspective

The institution of education has a set of manifest and latent functions. **Manifest functions** are intended goals or consequences of the activities within an institution. Education's primary manifest function should come as no surprise: It is to educate! The other manifest functions include socialization, personal development, and employment. Our educational system ensures that each of us will be appropriately socialized and adequately educated to become a contributing member of society (and the labor force). As Nicola Ansell (2008) writes, "Educational systems view children as 'human becomings' that they are explicitly preparing for work" (p. 808). We learn skills and knowledge, as well as about society's norms, values, and beliefs, which are necessary for our survival and, ultimately, the society's survival.

Education's **latent functions** may be less obvious. One unintended function that education serves is as a public babysitter. No other institution can claim such a monopoly over the total number of hours, months, and years of a child's life. From kindergarten through high school, parents can rely on teachers, administrators, and counselors for their child's education and for supervision, socialization, and discipline. In addition, education controls the entry of young women and men into the labor force and the timing of that entry. Consider the surge in employment rates after high school and college graduation. There is always a rush to get a job each summer; employers rely on the temporary labor of high school and college students during busy summer months. Finally, education establishes and protects social networks by ensuring that individuals with similar backgrounds, education, and interests are able to form friendships, partnerships, or romantic bonds.

Functionalists argue that education has been assigned so many additional tasks that it struggles in its primary task to educate the young. In addition to its own main functions, our educational system has taken over functions of other institutions. For example, the educational system provides services to students with family problems, emotional needs, or physical challenges. Schools also provide services for parents in the form of adult education or parenting classes.

Conflict Perspective

Conflict theorists do not see education as an equalizer; rather, they consider education a "divider"—dividing the haves from the have-nots in our society. From this perspective, conflict theorists focus on the social and economic inequalities inherent in our educational system and on how the system perpetuates these inequalities.

Conflict theorists highlight the socialization function of education as part of the indoctrination of Western bureaucratic ideology. The popular posters and books on "what I learned in kindergarten" could serve as the official list of adult life rules: Share everything, play fair, and put things back where you found them. Never mind kindergarten—the indoctrination can begin as early as nursery school. Rosabeth Moss Kanter (1972) describes a child's experience in nursery school as an "organizational experience" creating an organizational child. Carefully instructed and supervised by their teachers, students are guided through their day in ordered agendas; they are rewarded for conformity, and any signs of individuality are discouraged. The organizational child is sufficiently prepared for the demands and constraints of a bureaucratic adult world.

Although we consider education as the primary method of achieving equality and mobility in our society, conflict theorists argue that it actually sustains the structure of inequality. As Martin Marger (2008) explains, the relationship between education and socioeconomic status operates in a cycle perpetuated from one generation to the next. It begins with high-income and high-status parents who can ensure greater quality and amount of education for their children. Pierre Bourdieu (1977) argues that children from upper- and middle-class families are advantaged in our educational system due to their possession of cultural capital, linguistic and cultural competence, and familiarity with culture that is passed on by their parents and their social position. Children whose parents introduce them to a culture consistent with the class-based assumptions of education are more likely to succeed than those whose parents do not (Lareau 2003). There is another form of capital to consider. **Social capital** refers to investments in social relationships and networks (Lin 2011) and is also distributed unequally by social class. Young children who are more engaged in extracurricular activities and have increased opportunities to build personal relationships with adults outside of their immediate family demonstrate greater academic progress than children who lack access to these activities or opportunities (Freeman and Condron 2011).

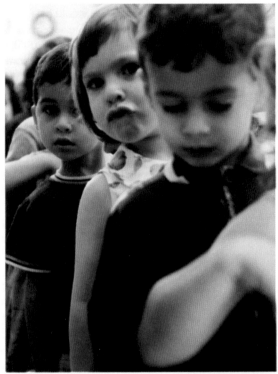

As family income increases, so does the likelihood of college attendance and the quality of education. Among the top 146 highly selective U.S. colleges, nearly 75% of students come from families in the top quarter of the socioeconomic distribution (Carnevale and Rose 2003). With this higher-quality education, the students continue to enjoy high income and status as adults, and in turn, they will pass their socioeconomic advantage on to their own children. Access to selective colleges is also skewed by race and ethnicity.

Jonathan Kozol, in his books *Savage Inequalities: Children in America's Schools* (1991) and *The Shame of the Nation: The Restoration of Apartheid School in America* (2005), presents a discouraging portrait of student learning in inner-city schools that are understaffed, undersupplied, and in disrepair. This educational inequality is created by public school systems that rely on property taxes to finance school staffing and operations. As a result, a caste system has emerged in our educational system. Despite the U.S. Supreme Court's 1954 *Brown v. Board of Education* ruling, de facto school segregation still exists. Income and residential segregation have led to greater differentiation in school quality and opportunities between rich and poor neighborhoods (Reardon 2011).

Photo 8.2

The title of a popular book claimed, "All I really need to know I learned in kindergarten." What did you learn in kindergarten that prepared you to be part of society?

Modern-Day Segregation

The gap between the haves and the have-nots is so wide it seems impossible to attain educational equity. As Kozol (1991) observes,

> Children in one set of schools are educated to be governors; children in another set of schools are trained to be governed. The former are given the imaginative range to mobilize ideas for economic growth; the latter are provided with the discipline to do the narrow tasks the first group will prescribe. (p. 176)

He introduces us to 8-year-old Alliyah, a third grader he met in 1997. At that time, the New York City Board of Education spent $8,000 for her education in a public school in the Bronx. She would have received a public education worth $12,000 had she been educated in a typical White suburb of New York, and $18,000 if she resided in a wealthy White suburb. According to Kozol (2005), what society chooses to spend on lower-class neighborhoods and schools "surely tells us something about what we think these kids are worth to us in human terms and in the contributions they may someday make to our society" (p. 44).

Feminist Perspective

Inequalities are based not just on social class but also on gender. Research reveals the persistent replication of gender relations in schools, evidenced by the privileging of males, their voices, and their activities in the classroom, on the playground, and in hallways (Smith 2000).

One of my favorite illustrations of the privilege given to a male voice comes from my own discipline. In sociology, there is a concept called the "definition of the situation," which refers to the phrase "If men define situations as real, they are real in their consequences" (Thomas and Thomas 1928:572). The concept is an important one to the symbolic interactionist perspective and is often attributed solely to sociologist W. I. Thomas. However, the correct acknowledgment is to Thomas and his wife, Dorothy Swaine Thomas. R. S. Smith (1995) investigated the citation in more than 244 introductory sociology textbooks and found that most attributed the concept solely to W. I. Thomas. One reason for the omission of Swaine Thomas is that she may not have contributed to the phrase (although there is no documented evidence to support this), but Smith (1995) suggests that the omission is because of a professional and structural ideology that historically represented sociology as a "male" domain. Smith notes that the citations began to include Swaine Thomas after the mid-1970s, a time when sociology and introductory texts began to respond to and to reflect the changes brought about by a growing women's movement and increasing numbers of female sociologists.

Gender bias and gender stereotypes work to exclude and alienate girls early in their educational experience (American Association of University Women 1992; Sadker and Sadker 1994). Males have favored status in education, particularly in their interactions with their teachers. In the classroom, girls are invisible, often treated as second-class educational citizens. This is how Myra and David Sadker (1994) explained the subtle yet consequential gender bias in the classrooms they visited. After observing teachers and their interactions with girls and boys in more than 100 elementary classrooms, the Sadkers found that teachers were more responsive to boys and were more likely to teach them actively. Overall, girls received less attention, whereas boys got a double dose, both negative and positive. Boys received more praise, corrections, and feedback, whereas girls received a cursory "OK" response from their teachers. Sadker and Sadker concluded that over time, the unequal distribution of teacher time and attention may take its toll on girls' self-esteem, achievement rates, test scores, and ultimately careers.

Photo 8.3

Are female faculty perceived as different from male faculty? Are there any gender stereotypes associated with female professors?

For example, Sian Beilock and her colleagues examined the effects of teacher math anxiety on student math anxiety in an elementary school setting (quoted in Schmid 2010). They found that students tend to model themselves after adults of the same sex. A female teacher who is anxious about math may pass on the same concerns to her female students, reinforcing the belief that boys are better at math than girls. Though student math anxiety was not related to teacher math anxiety at the beginning of the school year, by the end of the year, the more anxious teachers were about their math skills, the more likely their female students agreed that boys are good at math and girls are good at reading. Girls who agreed with this statement scored lower on math tests than boys and girls who had not developed this belief (Schmid 2010).

Structural factors along with interpersonal dynamics also contribute to the creation and maintenance of gender inequality on college and university campuses (Stombler and Yancey Martin 1994). Men and women experience college differently and have markedly different outcomes (Jacobs 1996). College women are subjected to male domination through their peer relations (Stombler and Yancey Martin 1994) in the classroom, in romantic involvements (Holland and Eisenhart 1990), and in organized activities. Even activities such as fraternity "little sister" programs, which Mindy Stombler and Patricia Yancey Martin (1994) studied, provide the structural and interpersonal dynamics necessary to create an atmosphere conducive to women's subordination.

Interactionist Perspective

In Sadker and Sadker's 1994 study, we identified the differential effects of teacher communication on female and male students. The interaction between teachers and students daily reinforces the structure and inequalities of the classroom and the educational system. From this microperspective, sociologists focus on how classroom dynamics and practices educate the perfect student and at the same time create the not-so-perfect ones. In what ways does classroom interaction educate and create?

Assessment and testing are standard practices in education. Students are routinely graded and evaluated based on their work and ability. Interactionists would argue that along with assessment come unintended consequences. Based on test results, students may be placed in different ability or occupational tracks. In the practice called tracking, advanced learners are separated from regular learners; students are identified as college bound versus work bound.

Advocates of tracking argue that the practice increases educational effectiveness by allowing teachers to target students at their ability level (Hallinan 1994). Yet placing students in tracks has been controversial because of the presumed negative effects on some students. Opponents argue that labels such as *upper* versus *lower* track or *"special"* or *slow learners* are used systematically to deny a group of students access to education (Ansalone 2004). In addition to creating unequal learning opportunities (Hallinan 1994), tracking may encourage teachers, parents, and others to view students differently according to their track, and as a result, their true potential may be hindered (Adams and Evans 1996). Although tracking is intended to aid students, it may lead to a self-fulfilling prophecy: Students will fail because they are expected to do so.

Sociological Perspectives on Education

Despite the documented negative consequences of tracking, the practice continues in approximately 60% of all elementary schools and 80% of all secondary schools (Ansalone 2001). Although interactionists do not assess the appropriateness of the label, they would address how the label affects students' identity and educational outcomes. Issues of inequality must also be addressed if the data suggest that students of particular gender or ethnic/racial categories are targeted for tracking. A summary of all sociological perspectives on education is presented in Table 8.2.

Table 8.2

Summary of Sociological Perspectives: Education

	Functional	Conflict/Feminist	Interactionist
Explanation of education	Using a macro perspective, functionalists examine the functions of the educational system. The educational system is strained from performing multiple functions.	Conflict and feminist theorists address how the educational system perpetuates economic, ethnic, and gender inequalities. Students, depending on their social backgrounds, are differentially treated by the educational system.	Using a micro perspective, an interactionist focuses on how the educational experience is created through interaction and shared meanings in the classroom.
Questions asked about education and its social problems	What manifest or latent functions does education serve? How is education affected by other social institutions?	How does education perpetuate social inequalities? Is one group more disadvantaged than another?	How do classroom dynamics determine the educational success of a student? What is the relationship between teacher–student interaction and student success? How does student tracking or labeling impact student achievement?

What Does It Mean to Me?

Refer to state rankings on public high school graduates and dropout rates. Which state ranks the highest in terms of the number of high school graduates? Which state ranks the highest in terms of high school dropouts? Where does your state fit? Are there any states that rank high in terms of graduates and dropouts?

Problems and Challenges in American Education

The idea that there is a public education crisis is not a new one. A 1918 government report referred to the "erosion of family life, disappearing fathers, working mothers, the decline of religious institutions, changes in the workplace, and the millions of newly arrived immigrants" as potential sources of the public education crisis (Meier 1995:9). At the time, the government's response was the creation of the modern school system with two tracks, one for terminal high school degrees and the other for college-bound students (Meier 1995).

The current call for educational reform was initiated during President Ronald Reagan's administration. In 1983, the National Commission on Excellence in Education released its report, *A Nation at Risk: The Imperatives for Educational Reform,* a scathing indictment of the education system. The commission was created by Secretary of Education T. H. Bell to respond to what he called the "widespread public perception that something is seriously remiss in our educational system" (National Commission on Excellence in Education 1983:7). Claiming that we are raising a scientifically and technologically illiterate generation, the commission noted the relatively poor performance of American students in comparison with their international peers, declining standardized test scores, the weaknesses of our school programs and educators, and the lack of a skilled American workforce (National Commission on Excellence in Education 1983).

Revising No Child Left Behind

The educational reform movement marches on, gaining momentum with each elected president. At one time or another, each president after Reagan has referred to himself as the "Education President," declaring an educational crisis and calling for change. Educators and reformers agree that this is an exciting time for American education (Ravitch and Viteritti 1997). Under George H. W. Bush's administration, Congress passed America 2000, which was followed by the Goals 2000: Educate America Act in 1994 during Bill Clinton's administration. Congress passed the No Child Left Behind (NCLB) Act of 2001 under George W. Bush's administration. All congressional acts call for coordinated improvements and sweeping reform of our educational system.

David Berliner and Bruce Biddle (1995) contend that the crisis in public education is a manufactured one, constructed by well-meaning or not-so-well–meaning politicians, educational experts, and business leaders. Berliner and Biddle don't believe that public schools are problem free; rather, by focusing on the manufactured crisis, they believe we're not addressing the real problems facing our schools, those based in social and economic inequalities. What is the evidence regarding these problems and challenges to our educational system? Let's first examine the basis of education: literacy.

Taking a World View

Educational Tracking and Testing in Japan

After World War II, Japan adopted a 6-3-3-4 model of education that includes 6 years of elementary school (*shogakko*), 3 years of junior high school (*chugakko*), 3 years of high school (*kotogakko*), and 4 years of university study. Tracking does not occur in Japanese elementary and junior high schools; instead, their educational system emphasizes effort and hard work, discounting differences in ability. No effort is made to identify below- or above-average children in the classroom. All elementary and junior high schools offer the same curriculum regulated by the national Ministry of Education, Culture, Sports, Science and Technology (MEXT; Ansalone 2004).

However, a highly competitive form of tracking (*ruikei*) begins at the high school level, separating students into two distinct tracks: general high schools leading to college and vocational high schools leading to jobs. Educational leaders argue that this system is able to accommodate students' different interests and talents and improves students' overall performance on national entrance exams (Ansalone 2004). Entrance examinations, also known as *jyuken higoku* (examination hell), serve as the major sorting mechanism for Japan's high schools and colleges (Bjork and Tsuneyoshi 2005).

Unintentionally, this tracking system has created a two-tier system of schools. Vocational high schools are students' second choices (Ono 2001). In his analysis of vocational high schools in the city of Kobe, Thomas Rohlen (1983) reports that one vocational high school draws students from the lower third of graduating ninth graders in the city. When asked if they had a choice, 80% of the students would have rather attended a general high school. Vocational high schools have developed a negative reputation for school violence, smoking, and drug abuse, and their students are considered second-class citizens (Rohlen 1983). In his comparative analysis of educational systems in Japan and the United States, George Ansalone (2004) concluded that tracking "promotes differentiation of the curricula, teacher expectations, school misconduct, race, class, gender bias, and the development of separate friendship patterns. When tracking is employed, upper-track students receive a higher quantity and quality of instruction from more qualified instructors who utilize a greater variety of instructional techniques" (p. 150).

During the last two decades of the twentieth century, several significant changes have occurred in the Japanese educational system. First, government leaders and educational scholars asserted that the emphasis on entrance examinations combined with the demands on students to learn large volumes of content had actually dulled students' interest in learning (Bjork and Tsuneyoshi 2005). Educational reforms began in the 1970s, reducing the amount of material covered by teachers, incorporating more student-centered and integrated learning in the classroom, and reducing the intensity of student learning and testing. MEXT referred to these reform policies as *yutori kyoiku* or reduced-intensity reforms. Response to the reforms has been mixed, with some applauding the new student-centered emphasis of the curriculum but others worrying about the impact of a "watered down" curriculum (Bjork and Tsuneyoshi 2005).

Second, admissions into Japan's universities have become less competitive. As its population of 18-year-olds has decreased by more than half a million since 1992, Japan's universities have trouble recruiting students. According to Rie Mori (2002), entrance examinations were expected to identify the best students for university education, but this is no longer necessary because there are more universities to accept students who do not score well on the exams. The universalization of higher education in Japan has led to a greater number of students entering universities who are not as high achieving as students of the past. Japanese higher education must figure out how to educate students with a broader range of learning styles and abilities (Mori 2002).

The Problem of Basic Literacy

The United Nations Educational, Scientific and Cultural Organization (UNESCO 2009) estimates that there are more than 774 million illiterate adults in the world. Most live in South and West Asia, East Asia, and sub-Saharan Africa. Multiple barriers restrict the achievement of widespread literacy: insufficient access to quality education, weak support for youth exiting the educational system, poorly funded and fragmented educational programs, and limited opportunities for adult learning. Literacy disparities are associated with gender, poverty, place of residence, ethnicity, language, and disabilities. Gender disparities are particularly pronounced in developing countries. Women account for 64% (UNESCO 2009) of adults worldwide who cannot read and write (refer to Table 8.3).

According to the Literacy Volunteers of America (2002), very few U.S. adults are truly illiterate, yet the United States is not a literacy superpower (ProLiteracy Worldwide 2006). What continues to be of concern is the number of adults with low literacy skills who are unable to find and retain employment, support their children's education, and participate in their communities. Basic literacy skills, such as understanding and using information in texts (newspapers, books, a warranty form) or instructional documents (maps, job applications) or completing mathematical operations (filling out an order form, balancing a checkbook), are related to social, educational, and economic outcomes (Sum, Kirsch, and Taggart 2002).

Data from the 2003 National Assessment of Adult Literacy (ProLiteracy Worldwide 2006) reveal that 30 million U.S. adults demonstrated skills in the "below basic" level (from being nonliterate in English to being able to follow written directions to fill out a form). About 63 million adults demonstrated skills in the basic level (having basic literary skills to read and understand information in short, simple documents). A total of 43% of all Americans are estimated to be in these two levels. In contrast, 57% of Americans were categorized in the higher levels—intermediate (able to complete moderately challenging literacy tasks, e.g., refer to a reference document for information) and proficient (able to read and integrate various materials; ProLiteracy Worldwide 2006).

Toppling Adult Illiteracy

Table 8.3

Estimated Number of Adult Illiterates (Age 15+) and Percentage Who Are Females, 2000 to 2006

Country	Total Number (in Thousands)	Female (%)
Sub-Saharan Africa	161,088	62
Arab States	57,798	67
Central Asia	784	68
East Asia and the Pacific	112,647	71
South and West Asia	392,725	63
Latin America and the Caribbean	36,946	55
North America and Western Europe	5,682	61
Central and Eastern Europe	8,235	80

Source: UNESCO 2009.

The U.S. Department of Education reports that individuals at higher levels of literacy are more likely to be employed, to work more weeks per year, and to earn higher wages than are individuals with lower levels of literacy (Kirsch et al. 2002). Education increases an individual's literacy skills, which determine educational success. Basic academic skills influence such educational outcomes as high school completion, college enrollment, persistence in college, field of study, and type of degrees obtained (Sum et al. 2002).

Although the United States spends more per capita on education than other high-income countries, our literacy scores are average in a world comparison. The literacy scores of native-born U.S. adults rank 10th among the 17 high-income nations. The nations that scored higher were Sweden, Norway, Denmark, Finland, the Netherlands, Germany, Canada, Belgium, and Australia. Moreover, the United States ranked first for the largest gap between highly and poorly educated adults, with immigrants and minorities among those poorly educated (Sum et al. 2002).

Inequality in Educational Access and Achievement

Social Class and Education

Socioeconomic status is one of the most powerful predictors of student achievement (College Entrance Examination Board 1999). The likelihood of dropping out of high school is five times higher among students from lower-income families than among their peers in high-income families (Laird, DeBell, and Chapman 2006). Dropping out of high school is related to negative economic outcomes. For example, the 2010 median income of persons who had not completed a high school degree was $19,369. In contrast, the median income of persons who had completed at least a high school credential (e.g., general equivalency diploma) was $28,070 (U.S. Census Bureau 2011).

Photo 8.4

Without the first two lines, how much of this sign do you understand? An estimated 43% of the U.S. population has literacy skills at or below the basic level, which includes reading maps or understanding directions to fill out a form.

Students from lower-income homes or who have parents with little formal education score lower on average than students from families earning more than $100,000 per year or who have parents with a bachelor's degree or higher. In 2009, the average critical reading SAT score was 434 for a student with a family income below $20,000 versus 525 for a student with a family income of $100,000–$120,000. For students with parental education less than a high school diploma, the average critical reading score was 420. In contrast, students with parental education of at least a bachelor's degree had an average score of 521 (College Board 2009).

High-income families can invest more time and resources into their children's cognitive development than lower-income families; high-income families have greater socioeconomic and social resources that benefit their children than lower-income families; and, according to Douglas Downey, Paul von Hippel, and Beckett Broh (2004), the primary source of inequality between children of high and low socioeconomic status lies in the children's disparate nonschool (home and neighborhood) environments. High-income families can invest more time and resources into their children's cognitive development than lower-income families; high-income families have greater socioeconomic and social resources that benefit their children than lower-income families (Reardon 2011). Yet Downey and his colleagues (2004) document how school enrollment serves as an equalizer. They examined reading scores among high- and low-socioeconomic-status students from kindergarten to first grade. Consistent with their theory, first-day-of-kindergarten reading scores were higher for children from high socioeconomic backgrounds than for those from low socioeconomic backgrounds. Though the gap continues to grow (and never disappears) after schooling starts, it grows more slowly between the two socioeconomic groups when school is in session than when it is not.

Achievement Gap in Schools

During the recession, almost all colleges and universities raised tuition fees to compensate for their shrinking operating budgets and endowments. For example, higher education in California, which includes the 23-campus California State University system and the 10-campus University of California system, not only adjusted its budgets with layoffs, furloughs, and reduced course offerings in the 2009–2010 academic year but also increased tuition and fees. The increasing cost of college tuition has reduced college access and affordability, leading many students to reassess the affordability of their college dreams. A national survey of college freshmen in 2009 revealed that students were more likely to have a parent who was unemployed and less likely to have found a job to support their college expenses in comparison with previous freshman classes (Zernike 2010). The cost of tuition and the offer of financial aid were identified as "very important" factors for choosing their college (Zernike 2010).

What Does It Mean to Me?

Refer to U.S. Data Map 8.1 for the percentage of the population with bachelor's degrees. What are the three highest-ranked states? What are the three lowest? Where does your home state rank?

STATE STATS

In research conducted by the Public Agenda organization (Johnson et al. 2009), the number-one reason students gave for leaving college is that they had to simultaneously balance work and school. College dropouts were less likely to report being bored or not enjoying their classes as the reason why they quit. More than half of those who left school identified the "need to work and make money" and the stress related to juggling both. Most students did not receive financial assistance from their families or from their schools. Public Agenda researchers suggest that today's college students are not leading the stereotypical college life of balancing classes and weekend parties; instead, they are balancing classes with working to pay rent.

What Does It Mean to Me?

Peter Sacks (2009) observes how our educational system, despite the promise of equal opportunity, is profoundly stratified. There is a growing concentration of lower- and working-class students in community colleges, while middle- and upper-class students are more likely to attend four-year colleges and universities. How would you describe the class composition of your school? Does it recruit or cater to a particular social class? How does this compare with other colleges or universities in your area?

In Focus

Controlling the Cost of Higher Education

A college education is still part of the American Dream. Sallie Mae, a financial service company specializing in education, annually releases a national report on how college tuition is managed by parents and their students. In the 2012 report, Sallie Mae and Ipsos (an independent marketing research company) found that 83% of college students and parents strongly agreed that higher education is an investment in the future, college is needed now more than ever (70%), and college is the path to earning more money (69%).

What Does It Mean to Me?

Refer to state rankings on average student costs at public institutions of higher education. What is the student cost of public higher education in your state? Which three states have the lowest costs for students for public higher education? Which three states have the highest costs?

But the truth is that most young adults do not attend a four-year college. According to Paul Taylor and his colleagues (2011), the main barrier to higher education is financial. Among individuals 18 to 34 years old who are not in school and do not have a bachelor's degree, about two thirds report that they are not continuing their education in order to support a family; more than half say they prefer to work and make money (Taylor et al. 2011).

In his 2012 State of the Union speech, Barack Obama called on the federal government, states, colleges, and universities to promote access and affordability in higher education. Obama proposed educational and legislative reforms tying federal campus aid to responsible tuition policies. Aiming primarily at state colleges and universities, Obama outlined financial incentives for schools to contain their tuition, enhance teaching and learning, and increase affordability and graduation rates (White House 2012).

The president's announcement received a mixture of praise and caution from educational leaders and college groups (Field 2012). David Warren (2012), director of the National Association of Independent Colleges and Universities, said, "The collective challenge facing the nation is to make college more affordable, without losing our position of having the best higher education system in the world. . . . The answer is not going to come from more federal controls on colleges or states, by telling families to judge the value of an education by the amount young graduates earn in the first few years after they graduate."

Warren, along with other academic leaders, warned about the unintended consequences of Obama's proposals—reducing educational quality, cutting back essential student services, and disproportionately harming schools that serve larger numbers of at-risk students (Field 2012).

Sallie Mae and Ipsos (2012) report that, in 2012, families adjusted how they paid for college in three ways. First, parents cut their contributions from income and savings. For 2012, parents spent an average of $5,955 from their income and savings, down from $6,664 in 2011. Second, fewer families utilized scholarships—35% in 2012 compared with 45% in 2011. Some of this decline is attributed to colleges reducing the amount of scholarships that they are able to offer. Finally, students paid more out of pocket through their savings and income and borrowing more in 2012 than in previous years. In 2012, students contributed 18% of the total cost of college through borrowing compared with 15% the previous year and 14% in 2008–2010.

What Does It Mean to Me?

Are finances the only barrier to higher education? What other barriers can you identify? Is a college degree still attainable for those in your generation? Why or why not?

 STATE STATS

Gender and Education

Female college enrollment has steadily increased since the 1970s. In 2000, females were the majority of undergraduate and graduate students (Freeman 2004). Table 8.4 provides a summary of enrollment data from 1970 to 2009. Undergraduate enrollment for women increased from 41.3% in 1970 to 55% in 2009. A similar increase occurred among women enrolled in graduate programs: 30.3% to 56%. A more substantial increase occurred among women enrolled in first professional programs (including dentistry, medicine, optometry, and pharmacy). Women constituted 8.5% of all those enrolled in these programs in 1970 but increased to 46.6% in 2000. Ryan and Siebens (2012) report that for the U.S. population ages 25 and older, about 85.9% of women and 84.9% of men completed high school; 27.4% of women earned a college degree or more, compared with 28.4% of men.

 State of the Union Speech

Table 8.4

Percentage Distribution of Full-Time College Students by Level and Sex, Fall 1970 to Fall 2009

Level	1970		1980		1990		2000		2009	
	Male	**Female**	**Male**	**Female**	**Male**	**Female**	**Male**	**Female**	**Male**	**Female**
Undergraduate	58.7	41.3	50.7	49.3	47.8	52.2	45.3	54.7	45.0	55.0
Graduate	69.7	30.3	57.9	42.1	53.6	46.4	46.4	53.6	44.0	56.0
First-professional	91.7	8.5	71.8	28.2	61.0	39.0	53.4	46.6	N/A	N/A

Note: N/A = not available.

Source: Freeman 2004, Synder and Dillow 2011.

Although more women are being awarded bachelor's degrees, fewer women than men complete bachelor's degrees in mathematics, engineering, physics, and other quantitative fields (College Entrance Examination Board 1999). By the time they leave high school, males are three times more likely to pursue careers in science, mathematics, or engineering than are females (Strand and Mayfield 2002). Is this because of natural ability? The answer is no, according to the American Association of University Women (AAUW). The 1992 AAUW study reported no differences in math performance between boys and girls at age 9, and only minimal differences at age 13. Boys have higher achievement scores in physics, chemistry, earth sciences, and space sciences than girls, and the differences are largest among 17-year-olds.

Gender Gap

Differences in mathematical and scientific abilities favoring boys do not appear until the intermediate grades. A study by Linda K. Silverman (1986) suggests that females will eventually achieve less than males because they are gradually conditioned by "powerful environmental influences" such as the educational system, peers, and parents to believe that they are less capable than males. A "hidden curriculum" perpetuates gender inequalities in math and science courses. This curriculum takes the form of differential treatment in the classroom, where boys tend to dominate class discussion and monopolize their instructor's time and attention, whereas girls are silenced and their insecurities reinforced (Linn and Kessel 1996). Research suggests that girls, especially gifted ones, fail to achieve their potential because of lower expectations of success, the attribution of any success to chance, and the belief that success will lead to negative social consequences (Silverman 1986).

In 2006, the media declared a "boy crisis" in education when published research revealed how girls had narrowed the gap in their participation and academic achievements in math and science and that more women were completing bachelor's degrees than men (Perkins-Gough 2006). Education Sector policy analyst Sara Mead concluded that the concern over boys' academic performance was misguided. Although the percentages of boys and girls taking higher-level mathematics and science courses in high school have increased significantly in the last 20 years, the percentage of girls taking advanced courses has increased more rapidly than has the percentage of boys. Men's higher educational attainment is not declining; rather, it is increasing at a slower rate than that of women. Mead cautioned instead about the growing gaps among students of different races and social classes, especially among Black and Hispanic boys (quoted in Perkins-Gough 2006).

Ethnicity/Race and Education

About 3.4 million students entered kindergarten in U.S. public schools last fall and already . . . researchers foresee widely different futures for them. Whether they are White, Black, Hispanic, Native American or Asian American will, to a large extent, predict their success in school. (Johnson and Viadero 2000:1)

Persistent academic achievement gaps remain between Black, Hispanic, and Native American students and their White and Asian peers. This was the conclusion made by the College Entrance Examination Board's (1999) National Task Force on Minority High Achievement. In the mid-1990s, underrepresented minorities received less than 13% of all the bachelor's degrees awarded. The College Entrance Examination Board noted that in the latter half of the 1990s, only small percentages of Black, Hispanic, and Native American high school seniors in the National Assessment of Educational Progress test samples had scores "typical" of students who are well prepared for college. Few students in these groups had scores indicating academic skills required for the most selective colleges or universities.

The educational attainment of the Hispanic population age 25 and over is lower than for other ethnic/racial groups. Though their high school and college graduation rates have steadily increased during the past decade, Hispanic students continue to trail behind all other groups in educational achievement. As indicated in Table 8.5, at least 80% of non-Hispanic Whites, Blacks, and Asians completed high school or more in 2010. In contrast, 62.9% of Hispanics (of any race) completed high school or more. Despite their lower high school graduation rates, there has been an increase in college enrollment among Hispanic students. Hispanic college enrollment increased 24% between 2009 and 2010 and 15% between 2010 and 2011, the largest among all ethnic and racial groups (Fry 2011; Fry and Lopez 2012). In 2011, 2.1 million Hispanics 18 to 24 years of age were enrolled in college, making Hispanics the largest minority group enrolled in college (Fry and Lopez 2012). Analysts are divided on the reasons for the increased enrollment—attributing the rate to demographics (Hispanics are one of the fastest growing ethnic groups) while acknowledging the real growth in Hispanic educational achievement and attainment (Fry 2011). Although the number of Hispanics receiving college degrees has grown, Hispanics continue to have the lowest rates of college graduation. At the bachelor's degree level, Asians have the highest proportion of college graduates (52.4%), followed by non-Hispanic Whites (30.3%), Blacks (19.8%), and Hispanics (13.9%).

California Dream Act

By 2015, there will be large increases in the number of Latino and Asian American youth, a substantial growth in the number of African American students, and a slight drop in the number of White students. The challenges to our educational system will only increase if demographic predictions hold true. The current educational gaps among racial and ethnic categories have the potential to grow into larger sources of inequality and social conflict (College Entrance Examination Board 1999).

Though male and female high school dropout rates have decreased since the 1970s, consistently the Hispanic dropout rate has been the highest since then (Freeman 2004). As reported in 2009, the total dropout rate was 9.1% for 16- to 24-year-old male students and 7.0% for females (Chapman et al. 2011). Dropout rates were highest for Hispanic males (19%) and females (16.1%). Second highest were the rates for Black, non-Hispanic students, 10.6% for males and 8.1% for females. Rates were lower for White, non-Hispanic students (males, 6.3%; females, 8.1%) and Asian/Pacific Islander students (males, 3.3%; females, 3.4%).

Ethnicity/race, along with poverty, defines major sources of disadvantage in educational outcomes (Maruyama 2003). Poverty among Latino families produces significant educational disadvantages: Parents may work multiple jobs, may not have the time to spend reading or going over homework with their children, and may not have the skills to read to their children. Economics also plays a role in dropout decisions. To support their families, Latino/a teens may leave school for a paying job. The power of parental and peer influence on

Race and Education

Table 8.5

Differences in Educational Attainment (In Percentages) by Race and Hispanic Origin for Adults Age 25 and Older, 2010

	Non-Hispanic White Alone	Black Alone	Asian Alone	Hispanic (of Any Race)
High school graduate or more	87.6	84.2	88.9	62.9
Bachelor's degree or more	30.3	19.8	52.4	13.9

Source: U.S. Census Bureau 2012.

Latino/a educational attainment has also been recognized. Parents may have expectations for their children that conflict with school expectations or requirements (AAUW 2001).

According to Claude Steele and Joshua Aronson (1995), the pressure to conform to an image or a stereotype is so strong that it can actually impair intellectual performance. Steele and his colleagues tested the effects of a stereotype threat among African American (Steele 1997; Steele and Aronson 1995) and female college students (Spencer, Steele, and Quinn 1999). The **stereotype threat** is the risk of confirming in oneself a characteristic that is part of a negative stereotype about one's group. The threat is situational, present only when a person can be judged, be treated in terms of the group, or self-fulfill negative stereotypes about the group (and the self; Spencer et al. 1999). In their studies, Steele and his colleagues investigated the effect of the stereotype that African Americans and women have lower academic abilities than do White or male students.

It doesn't matter if the individual actually believes the stereotype; if the stereotype demeans something of importance, such as one's intellectual ability, the threat can be disrupting enough to impair intellectual performance (Steele and Aronson 1995). Subjects were compared in test-taking situations using Graduate Record Examination (GRE), Scholastic Assessment Test (SAT), or American College Test (ACT) sample questions. In all study conditions where the tests were represented as affected by gender or race, African American and female students underperformed their comparison group. In situations where the stereotype threat was moderated (where subjects were not told that the tests produced gender differences or where subjects were not asked to report their race on the examination form), African American and female students performed as well as White or male students.

Violence and Harassment in Schools

Since a series of deadly school shootings in the late 1990s, part of the focus on education has revolved around safety in schools. School violence can be characterized on a continuum that includes aggressive behavior, harassment, property crimes, threats, and physical assault (Flannery 1997). Victims of school violence may include students, teachers, and staff members. From July 2007 to June 2008, 43 people died in school-related violent incidents. Of these deaths, 21 were homicides and 5 were suicides of school-age youth (ages 5 to 18), a rate of 1 homicide or suicide per 2.1 million school-age students during the 2007 to 2008 school year. During the 2006 to 2007 school year, 1,748 children ages 5 to 18 were victims of homicide while away from school. For this period, youth were 50 times more likely to be killed away from school than at school (Dinkes et al. 2009).

Although there have been fewer school-associated violent death events in recent years, there have been more deaths per event (Anderson et al. 2001). The deadliest U.S. incident took place in April 2007 at Virginia Polytechnic Institute and State University, where 33 students and faculty were killed by a student. The deadliest international incident occurred in 1996 when a gunman killed 16 primary school students and one teacher, as well as himself, in Scotland. We spend $200 million annually for school violence prevention and response (Flannery 1997). Though schools have been characterized as "battlegrounds" where both teachers and students fear for their safety (Kingery et al. 1993), they remain a safe place for students, with the risk of a violent death less than 1 in 2 million (Dinkes et al. 2009).

The 2009 national school-based Youth Risk Behavior Surveillance System (YRBSS) survey conducted annually by the Centers for Disease Control and Prevention found that nationwide about 5.0% of students had missed more than one day of school because they felt unsafe at school or on their way to or from school (Eaton et al. 2010). Hispanic and Black students were more likely than White students to have missed school because they felt unsafe. Among all students, 5.6% said they carried a weapon (a gun, knife, or club) on the school campus, with more male students (8%) than female students (2.9%) doing so. About 8% of all students reported being threatened or injured with a weapon on school property, and about 11% of students had been in a physical fight on school property (Eaton et al. 2010).

Lesbian, gay, bisexual, and transgendered (LGBT) youth are subject to verbal and physical harassment in high schools and middle schools. As reported by the Gay, Lesbian and Straight Education Network's 2011 National School Climate Survey, 63.5% of LGBT youth reported feeling unsafe in school because of their sexual orientation (Kosciw et al. 2012). About 40% experienced some form of physical harassment because of their sexual orientation; 18.3% were physically assaulted for the same reason. Almost 82% of the surveyed students reported being verbally harassed in school the past year. The majority of students who were harassed or assaulted did not report the incident to school staff or administrators. LGBT students' experience with harassment negatively affected their school attendance, their academic performance, and, ultimately, their college aspirations. Students who experienced more frequent harassment, either verbal or physical, were more likely to indicate that they were not planning to go on to college than were students who did not experience the same type of harassment (Kosciw et al. 2012).

LGBT Issues in Education

The extent of sexual harassment in schools has been documented by the AAUW Educational Foundation (Hill and Kearl 2011). According to its 2010–2011 report, 48% of students experience some form of sexual harassment during their school lives. Girls are more likely than are boys to experience sexual harassment. How is sexual harassment defined in schools? The definition offered by the Equal Employment Opportunity Commission (2001) under Title VII of the Civil Rights Act of 1964 reads,

> Unwanted sexual advances, requests for sexual favors, and other verbal or physical conduct of a sexual nature constitutes sexual harassment when submission or rejection of this conduct explicitly or implicitly affects an individual's employment, unreasonably interferes with an individual's work performance or creates an intimidating, hostile or offensive work environment.

Preventing Violence in Schools

Photo 8.5

The deadliest shooting in U.S. history occurred on the campus of Virginia Polytechnic Institute and State University (Blacksburg, Virginia) in April 2007. Cho Seung-Hui, a 23-year-old senior, killed 32 students and faculty members before turning the gun on himself. A state panel reviewing the incident concluded that several factors—confusion about state and federal privacy laws, weak enforcement of gun purchasing regulations, and inadequate funding of the state's mental health system—contributed to the tragedy.

In schools, sexual harassment can include such behaviors as sexual messages written on walls or in locker rooms, sexual rumors, being flashed or mooned, being brushed up against in a sexual way, or being shown sexual pictures or material of sexual content (Fineran 2002) and includes online harassment (e.g., receiving unwelcome comments or photos through texts, being the subject of sexual rumors or information) (Hill and Kearl 2011). Sexual harassment of students has serious consequences, including mental health symptoms (such as loss of appetite, disturbances in sleep, feelings of isolation, and sadness) and school performance difficulties (Fineran 2002).

Community, Policy, and Social Action

As a nation, we support the principle of educational excellence and, along with it, the assumption of educational opportunity for all, but in reality, we have an educational system that embraces these ideas yet fails to achieve them (Ravitch 1997). The educational experiences of poor and minority students fundamentally conflict with the principles of public education, namely that public schools should provide these children with opportunities so that all children can succeed as a result of hard work and talent (Maruyama 2003). Reformers argue that school choice, standardized testing, and school vouchers are improving our educational system. Critics argue that these strategies threaten to erode an already-weak public school structure. There is a deepening chasm between what the American public deems important in education (safety, skills, discipline) and the goals of the reform movement (access, standardization, multiculturalism; Finn 1997). Although we have not completely abandoned our public educational system, we still have not found a way to agree on what is appropriate or essential to save it.

Policy Responses—The Basis for Educational Reform

Educate America Act of 1994 and NCLB

Providing fuel to the reform movement have been congressional acts passed in 1994 and 2001. Although they were adopted under presidents from different political parties, both congressional acts provide strong support for school reform and, along with it, changes to our educational system.

The Goals 2000: Educate America Act introduced the notion of "standards-based reform" at state and community levels. This 1994 act, signed into law by President Clinton, provided the grounds for sweeping reform at all levels and from all angles: curriculum and instruction, professional development, assessment and accountability, school and leadership organization, and parental and community involvement. However, school reform hinged on the use of student performance standards and the creation of the National Education Standards and Improvement Council. A summary of the act reported, "Performance standards clearly define what student work should look like [at] different stages of academic progress and for diverse learners" ("Goals 2000" 1998:14). The act established performance and content standards in math, English, science, and social studies, and it encouraged participation from the entire community—local officials, educators, parents, and community leaders—in raising academic standards and achievement.

When George W. Bush signed the NCLB Act, he approved a plan that increased federal pressure on states to pursue a standards-based reform agenda. Under NCLB, states are required to institute a system of standardized testing for all public school students in Grades 3 to 8 and high school, about 45 million tests annually. Each state must have a plan for adequate yearly progress (AYP) toward the goal of academic proficiency for all students, a 100% rate regardless of economic status, ethnicity/race, gender, or disability, by 2014.

The more controversial elements of the act signed by George W. Bush included the provision for public school choice and charter schools. The act provided support to permit children in chronically failing public schools to transfer to other schools with better academic records. The bill also provided for annual testing of students in reading and math in the third to eighth grades, which would establish academic records for comparison. If there were no improvements in test results in two years, parents would have the option to move their children to another school. In such an event, the school district would be required to pay for the child's transportation to a better school, and the failing school would lose the per-pupil payment. Critics argued that such school choice provisions would only work if there were schools to choose from within a district and if there were room in these schools. The law does not provide school leaders with the means to create new slots for students (Schemo 2002).

Although expressing commitment to the basic intent of NCLB, many state leaders and educators expressed frustration in implementing the act's requirements and achieving its goals. In particular, school administrators and educators were critical of a key feature of NCLB: the one-size-fits-all accountability standard that assumes that all schools, districts, and groups of students will demonstrate progress according to the standardized measures. The standards, said critics, seriously compromise the abilities of schools to address the unique educational needs of special education students, low-income and minority students, and students with limited English proficiency.

In their 2010 proposal to reauthorize NCLB, the Obama administration set a new educational goal: "Every student should graduate from high school ready for college or a career regardless of their income, race, ethnic or language background, or disability status" by 2020 (U.S. Department of Education 2010:3). The proposal identified four policy and programming areas: improving teaching and principal effectiveness, providing information to families to evaluate and improve their children's schools and to educators to help improve student learning, implementing college- and career-ready standards and assessments, and improving student learning and achievement in the lowest-performing schools by providing support and effective interventions. In 2012, the Obama administration granted NCLB waivers to 24 states, in exchange for adopting the administration's educational standards and a new focus on accountability and teacher effectiveness. These states will need to set new performance targets for students and schools but will not be sanctioned as they were under the old law for schools failing or for not making adequate progress. More states will seek a waiver under the new plan (Hu 2012). Many characterized this as the beginning of the end of the NCLB era.

 Race to the Top

Promoting Educational Opportunities—Head Start

Called the most popular and most romantic of the War on Poverty efforts (Traub 2000), Head Start remains the largest early childhood program. More than 30 million poor and at-risk preschoolers have been served under Head Start since 1965. Head Start began with a simple model of service: organized preschool centers. At these centers, programs focused on the "whole child," examining and encouraging physical and mental health. Integrating strong parental involvement, Head Start provided a unique program targeting child development and school preparedness. Over the years, the Head Start program expanded to serve school-age children, high school students, pregnant women, and Head Start parents. In 1994, amendments to the Head Start Act established Early Head Start (EHS) services targeting economically disadvantaged families with children 3 years old or younger. EHS serves both children and their families through a comprehensive service plan that promotes child development and family self-sufficiency (Wall et al. 2000).

The effectiveness of Head Start programming, particularly the educational component, has been the focus of public and government debate (Washington and Oyemade Bailey 1995). Early program research and evaluation efforts were spotty, with the major findings pointing to short-term or "fade out" gains in student learning and testing (Washington and Oyemade Bailey 1995).

Recent research efforts have been more systematic, including longitudinal studies with larger cohorts of Head Start children. Evaluation data have identified a positive relationship between early childhood program enrollment and high school graduation, home ownership, school attendance, and motivation. For example, Diana Slaughter-Defoe and Henry Rubin (2001) noted that among African American middle school students and adolescents, Head Start graduates perceived themselves as more achievement oriented and motivated than did their non–Head Start peers. Head Start parents, Head Start teachers, and the family environment were important in sustaining the educational aspirations and expectations of Head Start graduates. Studies consistently indicate the effectiveness of strong parental involvement with the Head Start program. Head Start parents are more likely to remain involved in their children's education once they begin elementary school, and children whose parents have high participation rates perform better on achievement and development tests (Washington and Oyemade Bailey 1995).

In 1998, the congressional reauthorization of Head Start included an assessment component, requiring the Department of Health and Human Services (HHS) to document the program's effectiveness with low-income 3- and 4-year-old children. In its 2005 impact study report, HHS compared the performance of Head Start children with non–Head Start children from fall 2002 through summer 2005. For Head Start children in both age groups, small-to-moderate positive effects were found in prereading, prewriting, and vocabulary skills. Both groups also had significantly better access to health care; in addition, the 3-year-olds reported significantly better overall health than did the non–Head Start group. Positive parenting practices (e.g., reading to one's child) were also documented for children in both Head Start age groups (U.S. Department of Health and Human Services 2005). Head Start was reauthorized in 2007 with increased funding for Migrant and Seasonal Head Start and the Indian Head Start programs. The reauthorization also increased educational requirements for Head Start teachers.

Head Start Program

Mentoring, Supporting, and Valuing Networks

Women and Girls

In its 1992 report, the AAUW called on local communities and schools to promote programs that encourage and support girls studying science, technology, engineering, and mathematics (STEM). Studies indicate that most girls and women learn best in cooperative, rather than competitive, learning activities. With seed money from the W. K. Kellogg Foundation, the AAUW Educational Foundation initiated the Girls Can! Community Coalitions Project in 1996. The project funded 10 community-based projects that encouraged schools and community groups to improve girls' educational opportunities.

AAUW continues its support of STEM projects through the National Girls Collaborative Project established in 2005. The National Girls Collaborative Project goals include maximizing access to shared resources within projects and with public and private organizations interested in expanding girls' STEM participation, strengthening the capacity of existing and evolving projects by sharing promising research and program models, and using the collaboration of individual girl-serving STEM programs to create the tipping point for gender equity in STEM (National Girls Collaborative Project 2006).

Fourteen regional collaborative sites operate in California, Florida, Massachusetts, the mid-Atlantic, and the Northwest. Small minigrants help fund tutoring, career days, field trips, and special events to expose girls and boys to STEM education and careers. One such grant helped fund California State Summer School for Mathematics and Science (COSMOS), a monthlong residential academic experience for top California high school students in science and mathematics. Students reside at one of four University of California campuses—Davis, Irvine, San Diego, or Santa Cruz—while taking COSMOS classes in their areas of interest.

Mentoring can also begin in one's own community and among friends. In 1996, Michele Deane noticed that a number of girls in her Boyle Heights (Los Angeles, California) neighborhood did not have anything to do after school. She created a youth organization for local Mexican American and Latin American girls and women, beginning with a group of her friends, that now serves more than 200 girls and women each year. According to Deane, her organization, Girls Today, Women Tomorrow, created a state of consciousness for thinking "bigger":

> What do I want to do? Who can I become with the support of everyone around me? It's a state of consciousness coming from the world around you instead of seeing only the obstacles. Once they saw other people doing it, they started doing it for their friends, for the younger kids growing up. (quoted in Wiland and Bell 2006:187)

The volunteer program includes fitness activities, a computer lab, video shooting and editing classes, and a community garden. The garden serves as a connection to the environment and the girls' Latin culture and raises their awareness about the kind and quality of food they consume. Program graduates return to the program and serve as mentors and volunteers. Ginette Sanchez credits the program for her academic and life successes: "I always thought that I wouldn't have a future. Now that I have positive role models, I'm going to college and I'm being positive by thinking that I'm going to be someone in life as well" (quoted in Wiland and Bell 2006:189).

Voices in the Community

Wendy Kopp

Wendy Kopp

Wendy Kopp's vision for Teach for America began as her senior undergraduate thesis. This Princeton graduate is the youngest and only female to receive the university's Woodrow Wilson Award, the highest honor bestowed to alumni. In the following excerpt from her book, *One Day, All Children: The Unlikely Triumph of Teach for America and What I Learned Along the Way*, Kopp (2001) explains how Teach for America began with an idea:

> Princeton University was not the most likely place to become concerned about what's wrong in education, but it made me aware of students' unequal access to the kind of educational excellence I had previously taken for granted. I got to know students who had attended public schools in urban areas—thoughtful, smart people—as well as students who attended the East Coast prep schools. I saw the first group struggle to meet the academic demands of Princeton and the second group refer to it as a "cake walk." Clearly at Princeton I could not glimpse the depths of educational inequity in our country, but the disparities I did see got me thinking. It's really not fair, I thought, that where you're born in our country plays a role in determining your educational prospects.

In an effort to figure out what could be done about this problem, I organized a conference about the issue. At this time I led an organization called the Foundation for Student Communication. . . . So in November of my senior year, my colleagues and I gathered together fifty students and business leaders from across the country to propose action plans for improving our educational system. . . .

At one point during a discussion group, after hearing yet another student express interest in teaching, I had a sudden idea: Why didn't this country have a national teacher corps of top recent college graduates who would commit to teach in urban and rural public schools? A teacher corps would provide another option to the two-year corporate training programs and grad schools. It would speak to all college seniors who were searching for something meaningful to do with our lives. . . .

The more I thought about it, the more convinced I became that this simple idea was potentially very powerful. If top recent college graduates devoted two years to teaching in public schools, they could have a real impact on the lives of disadvantaged kids. Because of their energy and commitment, they would be relentless in their efforts to ensure their students achieved. They would throw themselves into their jobs, working investment-banking hours in classrooms instead of skyscrapers on Wall Street. They would question the way things are and fight to do what was right for children.

Beyond influencing children's lives directly, a national teacher corps could produce a change in the very consciousness of our country. . . .

In the end, I produced "A Plan and Argument for the Creation of a National Teacher Corps," which looked at the educational needs in urban and rural areas, the growing idealism and spirit of service among college students, and the interest of the philanthropic sector in improving education. The thesis presented an ambitious plan: In our first year, the corps would inspire thoughts of graduating college students to apply. We would then select, train, and place five hundred of them as teachers in five or six urban and rural areas across the country. (pp. 5–6, 10)

 Teach for America

In its first year, Teach for America received 2,500 applications, of which, as Kopp planned, 500 were selected and trained for two years of teaching. Since then, more than 33,000 teachers have been placed or are currently placed in 42 urban and rural sites throughout the United States. Corps members' salaries and health benefits are paid directly by the school districts they are placed in.

Source: Kopp 2001:5–6, 10. Published by PublicAffairs, a member of Perseus Books Group.

LGBT Students

 LGBT Youth

The best estimate of the number of LGBT students is about 5% to 6% of the total student population (Human Rights Watch 2001). LGBT youth have been a driving force behind creating change in their schools and communities. Support groups and organized student activities have emerged in states such as California, Illinois, and Washington, providing valuable support to LGBT teens and their friends and families (Bohan and Russell 1999; Human Rights Watch 2001).

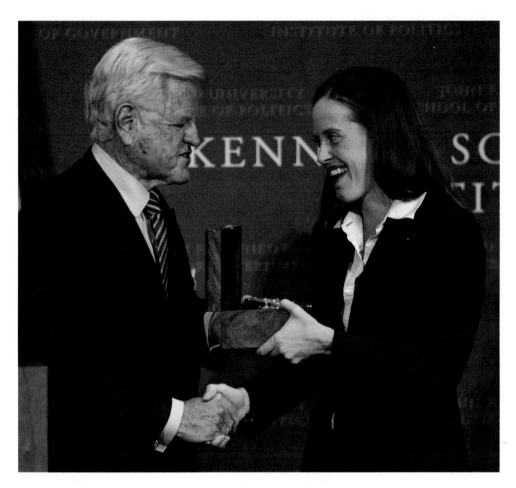

Photo 8.6

Wendy Kopp, founder of Teach for America, is pictured in 2004 with then–Senator Edward Kennedy (D-MA). Kopp was the first to receive the John F. Kennedy New Frontier Award, an honor presented to Americans under the age of 40 for their commitment to public service.

One such student group is the Gay-Straight Alliance (GSA) in East High School in Salt Lake City, Utah. As Janis Bohan and Glenda M. Russell (1999) chronicle, a group of students proposed creating a student alliance to provide a support network for LGBT students and their heterosexual friends in October 1995. In response to the students' proposal, the school board and the state legislature banned all noncurricular clubs rather than allow the GSA. The club continued to meet, paying rental and insurance fees for the use of school facilities. According to Bohan and Russell, students indicated how the club had a positive impact on their lives. The alliance served as a safe refuge, decreasing their feelings of isolation and vulnerability, students said, and they reported decreases in substance abuse, depression, suicidal impulses, truancy, and conflict with parents. The straight student members also reported positive effects. In September 2000, Utah's Salt Lake City School District Board of Education voted to permit noncurricular student groups to meet on school grounds, reversing its 1995 decision against the GSA (Human Rights Watch 2001). According to the Gay, Lesbian and Straight Education Network, there are more than 4,000 registered clubs for LGBT students and their friends throughout the United States.

Schools are allowing students to participate in the national Day of Silence in April. A vow of silence for the day symbolizes the silencing effect of antigay harassment and bullying. The event was founded in 1996 by students at the University of Virginia. In 2012, the day was observed in 9,000 schools in over 70 countries. Although some religious and parent groups object to what they consider "promotion" of homosexuality, most agree that it is important to create and promote a safe school environment for LGBT youth.

Antiviolence and Antibullying Programs in Schools

Prevention Programs

As awareness of school violence has increased, so have the calls for effective means of prevention (Aber, Brown, and Henrich 1999). The current focus is less on reacting to school violence and more on promoting school safety through prevention, planning, and preparation (Shaw 2001).

The largest and longest-running school program focusing on conflict resolution and intergroup relations is the Resolving Conflict Creatively Program (RCCP). Initiated in 1985 in New York City by the local chapter of Educators for Social Responsibility, the program is a research-based K–12 school program in social and emotional learning. RCCP is in 400 schools nationwide, serving 6,000 teachers and more than 175,000 students. RCCP begins with the assumption that aggression and violent behavior are learned and therefore can be reduced through education. The program teaches children conflict resolution skills, promotes intercultural understanding, and provides models and opportunities for positive ways of dealing with conflict and differences. For kindergarten students, puppets and other objects are used to illustrate how conflict can be resolved by talking rather than hitting. RCCP includes training for teachers, parents, administrators, and school staff.

An evaluation of the New York City programs indicated that students who received RCCP instruction developed more positively than did students without any RCCP exposure. RCCP students were more prosocial, perceived their world in a less hostile way, saw violence as unacceptable, and chose nonviolent ways to resolve conflict. Reading and math scores were higher for RCCP students, especially those who had 25 RCCP lessons over the school year. Evaluators concluded that the RCCP-intensive children were more able to focus on academics when there was less conflict with peers (Shaw 2001).

The Safe Schools Improvement Act and the Student Non-Discrimination Act were introduced in Congress in 2011 in an effort to support safe schools and enrich the learning environment. Both bills would require schools that accept federal funding to track, create policy, and demonstrate reduction in bullying and harassment incidents. Bullying and harassment data would be reported biennially. While ensuring the safety and well-being of all students, the bills were applauded for their focus on students with disabilities and LGBT students.

With the increase in school violence, more attention has been given to school safety through security screening or police-school liaison projects. Schools are more aware of the links between safety and violence and other student behaviors such as dropout rates, academic failures, bullying, and suicide (Shaw 2001). Violence prevention programs have become common throughout the country with the primary focus on early education. In addition to the RCCP, other national initiatives include the Office of Safe and Healthy Students and the Safe Schools/Healthy Students Initiative. Regional initiatives include the PeaceBuilders elementary program and Students Against Violence Everywhere. U.S. and international approaches focus more on school safety and less on school violence, use programs to serve students and the entire school population, develop school-community partnerships, and use evaluated program models (Shaw 2001). The most effective school-based violence prevention programs are those that include parental involvement and support, with parents backing school limits and consequences at home (Flannery 1997). Antiviolence programs have also been established on college and university campuses (refer to Table 8.6).

Table 8.6

What College and University Campuses Can Do to Make a Difference: Recommendations From the *ToolKit to End Violence Against Women*

The National Advisory Council on Violence Against Women (2001) released the following list of recommendations as part of its *Toolkit to End Violence Against Women*. The list includes recommendations for strengthening prevention efforts and improving services and advocacy for victims on campus:

- Institutionalize a campus-wide response to violence against women.
- Create an interdisciplinary task force to address violence against women.
- Establish a fair campus adjudication process.
- Administer sanctions for perpetrators that convey the seriousness of the offense.
- Invest in comprehensive and accessible on-campus and community services to victims.
- Provide training on violence against women for all campus law enforcement.
- Form partnerships with local victim service programs and criminal justice agencies.
- Highlight men's ability and responsibility to prevent violence against women.
- Enlist men in education efforts.
- Participate in full disclosure of campus crime data reports.

Source: National Advisory Council on Violence Against Women 2001.

Does Having a Choice Improve Education?

There is a new term now, *public school choice*. Data issued by the National Center for Education Statistics reveal that more parents are turning away from local public schools to private schools or charter schools (Zernike 2010). There were 4,694 charter schools in operation from 2008 to 2009, enrolling more than 1.4 million students (U.S. Department of Education, National Center for Education Statistics 2011). At least one in four children attends a school other than the one nearest home (Wilgoren 2001). In 2009, more students attended charter schools in the Los Angeles Unified School District than in any other school district in the country (Blume 2009).

Parents and children have two additional options within the public education system: magnet schools and charter schools. Magnet schools offer specialized educational programs from elementary school through high school. These schools are organized around a theme such as performing arts, science, technology, or business or around different instructional designs such as free (where students can direct their own education) or open schools (with informal classroom designs). Often, magnet schools are placed in racially isolated schools or neighborhoods to encourage students of other races to enroll. Magnet schools have been criticized for creating a two-tier system of education (Kahlenberg 2002).

Charter schools are nonsectarian public schools of choice that operate free from most state laws and local school board policies that apply to traditional public schools. Charter schools are funded with public funds, like public schools. A charter contract establishes the school's operation, usually limited to three to five years, detailing the school's mission and instructional goals, student population, educational outcomes, and assessment methods, along with a management and financial plan. These schools have grown in popularity since 1991, when Minnesota became the first state to pass an outcome-based school law. Charter schools are characterized by innovative teaching practices and accountability to students and families. If a school fails to meet its goals, it cannot be renewed under its charter.

School choice has become an even hotter topic with the idea of school vouchers. Simply stated, school vouchers allow the transfer of public school funds to support a student's transfer to a private school, which may include religious institutions. Supporters of school vouchers argue that the system would give parents more choice and freedom in school selection and would create incentives for school improvement (Good and Braden 2000; Kennedy 2001).

Opponents argue that vouchers would siphon money away from public schools, removing any ability to resolve the schools' problems, thus only increasing problems. Others argue that schooling is a public good and must be provided by the government to all children (Good and Braden 2000) equally and fairly. In June 2002, the U.S. Supreme Court ruled that school voucher programs did not violate any church-versus-state separation and upheld the constitutionality of using public funds to support private school systems (Bumiller 2002). Charter schools have been criticized for increasing income and racial school segregation. David Garcia (2008) documented how charter elementary school choosers enter charter schools that are more racially segregated than the schools they exited. High school choosers enter charter schools that are as racially segregated as or more integrated than the school districts they exited.

On the effectiveness of voucher programs and charter or magnet schools, the research remains mixed and ultimately divided according to political party lines. The same issues concerning charter schools and voucher systems continue to be the subject of inquiry and debate: defining clear systems of accountability, establishing comparable performance standards, and ensuring the racial and economic integration of students.

In 2006, data analysis based on the 2003 National Assessment of Educational Progress test by the U.S. Department of Education revealed that children in charter schools were performing worse than were their peers in public schools. Fourth graders in traditional public schools scored an average of 4.2 points better in reading and 4.7 points better in math than did comparable students in charter schools. The federal commissioner of education statistics, Mark S. Schneider, said at the release of the report that the department would not put its stamp on research comparing public and charter schools. Schneider admitted, "This is one of the most contentious issues with regard to the charter school research debate" (quoted in Schemo 2006). Most researchers agree that charter school performance has been mixed (Hill 2005) yet disagree about why this is the case and how best to measure the level of effectiveness of these schools (Scott and Villavicencio 2009).

A number of education and social science researchers have noted the paradox of charter school reform: Although these schools provide parents and educators with an opportunity to more actively participate in the content, organization, and governance of public schools, charter schools often benefit people who are able to gather private resources (Stambach and Becker 2006). According to researchers Salvatore Saporito and Annette Lareau (1999), if there is one consistent finding on school choice, it is that students from poorer families or with less-educated parents are less likely to apply to or participate in public choice programs than are those from middle-class families. In addition, the researchers raise questions about the school selection process for White and African American families. Although school choice advocates suggest that promoting racial equality is one of the by-products of school choice, Saporito and Lareau found that White families as a group are more likely to avoid schools with higher percentages of Black students, whereas African American families show no such sensitivity to race. African American families in their study were likely to select schools with lower poverty rates. The researchers concluded that race was a persistent factor in the choice process. Their findings have been confirmed by other researchers, suggesting the need to examine the social and political processes by which race and class stratification are perpetuated (Stambach and Becker 2006).

Main Points

- The educational attainment level of adults will continue to rise, as younger, more educated age groups replace older, less educated ones.

- The institution of education has a set of manifest and latent functions. Manifest functions are intended goals or consequences of the activities within an institution. Education's primary manifest function is to educate. The other manifest functions include personal development, proper socialization, and employment. Education's latent or unintended consequences may be less obvious.

- Conflict theorists do not see education as an equalizer; rather, they consider education a divider, dividing the haves from the have-nots in our society. From this perspective, conflict theorists focus on the social and economic inequalities inherent in our educational system and how the system perpetuates these inequalities. Inequalities are based not just on social class but also on gender. Research reveals the persistent replication of gender relations in schools, evidenced by the privileging of males, their voices, and their activities in the classroom, on the playground, and in hallways.

- From an interactionist perspective, the interaction between teachers and students reinforces the structure and inequalities of the classroom and the educational system. Sociologists focus on how classroom dynamics and tracking practices educate the perfect student and at the same time create the not-so-perfect ones.

- Although educational attainment is increasing, it is still unevenly distributed among social groups. Socioeconomic status is one of the most powerful predictors of student achievement. The likelihood of dropping out of high school is higher among students from lower-income families.

- Census data indicate slight differences in educational attainment for men and women. A hidden curriculum perpetuates gender inequalities in math and science courses. This curriculum takes the form of differential treatment in the classroom, where boys tend to dominate class discussion and monopolize their instructor's time and attention, whereas girls are silenced and their insecurities reinforced.

- Persistent academic achievement gaps remain between Black, Hispanic, and Native American students and their White and Asian peers. Latino/a students are at greater risk of not finishing school than any other ethnic/racial group.

- Part of the focus on education has revolved around safety in schools. School violence can be characterized on a continuum that includes aggressive behavior, harassment, threats, property crimes, and physical assault.

- Recent acts and initiatives to reform education include the Educate America Act of 1994 and the NCLB Act of 2001. Several education programs promote educational opportunities. Probably the most well-known early childhood program is Head Start.

- Programs such as the National Girls Collaborative Project support girls studying mathematics and science. LGBT youth have been a driving force behind creating change in their schools and communities. Support groups and organized student activities have emerged in states such as California, Illinois, and Washington, providing valuable support to LGBT teens and their friends and families.

- There is a new term now: *public school choice*. School vouchers allow the use of public school funds to support student transfers to private schools, which may include religious institutions. Supporters of school vouchers argue that the system would give parents more choice and freedom in school selection and would create incentives for school improvement. Opponents argue that vouchers would siphon money away from public schools, removing any ability to resolve the schools' problems, thus only increasing problems.

On Your Own

Log on to the open-access Student Study Site at www.sagepub.com/leonguerrero4e for these additional learning tools:

- Interactive quizzes
- Video clips
- NPR audio links
- Handbook articles

- E-flashcards
- Journal articles
- End-of-chapter web exercises
- Additional web resources and current events

Internet and Community Exercises

1. Contact your local ProLiteracy Worldwide volunteer program or search the organization's national website (log on to *Study Site Chapter 8*). Click on "Get Involved" and "Find a Program" to identify a program in your state. If a program does not exist in your community, find the one nearest you (your local library may have information on literacy programs). What services or activities does the program provide for students? Does the program have data regarding the number and types of students it has served? On its effectiveness? What skills are necessary to become a literacy tutor?

2. Interview a student who is a first-generation college student. The student can be from your social problems class or any of your other classes. What challenges do first-generation college students face? Do you believe their challenges are different from those of students who are second- or third-generation college students? Does your college provide programs for first-generation students? If not, what type of services or support might be valuable for this group of students?

3. Investigate whether your local school district supports educational outreach programs for girls or minority students. Select one program and answer the following: What group does the program serve? What educational "gaps" does the program address and how? How effective is the program? Contact the local school district, the Young Women's Christian Association, or the American Association of University Women (log on to *Study Site Chapter 8*) for more information.

4. In addition to public school choice, homeschooling has become an option for many families. It was estimated that 1.5 million children were homeschooled in 2007, about 2.9% of all students age 5 to 17 years (U.S. Department of Education, National Center for Education Statistics 2009). This figure includes students who were homeschooled only and students who were homeschooled and enrolled in school for 25 hours or less per week. Parents offered a variety of reasons for homeschooling their children: belief that they can give their child a better education at home, to provide religious or moral instruction, the poor learning environment at school, and family reasons (Planty et al. 2009). Homeschoolers are more likely to be located in rural and suburban areas of the western United States (Bauman 2001). Homeschool World provides a listing of all U.S. national and state homeschool organizations, including a listing of international organizations (under "Homeschool Organizations"). Log on to *Study Site Chapter 8*.

5. Log on the United Nations Human Development Report website and review the data for mean years of schooling (for adults ages 25 years and older) and public expenditures on education. Identify the top 10 countries for each measure. How does the United States rank in each list? Log on to *Study Site Chapter 8* for more information.

6. Investigate how many female and male students are declared majors in math, engineering, English, nursing, and sociology at your university. Is there a difference in the number of female majors in engineering versus English? Math versus nursing? What sociological perspective(s) might best explain the gender gap in majors?

Study Questions

1. Explain the shift in the educational standard from high school degree to college degree.

2. How does the educational system socialize children for adulthood and employment? Which theoretical perspectives support this argument?

3. Do you think tracking is a necessary educational practice? In your answer, consider evidence from Japan's tracking system.

4. Explain how social class, gender, and race/ethnicity contribute to educational inequality in the United States.

5. How effective are U.S. policies, including NCLB, on improving educational achievement?

6. Is public school choice a viable educational alternative? Why or why not?

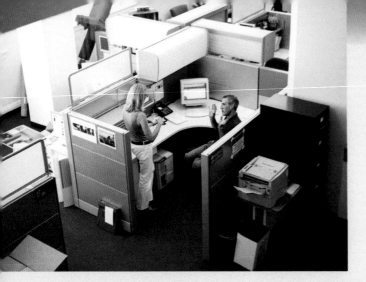

CHAPTER 9

Work and the Economy

Dubai Recession

I n November 2009, Dubai, a member of the United Arab Emirates federation, requested to delay payment on a $56 billion debt issued by conglomerate Dubai World and its main property subsidiary, Nakheel (a real estate developer of three luxurious, palm-shaped islands off the Dubai coast). The announcement set off stock market losses in Asia, Europe, and the United States, reinforcing the fragile and interconnected nature of our global economy. After all, the global economy is still in a recession that began in late 2007, after the U.S. economy crashed due to problems with subprime mortgages (mortgages offered to less-than-creditworthy borrowers), and housing prices and values began to decline.

A recession is when the overall state of the economy declines, measured by multiple indicators: a decline in the gross domestic product (GDP, the total production of goods and services) for two or more consecutive quarters, an increase in unemployment rates, and a decline in housing prices and values. In 2008, the failure or near-failure of several major financial firms, such as Merrill Lynch, AIG, and Lehman Brothers, caused many financial and credit markets to freeze (Bernanke 2009). The ripple effects were seen worldwide in countries such as Russia, Brazil, and Indonesia and some states in the Middle East, which had little to do with the U.S. subprime mortgage and housing crises but were vulnerable to the sudden halt in the flow of money and credit (Landler 2008).

Our current economic crisis has been referred to as "one of the most difficult financial and economic episodes in modern history" by U.S. Federal Reserve Chairman Ben Bernanke. The 2011 U.S. median household income was estimated at $50,054 (DeNavas-Walt, Proctor, and Smith 2012). The 2011 real household income was 8.1% lower than in 2007 ($54,489), the year before the recession.

News headlines in this country referred to unemployment as the biggest problem. Between 2008 and 2009, the United States lost 8.4 million jobs or about 6.1% of all payroll employment, the largest job loss since the Great Depression (Economic Policy Institute 2012). Unemployment is an experience no longer limited to people of color, immigrants, or the undereducated. Unique to this recession has been its impact on the educated and the (formerly) middle class. Many more people, across different demographic groups, are experiencing the hardships of unemployment. For March 2012, the U.S. Bureau of Labor Statistics (2012a) reported that 12.7 million women and men were unemployed, an overall rate of 8.2%. Similar concerns about unemployment were also expressed in Asia, in India, and throughout the European Union (EU). In the EU, the unemployment rate was 10.8% in February 2012, with rates highest in Greece, Spain, and Latvia (Eurostat 2012).

Though political and economic attention has shifted to job creation, economic stimulus packages, and unemployment, these aren't the only problems facing workers. For some, work remains a dangerous place, leading to injury or death. Others are victims of discrimination or harassment in the workplace. And for many men and women, even though they are employed, their paychecks do not provide a livable wage.

Work isn't just what we do; work is a basic and important social institution. It fuels our economy and provides economic support for individuals and families. In February 2012, more than 154 million women and men were employed in the United States, about 65% of the population aged 16 years or older (U.S. Bureau of Labor Statistics 2012b). But work is also important for our social and psychological well-being. Individuals find a sense of fulfillment and happiness, and for most, work provides a self-identity. Much of our social status is conferred through our occupation or the type of work we do. Because of the importance of work, problems related to work become categorized as social problems, as everyone's problem. In this chapter, we examine the work that we do, the social organization of work itself, and the social problems associated with our work and economy. We begin first with a review of the changing nature of work.

The Changing Nature of Work

During the late eighteenth century and early nineteenth century, the means of production shifted from agricultural to industrial. In agrarian societies, economic production was very simple, based primarily on family agriculture and hunting or gathering activities. Each family provided its own food, shelter, and clothing. This changed during the Industrial Revolution, an economic shift in how people worked and how they earned a living. Family production was replaced with market production, in which capitalist owners paid workers wages to produce goods (Reskin and Padavic 1994).

Industrial Revolution

As a whole, we don't produce goods anymore; we provide services. Since the late 1960s, the U.S. economy has shifted from a manufacturing to a service-based economy (Brady and Wallace 2001). In 1950, manufacturing accounted for 33.7% of all nonfarm jobs; by 2000, manufacturing's share had dropped to 14% (Pollina 2003). The **service revolution** is an economy dominated by service and information occupations. Examine Table 9.1, which lists the 10 fastest-growing projected occupations between 2008 and 2018. Notice that none of the occupations on the list involve manufacturing; instead, jobs in retail, food, and customer service dominate the list.

Table 9.1

10 Occupations With the Largest Projected Job Growth (in Thousands), 2008–2018

Industry Description	2008	2018
Retail salespersons	4,489	4,864
Office clerks, general	3,024	3,383
Combined food preparation and serving workers, including fast food	2,702	3,096
Registered nurses	2,619	3,200
Waiters and waitresses	2,382	2,533
Customer service representatives	2,252	2,652
Bookkeeping, accounting, and auditing clerks	2,064	2,276
Truck drivers, heavy and tractor-trailer	1,798	2,031
Postsecondary teachers	1,699	1,956
Executive secretaries and administrative assistants	1,594	1,799

Source: U.S. Bureau of Labor Statistics 2009a.

This shift has been referred to as **deindustrialization**, a widespread, systematic disinvestment in our nation's manufacturing and production capacities (Bluestone and Harrison 1982). Less manufacturing takes place in the United States because most jobs and plants have been transferred to other countries. The expansion of industrialization in other regions such as Asia, the Caribbean, Eastern Europe, and Africa has encouraged managers to reduce their manufacturing costs by exporting manufacturing jobs there (Sullivan 2004). In addition, U.S. factories have closed as a result of mergers or acquisitions as well as poor business. And thanks to technological advances, it takes fewer people to produce the same amount of goods.

Job losses in manufacturing have been particularly acute since early 2000: U.S. manufacturers have lost 2.7 million jobs since July 2000. Affected areas have experienced devastating social and economic losses, turning some into ghost towns (Brady and Wallace 2001) or leading cities to the brink of bankruptcy—the plight of Cleveland, Ohio, and Detroit, Michigan, since the 1980s. The phenomenon was also observed in Great Britain in the 1970s and 1980s in cities such as Birmingham and Manchester (Carley 2000). Lost manufacturing jobs are often replaced with unstable, low-paying service jobs or no jobs at all. As a result, cities may experience a significant loss of revenue to support basic public services such as police, fire protection, and schools (Bluestone and Harrison 1982).

In addition to the transformation in the type of work we do, there has been a transformation in who is doing the work. The first significant workforce change began in World War II with the entry of record numbers of women into the workplace. In 1940, the majority of 11.5 million employed women were working as blue-collar, domestic, or service workers out of economic necessity (Gluck 1987). White and Black women's entry into defense jobs signaled a major

Photo 9.1

Fellow workers and family members mourn the deaths of 29 coal miners killed by a methane gas explosion at the Massey Energy Company's Upper Big Branch Coal Mine in West Virginia. The 2010 explosion was the worst U.S. mining accident in 25 years.

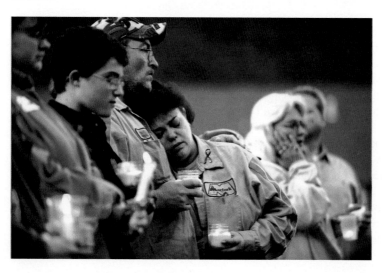

breakthrough. One fourth of all White women and nearly 40% of Black women were wage earners who previously worked in lower-paid clerical, service, or manufacturing jobs. By 1944, 16% of working women held jobs in war industries. At the height of wartime production, the number of married women in the workplace outnumbered single working women for the first time in U.S. labor history. Almost one in three women defense workers were former full-time homemakers. In Los Angeles, women made up 40% of the aircraft production workforce.

These heavy industry jobs may have paid better, but the jobs held an important symbolic value: These jobs were men's jobs. After the war, although the proportion of women workers in durable manufacturing increased in many cities, many women were forced back into low-paying, female-dominated occupations (Gluck 1987) or back to their homes.

Labor force participation rates have steadily increased for White, Black, and Hispanic women since World War II (see Table 9.2). In 2010, 72 million or 59% of women aged 16 years or older were labor force participants (working or looking for work; U.S. Department of Labor, Women's Bureau 2011). Women dominated secretarial, nursing, teaching, and retail sales occupations during that year (U.S. Department of Labor, Women's Bureau 2011). In 2010, for the first time in U.S. history, women outnumbered men in the workplace (nonfarm jobs)—50.3% versus 49.7%. Legislation ensuring gender equality, along with increasing higher education enrollment among women, has improved women's value and participation in the labor market (Economist 2009).

Women in the Workforce, 1940

What Does It Mean to Me?

Just for one week, count the number of times you hand cash, a credit card, or a check to someone for payment. How many times do you hand it to a woman? Mary Frank Fox and Sharlene Hesse-Biber (1984) offered the following description for the typical working woman—a working mother who attended high school and has little or no college experience, working in a retail, clerical, or service occupation. View the current list of the 20 leading occupations for employed women at the U.S. Department of Labor's Women's Bureau website. Has "women's work" changed? Why or why not?

 STATE STATS

Table 9.2

Civilian Labor Force Participation Rates (%) for White, Black, and Hispanic Women, 1930–2020

	All Women	White Women	Black Women	Hispanic Women
1930	24.3	n.a.	n.a.	n.a.
1940	25.4	n.a.	n.a.	n.a.
1950	31.4	n.a.	n.a.	n.a.
1960	37.1	36.2	n.a.	n.a.
1970	41.6	42.6	49.5	n.a.
1980	51.5	51.2	53.1	47.4
1990	57.5	57.4	58.3	53.1
2000	59.9	59.5	63.1	57.5
2010	58.6	58.5	59.9	56.5
2020 Projected	57.1	56.9	57.9	56.1

Source: U.S. Bureau of Labor Statistics 2012b; U.S. Census Bureau 1951, 1960, 1966.

Note: n.a. = not available.

In Focus

Recession 101

"Living With Less: The Human Side of the Global Recession" is a website for readers of the *New York Times* to post their recession survival strategies. Strategies are organized by food, health, home, work, transportation, and other categories. Derek, from Highland Park, New Jersey, wrote, "A day in the (frugal) life: home exercise, home coffee, pack lunch, bike to the train, then walk to the office. Rinse. Repeat. Save." Jeanne from Florida reported, "Got local job, got Prius; let my renter's insurance lapse; gave up land line; gave up hair salon, manicures, pedicures, shop Goodwill." And Maria from Chile, South America, shared her simple strategy: "Enjoy things you can do, and forget the others."

National and international polls confirm how individuals and families are spending less on nonessentials, buying fewer items (online and in stores), and, in the process, shifting their priorities from products to activities (Cave 2010). "Doing more with less" is this recession's mantra. In 2009, attendance at movies, art and science museums, and public parks grew from the previous year. Families turned to fun and healthy outdoor activities, such as camping, hiking, canoeing, and biking. Igor Montoya, describing his family's weekend canoe trips, said, "I'm trying to teach the kids that you don't need to have expensive toys to have fun. You can make it fun, from anything" (Cave 2010:12).

Unemployment is challenging. Laid-off workers usually try to find work in their original career field, or some, like Natasha Case, decide it's time to try something new. Case, laid off from Walt Disney Imagineering, started a business selling homemade ice cream sandwiches with her friend Freya Estreller, a laid-off real estate developer. Lisa Traina was a party planner in New York City. After being laid off, Traina began volunteering at the Bowery Mission homeless shelter (Bosman 2009). Nonprofit organizations across the country report an increase in the number of professional and skilled volunteers, most unemployed due to the economy. Debi van Zyl was laid off from a small residential design firm in Los Angeles. She said, "You think you're in charge of your profession, and then the recession hits and you realize that your career is market driven. . . . My motto is don't say no to anything" (quoted in Shevory 2010:6).

What Does It Mean to Me?

What effect has the recession had on you, your spending, and your postgraduation plans?

Work and Occupation

The second workforce change has been the record numbers of elderly Americans returning to work. Since the mid-1980s, the labor force participation rates of older Americans have consistently increased (Toossi 2005). In 2007, 25.7 million Americans aged 55 or older were employed in the labor force, reflecting a 38.6% participation rate (Rix 2008). The percentage of Americans aged 55 years or older staying employed or going back to work after retirement is projected to increase by 2018, more than for any other age group (refer to Figure 9.1).

Although Americans are working longer partly because they are living longer, additional factors contribute to the increase in 55-plus employment. Government policies have eliminated mandatory retirements and outlawed age discrimination in the workplace. In 2000, older Americans were also encouraged to go back to work with the removal of age restrictions and taxes on their earned wages (Toossi 2005). Stung by the economic recession, older Americans are delaying their retirement, deciding that they should work longer.

Changing Job Market

The final workforce shift began with the latest immigration boom between 1996 and 2000 from Latin America and Asia (Mosisa 2002). The number of foreign-born workers rose from a low of 4.3 million in 1970, to 11.6 million in 1990, to 17.3 million in 2000. For 2011,

Figure 9.1

Projected Percentage Change in Number of Labor Force Participants by Age Group, 2008–2014

Source: Toossi 2009.

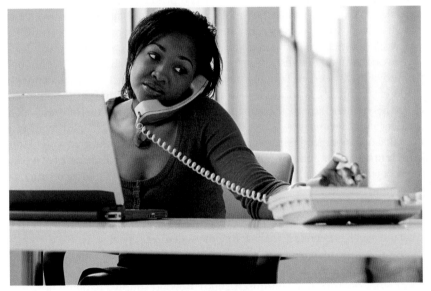

Photo 9.2

For the first time in U.S. history, women outnumber men in the workplace—50.3% versus 49.7%. The leading occupations for U.S. women continue to be in retail, administrative support, and service.

there were 24.4 million foreign workers in the United States, about 16% of the labor force (Newburger and Gryn 2009; U.S. Bureau of Labor Statistics 2012c). Foreign-born workers are more likely to be male, less educated, and younger (in their late 20s and early 30s) than native-born workers. More than 80% of the labor force increase among workers between 35 and 44 years of age can be attributed to the increase in foreign-born workers. Ronald Pollina (2003) predicted that, as our native population continues to age, the U.S. workforce will become increasingly dependent on foreign-born workers.

Foreign-born workers account for half or more of the increase in the job categories of administrative support, services, precision production, craft and repair, operators, fabricators, and laborers. Foreign-born workers are overrepresented in low-paying occupations that do not require a high school diploma. During 2011, about 40% of foreign workers lived in the West and the Northeast (U.S. Bureau of Labor Statistics 2012c). Immigrants settle in regions with perceived economic opportunities, seeking established ethnic enclaves providing interpersonal and job support (Mosisa 2002).

 Career Success

Sociological Perspectives on Work

Functionalist Perspective

According to the functionalist perspective, work serves specific functions in society. Our work provides us with some predictability about our life experiences. We can expect to begin paid employment around the age of 18 years or after high school graduation (or we could delay it for four or five more years by attending college and graduate school). Your work may determine when you get married, when you have your first child, and when you purchase your home. Work serves as an important social structure as we become stratified according to our occupations and our income. Finally, even for the most independent among us, the way we live depends on the work of thousands—for our food, clothing, safety, education, and health. Our lives are bound to the products and activities of the labor force (Hall 1994).

Recall that from this perspective, work can also produce a set of dysfunctions that can lead to social problems (or that may be problems themselves). Employers encourage workers to become involved with their work, hoping to increase their productivity as well as their quality of work (a function). However, getting too involved in one's work may lead to job stress, overwork, and job dissatisfaction for workers (all are dysfunctional). Although technology improves the speed and quality of work for some (a function), as machines replace human laborers, technology can also lead to job and wage losses (dysfunctions).

Job Satisfaction

As some researchers have focused on the functions and dysfunctions of work, others have tried to understand the nature of work itself. Frederick W. Taylor, a mechanical engineer, offered an analysis that revolutionized nineteenth- and twentieth-century industrial work. Using what he called **scientific management**, Taylor broke down the functional elements of work, identifying the most efficient, fastest, best way to complete a task. In one of his first research projects, Taylor determined the best shovel design for shoveling coal. He believed that with the right tools and the perfect system, any worker could improve his or her work productivity, all for the benefit of the company. In his book *The Principles of Scientific Management,* Taylor (1911) wrote, "In the past the man has been first; in the future the system must be first" (p. 5).

Although scientific management in its pure form has rarely been implemented, Taylor's principles continue to serve as the foundation for modern management ideology and technologies of work organization (Bahnisch 2000). Beyond simply changing how work was organized, Taylor offered his ideas about the organization of work: the need for defining a clear authority structure, separating planning from operational groups, providing bonuses for workers, and insisting on task specialization. In contrast, Max Weber ([1925] 1978) warned that in exchange for the efficiency and predictability of bureaucracy, workers would lose their individual freedom, ultimately dehumanizing their labor. Indeed, Taylor's model shifted power to management, forcing skilled workers to give up control of their own work (Hirschhorn 1984), which was a cause for concern expressed by theorists from the next theoretical perspective.

Conflict Perspective

Power, explained Karl Marx, is determined according to one's relationship to the means of production. Owners of the means of production possess all the power in the system, he believed, with little (probably nothing) left for workers. As workers labor only to make products and profits for owners, workers' energies are consumed in the production of things over which they have no real power, control, or ownership (Zeitlin 1997). According to Marx, man's labor becomes a means to an end; we work only to earn money. Marx predicted that eventually we would become alienated or separated from our labor, from what we produce, from our fellow workers, and from our human potential. Instead of work providing a transformation and fulfillment of our human potential, work would become the place where we felt least human (Ritzer 2000).

Modern systems of work continue to erode workers' power over their labor. Deskilling refers to the systematic reconstruction of jobs so that they require fewer skills and, ultimately, management can have more control over workers (Hall 1994). Although Taylor (1911) proposed scientific management as a means to improve production, sociologist Harry Braverman (1974) argued that by altering production systems, capitalists and management increase their control over workers. Once dependent on the workers' abilities, the nature of work shifts to managerial priorities. Management, according to Braverman (1974), "controls each step of the labor process and its mode of execution" (p. 119). Workers lose their power when their skilled labor is taken away.

Although Marx predicted that capitalism would disappear, capitalism has grown stronger, and at the same time, the social and economic inequalities in U.S. society have increased. Capitalism has become more than just an economic system; it is an entire political, cultural, and social order (Parenti 1988). Modern capitalism includes the rise and domination of corporations, large business enterprises with U.S. and global interests. Conflict theorists argue that capitalist and corporate leaders maintain their power and economic advantage at the expense of their workers and the general public.

 Enron

In the 1990s and early 2000s, energy trader Enron was the epitome of corporate power and success. The company bought and sold natural gas, power facilities, telecommunications, and other energy-related businesses. In 2000, Enron operated in 30 countries, employing 18,000 women and men (Enron Corporation 2000). *Fortune* magazine named Enron as the "Most Innovative Company in America" for six consecutive years (Enron Corporation 2001), and it was reportedly worth $70 billion at its peak (National Public Radio 2003). A great company to work for, a powerful and successful company, Enron was unstoppable—or was it?

Through a complex web of tax-sheltering partnerships, Enron hid millions of dollars in debts and company losses. Enron's accounting firm, Arthur Andersen, was a partner in the deception and was later convicted of obstruction of justice in the government's investigation. The company's losses were first made public in October 2001, when the Securities and Exchange Commission launched a formal investigation into the company's dealings (Fowler 2001). On December 2, 2001, Enron declared bankruptcy, the largest in U.S. history. Enron executives, including Chairman Kenneth Lay, left the company in disgrace.

Enron's employees lost their jobs and more than $1 billion in pension holdings. Several class action lawsuits have been filed against Enron executives, directors, and consultants, alleging that they knew about Enron's financial troubles but chose not to inform its employees or stockholders. Enron was not the only company involved in erroneous claims. In the 1990s, more than 700 companies were forced to correct misleading financial statements as a result of accounting failures or fraud (*Frontline* 2002). According to Lynn Turner, chief accountant of the Securities and Exchange Commission from 1998 to 2001 (*Frontline* 2002), Enron's demise is a symptom of something larger in our economic system:

> It's beyond Enron. . . . It's embedded in the system at this time. . . . There's been a change in culture that arose out of the go-go times of the 1990s. Some people call it greed. But I think it is an issue where we got a lot of financial conflicts built into the system, and people forgot, quite frankly, about the investors.

Feminist Perspective

From a feminist perspective, work is a gendered institution. Through the actions, beliefs, and interactions of workers and their employers, as well as the policies and practices of the workplace (Reskin and Padavic 1994), men's and women's identities as workers are created, reproduced, and then solidified in the everyday routines of informal work groups and formal workers' organizations (Brenner 1998). We already discussed the importance of World War II for women's employment; but recall that after the war, there was pressure on women to resume their roles as housewives or to assume more appropriate occupations. As a gendered institution, work defined the roles appropriate for World War II women and defines them for women today. The workplace does not treat women and men equally. Women are concentrated in different—and lower-ranking—occupations than men, and women are paid less than men (Reskin and Padavic 1994).

A fundamental feature of work is the gendered division of labor, the assignment of different tasks and work to men and women. This division of labor leads to a devaluing of female workers and their work, providing some justification for the differential compensation between men and women (Reskin and Padavic 1994). In the United States, as in most other countries, women earn less than men (England and Browne 1992). There is no country in the world where women make the same as or more than men (refer to Figure 9.2). In the early 1960s, U.S. women earned about 59 cents for every dollar earned by men (Armas 2004). By 2010, for every dollar a man earned, a woman made 77.4 cents (National Committee on Pay Equity 2011). (Refer to Table 9.3 for a comparison of women's median weekly earnings by race, for 2010.)

Ethical Blind Spots

In pay, compared with men, women are disadvantaged because they are in lower-paying feminized jobs or because they are paid less for the same work (Budig 2002). Sociologists and feminist scholars insist that no natural differences between men and women would lead to this. Instead, these researchers offer several structural explanations for the differences: differential socialization (women are socialized to pursue careers that traditionally pay less or are lower in status), differential training (men are better educated, so should be rewarded with higher pay), and workplace discrimination (Reskin and Padavic 1994). For additional discussion of these perspectives, refer to Chapter 4, "Gender."

One workplace problem feminist advocates and scholars have focused on involves exclusionary and discriminatory practices in the global field of information technologies (IT) (Rosser 2005). The IT workforce represents a vertically and horizontally gender-stratified labor market. Women are concentrated in the lowest paid positions—performing the tedious,

Figure 9.2

Women's Earnings as a Percentage of Men's Earnings, in U.S. Dollars, 2003

Source: UNICEF 2007.

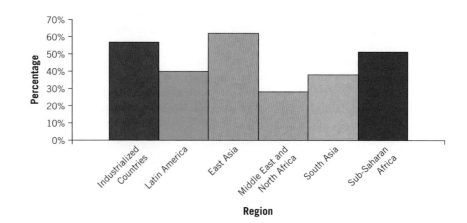

Table 9.3

2010 Median Weekly Earnings for All Full-Time Wage and Salary Workers

Women:	$669		
Men:	$824		
White women:	$684	Black women:	$592
White men:	$850	Black men:	$633
Hispanic women:	$508	Asian women:	$773
Hispanic men:	$560	Asian men:	$936

Source: U.S. Department of Labor, Women's Bureau 2011.

hands-on, eye-straining work of making hardware and software products on assembly lines. Their work is dangerous and menial, and it offers little economic or geographic mobility. Women of color are disproportionately represented in these jobs in China, India, Mexico, and Taiwan. Conversely, men dominate the IT field in positions with more creative and financial control, as venture capitalists, computer scientists, and engineers. Men are economically rewarded for their positions of power in the industry.

What Does It Mean to Me?

As recently as 1996, there was only one female CEO of a Fortune 500 company. In 2011, there were 12 female CEOs, 2.5% of all Fortune 500 CEOs. From a sociological perspective, why aren't there more women CEOs? Are women less qualified to lead a major corporation? What would it take to increase the number of female CEOs?

Interactionist Perspective

The sociologies of work and symbolic interaction were developed side by side in the 1920s and 1930s at the University of Chicago. There are strong similarities between the two sociological perspectives: In the same way that symbolic interactionists are interested in how individuals negotiate their social order, the sociologists of work are interested in the negotiated order of work (Ritzer 1989). Interactionists address norms in the workplace, how workers interact with their peers, how workers deal with stress, and how workers find meaning in the work they do. This perspective allows us to understand the process by which individuals understand, interpret, and create their work.

For example, Geraldine Byrne and Robert Heyman (1997) interviewed nurses in the United Kingdom, investigating the relationship between their perceptions of work and patients and how it influenced their communication with patients. The researchers noted how nurses distinguished their work with "major trauma" and "minor" patients. They defined their work as more valuable and satisfying in trauma cases, giving them an opportunity to feel technically expert and rewardingly useful. Their time with minor patients was described as boring or repetitive and a small part of their daily work. Although nurses felt that all patients experience some anxiety in the hospital, they felt that those with more serious illnesses or injuries would be more anxious than others. As a result, they spent more time with the seriously ill or injured patients, but they made sure to "pop in" with all patients as a way of demonstrating that they had not forgotten about them and providing some nursing contact.

According to symbolic interactionists, we attach labels and meanings to an individual's work (and major). If you meet a fellow student for the first time, one of the first questions you may ask is "What's your major?" Why ask about a major? Think of it as a shortcut for who you are. Based simply on whether you are a sociology major or a physics major, people make assumptions about how much you study or your academic quality. This is no different from asking someone what he or she does for a living. These social constructs create an order to our work and our lives, but they can also create social problems.

Problems arise when these social constructs serve as the basis of job discrimination. A study by researchers from the University of Chicago and Massachusetts Institute of Technology revealed discrimination in the recruiting process based only on what was perceived about someone's first name (Bertrand and Mullainathan 2003). Researchers sent 5,000 résumés in response to job advertisements in the *Boston Globe* and *Chicago Tribune*. First names were selected based on a review of local birth certificates. Fictional applicants with "White" first names—Neil, Brett, Emily, and Jill—received one callback for every 10 résumés mailed out. In contrast, equivalent "Black" applicants—with names such as Aisha, Rasheed, Kareem, and Tamika—received one response for every 15 résumés sent. Other aspects of discrimination were revealed in the study. If the résumé indicated that the applicant lived in a wealthier, more educated, or more-White neighborhood, the rate of callbacks increased. This effect did not vary by race.

Though employers report positive attitudes toward people with disabilities, actual hiring rates reveal an opposite trend. Since 1986, the jobless rate of people with disabilities has been around 66%. Researchers have attributed the persistence of stigma regarding the disabled and the negative impact on hiring them to a variety of reasons. For many, disability is associated with low or no ability, poor performance, or unsafe work behavior (Rubin and Roessler 2008). Employers are also concerned about the perceived costs of accommodations and the possibility of other workers demanding special consideration themselves (Schur, Kruse, and Blanck 2005). The stigma attached to disability is compounded by other personal characteristics such as age, race or ethnicity, or gender; these individuals are doubly disadvantaged in the workplace (McMahon et al. 2008). See Table 9.4 for a summary of all perspectives.

Problems in Work and the Economy

Unemployment and Underemployment

According to the U.S. Bureau of Labor Statistics (2010), about 154.7 million Americans were employed and 12.7 million were unemployed in March 2012. Compared with the unemployment rate of Whites, 7.3%, the rate was 14.0% for African Americans and 10.3% for Hispanics or Latinos. Nearly 5.2 million individuals were long-term unemployed or unemployed for 27 weeks or more (U.S. Bureau of Labor Statistics 2012a).

This recession has been characterized as a man's recession or a "man-cession." Since 2008, the U.S. unemployment rate for men has increased more steeply than the rate for

Table 9.4

Summary of Sociological Perspectives: Work and the Economy

	Functional	Conflict/Feminist	Interactionist
Explanation of work and the economy and its social problems	Sociologists use this perspective to examine the functions and dysfunctions of work and employment. Functionalists also analyze the functional elements of work itself.	Conflict or feminist theorists focus on how economic, ethnic, and gender inequalities are perpetuated in the economy and the workplace.	From this perspective, sociologists investigate how our work experiences are created through interaction and shared meanings. Social problems emerge from the meanings we associate with our work.
Questions asked about work and the economy	How does the institution of work help preserve the social order? How is economic and social stability maintained by the institution of work? How do other institutions affect our work or our economy?	What social inequalities are present in the institution of work? How do we become alienated from our work?	How is our work and workplace socially defined? How do we behave based on our meaning of work? Are there positive and negative meanings of work?

women, due largely to layoffs in manufacturing and construction, where men made up roughly 70% and 85% of the workforce, respectively (Cook 2009). On the other hand, women are concentrated in occupations that are more resistant to the economic decline, such as health, education, and public service. Health care employment has been among the strongest in this recession (Rampell 2010). As of March 2012, 8.3% of men aged 16 or older were unemployed compared with 8.1% of women in the same age group (U.S. Bureau of Labor Statistics 2012a). Comparative unemployment data for men and women are presented in Table 9.5, highlighting the higher rates of unemployment for men.

Table 9.5

Unemployment Rates for Men and Women, by World and Regions

	Men (%)	Women (%)
World	4.9	3.6
Developed Economies and European Union (EU)	5.6	4.6
Central and Southeastern Europe (non-EU) and Commonwealth of Independent States	7.3	5.0
East Asia	4.0	2.5
Southeast Asia and the Pacific	4.5	3.4
South Asia	3.9	2.3
Latin America and the Caribbean	5.5	5.2
Middle East	5.8	3.8
North Africa	6.6	4.3
Sub-Saharan Africa	6.3	5.5

Source: International Labour Office 2010.

During and after the Great Recession, the unemployment rate for young adults has been a concern in the United States and globally. In the United States, the unemployment for all four-year college graduates is 4.5%; however, the unemployment rate for recent four-year graduates is higher at 6.8% and for recent high school graduates is nearly 24% (Carnevale, Jayasundera, and Cheah 2012). A college degree has been described as "the best umbrella in this historic economic storm and the best preparation for the economy that is emerging in recovery" (Carnevale et al. 2012:1). For Europeans 15 to 24 years of age (level of education not identified), the rate of unemployment was 21.6% in 2011 (Eurostat 2012).

Underemployment

In addition to unemployment, we should be aware of another rate, underemployment. **Underemployment** is defined as the number of employed individuals who are working in a job that underpays them, is not equal to their skill level, or involves fewer working hours than they would prefer (taking a part-time job when a full-time job is not available). In March 2012, the number of people working part-time because of cutbacks or because they were unable to find a full-time job was 7.7 million (U.S. Bureau of Labor Statistics 2012a).

There is significant variation in unemployment and underemployment rates. People who are young, non-college-educated, and members of ethnic/racial minorities have higher underemployment rates (Bernstein 1997). Minority group underemployment is significantly higher than underemployment among non-Hispanic Whites. Min Zhou (1993) reports at least 40% of the members of each minority group he analyzed (Puerto Ricans, Blacks, Mexicans, Cubans, Chinese, and Japanese) were underemployed. In particular, Blacks and Puerto Ricans have the highest rates of labor force nonparticipation (were not in the labor force and had not worked in the last two years) and joblessness. Joblessness includes subemployment (individuals who were not in the labor force but worked within the last two years) and underemployment rates (based on either low wage or occupational mismatch). Recent immigrants, a large portion of the Asian and Hispanic minority groups, may have difficulty in securing employment because of lack of job skills or language proficiency and, as a result, are more likely underemployed than are native-born and non-Hispanic White workers (DeJong and Madamba 2001).

Scholars have documented the destructive effects of joblessness on overall health (Rodriguez 2001) and emotional well-being (Darity 2003). Unemployment has been consistently linked with higher levels of alienation, anxiety, and depression (Rodriguez 2001) and a lower sense of overall health (Darity 2003). Cross-national data reveal how long periods of unemployment are related to increased rates of suicide and spousal abuse (Darity 2003). Among Blacks and non-Hispanic Whites, long-term exposure to unemployment produces a "scarred worker effect." The experience of unemployment undermines the worker's will to perform, leading that person to become less productive and less employable in the future (Rodriguez 2001).

The Problem of Globalization

Globalization, introduced in Chapter 1, is a process whereby goods, information, people, communication, and forms of culture move across national boundaries. Though we tend to think of globalization as an economic phenomenon, we should not lose sight of its political, social, and cultural implications (Eitzen and Zinn 2006).

Globalization has transformed the nature of economic activity (Eitzen and Zinn 2006). It has been credited with bringing the world together—creating a world market where all businesses, employers, and employees must compete. This competition keeps corporations focused on innovation, quality, and production. Increasing productivity and output creates more jobs and stimulates economic growth (Weidenbaum 2006), creating a new middle class and reducing poverty in many countries (Yergin 2006). The United States has benefited from globalization, experiencing a doubling in foreign trade during the 1990s, which led to the creation of more than 17 million new jobs (Yergin 2006).

Yet, globalization has its dark side (Weidenbaum 2006). Foremost, worker security has declined everywhere, including in the United States. Skilled workers are threatened by the unfair competition of low-cost sweatshops, of cheaper labor to be found in other nations. More than 3 million U.S. manufacturing jobs were lost from 2001 to 2004 (Dobbs 2004). These high-paying jobs ($16 per hour) migrated to other countries, in a process characterized as the "race to the bottom." Corporations are moving to lower-wage economies, shifting their production from the United States to Mexico to China (where the average manufacturing wage is 61 cents per hour) (Eitzen and Zinn 2006).

There are conflicting assessments on the relationship between globalization and poverty. Some highlight how progress in poverty reduction has been limited and geographically isolated (Weller and Hersh 2006). Others conclude that globalization has reduced global poverty (pointing to the overall reduction of the number of poor according to the World Bank standard, discussed in Chapter 2), while also warning about the threat from the persistent inequality between rich and poor countries. Developed (rich) countries are able to reap more economic benefits from less developed (poor) countries through the system of globalization (Shin 2009).

Women are particularly vulnerable in the new global economy. The global assembly line is filled with girls and women engaged in work that is low-wage, temporary, part-time, or home-based and usually performed under unsafe working conditions. More than half the world's legal and illegal immigrants are women—Third World women moving to postindustrial societies for jobs as nannies, maids, and sex workers (Eitzen and Zinn 2006).

Contingent or Temporary Workers

Contributing to the increase in unemployment and underemployment is the use of **contingent workers**. A contingent workforce is composed of full-time or part-time temporary workers who do not expect their jobs to last. There were about 5.7 million contingent workers in 2005 (U.S. Bureau of Labor Statistics 2005), with more than half (55%) reporting that they would have preferred to have a permanent job.

 Contingent Work

Companies rely on temporary workers to handle short-term projects and work overloads or to fill in for employees who are vacationing, sick, or on family leave (Saftner 1998). Companies have also used temporary workers to eliminate positions and to reduce costs (Davidson 1999). Overall, temp workers are less likely to have health insurance or pension coverage. In addition, they are not covered by health and safety regulations and may not be qualified for workers' compensation if injured on the job (Davidson 1999). Many temps feel like second-class corporate citizens (Eisenberg 1999).

 Outsourcing

The term **outsourcing** refers to a practice by businesses of hiring external contractors to do the jobs that a regular work staff once completed. One common task that is outsourced is accounting. In the past, businesses would have an in-house accountant, someone who did the books and took care of accounts receivable or payable. But businesses began to contract with external accountants or accounting firms to handle their accounts. By paying accountants as contract workers, companies avoid providing them with employee or medical benefits. In fall 2009, Hyatt Hotels made a controversial decision to lay off 98 members of its housekeeping staff at three of its hotels in Boston, replacing them with subcontracted workers at half the wage level ($14–$16 vs. $8 per hour). Hyatt management said the decision was based on economic challenges facing the company and described the layoffs as a major cost-cutting strategy.

U.S. companies also outsource internationally, a strategy referred to as **offshore outsourcing** or **offshoring**. By 2015, more than 3.3 million U.S. jobs will have been sent overseas, about 2.5% of the total U.S. employment. European companies, motivated by their own need to reduce costs, are also practicing offshoring, sending work to China and parts of Central and Eastern Europe. It has been estimated that more than a million EU jobs will be sent outside of Europe by 2015 (Parker 2004).

India, with its large number of English-speaking college graduates, is expected to receive more than half of the U.S. and European jobs. Indian labor is used for what is referred to as "back office" work—call center support, research and development, tax return preparation, health insurance claim processing, and medical transcription (Waldman 2003)—usually at wages substantially lower than their U.S. counterparts receive. In 2005, Indian outsourcing businesses generated more than $17.7 billion in software and IT services exports (King 2006). Back office locations have sprung up in China, Morocco, Brazil, Chile, and Mexico—some established by the same Indian outsource companies who started it all.

But offshore outsourcing isn't the perfect solution. Employees in India work 10- to 12-hour night shifts to be at their desks at the same time as colleagues in the United States (India is 10.5 hours ahead of U.S. Eastern Standard Time). Doctors in India report high levels of substance abuse and relationship breakups among outsourcing workers. India's outsourcing industry has a rate of 60% employee turnover per year (Thottam 2004).

Photo 9.3

By 2015, more than 3.3 million U.S. jobs will be sent overseas, about 2.5% of the total U.S. employment. India is expected to receive most of the U.S. jobs, characterized as "back office" work, which includes call center support, processing and transcription, and research and development.

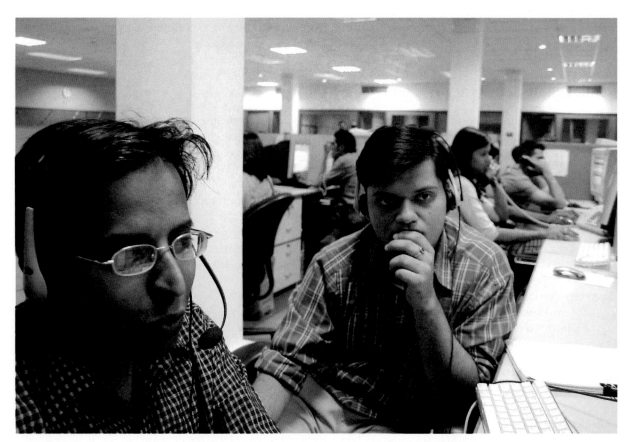

A Livable Wage

One way the United States addresses inequality is through the federal minimum wage. A three-step wage increase was passed by Congress in 2007, when the minimum hourly wage was $5.15. The current federal minimum wage is $7.25. However, when adjusted for inflation, the current federal minimum is still less than the minimum wage from 1961 to 1981 (Filion 2009). Eighteen states have a minimum wage above the federal minimum (refer to U.S. Data Map 9.1).

While the minimum wage raises the wages of low-income workers in general, many low-income families continue to move in and out of poverty. Data indicate that low-wage

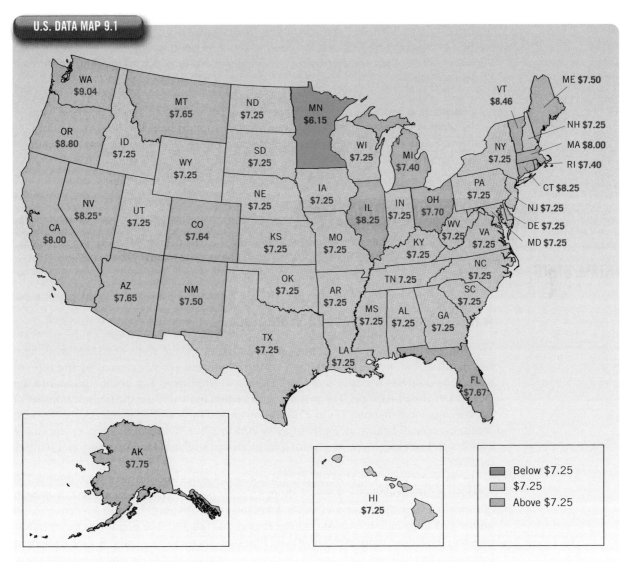

U.S. DATA MAP 9.1

WA $9.04
MT $7.65
ND $7.25
MN $6.15
ME $7.50
VT $8.46
NH $7.25
MA $8.00
RI $7.40
CT $8.25
NY $7.25
OR $8.80
ID $7.25
SD $7.25
WI $7.25
MI $7.40
PA $7.25
NJ $7.25
DE $7.25
MD $7.25
WY $7.25
NE $7.25
IA $7.25
OH $7.70
WV $7.25
VA $7.25
NV $8.25*
UT $7.25
CO $7.64
IL $8.25
IN $7.25
KY $7.25
NC $7.25
CA $8.00
KS $7.25
MO $7.25
TN 7.25
SC $7.25
AZ $7.65
NM $7.50
OK $7.25
AR $7.25
MS $7.25
AL $7.25
GA $7.25
TX $7.25
LA $7.25
FL $7.67

AK $7.75

HI $7.25

Legend:
- Below $7.25
- $7.25
- Above $7.25

Minimum Hourly Wage by State, 2012

Source: Labor Law Center 2012.

*only when the employer does not provide health insurance; otherwise $7.25

or poverty-level workers are likely to be minority, female, non-college-educated, and nonunion, working in low-end sales and service occupations (Bernstein 1997; Bernstein, Hartmann, and Schmitt 1999; Mishel, Bernstein, and Shierholz 2009; U.S. Department of Labor 2002).

American Dream

In her 2001 book, *Nickel and Dimed: On (Not) Getting By in America,* Barbara Ehrenreich explored life and work on minimum wage in three states: Florida, Maine, and Minnesota. Working as a hotel maid, a nursing home aide, a sales clerk, a waitress, and a cleaning woman, Ehrenreich rated her work performance as a B or maybe even a B+. In each new job, Ehrenreich had to master new terms, new skills, and new tools (and not as quickly as she thought she would be able to master them). How did Ehrenreich survive on minimum wage? She discovered that she needed to work two jobs or seven days a week to achieve a "decent fit" between her income and her expenses. She describes getting her meals down to a "science": chopped meat, beans, cheese, and noodles when she had a kitchen in which to cook; if not, fast food at about $9 per day. For housing, she shuffled between motel rooms and apartments, moving to a trailer park at one point. Ehrenreich (2001) concluded,

Low-Wage Workers

> Something is wrong, very wrong, when a single person in good health, a person who in addition possesses a working car, can barely support herself by the sweat of her brow. You don't need a degree in economics to see that wages are too low and rents too high. (p. 199)

What Does It Mean to Me?

Refer to the rankings on state minimum wage rates in U.S. Data Map 9.1 on page 241. In your state, what is the minimum wage rate? Does that seem like a livable wage to you? Why or why not?

A Hazardous and Stressful Workplace

According to the U.S. Bureau of Labor Statistics (2012d), there were 4,690 fatal work injuries in 2010. The majority of fatalities occurred in men, mostly caused by the type of work they do. Data for 2010 include incidents at the Upper Big Branch mine and the Deepwater Horizon oil rig. The private construction industry had the highest number of fatal occupational injuries, 774 in 2010. Highway or transportation incidents are the most common cause of fatal work injuries (about 20% in 2010). Workplace violence—including assaults and suicides—accounted for 17% of all work-related fatal occupational injuries in 2010.

In the same year, a total of 3.1 million nonfatal injuries and illnesses were reported in private industry workplaces, a rate of about 3.5 cases per 100 full-time workers (U.S. Bureau of Labor Statistics 2011). Approximately 2.9 million were injuries, the most occurring in the service-providing industries (trade, transportation, and utilities). The goods-producing industries had the largest share of occupational illnesses, about 36.3%. The U.S. Department of Labor monitors illnesses such as skin diseases, respiratory conditions, and poisonings. New reported workplace illnesses were related directly to work activity, such as contact dermatitis or carpal tunnel syndrome. Some conditions, such as long-term illnesses related to exposure to carcinogens, are usually underreported and not adequately recognized (U.S. Bureau of Labor Statistics 2009b).

Taking a World View

Mexico's Maquiladoras

Maquiladoras are textile, electronics, furniture, chemical, processed food, or machinery assembly factories where workers assemble imported materials for export (Abell 1999; Lindquist 2001). The maquiladora program allows imported U.S. materials to enter Mexico without tariffs; when the finished goods are sent back to the United States, the shipper pays duties only on the value added by the manufacturer in Mexico (Abell 1999; Gruben 2001). The program began in 1965 as an employment alternative for Mexican agricultural workers. Drawn to Mexico because of its proximity to U.S. borders and by low labor costs, nearly every large U.S. manufacturer has a maquiladora location. Several Asian and European companies including Sony, Sanyo, Samsung, Hitachi, and Philips also have maquiladora locations (Lindquist 2001). There are an estimated 5,000 export manufacturers along Mexico's border with the United States, employing over 1.3 million workers (Bacon 2011).

The maquiladora program became controversial as soon as it appeared (Gruben 2001). Supporters of the maquiladora program argue that if these plants had not located in Mexico, they would have gone to other low-wage countries. Opponents argue that the program helped U.S. firms and others take advantage of the low-wage Mexican labor force. The maquiladoras have been criticized for their treatment of female workers, dangerous work conditions, and impact on the physical and social environment of border towns.

Most maquiladora workers are women. Yolanda is a worker from Piedras Negras.

As the sun rises, Yolanda is already awake and working—carrying water from a nearby well, cooking breakfast over an open fire, and cleaning the one-room home that she and her husband built out of cardboard, wood, and tin. She puts on her blue company jacket and boards the school bus that will take her and her neighbors across Piedras Negras to a large assembly plant. Yolanda and 800 co-workers each earn US $25–35 a week for 48 hours' work, sewing clothing for a New York-based corporation that subcontracts for Eddie Bauer, Joe Boxer, and other U.S. brands. These wages will buy less than half of their families' basic needs. (Abell 1999:595)

Yolanda's job provides a wage, but it is not adequate to support her or her family. The daily salary for maquiladora women is about $4.67, described not as a standard of living but, rather, as a standard for survival (Moffatt 2005). According to Elizabeth Fussell (2000), early maquiladora factories attracted the "elite" of the Mexican female labor force: young, childless, educated women. Current maquiladora laborers are likely to be the least-skilled Mexican women: slightly older, poorly educated women with young children (Fussell 2000).

Yolanda's town of Piedras Negras is no different from other maquiladora towns such as Tijuana and Matamoros. Once-quaint border towns have been transformed by maquiladora activity. Despite their profits, companies do not invest in the physical and social infrastructure of these border towns. As a result, most factory neighborhoods lack basic health and public services such as clean drinking water or sewage systems, electricity, schools, health facilities, and adequate housing (Abell 1999).

Sexual harassment is often used as a method of intimidation in the maquiladora. Supervisors taunt female workers and proposition them by offering lighter workloads in exchange for dates and sexual favors. Supervisors have also sexually assaulted female workers. Women, on and off their jobs, are subject to intimidation and violence. For example, since 1993 in the town of Ciudad Juárez, approximately 300 women have been found murdered. Although it is unclear how many of these women were maquiladora workers, all of them have been identified as victims of an unsafe environment, easy targets for serial killers, drug traffickers, and even police officials (Moffatt 2005).

Under the 1994 North American Free Trade Agreement (NAFTA), tariff breaks formerly limited to all imported parts, supplies, and equipment used by Mexican maquiladoras now also apply to manufacturers in Canada and the United States (Lindquist 2001). During the recent national debate about immigration, NAFTA and the maquiladora program were blamed for failing to improve Mexico's economic and business infrastructure and thus failing to reduce illegal immigration in the United States.

In 2009, Monica Gonzalez Greer was appointed the first woman president of the Mexican National Maquiladora Association. Greer's organization represents 1.3 million employees working in 5,000 Mexican firms.

The 2010 explosions at the Upper Big Branch Mine in West Virginia and the *Deepwater Horizon* oil platform in the Mississippi River delta heightened concerns about the safety of industrial workers. In West Virginia, 29 were killed in an explosion in the country's worst mine disaster in 40 years. These incidents led to an ongoing reevaluation of mine regulation, employee training, and safety and the development of emergency response teams, along with improvements in underground communications technology. Coal mining is an inherently dangerous occupation with deaths and injuries documented worldwide. China and Russia have the largest number of coal mine fatalities annually. The *Deepwater Horizon* explosion resulted in the deaths of 11 operators and is the largest marine oil spill in U.S. history.

The National Institute for Occupational Safety and Health (NIOSH) (2003) defines job stress as the harmful emotional or physical response that occurs when a job's characteristics do not match the capabilities, resources, or needs of the worker. Certain job conditions are likely to lead to job stress: a heavy workload, little sense of worker control, a poor social environment, uncertain job expectations, or job insecurity. Eventually, job stress can lead to illness, injury, or job failure. Studies have analyzed the impact of stress on our physical health, noting the relationship of stress to sleep disturbances, ulcers, headaches, or strained relationships with family or friends. Recent evidence suggests that stress also plays a role in chronic diseases such as cardiovascular disease, musculoskeletal disorders, and psychological disorders (NIOSH 2003).

Discrimination at the Workplace

The Equal Employment Opportunity Commission (EEOC) was established in 1964 by Title VII of the Civil Rights Act. The EEOC monitors and enforces several federal statutes regarding employment discrimination. Under Title VII of the Civil Rights Act of 1964, employment discrimination based on race, religion, sex, or national origin is prohibited. Discrimination based on age was added to the prohibited activities in 1967 with the passage of the Age Discrimination in Employment Act, and employment discrimination against individuals with disabilities was prohibited in Title I and Title V of the Americans with Disabilities Act of 1990. Under current federal law, discrimination based on sexual orientation is not prohibited. The EEOC (2012) has received between 95,000 and 99,000 charges annually since 2008.

 Disabilities

Of the 99,000 cases that were filed during 2011, about 12% were based on national origin discrimination. Cases in this category and those involving religious discrimination increased after September 11, 2001, whereas discrimination charges based on race and sex declined slightly (McDonough 2003). According to EEOC spokesman David Grinberg, "Most people think about race and gender discrimination—national origin discrimination doesn't come to mind, but it's having a greater impact on the workplace" (McDonough 2003). Under this category, discrimination based on birthplace, ancestry, culture, or linguistic characteristics shared by a specific ethnic group is unlawful. Many incidents of national origin discrimination may still be unreported because of fear of retaliation or lack of awareness about EEOC laws.

Sweatshop Labor

 Sweatshops

According to Sweatshop Watch (2003), there is no legal definition of a "sweatshop." The GAO (1994) defines a sweatshop as a workplace that violates more than one federal or state labor law. The term has come to include exploitation of workers, for example, with no livable wages or benefits, poor and hazardous working conditions, and possible verbal or physical abuse (Sweatshop Watch 2003); employers who fail to treat workers with dignity and violate basic human rights (Co-Op America 2003); and businesses that violate wage or child labor laws and safety or health regulations (Foo 1994). The term **sweatshop** was first used in the nineteenth century to describe a subcontracting system in which the contractors earned profits from the margin between the amount they received for a contract and the amount paid to their workers. The margin was "sweated" from the workers because they received minimal wages for long hours in unsafe working conditions (Sweatshop Watch 2003).

Jill Esbenshade (2008) describes the networks of production that promote sweatshops and labor exploitation. She identifies how a single company, like the Gap or Levi's, relies on manufacturing in dozens of countries on four or five continents supported by an extensive competitive network of agents, factories, and small subcontractors. This type of production arrangement severs the legal liability of the brand-name companies from the workers who make their products. For example, in 2012, Apple was scrutinized for poor working conditions among iPad production workers in China. Esbenshade (2008) explains, "For garment workers this means they have little leverage in the production system, and in general have not been able to successfully organize to change their conditions. Garment factories, with little capital investment, close down and more on when confronted with an organized and demanding labor force" (p. 457). Clothing and other lightly manufactured products sold in the United States are made in more than 100 countries (International Labor Rights Forum 2011).

All U.S. manufacturers must follow the Fair Labor Standards Act (FLSA), which establishes federal minimum wage, overtime, child labor, and industrial homework standards. The Department of Labor's Wage and Hour Division makes routine enforcement sweeps in major garment centers, fining businesses that are in violation of the FLSA. Globally, antisweatshop activists have increased regulatory and monitoring systems in producing countries and have pressured contractors to improve working conditions and to recognize unions (Esbenshade 2008).

Photo 9.4

A California garment factory worker wears a face guard to protect herself from dust while she sews. An estimated 7,439 apparel or textile businesses operated in the United States in 2011.

 Labor Unions

Community, Policy, and Social Action

Federal Policies

When President William Howard Taft signed Public Law 426-62 in March 1913, he created the U.S. Department of Labor. From the beginning, the department was intended to foster and promote the welfare of U.S. wage earners, to improve working conditions, and to advance opportunities for profitable employment. In its current mission statement, the department includes improving working conditions, advancing opportunities for profitable employment, protecting retirement and health care benefits, helping employers find workers, and strengthening fee collective bargaining as part of its charge. The department administers and enforces more than 180 federal laws that regulate workplace activities for about 10 million employers and 125 million workers.

Workers' Rights

In addition to the FLSA, the Department of Labor enforces several statutes applicable to most workplaces. It regulates the Employee Retirement Income Security Act (pension and welfare benefit plans), the Occupational Safety and Health Act (ensuring work and a workplace free from serious hazards), the Family and Medical Leave Act (granting eligible employees as many as 12 weeks of unpaid leave for family care or medical leave), and several acts that cover workers' compensation for illness, disability, or death resulting from work performance.

There have been two legislative responses to the labor market and income consequences of the recent recession. In 2009 the American Recovery and Reinvestment Act (ARRA) was signed into law. ARRA was a stimulus package that allowed for benefit increases and tax cuts for households, along with federal investments in infrastructure and technology. A second stimulus package, the Tax Relief, Unemployment Insurance Reauthorization, and Job Creation Act, was signed into law in 2010. This package extended temporary income and payroll tax cuts and provided additional funding for emergency unemployment compensation. The nation's long-term recovery after the recession was a primary focus of the 2012 presidential election.

Two labor issues continue to be debated in Congress. The first is raising the minimum wage. In 2001, Senator Ted Kennedy of Massachusetts and Representative David Bonior of Michigan, both Democrats, introduced legislation that proposed a $1.50 raise in the minimum wage over three years. Efforts to increase the minimum wage are supported by unions and poverty organizations that argue that doing so will help the nation's working poor and low-income families. Opponents, who include members of the business community and the U.S. Chamber of Commerce, argue that increasing the minimum wage would put an unnecessary stress on medium-size and small businesses but would not decrease poverty. Some predict that businesses would be forced to eliminate jobs, reduce work hours, or close altogether. Results from policy analyses and academic research have not provided conclusive evidence for either argument (Information for Decision Making 2000). In 2007, the U.S. Congress passed legislation that would increase the minimum wage to $7.25 over two years. States, unwilling to wait for congressional action, have passed higher minimum wage laws during the past decade (Uchitelle 2006).

Maryland became the first state to require a living wage, effective October 2007. For 2011, Maryland employers with state contracts were required to pay workers a minimum of $12.49 an hour in the Baltimore-Washington areas and $9.39 an hour in rural counties (Maryland Department of Labor, Licensing and Regulation 2011).

The second issue involves protection against workplace discrimination based on sexual orientation. Several congressional actions provide protection against forms of discrimination: Title VII of the Civil Rights Act of 1964 (race, color, gender, national origin, or religion), the Age Discrimination in Employment Act (1967), the Vocational Rehabilitation Act (1973), and the Americans with Disabilities Act (1990). The Employment Non-Discrimination Act, which prohibits employment discrimination based on sexual orientation, has been introduced in every Congress (except the 109th) since 1994. The bill has yet to pass. Twenty-one states and the District of Columbia have passed laws prohibiting employment discrimination based on sexual orientation, and 16 states and Washington, D.C., also prohibit discrimination based on gender identity (Human Rights Campaign 2012).

Expanding Employment Opportunities for Women

In 1992, Congress passed the Nontraditional Employment for Women (NEW) Act to broaden the range of Job Training Partnership Act (JTPA) efforts on behalf of women (U.S. Department of Labor, Women's Bureau 2000). Also enacted in 1992 was the Women in Apprenticeship and Nontraditional Occupations (WANTO) Act, designed to provide technical assistance to employers and labor groups. Through both programs, the federal government has provided support to more than 20 state and 32 community-based initiatives to provide technical assistance to employers and labor organizations, to improve JTPA programs, to promote apprenticeships in nontraditional occupations, and to provide information through community workshops, seminars, and outreach. According to the U.S. Department of Labor, Women's Bureau (2000), almost 5,000 women participated in training or job placement programs, 30,000 women were reached through community programs, and 3,000 employers and labor groups were provided technical assistance through NEW and WANTO initiatives. Funding for WANTO ended in 2003.

Hard Hatted Women, based in Cleveland, Ohio, received a WANTO 2002–2003 grant to increase the employment of women in a variety of blue-collar jobs in building and manufacturing trades. With WANTO funding, the program provided technical assistance to employers and labor unions, on-site counseling for women, a job search networking club, and training (U.S. Department of Labor 2003). Hard Hatted Women continues as the only community non-profit organization dedicated to supporting women in high-wage, nontraditional, blue-collar careers. The program maintains two areas of focus: education and training and supporting economic equity policy initiatives. Between 1992 and 2005, in its Pre-Apprentice Training Program, Hard Hatted Women graduated 441 women, placing almost 60% of graduates in jobs (Hard Hatted Women 2006).

Funded by the Women's Foundation of California (a 501[c][3] private organization that funds community-based organizations), La Cocina is a nonprofit kitchen incubator for women entrepreneurs. La Cocina provides its commercial kitchen facilities to women, about half Latina, to produce specialty foods for their businesses. According to Valier Perez Ferreiro, participants are selected because "we are finding amazing entrepreneurs who are already cooking or have a product that is so promising that it deserves to be seen in the market and that we think has a chance for success" (Novak 2007:B4). For $10 per hour or less, women can use La Cocina's facilities and equipment. There are kitchen incubators throughout the United States, some based in such urban areas as Denver, New York City, and Minneapolis. La Cocina also provides training from local experts in business operations and management, banking, and food science. Jill Litwin brought her Peas of Mind line of organic foods to La Cocina, which introduced her to a buyer for Whole Foods Market. As of 2012, Litwin's company had developed three product lines and was represented in stores throughout the United States.

Worker-Friendly Businesses—Conducting Business a Different Way

Each year *Fortune* magazine releases a list of the "100 Best Companies to Work For." For 2007, the magazine wrote,

> Ten years ago, when we began compiling this list, the idea that your employer would deliver your groceries (a new perk at Microsoft) or allow you to do your laundry at work (Google) might have seemed crazy. . . . Indeed, much has changed in the American workplace over the past decade. (Levering and Moskowitz 2007:94)

No. 1 on Fortune's 2012 list was Google. This employer features 25 free gourmet cafeterias in its Mountain View, California, headquarters. But Google was named number one for more than its food. This business rewards its 32,000 employees with benefits that include competitive salaries and stock options, on-site laundry and dry-cleaning, outdoor and indoor recreational facilities, a community-supported fishery program, and a generous parental leave program (18 weeks for new mothers and 12 weeks for new fathers) (CNN Money 2012).

 Google

There is no big secret to creating worker-friendly organizations, although some organizations are slow to learn their values. Beyond the standard employee benefit package of vacations, health care, retirement plans, and life insurance, innovative employers have used dependent care, flexible work options, expanded leave time, and enhanced traditional benefits to attract and retain employees. As a result, these employers have reduced employee turnover, increased employee satisfaction, and improved worker productivity (Schmidt and Duenas 2002).

Voices in the Community

Judy Wicks

Judy Wicks

Businesses have also found a way to give back to their communities, to combine their work with their social activism. Judy Wicks accomplished this as the owner of Philadelphia's White Dog Café between 1983 and 2009. In an interview with Maryann Gorman (2001), Wicks examined how her business and activist philosophies merged at the White Dog.

A person could go to the White Dog Café just to eat. Many customers do—at least for the first time. . . . But many of the diners who come just for the food end up staying for the activism. Wicks tells of a salesman who sold the restaurant its insurance, then attended a Table Talk on the School of the Americas and became a regular at the annual protests held at the School. Wicks jokes, "I use food to lure innocent customers into social activism."

The Dog offers diners an array of learning experiences in lecture or hands-on formats as well as field trips to other countries. There are Table Talks on a variety of topics: the American war on drugs, the Supreme Court's decision in the 2000 election, racism. And the White Dog often organizes rides to rallies and marches, like the demonstrations against Clinton's impeachment that Jesse Jackson called for, the Million Mom March, Stand for Children and more. . . .

Wicks' White Dog venture began when she sensed the dissonance between her profession and her activism. Her energies drained by splitting her values into the commercial and nonprofit worlds, she sought a simpler solution, which first led her to managing someone else's restaurant. "I realized with the nonprofit and the for-profit that in order to really be effective, I needed to focus on one organization," Wicks says. "So I eventually abandoned the publishing work and focused on the restaurant. But it wasn't all my restaurant, and when I started experimenting with bringing my values to work, like having a breakfast for Salvadoran refugees, I had to part ways with my partner there. This idea of compartmentalizing your life, and having certain values in one area and other values in another, has never worked for me."

The first step, Wicks says, was simply to change her life so that she lived where she worked. "I think that society teach[es] us, 'Separate work from home; don't mix them together. That'll be too stressful.' And I've always worked against that." So the White Dog, located in a block of row houses near the University of Pennsylvania, became both her home and her business. "I'm kind of a holistic person," she says. "I live where I work. I live 'above the shop,' in the old-fashioned way of doing business." . . .

Not only does she not have to commute, . . . but she doesn't have to go food shopping or do the dishes. "But it's more than that," she says, "It's about energy and focus. And relationships. Being able to foster all these relationships."

The relationships she speaks of are those with her staff. One of the White Dog's missions is "Service to Each Other," an in-house goal of creating a tolerant and fair workplace. . . . Moving past standard business boundaries in this way has informed Wicks' creative development of the White Dog's missions. From encouraging her employees to re-create their job descriptions to fostering a sense of community among other Philadelphia restaurants, Wicks has shown that profitable businesses don't have to be stark-raving competitive.

In 2009, Wicks sold the White Dog Café to allow her to focus full-time on her social and humanitarian efforts. In 2001, Wicks cofounded the national organization Business Alliance for Local Living Economies. The organization brings together more than 22,000 independent U.S. and Canadian businesses to build economies that are community-based, green, and fair (Business Alliance for Local Living Economies 2012).

Log on to the Study Site, Chapter 9, at www.sagepub.com/leonguerrero4e for more information.

Source: Gorman, Maryann. 2001. "The White Dog's Tale" YES! Magazine, Spring 2001. Reprinted from YES! Magazine, Bainbridge Island, WA 98110. Subscriptions: 800/937-4451. Web: www.yesmagazine.org

Organized and Fighting Back

Historically, labor unions have served as bargaining agents for workers, fighting for fair wages, safe work environments, and benefits from employers. Many of the worker benefits advocated by early labor unions are now mandated through federal, state, or local labor laws. In our changing and global economy, unions cannot sustain themselves by simply negotiating pay, benefits, and working rights. To remain vital and relevant, unions need to develop multilevel strategies and use new skills (Lazes and Savage 2000). In 1983, the first year when union membership data were available, the rate of membership was 20.1%, accounting for 17.7 million union members. For 2011, the rate of membership was 11.8%, with a total of 14.8 million members (U.S. Bureau of Labor Statistics 2012d).

 Union Workers

In the 1990s, following years of declining membership, U.S. unions shifted their membership strategy (Fantasia and Voss 2004). Changing their focus from the declining U.S. manufacturing sector, union organizers began to successfully rebuild their membership in the service and public sectors dominated by female, immigrant, and minority workers. During 2011, membership in the manufacturing industries was 11.2%, while employees in the utilities industry had the highest rate of membership, 25.7% (U.S. Bureau of Labor Statistics 2012d). Unions are presented as organizational vehicles of social solidarity, "emphasizing direct [worker] action as an important source of collective power" (Fantasia and Voss 2004:128). In addition, these unions have a strong orientation toward social justice that appeals to their new members, connecting the labor movement with the movement for social citizenship and universal civil rights (Fantasia and Voss 2004).

In recent years, innovative collaborations have been forged. Unions have collaborated with other types of social movements to better support workers and their families. Non-union social movements include worker advocacy groups representing women, immigrants, racial and ethnic groups, and working families. Living-wage campaigns and worker centers have also been part of the effort to increase worker power (Kalleberg 2011).

One example of union innovation is the Union of Needletrades, Industrial, and Textile Employees (UNITE). In 1996, it launched a "Stop Sweatshops" campaign linking union, consumer, student, civil rights, and women's groups in the fight against sweatshops. UNITE helped form United Students Against Sweatshops (USAS) in 1997, bringing together a coalition

Photo 9.5

Why is there poverty at the world's richest university? In 2001, Harvard University students demanded answers to this question, staging a 21-day sit-in at the president's office. Students demanded a better living wage for lower-paid university workers. While achieving salary increases for workers, the Harvard Living Wage Campaign also advocated for better labor practices and salaries for the university's service, janitorial, and dining staff.

of student groups to raise awareness about the problem of sweatshop labor in the manufacturing of collegiate clothing (caps, shirts, and sweatshirts sold in campus stores). In March 1998, Duke University adopted the nation's first code of conduct for university trademark licensees. Under the code, any clothing with the Duke logo would be subject to labor and human rights standards. The student group Duke Students Against Sweatshops played a key role in shaping the antisweatshop code (Sweatshop Watch 2000). In 2004, UNITE announced that it was merging with the Hotel Employees and Restaurant Employees International Union. The new union, called UNITE HERE (2012), represents workers in the hotel, gaming, food service, manufacturing, textile, distribution, laundry, and airport industries.

Also working with USAS is the Student Labor Action Project (SLAP). This campus-based coalition supports the growing economic justice movement among college students by "making links between campus and community organizing, providing skills training to build lasting student organizations, and developing campaigns that win concrete victories for working families" (Student Labor Action Project 2007). The organization sponsors a national student labor week of action each year, highlighting issues such as the DREAM Act, fair contracts for campus employees, environmental and workforce sustainability, and living wages. In recent years, SLAP has also organized against educational cuts in state budgets and increasing tuition.

Main Points

- In March 2012, about 65% of the U.S. population 16 years of age or older was employed. Work isn't just what we do; work is a basic and important social institution. Because of the importance of work, problems related to work quickly become

- categorized as social problems—as everyone's problem.

- During the late eighteenth century and early nineteenth century, the means of production shifted from agricultural to industrial. In agrarian societies, economic production was very simple, based primarily on family agriculture and hunting or gathering activities. During the Industrial Revolution, an economic shift occurred in how people worked and how they earned a living. Family production was replaced with market production, in which capitalist owners paid workers wages to produce goods.

■ Since the 1960s, there has been another shift, referred to as deindustrialization, a widespread, systematic disinvestment in our nation's manufacturing and production capacities. Most manufacturing jobs and plants have been transferred to other countries. Local U.S. factories have closed as a result of globalization, mergers, or acquisitions and poor business.

■ At the same time, more women are working, and more elderly people are returning to work. A very recent shift includes an immigration boom and the presence of more foreign-born workers, often working in low-paying jobs.

■ According to the functionalist perspective, work serves specific functions in society. Our work provides us with some predictability about our life experiences.

■ Conflict theorists argue that capitalist and corporate leaders maintain their power and economic advantage at the expense of their workers and the general public.

■ From a feminist perspective, work is a gendered institution. Through the actions, beliefs, and interactions of workers and their employers, as well as the policies and practices of the workplace, men's and women's identities as workers are created, reproduced, and then solidified in the everyday routines of informal work groups and formal workers' organizations.

■ According to symbolic interactionists, we attach labels and meanings to an individual's work. These social constructs create an order to our work and our lives but can also create social problems.

■ Problems related to work include unemployment and underemployment (the number of employed individuals who are working in a job that underpays them, is not equal to their skill level, or involves fewer working hours than they would prefer), globalization, contingent (temporary) work, outsourcing (including offshore outsourcing), sweatshop labor, discrimination in the workplace, and hazardous work.

■ Several federal policies and institutions have been created with regard to the workforce. These include the U.S. Department of Labor, which oversees several laws and organizations relevant to the workforce. Two labor issues continue to be debated in Congress: raising the minimum wage and workplace discrimination.

■ In addition to government efforts, some companies have independently tried to make the atmosphere at work more worker-friendly through such areas as enhanced traditional benefits, flexible time, and expanded leave. Others try to follow a no-layoff policy.

■ Labor unions, which historically have attempted to defend worker rights and whose efforts have led to many federal laws, still attempt to help workers, often in innovative ways. Student groups have provided strong support for unions and living wage organizations on campus.

On Your Own

Log on to the open-access Student Study Site at www.sagepub.com/leonguerrero4e for these additional learning tools:

- Interactive quizzes
- Video clips
- NPR audio links
- Handbook articles

- E-flashcards
- Journal articles
- End-of-chapter web exercises
- Additional web resources and current events

Internet and Community Exercises

1. The *Occupational Outlook Handbook,* published by the U.S. Bureau of Labor Statistics, provides career descriptions, earning information, and job prospects for a range of occupational groups. For information about sociologists and other social scientists, go to *Study Site Chapter 9*. Research other occupations that might be of interest to you.

2. Do you know what the fourth Thursday in April is? It is "Take Our Daughters and Sons to Work Day." The program is sponsored by the Ms. Foundation for Women, which first created the "Take Our Daughters to Work Day" in 1993. "Take Our Daughters and Sons to Work" is a program that explores career opportunities and work/life issues with girls and boys. To find out more about the national program and related activities, log on to *Study Site Chapter 9*. Does your school or workplace support this program? Why or why not? Do you believe that these or similar activities are effective in changing girls' and boys' definitions of work and family life? Why or why not?

3. The Kheel Center at the Cornell University library presents an on-site historical exhibit of the Triangle Factory Fire. On March 25, 1911, a fire at the Triangle Shirtwaist Factory in New York City killed 146 immigrant workers. In 2003, the factory site was recognized as an official landmark by New York's Landmarks Preservation Commission. This tragedy led to the creation of local and federal policies prohibiting sweatshop conditions and ensuring worker health and safety. Log on to *Study Site Chapter 9* for more information. The website provides a history of early industrial sweatshops, along with a detailed narrative of how the community, workers, and unions responded to the tragedy. The website includes photographs, interviews, and documents from the period.

4. The United Nations' *Human Development Report* tracks the labor force participation ratio of females to males. Log on to *Study Site Chapter 9* to compare the U.S. rate with rates in the other listed countries. How does our rate compare with those of other developed countries? Which countries have the lowest rates?

Study Questions

1. Which population of workers has changed the U.S. workplace the most—women or foreign-born workers? Explain the reason for your answer.

2. Using a coffee barista as an example, identify and explain Karl Marx's theory of worker alienation.

3. Why and how are women disadvantaged in the workforce—in both the types of jobs they occupy and their salary level?

4. Identify the positive and negative consequences of globalization.

5. From a functionalist and conflict perspective, examine the role of a contingent workforce in the U.S. economy.

6. Why have labor unions declined in membership since 2005? How can labor unions expand their appeal and membership to workers, and how can they do this during the economic recession?

7. Human trafficking includes the involuntary movement of individuals within one country or from one country to another for exploitation. Exploitation may include physical labor or sexual exploitation (United Nations Office on Drugs and Crime—Anti-Human Trafficking Unit 2006). In 2012, the United Nations reported that 2.4 million people are victims of human trafficking at any one time, with the majority exploited as sexual slaves (Lederer 2012). The United States is reported to be a frequent destination country where victims are brought to be exploited, yet not much is discussed about our country's role in human trafficking. Is trafficking a U.S. social problem? Why or why not?

CHAPTER 10

Health and Medicine

Preventative Medicine

T he Centers for Disease Control and Prevention (CDC) releases an annual report of health trends. In *Health, United States, 2011* (National Center for Health Statistics 2012), the CDC reported that life expectancy had reached 78.5 years, with gaps between Blacks and Whites and men and women narrowing (see Table 10.1). The report concluded that higher education and income levels were related to lower rates of many chronic diseases compared to lower education and income levels.

The CDC reported on additional aspects of our nation's health:

- Heart disease remains the leading cause of death, accounting for 617,000 deaths in 2008.
- There was little progress in lowering the U.S. infant mortality rate from 2000 to 2007. The rate was 6.9 infant deaths per 1,000 live births in 2000 versus 6.8 in 2007.
- Within each racial or ethnic group, adults living below 200% of poverty were more likely to be uninsured than those with higher income. Hispanic adults were more likely to be uninsured than any other race or ethnic group.
- The United States spends more on health per capita than any other country, and health spending continues to increase.

Universal Health Care

Before we discuss health inequalities and challenges, let's use our sociological imagination to better understand the relationship between health, illness, and medicine.

Table 10.1

Life Expectancy at Birth in Years According to Race and Sex in the United States, Selected Years

	All Races		White		Black	
	Male	**Female**	**Male**	**Female**	**Male**	**Female**
1900	46.3	48.3	46.6	48.7	32.5	33.5
1950	65.6	71.1	66.5	72.2	59.1	62.9
1960	66.6	73.1	67.4	74.1	61.1	66.3
1970	67.1	74.7	70.7	78.1	60.0	68.3
1980	70.0	77.4	70.7	78.1	63.8	72.5
1990	71.8	78.8	72.7	79.4	64.5	73.6
2000	74.3	79.7	74.9	80.1	68.3	75.2
2007	75.4	80.4	75.9	80.8	70.0	76.8

Source: National Center for Health Statistics 2011.

Sociological Perspectives on Health, Illness, and Medicine

If you are thinking that this is going to be a discussion about human physiology and theories about germs and viruses, full of medical terms, you're wrong. Although medicine can identify the biological pathways to disease (Wilkinson 1996), we will need a sociological perspective to address the social determinants of health. "Health is a result of an individual's genetic makeup, income and educational status, health behaviors, communities in which the individual lives, and the environments to which he or she is exposed" (Lurie and Dubowitz 2007: 1119).

Consider the gross inequalities in health between and within countries. For example, life expectancy at birth is highest for a child born in Japan (81.9 years) and lowest for one born in Sierra Leone (34 years). Within the United States, there is a 20-year gap in life expectancy between most and least advantaged populations (Marmot 2005). There is no biological reason why life expectancy should be 48 years longer in Japan than in Sierra Leone or why there is a gap in life expectancy between the rich and the poor in the United States. To better understand the connection between our social structure and health, we must investigate how our political economy, our corporate structure, and the distribution of resources and power influence health and illness (Conrad 2001a).

The sociology of health and illness includes the field of epidemiology. **Epidemiology** is the study of the patterns in the distribution and frequency of sickness, injury, and death and the social factors that shape them. Epidemiologists are like detectives, investigating how and why groups of individuals become sick or injured (Cockerman and Glasser 2001). They don't focus on individuals; rather, epidemiologists focus on communities and populations, addressing how health and illness experiences are based on social factors such as gender, age, race, social class, or behavior (Cockerman and Glasser 2001). Epidemiology has successfully increased public awareness about the risk factors associated with disease and illness, leading many to quit smoking, to participate in more physical exercise, and to eat healthier diets (Link and Phelan 2001).

 Health & Dieting

For example, type 2 diabetes, the most common form of the disease, occurs when the body does not produce enough insulin or when the cells ignore the insulin. An estimated 25.8 million Americans have type 2 diabetes (diagnosed or undiagnosed). However, the disease can be effectively managed with healthy behaviors such as meal planning, exercise, and weight management (American Diabetes Association 2012). Modernization, fast foods, and physical inactivity have led to significant increases in the number of type 2 diabetes cases in countries such as Brazil and India. Indian public health officials project that in 20 years there may be 78 million diabetics in their country. A disease that usually affects the old is affecting the younger Indian population primarily because they have adopted a modern lifestyle and diet (Kleinfield 2006).

What Does It Mean to Me?

All of us practice healthy behaviors we believe or were told can prevent or cure illness or disease. Brushing our teeth is one practice that we routinely do without really remembering why we do it. What other healthy behaviors do you practice? Why do you do them? Where did you learn them?

Epidemiologists use three primary measures of health status: fertility, mortality, and morbidity. These data are routinely collected by the National Center for Health Statistics, CDC. **Fertility** is the level of childbearing for an individual or a population. The basic measure of fertility is the crude birthrate, the number of live births per 1,000 women ages 15 to 44 in a population. The U.S. crude birthrate for 2009 was 13.5 births per 1,000 women (Martin et al. 2012). Related to this is the measure of **fecundity**, the maximum number of children that could be born (based on the number of women of childbearing age in the population).

In the early 1900s, a woman could expect to give birth to about four children, whereas a woman during the Great Depression of the 1930s could expect to have only two (U.S. Census Bureau 2002). The lowest number of births per woman was 1.8 children in the mid-1970s. Since then, the rate has averaged around two births per woman (U.S. Census Bureau 2002). Fertility is determined by a set of biological factors, such as the health and nutrition of childbearing women. But innovations in medicine, in the form of infertility treatments, have also made childbirth possible for women who once considered it impossible. Social factors, such as our social values and definitions of the role of women, the ideal family size, and the timing of childbirth, can influence fertility. Fertility rates have also been determined by the ethnic and foreign-born composition of the population. Demographer Kenneth Johnson explains, "You could shut off immigration tomorrow and the impact of the foreign born on U.S. demographic trends would still be a powerful force" (quoted in Roberts 2010:A13). Hispanics are not only the largest minority group in the United States but also the youngest. One in four newborns is Hispanic (Pew Hispanic Center 2009).

Mortality is the incidence of death in a population. The basic measure of mortality is the crude death rate, the number of deaths per 100,000 people in a population in a given year. For 2010, the U.S. death rate was 798.7 deaths per 100,000 people (Murphy, Xu, and Kochanek 2012). In the United States, it is unlikely that we'll die from acute infectious diseases, such as an intestinal infection or measles. Rather, the leading causes of death are chronic conditions such as coronary heart disease, cancer, stroke, and chronic lower respiratory disease, all of which have been linked to heredity, diet, stress, and

Photo 10.1

Ogimi, a village on Japan's southern island of Okinawa, is known as "longevity village" because of the long life span of residents. Pictured here is a 105-year-old female resident. As a whole, Japan has one of the world's oldest populations.

exercise. The leading causes of death vary considerably by age. The leading cause of death of college-age Americans is unintentional injuries, followed by homicide and suicide. Among the elderly, mortality caused by chronic diseases (heart disease, cancer, chronic bronchitis, diabetes) is more prevalent.

Infant mortality is the rate of infant death per 1,000 live births. For 2010, the infant mortality rate was 6.14 deaths per 1,000 live births (Murphy et al. 2012). The three leading causes of death among U.S. infants were congenital birth defects, low birth weight, and sudden infant death syndrome. Infant mortality is considered a basic indicator of the well-being of a population, reflecting the social, economic, health, and environmental conditions in which children and their mothers live. Though infant mortality rates in the United States have declined, rates are disproportionately higher for minority children. In 2010, the highest rate, 11.61 deaths per 1,000 live births, for infants of non-Hispanic Black mothers was more than double the death rate of infants born to White mothers (5.19; Murphy et al. 2012).

The U.S. infant mortality rate is historically higher than in other industrial societies. For 2010, UNICEF (2012a) identified six industrialized countries with the lowest infant mortality rate—2 deaths per 1,000 births. (Refer to Table 10.2 for a list of industrialized countries with the lowest rates.) When comparing U.S. infant mortality rates with the rates of other countries, researchers noted that maternal health care is more widely and uniformly available in countries with national health care programs. The U.S. rate is 7 deaths per 1,000 live births.

Morbidity is the study of illnesses and disease. Illness refers to the social experience and consequences of having a disease, whereas disease refers to a biological or physiological problem that affects the human body (Weitz 2001). Epidemiologists track the **incidence rate**, the number of new cases within a population during a specific period, along with the **prevalence rate**, the total number of cases involving a specific health problem during a specific period (Weitz 2001). For example, the 2010 incidence rate for diabetes was 1.9 million

Table 10.2		

Infant Mortality (under age 1) in the Industrialized World, 2010

Country	Infant Mortality Rate (per 1,000 Live Births)
Finland, Iceland, Ireland, Japan, Luxembourg, Sweden	2
Czech Republic, Denmark, France, Germany, Greece, Ireland, Israel, Norway, Portugal	3
Australia, Austria, Belgium, Estonia, Italy, Netherlands, Spain, Switzerland	4

Source: UNICEF 2012a.

people age 20 years or older; the prevalence rate was 25.8 million or 8.3% of the population (American Diabetes Association 2012). Incidence rates help measure the spread of **acute illnesses**, which strike suddenly and disappear quickly, such as chicken pox or the flu. The prevalence rate measures the frequency of long-term or chronic illnesses, such as diabetes, asthma, or HIV (Weitz 2001). The National Center for Health Statistics publishes the *Morbidity and Mortality Weekly Report,* a weekly summary of surveillance information on reported diseases and deaths.

In addition to epidemiological analyses, sociologists have applied theoretical perspectives to better explain the social problems of health and illness.

Functionalist Perspective

Émile Durkheim conducted the first empirical analysis of suicide in the late 1800s. Before Durkheim's work, scientists attributed suicide primarily to psychological or individual factors. However, Durkheim treated suicide as a social fact and identified the relationship between suicide and the level of social attachment or regulation between an individual and society. His research is the first true epidemiological analysis, and, most important, it revealed the relationship between illness and the larger social structure. The stability of society is paramount from a functionalist's perspective. Consider for a moment what happens when you become sick. When are you sick enough not to attend class? How do others begin to treat you? According to the functionalist perspective, illness has a legitimate place in society. The first sociological theory of illness was offered by Talcott Parsons (1951); the theory addresses how individuals are expected to act and to be treated while sick (Weitz 2001). This set of behaviors is part of Parsons's theory of the sick role.

Photo 10.2

In Kampala, Uganda, a nurse (left) provides counseling to a patient (right) who is affected by cancer as a result of HIV. The nurse is a volunteer trained by The AIDS Support Organisation (TASO). Uganda has been called a pioneer in the battle against AIDS in Africa, reducing the prevalence of the disease in the country from a high of 18.3% to 6.5% in 2009 (UNICEF 2012b).

The **sick role** has four parts. In the first, sick people are excused from fulfilling their normal social role. Illness allows them to be excused from work, from chores around the house, or even from attending class! Second, sick people are not held responsible for the illness. The flu that's going around is no one's fault, so you aren't personally blamed if you catch it (although your roommates may blame you if they catch what you have). Third, sick people must try to get well. Illness is considered a temporary condition, and sick people are expected to take care of themselves with appropriate measures. In relation to this, Parsons offers the last part, that sick people are expected to visit medical authorities and to follow their advice.

Although Parsons legitimized the social role of illness, he also identified a critical source of the problem in health care today. In the fourth element, Parsons identified the authority and control of the physician. Even though you're the one who is sick, the doctor has the ultimate power to diagnose your condition and to tell you that you're "really" sick. Doctors play a prominent role in managing our illnesses, but they don't do it alone. Doctors, along with nurses, pharmaceutical corporations, hospitals, and health insurers, form a powerful medical industry. The medical industry has served us well with its technological and scientific advances, offering a wider array of medical services and treatment options. However, this industry has also created a set of problems, or dysfunctions, as functionalists like to refer to them. Medicine has shifted from a general practitioner model (a family doctor who took care of all your needs) to a specialist model (where one doctor treats you for a specific ailment). You are receiving quality care, but at a price (and you are paying to be treated by many different doctors, instead of just one). As a result, health care costs have become less affordable, leaving many without adequate coverage and care. The system intended to heal us does not treat everyone fairly. We will explore this further in the next perspective.

Conflict Perspective

According to conflict theorists, patterns of health and illness are not accidental or solely the result of an individual's actions. Conflict theorists identify how these patterns are related to systematic inequalities based on ethnicity/race or gender and on differences in power, values, and interests.

The experience of AIDS treatment in Africa highlights the inequality of health care delivery and access. The World Health Organization (WHO) reports that though antiretroviral treatments for AIDS are available, most HIV-positive children from poor countries are not receiving these drugs. An estimated 2.3 million children under the age of 15 are infected with HIV, and 800,000 of them need antiretroviral drugs to stay alive, yet only 60,000 to 100,000 are being treated (Altman 2006). Fewer than 10% of pregnant women with HIV in poor or middle-income countries are receiving medication to prevent the transmission of the virus to their newborns (Altman 2006). So why have rich(er) countries been able to virtually eliminate pediatric AIDS? Observers note that the disease would and could have been eradicated earlier if there were stronger health systems in African countries, a stronger commitment from the global community, and more money to be made helping these poorer countries (Altman 2006).

Conflict theorists may take a traditional Marxist position and argue that our medical industry is based on a capitalist system, founded not on the value of human life, but on a pure profit motive. Studies consistently find that those in upper social classes have better health, health insurance, and medical access than men and women of lower socioeconomic status. A conflict theorist argues that instead of defining health care as a right, our capitalistic system treats health care as a valuable commodity dispensed to the highest bidder. The alternative would be a dramatic change in the medical system, ensuring that health care is provided to all regardless of their race, class, or gender.

Instead, what we have in place is a medical system responsive to middle- or upper-class patients and their needs. According to Ken Silverstein (1999), 6.1 million people have died worldwide of malaria or of acute lower-respiratory infections because there were no drugs available to treat these illnesses. Silverstein notes that pharmaceutical companies have pursued drugs that maximize their profitability, focusing less on diseases of the poor or on drugs that are commercially unviable. As he explains, the interest is in lifestyle drugs, "remedies that may one day free the world from the scourge of toenail fungus, obesity, baldness, face wrinkles, and impotence" (Silverstein 1999:14).

The medical system itself ensures that those already in charge maintain power. In health care, no other group has greater power than medical physicians and their professional organization, the American Medical Association (AMA), established in 1847. On its website, the AMA identifies itself as "the nation's most influential medical organization." In his book *The Social Transformation of American Medicine,* Paul Starr (1982) explains how the AMA's authority over

Health Care Reform

the medical profession and education was secured in the early 1900s, with a series of events that culminated with the Flexner Report. The 1910 report was written by Abraham Flexner and was commissioned by the Carnegie Foundation and supported by the AMA. Through the report, Flexner and the AMA were able to pass judgment on the quality of each medical school, based on an assessment of its curriculum, facilities, faculty, admission requirements, and state licensing record. This report eventually led to strict licensing criteria for all medical schools, which led to the closure of schools that could not meet the new standards. Starr reveals that although the increased standards and school closures may have improved the quality of medical training and care, they also increased the homogeneity and cohesiveness of the profession. From 162 schools in 1906, the number of medical schools dropped to 81 by 1922. Some of the closed schools were exclusively for African Americans and women. According to Rose Weitz (2001), with the increasing cost of education and higher educational prerequisites, fewer minorities, women, immigrants, and poor students could meet the requirements. As a result,

> Fewer doctors were available who would practice in minority communities and who understood the special concerns of minority or female patients. At the same time, simply because doctors were now more homogenously White, male, and upper class, their status grew, encouraging more hierarchical relationships between doctors and patients. (Weitz 2001:327)

The legacy of the Flexner Report—higher medical standards and more limited access to medical education and care—continues to this day. Examinations of the social and economic backgrounds of medical students in the United States, Canada, and Great Britain confirm that medical students tend to be recruited from families with higher socioeconomic standing and with medical professionals among their members (Magnus and Mick 2000).

 Future Physicians

The AMA (2003) continues its lobbying and legislative efforts today, pursuing several legislative goals including medical liability reforms (asking for limits on punitive or noneconomic damages), preserving Medicare physician payments, expanding health insurance options, and obtaining regulatory relief from Medicare administration.

What Does It Mean to Me?

The consumer movement has shifted some of the power in the doctor-patient relationship to the patient. Drug ads, previously reserved for professional medical journals, are now commonly featured in popular magazines and in television advertisements. Pharmaceutical companies routinely take two or three full-page ads, featuring drug warnings, side effects, and precautions, along with a description of their drug and its benefits. It sometimes is difficult to figure out what the drug is for. How do you think this popular diffusion of pharmaceutical information has redefined the relationship between doctor and patient? Between your doctor and you?

Feminist Perspective

According to Peter Conrad (2001b), illness and how we treat it can reflect cultural assumptions and biases about a particular group. Take, for example, the case of women and their medical care. Conrad explains that throughout history, there are examples of medical and scientific explanations for women's health and illnesses that reflect dominant and often negative conceptions of women. Since the 1930s, women's natural physical conditions and experiences, such as childbirth, menopause, premenstrual syndrome, and menstruation, have been medicalized. **Medicalization** refers to the process through which a condition or behavior becomes defined as a medical problem (Weitz 2001). Although the medicalization of these conditions may have been effective in treating women, various feminist theorists see it as an extension of medicine's control of women (Conrad 2001b), specifically normal female experiences linked with the female reproductive system (Markens 1996), inappropriately emphasizing the psychological, biomedical, or sociocultural origins (Hamilton 1994). Once a condition is defined as a medical problem, medicine, rather than the woman herself, gains control of its diagnosis and treatment.

Menopause, a natural physiological event for women, was defined in the medical community as a "deficiency disease" in the 1960s when commercial production of estrogen replacement therapy became available (Conrad 2001b; Lock 1993). Although a few medical writers refer to menopause as a natural process, many continue to describe it as a "hormonal imbalance" that leads to a "menopausal syndrome" (Lock 1993). Although estrogen replacement treatment has been presented as a means for women to retain their femininity and to maintain good health, feminists argue that menopause is not an illness; actually, estrogen therapy may not be necessary and may actually be dangerous (Conrad 2001b). A recent study indicated that although estrogen is an effective short-term treatment for hot flashes or night sweats, estrogen does little to improve the quality of older women's lives (Haney 2003).

Studies have suggested that the meanings and experiences of menopause may also be bound by cultural definitions. In North America, where women are defined by their youth and beauty, aging women are set up as a target for medicalization. In Japan, however, public attention focuses on a woman's life course experience. For a middle-aged Japanese woman, what matters is how well she fulfills her social and familial duties, especially the care of elderly family members, rather than her physical or medical experiences. The Japanese medical community has a different perspective on menopause than its American colleagues do: Most doctors in Japan define menopause as natural and an inevitable part of the aging process (Lock 1993).

Interactionist Perspective

Medical Sociology

From the interactionist perspective, health, illness, and medical responses are socially constructed and maintained. In the previous sections, we discussed how health issues are defined by powerful interest or political groups. We just reviewed how the medicalization of women's conditions reflects our cultural assumptions or biases about women. Each example demonstrates how social, political, and cultural meanings affect our definition and response to health and illness.

A patient's experience with the medical system can be disempowering (Goffman 1961), but the experience can be mediated by social meaning and interpretations (Lambert et al. 1997). According to Suni Peterson, Martin Heesacker, and Robert C. Schwartz (2001), when people contract a disease, they define their illness according to a socially constructed definition of the disease, which includes a set of images, beliefs, and perceptions. Patients use these definitions to create a personal meaning for their diagnosis and to determine their subsequent behavior. The authors argue that these social constructs have a greater influence on the patient's actions and decisions about his or her health than recommendations from health professionals do.

Sociologists also examine how the relationship between doctors and their patients is created and maintained through interaction. In particular, sociologists focus on how medical professionals use their expertise and knowledge to maintain control over patients. Research indicates that doctors' power depends on their cultural authority, their economic independence, cultural differences between patients and doctors, and doctors' assumed superiority to patients (Weitz 2001). Studies consistently demonstrate the systematic differences in the level of information provided by physicians to their patients. Although differences might be attributed to the doctor responding to a patient's particular communication style, researchers argue that information varies according to the doctor's impressions of a patient (e.g., intelligence) or according to subjective judgments about what information the patient needs (Street 1991) or based on status differentials between doctor and patients (male vs. female or White vs. non-White) (Peck and Conner 2011). Educated and younger patients tend to receive more diagnostic information, as do patients who ask more questions and express more concerns; doctors are likely to communicate as equals with their educated, older male patients (Street 1991). African Americans, Asian Americans, and Hispanics are more likely than Whites to experience difficulties in communicating with their doctors. The difficulties include not understanding their doctors, not feeling that their doctors listened to them, or having questions for their doctors that they did not ask (Collins et al. 2002).

African American Women

Interactionists and social constructionists also investigate how a disease is socially constructed. This doesn't mean that disease and illness do not exist. Rather, the focus is on how illness is created and sustained according to a set of shared social beliefs or definitions. In his essay "The Myth of Mental Illness," Thomas Szasz (1960) argues that mental disorders are not actually illnesses. He considers mental illness a convenient myth to cover up the "everyday fact that life for most people is a continuous struggle" (Szasz 1960:118). The disease of mental illness is constructed and maintained through a set of medical, legal, and social definitions. The social construction of disease has also been applied to anorexia nervosa (Brumberg 1988), black lung disease (Smith 1987), and chronic fatigue syndrome (Richman and Jason 2001).

For a summary of sociological perspectives on health and medicine, see Table 10.3.

Table 10.3

Summary of Sociological Perspectives: Health and Medicine

	Functional	Conflict/Feminist	Interactionist
Explanation of the social problems of health and medicine	Although illness may threaten the social order, it does have a legitimate place in society. This perspective also addresses the functions and dysfunctions of the medical industry.	Patterns of health and illness reflect systematic inequalities based on ethnicity/race or gender, and on differences in power, values, and interests. Conflict theorists examine the power of the medical industry and its consequences. Feminist theorists examine medicine's control of women, specifically of normal female experiences linked with the female reproductive system.	This perspective acknowledges how illness is created and sustained according to a set of shared social beliefs or definitions. Theorists in this perspective address how social, political, and cultural meanings affect our definition and response to health and illness.
Questions asked about health and medicine	What is the role of illness in our society? What functions and dysfunctions does the medical industry provide?	How does the medical industry exert control over its patients? Is everyone treated fairly and equally by the medical system?	Who or what defines what it means to be "sick" in our society? How do our definitions of disease and illness shape our beliefs and behaviors?

Health Inequalities

Gender

As noted in Table 10.1, women live about five years longer than men. The three lead-ing causes of death for males and females are identical: heart disease, cancer, and stroke. Although women live longer than men, women experience higher rates of nonfatal chronic conditions (Waldron 2001; Weitz 2001). Men experience higher rates of fatal illness, dying more quickly than women when illness occurs (Waldron 2001; Weitz 2001).

These differences in mortality have been attributed to three factors: genetics, risk taking, and health care (Waldron 2001). Biological differences seem to favor women; more females than males survive at every age (Weitz 2001). Because of differences in gender roles, men are more likely to engage in risk-taking behaviors or potentially dangerous activities: driving too fast or incautiously, using legal or illegal drugs, or participating in dangerous sports (Waldron 2001). The workplace offers more dangers for men. More men than women are employed, and men's jobs tend to be more hazardous (Waldron 2001); about 9 of every 10 fatal work-place accidents occur to men (U.S. Bureau of Labor Statistics 2012). Finally, because women obtain more routine health examinations than men do, their health problems are identified early enough for effective intervention (Weitz 2001). Typically, women eat healthier diets and smoke and drink less alcohol than men do (Calnan 1987).

According to the Men's Health Network (2002), "No effective program exists which is devoted to awareness and prevention of the leading killers of men." Although men die of can-cer at twice the rate of women by the age of 75, there is little education for men in cancer self-detection and prevention. Whereas there is a popular national campaign for breast cancer, there is no national educational campaign teaching men how to self-examine for testicular cancer, a leading killer of men from 15 to 40 years of age. In addition, there are no qual-ity educational programs regarding prostate cancer, a cancer that strikes one in five men (Men's Health Network 2002).

Social Class

Low Income and Health

Regardless of the country where a person lives, social class is a major determinant of one's health and life expectancy (Braveman and Tarimo 2002); those lower on the socioeconomic ladder have worse health than those above them (Marmot 2004). The link between class and health has been confirmed in studies conducted in Australia, Canada, Great Britain, the United States, and Western Europe (Cockerman 2004). Although no factor has been singled out as the primary link between socioeconomic position and health, scholars have offered many factors—standard of living, work conditions, housing conditions, access to better-quality food, leisure activities, and the social and psychological connections with others at work, at home, or in the community—to explain the relationship (Krieger, Williams, and Moss 1997).

Poverty & Illness

Weitz (2001) offers several explanations for the unhealthy relationship between pov-erty and illness. The type of work available to poorly educated people can cause illness or death by exposing them to hazardous conditions. Poor and middle-class individuals who live in poor neighborhoods are exposed to air, noise, water, and chemical pollution that can increase rates of morbidity and mortality. Inadequate and unsafe housing contributes to infectious and chronic diseases, injuries, and illnesses, including lead poisoning when children eat peeling paint. The diet of the poor increases the risk of illness. The poor have little time or opportunity to practice healthy activities such as exercise, and because of life stresses, they may also be encouraged to adopt behaviors that might further endanger their health. Finally, poverty limits individual access to preventative and therapeutic health care.

The relationship between health and social class afflicts those most vulnerable, the young. Children in poor or near-poor families are two to three times more likely not to have a usual source of health care than are children in nonpoor families (Federal Interagency Forum on Child and Family Statistics 2007). Access to a regular doctor or care facility for physical examinations, preventative care, screening, and immunizations can facilitate the timely and appropriate use of pediatric services for youth. Even children on public insurance (which includes Medicaid and the State Children's Health Insurance Program) were more likely not to have a usual source of care than were children with private insurance. Children in families below the poverty level had lower rates of immunization and yearly dental checkups (both basic preventative care practices) than did children at or above the poverty level (Federal Interagency Forum on Child and Family Statistics 2007). More than 9 million U.S. low-income children are uninsured (Kaiser Family Foundation 2007).

The cost of medical care, particularly out-of-pocket expenses, is a financial burden even to those with health insurance. Harvard researchers concluded that illness or medical bills contributed to 62% of all bankruptcies in 2007 (Sack 2010). More than three fourths of those with medical debt had medical insurance (Sack 2010). Though spending on prescription drugs in the United States is the highest in the world, economic hard times have caused some patients to alter their spending or their dosage of prescription drugs (Saul 2008). Through the first eight months of 2008, the number of all dispensed prescriptions was lower than in the same period of time in 2007 (Saul 2008). The decrease was attributed to individual cost-cutting measures, causing concern among physicians about the health and well-being of their patients. Patients reduced their medications (cutting their pills in half or taking medications every other day) or, among those who could no longer afford their medications, stopped taking their medicine altogether without consulting with their physician (Saul 2008).

 Health Care

Education

A similar relationship has been documented between education and health—the higher your education, the better your health (no matter how it is measured—mortality, morbidity, or other general health measures). Schooling might be a more important correlate to good health than is one's occupation or income (Grossman and Kaestner 1997).

Recent studies on the effects of compulsory education in Sweden, Denmark, England, and Wales consistently identify that a longer educational experience leads to better health (Kolata 2007). Michael Murphy and his colleagues (2006) identified mortality trends by educational level for Russian men and women between 1980 and 2001. Murphy et al. concluded that better-educated men and women had a significant mortality advantage over less-educated men and women. In 1980, life expectancy at age 20 for university-educated men was three years greater than for men with only an elementary education. By 2001, however, the gap between university- and elementary-educated men had increased to 11 years. Similar differentials were also noted among Russian women.

Researchers suggest that education helps individuals choose and practice a healthier lifestyle regarding diet, exercise, and other health choices. Highly educated men and women are likely to visit their primary physicians more often and regularly and may be more willing to use new medical technologies or medicines. Knowledge about the health consequences of smoking and drinking has been shown to decrease smoking and excessive alcohol consumption. Educated parents will also transmit their healthier lifestyle to their children (Grossman and Kaestner 1997). Education represents both the long-term influence of early life circumstances and the influence of adult circumstances on adult health (Beckles and Truman 2011).

Researchers have demonstrated the link between education and future orientation. Future-oriented individuals attend school for longer periods. Educated individuals are able to link their current actions to their future, not only for their education but also for preventative health care practices. For example, a future-oriented person will say, "I'm going to college now so that I can have a good job when I graduate." Applied to health behaviors, the same person will say, "I won't start smoking because I know there are long-term health consequences of smoking." Studies have shown that men and women who discount the future are more likely to become addicted to alcohol or other drugs (Becker and Mulligan 1994).

Other Health Care Problems

The Rising Cost of Health Care

The United States spends about 18% of its gross domestic product (GDP) on health care—the largest expenditure in this category among industrialized countries. (A per-capita spending comparison with other countries is presented in Figure 10.1.) In 2010, total health care spending reached $2.6 trillion (equivalent to France's GDP), with an average of $8,086 spent

Figure 10.1

Total Health Expenditures per Capita, United States and Selected Countries, 2011

Source: Organisation for Economic Co-operation and Development 2011.

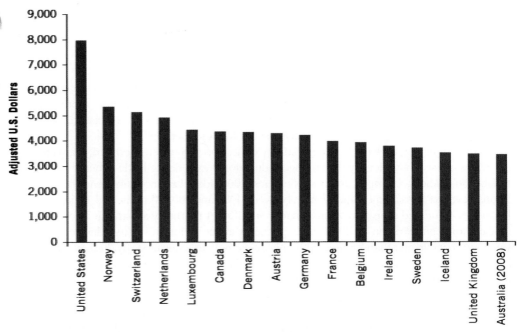

per person in health expenses (Centers for Medicare and Medicaid Services 2012). Ezekiel Emanuel (2011), a former Obama health care adviser, offered the following perspective about our health care spending: "The United States spends on health care alone what the 65 million people of France spend on everything: education, defense, the environment, scientific research, vacations, food, housing, cars, clothes and health care" (p. 5). However, U.S. national health care spending grew more slowly between 2009 and 2010 as more Americans delayed visits to their doctors or hospitals, reduced their prescription drug purchases (Pear 2012), or lost their insurance coverage along with their jobs (Lowrey 2012). (Refer to the In Focus discussion for a summary of health insurance plans.)

In Focus

U.S. Health Insurance and Health Care Delivery Systems

The U.S. health care system is often referred to as a private health care system, but in reality, it is a mixed system of public and private insurance (Oberlander 2002). Refer to the Taking a World View section of this chapter for more information. Most Americans receive health insurance from their employers. This type of insurance is referred to as group insurance or as employment-based private insurance. Employers buy into a health insurance program, paying for part or all of the cost of the insurance premiums. A premium is a monthly fee to maintain your health coverage.

Most college students are probably covered by their parents' insurance plan. That handy insurance card in your wallet identifies your insurance provider, the amount of your deductible (payment due at the time of service), and the amount of coverage for prescription drugs or emergency services. There are many different types of group insurance programs:

- *Fee-for-service plan.* Under this plan, also known as an indemnity health plan, insurance companies pay fees for services provided to the people covered by the policy. This type of program emphasizes patient choice and immediate patient care.
- *Health maintenance organization (HMO).* These organizations operate as prepaid health plans. For your premium, the HMO provides you and your family comprehensive care. This plan is also known as managed health care, a plan that controls costs by controlling access to care. You'll be assigned to a primary care provider who will provide most of your medical care, but if necessary, that doctor will refer you to specialists within the HMO practice or to providers contracted by the HMO. Under the plan, there is limited coverage for any treatment outside the HMO network.
- *Preferred provider organization (PPO).* A PPO is a combination of the fee-for-service and HMO plan. With a PPO, you can manage your own health care needs by selecting your own doctors. These specialists will be on a preferred provider list supported by the PPO plan. If you use a provider outside of your plan, you may have to pay a larger percentage of your health care expenses.
- *Federal health plans.* Medicare is available to Americans 65 years or older or those with disabilities, whereas Medicaid pays for medical and long-term care for the poor; low-income children, pregnant women, and elderly; the medically needy; and people requiring institutional care.

Even though the U.S. health system is the most expensive in the world, "comparative analyses consistently show the United States underperforms relative to other countries on most dimensions of [health] performance" (Davis et al. 2007:viii). The United States remains the only major industrial country without some form of universal health coverage. In their analyses of health care systems and outcomes in Australia, Canada, Germany, New Zealand, the United Kingdom, and the United States, Karen Davis and her colleagues (2007) concluded that the United States failed to achieve better health outcomes and scored last on the dimensions of access, quality, efficiency, and equity despite spending the most per capita on health care.

Given our lack of universal health care coverage, when compared with these other nations, more Americans are uninsured or underinsured and are more unlikely to seek necessary care because of costs. Davis and her colleagues (2007) identify how "other nations ensure the accessibility of care through universal health insurance systems and through better ties between patients and the physician practices that serve as their long term 'medical home.' . . . It is also apparent that the U.S. is lagging in adoption of information technology and national policies that promote quality improvement" (p. viii). (Information systems in countries such as Germany, New Zealand, and the United Kingdom enhance the ability of physicians to monitor patients' chronic conditions and medication use. These countries also routinely use nonphysician clinicians to assist with patients with chronic diseases.) Germany ranked first on access to health care (the ability of patients to obtain affordable care in a timely manner), and the United Kingdom ranked first for health care quality (safe, coordinated, and patient-centered health care), efficiency (maximizing the quality of care and outcomes given the system's resources), and equity (providing care that does not vary in quality because of personal characteristics, such as gender, ethnicity, and socioeconomic status). The United States ranked last on both measures.

Policy makers and consumers have been keeping an eye on the cost of prescription drugs, one of the fastest-growing sectors of medical care. Increases in drug costs are expected to outstrip the overall growth in health care spending for the next 10 years. Spending for prescription drugs in 2010 totaled $259.1 billion, about 10 cents of every dollar spent on health care (Centers for Medicare and Medicaid Services 2012).

The cost of prescription drugs remains a significant burden for elderly Americans. AARP annually examines prices for 112 brand-name and generic specialty prescription drugs used by Americans 50 years of age or older. AARP reported that in 2009, manufacturer prices increased 8.9% (while the general inflation rate was −0.3% for the same period) (Schondelmeyer and Purvis 2011). The cost of 87 drugs most commonly used by older Americans had retail price changes that met or exceeded the rate of general inflation for 2009.

Photo 10.3

The fastest-growing sector of medical care is prescription drug spending. In 2010, $259.1 billion was spent on prescription drugs. The cost of drugs remains a significant burden for elderly Americans.

Inequalities in Health Insurance

Access to health care is unevenly distributed across the U.S. population (Conrad and Leiter 2003). Data from the U.S. Census Bureau reveal that 48.6 million Americans or 15.7% of the U.S. population had no health insurance at any time during 2011 (DeNavas-Walt, Proctor, and Smith 2012). (Refer to U.S. Data Map 10.1.) Although most Americans receive health insurance through their employers, about 60% of the uninsured have at least one full-time worker in their family (Kaiser Family Foundation 2011). Uninsured workers are more likely to be low-wage or blue-collar workers or work for small firms or in service industries than insured workers (Kaiser Family Foundation 2011). Most of the working poor are not eligible for public-assistance medical programs (e.g., Medicaid) even though their employers do not provide health insurance (Seccombe and Amey 2001; Kaiser Family Foundation 2011). Among households with incomes less than $25,000, only 74.6% received health insurance (DeNavas-Walt et al. 2012).

What Does It Mean to Me?

How does your state rank in terms of the number of people with health insurance? Refer to the state rankings of persons not covered by health insurance (U.S. Data Map 10.1). Why do you think your state is positioned where it currently is in the state rankings?

U.S. DATA MAP 10.1

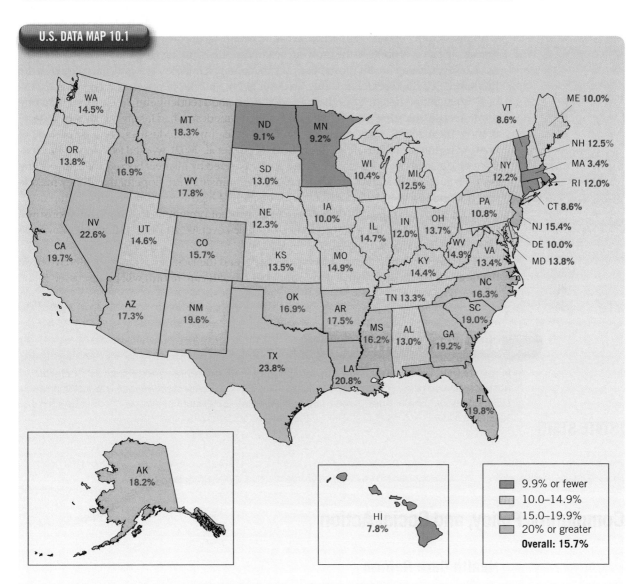

Percent of Population Not Covered by Health Insurance by State, 2011

Source: DeNavas-Walt et al. 2012.

Several social factors are related to health coverage. About 9.4% or 7.0 million children under the age of 18 do not have health insurance (DeNavas-Walt et al. 2012). When parents lose jobs, children lose health insurance coverage. Children in poverty, with an uninsured rate of 13.8%, are more likely to be uninsured than are children generally.

Among all minority groups, Hispanic Americans are most likely not to have insurance. Thirty percent of Hispanics do not have any health insurance compared with 19.5% of Blacks, 11.1% of Whites, and 16.8% of Asians (DeNavas-Walt et al. 2012). Hispanics are three times as likely as Whites and twice as likely as African Americans to be employed full-time, but lacking health insurance (National Institutes of Health 2006). Most Hispanics obtain health insurance through their employers; however, lower-income or part-time workers or those employed in particular industries are less likely to be offered health coverage through their employment (National Institutes of Health 2006). According to Michelle Doty (quoted in Commonwealth Fund 2003a), "Lack of insurance, unstable coverage, language barriers, and low income all contribute to the growing health care crisis among Hispanics."

However, losing health insurance is also becoming a middle-class issue, according to the Employee Benefit Research Institute. In 2001, about 800,000 people had incomes in excess of $75,000 but no health insurance (Broder, Pear, and Freudenheim 2002). More than one third of those uninsured in 2007, about 17 million Americans, had family incomes of $40,000 or more (Pear 2007a). They either lost their jobs in high-wage industries, were employed but unable to afford health insurance premiums (Broder et al. 2002), worked as independent contractors (e.g., real estate agents), or would not be covered by insurers because of a preexisting health condition (Pear 2007a). Advocates for the uninsured are hopeful that policy makers will respond to a more effective lobbying coalition of high-wage workers, the unemployed, the poor, and minorities (Broder et al. 2002). Annual premiums for employer-sponsored health insurance for 2012 averaged $5,615 for single coverage and $15,745 for family coverage (Kaiser Family Foundation 2012).

The structure of the health insurance system and the lack of coverage for all have been the target of recent presidential administrations. Health care reform will be discussed in the next section.

What Does It Mean to Me?

Policy analysts, advocates, and health care professionals sharply criticized President George W. Bush for stating in 2007, "People have access to health care in America. After all, you just go to an emergency room." From a sociological perspective, was the president's statement correct? Does his statement address access as discussed in the previous section? Why or why not?

 STATE STATS

Community, Policy, and Social Action

Health Care Reform

According to Stuart Altman and Uwe Reinhardt (1996), although Americans in general are pleased with the quality of health care they receive, they are troubled by other aspects of health care. Americans are upset primarily about the cost of health care, both out-of-pocket costs and the cost of the health care system as a whole. Second, the structure of the health insurance system is viewed as having a number of shortcomings, foremost among them the lack of universal coverage. Finally, although the quality of health care is high, people believe it is not uniformly so.

During his first administration, President Bill Clinton said problems connected with the U.S. health care system were the most pressing in the United States. In 1993, Clinton pushed for passage of the Health Security Act, an attempt at comprehensive health care reform. The act would have required all employers to provide health insurance to their employees and would have given small businesses and unemployed Americans subsidies to purchase insurance. After Congress rejected Clinton's health care plan, Americans looked to the private market to restrain health care costs and to enhance patient care and choice. U.S. medicine moved aggressively toward managed care arrangements, HMOs, and for-profit health plans (Oberlander 2002).

Sixteen years later, with Democratic majorities in the U.S. House of Representatives and the Senate, President Barack Obama declared "a season for action. . . . Now is the time to deliver on health care" (Obama 2009). After months of contentious and politically charged debate, Congress passed a compromise health reform bill in March 2010. Obama signed the Patient Protection and Affordable Care Act, along with the Health Care and Education Reconciliation Act of 2010, into law. The law is most often referred to as the Affordable Care Act (ACA). As of 2012, several ACA elements are in effect: Young adults up to age 26 remain covered by their parents' health insurance, plans are available for those with preexisting conditions, and lifetime limits on coverage have been eliminated. The U.S. Census Bureau measured an overall decline in the percentage of uninsured from 16.5% in 2010 to 15.7% in 2011 (DeNavas-Walt et al. 2012). Most notable was the decline among those ages 19 to 25 years from 29.8% in 2010 to 27.7% in 2011, attributed to the ACA provision. By 2014, all citizens and legal residents must purchase health insurance or face an annual fine. Additionally, states are required to expand Medicaid coverage to those with incomes 133% of the federal poverty line. Another feature of the law is elimination of gender rating, using gender as a factor in setting health insurance rates. In 2010, Obama said he was signing the bill on behalf of his mother, along with others who struggled to find affordable and comprehensive health coverage. The signing of the bill enshrined "the core principle that everybody should have some basic security when it comes to their health care" (Obama 2010). It is estimated that by 2016, the ACA will increase the number of nonelderly people with health insurance by 30 to 33 million (Congressional Budget Office 2012a).

 Health Care Reform

In 2012, the U.S. Supreme Court upheld the constitutionality of the ACA, examining specifically the individual health insurance mandate and the portion of the law that will require states to expand their Medicaid rolls by 2014. The majority of justices likened the penalty for not obtaining health insurance to a tax. "Because the Constitution permits such a tax, it is not our role to forbid it, or to pass upon its wisdom or fairness," wrote Chief Justice John G. Roberts Jr. (quoted in Liptak 2012:A1). The Medicaid expansion was upheld by the Court, but states would be permitted to keep their current federal money for Medicaid while refusing to expand the program. The Court ruled that states could decide whether to go along with the expansion without penalties to their existing Medicaid payments (Liptak 2012).

 Affordable Care Act

The expansion of Medicaid has been controversial, not only for the increased cost to states, but also because of claims that the program is ineffectual and may also be associated with worse health (Belluck 2012). More than a dozen Republican governors announced that their states would not comply with the Medicaid expansion. However, most governors from both parties responded to the ruling with caution, stating that they would need to study the impact of Medicaid expansion on their state's budget and on their uninsured population (Cooper 2012). The Congressional Budget Office (2012b) estimated that the Supreme Court's decision would lead to about 6 million fewer people covered by the federal Medicaid program, yet half of them should gain private insurance coverage through health insurance exchanges established by ACA. The other half, a predicted 3 million, would be uninsured.

State Health Care Reforms

Several states aggressively moved forward on health reform, and several—Florida, Hawaii, Massachusetts, Minnesota, Oregon, and Washington—are committed to providing health coverage for all of their citizens. At this time it is unclear how implementation of the ACA will impact these state plans. Following are summaries of four state plans.

Hawaii was one of the first states to act on health care reform. In 1974, the state passed the Hawaii Prepaid Health Care Act, requiring employers to provide health insurance for all employees working more than 20 hours per week and to pay at least 50% of the cost. Hawaii is the only state that requires employer payments to medical insurance under a congressional exemption of the Employee Retirement Income Security Act (ERISA). ERISA bars states from requiring all employers to offer health insurance, from regulating or taxing self-insured plans, and from mandating the specific benefits to be covered by employer health plans (Beatrice 1996). Hawaii's plan also limits employees' share of the insurance premium expenses to no more than 1.5% of their income. Recently, there has been a call to repeal or at least revise the Prepaid Health Care Act because of increasing health care costs. The percentage of uninsured Hawaiians is 7.8% (DeNavas-Walt et al. 2012).

Massachusetts became the first state to provide universal health care coverage to all its residents in 2006. The plan reduced the number of uninsured in the state to 3.4% (DeNavas-Walt et al. 2012), the lowest in any state. The plan allows the state to provide sliding-scale coverage, low-cost coverage, and free insurance coverage to uninsured residents depending on their income, age, or employment status. Individuals who can afford health insurance will be penalized on their state income taxes if they do not purchase it. There were modest provisions included in the plan to control costs, but not enough. Massachusetts spends 23% more per person on health care ($9,000) than the national average ($8,000). By 2010, 94.2% of all nonelderly adult state residents had health insurance coverage, an increase from 86.6% coverage in 2006. While spending continues to be a concern, analysts have noted how health care reform has led to gains in access to and use of health care in the state (Long, Stockley, and Dahlen 2012). Massachusetts government and health industry officials agreed that universal coverage would not be sustainable if they did not address the growth of health care spending (Sack 2009). In 2012, the state legislature passed a bill that would not allow health care spending to grow any faster than the state's economy through 2017 (Goodnough 2012).

MinnesotaCare became law in Minnesota in 1992. Also known as the Health Right Act, the legislation included a variety of laws aimed at reducing costs and expanding access to health care for the uninsured (Beatrice 1996). MinnesotaCare is funded through a tax on health care providers and through enrollee premiums (based on family size, number of people covered, and income) (Sacks, Kutyla, and Silow-Carroll 2002). The act set price controls for health care spending (repealed in 1997), set statewide managed care guidelines, initially mandated that all non-HMO physicians follow a state fee structure (repealed in 1995), placed all HMOs under the regulation of the Commission of Health, and mandated that HMOs be nonprofit (Citizens Council on Health Care 2003). The act also subsidized health insurance for low- and middle-income uninsured families and individuals. Minnesota placed all MinnesotaCare recipients into HMOs (Beatrice 1996; Citizens Council on Health Care 2003). A small number of Minnesotans, about 9.2%, are uninsured (DeNavas-Walt et al. 2012).

In 2008, Oregon's Medicaid agency realized that it had enough funds to provide health insurance to an additional 10,000 adults (Oregon Health Study 2012). The agency decided to distribute the extra funds via a lottery system, drawing names to determine who would receive the Medicaid coverage. As part of the implementation, the Oregon Health Study was initiated to track the social, economic, and health outcomes among those enrolled in Medicaid and those who were not. Results of the study will provide policy makers with data on the effects of expanding health insurance on both individual and system levels. After a year of tracking the two study groups, Amy Finkelstein and her colleagues (2011) concluded that enrollment in Medicaid increased access to and use of health care (including preventative care and regular office or clinic visits), increased financial security (decreasing the probability of having an unpaid medical pill sent to a collection agency), and improved health and well-being (reporting to be in good to excellent health, increased probability in not screening positive for depression) compared to those who were not enrolled in the Oregon Medicaid program.

State Children's Health Insurance Program

The State Children's Health Insurance Program (SCHIP) was adopted in 1997 as an amendment to the Social Security Act, Title XXI. The program is administered under the Centers for Medicare and Medicaid Services (CMS). SCHIP enables states to implement their own children's health insurance programs for uninsured low-income children 18 years old or younger and targets the children of working parents or grandparents. For example, a family of three that earns as much as $52,800 a year (in 2008) is eligible. The insurance plan pays for regular checkups, immunizations, prescription medicines, and hospitalizations. SCHIP uses comprehensive outreach materials and educational programs to recruit eligible children and their families, especially through elementary and secondary schools. In many states, as SCHIP enrollments began, so did Medicaid enrollments. By 2008, the number of children enrolled in SCHIP had reached a record high of more than 7 million. State officials expected SCHIP enrollment increases to continue.

SCHIP

Based on his concern that SCHIP expansion would be too costly and would be a step toward universal health coverage, in fall 2007, George W. Bush vetoed a House bill that proposed coverage for more than 10 million children as well as expansion of coverage to include dental services, mental illness, and pregnant women with low incomes. The expansion bill was supported by many state governors whose states were running out of federal funds to support the program (Pear 2007b). SCHIP advocates accused the president and his congressional supporters of placing their concerns for socialized medicine over the necessary expansion of health coverage for children. With the House unable to override the president's veto, the administration promised to work with Congress on a bill compromise.

SCHIP Effects

In 2009, Obama signed the SCHIP expansion bill. The measure provides coverage to an additional 4 million uninsured children over the next five years, raising the total number of uninsured children covered by the program to 11 million. Obama praised the program for providing access to quality affordable health care and emphasized the program's importance during a time when families have lost their jobs and health insurance. The bill was passed with partisan support from House and Senate Democrats. The expansion will be financed with a 62-cent-per-pack increase in the federal tax on cigarettes.

State Prescription Drug Plans

In an effort to control drug costs for their residents, several states have offered innovative cost-control models. Pennsylvania is second to Florida in the proportion of its population that is 65 years or older (Pear 2002). More than 300,000 people in Pennsylvania are enrolled in Pharmaceutical Assistance Contract for the Elderly (PACE). Men and women 65 years or older can enroll in the program if they have annual incomes less than $25,100 for an individual or $33,800 per couple. The program costs patients a $16.25 co-payment per filled prescription and is financed largely from state lottery proceeds. The program requires the use of low-cost generic drugs, which account for about 45% of all filled prescriptions. PACE was established in 1984 with strong bipartisan support, but with the rising cost of drugs and the increasing number of patients, lawmakers are looking for more cost-cutting strategies (Pear 2002). Pennsylvania also supports PACENET, an assistance program available for elderly individuals with household incomes between $14,500 and $23,500 or between $17,700 and $31,500 per couple (with a $40 deductible and an $8 co-payment).

In 2003, Pennsylvania joined eight other states and the District of Columbia to form a nonprofit consortium to buy drugs in bulk, passing on the savings to their citizens (Freudenheim 2003). The consortium includes a drug benefit manager who will help states maximize their drug benefits by receiving full-price discounts and rebates, determining the most cost-effective and appropriate drugs, and including coverage for mail-order prescriptions and for importing drugs from Canada. The program is supported by the Heinz Family Philanthropies, a charitable organization.

U.S. laws prohibit the importation of Canadian drugs into the United States, unless their safety is certified by the U.S. Department of Health and Human Services. Despite this law, Boston, Massachusetts, and the state of New Hampshire announced in 2003 that they would begin buying prescription drugs from Canada. Springfield, Massachusetts, was the first city to import Canadian drugs for city employees in 2003. Boston plans to

Photo 10.4

In one of the first bills he signed as president, Barack Obama reauthorized the State Children's Health Insurance Program in 2009. While continuing medical coverage for 7 million children, the reauthorization also expanded coverage to an additional 4 million children.

do the same for its city employees and retirees, estimating a savings of about $1 million annually. For example, 90 pills of Lipitor, a popular cholesterol drug, cost $183.97 in the United States, but the Canadian price is $136.70, a savings of $47.27 per prescription (Testa 2003). The Nevada State Board of Pharmacy approved regulations in 2006 that would allow Nevada residents to purchase online prescriptions filled by state-approved Canadian pharmacies.

Taking a World View

Not-So-Foreign Models of Health Care

Opponents of health care reform equated Obama's plan to "socialized medicine," believing that increasing government control of health care is intrusive and restrictive. Journalist T. R. Reid (2009) describes the term as a powerful political weapon, first used in 1947 to disparage President Truman's national health care proposal. But as Reid explains, the argument against socialized medicine is flawed. First, most national health care systems are not socialized. Many countries provide universal health care using private doctors, hospitals, and insurance plans. In fact, there is no single health care system in the world that is exclusively government owned and operated. Second, the United States already has socialized medicine, government-run medicine, in the form of the Department of Veterans Affairs and the Medicare system.

As Reid (2009) describes, "We're like no other country, because the United States maintains so many separate systems for separate classes of people" (p. 21). In his 2009 book, *The Healing of America: A Global Quest for Better, Cheaper, and Fairer Health Care,* Reid identifies the four separate systems of health care in our country:

1. Bismarck Model. For most working Americans under 65 years of age, their health care coverage is similar to the health systems in Germany, France, and Japan. Under this model, the worker and the employer share the cost of health insurance premiums.

2. Beveridge Model. Native Americans, military personnel, and veterans are covered under health care systems much like Great Britain and Cuba. Care is provided by doctors who are government employees working in government-owned clinics and hospitals. Patients who use this system never receive a medical bill.

3. National Health Insurance Model. Americans over the age of 65 are covered under Medicare, a system similar to the Canadian health system. Most health care providers are private, but the payer is a single government-run insurance program that every citizen pays into.

4. Out-of-Pocket Model. Americans without a health insurance policy are no different from citizens from poor countries such as Cambodia or parts of rural China or India. If medical care is available, individuals will have to pay the bill out of their own pocket. Care is often available from emergency rooms or community-based free clinics.

In his analysis of these different models of care, Reid (2009) concludes that no system is perfect. Health care reform debates are taking place in other countries.

In 2004, the Health and Human Services Task Force on Drug Importation concluded that savings on foreign drugs were not as much as consumers would expect and warned about significant risks to consumers purchasing imported drugs. The report questioned the safety and effectiveness of foreign-made drugs. At the release of the report, consumer and health advocates weighed in, criticizing the task force for failing to address the fundamental problem of providing affordable prescription drugs to those who cannot afford them.

Voices in the Community

Victoria Hale

Victoria Hale

In 2005, Victoria Hale was named by *Esquire* magazine as its businesswoman of the year. She is the director and founder of OneWorld Health, the first nonprofit pharmaceutical company in the United States.

Hale worked as an analyst for the U.S. Food and Drug Administration's Center for Drug Evaluation and Research and then at Genentech (a biotechnology firm) when she first envisioned her company. Her position in the pharmaceutical industry allowed her to see how drugs were being set aside simply because they were not making enough money. The industry dedicates less than 10% of its total research and development budget to eradicating diseases of the developing world, which account for 90% of the world's total infections (Heffernan 2005). Of the more than 1,500 drugs marketed worldwide between 1974 and 2004, only 21, or 1.3%, were used to treat diseases of the developing world (Buse 2006).

She established OneWorld Health to accomplish what she believed the industry should be doing—investing in the development and distribution of drugs that could be used to eradicate diseases in the developing world. Says Hale, "We deliberately chose neglected diseases that others were not working on. . . . There has been little research done on these diseases, and limited money for research or development. We don't choose projects because money is available, we choose projects and then we go find funding" (Roth 2006:2). OneWorld Health is funded by charitable contributions.

Hale's strategy was simple. She searched for drugs whose patents had expired or were not being used because of low profit margins. The first drug OneWorld Health invested in was paromomycin, an antibiotic that cures a parasitic disease called visceral leishmaniasis, also known as black fever or kala-azar. The disease afflicts a half a million people annually worldwide, particularly in Bangladesh, Brazil, India, Nepal, and Sudan. Hale discovered that the development of paromomycin had been shelved before its clinical trials were completed. After continuing and completing clinical trials with the drug, Hale found a company, Gland Pharma, based in Hyderabad, India, that agreed to produce paromomycin and sell it for $10 per full course of treatment, affordable for the poor people of India.

The use of paromomycin was approved in India in late 2006. The government publicly announced its goal of eradicating the disease by 2010. Eradication dates have also been set in Bangladesh and Nepal for 2015. After dealing with the initial skepticism of the pharmaceutical industry and its executives, Hale's OneWorld Health has been heralded as an innovative, socially minded organization. Hale's work will continue: "You can't take care of all two billion of the world's poorest poor at one time. But you can go disease by disease and determine which one you can succeed with" (Roth 2006:2). OneWorld Health is working on three additional drugs—for malaria (the most severe parasitic disease), diarrhea (the number-two killer of children in the developing world), and soil-transmitted hookworm infection (nearly 2 billion people have active infections).

For more information about OneWorld Health, go to *Study Site Chapter 10* at www.sagepub.com/leonguerrero4e.

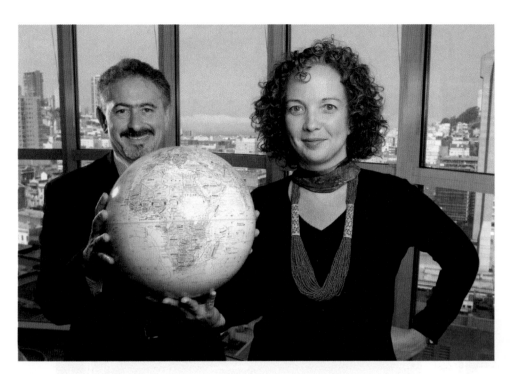

Photo 10.5

The Institute for OneWorld Health's CEO and founder Victoria Hale is photographed with the institute's chief medical officer Ahvie Herskowitz.

Work-Based Health Clinics

In an effort to manage and control the cost of their health care expenses, more U.S. corporations are providing on-site medical care. Since 2005, Cigna, Sprint Nextel, Credit Suisse, and Walt Disney World have opened on-site health clinics. More than 100 of the nation's largest 1,000 employers now provide primary care clinics or preventative health services on-site for their employees (Freudenheim 2007). One such company, Pepsi Bottling Group, operates 11 employee clinics in the United States with plans to add more in the future. Toyota's San Antonio, Texas, primary care center is open for workers and their families, complete with two full-time doctors, a blood test lab, and an X-ray center.

On-site clinics are a "modern model that is . . . proving to be cost-effective. . . . Not only does it pick up health issues earlier, but it doesn't require time away from work and at the same time creates a culture of caring," says Sean Sullivan, president of the Institute for Health and Productivity Management (Wells 2006:48). The health care savings from these clinics is estimated to be between 5% and 20%. The range of services includes routine physical examinations, allergy and flu shots, routine monitoring for chronic diseases, prescriptions, and advice on weight loss or smoking cessation (Freudenheim 2007; Wells 2006). On-site medical facilities and staff can be outsourced or company managed and hired; both models allow companies to customize their clinics and range of services to meet the needs of their workforce (Wells 2006).

Community-Based Health Care for Minorities

Regardless of their health insurance status, minority Americans are more likely than Whites to be disconnected from the health care system and a regular doctor (Commonwealth Fund 2003b). Unique community-based health care approaches have emerged to serve these groups.

Photo 10.6

Community health centers bring health care to the people. This remote area medical (RAM) clinic is an annual medical clinic set up at the Wise County Fairgrounds in Wise, Virginia. Over three days, the clinic will assist more than 7,000 rural residents. All services, equipment, and supplies are donated.

 Project Brotherhood

Community health centers (CHCs) were based on neighborhood health clinics first established during the War on Poverty in the 1960s. CHCs are operated by a variety of nonprofit organizations, health departments, religious and faith-based organizations, medical organizations, and schools. Costs are covered through a variety of sources, ranging from private insurance to government contracts or grants. These centers have been called the most effective tool to reduce health disparities and can increase access to health care to an estimated 14 million individuals, two thirds of whom are minority group members (Hargreaves, Arnold, and Blot 2006).

One example of a community health center is the Project Brotherhood Black Men's Clinic, located on Chicago's South Side. The clinic was created to address the disproportionate disease burden and shorter life expectancy for Black men (Tanner 2003). Eric Whitaker, cofounder of the clinic, explained how many men avoid traditional health care providers because they never find doctors who look and talk like them. Focus groups indicated that Black men need a reason other than their health to go to the clinic, so program administrators latched onto a cornerstone of Black cultural life: the barbershop.

Project Brotherhood opened a barbershop alongside the community health clinic, where men are able to get free haircuts and listen to informal presentations by the clinic staff on HIV, heart disease, and cancer. In addition, the clinic offers job search and résumé writing information and parenting classes. As Whitaker describes it, "It's a place where information is exchanged, it's a place of familiarity. . . . We just transported that idea to the clinic setting" (quoted in Tanner 2003:A12). He explains, "We want to learn how to listen to our community and discover its own perception of needs and assets" (Whitaker quoted in Phalen 2000). The organization has developed a network of a dozen barbershops where the barbers are trained to address colon and prostate cancer and HIV education (Project Brotherhood 2010). In 1999, the clinic averaged about four medical visits per week; by 2005, the average number of medical visits increased to 27 per week (Project Brotherhood 2006).

Using the same strategy of bringing care to community members, the American Diabetes Association (2003) has enlisted the help of African American churches to educate their parishioners about the disease. Recognizing the importance of the African American church as a source of community support and a vehicle for communication, "Diabetes Sunday" began in 1996. Diabetes Sunday is often held during Black History Month. Church pastors discuss diabetes and distribute education materials. Certified diabetes educators are on hand to answer questions after the service. Similar community-based programs target Latino, Asian Pacific Islander, and immigrant populations.

Main Points

- Although medicine can identify the biological pathways to disease, we need a sociological perspective to address the social determinants of health. Research continues to demonstrate the relationship between the individual and society and the structural effects on health: how our health is affected by our social position, work, families, education, and wealth and poverty.

- Epidemiology is the study of the patterns in the distribution and frequency of sickness, injury, and death and the social factors that shape them. Epidemiologists focus on communities and populations, addressing how health and illness experiences are based on social factors such as gender, age, race, social class, and behavior.

- According to the functionalist perspective, illness has a legitimate place in society.

- Conflict theorists believe that patterns of health and illness are not accidental or solely the result of individuals' actions. Theorists identify how these patterns reflect systematic inequalities based on ethnicity/race or gender and differences in power, values, and interests.

- Although the medicalization of such conditions as premenstrual syndrome and menopause may have been effective in treating women, various feminist theorists see this trend as an extension of medicine's control of women.

- From an interactionist's perspective, health, illness, and medical responses are socially constructed and maintained.

- Women live longer than men, but women experience higher rates of nonfatal chronic conditions. Men experience higher rates of fatal illness. These differences in mortality have been attributed to three factors: genetics, risk taking, and health care.

- Data consistently support the notion that those with higher education, income, and occupational prestige have lower rates of morbidity and mortality. No factor has been singled out as the primary link between socioeconomic position and health; however, scholars have offered many factors—standard of living, work conditions, housing conditions, and the social and psychological connections with others at work, at home, and in the community—to explain the relationship.

- Another problem with health is access to health care and insurance; many groups do not have insurance or access to it, and now the middle class is experiencing problems in retaining health insurance. Illegal immigrants also do not have insurance and often use the emergency room as their place of primary care.

- Among industrialized countries, the United States spends the greatest proportion of its GDP on health care. The rising cost of health care in the United States has been attributed to various factors:

increases in the application of high technology for medical treatment and diagnosis, the aging population, the overall demand for health care, the amount of uncompensated care, and the cost of prescription drugs (the fastest-growing spending category and a particular problem for the elderly).

■ Health care reform has been a topic of debate in Congress and the White House for several years. Recent federal health care initiatives include the Affordable Care Act, Medicare reform, and the State Children's Health Insurance Program. But as health care continues to be debated at the federal level, some states are taking action to make reforms. Local communities and organizations are also becoming involved.

On Your Own

Log on to the open-access Student Study Site at www.sagepub.com/leonguerrero4e for these additional learning tools:

■ Interactive quizzes
■ Video clips
■ NPR audio links
■ Handbook articles

■ E-flashcards
■ Journal articles
■ End-of-chapter web exercises
■ Additional web resources and current events

Internet and Community Exercises

1. Based on the American Medical Association website, review the organization's mission statement, history, and legislative initiatives. Log on to *Study Site Chapter 10.* Is there evidence to demonstrate how the AMA maintains its power and influence on the medical profession?

2. Select a specific disease or illness that you believe affects college-age men and women. Identify several Internet websites and support groups related to the disease or illness. How is the disease defined? Are there objective and subjective aspects of the disease? Does it vary by gender? By ethnicity/race?

3. Select one local hospital or health care system in your area or state. Through the Internet (or by visiting the hospital), identify the organization's mission statement, its patient bill of rights, and community-based programs. How does this organization define *care*? Does its definition appear to be consistent with the community's population and needs? Why or why not?

4. The United Nations Human Development Report tracks several health indicators: life expectancy at birth, expenditure on health (percentage of GDP), and maternal mortality ratio. Log on to *Study Site Chapter 10* for the UN link and compare the United States with Canada, Germany, Mexico, Sweden, and the United Kingdom.

5. In an effort to improve the quality of food served at local schools, some parent, health, and medical advocacy groups have rejected the National School Lunch Program, promoting instead a healthier and local school lunch program. Legislation introduced in 2010 by the Obama administration would ban candy and sugary beverages from schools, replacing them with healthier options. Each school day about 32 million children participate in a meal program. Select one local elementary or high school in your area. Investigate its school lunch program. Does its menu feature healthy options? Does it rely on food products from local or regional farmers?

Study Questions

1. How is health examined from a sociological perspective?

2. How is illness functional in society? What behavior is expected from someone who is sick?

3. Explain from a conflict perspective how health inequalities are shaped by conflict and competing interests between groups.

4. Using eating disorders as the basis for your answer, examine how illness and disease are socially constructed.

5. Review the inequalities of health and health care access by gender, race/ethnicity, and social class.

6. Why is the United States the last industrial country to adopt a national health care program? Which sociological perspective(s) best explains why public and political support for health care reform has been difficult to achieve?

7. Do you know what a "mommy job" is? Mentioned on ABC's *Brothers and Sisters* program and featured in print and television advertisements, a mommy job is a cosmetic surgical procedure that may include a breast lift, a tummy tuck, and liposuction to reduce the stretch marks, slackened skin, and excess fat that result from pregnancy and childbirth. Targeting women of childbearing age, the marketing of mommy makeovers has been described as an attempt to "pathologize the postpartum body, characterizing pregnancy and child birth as maladies with disfiguring aftereffects that can be repaired with the help of scalpels" (Singer 2007:E3). From a sociological perspective, is a mommy job a surgical necessity or an invention? What do you think?

CHAPTER 11

The Media

> *Imagine that you wake up tomorrow in a sort of "Twilight Zone" parallel society where everything is the same except that media do not exist: no television, no movies, no radio, no recorded music, no computers, no Internet, no books or magazines or newspapers.*
>
> —Croteau and Hoynes (2000:5)

 Growing Up Online

What would your life be like without the media? Without communication, and the media to communicate with, there would be no society. The term *media* is the plural of *medium,* derived from the Latin word *medius,* which means middle. A *medium* is a method of communication—television, telephone, cable, Internet, radio, or print—between (or in the middle of) a sender and a receiver. But taken all together, the **media**, as defined by David Croteau and William Hoynes (2000), are the "different technological processes that facilitate communication between the sender of the message and the receiver of that message" (p. 7).

Communication is a basic social activity (Seymour-Ure 1974). It is impossible not to communicate and not to come in contact with the media. According to the U.S. Census Bureau (2010), in 2007, the average U.S. adult watched 1,613 hours of television, listened to 177 hours of recorded music, and watched 61 hours of home videos. The average U.S. adult also spent 171 hours reading the daily newspaper, 125 hours reading magazines, and 189 hours on the Internet.

What Does It Mean to Me?

For at least a week, monitor your own media usage. How many hours of television do you watch? How many hours are you on the Internet and on your phone? Would it be possible for you to live a day without media?

 STATE STATS

Photo 11.1

In 2007, for the first time, Americans spent more time on their cell phones than on landlines and pay phones. People are using their cell phones in various ways—for phone calls, text messaging, video messages, e-mail, and web access.

The media reflect "the evolution of a nation that has increasingly seized on the need and desire for more leisure time" (Alexander and Hanson 1995:i). Technological developments have increased our range of media choices, from the growing number of broadcast and cable channels to the ever-increasing number of Internet websites. New technologies have also increased our viewing control of and access to the media. For example, technology allows us to choose where and when we want to see a recent film. Are you taking a long road trip? You can download your favorite movie to your notebook or your phone and watch it on the road. Need to access your e-mail? You can check e-mail with a wireless connection in your classroom or with your phone from nearly any location. In fact, u cn comnC8 w/yr F W txt msgN A3 (translation: You can communicate with your friends with text messaging anytime, anywhere, anyplace). As Croteau and Hoynes (2001) observed, "We navigate through a vast mass media environment unprecedented in human history" (p. 3).

Yet, the media have been blamed for creating and promoting social problems and accused of being a problem themselves. The most commonly identified problem is the media's content: controversial programming that features violence, racism, and sexism. Media critics have expressed concern about the highly controlled process by which the images that we see are conceived, produced, and disseminated by media conglomerates. Social researchers and policy makers have identified the unequal advantage some social groups have over others in our increasingly high-tech media environment. Before we review the media and their related social problems, we first examine the media from a sociological perspective.

 Social Media

What Does It Mean to Me?

The digital equivalent of hanging out can be found on social networking sites such as Facebook and Twitter. Also referred to as **social media**, these sites provide teens and adults opportunities for personal expression and connection. How do these sites provide a way to connect with others? If you have your own page, how does it work for you? Are there any dysfunctions related to these social networking sites? Are you concerned about your privacy when using these sites?

 STATE STATS

Sociological Perspectives on the Media

Functionalist Perspective

Functionalists examine the structural relationship between the media and other social institutions. Even before the content is created, political, economic, and social realities set the stage for media content. The media are shaped by the social and economic conditions of American life and by society's beliefs about the nature of men and women and the nature of society (Peterson 1981). The first American printing press arrived in Boston along with a group of Puritans fleeing England in 1638. The press became an instrument of religion and government, used to print a freeman's oath that presented the conditions of citizenship in this new country, as well as an almanac and a book of hymns (Peterson 1981).

Through electronic and print messages, the media continue to frame our understandings about our lives, our nation, and our world. The media serve as a link between individuals, communities, and nations. They help create a collective consciousness, a term used by Émile Durkheim to describe the set of shared norms and beliefs in a society. The mass media provide people with a sense of connection that few other institutions can offer. Live media events, such as the Olympics, the Super Bowl, or the Oscars, are set off from other media programs. People gather in groups to watch, they talk about what they see, and they share the sense that they are watching something special (Schudson 1986). News events captured by the media, such as the terrorist attacks of September 11, 2001, the 2011 Egyptian protests, or the 2012 Summer Olympic games, connect a nation and even the world.

What Does It Mean to Me?

How does the mass media provide a sense of connection for you—for instance, how did the media do so for the 2011 royal wedding of Prince William and Kate or the 2012 presidential election?

 LGBT Content

In particular, television has contributed to a corresponding nationalization of politics and issues, taking local or regional events and turning them into national debates. Socially and politically, the media make our world smaller. In 2004, the entire nation watched as gay and lesbian couples were allowed to marry in San Francisco. Other mayors and cities began to follow their lead, and the number of gay and lesbian wedding ceremonies increased across the country, along with the growing debate about how same-sex marriages would affect the institution of marriage. Thanks to various forms of social media, the world watched as millions of Egyptians converged on Tahrir Square in 2011 demanding the overthrow of the regime of President Hosni Mubarak. Mubarak resigned after 18 days of demonstrations. Facebook and Twitter are credited with unifying protestors and ultimately shaping the political debate.

The media have been accused of creating serious dysfunctions and social problems in society. Research has documented the link between viewing of media violence and the development of aggression, particularly among children who watch dramatic violence on television and film. Television has been called the "other parent" or the "black box," accused of draining the life and intelligence out of its young viewers. Popular media culture has been accused of undermining our educational system and subverting traditional literacy (Postman 1989). Public health studies have documented the link between television viewing and poor physical health among children and adults. The one thing television viewers seem to do while watching television is eat, and the danger is in what they choose to eat and drink—unhealthy snack foods or high-calorie drinks (Van den Bulck 2000). We examine these dysfunctions more closely in the section titled "Do the Media Control Our Lives?"

Conflict Perspective

The media, says Noam Chomsky (1989), are like any other businesses. The fundamental principle in American media is to attract an audience to sell to advertisers. Yes, you read that correctly. Commercial television and radio programming depend on advertising revenue, and in turn, the networks promise that you, the consumer audience, will buy the advertisers' products. "The market model of the media is based on the ability of a network to deliver audiences to these advertisers" (Croteau and Hoynes 2001:6).

Persuasive Marketing

In the United States, media organizations are likely to be part of larger conglomerates where profit making is the most important goal (Ball-Rokeach and Cantor 1986). Since the very beginning of mass communications, ideas, information, and profit have mixed. The first books printed in the colonies may have been devoted to religion, but the printers made money (Porter 1981). The media, according to conflict theorists, can only be fully understood when we learn who controls them.

One of the clearest, and some say most problematic, trends in the media is the increasing consolidation of ownership. The corporate media play a major role in managing consumer demand, producing messages that support corporate capitalism, and creating a sense of political events and social issues (Kellner 1995). In 1984, more than 50 corporations controlled most of our newspapers, magazines, broadcasting, books, and movies. By 1997, Ben Bagdikian reported that there were 10 media giants. Bagdikian (1997) declared, "Media power is political power" (p. xiii). The top five entertainment multinational conglomerates controlling the media for 2011 are listed in Table 11.1. These companies are truly multimedia corporations, producing movies, books, magazines, newspapers, television programming, music, videos, toys, and theme parks in the global marketplace. Under this increasing media consolidation, women- and minority-owned broadcasting has declined. People of color own only 3% of commercial television stations (Wade 2008).

Table 11.1

Five Largest Entertainment Companies

1. Walt Disney (United States)
2. News Corporation Ltd. (Australia)
3. Time Warner Inc. (United States)
4. CBS (United States)
5. Viacom (United States)

Source: CNN Money 2011.

Note: For more information about these media companies, visit the website "Who Owns What," sponsored by the Columbia Journalism Review. *Log on to the Study Site, Chapter 11, at www.sagepub.com/leonguerrero4e for a link.*

Media Bias

Mass Communication

Media & Revolution

Stereotypes

Miller (2002) warned that the most corrosive influence of the 10 media conglomerates cited by Bagdikian (1997) was their impact on journalism. Journalism has traditionally been referred to as the fourth estate, an independent institutional source of political and social power that monitors the actions of other powerful institutions such as politics, economics, and religion. However, conflict theorists remind us that someone is in charge of the fourth estate. Those who control the media are able to manipulate what we see, read, and hear. The media, serving the interest of interlocking state and corporate powers, frame messages in a way that supports the ruling elite and limits the variety of messages that we read, see, and hear (Chomsky 1989).

Edward Jay Epstein (1981) reveals that what we consider news is not the product of chance events; "it is the result of decisions made within a news organization" (p. 119). He explains that the crucial decisions on what constitutes news—what will and won't be covered—are made not by the journalists but by executives of the news organization. Although the public expects news reporters to act like independent fair-minded professionals, reporters are employees of corporations that control their hiring, firing, and daily management (Bagdikian 1997). News executives are in control of the selection and deployment of specific reporters, the expenditure of time and resources for gathering the news, and the allocation of space for the presentation of news (Epstein 1981). And because they are economically motivated, news organizations are mindful of their audiences' preferences and try to cater to those preferences as much as possible (Baron 2006).

Regina Branton and Johanna Dunaway concluded that audience preferences and newspaper profit motives result in differences between English and Spanish news coverage of immigration in the United States. In their 2008 study, Spanish-language news outlets generated a larger volume of immigration coverage than English-language outlets. On the other hand, English-language news media were more likely to focus on negative aspects of immigration than Spanish-language media outlets. Both patterns, according to the researchers, are motivated by profit and the desire to satisfy their different target audiences. Branton and Dunaway suggest that conflicting media coverage may even contribute to the differences in immigration attitudes between Anglos and Latinos.

Feminist Perspective

Douglas Kellner (1995) says that the media represent "a contested terrain, reproducing on the cultural level the fundamental conflicts within society" (p. 101). Feminist theorists attempt to understand how the media represent and devalue women and minorities. This perspective examines how the media either use stereotypes disparaging women and minorities or completely exclude them from media images (Eschholz, Bufkin, and Long 2002).

One of the most important lessons young children learn is expected gender roles, learning masculine versus feminine behaviors. Although these lessons are taught by parents and teachers, a significant source of cultural gendered messages is television programs (Powell and Abels 2002). As Leah R. VandeBerg (1991) explains, television programs are "designed to . . . evoke, activate, reference, and occasionally challenge mainstream social myths, policies and beliefs, including those concerning gender" (p. 106).

In his analysis of children's programming, Mark Barner (1999) found that women are typically portrayed in passive roles as housewives, waitresses, and secretaries, whereas men are seen in active roles as construction workers or doctors. In their study of children's shows *Barney and Friends* and *Teletubbies,* Kimberly Powell and Lori Abels (2002)

Photo 11.2

According to a 2007 survey from the Pew Research Center for the People and the Press, viewers of *The Daily Show with Jon Stewart* (and *The Colbert Report*) were the most well-informed about current events. When asked to name national and international political leaders or list current news stories, more *Daily Show* and *Colbert Report* viewers were able to correctly answer the questions than were viewers who relied on broadcast television (network and local news) or those who obtained their news from the Internet or newspapers.

reported that neither popular program showed men and women in nonstereotypical roles. The female characters were followers most of the time, were underrepresented in a variety of occupations, and played feminine roles. The male characters on these children's programs were leaders or directors of action and were larger and stereotypically male in appearance.

Feminist scholarship demonstrates how the media undermine women, particularly those who challenge traditional gender roles (Gibson 2009). In 2006, Katie Couric made history when she debuted as the first woman to solo anchor a major network newscast. Her debut and performance, according to Katie Gibson (2009), was critiqued in the media through a sexualized frame. By focusing primarily on her body and her appearance (her hair style, legs, and fashion), the media objectified Couric and undermined her as a legitimate news professional.

Researchers have identified how female political candidates receive different attention from their male counterparts. News reports focus on political women's physical appearance, lifestyle, and family life rather than on campaign issues and how women are the targets of negative coverage regarding their lack of experience and knowledge (Wasburn and Wasburn 2011). Coverage about a female candidate's political positions will feature women's topics such as abortion, child care, or education as opposed to men's issues such as the economy or national security. Wasburn and Wasburn (2011) in their analysis of media coverage of Governor Sarah Palin's vice presidential campaign concluded that "with respect to the coverage of political women, the political culture of America's commercial media remained largely unchanged through decades of election cycles" (p. 1039). Though there was more coverage of Palin than Joe Biden, the Democratic vice presidential candidate, Palin was objectified by the media and treated as a sex object through references to her beauty queen background, her appearance, and her wardrobe. There was frequent mention of her lack of national and global political experience, and policy coverage was focused on her take on women's issues.

Interactionist Perspective

In what they tell us and what they choose not to tell us, the media define our social world (McNair 1998). The interactionist perspective focuses on the symbols and messages of the media and how the media come to define our "reality." It might be best to view the media, as Michael Gurevitch and Mark Levy (1985) suggest, as "a site on which various social groups, institutions, and ideologies struggle over the definition and construction of social reality" (p. 9).

The mass media become the authority at any given moment for "what is true and what is false, what is reality and what is fantasy, what is important and what is trivial" (Bagdikian 1997:xliv). The mass media define what events are newsworthy. The first criterion is proximity; events happening close are more newsworthy than those happening at a greater distance. Second, deviation is an important criterion. Events that can be reported as disruptions (natural disasters, unexpected deaths, murders), deviations from cultural or social norms of behavior (especially sexual, e.g., philandering clergy or politicians), and lifestyle deviance (alternative lifestyle reports) make the news (Galtung and Ruge 1973).

Sociologist Herbert Gans (1979) explained that the news isn't about just anyone; it is usually about "knowns." Women and men identified by their position in government or their fame and fortune are automatically newsworthy. Knowns are elites in all walks of life, but especially from politics, the entertainment industry, and sports. Incumbent presidents appear in the news most often. The president is the only individual whose routine activities are noteworthy. (When was the last time that a news crew followed your every move?) In recent years, "celebutantes" (daughters from wealthy or famous families), such

Photo 11.3

During the 2008 U.S. presidential campaign, media reports addressed Governor Sarah Palin's lack of political experience, but also focused on her appearance and her beauty pageant background.

as Paris Hilton and Nicole Richie, have been deemed newsworthy by the media with their every move and fumble chronicled.

One of the biggest news stories of the late twentieth century was the death of Princess Diana. The facts and circumstances of her 1997 death and the fairy-tale life that preceded it conformed to all the criteria of newsworthiness. Although it occurred in France, her death involved cultural proximity: Princess Diana was a worldwide celebrity. The nonstop coverage of her life and death began as a story of celebrity fascination but ended as an international tragedy (McNair 1998). Shortly after Princess Diana's death, Mother Teresa, a renowned humanitarian, died. Although Mother Teresa's death was a news story, it never got the same attention and coverage as the death of Princess Diana did. As journalist Daniel Schorr (1998) says, the difference between the two women's lives was "the difference between a noble life well lived and a media image well cultivated. . . . Mother Teresa was celebrated, but was not a celebrity" (p. 15).

Media Hype

Taking a World View

Women's Feature Service, New Delhi, India

In New Delhi, India, is the headquarters of Women's Feature Service, an international news organization directed and staffed by women who produced articles reported from 40 countries for newspapers, magazines and Web sites. By gathering and providing access to these stories about women's lives, Women's Feature Service (WFS) seeks to create "space" for women's voices and experiences in mainstream media, where such topics don't usually receive this same kind of attention. WFS produces and markets women-centric articles. It also lobbies with decision makers in newspapers and magazines about such coverage and trains journalists to be able to recognize stories about women's concerns, to use gender-correct language, and to ask the right questions of appropriate sources.

WFS exists because of the felt need for a gender balance in news coverage and because of dissatisfaction about

the ways in which news organizations—in India and elsewhere—treat news coverage about women. Often, the media either ignore important stories altogether, relegate reporting to obscure places in the newspaper, or sensationalize incidents without examining the underlying context or causes. The media tend to focus on women only when it comes to "women's issues," forgetting that women also have an equal stake in so-called "male concerns" such as the budget, economy, globalization, agriculture, and conflict resolution. . . .

Photo 11.4

An estimated 18.6 million U.S. households watched television coverage of the 2011 royal wedding of Prince William and Kate Middleton. In addition to network and cable television programming, the ceremony was streamed live online via Facebook, Yahoo, and Hulu. iPad and iPhone apps also allowed fans to follow the royal nuptials.

(Continued)

(Continued)

Despite the presence of women journalists on the crime beat, incidents of rape and dowry deaths (shockingly regular occurrences in the Indian subcontinent) are usually reported in a routine manner, with the police being the sole source of information. Deadline pressure is one reason, but the other is that editors rarely insist that reporters get more information from other sources. Nor is there any follow-up to an incident.

When it comes to issues that impact most directly on women, news that should cause concern and lead to analytical articles that examine a particular issue in depth, is often dismissed in a couple of paragraphs on an inside page.

The other drawback is that there are only a few women writers—and fewer men—who can give a fresh perspective or insights into issues that concern women. Many women journalists have been conditioned (both socially and through the competitiveness of this profession) to adopt masculine attitudes and values. For instance, for a month after the United States declared its "war on terror" and began bombing Afghanistan, none of the leading newspapers in India wrote on its editorial page about the women in the conflict.

In India, there is a glass ceiling that women journalists have yet to break. Not a single mainline newspaper in India has a woman chief editor. One reason, of course, is that women joined the profession late—the first batch of women entered the profession in the 1960s—and took to covering politics even later. But it must be pointed out that there are male chief editors who are much younger than many senior women journalists are. Though women journalists have proven as competent, if not more, than men, they still lag behind in the power game. Two women who are at the top—Shobhana Bhartia (managing editor of *The Hindustan Times*) and Malini Parthasarathy (executive editor of *The Hindu*)—both belong to the families that own the newspapers. They've had to work hard to prove themselves and overcome some amount of intra-office opposition, but the fact remains they would not have risen this far but for their family connections. Interestingly, both do not have brothers, giving rise to the question: Would they have been given these opportunities had there been male siblings?

Source: This is an excerpt from Angana Parekh's "Bringing Women's Stories to a Reluctant Mainstream Press," Nieman Reports, 2001.

Advertising Influence

The mass media play a large role in shaping public agendas by influencing what people think about (Shaw and McCombs 1997) and, ultimately, what people consider a social problem (Altheide 1997). David Altheide (1997) describes the news media as part of the "problem-generating machine" produced by an entertainment-oriented media industry. The news informs the public, but its message is also intended to serve as entertainment, an opportunity for voyeurism, and a "quick fix" rather than providing an understanding of the underlying social causes of the problem.

Media Success

Altheide (1997) argues that the fear pervasive in American society is mostly produced through messages presented by the news media. According to Barry Glassner (1997), the disproportionate coverage of crime and violence in the news media affects readers and viewers. Despite evidence that Americans have a comparative advantage relative to diseases, accidents, nutrition, medical care, and life expectancy, American women and men perceive themselves to be at greater risk than do their counterparts elsewhere and express fears about this (Altheide 1997). In a national poll, respondents were asked why they believe the country has a serious crime problem. About 76% said they had seen serious crime in the media whereas only 22% said they had a personal experience with crime (Glassner 1997). In a study of 56 local news programs, crime was the most prominently featured subject, accounting for more than 75% of all news coverage in some cities (Klite, Bardwell, and Salzman 1997).

For a summary of sociological perspectives, see Table 11.2.

Table 11.2

Summary of Sociological Perspectives: The Media

	Functional	Conflict/Feminist	Interactionist
Explanation of the media and social problems	Functionalists examine the structural relationship between the media and other social institutions. Sociologists using this perspective also examine the functions and dysfunctions of the media.	Conflict theorists focus on the media and how their messages are controlled by an elite group. Feminist theorists address how the media use stereotypes disparaging women and minorities or completely exclude them from media images.	From this perspective, sociologists investigate how the media define our social reality.
Questions asked about the media	How do other institutions affect the media and their content? What functions do the media serve in society? What are their dysfunctions?	Who owns the media? How are the media's messages manipulated? What images of women and minorities are presented by the media?	How do the media define what is newsworthy? How do the media define the public agenda? How do the media define what we believe is a social problem?

The Media and Social Problems

Big Brother Is Watching

"Before our children can walk or talk, we teach them to share. So it is no wonder that we have flocked to social media, a platform based on sharing, to share everything from our birth dates to films of our child's birth," said Julie Brill, commissioner of the Federal Trade Commission (FTC), during a discussion on how the media industry should protect consumer privacy (quoted in Naoum 2012).

Jimmy Nguyen (2011) reports how websites track your personal information and online activities. Websites and online applications use cookies to track information about users. Cookies allow website operators to see your browsing history, store your log-in information, and help personalize sites by remembering your preferences and searches from previous visits. Though many Intern users have learned how to disable cookies through control panels, most Internet users do not do so. Facebook and other social media networks also maintain and track personal data about their users, including where the users live and users' personal interests and activities. Many Facebook applications (including Zynga, the creator of the online game FarmVille) were transmitting Facebook user IDs to advertisers and Internet tracking firms. Facebook and Zynga both pledge not to share personally identifiable information with third parties (Nguyen 2011).

Google's and Facebook's privacy policies have been scrutinized by media watch groups, politicians, and consumers. In 2011, Facebook settled FTC charges that it deceived users by

Sociology of Entertainment

telling them that it would keep their Facebook information private, though it was sharing users' personal data with others. According to its settlement, Facebook must not make any deceptive privacy claims, is required to get consumers' approval before making changes in data sharing, and is required to obtain assessments of its privacy practices by independent, third-party auditors though 2031 (FTC 2011). In 2012, Google announced plans to unify data collections across all its services, including its search engine, YouTube, and Gmail. Consumer privacy groups expressed concern that the data consolidation would reveal information about a person's location, religion, sexual orientation, health status, and personal interests. Google claims that it maintains a priority on user security, transparency, and control.

The Digital Haves and Have-Nots

The term **digital divide** was first used in the mid-1990s by policy leaders and social scientists concerned about the emerging split between those with and those without access to computers and the Internet. The term refers to the gap separating individuals who have access to new forms of technology from those who do not. In addition, others have identified a gap between those who can effectively use new information and communication tools and those who cannot (Gunkel 2003). Despite the increasing diffusion of computers and an overall increase in Internet use, a deep divide remains "between those who possess the resources, education and skills to reap the benefits from the technology and those who do not" (Servon 2002:4). President Obama has pledged to make high-speed Internet service available to most Americans, raising access to 90% in the coming decade.

The divide is also a global phenomenon. Less than 10% of the world's population uses the Internet (Guillén and Suárez 2005). According to data collected by the Central Intelligence Agency (2012), China and the United States rank the highest with Internet users—each has more than 200 million users (refer to Figure 11.1). Developing non-Western countries such as those in Africa, South America, and South Asia have fewer than a million Internet users.

The Internet has been described as both empowering and discriminating, enabling residents in some countries to pursue a better life while others are left behind (Guillén and

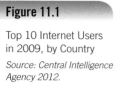

Figure 11.1

Top 10 Internet Users in 2009, by Country

Source: Central Intelligence Agency 2012.

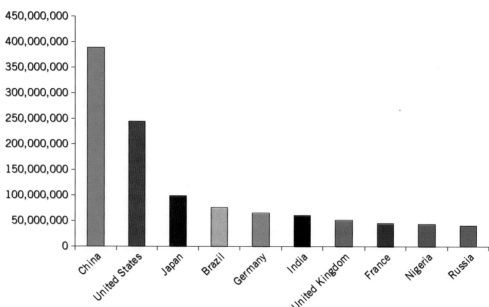

Suárez 2005). Cross-national research has linked the diffusion of Internet technology with developed service sector economies, an educated population, economic development, and significant research and development investment. Users in less-developed countries have basic access problems: economic (cost of basic necessities vs. cost of Internet access), technological (varying ability of local networks), and geographical (limited access outside urban areas) aspects (Vartanova 2002). Mainly because of income differentials, the Internet is beyond the reach of global citizens. For example, in countries with low human development, the average annual income is about $1,200 (in U.S. dollars); the cost of owning a cheap personal computer would take more than half of that income, about $700 (Drori 2004; United Nations Development Programme 2001). On the other hand, pay-as-you-go plans have made cellular phones more affordable. Nearly 40% of all adults living in poverty are cellular-only users compared with 21% of adults with higher incomes (Blumberg et al. 2011). Some states also provide cellular phone subsidies for low-income residents.

The digital divide implies a chain of causality. Access and ability to use computers and Internet technology help improve one's social and economic well-being; lack of access to computers and the Internet harms one's life chances. But it is also true that those who are already marginalized in society will have fewer opportunities to access and use computers and the Internet (Warschauer 2003). Among persons with incomes of $15,000 or less, only 32.1% have broadband access compared with 89.6% of individuals with incomes more than $150,000. Data also indicate that rates of broadband usage are higher among individuals with a bachelor's degree or more (84.2%) than among those

Table 11.3

Demographics of Internet Users in 2000 and 2011, Percentage of Adults (Age 18+) Who Use the Internet

Characteristic	June 2000	August 2011
Race/Ethnicity		
White, Non-Hispanic	49	80
Black, Non-Hispanic	35	71
Hispanic	40	68
Educational Attainment		
No high school diploma	16	43
High school graduate	33	71
Some college	62	88
College +	76	94
Household Income		
Less than $30,000/year	28	62
$30,000–$49,999	50	83
$50,000–$74,999	67	90
$75,000+	79	97
Age		
18–29	61	94
30–49	57	87
50–64	41	74
65+	12	41

Source: Pew Internet & American Life Project 2012.

with a high school degree (54.1%) (U.S. Department of Commerce 2011). The U.S. Census Bureau (2010) projected that the average consumer would spend almost $1,000 for media usage (e.g., television, Internet, cell phone, and radio) in 2010. In contrast, in 2004, the average consumer spent $770.

The digital divide is a symptom of a larger social problem in the United States: social inequality based on income, educational attainment, and ethnicity/race. Data from the Pew Internet & American Life Project (2012) reveal how Internet use is divided along demographic and socioeconomic lines. Internet use is higher among Whites and Blacks than among Hispanics. Higher Internet use is positively associated with higher incomes and educational attainment. (Refer to Table 11.3 for a summary of the Pew Internet & American Life Project data. U.S. Data Map 11.1 reports the percentage of households with Internet

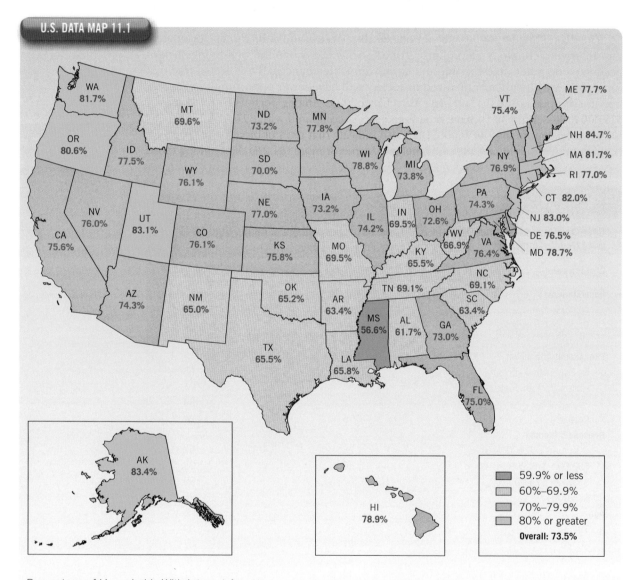

U.S. DATA MAP 11.1

WA 81.7%
OR 80.6%
MT 69.6%
ID 77.5%
WY 76.1%
ND 73.2%
SD 70.0%
MN 77.8%
WI 78.8%
MI 73.8%
NV 76.0%
UT 83.1%
CO 76.1%
NE 77.0%
IA 73.2%
IL 74.2%
IN 69.5%
OH 72.6%
CA 75.6%
AZ 74.3%
NM 65.0%
KS 75.8%
MO 69.5%
OK 65.2%
AR 63.4%
KY 65.5%
WV 66.9%
VA 76.4%
TN 69.1%
NC 69.1%
SC 63.4%
MS 56.6%
AL 61.7%
GA 73.0%
TX 65.5%
LA 65.8%
FL 75.0%
PA 74.3%
NY 76.9%
VT 75.4%
ME 77.7%
NH 84.7%
MA 81.7%
RI 77.0%
CT 82.0%
NJ 83.0%
DE 76.5%
MD 78.7%

AK 83.4%

HI 78.9%

Legend:
- 59.9% or less
- 60%–69.9%
- 70%–79.9%
- 80% or greater

Overall: 73.5%

Percentage of Households With Internet Access

Source: U.S. Census Bureau 2009.

access per state.) However, as digital access has improved, researchers have noted an overall increase in the use of media for time wasting among youth and continuing disparities. As reported by the Kaiser Family Foundation (Rideout, Foehr, and Roberts 2010), youth whose parents attained a high school degree or less spend more time per day exposed to media (television, music, video games, and movies) than youth whose parents have a college degree.

Internet access is not the only issue facing underserved communities. Wendy Lazarus and Francisco Mora (2000) identified four online content barriers. The greatest barrier is the lack of locally relevant information. They discovered that low-income users seek practical and relevant information that affects their daily lives, topics such as education (adult high school degree programs), family (low-cost child care), finances (news on public benefits, consumer information), health (local clinics, low-cost insurance resources), and personal enrichment (foreign-language newspapers). In some instances, information may be available in printed documents, but these may be difficult to locate or obtain. General information may exist online, but it might not be suitable to low-income audiences. For example, online housing services might list high-end rental units rather than lower-rent housing.

The second barrier identified by Lazarus and Mora (2000) was the lack of information at a basic literacy level. According to the authors, a number of online tutorials that review computer program and Internet skills are written at a higher level of literacy. The third barrier was the need for content for non-English speakers. There is little government material (e.g., on voting, Medicare, or taxes) translated into Spanish. Last, there is a need for more websites that reflect diverse cultural heritages and practices.

What Does It Mean to Me?

Is there a digital divide among students at your school? What advantages are there for students who own and use laptops and/or smartphones? What do you think is the minimum equipment requirement for staying digitally connected or for being technologically literate?

 STATE STATS

Do the Media Control Our Lives?

Internet Abuse and Addiction

Researchers define **Internet addiction** as the excessive use and nonproductive use of the Internet. The literature suggests that addiction does exist but that it affects very few users (Griffiths 2003). Ina Blau (2011) reports that the incidence rate of Internet addiction varies by culture and participant age, from less than 1% of U.S. adults (Aboujaoude et al. 2006) to 11.7% of high school students in Taiwan (Lin and Tsai 2002). Internet addiction is a broad term that covers a variety of behaviors and impulse controls (Griffiths 2002). Five types of addiction have been identified: cybersexual addiction (compulsive use of adult websites for cybersex and cyberporn), cyberrelationship addiction (overinvolvement in online relationships), net compulsions (online gambling, shopping, or trading), information overload (compulsive web searching), and computer addiction (computer game playing) (Griffiths 2002).

Internet use, including web surfing, instant messaging, shopping, and visiting chat rooms, can become a problem when it begins to interfere with one's job or social life ("Doctors Diagnose" 2003). Online computer games, such as Sims Online, EverQuest, or Ultima Online, attract an estimated hundreds of thousands of players each day. Aaron Hazell (quoted in

Snider 2003) admits to playing Ultima Online for as many as 18 hours per day, even skipping his job as a software developer a few times so that he could continue playing the game. According to Hazell, "These games have an amazing amount of depth. You can buy a boat and sail to another continent. Or you can buy a house and then chop wood and make furniture for your home. The possibilities are endless" (Snider 2003:23).

Employers have identified Internet abuse as a serious work problem. According to a recent SurfControl study, office workers who spend one hour a day at work on nonwork Internet activities (shopping online, booking vacations) could cost businesses as much as $35 million per year. The study found that 5% of the Internet use at the office was not work-related (Griffiths 2003). Unlike Internet addiction, Internet abuse has no negative effects for the user, except for a decrease in work productivity if occurring at the workplace (Griffiths 2003).

A survey of human resource management directors revealed that 83% of their companies have Internet access policies regulating how much Internet time employees can have during their workday. Despite the existence of such policies, 64% of companies disciplined employees and more than 30% terminated employees for inappropriate use of the Internet. The leading causes for disciplinary action or termination included accessing pornography, chatting online, gaming, visiting sports sites, investing, and shopping (Case and Young 2002).

The Problem With Television

In his 1932 book *Brave New World,* Aldous Huxley writes about a society in which the pain of living is eased by the "television box." In Huxley's world, the television is constantly on, like a "running tap." Although TV may not be on 24/7, individuals in the industrialized world devote an average of three hours per day to television viewing. About 40% of families always watch television while eating dinner (TV Turnoff Network 2004). In 2006, Nielsen Media Research reported that the average American home had more television sets than people—2.73 TV sets versus 2.55 people (Bauder 2006).

The average child or adolescent watches nearly three hours of television per day, not including time spent watching videotapes or playing video games. A recent study indicated that children spend more than six hours a day with various media combined (American Academy of Pediatrics, Committee on Public Education 2001a). By the time the average young person graduates from high school, he or she will have spent about 12,000 hours in the classroom and about 18,000 hours watching television (Greeson and Williams 1986).

A large body of scholarly literature has consistently confirmed the negative impact of television on children and adolescents, who are particularly vulnerable to the messages conveyed through television (American Academy of Pediatrics, Committee on Public Education 2001a). Exposure to violence in the media, including television, poses a significant risk to the health of children and adolescents (American Academy of Pediatrics, Committee on Public Education 2001b). It is estimated that by age 18, the average young person will have viewed more than 200,000 acts of violence on television (American Academy of Pediatrics, Committee on Public Education 2001b). Girls and boys who are exposed to violent behavior on film or TV behave more aggressively immediately afterward, are more tolerant of aggressive behavior (Huesmann et al. 2003), and are desensitized to the pain of others (American Academy of Pediatrics, Committee on Public Education 2001b). Researchers have also linked high levels of exposure to violent television programs to aggression in later childhood, adolescence, and young adulthood (Anderson et al. 2003).

Exposure to violent video games has been linked with heightened levels of aggression in young adults and children (Anderson and Bushman 2001). Interactive video games are the preferred leisure activity for children and adolescents, yet about 80% of today's most popular games contain violence (Vessey and Lee 2000). Playing violent video games has been found to account for a 13% to 22% increase in violent adolescent behavior (American Academy of Pediatrics, Committee on Public Education 2001b).

Simply stated, television may be bad for your physical health. Elevated television viewing and physical inactivity have been found to promote obesity in children (Faith et al. 2001). In addition to the unhealthy snacking that may occur while watching television, when people watch television, they burn fewer calories (Van den Bulck 2000). TV watching reduces the amount of time spent on more physical activities (Dietz and Gortmaker 1985). David Dunstan and his colleagues (2010) examined the relationship between time spent watching television and cardiovascular disease among more than 8,000 Australian men and women age 25 years or older. They found that each hour increment of television viewing was associated with an 18% increased risk of cardiovascular disease mortality. Among those watching four or more hours of television, there was an 80% risk of cardiovascular disease mortality compared with those who watched less than two hours of television per day. Even when the researchers controlled for smoking, high blood pressure, high cholesterol, and diet, they still found the same relationship between television viewing and cardiovascular disease mortality.

Television viewing by children is also correlated with between-meal snacking, consumption of foods advertised on television, and children's attempts to influence their mothers' food purchases (Dietz and Gortmaker 1985). The Kaiser Family Foundation study (Gantz et al. 2007) of advertising time during children's programming found that 50% of television ads were devoted to food; 72% were for candy, snacks, cereals, or fast food. The food industry has attempted to self-regulate the content of its commercials aimed at young audiences. The Kellogg Company, makers of breakfast cereals such as Froot Loops and Apple Jacks, announced in 2007 that it would phase out advertising products to children under 12 years of age unless the food products met specific nutrition guidelines for calories, sugar, fat, and sodium (Martin 2007). Sweden, France, and the Quebec province of Canada have banned the advertising of food to children; the need for similar federal regulations has been suggested in the United States (Martin 2007).

Driving Distracted

In 2007, a 53-year-old male driver was checking his e-mail while driving and caused a five-car pileup on Interstate 5 outside of Seattle, Washington. Driving while texting (DWT) is part of the growing phenomenon of distracted driving. Texting, along with the use of cell phones while driving, has been attributed to at least 1.6 million traffic accidents. Cell phone use causes more crashes than texting—1.4 million versus 200,000. According to the National Safety Council (2010), 28% of all traffic accidents involve talking and texting on cell phones. Drivers who use a cell phone—handheld or hands-free—are four times more likely to be involved in an accident.

The Seattle incident led to the passage of two laws, the first of their kind in the nation. One law prohibits driving while texting, and the second prohibits the use of a handheld phone while driving. Both laws are secondary enforcement laws, which means a driver will be ticketed for the offense only if pulled over for another driving violation. Public support for laws banning cell phone use while driving is gaining momentum (National Safety Council 2010). Since 2009, 29 states have enacted bans on texting while driving, and 15 states have enacted total cell phone bans for young drivers. Ten states ban the use of handheld devices while driving (National Safety Council 2012).

In an executive order signed by President Obama, federal employees are not allowed to text while driving. The federal government also plans to ban texting by interstate bus drivers and truckers. The use of cell phones may be limited to emergency situations.

Photo 11.5

Texting, along with the general use of cell phones while driving, has been attributed to at least 1.6 million traffic accidents.

Newpaper
Journalism

In Focus

The Death of the Newspaper?

As the fourth estate, journalism serves as a watchdog for government activities. Independent reporters, especially through print media, keep the public informed about political issues and activities. According to Robert McChesney and John Nichols (2010), citizens should have "media that regard the state secret as an assault to popular governance, that watch the politically and economically powerful with a suspicious eye, that recognize as their duty the informing and enlightening of citizens" (p. 2).

Yet, in our increasingly digital age, newspaper readership has declined while the use of online news sources has increased. In 2010, 37% of Americans said they read a paper yesterday (compared with 43% in 2006), while the number who said they read news online yesterday was 34% (compared with 29% in 2006) (Project for Excellence in Journalism 2011).

This transition has caused concern among those in the newspaper industry: owners and employees. According to the Newspaper Association of America (2010), in 2000, there were 1,468 daily papers. By 2009, the number of daily papers declined to 1,397. In 2009, more than 100 papers closed or shifted to an online format. Nearly every large paper has fewer pages and fewer articles; some have eliminated entire sections (Pérez-Peña 2009). In 2011, 1,000 full-time newsroom jobs were cut. While some argue that news is more accessible via the Internet, the quality and content of the news is changing. According to the Pew Research Center's Project for Excellence in Journalism (2012), the decline in print newspapers will mean "less coverage of government in suburbs or remote cities, pulling back on state government coverage, the decimation of specialty beats like science or religion, fewer feature stories and elimination of many weekday feature sections."

So what will take the place of your local newspaper? Several online companies have created hyperlocal news sites that allow readers to create their own neighborhood-focused news site—with stories, information, and advertising catering to their specific interests and needs. But some think that online news services are not the same. In a 2009 Senate hearing on journalism, Senator Benjamin Cardin (D-Md.) testified, "As local newspapers disappear, we lose an important check on local governments, state governments, the federal government, elected officials, corporations, school districts, businesses, individuals and more. Newspapers and the investigative journalism they provide are essential in a free, democratic society and must be preserved" (as quoted in Tucker 2009:8). According to Gary Kebbel, journalism program director for the Knight Foundation, the news business "is in a difficult time period right now, between what was and what will be" (quoted in Miller and Stone 2009:B1).

Do You Trust the News Media?

Whether we are watching CNN, ABC, NBC, CBS, or Fox, we rely on reporters for most if not all of our information about our community and our world. According to the Project for Excellence in Journalism (2004), public attitudes about the press have been growing less positive for about 20 years. In its report, *The State of the News Media 2004,* the Project for Excellence in Journalism identified the disconnection between the public and the news media over motive as the fundamental reason for the decline in public support. Whereas journalists believe they are working in the public interest, the public believes that news organizations are working primarily for profit and that journalists are motivated by professional ambition. In 2011, reporters from the *News of the World,* a tabloid newspaper in Great Britain, were exposed for phone hacking practices used to gather information about celebrities, politicians, and other people in the news.

The Future of Journalism

The public debate about whether U.S. media are liberal or conservative also sensitizes the public to how the media could be manipulative or subjective in content. In addition, people are increasingly distrustful of the large multinational corporations that own and control most of the news media (Project for Excellence in Journalism 2004). These findings are confirmed by the Pew Research Center for the People and the Press (2005). More than 70% of the public feels that news organizations are influenced by powerful people and organizations rather than being independent. Approximately 60% of Americans consider news organizations politically biased. In addition, more than 70% believe news organizations tend to favor one side rather than treat all sides fairly.

Public Trust

In addition, the Pew Research Center examined how Americans regard their news organizations. The center documented how, after the media's focus shifted away from terrorism, Americans grew increasingly skeptical. In July 2009, 59% of respondents thought that news organizations were highly professional, down from 73% in November 2001. About 29% felt that the news media usually get their facts straight, and 63% believed that news organizations usually provide inaccurate reports. And if the news organizations do make a mistake, 70% of respondents believed that the news organizations were likely to try to cover up their mistakes; only 21% believed that media are willing to admit their mistakes (Pew Research Center for the People and the Press 2009). Recent accounts exposing untrue or falsified reporting have contributed to the public's mistrust of the media.

During the early months of the 2008 presidential campaign, a news report claimed that Democratic candidate Senator Barack Obama had attended a madrassa (a Muslim religious school) while living in Indonesia. The allegation was first raised in *Insight,* a conservative Internet magazine owned by the *Washington Times,* and it was repeated by other news services. The magazine alleged that Obama was raised as a Muslim and that the sources of its information were researchers close to rival Senator Hillary Rodham Clinton's campaign. The deputy headmaster of the school Obama attended stated that the school is a public one that does not focus on religion. Obama's campaign staff maintained that the story was "completely ludicrous" and identified the candidate as a committed Christian. Clinton's staff claimed that they had nothing to do with the story.

Community, Policy, and Social Action

Federal Communications Commission and the Telecommunications Act of 1996

The Federal Communications Commission (FCC) was established by the Communications Act of 1934 and is charged with regulating interstate and international communications by radio, television, wire, satellite, and cable. As an independent agency, the FCC oversees violations of federal law and policies and reports directly to the U.S. Congress (FCC 2004). Under current FCC rules, radio stations and broadcast television channels cannot air indecent language or material that shows or describes sexual or excretory functions between 6 a.m. and 10 p.m., when children may be watching. In response to a violation, the FCC may issue a warning, revoke a station's license, or impose a monetary fine. In the entire history of the FCC, the commission has fined two television stations for indecency (Kelly, Clark, and Kulman 2004).

Introduced a week before the Super Bowl in 2004, the Broadcast Decency Enforcement Act was designed to amend the Communications Act of 1934. The bipartisan bill increased penalties to $500,000 for violating FCC regulations. Broadcasters could also lose their license if they violated indecency standards three times. The act would not apply to cable television programming. In the case of the 2004 Super Bowl halftime show, each CBS station that aired the program could have been fined as much as $27,500. After the 2004 Super Bowl halftime show (and Janet Jackson's wardrobe malfunction) television broadcasters began to police their programming more closely.

Through the FCC, the public can file complaints on a range of issues: billing disputes, wireless questions, telephone company advertising practices, telephone slamming (switching a consumer's telephone service without permission), unsolicited telephone marketing calls, and indecency and obscenity complaints. Along with the FTC, the FCC is enforcing the National Do Not Call Registry, which went into effect in October 2002. The FCC and FTC report that more than 55 million people have signed up for the registry.

The first major overhaul of the original 1934 act, the Telecommunications Act of 1996, was seen as a way to encourage competition in the communications industry. The law specified how local telephone carriers may compete, how and under what circumstances local exchange carriers can provide long-distance services, and ways to deregulate cable television rates. Also included in the act were provisions to make telecommunications more accessible to disabled Americans. A Decency Act makes it a crime to knowingly convey pornography over the Internet on a website accessible to children.

Although the act was presented as an opportunity to encourage competition and break down media monopolies, industry watchers noted that the 1996 law swept away the minimal consumer and diversity protections of the original 1934 act. The 1996 act reduced competition and allowed more cooperation between media giants. Data we reviewed in an earlier section of this chapter seem to support this. The new law permitted some of the largest industries—those not active in creating media content, such as telephone companies—to enter the television, radio, and cable industry. New industries joined older media companies to form interlocking partnerships, rather than become independent competitors as the act had predicted. For example, U.S. West, one of the largest telephone companies in the country, acquired Continental Cablevision, the third-largest cable system. Sprint, the long-distance telephone company, formed a joint venture with TCI, a cable company. The merger between Disney, ABC Broadcasting, and Capital Cities was made possible only through the passage of the 1996 law (Bagdikian 1997).

Who Is Watching the Media?

Numerous organizations have emerged as watch groups monitoring media accuracy and content. Groups such as Accuracy in Media (AIM) and the Center for Media and Public Affairs (CMPA) are nonprofit, grassroots organizations that attempt to expose biased and inaccurate news coverage while encouraging members of the media to report the news fairly and objectively. AIM publishes a newsletter and weekly newspaper column, broadcasts a daily radio commentary, and promotes a speaker's bureau to expose faulty reporting. On its website, current news stories are posted, along with AIM's analysis of the story's accuracy. CMPA conducts scientific research of the news and entertainment events, such as coverage of the presidential elections, the current presidential administration, international media, science and health, and religion (Center for Media and Public Affairs 2012).

Several organizations attempt to improve and protect the integrity of journalists in print, electronic, and Internet media. The Project for Excellence in Journalism (2004) began as an initiative by journalists to clarify and raise the standards of American journalism. The project serves as a research organization, conducting an annual review of local television news, producing a series of content studies on press performance, and offering educational programs for journalists. The project also provides information to the public about what to expect from the press, how to write a letter to the editor, and how to talk to the news media. Another organization, the Committee to Protect Journalists, is an independent, nonprofit organization promoting press freedom worldwide by defending the rights of journalists to report the news without fear of reprisal. The organization documents attacks on the press worldwide, including the number of journalists killed, missing, or imprisoned. For 2011, the committee reported that 46 journalists were killed (Committee to Protect Journalists 2012).

 Conflict Zones

Voices in the Community

Geena Davis

 Geena Davis

Responding to the lack of female characters in television and motion picture programming, Geena Davis founded the See Jane program to promote and advance gender balance in media for children 11 years of age or younger. Davis (2006) explains that after she gave birth to her daughter and began to watch preschool programs, she did a study of her own, examining the characters in her daughter's videos, and she realized that the programming was dominated by male characters.

Where the Girls Aren't is the first research project sponsored by the program, using content analysis to examine 101 top-grossing G-rated animated and live action films from 1990 to 2004 (Kelly and Smith 2006). In these films, researcher Stacy Smith found that there were three male characters for every one female character. Twenty-three percent of speaking characters were female, and more than 80% of film narrators were male. This gender imbalance can affect children's gender development, reinforcing children's stereotypical attitudes and beliefs about gender. According to Davis, "By making it common for our youngest children to see everywhere a balance of active and complex male and female characters, girls and boys will grow up to empathize with and care more about each others' stories" (quoted in Kelly and Smith 2006:9–10).

Certainly Davis's experience on the film *Thelma and Louise* helped her recognize the impact of a strong female character on women and men. She acknowledges the effect of media images on adults, but her concern is on the impact on children. "We know that kids learn their value by seeing themselves reflected in the culture. They say, 'I see myself! I must matter. I must count.'" Her goal is for media portrayals to be "normal and natural for children to see worlds and characters—be they Martians or dinosaurs or talking toaster ovens—that are roughly half female and male. Just like the real world that our kids live in" (Davis 2006).

The See Jane program was renamed the Geena Davis Institute on Gender in Media. In addition to ongoing research, the institute continues to educate education professionals, parents, and child professionals about the importance of gender equity in the media. The program's goal is to see females constituting half of all characters in media made for young children.

Media Literacy and Awareness

Evidence shows that media education can help mitigate the harmful effects of the media. Parents can mount the most effective intervention to reduce the effects of media violence on children. Amy I. Nathanson (1999) reported that parental co-viewing of and commenting on the programs seem to reduce the effects of TV violence on the child, probably because they reduce the child's perception that the violence is real and the likelihood that the child will act out the violence. Leonard Rowell Huesmann et al. (2003) also reported on the effectiveness of a school-based intervention that teaches children that violence on television is not real and should not be imitated.

 Media Awareness

According to the Media Awareness Network (2004), **media literacy** is the ability to sift through and analyze the messages that inform, entertain, and sell to us every day. It is about shifting from the role of a passive receiver of media to an active critical receiver. Media literacy includes asking several questions: For whom is this media message intended? Who wants to reach this audience, and why? From whose perspective is this story being told? Whose voices are being heard, and whose are absent? (Media Awareness Network 2004). This type of literacy develops one's abilities to examine the social and commercial context of media messages as well as the consequences of those messages (Considine, Horton, and Moorman 2009). The Action Coalition for Media Education offers 10 basic principles for media literacy, which are presented in Table 11.4.

Table 11.4

The 10 Basic Principles of Media Literacy Education

1. Medium. The form of communication that transmits messages, tells stories, structures learning, and constructs a "reality" about the world.

2. Media literacy. An educational approach that seeks to give media users greater freedom and choice by teaching them how to access, analyze, evaluate, and produce media.

3. Construction of reality. Media construct our culture, which involves trade-offs. Ask yourself: What are the trade-offs in this media experience? Who produced this media? What kind of reality does this media create? How accurate is this "reality"? What stories are NOT being told and why?

4. Production techniques. Media use identifiable production techniques (camera angles, editing, sound effects, colors and symbols, etc.). Ask: What kinds of production techniques does this media employ?

5. Value messages. Media contain ideological and value messages. Ask: What kinds of value messages does this media promote?

6. Commercial motives. Media are commercial and business interests. Ask: What are the commercial motives behind this media? Who or what paid for this media and why? Who or what owns this media product?

7. Individual meanings. Individuals construct their own meaning of media. Ask: What meanings do YOU find in this media? What different meanings might other individuals or groups find?

8. Emotional transfer. Commercials and other multimedia experiences operate primarily at an emotional level and are usually designed to transfer the emotion from one symbol or lifestyle onto another. Ask: What emotions does this media tap? What might we consider if we think more deeply about this media?

9. Pacing. TV runs at 30 frames per second; movies at 24 frames per second. The conscious mind can process about 8 frames per second; hence, television and movies tend to keep us from conscious analysis and reflection about individual messages and larger industry contexts. Ask: What do you observe about this media upon reflection?

10. Symbolic rhetoric/techniques of persuasion. Symbols, flattery, repetition, fear, humor, words, and sexual images are common and effective techniques of media persuasion. Ask: What persuasive techniques is this media using?

Source: Action Coalition for Media Education (ACME) 2004. Reprinted with permission of ACME.

Main Points

- Media are the technological processes facilitating communication, and they have increased to include more broadcast and cable channels and Internet websites. Yet, the media have been blamed for directly creating and promoting social problems and have been accused of being a problem themselves through controversial programming and manipulating how we see events.

- Functionalists examine the structural relationship between the media and other social institutions that affect content, including the social and economic conditions of American life and society's beliefs about the nature of men, women, and society. Research has documented the link between viewing media violence and the development of aggression, particularly among children who watch dramatic violence on television and film.

- Conflict theorists believe that the media can be fully understood only when we learn who controls them. The media, serving the interest of interlocking state and corporate powers, frame messages in a way that supports the ruling elite and limits the variety of messages that we read, see, and hear.

- Feminist theorists attempt to understand how the media represent and devalue women and minorities. They examine how the media either use stereotypes disparaging women and minorities or completely exclude them. One of the most important lessons young children learn is expected gender roles.

- The interactionist perspective focuses on the symbols and messages of the media and how the media come to define our "reality." The mass media define what events are newsworthy, using proximity (nearness of events) and deviation (something different from what we are accustomed to) as criteria. The mass media play a large role in shaping public agendas by influencing what people think about and, ultimately, what people consider a social problem.

- The term *digital divide* refers to the gap separating individuals who have access to and understanding of new forms of technology from those who do not. This divide is a symptom of a larger social problem: social inequality based on income, educational attainment, and ethnicity/race. Internet access is not the only issue facing underserved communities. A lack of locally relevant information, a lack of information at a basic literacy level, and English-only content are also barriers.

- Although the media are owned and operated by private organizations, their content is regulated by federal standards enforced by the Federal Communications Commission (FCC). The FCC enforces federal law and commission rules regarding indecency.

- Other social problems include Internet addiction, a broad term that covers a variety of behaviors and impulse controls. Internet use can become a problem when it begins to interfere with one's job or social life. Employers have identified Internet abuse as a serious work problem.

- The average child or adolescent watches nearly three hours of television per day. Research confirms the negative impact of television on children and adolescents, including more aggression and physical problems such as poor health and obesity.

- Public attitudes about the press have been growing less positive. The public believes that news organizations are working primarily for profit and that journalists are motivated by professional ambition; doubts about the political bent of the media and the motives of the multinational corporations that own and control them also lead to distrust.

- Aside from the FCC, numerous organizations have emerged as watch groups monitoring media accuracy and content, including the Project for Excellence in Journalism and the Committee to Protect Journalists.

- Evidence shows that media education can help mitigate the harmful effects of the media. Parents can provide the most effective intervention to reduce the effects of media violence on children, and school-based intervention also seems to help. The goal is media literacy, shifting the viewer from the role of passive receiver to active critical receiver.

On Your Own

Log on to the open-access Student Study Site at www.sagepub.com/leonguerrero4e for these additional learning tools:

- Interactive quizzes
- Video clips
- NPR audio links
- Handbook articles

- E-flashcards
- Journal articles
- End-of-chapter web exercises
- Additional web resources and current events

Internet and Community Exercises

1. Interview the editorial staff of your school newspaper. Ask the editor how decisions are made regarding the leading stories in the paper. What qualifies as news? Who makes decisions about the content of the paper and what appears as the lead story on the front page? Is it done by the entire news staff or by a small group?

2. Media watchdog groups such as the Center for Media and Public Affairs (CMPA) and Accuracy in Media (AIM) track major news stories, checking reporters' facts or exposing their biases. Select a current news story and observe how these groups examine it. Do they reveal any different or new information about the story?

3. Project Censored is a media research group based at Sonoma State University. The group of faculty, students, and community members publishes an annual list of 25 news stories of social significance that have been overlooked, underreported, or self-censored by the major national news media. Go to the Project Censored website (see *Study Site Chapter 11*) to review the most recent list of news stories. What social problems are identified by these stories? What might be done to promote these stories in mainstream media?

4. Research suggests that women's magazines also promote a traditional gender ideology. Review four women's magazines, *Ms., More, New Woman,* and *Essence,* and identify the images of women presented. Through the articles and advertisements, how do these magazines promote feminism, independence, beauty, or social class?

5. File sharing is restricted by U.S. copyright law. Under this law, copyright owners have the right to control copies and distribution of their original material. Throughout the United States, colleges and universities have implemented policies for P2P (person-to-person) file sharing including documents, software, music, and movies. What is your university's policy regarding file sharing? How is it enforced? Do you believe it is an effective policy? Why or why not?

Study Questions

1. Explain how the media serve to unite and divide members of society.
2. How is control over the content of the media (according to conflict and feminist perspectives) problematic? What groups are in conflict?
3. From an interactionist perspective, examine how Michael Jackson's death met the three criteria for newsworthiness.
4. How is one's access to media and technology related to one's life chances?
5. Which sociological perspective could best explain how trust is earned by new agencies and outlets? Do you trust the news media? Why or why not?
6. Define what is meant by media literacy. How does media literacy mitigate the harmful effects of the media?

PART IV

Our Social and Physical Worlds

D rug abuse and criminal behavior are usually perceived as personal troubles. Both are considered deviant behavior, deviating from the normal expectation of not abusing drugs or engaging in criminal activity. We tend to believe that someone turns to drug use or criminal activity because of some personal defect, individual failure, or weakness. Yet both can be defined as public issues, emerging from the social structure and threatening the quality of human life.

Drug abuse is a serious personal and social problem. It can kill. It can impair an abuser's ability to effectively function in the workplace, among friends, and at home. Treatment and prevention of drug abuse cost society billions of dollars and divert needed funds and support from other social problems. Drug activity in a neighborhood can increase violence and decrease personal safety for all residents, even those not directly involved with drugs. The quality of human life, beyond the abuser, is threatened by or damaged by the use of drugs (Goode 2004).

What Does It Mean to Me?

Like drug abuse, criminal activity has collateral effects, unintended effects on offenders, their families, and their communities (Tonry 2004). What collateral effects of crime can you identify?

Drug abuse and crime are the subject and focus of extensive scholarly research attempting to understand the extent and origins of both. Both problems also receive global attention, including from governments and public agencies monitoring and combating drug abuse and crime in their part of the world. These issues will be discussed in Chapters 12 and 13.

In the last three chapters of Part IV, we will review social problems that affect our physical and natural worlds—problems related to urbanization, the environment, and war and terrorism. Sociologists acknowledge that our physical and natural environments influence and are influenced themselves by human societies and behavior.

Yet some of you may be wondering why a discussion on urban sprawl or global climate change should be included in this textbook. Though these issues deal with our physical and natural worlds, both have definite human connections—humans cause these problems or experience consequences as a result of them. Environmentalist Paul Hawken (1993) explains, "Human activity *is* part of the natural world, in the largest sense, but human activity ignores the means-and-ends, give-and-take factors that are inherent in any maturing ecosystem" (p. 26). The Industrial Revolution brought great human growth and prosperity at an immense cost to the Earth (Hawken 1993). Almost every living system on the planet has lost some capacity to sustain itself. We consume our natural commodities, such as water, air, soil, and minerals, without much thought to their true cost.

However, our understanding of the relationship between our actions and our natural and physical worlds has considerably improved. Former Vice President Al Gore increased public awareness about climate change through his 2006 documentary, *An Inconvenient Truth*. Gore and others from the scientific community have documented how environmental problems are caused by human action (or inaction), our social policies, and our priorities. We have also been cautioned about how urbanization and population growth have fueled our consumption of natural resources, particularly in developing parts of the world. Scientists warn us that we are about to run out of these natural commodities, leading to irrevocable global damage. The consequences of human action on our urban landscape and environment will be discussed in Chapters 14 and 15.

The terrorist attacks on September 11, 2001, were the result of human action. Since then, the Iraq and Afghanistan wars have been part of our nation's psyche, significantly affecting many aspects of our lives—socially, economically, and politically. Our country's response to terrorism has been accused of creating and exacerbating problems here and abroad. War and terrorism as a social problem will be discussed in Chapter 16.

Responding to Environmental Problems

▶ We are increasingly aware of the human impact on our environment and have responded by adopting new earth-friendly technologies and practices. Using a water bottle or driving a hybrid car can be considered part of a movement, becoming part of a solution.

What earth-friendly technologies or practices are a part of your life? How have you reduced your impact on the environment?

CHAPTER 12

Alcohol and Drug Abuse

The Story of a Heroin Addict

A s a nation, we have been in the War on Drugs for the past 40 years. Some refer to it as a war with "no rules, no boundaries, no end" (PBS 2000). Since the mid-1980s, the United States has adopted a series of aggressive law enforcement strategies and criminal justice policies aimed at reducing and punishing drug abuse (Fellner 2000). Changes in federal law require all sentenced federal offenders to serve at least 87% of their court-imposed sentences. Many drug offenders are subject to mandatory minimum sentences based on the type and quantity of drugs involved in their arrest (Scalia 2001). According to the most recent Uniform Crime Report (Federal Bureau of Investigation 2011), 1,531,251 drug arrests were made in 2011, a decrease from 1,638,846 in 2010. Although some consider the large number of drug arrests a good sign, critics charge that mandatory sentencing denies drug users what they really need, access to treatment. Tougher sentencing has failed to decrease the availability of drugs and has failed to reduce illicit drug use. In addition, some argue that the focus on drug-related crimes has distracted law enforcement from monitoring more serious crimes.

There seems to be no argument about the seriousness of the drug problem in the United States and worldwide. According to the 2010 National Survey on Drug Use and Health, 22.6 million Americans (or 8.9%) age 12 or older reportedly were current users of illicit drugs other than marijuana (Substance Abuse and Mental Health Services Administration [SAMHSA] 2011). (Refer to Figure 12.1 for illicit drug use by age and U.S. Data Map 12.1 for the percentage of illicit drug use by state.) Nearly 18 million American adults abuse alcohol or are alcoholics (National Institute on Alcohol Abuse and Alcoholism [NIAAA] 2004). Globally, more than 76 million individuals have diagnosable drinking problems (World Health Organization 2004), and between 15 and 39 million are problem drug users (United Nations Office on Drugs and Crime [UNODC] 2012). The most widely produced and consumed illicit drug is cannabis or marijuana. Refer to Figure 12.2 for more information.

Although we might focus first on one drug user and his or her personal trouble with drugs, it doesn't take long to recognize how drug use affects the user's family and friends, workplace or school, and neighbors and community. Throughout this chapter, we will examine the social problem of drug abuse, reviewing its extent, its social consequences, and our solutions. We begin first with a look at how the sociological perspectives address the problem of drug abuse.

Figure 12.1

Past-Month Illicit Drug Use Among Persons Age 12 or Older, by Age, 2010

Source: Substance Abuse and Mental Health Services Administration 2011.

Sociological Perspectives on Drug Abuse

Biological and psychological theories attempt to explain how drug abuse is based on the individual. Both perspectives assume that there is little a person can do to escape from his or her abuse: A person's abuse is genetic or inherited. Abuse may emerge from a biological or chemical predisposition or from a personality or behavioral disorder. Such explanations also have consequences for treatment. Programs focus on the individual, arguing that the abuser needs to be "fixed." Although both perspectives have been important in shaping our understanding of drug abuse, these perspectives cannot explain the social or structural determinants of drug abuse. In this next section, we will examine how sociological perspectives address the problems of drug abuse.

Sociology of Drug Use

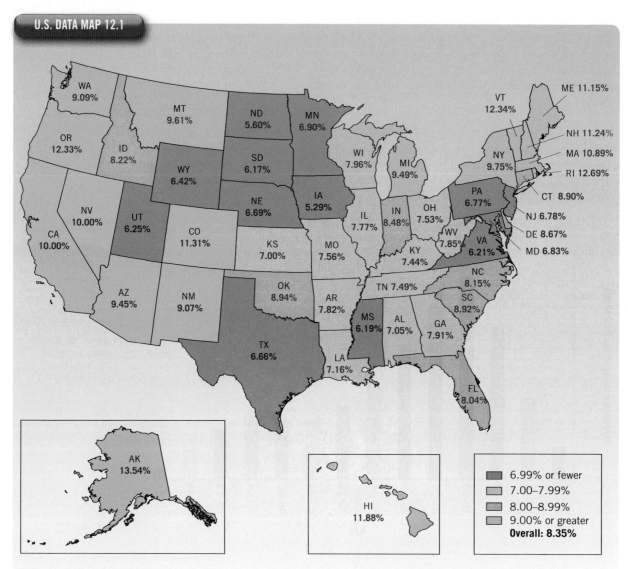

U.S. DATA MAP 12.1

WA 9.09%
MT 9.61%
ND 5.60%
MN 6.90%
VT 12.34%
ME 11.15%
OR 12.33%
ID 8.22%
WI 7.96%
NH 11.24%
NY 9.75%
MA 10.89%
SD 6.17%
MI 9.49%
RI 12.69%
WY 6.42%
PA 6.77%
CT 8.90%
NV 10.00%
UT 6.25%
NE 6.69%
IA 5.29%
IL 7.77%
IN 8.48%
OH 7.53%
NJ 6.78%
CA 10.00%
CO 11.31%
KS 7.00%
MO 7.56%
WV 7.85%
VA 6.21%
DE 8.67%
KY 7.44%
MD 6.83%
AZ 9.45%
NM 9.07%
OK 8.94%
AR 7.82%
TN 7.49%
NC 8.15%
SC 8.92%
TX 6.66%
MS 6.19%
AL 7.05%
GA 7.91%
LA 7.16%
FL 8.04%
AK 13.54%
HI 11.88%

Legend:
- 6.99% or fewer
- 7.00–7.99%
- 8.00–8.99%
- 9.00% or greater
- **Overall: 8.35%**

Any Illicit Drug Use in the Past Month, Percentage by State, Annual Averages Based on 2010 National Survey on Drug Use and Health

Source: Substance Abuse and Mental Health Services Administration 2011.

Functionalist Perspective

Functionalists argue that society provides us with norms or guidelines on drug use. Cross-cultural studies reveal that there is variation in the way people expect to behave when they drink. For example, violent behavior is associated with alcohol consumption in the United States, Great Britain, and Australia; yet drinking behavior is described as "peaceful and harmonious" in Mediterranean and South African countries (Social Issues Research Center 1998).

A set of social norms identifies the appropriate use of drugs and alcohol. The use of prescription drugs, as directed by a physician, is considered acceptable behavior. Prescription drugs alleviate pain, reduce fevers, and curb infections. Alcohol in moderation may be routinely consumed with meals, for celebration, or for health benefits. One glass of red wine a day has been shown to reduce one's risk of heart disease.

Yet society also provides norms regarding the excessive use of drugs. For example, college students share the perception that excessive college drinking is a cultural norm (Butler 1993); this perception is enforced by the media and advertisers (Lederman et al. 2003). Aaron Brower (2002) argues that binge drinking is determined by and is a product of the college environment. Unlike alcoholics, college students are able to turn their willingness to binge drink on and off depending on their circumstances (e.g., whether they have to study for an exam).

To explain drug abuse, functionalists identify a culture or the social structure as the cause. In examining substance abuse among adolescents, researchers contend that peers may be the most influential (Allen et al. 2003). Howard Kaplan, Steven Martin, and Cynthia Robbins (1984) write, "The use of illicit drugs persists in part of ongoing peer subculture(s) which may endorse, if not require, use of illicit drugs" (p. 271). Peer influence may be direct or indirect: Peers provide social opportunities to engage in substance abuse, and peers shape attitudes toward substance abuse (Leventhal and Cleary 1980; Prinstein and Wang 2005).

Émile Durkheim believed that under conditions of rapid cultural change, there would be an absence of common social norms and controls, a state he called anomie. If people lack norms to control their behavior, they are likely to pursue self-destructive behaviors such as alcohol abuse (Caetano, Clark, and Tam 1998). During periods when individuals are socially isolated (such as moving to a new neighborhood, experiencing a divorce, or starting a new school year), they may experience high levels of stress or anxiety, which may lead to deviant behaviors, including drug abuse. Society can also be the source of **role strain**—when an individual has insufficient resources to deal with demanding social situations or circumstances. The strain occurs when the demands of one's role exceed one's ability and resources to fulfill that role (Wheaton 1990). Illicit drug use or self-medication can be perceived as an adaptive coping response to stress—people turn to drug use to reduce their level of stress (Crutchfield and Gove 1984).

 Impaired Control

Conflict Perspective

 Weak Drug Laws

Although many drugs can be abused, conflict theorists argue that intentional decisions have been made over which drugs are illegal and which ones are not. Powerful political and business interest groups are able to manipulate our images of drugs and their users.

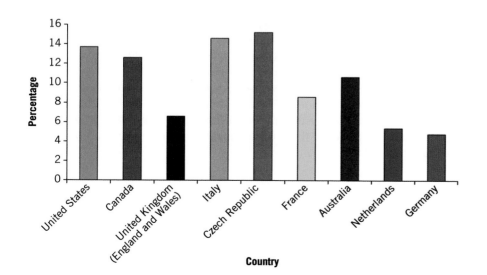

Figure 12.2

Annual Prevalence of Cannabis Use as a Percentage of the Population Ages 15–64, Selected Countries, Estimates From 2007 to 2009

Source: United Nations Office on Drugs and Crime 2012.

Arthur Benavie (2009) explains how the War on Drugs in this country is defined by subjective social, religious, and political positions. For example, drugs are classified by five schedules, categories that define their susceptibility to abuse and medical application. Criminal penalties are applied to the drugs in Schedules I and II, dangerous drugs with a high potential for abuse. Benavie highlights how the classification of these drugs is determined by the U.S. Drug Enforcement Administration (DEA) of the U.S. Department of Justice (DOJ) rather than the Food and Drug Administration (FDA) or the Surgeon General.

Our history of drug laws, concludes Benavie (2009), has little to do with objective information about the effects or dangers of illicit drugs. Drug policy has been fueled by racial, ethnic, and economic antagonisms. For example, heroin, opium, and marijuana were considered legal substances in the late eighteenth and early nineteenth centuries, but public opinion and law changed when their use was linked to ethnic minorities and crime. Opium smoking, most associated with Chinese immigrants brought here to work on the railroads, became the subject of intense antidrug efforts after completion of the railroad system. At the same time, the oral consumption of opium, more widespread among Whites, was never considered as problematic (Reinarman and Levine 1997).

According to Benavie (2009), the War on Drugs is a crusade, fueled by a fear of social disorder and disease, a perceived threat to our capitalistic economic structure, and a religious crusade against sin and vice.

Feminist Perspective

Theorists and practitioners in the field of alcohol and drug abuse have ignored the experiences unique to women, ethnic groups, gay and lesbian populations, and other marginalized groups. Women face unique social stigmatization as a result of their drug use and may also experience discrimination as they attempt to receive treatment (Drug Policy Alliance 2003b).

Katherine Beckett (1995) and Dorothy Roberts (1991) describe how women of color have been unfairly targeted in the War on Drugs. As crack cocaine use spread throughout the inner cities in the 1980s, prosecutors shifted their attention to drug use among pregnant women, making drug and alcohol abuse during pregnancy a crime. The approach treated pregnant drug users as criminals and was "aimed at punishing rather than empowering women who use drugs during their pregnancy" (Beckett 1995:589). As Beckett (1995) explains, "Prosecutions of women for prenatal conduct thus create a gender specific system of punishment and obscure the fact that male behavior, socio-economic conditions, and environmental pollutants may also affect fetal health" (p. 588). Roberts (1991) argues that poor Black women are the primary targets for prosecutors. Research indicates that African American women are about 10 times more likely than are other women to be reported to civil authorities for drug use.

The scientific literature did not address women's addiction until the 1970s. Specifically, there has been a lack of sensitivity to the range of drug abuse experiences beyond the male or White perspective. Early prevention and treatment models treated female abusers no differently than men were treated, failing to provide comprehensive services for women such as prenatal and gynecologic care, contraceptive counseling, job training, and abuse counseling (Roberts 1991). However, there is increasing recognition of the importance of gender-specific and gender-sensitive treatment models, including the development of separate women's treatment programs. Female users have a variety of different treatment and psychosocial needs, influenced by their backgrounds, experiences, and drug problems. Most outpatient clinics do not provide child care, and many residential programs do not admit children (Roberts 1991). And single, career-oriented women without children will have different treatment needs and priorities than will single mothers or married mothers (National Clearinghouse for Alcohol and Drug Information [NCADI] 2003a).

Gail Unterberger (1989) offers a feminist revision of the traditional 12-step statement used by Alcoholics Anonymous. As originally written, the 12 steps send a negative message for women, reinforcing feelings of powerlessness and hopelessness during recovery. Unterberger believes that alcoholic women are more likely to suffer from depression than their male counterparts are, and unlike men, women alcoholics may turn their anger on themselves rather than on others. Unterberger's revised 12-step statement is presented in Table 12.1.

Interactionist Perspective

Glamorizing Drugs

Sociologists Edwin Sutherland and Howard Becker argue that deviant behavior, such as drug abuse, is learned through others. Sutherland (1939) proposed the theory of **differential association** to explain how we learn specific behaviors and norms from the groups we have contact with. Deviance, explained Sutherland, is learned from people who engage in deviant behavior. In his study "Becoming a Marijuana User," Becker (1963) demonstrated how a novice user is introduced to smoking marijuana by more experienced users. Learning is the key in his study:

> No one becomes a user without (1) learning to smoke the drug in a way which will produce real effects; (2) learning to recognize the effects and connect them with drug use . . . ; and (3) learning to enjoy the sensations he perceives. (Becker 1963:58)

Native Americans

This perspective also addresses how individuals or groups are labeled *abusers* and how society responds to them. For example, consider alcohol abuse among the Native American population. Alcohol abuse and alcoholism are leading causes of mortality among Native Americans, and there are disproportionately higher rates of alcohol-related crimes among Native Americans. Yet Malcolm Holmes and Judith Antell (2001) argue that alcohol abuse and its related problems are not entirely objective phenomena; they also involve interpretation and stigmatization of deviant behavior. One persistent societal myth maintains that as a

Table 12.1

The 12 Steps for Women Alcoholics

1. We have a drinking problem that once had us.

2. We realize that we need to turn to others for help.

3. We turn to our community of sisters and our spiritual resources to validate ourselves as worthwhile people, capable of creativity, care, and responsibility.

4. We have taken a hard look at our patriarchal society and acknowledge those ways in which we have participated in our own oppression, particularly the ways we have devalued or escaped from our own feelings and needs for community affirmation.

5. We realize that our high expectations for ourselves have led us either to avoid responsibility and/or to overinvest ourselves in others' needs. We ask our sisters to help us discern how and when this happens.

6. Life can be wondrous or ordinary, enjoyable or traumatic, danced with or fought with, and survived. In our community we seek to live in the present with its wonder and hope.

7. The more we value ourselves, the more we can trust others and accept how that helps us. We are discerning and caring.

8. We affirm our gifts and strengths and acknowledge our weaknesses. We are especially aware of those who depend on us and our influence on them.

9. We will discuss our illness with our children, family, friends, and colleagues. We will make it clear to them (particularly our children) that what our alcoholism caused in the past was not their fault.

10. As we are learning to trust our feelings and perceptions, we will continue to check them carefully with our community, which we will ask to help us discern the problems we may not yet be aware of. We celebrate our progress toward wholeness individually and in community.

11. Drawing upon the resources of our faith, we affirm our competence and confidence. We seek to follow through on our positive convictions with the support of our community and the love of God.

12. Having had a spiritual awakening as a result of these steps, we are more able to draw upon the wisdom inherent in us, knowing we are competent women who have much to offer others.

Source: Copyright © 1989 by The Christian Century. *"Twelve Steps for Women Alcoholics," by Gail Unterberger is reprinted by permission from the December 6, 1989, issue of* The Christian Century.

group, Native Americans have problems handling alcohol. However, research indicates that factors such as demography (a young population) and geography (rural Western environment) may explain high rates of alcohol-related problems in Native American populations.

The authors highlight the considerable variation in drinking patterns within and between tribal communities; in other words, not all Native Americans have drinking problems. The social construction of the "drunken Indian" stereotype links alcohol abuse to the perceived "weaker" cultural and individual characteristics of Native Americans. Holmes and Antell (2001) explain, "The persistence of such myths in the symbolic-moral universe of the dominant White culture, despite evidence to the contrary, suggests that alcohol use by Native Americans still documents allegations of weak will and moral degeneracy" (p. 154). For a summary of these four sociological perspectives, see Table 12.2.

What Is Drug Abuse?

Drug abuse is the use of any drug or medication for a reason other than the one it was intended to serve or in a manner or in quantities other than directed, which can lead to clinically significant impairment or distress. **Drug addiction** refers to physical or psychological dependence on the drug or medication. Although many drugs can be abused, five drugs will be reviewed in the following section: alcohol, nicotine, marijuana, methamphetamine, and cocaine. Marijuana, methamphetamine, and cocaine are considered illicit (illegal) drugs. Most of the information presented in this section is based on data from the National Institute on Drug Abuse (NIDA) and the Office of National Drug Control Policy (ONDCP). For more information, log on to the Study Site, Chapter 12, at www.sagepub.com/leonguerrero4e.

Alcohol

Alcohol is the most abused drug in the United States. Although the consumption of alcohol by itself is not a social problem, the continuous and excessive use of alcohol can become problematic. Four symptoms are associated with alcohol dependence or **alcoholism**: craving (a strong need to drink), loss of control (not being able to stop drinking once drinking begins), physical dependence (experiencing withdrawal symptoms), and tolerance (the need to drink greater amounts of alcohol to get "high") (NIAAA 2003b). Alcohol use is related to a wide range of adverse health and social consequences, both acute (traffic deaths or other injuries) and chronic (stroke, alcohol dependence, liver damage) (NIAAA 2005).

 Alcohol Abuse

Current drinking (12 or more drinks in the past year) and heavy drinking (five drinks on a single day at least once a month for adults) among adults is highest for Native Americans and Alaska Natives, followed by Native Hawaiians. Prevalence of deaths from chronic liver disease and cirrhosis is about four times higher, and of fatal car accidents caused by alcohol three times higher, among Native Americans and Alaska Natives than among the rest of the U.S. population. Adult drinking is lowest among Asian Americans and Pacific Islanders, but alcohol use is increasing significantly in this group.

 World Health Organization

Table 12.2

Summary of Sociological Perspectives: Drug Abuse

	Functional	Conflict/Feminist	Interactionist
Explanation of drug abuse	Drug abuse is likely to occur when society is unable to control or regulate our behavior.	Powerful groups decide which drugs are illegal. Certain social groups are singled out for their drug abuse. There has been a lack of sensitivity to the range of drug abuse experiences.	Drug abuse is learned through interaction with others. The perspective also focuses on society's reaction to drug abuse, noting that certain individuals are more likely to be labeled as drug users than others.
Questions asked about drug abuse	What rules exist to control or encourage drug abuse? Are some groups or individuals more vulnerable to drug abuse than others?	What groups are able to enforce their definitions of the legality or illegality of drug use? How are they able to enforce their definitions? How are the experiences of women and minority drug users different from those of White males?	How is drug abuse learned through interaction? How are drug users labeled by society? Why are specific groups targeted?

Among adolescent minorities, African Americans have the lowest rates of drinking and the lowest frequency of being drunk. Hispanic adolescents have the highest rates of heavy drinking, followed by White adolescents. Decline in alcohol abuse with increased age is called "aging out" or simply part of the maturation process. Although studies suggest that White adolescents drink alcohol more heavily and frequently than other ethnic/racial groups do, White adolescents are also more likely to age out. During early to middle adulthood, the frequency of heavy drinking stabilizes among Whites, increases among African Americans, and declines but remains high for Hispanics (Caetano and Kaskutas 1995; Chen and Kandel 1995).

Alcohol researchers have begun to identify the importance of individual attributes, cultural factors, and structural factors in minority drinking. Studies suggest that ethnic/racial groups have different sets of norms and values regulating drinking. For example, some groups exhibit low rates of problem drinking because their culture associates the use of alcohol primarily with eating, social occasions, or rituals (Herd and Grube 1996). However, other ethnic/racial groups may consider drinking as an activity separate from eating or ritual celebrations, leading to higher rates of problem drinking. Researchers have attributed alcoholism among ethnic minorities to three different sources of stress: **acculturative stress**, experienced by most immigrants who are faced with leaving their homeland and adapting to a new country; **socioeconomic stress**, experienced by ethnic minorities who feel disempowered because of social and economic inequalities in U.S. society; and **minority stress**, which refers to the tension that minorities encounter because of racism (Caetano et al. 1998).

Although social class, occupational and social roles, and family history of alcohol all play a role in determining the drinking patterns of people in general, specific factors put women particularly at risk (Collins and McNair 2003). Research indicates that a woman's risk for drinking increases with the experience of negative affective states, such as depression (Hesselbrock and Hesselbrock 1997) or loneliness, and negative life events, such as physical or sexual abuse during childhood or adulthood (Wilsnack et al. 1997). Other factors decrease women's chances of developing alcohol problems. Traditionally, women are socialized to abstain from alcohol use or to drink less than men (Filmore et al. 1997). Women who do not participate in the labor force may have less access to alcohol than men do (Wilsnack and Wilsnack 1992), and women's roles as wife and mother may also discourage alcohol intake (Leonard and Rothbard 1999).

Juvenile Drinking

Research confirms how drinking accelerates during adolescence, peaking at young adulthood and then decelerating to moderate levels in adulthood (Muthén and Muthén 2000). People who begin drinking before age 15 are four times more likely to develop alcohol dependence at some time in their lives as are people who have their first drink at age 20 or older (NIAAA 2003a). Patrick O'Malley, Lloyd Johnston, and Jerald Bachman (1998) report that adolescents who use alcohol are at higher risk for social, medical, and legal problems, such as poor school performance; interpersonal problems with friends, family, and others; physical and psychological impairment; drunk driving; and death. The rate of fatal crashes related to alcohol among drivers ages 16 to 20 is more than twice the rate among drivers age 21 or older (NIAAA 2003a). The most common alcohol-related problem reported by adolescent drinkers is that alcohol use causes them to behave in ways that they later regret (O'Malley et al. 1998). Underage use of alcohol is more likely to kill young people than all illegal drugs combined (NIAAA 2003a).

What Does It Mean to Me?

How would you describe the drinking culture on your campus? Is alcohol consumption an acceptable and normal part of college life? Why or why not?

Taking a World View

The Scottish Drinking Problem

Some have noted that "Scotland has a special relationship with alcohol" (Ritson 2002). Scotland is known for its Scotch whisky, a national beverage that is more than just a drink or a means of getting drunk. According to Sharon MacDonald (1994), whiskey is "a symbolic distillation of many images of Scottishness, especially hospitality, camaraderie, joviality, and masculinity" (p. 125).

Alcohol abuse in Scotland is increasing because of excessive drinking levels among adults and the frequency and level of drinking among teenagers. In recent studies, 27% of Scottish men and 14% of Scottish women between 16 and 64 years old were drinking more than the recommended weekly limits of less than 21 units for men and 14 units for women (a unit of alcohol is 8 grams by weight) (Alcohol Information Scotland 2007). Younger Scots, between the ages of 16 and 24, were more likely to exceed the weekly limits—62% of males and 56% of females. Cirrhosis mortality rates in Scotland were among the highest in Western Europe. In 2002, the rate per 100,000 per year was 45.2 for men and 19.9 for women. Between 1987 and 1991 and between 1997 and 2001, cirrhosis mortality increased among Scottish men by 69% and increased among Scottish women by 46% (Leon and McCambridge 2006).

Men's and women's drinking are not viewed as equally problematic by Highland residents or the Scottish population in general. According to MacDonald (1994), in the Highlands, although more men abuse alcohol, their drinking is viewed as a lesser problem than the problem of women who drink. Drunkenness is accepted, even expected, of Scottish males, but a drunken woman is considered unrespectable, slovenly, and loose. The drunk Scottish woman is a pathetic figure rather than the humorous figure of a drunk Scot male. It is likely, says MacDonald, that the number of women who abuse alcohol is underestimated because of the added stigma associated with women's drinking. In her research, MacDonald was told of female alcoholics in "hushed, conspiratorial" tones. Women were desperate to conceal their drinking problem. Women's drinking was more likely to be confined to home than men's drinking was (MacDonald 1994).

In February 2009, the Scottish government launched a *Framework for Action,* a national legislative and cultural program aimed at reducing alcohol abuse and harm. The plan focused on correcting harmful drinking patterns and influencing the habits and attitudes of children, young people, and adults through prevention and treatment programs. "We are embarked on a journey which will challenge many of us to re-think some deeply held assumptions and beliefs. But attitudes to smoking are changing. We believe that attitudes to alcohol misuse can change too" (Scottish Government 2009:7).

Tobacco and Nicotine

Tobacco is the world's number-one problem drug, killing more people than all other drugs combined (Goode 2004). According to the World Health Organization (2007a), if current smoking patterns continued, by 2010 10 million people per year worldwide would die of diseases caused by cigarette smoking. Cigarette smoking is the most prevalent form of nicotine addiction, and tobacco is the most frequently used addictive drug in the United States (NCADI 2003b). Nicotine is both a stimulant and a sedative to the central nervous system. An average cigarette contains about 10 milligrams of nicotine. Through inhaling the cigarette smoke, the smoker takes in 1 to 2 milligrams of nicotine per cigarette. In 2010, 69.6 million Americans reported current use of a tobacco product (SAMHSA 2011).

In the United States, the prevalence of smoking is highest among Native Americans and Alaska Natives (35.8%), followed by persons who reported two or more races (32%),

Whites (29.5%), Blacks (27.3%), and Hispanics (21.9%) (SAMHSA 2011). Eleven percent of youths ages 12 to 17 were current smokers (SAMHSA 2011).

Cigarette smoking is the most important preventable cause of cancer in the United States. It has been linked to most cases of lung cancer in Europe and in the United States (Crispo et al. 2004). Smoking has also been linked to other lung diseases, such as chronic bronchitis and emphysema, and to cancers of the mouth, stomach, kidney, bladder, cervix, pancreas, and larynx. The overall death rates from cancer are twice as high among smokers as nonsmokers (NIDA 1998). It is estimated that 438,000 annual deaths are attributable to cigarette smoking in the United States (American Lung Association 2006).

Passive or secondhand smoke is a major source of indoor air contaminants. Nonsmokers exposed to secondhand smoke at home or work increase their risk of developing heart disease by 25% to 30% and lung cancer by 20% to 30% (NIDA 2006). Secondhand smoke is estimated to cause about 3,000 lung cancer deaths per year and may contribute to as many as 40,000 deaths related to cardiovascular disease in the United States (NIDA 1998). More than 79,000 adults die each year as a result of passive smoking in the European Union countries (European Lung Association 2006).

Despite the persistent public health message that smoking is bad for your health, smoking among teenagers has been on the rise since 1991 (Lewinsohn et al. 2000). In a study comparing adolescent smokers with nonsmokers, adolescent smokers were found to have more stressful environments, more academic problems, and poorer coping skills than nonsmokers have. Adolescent smoking has also been associated with a number of environmental factors, such as disruptive home environment, parental and peer smoking, low social support from family and friends, conflict with parents, and stressful life events (Lewinsohn et al. 2000).

Data indicate that the use of smokeless chewing tobacco products (referred to as "snuff," "dip," or "chew") occurs at a significantly younger age than cigarette smoking does. Smokeless tobacco products are consumed orally, with packets of the tobacco tucked in a front lip or cheek. An average size chew kept in the mouth for 30 minutes provides the same amount of nicotine as three cigarettes (National Cancer Institute 2003). Smokeless tobacco may cause permanent gum recession, mouth sores, lesions, and cancers of the mouth and throat. Most adolescent users are White, male, and from a rural area (Newman 1999). Experimentation with chewing tobacco has been associated with personal factors (such as risk taking, physical fighting, and low satisfaction in school) and weak family structure or support (e.g., a one-parent family). Regular use of chew has been linked to adult modeling, peer influences, and certain sports teams' membership (Campbell-Grossman, Hudson, and Fleck 2003).

Marijuana

Teen Substance Abuse

Marijuana is the most commonly used illicit drug, widely used by adolescents and young adults (NIDA 2002a), with an estimated 141 million people or 2.45% of the world's population consuming it (UNODC 2006). It is a favorite drug among youth and adolescents, with use (at least once in a lifetime) estimated as high as 37% in some countries (UNODC 2006). The major active chemical in marijuana is THC or delta-9-tetrahydrocannabinol, which causes the mind-altering effects of the drug. THC is also the main active ingredient in oral medications used to treat nausea in chemotherapy patients and to stimulate appetite in AIDS patients (ONDCP 2006a).

According to the Centers for Disease Control and Prevention, 38.4% of surveyed high school students and 49% of college students reported lifetime use of marijuana. Longitudinal data show increases in marijuana use during the 1960s and 1970s, declines in the 1980s, and increasing use since the 1990s (NIDA 2002a). In 2010, there were a reported 17.4 million current (past month) users of the drug, or 6.9% of the population (SAMHSA 2011).

Acute marijuana use can impair short-term memory, judgment, and other cognitive functions, as well as a person's coordination and balance, and it can increase heart rate. Chronic abuse of the drug can lead to addiction, as well as increased risk of chronic cough, bronchitis, or emphysema. Addictive use of the drug may interfere with family, school, or work activities. Smoking marijuana increases the risk of lung cancer and cancer in other parts of the respiratory tract more than smoking tobacco does (NIDA 2002a). Marijuana smoke contains 50% to 70% more carcinogenic hydrocarbons than tobacco smoke does (ONDCP 2006a). Because marijuana users inhale more deeply and hold their breath longer than cigarette smokers do, they are exposed to more carcinogenic smoke than cigarette smokers are. In 2005, marijuana use was a contributing factor in more than 240,000 emergency room visits (SAMHSA 2008).

What Does It Mean to Me?

As of 2012, 16 states and the District of Columbia have passed medical marijuana programs, and 13 have enacted versions of marijuana decriminalization (meaning no prison time or criminal record for first-time possession of a small amount of the drug). Opponents of these laws argue that marijuana is not a safe or benign substance, characterizing it as a gateway drug to other more serious drug abuse. What do you think? Is marijuana a safe drug or not?

 STATE STATS

Methamphetamine

 Methamphetamines

Methamphetamine or "meth" is a highly addictive central nervous system stimulant that can be injected, snorted, smoked, or ingested orally. A derivative of amphetamine, methamphetamine was therapeutically used in the 1930s to treat asthma and narcolepsy (a sleeping disorder) (Pennell et al. 1999). It is the most prevalent synthetic drug manufactured in the United States. The drug is commonly referred to as "speed," "crystal," "crank," "go," and "ice" (a smokable form). Approximately 13 million Americans age 12 or older (or 5%) reported methamphetamine use at least once during their lifetimes (Rose 2009).

Chronic methamphetamine use can cause violent behavior, anxiety, confusion, and insomnia. Users may also exhibit psychotic delusions, including homicidal or suicidal thoughts. Long-term use of the drug can lead to brain damage, similar to damage associated with Alzheimer's disease, stroke, or epilepsy (ONDCP 2006b).

The increase in methamphetamine use has been attributed to the ease of manufacturing the drug and to its highly addictive nature (ONDCP 2006b). In the early 1990s, the primary sources of methamphetamines were super laboratories in California and Mexico. Super labs are able to produce 10 pounds of meth in a 24-hour production cycle.

Certain aspects of the manufacturing and use of methamphetamines, compared with other illegal drugs, have different consequences. Unlike other drugs, meth is easy to make with common chemicals that are easy to obtain (Pennell et al. 1999). The drug can be manufactured illicitly in laboratories set up in homes, motels, trailers, cars, or public storage lockers operated by independent "cooks." Meth produced in these labs is primarily for personal use or limited distribution. Of the 32 chemicals that are used to make or "cook" meth, about one third are toxic (Snell 2001). The waste and residue remaining from meth cooking can contaminate water supplies, soil, and air, causing danger to people, animals, and plant life in the area. Many of the chemicals are explosive, flammable, and corrosive.

Production in these small-scale labs peaked in the late 1990s and early 2000s. Drug officials reported that between 2004 and 2007, the number of small-lab seizures declined, though domestic production increased in 2008. The DEA credits efforts by states and drugstore chains to limit access to the ingredients used to make the drug.

Items used in the production of methamphetamine are displayed on a table. The increase in methamphetamine use has been attributed to how easy the drug is to make with common chemicals and household items.

Cocaine

Cocaine is one of the oldest known drugs, derived from the leaves of the coca bush. Cocaine is listed as a Schedule II drug, a drug with a high potential for abuse. The drug is a strong central nervous system stimulant and can be snorted, smoked, or injected. Crack is the street name for cocaine that has been processed from cocaine hydrochloride into a smokable substance. Because crack is smoked, the user experiences a high in less than 10 seconds.

Prevalence rates for lifetime use of cocaine are between 1% and 3% in developed countries (World Health Organization 2007b). In the United States, 1.5 million Americans were current cocaine users in 2010 (SAMHSA 2011). Adults 18 to 25 years old have a higher rate of use than any other age group. Overall, men have higher rates of use than women do. Cocaine initiation is more likely to occur among adults than among youths under 18. In 1968, the average age of a new user was 18.6 years; it was 23.8 years in 1990 and 21 years from 1995 to 2001 (SAMHSA 2003a). For 2005, the average age of a new user was reported at 19.7 years of age (NIDA 2007).

Some of the most common complications of the drug include cardiovascular disease (disturbances in heart rhythm and heart attacks), respiratory effects (chest pain and respiratory failure), neurological effects (strokes, seizures), and gastrointestinal complications (NIDA 2002b).

The full effect of prenatal drug exposure is not completely known. Babies born to mothers who abuse cocaine are often premature, have low birth weights, and are often shorter in length. It has been predicted that "crack babies" will suffer severe irreversible damage. However, it appears that most crack babies recover, although there is indication of some learning deficits, such as the child's inability to block distractions or to concentrate for long periods of time (NIDA 2002c).

The Problems of Drug Abuse

The Relationship With Crime and Violence

War on Drugs

According to Bureau of Justice Statistics researchers Jennifer Karberg and Doris James (2005), more than two thirds of jail inmates were found to be dependent on or to abuse alcohol or drugs. A larger percentage of inmates were dependent on or abused drugs (53%) than alcohol (47%). Fifty-two percent of female jail inmates were found to be dependent on alcohol or drugs compared with 44% of male inmates. Karberg and James also reported that White and middle-aged inmates had higher rates of substance abuse or dependence. Half of all convicted jail inmates were under the influence of drugs or alcohol at the time of their offense. Only 16% of inmates said they committed their offense to get money for drugs (Karberg and James 2005).

Drinking- and alcohol-related problems have been associated with intimate partner violence among White, Black, and Hispanic couples. This does not mean that violence can occur only when drinking is involved or that alcohol is the prime cause of the violence. Rather, some people may consciously use alcohol as an excuse for violent behavior. Also, alcohol may be related to violence because heavier drinking and violence have common predictors, such as impulsive personalities (Caetano, Schafer, and Cunradi 2001).

Alcohol use has also been associated with child abuse as both a cause and a consequence (Widom and Hiller-Sturmhofel 2001). Parental alcohol abuse may increase a child's risk of experiencing physical or sexual abuse, either by a family member or by another person. Parental alcohol abuse may also lead to child neglect. Studies indicate that girls who were abused or neglected are more likely to have alcohol problems as adults than are other women (Widom and Hiller-Sturmhofel 2001).

Drug Use in the Workplace

Employers have always been concerned about the impact of substance abuse on their workers and their businesses because drug use may undermine employee productivity, safety, and health (Frone 2004). About 8% of full-time workers between the ages of 18 and 64 years used an illicit drug in the past month (Larson et al. 2007). Illicit drug use was higher among White workers, male workers, workers with less than a college degree, and workers with lower family incomes (Larson et al. 2007). Drug abuse cost American businesses $81 billion in lost productivity, $37 billion because of premature death, and $44 billion because of illness in 2002. Alcohol abuse contributed to about 86% of the costs (U.S. Department of Labor 2003).

In their examination of occupational risk factors for drug abuse, Scott MacDonald, Samantha Wells, and T. Cameron Wild (1999) found that problem drinking or drug use was linked to the quality and organization of work, drinking subcultures at work, and the safety of the workplace. Respondents reporting alcohol problems were more likely to have jobs involving repetitive tasks and dangerous working conditions. Respondents with alcohol problems were also more likely to drink with coworkers and experience some social pressure to drink. The same pattern was true for workers with drug problems: They considered their jobs "boring" or repetitive, they identified their job as dangerous, they experienced stress at work, or they were likely to be part of a drinking subculture at work. Among all factors they identified, the presence of a drinking subculture at work was the strongest risk factor for alcohol and drug abuse.

By occupation, the highest rates of current illicit drug use and heavy drinking were reported by food preparation workers, waiters/waitresses, and bartenders (19%); construction workers (14%); service occupations (13%); and transportation and material moving workers (10%) (U.S. Department of Labor 2003). Among employed adults, White, non-Hispanic males between the ages of 18 and 25 who have less than a high school education are likely to report the highest rates of heavy drinking and illicit drug use (U.S. Department of Labor 2003).

Problem Drinking Among Teens and Young Adults

For 2010, the National Survey on Drug Use and Health (NSDUH) reported that the highest prevalence of binge drinking (drinking five or more drinks within a few hours or within one sitting) was for young adults aged 21 to 25 (30.3%), followed by 26- to 29-year-olds (27.2%). Heavy drinking (five or more drinks on the same occasion on at least five different days in the past 30 days) was reported by 15.2% of those 21 to 25 years of age (SAMHSA 2011). See Figure 12.3 for a summary of 2010 alcohol use by age.

An international comparative study on drinking trends among 15- and 16-year-olds revealed that teens in the United Kingdom were among those most likely to drink heavily and to experience intoxication. In 2003, 52% of boys and 56% of girls reported binge drinking in the past 30 days (Plant, Miller, and Plant 2005). From 1995 to 2003, although there was no significant increase in the proportion of boys engaging in binge drinking, researchers observed a sharp increase in the proportion of girls binge drinking since 1999. The rise in binge drinking among girls is consistent with recent reports documenting the increase in heavy episodic or binge drinking among young women in Britain. The majority of surveyed teens, 75%, reported that they had at some time "been drunk" in 2003. Researchers concluded that U.K. teenagers drink in ways that are potentially harmful and that binge drinking among U.K. teens is a matter of real concern (Plant et al. 2005).

Figure 12.3

Current, Binge, and Heavy Alcohol Use Among Persons Ages 12 and Older, by Age, 2010

Source: Substance Abuse and Mental Health Services Administration 2011.

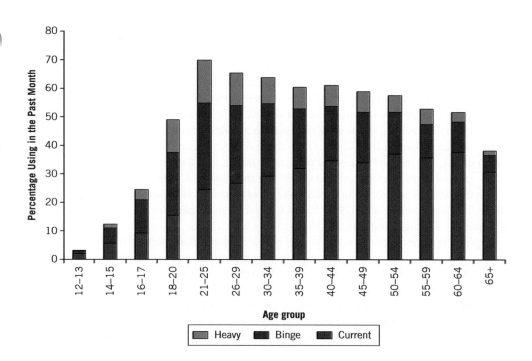

By the time they reach the eighth grade, nearly 50% of U.S. adolescents report having had at least one drink, and more than 20% report having been drunk (NIAAA 2003b). Underage drinkers account for nearly 20% of the alcohol consumed in the United States (Tanner 2003). In 2010, among youth ages 12 to 17, 13.6% used alcohol in the month before the National Survey on Drug Use and Health, lower than the rate of youth alcohol use reported in 2009, 14.7%. Among all youth, 7.8% were binge drinkers, and 1.7% were heavy drinkers (SAMHSA 2011). Adolescent binge drinking is one of the stronger predictors of bingeing through college (Wechsler et al. 1995).

Binge drinking among college students has been called a major U.S. public health concern (Clapp, Shillington, and Segars 2000). (Refer to Figure 12.4 for a comparison of heavy drinking among those enrolled full-time in college and those who are not. Drinking rates are consistently higher for those enrolled full-time.) Henry Wechsler (1996) reported results from the 1996 Harvard School of Public Health College Alcohol Study, highlighting how binge drinking has become widespread among college students. In the Wechsler study, binge drinking was defined as five or more drinks in a row one or more times during a two-week period for men and four or more drinks in a row one or more times during a two-week period for women. The author explains that men, students younger than 24, fraternity and sorority residents, Whites, students in athletics, and students who socialize more are most likely to binge drink. On average, students who engaged in high-risk behaviors such as illicit drug use, unsafe sexual activity, and cigarette smoking were more likely to be binge drinkers. In contrast, students who were involved in community service, the arts, or studying were less likely to be binge drinkers (Wechsler 1996).

Although the demographic and social correlates of college drinking have been consistently identified in many studies, attempts to explain the behavior through various sociological perspectives have been limited. Most prevalent in the literature are theories that identify drinking as part of the social learning process: addressing the role of peer groups, students' attitudes, and perceptions as well as the social construction of drinking norms related to alcohol consumption. Similar social learning theories have also been linked to substance abuse (Durkin, Wolfe, and Clark 2005).

Binge Drinking

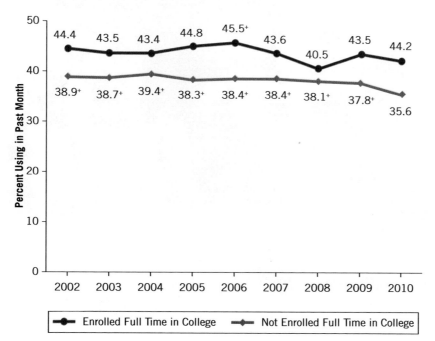

Figure 12.4

Heavy Alcohol Use Among Adults Ages 18 to 22, by College Enrollment: 2002 to 2010

Source: Substance Abuse and Mental Health Services Administration 2011.

+Difference between this estimate and the 2010 estimate is statistically significant at the .05 level.

Access to alcohol is also related to problem drinking. Weitzman et al. (2003) reported a positive relationship between alcohol outlet density (number of bars and liquor stores near campus) and frequent drinking (drinking on 10 or more occasions in the past 30 days), heavy drinking (five or more drinks at an off-campus party), and drinking problems (self-reported).

The Task Force of the National Advisory Council on Alcohol Abuse and Alcoholism (2010) concluded that 1,825 college students between the ages of 18 and 24 die each year from alcohol-related unintentional injuries, including motor vehicle crashes. About half a million students between the ages of 18 and 24 are unintentionally injured while under the influence of alcohol, and more than 600,000 students are assaulted by another student who has been drinking. In addition, the task force reports that 25% of college students report academic consequences (poor grades, poor performance, missing classes) as a result of their drinking, and more than 150,000 develop an alcohol-related health problem. Based on self-reports about their drinking, 31% of college students meet the criteria for alcohol abuse, and 6% meet the criteria for alcohol dependence (Task Force of the National Advisory Council on Alcohol Abuse and Alcoholism 2010).

Brower (2002) explains that there is no evidence that drinking in college leads to later-life alcoholism or long-term alcohol abuse. He writes, "Real life is a strong disincentive for the kind of binge drinking that college students do" (Brower 2002:255). He suggests using the term *episodic high-risk drinking* to describe more accurately how college students drink: infrequently drinking a large quantity of alcohol in a short period.

Photo 12.3

Binge drinking among college students has been called a major U.S. public health concern. According to the Task Force of the National Advisory Council on Alcohol Abuse and Alcoholism (2010), 1,825 college students between the ages of 18 and 24 die each year from alcohol-related unintentional injuries, including motor vehicle crashes.

What Does It Mean to Me?

What is the drinking policy on your campus? Does your campus culture promote safe drinking? What educational or service programs are provided for students who abuse alcohol?

 STATE STATS

In Focus

Alcopops

Flavored alcoholic beverages, sugary fruit-flavored alcoholic beverages such as Mike's Hard Lemonade and Bacardi Silver, have become popular with young drinkers. Though the alcohol content must be included in the packaging, some packaging makes these beverages appear more like nonalcoholic soft drinks or energy drinks than an alcoholic beverage containing 5% to 7% alcohol per volume. State lawmakers and parents have increasingly grown concerned about the popularity of these drinks, believing that these beverages contribute to underage drinking (Marshall 2007) and referring to them as "gateway" drugs (leading youth to more traditional alcoholic beverages).

A 2001 national poll revealed that 41% of all teens ages 14 to 18 have tried an alcopop, with twice as many 14- to 16-year-olds preferring them to beer or mixed drinks. When asked why they would choose these beverages over beer, wine, or liquor, teens reported that they liked the sweet taste of the drinks and the disguised taste of alcohol. Most surveyed teens believed the products were marketed to their age group (Alcohol Policies Project 2001).

However, there appears to be more concern about the growing consumption of these beverages among young girls.

Photo 12.4

Girls are more likely to consume alcopops than boys. The American Medical Association's 2004 survey revealed that a third of all teen girls older than age 12 have tried alcopops. Pictured here are two girls drinking alcopops in a club in Great Britain.

The American Medical Association released 2004 poll results that indicated that a third of all teen girls older than age 12 have tried alcopops. As part of an effort to urge then Governor Arnold Schwarzenegger to reclassify these beverages as hard liquor, Cinthya Luis, a high school senior and member of the San Diego Youth Council, explained, "Kids all over the state and the nation call these products 'cheerleader beer' and 'girlie beer' because they are so popular with underage girls—their sweet taste is designed to appeal to young drinkers." Though Schwarzenegger vetoed the bill in 2005, the California State Board of Equalization voted to reclassify alcopops as distilled spirits (taxable at $3.30 per gallon) rather than beer (taxable at $0.20 per gallon). Prevention and youth advocates applauded the decision, hoping the higher cost would discourage underage consumption.

In addition to California, several other states, such as Arkansas, Illinois, and Nebraska, have considered reclassifying these beverages as hard liquor. Critics argue that these beverages are no different from beer, which contains 4% to 6% alcohol per volume. Maine and Utah have already reclassified these beverages as hard liquor.

The Increase in Club Drugs

MDMA (3,4-methylenedioxymethamphetamine) is a synthetic psychoactive drug with stimulant and hallucinogenic properties. The pill—popularly known as Ecstasy, Adam, X, XTC, hug, beans, and love drug—first gained popularity at dance clubs, raves, and college scenes.

The 2009 NSDUH reported that 4.3% or 10.2 million Americans have used MDMA at least once during their lifetime (NIDA 2010). MDMA is usually taken in pill form at the cost of about $25 per tablet, but the drug can also be snorted, injected, or used in a suppository.

Rohypnol, GHB, and ketamine are other drugs commonly used in club and rave scenes. All three are also known as "date rape" drugs. Previously confined to the club or rave subculture, Ecstasy has become a mainstream drug (NIDA 2003a), second only to marijuana as the most frequently used illicit drug among young adults (Johnston, O'Malley, and Bachman 2001).

From 2002 to 2004, a public service announcement sponsored by the Partnership for a Drug Free America featured Jim and Elsa Heird. The Nevada couple's 21-year-old daughter, Danielle, took Ecstasy on three occasions; the last time it resulted in her death. After taking one or one and a half pills, Danielle began to feel ill and decided to stay home to rest. A few hours later when her friends came home, they found her dead. There were no other controlled substances or alcohol in her body at the time of her death (Vaughn 2002). Ecstasy-related deaths like Danielle Heird's are rare. During the third and fourth quarters of 2003, MDMA use was reported in more than 2,000 drug abuse–related emergency room cases (ONDCP 2006d).

Even when they are not fatal, Ecstasy and other related drugs, known collectively as methylated amphetamines, are not harmless. Ecstasy produces an intense release of serotonin in a user's brain, which can cause irreparable damage to the brain and memory functions. Research indicates that long-term brain damage, especially to the parts of the brain critical to thought and memory, may result from its use. Users may also experience psychological difficulties (such as confusion, depression, and sleeping problems) while using the drug and sometimes for weeks after. As a result of using the drug, individuals can also experience increases in heart rate and blood pressure and physical symptoms such as nausea, blurred vision, or faintness (NIDA 2003a). When users overdose, they can experience rapid heartbeat, high blood pressure, faintness, panic attacks, and even loss of consciousness (Vaughn 2002).

In a study of undergraduates at a large midwestern university, Carol Boyd, Sean E. McCabe, and Hannah d'Arcy (2003) found that men and women were equally likely to have used Ecstasy, and that several factors predicted its use. White students were more likely to report lifetime Ecstasy use than were African American or Asian students. According to the researchers, sexual orientation was also related to Ecstasy use: Those who identified themselves as gay, lesbian, or bisexual were more likely to report lifetime, annual, or past-month Ecstasy use than were heterosexual students. Students with a grade point average (GPA) of 3.5 or higher were consistently less likely to have used Ecstasy in the past year or their lifetime than were students with GPAs below 2.5. Students who reported binge drinking within the past two weeks were also more likely to report past-month Ecstasy use.

Community, Policy, and Social Action

Federal Programs

Throughout the first part of this chapter, I have already referred to three U.S. offices: NIDA, the ONDCP, and the NIAAA. All three programs are federally funded.

The NIAAA was established after the passage of the Comprehensive Alcohol Abuse and Alcoholism Prevention, Treatment, and Rehabilitation Act of 1970. Signed into law by President

Richard Nixon, the legislation acknowledged alcohol abuse and alcoholism as major public health concerns. The law instructed the NIAAA to "develop and conduct comprehensive health, education, research, and planning programs for the prevention and treatment of alcohol abuse and alcoholism and for the rehabilitation of alcohol abusers and alcoholics" (NIAAA 2003a). Since then, the NIAAA's mission has been revised to include support and implementation of biomedical and behavioral research, policy studies, and research in a range of scientific areas to address the causes, consequences, treatment, and prevention of alcoholism and alcohol-related problems (NIAAA 2003b).

NIDA was established in 1974 as the federal office for research, treatment, prevention, training services, and data collection on the nature and extent of drug abuse. Like the NIAAA, NIDA is part of the National Institutes of Health, the federal biomedical and behavioral research agency. NIDA's stated mission is to bring "the power of science to bear on drug abuse and addiction" (NIDA 2003b). NIDA supports more than 85% of the world's research on the health aspects of drug abuse and addiction.

The ONDCP is the newest federal drug program, operated through the White House. Established in 1988 through the Anti-Drug Abuse Act, the ONDCP's mission was to set national priorities, design comprehensive research-based strategies, and certify federal drug control budgets. According to the act, the purpose of the office was to prevent young people from using illegal drugs, reduce the number of drug users, and decrease the availability of drugs (ONDCP 2003). Ten years later, the ONDCP's mission was expanded under the Reauthorization Act of 1998. Some of the legislative requirements included a commitment to a five-year national drug control program budget, the establishment of a parents' advisory council on drug abuse, development of a long-term national drug strategy, and increased reporting to Congress on drug control activities (ONDCP 2003). The act also provided support for the High Intensity Drug Trafficking Areas (HIDTA) program, coordinating local, state, and federal law enforcement drug control efforts.

Use of illegal drugs continues despite the efforts of these three lead agencies. And the War on Drugs comes with huge economic costs, with the Obama administration having requested $10.1 billion for prevention and treatment programs and $9.4 billion for law enforcement and incarceration (ONDCP 2012).

Drug Legalization

The contemporary debate about the legalization of drugs emerged in 1988 during a meeting of the U.S. Conference of Mayors. Baltimore's Kurt L. Schmoke called for a national debate on drug control policies and the potential benefits of legalizing marijuana and other illicit substances (Inciardi 1999). Proponents present several arguments for the legalization of drugs: Current drug laws and law enforcement initiatives have failed to eradicate the drug problem, arresting and incarcerating individuals for drug offenses does nothing to alleviate the drug problem, drug crimes are actually victimless crimes, legalization will lead to a reduction in drug-related crimes and violence and improve the quality of life in inner cities, and legalization will also eliminate serious health risks by providing clean and high-quality substances (Cussen and Block 2000; Silbering 2001). Many supporters of legalization argue that drugs should be legalized based on the libertarian legal code (Trevino and Richard 2002), namely that the legalization of drugs would give a basic civil liberty back to citizens by granting them control over their own bodies (Cussen and Block 2000).

The term *legalization* is often used interchangeably with another term, *decriminalization*. The terms vary in the extent to which the law can regulate the distribution and consumption of drugs. In general, **decriminalization** means keeping criminal penalties but

**Colorado Drug
Legalization**

reducing their severity or removing some kinds of behavior from inclusion under the law (e.g., eliminating bans on the use of drug paraphernalia). Some would support regulating drugs in the same way alcohol and tobacco are regulated, whereas others would argue for no restrictions at all. **Legalization** suggests removing drugs from the control of the law entirely (Weisheit and Johnson 1992).

Several European countries including Portugal, the United Kingdom, and Switzerland have moved toward drug legalization or decriminalization in some form. The country most identified with liberal drug policies is the Netherlands. Since the mid-1970s, Netherlands coffee shops have been allowed to sell marijuana products. Though possession and sale of marijuana are not legal, in practice sales through these shops are not prosecuted, and buyers (18 years of age or older) are not prosecuted for possession of small (personal use) amounts. As of 2012, medical marijuana was legal in 18 states and the District of Columbia. In 2012, voters in Colorado and Washington approved legislation that legalized the possession and sale of marijuana for recreational use. Personal possession of an ounce of marijuana is legal in both states for anyone 21 years of age or older.

Psychedelic Drugs

In the United States, drug legalization is generally opposed by the medical and public health community (Trevino and Richard 2002). The American Medical Association has consistently opposed the legalization of all illegal drugs, arguing that most research shows drugs, particularly cocaine, heroin, and methamphetamines, are harmful to an individual's health. Opponents charge that drug use is a significant factor in the spread of sexually transmitted diseases such as HIV, and drug users are more likely to engage in risky behaviors and in criminal activity (Trevino and Richard 2002). The DEA has also been clear about its opposition to drug legalization, citing concerns about potential increases in drug use and addiction, drug-related crimes, and costs related to drug treatment and criminal justice.

In the 1990s, the drug debate began to change, with legalization proponents advocating a "harm reduction" approach. Many opposed to legalization began to accept aspects of the harm reduction approach. Harm reduction is a principle suggesting that "managing

Photo 12.5

In the Netherlands, though possession and sale of marijuana are not legal, coffee shops are permitted to sell limited amounts of the drug to adults (18 years of age or older) for personal use. Smoking marijuana is permitted in these shops.

drug misuse is more appropriate than attempting to stop it all together" (Inciardi 1999:3). Proponents acknowledge that current drug policies are not working, but they are still not in favor of full decriminalization (McBride, Terry, and Inciardi 1999). The harm reduction approach emphasizes treatment, rehabilitation, and education (McBride et al. 1999), including advocacy for changes in drug policies (such as legalization), HIV/AIDS-related interventions, broader drug treatment options, counseling and clinical case management for those who want to continue using drugs, and ancillary interventions (housing, healing centers, advocacy groups) (Inciardi 1999).

What Does It Mean to Me?

What is your position on the legalization of drugs? What are the intended and unintended consequences of drug legalization?

The Drug Policy Alliance (2003a) is an organization "working to broaden the public debate on drug policy and to promote the realistic alternatives to the war on drugs based on science, compassion, health, and human rights." Since 1996, 46 states have enacted more than 150 drug policy reforms. The reforms usually target drug sentencing and the legalization of medical marijuana. For more information on drug policies in your state, go to the Study Site, Chapter 12, at www.sagepub .com/leonguerrero4e.

Punishment or Treatment?

Criminal Sentencing

Stricter federal policies have increased the number of men and women serving jail or prison time for drug-related offenses. As conflict and symbolic interaction theories suggest, drug laws are not enforced equally, with certain groups being singled out. Although most illicit drug users are White, Blacks constitute about 80% to 90% of all people sent to prison on drug charges (Fellner 2000). Nationwide, Black men are sent to state prison on drug charges at 13 times the rate of White men (Fellner 2000). Most women in prison are untreated substance abusers incarcerated for nonviolent offenses (Alleyne 2007). Drug enforcement usually targets urban and poor neighborhoods while ignoring drug use among middle- or upper-class people. Whereas our society treats middle- or upper-class drug use as a personal crisis, lower-class drug use is defined as criminal. Consider, for example, how the media reported the drug treatment of celebrities Lindsay Lohan and Britney Spears—was either referred to as a criminal?

Sasha Abramsky (2003) explains that with tougher drug laws, the U.S. drug war was taken away from public health and medical officials and placed into the hands of law enforcement and the courts. The notion that drug abuse is a disease was replaced with the idea that drug abuse is a crime. A punishment model has also been adopted in China, where its rehabilitation centers serve as forced labor camps punishing, not treating, addicts (Jacobs 2010). In contrast, the Netherlands defines drug abuse as a public health issue and has implemented harm reduction strategies, placing the priority on drug education and treatment, rather than on punishment.

However, as overall crime rates began to decline, public support for the get-tough-on-drugs policy began to wane. Research conducted by the Pew Research Center in 2001 found 47% of Americans favored rolling back mandatory minimum sentences for nonviolent drug offenders and 52% believed drug use should be treated as a disease rather than as a crime.

Abramsky (2003) identified key legislative changes in several states. Arizona and California passed legislation that diverted thousands of drug offenders into treatment programs instead of prisons. In 1998, Michigan repealed its mandatory life sentence law for those caught in the possession of more than 650 grams of certain narcotics. In 2002, Michigan Governor John Engler signed legislation that rolled back the state's tough mandatory-minimum drug sentences. The Kansas Sentencing Commission proposed reforms of the state's mandatory sentencing codes, along with expansion of treatment programs. The reforms were accepted in March 2003. Though California's 2010 ballot initiative to legalize marijuana did not pass, that same year Governor Arnold Schwarzenegger signed into law a bill that reduced the penalty for marijuana possession from a misdemeanor to a nonarrestable infraction (e.g., a traffic ticket).

At the federal level, the Obama administration, through the ONDCP, has focused on addiction as a disease and has called for increases in drug prevention and treatment programs for all who need them, including drug-involved offenders. In 2010, President Obama signed the Fair Sentencing Act into law, reducing the disparity in the amounts of powder cocaine and crack cocaine required for the imposition of mandatory minimum sentences.

Drug Treatment and Prevention Programs

Individual Approaches

Drug Addiction

Drug addiction is a "treatable disorder" (NIDA 2003b). Traditional treatment programs focus on treating the individual and his or her addiction. The ultimate goal of treatment is to enable users to achieve lasting abstinence from the drug, but the immediate treatment goals are to reduce drug use, improve the users' ability to function, and minimize their medical and social complications from drug use.

Treatment may come in two forms: Behavioral treatment includes counseling, support groups, family therapy, or psychotherapy; medication therapy, such as maintenance treatment for heroin addicts, may be used to suppress drug withdrawal symptoms and craving. Short-term treatment programs can include residential treatment, medication therapy, or drug-free outpatient therapy. Long-term programs (longer than six months) may include highly structured residential therapeutic community treatment or, in the case of heroin users, methadone maintenance outpatient treatment. Research conducted during the past 25 years indicates that treatment does work to reduce drug intake and drug-related crimes. Patients who stay in treatment longer than three months have better outcomes than do people who undergo shorter treatments (NIDA 2003b).

Workplace Strategies

Certain employers, such as employers in the transportation industry and organizations with federal contracts in excess of $100,000, are required by law to have drug-free workplace programs. The federal government, through the Drug Free Workplace Program, also encourages private employers to implement such programs in an effort to reduce and eliminate the negative effects of alcohol and drug use in the workplace (SAMHSA 2003b). The American Management Association reported that the percentage of companies that test employees for drugs increased from 22% in 1987 to more than 81% in 1997 (Hoffman and Larison 1999). After implementing a drug free workplace program, employers, unions, and employees are likely to see a decrease in administrative work losses (sick leave abuse, health insurance claims, disability payments, and accident costs), hidden losses (poor performance, material waste, turnover, and premature death), legal losses (grievances, threat to public safety, work-site security), and costs of health and mental health care services (SAMHSA 2003c).

Drug-testing programs have been subject to lawsuits during the past decade for challenging the employees' right to privacy and their constitutional freedom from unreasonable searches by the government (SAMHSA 2003b). There have also been challenges to the accuracy of drug tests. Critics have asserted a positive test does not always correlate with poor job performance, a criterion for assessing the adverse effects of drugs (Klingner, Roberts, and Patterson 1998). Consistent with conflict theories on drug use, some have argued that drug testing promotes various political agendas and reflects the manipulation of interest groups that market and sell drug testing and security services (Klingner et al. 1998). Yet many U.S. companies consider drug-testing programs part of an effective policy against substance abuse among workers (Hoffman and Larison 1999). Drug testing is also part of a preventative strategy, as the U.S. Department of Labor (2007) reports that between 10% and 20% of workers who die on the job test positive for alcohol or other drugs.

Paul Roman and Terry Blum (2002) report that employee assistance programs (EAPs) are the most common intervention used in the workplace to prevent and treat alcohol and other drug abuse among employees. The primary goal for many of these programs is to ensure that employees maintain their employment, productivity, and careers. These EAPs usually include health promotion, education, and referral to abuse treatment as needed. Most of these programs do not target the general workplace population; rather, services are directed to those already affected by a problem or in the early stages of their abuse. There is some evidence of the effectiveness of these programs, returning substantial proportions of employees with alcohol problems to their jobs (Roman and Blum 2002).

Campus Programs

The U.S. Supreme Court ruled that drug testing in schools is legal for student athletes (1993) and for students in other extracurricular activities (2002). In both rulings, the Court stated that drug screenings play an important role in deterring student drug use.

However, a national study of 76,000 high school students reported no significant difference in drug use among students in schools with testing versus students in schools without testing. Researchers Ryoko Yamaguchi, Lloyd Johnston, and Patrick O'Malley (2003) reported that 37% of 12th graders in schools that test for drugs said that they had smoked marijuana in the previous year, compared with 36% of 12th graders in schools that did not test. In addition, 21% of 12th graders in schools with testing reported that they had used illicit drugs (cocaine or heroin) in the previous year compared with 19% of 12th graders in schools without drug screenings. The study found that only 18% of schools did any kind of drug screening between 1998 and 2001. Large schools (22.6%) reported more testing than did smaller schools (14.2%). Most drug tests were conducted in high schools. The study did not compare schools that conducted intensive regular screenings with those that occasionally tested for drugs. The study indicated that education, rather than testing, may be the most effective weapon against abuse (Winter 2003).

In their review of 94 college drug prevention programs, Andris Ziemelis, Ronald Buckman, and Abdulaziz Elfessi (2002) identified three prevention models that produced the most favorable outcomes in binge-drinking prevention efforts. The first model includes student participation and involvement, such as volunteer services, advisory boards, or task forces, to discourage alcohol or other drug use or abuse. The researchers documented how these activities reinforce students' beliefs that they are in control of the outcomes in their lives and that their efforts and contributions are valued. This model encourages student ownership and development of the program. The second model includes educational and informational processes, such as instruction in classes, bulletin boards and displays, and resource centers. The most effective informational strategies were those that avoided coercive approaches but instead encouraged interactive communication between students and professionals on campus. The last model includes efforts directed at the larger structural environment, changing the campus regulatory environment and developing free alternative programming, such as providing alcohol-free residence halls or mandatory alcohol and drug abuse classes as part of campus intervention. In general, models that discourage or deglamorize alcohol and drug use were associated with better outcomes than were those that merely banned or restricted substance use (Ziemelis et al. 2002).

Voices in the Community

Jill Ingram

This article about Jill Ingram, of the National College Commission of Mothers Against Drunk Driving (MADD), was taken from MADD's website (Glenn 2000).

Ingram became involved in underage drinking prevention after her brother was hit by a drunk driver in 1996.

Ingram's brother, Dan, and his date were on their way home from a college sorority formal when the drunk driver—who [was] driving her van, headlights off, on the wrong side of a divided highway—hit their car head-on. Dan sustained multiple injuries to his ankle, knee, and wrist in the crash.

"There were several witnesses who saw [the drunk driver] and honked to get her attention, but she was too drunk to notice," said Ingram. "Later it was determined that her blood alcohol content was two times over the legal limit."

"I can't even bear to think about what my brother must have gone through during and in the moments that followed the crash," Ingram said. "But I do know what my family went through in the aftermath of the crash. It was then that I knew I had to do something to prevent another family from going through that kind of pain."

Ingram responded by taking action. Her first step was to attend the 1997 MADD National Youth Summit to Prevent Underage Drinking as a youth delegate. While Ingram was at the Summit, a cheerleading squad teammate back home nearly lost her life in an impaired driving crash. This second alcohol-related crash fueled Ingram's fire for preventing the senseless tragedy from happening to anyone else.

Armed with the knowledge and driven by the passion of a true activist, Ingram set out to make a difference. Working in conjunction with the MADD Northern Virginia chapter, she began speaking at high schools and local community colleges to educate students about the dangers of alcohol and impaired driving. She also co-founded the student-led Alcohol and Drug Abuse Prevention Team (ADAPT) on her university's campus.

"Underaged students like myself who choose not to drink didn't seem to have the same options to have fun and get together with friends as the students who do drink," Ingram said of her impression upon arriving at [the University of Virginia] her first year. "The drinkers and partyers at the university had an outlet that was not available to students like me on campus. Students need an outlet for their energies and their leadership abilities," she continued. "Our campus alcohol awareness program is

10 years old, but student involvement this year is the highest it has ever been because we have created new and different options for alcohol-free lifestyles."

ADAPT continues to operate on the University of Virginia campus, sponsoring a safe spring break activities program and educational presentations on alcohol safety, alcoholism, and hazing.

Community Approaches

In 1997, the Drug-Free Communities Act became law. The act was intended to increase community participation in substance abuse reduction among youth. The program is currently directed by the White House's ONDCP. The program supports more than 700 coalitions of youth; parents; law enforcement; schools; state, local, and tribal agencies; health care professionals; faith-based organizations; and other community representatives. The coalitions, such as Project Northland, rely on mentoring, parental involvement, community education, and school-based programs for drug prevention and intervention.

Based in northern Minnesota, Project Northland was the largest community trial in the United States to address the prevention of alcohol use and alcohol-related problems among adolescents (Williams and Perry 1998). Adopting a holistic approach, the project assumed that prevention efforts should be directed at adolescents and their immediate social environment (family, peers, friends) and should include larger peer groups (teachers, coaches, religious advisers) as well as the broader community of businesses and political leaders. The project was recognized for its programming by SAMHSA, the U.S. Department of Health and Human Services, and the U.S. Department of Education.

Project Northland included youth participation and leadership, parental involvement and education, community organizing and task forces, media campaigns, and school curriculum as part of its strategies for alcohol use prevention. The program included two phases. Phase 1 focused on strategies to encourage adolescents not to use alcohol. Phase 2 emphasized changing community norms about alcohol use, reducing the availability of alcohol among high school students, and adopting a functionalist approach in reinforcing community norms and boundaries. Community strategies included making compliance checks of age-of-sale laws (coordinated through local police departments), holding training sessions for responsible beverage servers at retail outlets and bars, and encouraging businesses to adopt "gold card" programs where discounts are provided to students who pledge to remain free of alcohol. At the end of Phase 2, significant differences between the intervention and comparison groups were observed. The rates of increase in underage drinking were lower among the intervention students (Perry et al. 2002). In 2002, Project Northland was implemented internationally. First-year program data from primary and secondary schools in Croatia reveal that Project Northland was effective in increasing dialog between Croatian students, parents, and teachers about students' actual use of alcohol (Abatemarco et al. 2004).

 Anti-Drug PSA

The Community Anti-Drug Coalitions of America (CADCA) is a nonprofit organization that provides technical assistance and training to community-based coalitions. The organization was established in 1992 by Jim Burke and Alvah Chapman and currently serves more than 5,000 antidrug coalitions. The program provides community groups with lobbying handbooks, alerts on drug-related legislation, funding information, and coalition training on various drug abuse topics. One CADCA affiliate is the Van Buren County SAFE Coalition in Keosauqua, Iowa, established in 2002. The organization focuses on prevention strategies targeting substance use and domestic violence. The coalition supported the passage of Iowa's Smokefree Air Act in 2008. The act prohibits smoking in nearly all enclosed public spaces and workplaces.

Main Points

- There seems to be no argument about the seriousness of the drug problem in the United States and throughout the world. In 2009, 21.8 million Americans age 12 and older reported they were current users of illicit drugs other than marijuana.

- Functionalists argue that society provides us with norms or guidelines on alcohol and drug use. A set of social norms identifies the appropriate use of drugs and alcohol.

- Conflict theorists argue that powerful political and business interest groups have made intentional decisions about which drugs are illegal.

- Feminists argue that theorists and practitioners in the field of alcohol and drug abuse have ignored experiences unique to women and other marginalized groups. However, there is increasing recognition of the importance of gender-sensitive treatment models.

- The interactionist perspective argues that drug abuse is learned from others; it addresses how individuals or groups are labeled abusers and how society responds to them.

- Alcohol is the most abused drug in the United States. Other abused drugs include nicotine, marijuana, methamphetamine, and cocaine. Alcohol problems can be both a cause and an excuse for intimate partner violence and child abuse. Alcohol abuse is more often suspected in crimes than abuse of any other drug.

- Employers have always been concerned about the impact of substance abuse. About 8% of full-time workers between the ages of 18 and 64 years used an illicit drug in the past month, costing businesses billions of dollars a year.

- Binge drinking among college students has been called a major public health problem. Some research shows that students who engaged in high-risk behaviors were more likely to be binge drinkers, whereas students who were involved in community service, the arts, or studying were less likely to be binge drinkers. Thousands of college students are injured or die each year from alcohol-related driving or injuries.

- In the early 1990s, the primary sources of methamphetamines were super laboratories. More recently, there has been an increase in the number of small-scale labs operated by independent cooks. The waste and residue remaining from meth cooking can contaminate the surrounding area, and cleanup is very dangerous and costly.

- Ecstasy, Rohypnol, GHB, and ketamine are drugs commonly used in club and rave scenes. Ecstasy has become a mainstream drug and can cause physical problems, irreparable damage to the brain and memory, psychological difficulties long after use, and death.

- Three offices—NIDA, the ONDCP, and the NIAAA—are federally funded agencies that research and educate about drug and alcohol abuse. Extensive use of illegal drugs continues despite the efforts of these three lead agencies and the War on Drugs.

- Some have explored alternatives to the War on Drugs, including legalization (removing drugs from the control of the law). Proponents argue that current laws fail to eradicate the problem; incarceration does not alleviate the drug problem, they say, and drug crimes are victimless. Proponents argue that legalization would reduce drug-related crimes and violence, make drugs cleaner, and return to citizens a basic civil liberty. Legalization is generally opposed by the medical and public health community because research shows that drugs are harmful and cause risky behaviors and criminal activity.

- As conflict and symbolic interaction theories suggest, drug laws are not enforced equally, with certain minority groups (particularly Blacks) and the lower class being singled out. Recently, however, key legislative changes suggest a shift in thinking to treatment rather than incarceration.

- Drug addiction is considered a "treatable disorder." Treatment may be either behavioral or medical and either short or long term. Research in the past 25 years indicates that treatment works to reduce drug intake and drug-related crimes.

- Certain employers are required by law to have drug-free workplace programs. A drug-free workplace program likely decreases administrative work losses, hidden losses, legal losses, and health care services.

- Drug-testing programs have been subject to lawsuits in the past decade over constitutional issues. There have also been challenges to the accuracy of drug tests. Consistent with conflict theories, some have argued that drug testing promotes various political agendas and reflects the manipulation of interest groups. Yet many U.S. companies consider drug-testing programs part of an effective policy against substance abuse.

■ Employee assistance programs are the most common intervention used in the workplace to prevent and treat alcohol and other drug abuse among employees. There is some evidence of the effectiveness of these programs.

■ The U.S. Supreme Court ruled that drug testing in schools is legal and an important deterrent to drug use for student athletes (1993) and for students in other extracurricular activities (2002). However, a national study of 76,000 high school students indicated that education, not testing, may be the most effective weapon against abuse.

■ In general, prevention models that discourage or deglamorize alcohol and drug use are associated with better outcomes than are those that merely ban or restrict substance use.

■ Recent acts and initiatives to reduce substance abuse include the Drug Free Communities Act and the Community Anti-Drug Coalitions of America.

On Your Own

Log on to the open-access Student Study Site at www.sagepub.com/leonguerrero4e for these additional learning tools:

- ■ Interactive quizzes
- ■ Video clips
- ■ NPR audio links
- ■ Handbook articles

- ■ E-flashcards
- ■ Journal articles
- ■ End-of-chapter web exercises
- ■ Additional web resources and current events

Internet and Community Exercises

1. Several advocacy groups are committed to promoting alternative solutions to the drug problem in the United States. Two groups are Students for Sensible Drug Policy and Stop the Drug War. Log on to *Study Site Chapter 12* for links to their websites. Examine how both organizations define the drug problem. Are there any differences in their definitions? What solutions does each group support?

2. According to the U.S. Drug Enforcement Administration, the illegal drug market in the United States is one of the most profitable in the world. The trafficking of illegal drugs has benefited from globalization, linking producers, dealers, and users more easily. The High Intensity Drug Trafficking Areas program provides assistance to enforcement agencies operating in critical drug-trafficking regions of the United States. For information about drug trafficking in your state, go to *Study Site Chapter 12*.

3. According to Maria Alaniz (1998), "Alcohol outlet density is an important determinant of the amount of alcohol advertising in a community. Merchants use storefronts and the interiors of alcohol outlets to advertise alcohol products. Therefore, areas with a high density of outlets have a greater number of advertisements" (p. 286). Alaniz cites a study showing that a student walking home from school in a predominantly Latino neighborhood in northern California may be exposed to between 10 and 60 storefront alcohol advertisements. The same study found that there are five times more alcohol advertisements in Latino neighborhoods than in predominantly White neighborhoods. Count the number of alcohol outlets around

your college or university, along with billboard advertising within a 5-mile radius. Do these ads target college students? Do you think exposure to alcohol advertising increases alcohol consumption? Why or why not?

4. The Campaign for Tobacco-Free Kids is a national campaign effort to protect children from tobacco addiction and exposure to secondhand smoke.

The campaign's website includes information on state initiatives, as well as statistics on tobacco use. Log on to *Study Site Chapter 12*.

5. The World Health Organization supports a global alcohol database. It reports trends in alcohol use and related mortality for selected countries since 1961, allowing you to compare international data. Log on to *Study Site Chapter 12*.

Study Questions

1. How are sociological explanations of drug abuse different from biological or psychological approaches?

2. From a functionalist perspective, explain how the social structure contributes to drug use.

3. Explain how stereotypes of drug use and abusers influence how specific individuals and groups are labeled *abusers* and how society responds to them.

4. Define drug abuse and drug addiction.

5. Is drinking a problem among teens and young adults? Why or why not?

6. Define drug legalization. Would it be effective in reducing the amount of drug use? Why or why not?

7. What treatment programs are available to drug users? What type of prevention programs?

CHAPTER 13

Crime and Criminal Justice

Think of a crime, any crime. Picture the first "crime" that comes into your mind. What do you see? The odds are you are not imagining a mining company executive sitting at his desk, calculating the costs of proper safety precautions and deciding not to invest in them. Probably what you see with your mind's eye is one person physically attacking another or robbing something from another via the threat of a physical attack.

—Reiman (1998:57)

 Crime

hen we think of crime, we imagine violent or life-threatening acts, not white-collar crimes committed by men and women using accounting ledgers and calculators as deadly weapons. Yet, an act does not have to be violent or bloody to be considered criminal. For our discussion, a crime is any behavior that violates criminal law and is punishable by fine, jail, or other negative sanctions. Crime is divided into two legal categories. **Felonies** are serious offenses, including murder, rape, robbery, and aggravated assault; these crimes are punishable by more than a year's imprisonment or death. **Misdemeanors** are minor offenses, such as traffic violations, that are punishable by a fine or less than a year in jail. In this chapter, we examine crimes as a social problem. We consider a full range of crimes, not just violent events that make the headlines on your evening news. Before we review the specifics about crimes, let's review sociological explanations of why people commit crime.

Sociological Perspectives on Crime

Biological explanations of crime tend to address how criminals are "born that way." Early explanations were intended to classify criminal types by appearance and genetic factors, such as Cesare Lombroso's nineteenth-century theory of "born criminal" types. Lombroso argued that criminals could be easily identified by distinct physical features: a huge forehead, a large jaw, and a longer arm span. Contemporary biological explanations focus on biochemical (diet and hormones) and neurophysical (brain lesions, brain dysfunctions) characteristics related to violence and criminality. Like biological theories, psychological perspectives focus on inherent criminal characteristics. Researchers link personality development, moral development, or mental disorders to criminal behaviors. Both biological and psychological theories address how crime is determined by individual characteristics or predispositions to crime, but they fail to explain why crime rates vary between urban and rural areas, different neighborhoods, or social or economic groups (Adler, Mueller, and Laufer 1991). Sociological theories attempt to address the reasons for these differences, highlighting how larger social forces contribute to crime.

Functionalist Perspective

Drug Use

Functionalists offer several explanations for criminal behavior. For the first explanation, we return to one of the first sociologists, Émile Durkheim. Criminal behavior, according to Durkheim, is normal and inevitable. Criminal behavior is functional because it separates acceptable from nonacceptable behavior in society. Though not a criminologist, Durkheim provided the field with one of its most enduring concepts—anomie (Walsh and Ellis 2007). Recall from our discussion in Chapter 1 that Durkheim argued that society and its rules are what make people human; without any social regulation, people are able to pursue their own desires (even criminal ones). He defined anomie as a state of normlessness, a structural condition where there is no or little regulation of behavior, which leads to deviant or criminal behavior.

Robert K. Merton applied Durkheim's theory of anomie to develop the strain theory of criminal behavior. He argued that we are socialized to attain traditional material and social goals: a good job, a nice home, or a great-looking car. We assume that society is set up in such a way that everyone has the same opportunity or resources to attain these goals. Merton explains that society isn't that fair; some experience blocked opportunities or resources because of discrimination, social position, or talent. People feel strained when they are exposed to these goals but do not have the access or resources to achieve them. This disjunction between cultural goals and structural impediments is anomic, and this is where crime is bred (Walsh and Ellis 2007).

This anomie creates an opportunity to establish new norms or break the old ones to attain these goals. Merton's **strain theory** explains how people adapt to life in this anomic situation. Merton presents five ways in which people adapt to society's goals and means, as presented in Table 13.1. Most individuals fit under the first category, conformity. Conformers accept the traditional goals and have the traditional means to achieve them. Attending college is part of the traditional means to attain a job, an income, and a home. Criminal behavior comes under the innovation category. Innovators accept society's goals, but they don't have the legitimate means to achieve them. Individuals in this category innovate by stealing from their boss, cheating on their taxes, or robbing a local store to achieve these goals.

Working from Merton's assumptions, scholars argue that criminal activity would decline if economic conditions improved. Solutions to crime would target strained groups, providing access to traditional methods and resources to attain goals. Actually, several studies have confirmed that when anomie is reduced among the poor, lower crime rates may result. Factors usually associated with anomie—the prevalence of female-headed families, the percentage of the population that is African American, and family poverty rates—are more weakly related to crime in areas with higher levels of welfare support (Hannon and Defronzo 1998).

Robert Agnew (1992) expanded upon Merton's strain theory to consider multiple individual and structural sources of strain, asserting that negative experiences and relationships motivate and promote criminal behavior (Kaufman et al. 2008). In his general strain theory, he identified three types of social-psychological sources of strain: the failure to achieve positively valued outcomes (not only due to blocked opportunities as explained by Merton, but also because of individual inadequacies due to ability or skill), the removal of positive or desired stimuli from the individual (e.g., the loss of something or someone of great worth), and the confrontation with negative action (or stimuli) by others (e.g., child abuse, adverse school experiences) (Akers and Sellers 2009). Agnew's theory is able to explain criminal offending differences by gender, class, race/ethnicity, communities, and those that occur over the life course, as well as situational variations in crime (Akers and Sellers 2009).

The second functionalist explanation links social control (or the lack of it) to criminal behavior. Whereas Merton's and Agnew's theories ask why someone commits a crime, social control theorists ask why someone *doesn't* commit crime. Society functions best when everyone behaves. Durkheim identified how well society provides us with a set of norms and laws to regulate our behavior. According to sociologist Travis Hirschi (1969), society controls our behavior through four elements: attachments, our personal relationships with others; commitment, our acceptance of conventional goals and means; involvement, our participation in conventional

---

Table 13.1

Robert Merton's Strain Theory

Mode of Adaptation	Agrees With Cultural Goals	Follows Institutional Means	Method of Adaptation
Conformity	+	+	Nondeviant Agrees with cultural goals and institutional means to achieve them
Innovation	+	−	Criminal Agrees with cultural goals, adopts nontraditional means to achieve them
Ritualism	−	+	Deviant, noncriminal Rejects cultural goals but continues to conform to institutional means
Retreatism	−	−	Deviant, could be criminal Rejects cultural goals and the approved means to achieve them
Rebellion	−/+	−/+	Deviant Challenges cultural goals and the approved means to achieve them; offers alternative goals and means

activities; and beliefs, our acceptance of conventional values and norms. Delbert Elliot, Suzanne Ageton, and Rachelle Canter (1979) redefined Hirschi's elements as integration (involvement with and emotional ties to external bonds) and commitment (expectations linked with conventional activities and beliefs). They believe that when all these elements are strong, criminal behavior is unlikely to occur.

Conflict Perspective

Sociologist Austin Turk (1969) explains that criminality is not a biological, psychological, or behavioral phenomenon; rather, it is a way to define a person's social status according to how that person is perceived and treated by law enforcement. An act is not inherently criminal; society defines it that way. Theorists from this perspective argue that criminal laws do not exist for our own good; rather, they exist to preserve the interests and power of specific groups.

In this view, criminal justice decisions are discriminatory and designed to sanction offenders based on their minority or subordinate group membership (race, class, age, or gender) (Akers and Sellers 2009). Turk (1969, 1976) states that criminal status is defined by "authorities" or members of the dominant class.

Photo 13.1

In 2009, financier Bernard Madoff pled guilty to 11 counts of fraud, money laundering, and perjury. In the largest Ponzi scheme in U.S. history, Madoff was accused of stealing an estimated $65 billion from individual, foundation, and corporate investors. Madoff is serving a life sentence.

Criminal status is imposed on "subjects," members of the subordinate class, regardless of whether a crime has actually been committed. Laws serve as a means for those in power to promote their ideas and interests against others. Law enforcement agents protect the interests and power of the dominant class at the expense of subjects. Police may use force, sometimes excessive; "when economic inequality is extreme, elites and polity as a whole may see a need for show of violent force to discourage civil disturbances" (Liska 1992:13). Excessive police force in Brazil is featured in this chapter's "Taking a World View" section.

From this perspective, problems emerge when particular groups are disadvantaged by the criminal justice system. Although the powerful are able to resist criminal labels, the labels seem to stick to minority power groups—the poor, youth, and ethnic minorities. Minority power groups' interests are on the margins of mainstream society, so most of their activities can be criminalized by dominant authorities (Walsh and Ellis 2007). Conflict theorists argue that the criminal justice system is intentionally unequal and serves as the vehicle for conflicts between opposing groups. We discuss this further in the section titled "The Inequalities of Crime."

Feminist Perspective

Criminology

For a long time, criminology ignored the experiences of women, choosing to apply theories and models of male criminality to women. Feminist researchers have been credited with making female offenders visible (Naffine 1996) and with documenting the experiences of women as the victims or survivors of violent men and as victims of the criminal justice system (Chesney-Lind and Pasko 2004). Feminist scholarship has attempted to understand how women's criminal experiences are different from those of men and how experiences of women differ from each other based on race, ethnicity, class, age, and sexual orientation (Chesney-Lind and Pasko 2004; Flavin 2001).

Freda Adler (1975) was one of the first to explain that women were "liberated" to commit crime when they were no longer restrained by traditional ideals of feminine behavior and could take on more masculine traits including criminal behavior. Called the "liberation approach," the logic of the argument is that as gender equality increases, women are more likely to commit crime. Although the approach was met with wide public acceptance, it has been discredited because of lack of empirical evidence (Chesney-Lind and Pasko 2004).

Recently, gender inequality theories have been presented as explanations of female crime. According to Darrell Steffensmeier and Emilie Allan (1996), patriarchal power relations shape gender differences in crime, pushing women into criminal behavior through role entrapment, economic marginalization, and victimization or as a survival response. The authors point out, "Nowhere is the gender ratio more skewed than in the great disparity of males as offenders and females as victims of sexual and domestic abuse" (p. 470). The logic of the inequality argument is that female crime increases as gender inequality increases.

Women are more likely to kill intimate partners, family members, or acquaintances than men are, "so the connection between women's overall homicide offending rates and gender inequality lies largely in the connection between gender stratification and women's domestic lives," explains Vicki Jensen (2001:8). Jensen describes gender inequality as being composed of economic, political-legal, and social inequalities experienced by women. Lower gender equality can negatively affect women's freedom and opportunities; these situations can push women into situations in which lethal violence seems to be the only way out. In the case of women killing abusive intimate partners, low levels of economic security limit women's opportunities to escape abusive situations. Low levels of gender equality can increase the emphasis on traditional gender norms, placing the responsibility on women to please men and requiring that women must be submissive and accept whatever their partner does (including violence). Jensen explains that most women who kill an intimate partner do so in response to abuse situations, in imminent self-defense, or when all other strategies have failed.

Economic Inequality

Research indicates that the surge in women's incarceration has little to do with any major change in women's criminal behavior. In comparison to men's, women's crime participation rates have remained stable over time (Becker and McCorkel 2011). Since 1995, the annual rate of growth in the number of U.S. female prisoners averaged 5%, higher than the 3% for male prisoners (refer to Table 13.2). The public's "get tough with crime" approach, along with a legal system that encourages treating women equally to men, has resulted in the greater use of imprisonment as punishment for female criminal behavior (Chesney-Lind and Pasko 2004).

Women Incarceration

Sarah Becker and Jill McCorkel (2011) examined how gender affects access to criminal opportunities, specifically looking at the types of crime committed by men and women and considering how the presence of a male co-offender alters women's crime participation. They found that most men and women co-offend with men; all-female offender groups are rare. Their analysis of national crime data revealed how women are more likely to be involved in gender-atypical offenses like drug trafficking, homicide, gambling, kidnapping, and weapons offenses when they have at least one male co-offender compared to when they work alone or in a same-sex group. The range of women's crime participation increases with the presence of a male co-offender.

During 2008, 112,826 females were in prison, accounting for 6.8% of all U.S. prisoners (Guerino, Harrison, and Sabol 2011). The International Centre for Prison Studies analyzed data on the number of incarcerated women worldwide at the end of April 2006. Based on data from 187 prison systems in countries and dependent territories, the center reported that more than half a million women and girls were currently being held in penal institutions as pretrial detainees or having been convicted and sentenced. The highest numbers of female

Table 13.2

Number of Prisoners Under the Jurisdiction of State or Federal Correctional Authorities and Incarceration Rate by Gender, 2000, 2004, 2008, and 2010

	Males	Females
All inmates—2000	1,298,027	93,234
All inmates—2004	1,392,278	104,822
All inmates—2008	1,495,594	114,852
All inmates—2010	1,499,573	112,822
Incarceration Rate*—2000	904	59
Incarceration Rate—2004	926	64
Incarceration Rate—2008	952	68
Incarceration Rate—2010	943	67

*The number of persons with a sentence of more than 1 year per 100,000 U.S. residents.

Source: Guerino, Harrison, and Sabol 2011; Sabol, West, and Cooper 2009

detainees or prisoners were in the United States (183,400), China (71,280), the Russian Federation (55,400), and Thailand (28,450) (Walmsley 2006).

The increase in the number of women inmates has caused prison officials to reconsider custody procedures for women, especially specific programs and services available to women. Also there are major differences between male and female prisoners, which have implications for women's confinement and release (Galbraith 2004). In particular, women are more likely (a) to be serving their first sentence, (b) to be the primary caregiver of their children, (c) to be victims of sexual abuse and trauma (Morash, Byrum, and Koons 1998), and (d) to suffer from depression. Parenting has become a focus of many programs. In 2000, 80,000 women in prisons and jails were estimated to have about 200,000 children under the age of 18 (Amnesty International 2000).

Photo 13.2

Female inmates wait to be chained together before being transported for "burial duty," where they will bury dead homeless and indigents at White Tanks Cemetery, 40 miles west of Estrella Jail in Phoenix, Arizona. Approximately 4 feet of chain separates each inmate, and there are four or five inmates to a group. Estrella Jail, in Maricopa County, is home to the only female chain gang in America.

Interactionist Perspective

Interactionists examine the process that defines certain individuals and acts as criminal. The theory is called **labeling theory**, highlighting that what's important isn't the criminals or their acts, but rather the audience that labels the persons or their acts as criminal. As Kai Erickson (1964) explains, "Deviance is not a property inherent in certain forms of behavior; it is a property conferred upon these forms by audiences which directly or indirectly witness them" (p. 11).

 Labeling

The basic elements of labeling theory were presented by sociologist Edwin Lemert (1967), who believed that everyone is involved in behavior that could be labeled delinquent or criminal, yet only a few are actually labeled. He explained that deviance is a process, beginning with primary deviation, which arises from a variety of social, cultural, psychological, and physiological factors. Although most primary acts of deviance go unnoticed, they may lead to a social response in the form of an arrest, punishment, or stigmatization. Secondary deviation includes more serious deviant acts, which follow the social response to the primary deviance. Once a criminal label is attached to a person, a criminal career is set in motion.

John Braithwaite (1989) observed that nations with low crime rates are those where shaming has great social power. Braithwaite defined shaming as all processes of "expressing disapproval which have the intention or effect of invoking remorse in the person being shamed and/or condemnation by others who become aware of the shaming" (p. 9). Braithwaite agreed with Lemert that shaming could be "stigmatizing" (increasing the distance between the offender and society) and lead to additional criminal acts. However, he proposed that shaming should be "reintegrative" (restoring the link between the offender and society) and lead to less crime.

 Labeling Theory

Henry Brownstein (2001) argued that race and class matter in how we conceptualize victims and offenders. News coverage of local crime stories contributes to how we define victims and offenders. Travis Dixon and Daniel Linz (2000) found that Blacks and Latinos were more likely to be portrayed in television news as criminal perpetrators than as victims. In contrast, Whites were more likely to be portrayed as victims than as perpetrators. Katherine Beckett and her colleagues (2005) demonstrated that the racial composition of drug arrests in a city could be attributed to police officers' mental image of drug dealers and the neighborhoods in which they chose to look for them. Racialized imagery related to the crack epidemic led officers to think and act as though drug possession was a Black crime.

What Does It Mean to Me?

What are your perceptions of a typical victim or perpetrator? What roles do the media—news, television, and movies—play in creating these perceptions? From what other sources are these perceptions learned?

Interactionists also attempt to explain how deviant or criminal behavior is learned through association with others. Edwin Sutherland's (1949) theory of differential association states that individuals are likely to commit deviant acts if they associate with others who are deviants. This criticism is often raised about our jail and prison systems; instead of rehabilitation, prisoners are able to learn more criminal activity and behavior while serving their sentences. Psychologists Craig Haney and Philip Zimbardo (1998) noted how "department of corrections data show that about a fourth of those initially imprisoned for nonviolent crimes are sentenced a second time for committing a violent offense. Whatever else it reflects, this pattern highlights the possibility that prison serves to transmit violent habits and values rather than to reduce them" (p. 721). Sutherland's theory does not address how the first criminal learned criminal behavior, but he does highlight how criminal behavior emerges from interaction, association, and socialization.

For a summary of sociological perspectives, see Table 13.3.

Table 13.3

Summary of Sociological Perspectives: Crime and Criminal Justice

	Functional	Conflict/Feminist	Interactionist
Explanation of crime and criminal justice	Crime emerges from the social order. People experience "strain" when they are exposed to cultural goals but do not have the access or resources to achieve them. Individuals are likely to make some new rules (or break the old ones) to attain these goals. Society also controls criminal behavior through four elements: attachments, commitment, involvement, and beliefs.	Criminal justice decisions are discriminatory and designed to sanction offenders based on their minority or subordinate group membership (race, class, age, or gender). Problems emerge when particular groups are disadvantaged more than others by the criminal justice system.	Interactionists examine the process that defines certain individuals and acts as criminal. Interactionists also examine how criminal or deviant behavior is learned through association with others.
Questions asked about crime and criminal behavior	How/why are individuals denied access to resources to achieve their goals? What social controls are in place to reduce criminal behavior?	How do our criminal justice policies reflect political, economic, and social interests? Why/how are particular groups targeted as "criminals"? How do women's experiences as crime victims and offenders differ from men's?	Is criminal behavior the result of being labeled a "criminal"? Is criminal behavior learned? How are our perceptions of criminals and victims socially created?

Sources of Crime Statistics

We rely on three sources of data to estimate the nature and extent of crime in the United States. The primary source is annual data collected by the Federal Bureau of Investigation (FBI). Since 1930, the FBI has published the Uniform Crime Report (UCR), data supplied by 17,000 federal, state, and local law enforcement agencies. The UCR reports two categories of crimes: index crimes and nonindex crimes. **Index crimes** include murder, rape, robbery, assault, burglary, motor vehicle theft, arson, and larceny (theft of property worth $50 or more). All other crimes except traffic violations are categorized as nonindex crimes. The UCR provides law enforcement officers and agencies with useful data about serious rates across states, counties, and cities, as well as trend and longitudinal data since its inception. The second source of crime data emerged in 1982, when the FBI began to use the National Incident-Based Reporting System (NIBRS), which adds detailed offender and victim information to the UCR data. Currently 31 states provide NIBRS information.

However, the often-cited problem with the UCR and the NIBRS is that the data only reflect reported crimes. The FBI cannot collect information on crimes that have not been reported, but it is estimated that only 3% to 4% of crimes are actually discovered by police (Kappeler, Blumberg, and Potter 2000). Also, being reported doesn't mean that a crime has actually occurred. The FBI does not require that a suspect has been arrested or that a crime is investigated and found to have actually occurred; it only needs to be reported (Kappeler et al. 2000).

In addition to the UCR, the FBI releases the Crime Clock, a graphic display of how often specific offenses are committed. Although it may make for good newspaper copy or give law enforcement and political officials clout (Chambliss 1988), the Crime Clock has been accused of exaggerating the amount of crime, leaving the public with the impression that they are in imminent danger of being victims of violence (Kappeler et al. 2000).

The third data source about crime is the National Crime Victimization Survey (NCVS or NCS), which has been published by the Bureau of Justice Statistics since 1972. The survey is based on victimization surveys first conducted in Denmark (in 1720) and Norway (in the late 1940s). Twice a year, the U.S. Census Bureau interviews members of about 77,200 households regarding their experience with crime. The NCVS identifies crime victims whether or not the crime was reported. The survey includes information about victims and crimes but covers only six offenses (compared with the eight index crimes reported by the UCR). Also included is information on the experiences of victims with the criminal justice system, self-protective measures used by victims, and possible substance abuse by offenders. NCVS crime victim data for 2008 are presented in Table 13.4.

 Reporting Crime

The results of the NCVS are often compared with the UCR to indicate that the number of crimes committed is actually higher than the number of crimes reported, suggesting that the UCR may not be an adequate measure of violent crime. However, "a more thoughtful interpretation of the inconsistency between these statistical reports concludes that while neither the UCR nor the NCVS is by itself an adequate measure of violence, each is an estimate of the scope and nature of violent crime" (Brownstein 2001:8–9).

 Mass Incarceration

Table 13.4

Number of Crime Victims, Personal and Property Crimes, 2010

Type of Crime	Number of Incidents
All crimes	18,725,710
Violent crimes	3,817,380
Rape/sexual assault	188,380
Robbery	480,750
Assault	3,148,250
Personal theft	138,340
Property crimes	14,769,990
Household burglary	2,923,430
Motor vehicle theft	606,990
Theft	11,239,560

Source: Truman 2011.

Types of Crime

Violent Crime

Violent crime is defined as actions that involve force or the threat of force against others and includes aggravated assault, murder, rape, and robbery. The victimization rate for crimes of violence in 2010 was 14.9 victimizations per 1,000 people age 12 or older, declining from 17.1 in 2009 (Truman 2011). The number of victimizations declined as well from 4.3 million in 2009 to 3.8 million in 2010.

In 2010, for the first time since the NCVS calculated violent victimization rates, males and females had similar rates—15.7 per 1,000 males and 14.2 per 1,000 females (Truman 2011). Male homicide victimization rates are higher than female rates worldwide. Comparing homicide victimization rates from 1950 to 2001, the countries with the highest male homicide victimization rates were Mexico, 35.13 per 100,000, followed by Puerto Rico, 24.64. For female homicide, the highest victimization rate was in Puerto Rico, 3.53 per 100,000; Mexico was second at 3.40. For the same period, rates for the United States were reported at 11.88 for males and 3.37 for females (LaFree and Hunnicutt 2006). For 2010, the victimization rate for U.S. males (11.6 per 100,000) was three times higher than the rate for females (3.4 per 100,000) (Cooper and Smith 2011).

Males are more likely to be victimized by a stranger, whereas women are more likely to be violently victimized by a friend, an acquaintance, or an intimate partner (Bureau of Justice Statistics 2003a). In 2008, women reported being raped or sexually assaulted in 47% of cases by a friend or an acquaintance, 27% by an intimate partner, and 17% by a relative (Truman 2011). In 2012, the federal government expanded the definition of forcible rape to include male victims and the types of sexual assault that would be counted by the FBI's Uniform Crime Report. The revised definition includes forcible oral or anal penetration, along with nonconsensual sex (Savage 2012).

 Victimology

Intimate violence (violence at the hands of someone known to the victim) is primarily committed against women in both the developed and developing worlds. The World Health Organization (WHO 2005), in its study of women from 10 different countries, revealed that violence by an intimate partner is "common, widespread, and far-reaching in its impact" (WHO 2005:viii). WHO reports that the proportion of ever-partnered women who had experienced physical or sexual violence or both by an intimate partner ranged from 29% to 62% in most studied countries. Women in Japan were the least likely to experience either type of violence, and the greatest amount of violence was reported by women living in provincial rural areas of Bangladesh, Ethiopia, Peru, and the United Republic of Tanzania (WHO 2005). In 2010, U.S. women experienced 407,700 rape, sexual assault, robbery, aggravated assault, and simple assault victimizations at the hands of an intimate partner; among men, 101,530 were victims of violent crimes by an intimate partner (Truman 2011).

Since 1973, Blacks have had the highest violent crime victimization rates. In 2010, 21 of 1,000 Black people experienced a violent crime versus 14 out of 1,000 Whites and 16 out of 1,000 Hispanics (Truman 2011). Research by William Julius Wilson (1996) and Robert Sampson and Wilson (1995) revealed that structural disadvantages, rather than race, contribute to higher levels of crime and victimization in Black communities (Ackerman 1998). The structural factors include neighborhood poverty, unemployment, social isolation, and economic disadvantage.

Data collected for 2008 reveal that disabled persons are more likely to experience higher rates of violence (40 crimes per 1,000 persons age 12 or older) than those without a disability (2% or 20 crimes per 1,000 persons). The violent crime rate was approximately

86% for youth ages 16–19 years with disabilities versus 34% for youth without. Females with a disability had a higher victimization rate than males with a disability (Harrell and Rand 2010). Refer to Table 13.5 for a summary of violent crime rates by selected social characteristics.

Table 13.5

Violent victimizations per 1,000 People Age 12 or Older by Selected Social Characteristics, 2011

	Rate per 1,000 Persons Age 12 or Older
Gender	
Male	15.7
Female	14.2
Race/Hispanic Origin	
White*	13.6
Black*	20.8
Hispanic	15.6
American Indian or Alaska Native*	42.2
Asian or Pacific Islander*	6.3
Two or more races*	52.6
Age	
12–14	27.5
15–17	23.0
18–20	33.9
21–24	26.9
25–34	18.8
35–49	12.6
50–64	10.9
65 or older	2.4

*Excludes persons of Hispanic origin.

Source: Truman 2011.

What Does It Mean to Me?

Crime rates have dropped significantly in most large cities since the 1990s. Take, for example, the homicide rate. The rate peaked in 1980 at 10.2 homicides per 100,000 people (Blumstein and Rosenfeld 1998). For 2010, the homicide rate was 4.8 homicides per 100,000 (Cooper and Smith 2011). In 1994, about 25.1 million households or household members experienced one or more violent or property crimes (Klaus 2004), but by 2010, the number had dropped to 18.7 million households (Truman 2011). There is less violent crime, but do we still live in fear? Why or why not?

 STATE STATS

Property Crime

Property crime consists of taking money or property from another without force or the threat of force against the victims. Burglary, larceny, theft, motor vehicle theft, and arson are examples of property crimes. Property crimes make up about three fourths of all crime in the United States. In 2010, there were an estimated 14.8 million property crimes, including

3.1 million household burglaries and 735,770 motor vehicle thefts. Households earning less than $7,500 and larger households (at least four or more individuals present) had higher rates of property victimization (burglary, motor vehicle theft, and theft) (Truman 2011).

Juvenile Delinquency

Juvenile Delinquency

The term **juvenile delinquent** often refers to a youth who is in trouble with the law. Technically, a **juvenile status offender** is a juvenile who has violated a law that only applies to minors 7 to 17 years old, such as cutting school or buying and consuming alcohol (Sanders 1981). In certain cases, minors can be tried as adults. Crimes committed by juveniles are more likely to be cleared by law enforcement than crimes committed by adults.

Inside Juvenile Prison

The Office of Juvenile Justice and Delinquency Prevention monitors data on rates of **juvenile crime**. For 2008, the total number of juvenile arrests was 2.11 million. Females accounted for 30% of juvenile arrests. Almost half of all juvenile arrests involved larceny-theft, simple assault, drug abuse violations, disorderly conduct, or liquor law violations. Only 12% of all violent crimes involved offenders younger than age 18 (Puzzanchera 2009). Unlike the United States, many countries do not collect systematic data on delinquency, and among the countries that do, their data are described as "incomplete because of faulty record keeping" (Stafford 2004:486).

Though the majority of juvenile offenders are male (70% in 2008), juvenile justice researchers have noted an increase in the number and percentage of female juvenile offenders. In 1980, 20% of all juvenile arrests involved female offenders, increasing to 30% in 2008. Although male juvenile arrests have declined in several crime index categories, arrests for female juvenile offenders decreased less than male arrests in most categories but increased in some (e.g., simple assault, larceny-theft, and DUI) between 1999 and 2008. Refer to Table 13.6 for a comparison of the percentage changes in male and female juvenile arrest rates.

Table 13.6

Percentage Changes in Arrest Rates for Juvenile Males and Females, 1999–2008

Offense or Charge	Females (%)	Males (%)
Violent Crime Index	−10	−8
Robbery	+38	+24
Aggravated assault	−17	−22
Simple assault	+12	−6
Property Crime Index	+1	−28
Burglary	−3	−16
Larceny-theft	+4	−29
Motor vehicle theft	−52	−50
Vandalism	+3	−9
Weapons	−1	−3
Drug abuse violations	−2	−8
Liquor law violations	−6	−29
DUI	+7	−34
Disorderly conduct	+18	−5

Source: Puzzanchera 2009.

For 2008, the racial composition of the U.S. juvenile population was 78% White (Hispanics are also classified as White), 16% Black, 5% Asian/Pacific Islander, and 1% American Indian. Although Black youth accounted for 16% of the youth population between the ages of 10 and 17, they were involved in 52% of the arrests for violent crimes and 33% of property crimes (Puzzanchera 2009).

Delinquency is often explained by the absence of strong bonds to society or the lack of social controls. In studies of serious adolescent crime, research indicates that the economic isolation of inner-city neighborhoods, along with the concentration of poverty and unemployment, leads to an erosion of the formal and informal controls that inhibit delinquent behavior (Laub 1983). Juveniles without any or much social control are likely to engage in illegal behavior when they live in any environment that offers opportunities for illegal activities. Youth who are strongly bonded to conventional role models and institutions (parents, teachers, school, community leaders, and law-abiding peers) are least likely to engage in delinquent behaviors.

Ex L.A. Gang Member

White-Collar Crime

The term **white-collar crime** was first used by Sutherland in 1949. He used the term to refer to "a crime committed by a person of respectability and high social status in the course of his occupation" (Sutherland 1949:9). Since then, the term has come to include three categories of offense: crimes committed by an offender as described by Sutherland (someone of high social status and respectability), crimes committed for financial or economic gain, and crimes taking place in a particular organization or business (Barnett n.d.).

White Collar Crime

The FBI (1989) has defined white-collar crime by the type of crime:

[White-collar crime includes] illegal acts which are characterized by deceit, concealment, or violation of trust and which are not dependent upon the application or threat of physical force or violence. Individuals or organizations commit these acts to obtain money, property or services; to avoid payment or loss of money or services; or to secure personal and business advantage. (p. 3)

Such acts include credit card fraud, insurance fraud, mail fraud, tax evasion, money laundering, embezzlement, and theft of trade secrets. Corporate crime may also include illegal acts committed by corporate employees on behalf of the corporation and with its support. Corporate fraud has been identified as the highest priority of the FBI's Financial Crimes Section. As of the end of fiscal year 2008, 545 fraud cases had been pursued by the FBI; several involved losses to public investors that individually exceeded $1 billion (FBI 2009). White-collar crimes cost taxpayers more than all other types of crime.

One of the most widespread forms of white-collar crime is Internet fraud and abuse, also known as **cybercrime**. In 2010, the Internet Crime Complaint Center (IC3) received 314,587 complaints (National White Collar Crime Center 2010). The complaints and crimes include identity theft, online credit card fraud schemes, theft of trade secrets, sales of counterfeit software, and computer intrusions (a hacker breaking into a system). The cost of online fraud was estimated at $617 million. Years ago, when computer systems were relatively self-contained, there was no concern about cybercrime. Committing cybercrime is easier with the growth of the Internet, increasing computer connectivity, and the availability of break-in programs and information. As computer-controlled infrastructure and networks have expanded, many systems—power grids, airports, rail systems, hospitals—have become vulnerable (Wolf 2000).

In response to Internet crimes, the FBI and the Department of Justice established computer crime teams or offices. Some states, such as Massachusetts and New York, have created high-technology crime units. Despite the increasing attention to cybercrime, "law enforcement at all levels is losing the battle" (Wolf 2000). Law enforcement does not have enough resources or technical support to detect and prosecute a significant number of cyberthieves. The government catches only 10% of those who break into government-controlled computers and fewer who break into computers of private companies (Wolf 2000).

What Does It Mean to Me?

Dharun Ravi, a former Rutgers University student, was convicted in 2012 of using a webcam to spy on his roommate kissing another man. Using Twitter and text messages, he encouraged others to watch the video. His roommate, Tyler Clementi, committed suicide after learning of the video. Because he had targeted Clementi, a gay man, his crime was classified as a hate crime. Ravi was sentenced to 30 days in jail, along with three years of probation and 300 hours of community service. Ravi served a total of 20 days, having earned early release for good behavior and his work in jail. Does this punishment fit his crime? Why or why not?

The Inequalities of Crime—Offenders and Victims

Offenders

Reports consistently reveal that African American males are overrepresented in incarceration statistics. Most jail or prison inmates are male and African American (refer to Table 13.7). As reported by Thomas Bonczar (2003), the lifetime chances of a person going to state or federal prison are higher for men (11.3%) than women (1.8%) and higher for Black males (16.6%) and Hispanic males (7.7%) than White males (2.6%). For U.S. residents born in 2001, an estimated 33% of Black males will enter prison during their lifetime, compared with 16% of Hispanic males and 6% of White males (Bonczar 2003). That a category of people is overrepresented among violent offenders does not necessarily mean that this group is responsible for more violent acts (Brownstein 2001). Keep in mind that these statistics are based only on those who were caught by the criminal justice system.

A number of studies confirm that regardless of the seriousness of the crime, racial and ethnic minorities, particularly African Americans and Hispanics, are more likely to be arrested or incarcerated than are their White counterparts. Though Latinos make up only 13% of the U.S. adult population, they account for one third of federal prison inmates, due in part to tougher enforcement of immigration laws (Moore 2009). This is also true for minority juvenile delinquents. Minority youth are overrepresented at every stage in the juvenile justice system; they are arrested more often, detained more often, overrepresented in referrals to juvenile court, and institutionalized at a disproportionate rate compared with White youth (Joseph 2000). In its analysis of contacts between police and the public for 2008, the U.S. Bureau of Justice Statistics reported that Black (12.3%) and Hispanic (5.8%) motorists were more likely to be searched during a traffic stop than White drivers (3.9%) (Eith and Durose 2011). Blacks and Hispanics were more likely than Whites to report being involved in an incident where police force was used (Eith and Durose 2011).

Table 13.7

Percentage of Prisoners Under State or Federal Jurisdiction by Gender and Race, Based on Inmates With Sentences of More Than 1 Year, December 2010

	Males	Females
White	31.2	45.9
Black	38.8	25.4
Hispanic	22.6	17.9
Other*	7.4	10.8

*Other includes American Indians, Asians, Native Hawaiians, other Pacific Islanders, and persons identifying two or more races.

Source: Guerino, Harrison, and Sabol 2011.

An early criminological explanation was offered by Marvin Wolfgang and Franco Ferracuti (1967), who argued that Blacks have adopted violent subcultural values, creating a "subculture of violence." Although this is an often-cited theory, there is insufficient empirical evidence to support the idea that Blacks are more likely to embrace a violent value system. Actually, studies have indicated that White males are more likely to express violent beliefs or attitudes than Black males (Cao, Adams, and Jensen 2000).

Family structure, specifically the presence of female-headed households in African American communities, has also been identified as a potential source for racial crime dispari-ties. Yet, criminological research has not articulated how family structure or family processes are related to crime (Morenoff 2005). Does the structure of the family itself increase the likeli-hood of crime? Is the incidence of crime related to the amount of parental supervision, the level of parental effectiveness, or the nature of the parent-child relationship? These questions remain the focus of researchers.

Criminologists and sociologists have examined patterns of racial bias or discrimination in the law enforcement and criminal justice system. Michelle Alexander (2010) character-izes mass incarceration as a caste system, much like the Jim Crow laws (1876–1965) that defined permanent second-class status for Black Americans. Specifically the War on Drugs served as a form of legalized discrimination entrapping African Americans in the criminal justice system. The harm to individuals and families only intensifies when prisoners are released. She explains, "They enter a separate society, a world hidden from public view, governed by a set of oppressive and discriminatory rules and laws that do not apply to everyone else. They become members of an undercaste—an enormous population of pre-dominately black and brown people who, because of the drug war, are denied basic rights and privileges of American citizenship and are permanently relegated to an inferior status" (Alexander 2010:181–82).

Victims

Early studies on crime victims tended to perpetuate the image that the victim was simply at the "wrong place at the wrong time" (Davis, Taylor, and Titus 1997). Following that reasoning, not being a victim of crime could be explained simply as good luck. However, research indicates that some individuals, by virtue of their social group or social behav-ior, are more prone than others to become victims (Davis et al. 1997). What people do, where they go, and with whom they associate affect their likelihood of victimization (Laub 1997).

Victimization is distributed across key demographic dimensions (Laub 1997). We reviewed some of the characteristics of crime victims in the "Types of Crime" section. Victimization rates are substantially higher for the poor, the young, males, Blacks, single people, renters, and central city residents (Davis et al. 1997). The likelihood of being injured because of a violent crime is higher among the young, the poor, urban dwellers, Blacks, Hispanics, and American Indians (Simon, Mercy, and Perkins 2001). Injury rates are lower for the elderly, for people with a higher income or higher educational attainment, and for people who are married or widowed (Simon et al. 2001).

Black males have the highest rate of violent victimization, and White females have the lowest (Laub 1997). Blacks also have the highest rate of overall household victimization. Although rates of violent crimes declined during the 1990s, mortality from homicide among minority groups is still high. Homicide is the leading cause of death among Black males between the ages of 15 and 24, and it is the second leading cause of death for Latino males in the same age group (Rich and Ro 2002). People who have been victims once are at an elevated risk of becoming victims again. Repeat victimization is likely to occur in poor, predominantly Black areas (Davis et al. 1997).

What Does It Mean to Me?

Have you ever been a victim of motor vehicle theft? Does car theft happen often on your college campus? Refer to the state rankings on motor vehicle theft. Which state is ranked #1, and what do you think might be contributing to its designation? Why do you think your state is positioned where it currently is in the state rankings?

 STATE STATS

Our Current Response to Crime

The Police

For 2008, there were more than a million full-time law enforcement employees. About 77% were sworn officers. Local police departments were the largest employer (60% of all employees) (Reaves 2011).

We rely on the police force to serve as the first line of defense against crime, and some officers lose their lives in the line of duty. In 2010, 56 law enforcement officers were feloniously killed in the line of duty, and 72 were killed in accidents. From 2001 through 2010, 23% of officers who were killed were involved in arrest situations at the time, 22% were involved in ambush situations or traffic stops, and 14% were responding to disturbance calls (FBI 2010).

American policing has gone through substantial changes during the past several decades (MacDonald 2002). Traditional models of policing emphasized high visibility and the use of force and arrests as deterrents to crime. Policing under these models relies on three tactics: police patrols, rapid response to service calls, and retrospective investigations (Moore 1999). These models reinforce an "us" versus "them" division, sometimes pitting the police against the public they were sworn to protect. High-profile incidents of police brutality and violence, such as the cases that involved Rodney King in Los Angeles and Amadou Diallo and Sean Bell in New York City, increased public distrust and tainted the image of policing.

Studies indicate that Whites trust police more and have more positive interactions with them than do Blacks and that Hispanics fall between these two groups (Norris et al. 1992). Black youth tend to have the most negative or hostile feelings toward police (Norris et al. 1992). Residents from poor or disadvantaged areas have a much lower regard for the police than does the general public. However, research has also indicated that when citizens believe that they are treated fairly, they tend to grant police more legitimacy and are more likely to comply with police (Stoutland 2001).

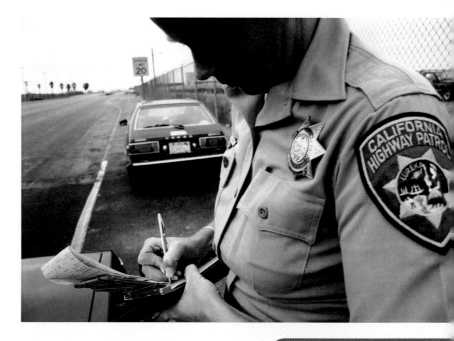

Photo 13.3

For most individuals, their interaction with police officers is limited to traffic violation stops. Police departments are incorporating new methods of policing based on community and problem-solving approaches, hoping to increase the interaction between officers and citizens.

Police departments are now incorporating new methods of policing based on the community and problem-solving approaches (Goldstein 1990; MacDonald 2002). The community policing approach refers to efforts to increase the interaction between officers and citizens, including the use of foot patrols, community substations, and neighborhood watches (Beckett and Sasson 2000). By 2000, two thirds of all local police departments and 62% of sheriff's offices had full-time sworn personnel engaged in community policing activities (Bureau of Justice Statistics 2003c). We learn more about community policing in the section titled "Community, Policy, and Social Action."

Prisons

Despite the decline in crime rates, prison populations are increasing (Anderson 2003), though the rate of new admissions has declined in recent years (Sabol, West, and Cooper 2009). At the end of 2010, the federal and state inmate population was more than 1.6 million (see U.S. Data Map 13.1). Though the United States represents 5% of the world's population, the number of incarcerated in our country represents nearly 25% of the world's prison population (Rosen 2010). Data reveal that the United States has the highest prison population rate in the world (refer to Figure 13.1).

Mandatory sentencing, especially for nonviolent drug offenders, is a key reason why inmate populations have increased for the past 30 years. Drug offenders now make up more than half of all federal prisoners (Anderson 2003). The United States incarcerates more people for drug offenses than any other country (Justice Policy Institute 2008). The majority of men and women sentenced under these laws are nonviolent, low-level drug offenders—couriers, street dealers, bystanders, or drug addicts—convicted for possession or sales of small amounts of drugs (Human Rights Watch 1999, 2000).

Additionally, probation and parole revocations are a growing source of prison admissions. In 2008, approximately 683,000 prisoners were released, an average of 1,800 per day (Sabol et al. 2009). Parolees were more likely to have served a sentence for a drug offense

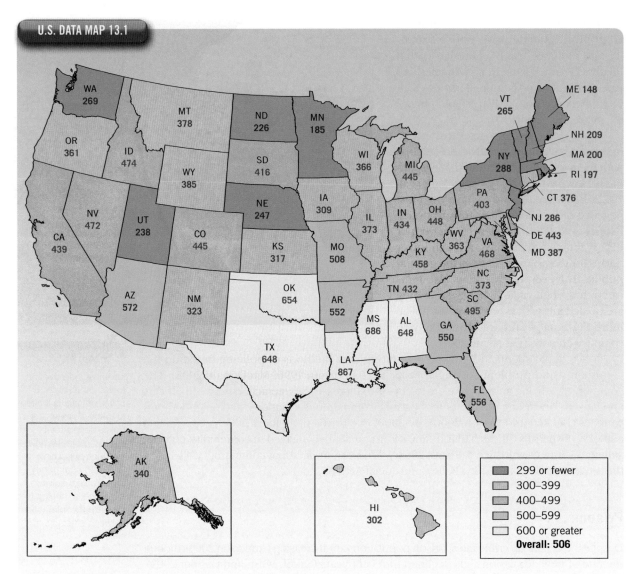

U.S. DATA MAP 13.1

	299 or fewer
	300–399
	400–499
	500–599
	600 or greater
	Overall: 506

Imprisonment Rates of Sentenced Prisoners, per 100,000 U.S. Residents, Year End 2010

Source: Guerino, Harrison, and Sabol 2011.

(37%) than any other type of offense (Glaze and Bonczar 2009). Parole violators accounted for 34% of all prison admissions in 2008 (Sabol et al. 2009). The problem is especially acute in California, the national leader in returning parolees to prison. Nearly 1 in 5 parolees in America lives in California (Travis and Lawrence 2002).

Along with the increase in the number of prisoners comes an increase in prison budgets. In 2001, the average state inmate cost about $22,650 per year while the average federal inmate cost about $22,632 (Stephan 2004). For each U.S. resident, the state prison costs were about $104 for 2001. Average operating costs per inmate varied by state, indicating differences in costs of living, wage rates, and other related factors. The five states with the highest annual

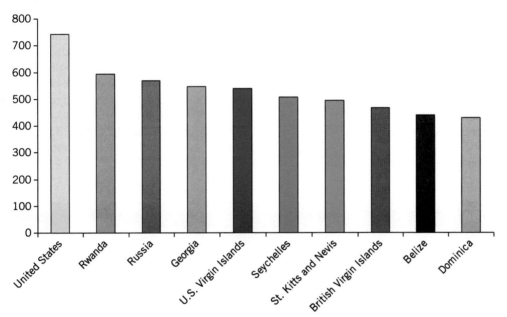

Figure 13.1

Highest Prison Population Rates in the World, 2011*

Source: Walmsley 2011.

*Per 100,000 of the national population.

operating costs per inmate were Maine ($44,379), Rhode Island ($38,503), Massachusetts ($37,718), Minnesota ($36,836), and New York ($36,835).

Human Rights Watch (2012) documented the aging of the U.S. prison population, reporting that the number of prisoners age 65 or older increased by 63% between 2007 and 2010. For 2012, there were 26,200 prisoners in this age group. Providing medical care to older prison populations suffering from chronic, disabling, and terminal illnesses will be expensive, no different from the level of care and spending required for an older non-prison population. While no systematic data are available regarding the annual cost of care, Human Rights Watch (2012) reported a range of state expenses from $4,000 to $8,500 per elderly prisoner per year.

What is the purpose of the prison system? Some argue that the system is intended to rehabilitate offenders, to prevent them from committing crime again. However, beginning in the mid-1970s, U.S. rehabilitation programs and community-based programs began to lose funding. Probation and parole offices redefined their core missions from treatment to control and surveillance (Tonry 2004). Other Western governments, such as Germany, the Netherlands, and the Scandinavian countries, continue to make large investments in treatment and educational programs in comparison with the United States (Albrecht 2001), with evidence revealing that some programs are able to reduce future reoffending (Gaes et al. 1999). For example, Belgium, Denmark, England, France, the Netherlands, and Sweden have established crime prevention agencies that develop programs for developmental, community, and situational crime prevention (Tonry and Farrington 1995); there are no comparable agencies in the United States (Tonry 2004).

Photo 13.4

Pictured here is an inmate in Liberia's Monrovia Central prison. In 2011, Amnesty International reported how Liberian prison conditions violate basic human rights, depriving prisoners of running water, food, bedding, and medical care.

The U.S. record of recidivism (or repeat offenses) indicates how badly our prison system is working. Data analyzed by the Pew Center on the States (2011) found that the three-year return-to-prison rate for inmates released in 1999 was slightly higher than the recidivism rate for inmates released in 2004, 45.4% versus 43.3%. Released offenders returned to prison for committing a new crime or for a technical violation (not reporting to their parole officer or failing a drug test). Previous studies indicate that men, Blacks, non-Hispanics, and prisoners with longer prior records were more likely to be rearrested. Younger prisoners were also more likely to reoffend than were older prisoners (Langan and Levin 2002). The Bureau of Justice Statistics released data for 2007, noting that 15.5% of 1.2 million parolees returned to incarceration that year (Glaze and Bonczar 2009).

Drug Cartels

Taking a World View

Policing in Brazil

Policing in Brazil has a dark and ugly history. The death squads of Brazil began in 1958, when Army General Amaury Kruel, chief of the police forces in Rio de Janeiro, handpicked a group of special policemen to combat rising theft and robberies in the city. These "bandit hunters" were given permission to hunt and kill these criminals. In other states and cities, teams of police hunters were formed to pursue *pistoleiros* (armed criminals), undesirables, and gangsters. Each new death squad, whether targeting economic or political criminals, became more distant from the formal criminal justice system (Huggins 1997). Through several political regimes, Brazilian police have never abandoned their practices of violent enforcement and vigilantism.

After 21 years of military dictatorship (1964–1985), the civilian government (inaugurated in 1985) set out to reform Brazil's authoritarian practices. In 1988, armed with a new constitution, the democratic leadership lifted the barriers to political participation and attempted to restore the legal premises of universal citizenship rights (Mitchell and Wood 1999). In 1996, President Fernando Henrique Cardoso released the National Human Rights Plan, a comprehensive set of measures to address human rights violations in Brazil, including cases of police abuses (Human Rights Watch 1997).

Yet, police violence and human rights violations all increased dramatically under democratic rule (Caldeira and Holston 1999). Police are some of the primary agents of violence in Brazil. According to organizations such as Amnesty International and Human Rights Watch, many citizens continue to suffer systematic abuse and violations at the hands of their own police force. Police in Rio de Janeiro and São Paulo have killed more than 11,000 people since 2003. For 2008, there were 1,137 police killings in Rio de Janeiro and 397 in São Paulo compared with 371 in the United States (Human Rights Watch 2009).

Although Brazilian law endorses due process, criminal proceedings and police methods subvert this principle (Mitchell and Wood 1999), supporting extralegal conduct in the majority of cases (Huggins 1997; Mitchell and Wood 1999). Government leaders also offer their support of extralegal activities. Three days after state civil police officers killed 13 suspected drug traffickers, Marcello Alencar, governor of Rio de Janeiro, was quoted as saying, "These violent criminals have become animals. They are animals. They can't be understood any other way. These people don't have to be treated in a civilized way. They have to be treated like animals" (Human Rights Watch 1997).

According to Martha Huggins (1997), police violence in Brazil comes in two forms: on-duty police violence and death squads. Highly organized, elite police units carry out extralegal killings while on duty. The police violence is usually deliberately planned and conducted during routine street sweeps and dragnets, actions justified by the state's war on drugs and crime. There is also death squad violence conducted by a group of murderers, usually off-duty police, who are paid by local businesses or politicians for their services.

Huggins calls them privatized security guards serving commercial or political interests.

In 1985, Brazil implemented women's police stations, *Delegacias de Policia dos Direitos da Mulher* (DPMs or *delegacias*). The DPMs were created in response to pressure from feminist groups demanding that violence against women be addressed. The first groups were formed in Rio de Janeiro and São Paulo, where the first DPM was established in 1985 (Hautzinger 1997). The female officers at each station are conventionally trained police, with no specialized training or qualifications for serving at the DPM except for the fact that they are women. There are more than 250 DPMs in Brazil today (Hautzinger 2002). Although domestic violence complaints were the original mission of the DPMs, these account for only 80% of the caseloads (Hautzinger 2002). Human Rights Watch (1995) reports that despite the presence of DPMs, "many rural and urban women have found police to be unresponsive to their claims and have encountered open hostility when they attempted to report domestic violence."

The Death Penalty

Twelve states executed 46 inmates in 2010 (Snell 2011). For the year, there were 3,158 inmates serving death sentences. The majority of death row inmates were White (55% or 1,750); Blacks accounted for 42% (1,316) of the inmate population. Since 1997, a total of 1,234 prisoners have been executed.

The death penalty was instituted as a deterrent to serious crime. The penalty applies only to capital murder cases, where aggravating circumstances are present. However, research indicates that capital punishment has no deterrent effect on committing murder. In fact, states with the death penalty have murder rates significantly higher than states without the death penalty. Kappeler and his colleagues (2000) explained that only a small proportion of people charged with murder can be sentenced to death. For example, between 1980 and 1989, 206,710 murders were reported to the police, but during the same period, only 117 executions were carried out. This is about 1 execution for every 1,767 murders committed during the same period (Kappeler et al. 2000).

Death Row

Worldwide, 139 countries have abolished the use of the death penalty. In 2011, there were 18,750 individuals reported on death row, and 676 were executed around the world in at least 20 countries. The number of executions in China, believed to be in the thousands, cannot be confirmed (Amnesty International 2012).

The Innocence Project

Opponents of the death penalty point out the racial disparities in its application. The most significant studies of racial disparities point to the race of the victims as the critical factor in sentencing. Those convicted of committing a crime against a White person are more often sentenced to death. Data reported by the Death Penalty Information Center (2012) reveal that the majority of victims in death penalty cases were White (76%), followed by Blacks (15%). Nationally, only 50% of murder victims are White. In their analysis of 1990–1999 California death penalty cases, Michael Radalet and Glenn Pierce (2005) reported that those who killed a non-Hispanic African American were 56% less likely to be sentenced to death than were those who killed non-Hispanic Whites. The difference increases to 67% when comparing those sentenced to death for killing Whites versus killing Hispanics.

In federal cases, racial minorities are being prosecuted beyond their proportion in the general population or in the population of criminal offenders. In an analysis of prosecutions under the federal death penalty provisions of the Anti-Drug Abuse Act of 1988, 89% of defendants were either African American or Mexican American (Subcommittee on Civil and Constitutional Rights, Committee on the Judiciary 1994).

Community, Policy, and Social Action

U.S. Department of Justice

We may perceive our criminal justice system as a single system when, actually, we have 51 different criminal justice systems: 1 federal and 50 state systems. The federal system is led by the U.S. Department of Justice. Headed by the Attorney General of the United States, the Department of Justice comprises 39 separate component organizations, including the FBI; the Drug Enforcement Administration (DEA); the Bureau of Alcohol, Tobacco, Firearms and Explosives; U.S. Citizenship and Immigration Services, which controls the border and provides services to lawful immigrants; the Antitrust Division, which promotes and protects the competitive process in business and industry; and the Bureau of Prisons, which oversees correctional operations and programs (U.S. Department of Justice 2002).

Funding for the U.S. Department of Justice and its organizations comes from federal legislation. The 1994 Violent Crime Control and Law Enforcement Act was the largest crime bill in history, providing funds for 100,000 new officers, $9.7 billion for prisons, and $6.1 billion for prevention programs. Under the Violence Against Women Act, the Office on Violence Against Women, administered by the Department of Justice, has awarded more than $4 billion in grant funds to U.S. states and territories. These grants have helped state, tribal, and local governments and community-based agencies to train personnel, establish domestic violence and sexual assault units, assist victims of violence, and hold perpetrators accountable (Office on Violence Against Women 2010).

Juvenile Justice and Delinquency Prevention Programs

The U.S. Department of Justice also supports the Office of Juvenile Justice and Delinquency Prevention. As its mission, the office attempts to provide national leadership, coordination, and resources to prevent and respond to juvenile delinquency and victimization. The office is guided by the Juvenile Justice and Delinquency Prevention Act of 1974. As stated in the 2002 reauthorization bill, "Although the juvenile violent crime arrest rate in 1999 was the lowest in the decade, there remains a consensus that the number of crimes and the rate of offending by juveniles nationwide is still too high" (U.S. Congress 2002).

The office sponsors more than 20 programs targeting juveniles and their communities. Through the Gang Reduction Program, four pilot sites have been funded in East Los Angeles, California; Milwaukee, Wisconsin; North Miami Beach, Florida; and Richmond, Virginia. Each program incorporates prevention, intervention, and suppression in attempts to reduce gang activity. The Tribal Youth Program is part of the Indian Country Law Enforcement Initiative to support tribal efforts to prevent and control juvenile delinquency. The Child Protection Division administers programs related to crimes against children, such as the National Center for Missing and Exploited Children and the Internet Crimes Against Children Task Force.

Faith-based and community organizations have also been involved in delinquency prevention programs. One such program is the Blue Nile rites-of-passage program based in Harlem's Abyssinian Baptist Church (established before President George W. Bush's initiative). Since 1994, the program has relied on a community-based mentoring component to address the spiritual, cultural, and moral character development of African American youth (Harlem Live 1999). In general, the program was designed to have "a positive impact on the family relationships, self-esteem, sexual behaviors, drug use, peer and sibling relationships, and the religious and social values of the youth" (Irwin 2002:30). Darrell Irwin (2002) says that faith-based initiatives contain much of what has been found to be valuable in traditional mentoring programs, with the church as a backdrop. In the Harlem program, students are assigned to a mentor, either a church minister or a congregation member. During weekly meetings, mentors work with their partnered youth, emphasizing problem-solving and decision-making skills. In addition, the mentors introduce the youth to different educational and cultural activities as examples of potential community interactions. The program also includes a media literacy component where students learn how to film, edit, direct, and produce their own videos (Harlem Live 1999).

The New American Prison

In an effort to reduce the costs of incarceration to state and federal correctional agencies, the idea of private correctional institutions has gained momentum. The perception that public prisons were deteriorating and overcrowded helped to encourage the growth of private prisons in the 1980s (Pratt and Maahs 1999). Private prisons incarcerate about 5% of the sentenced adult population (Camp and Gaes 2002), usually housing low-risk offenders. It has been argued that private correctional institutions save taxpayers' money, providing more services with fewer resources; studies reveal a slight advantage to private prisons and demonstrate a reduction in per-inmate cost over time (Larason Schneider 1999). State correction officials are also responding to the problem of chronic prison overcrowding. For example, one third of Hawaii's 6,000 state inmates are jailed in private prisons in Arizona, Kentucky, Mississippi, and Oklahoma because Hawaii does not have enough room in its own state facility (Moore 2007). Studies have indicated that the savings from private prisons are likely to come from lower wages and benefits, fewer staff, more efficient uses of staff, or a combination of these factors (Camp and Gaes 2002).

Scott Camp and Gerald Gaes (2002) found that private prisons did not perform better than public ones and in some cases did worse. According to the researchers, one of the most reliable indicators of prison operations is the rate at which inmates test positive for use of drugs or alcohol. If substance abuse is high, it indicates a pattern of poor security practices. For the private institutions, tests showed no drug use in 34% of the facilities and low to high drug use in 66% of the facilities. Nearly 62% of public prisons showed no evidence of drug use. In their analysis of another important performance measure, William Bales et al. (2005) found no significant difference in recidivism rates between public and private prisoner offenders. There were no significant differences among three groups in their study: adult males, adult females, and youth offender males.

Passed in 1996, the Prison Litigation Reform Act requires prisoners to exhaust all internal and administrative remedies before they can file federal lawsuits to challenge the conditions of their confinement or to report civil rights violations. The act was intended to prevent frivolous or unfounded lawsuits, but it has made it impossible for prisoners with valid complaints to be heard. Prisoners cannot file lawsuits for mental or emotional injury unless they can also show that physical injury occurred. Prisoners are required to pay for their own court filing fees; monthly installments can be taken out of their prison commissary account (American Civil Liberties Union [ACLU] 1999). The act also prohibits prison officials from settling lawsuits by agreeing to make changes in unconstitutional prison conditions. The ACLU and its National Prison Project have challenged the constitutionality of the Prison Litigation Reform Act, claiming that it "slams the courthouse door on society's most vulnerable members" (ACLU 1999). Despite its questionable constitutionality, many government leaders and courts have applauded the act.

In Focus

A Public Health Approach to Gun Control

The most deadly U.S. shooting occurred on April 16, 2007, when Virginia Polytechnic Institute and State University student Cho Seung-Hui shot and killed 32 people, including himself. In 2005, a Virginia court had declared Cho mentally ill and a danger to himself and sent him for psychiatric treatment. A month before the shooting, he purchased two semiautomatic pistols and 50 rounds of ammunition. Under federal law, Cho should have been prohibited from purchasing a gun after the Virginia court declaration. Federal law prohibits anyone who has been "adjudicated as a mental defective," as well as those who have been involuntarily committed to a mental health facility, from purchasing a gun.

Since the shooting at Virginia Tech, there have been several other deadly incidents. In July 2011, confessed killer Anders Behring Breivik killed 77 in Norway in two attacks, a bombing in downtown Oslo and a shooting massacre at a youth camp. A year later, James Holmes opened fire in a movie theater in Aurora, Colorado, during a premiere of *The Dark Knight Rises*. Holmes killed 12 and injured 56 others. Holmes amassed his weapons over several months, purchasing much of his ammunition via the Internet. In December 2012, gunman Adam Lanza killed 26 people, 20 of them children between the ages of 5 and 10 years, at Sandy Hook Elementary School in Newtown, Connecticut. The guns used by Lanza were legally registered to his mother Nancy, also one of his victims. Each tragedy reignited the debate over the regulated sale of firearms in the United States.

According to David Hemenway (2004),

> The United States has more firearms in civilian hands than any other high income nation. About 25 percent of adults in the United States personally own a firearm. Many gun owners have more than one firearm; some 10 percent of adults own over 75 percent of all firearms in the country. The percentage of households with a firearm has declined in the past two decades; about one in three households now contains a firearm. (p. 85)

He notes that public health approaches have reduced the burden of infectious disease, tobacco-related illness, and motor vehicle injuries, suggesting that a similar approach could be successfully applied to reducing gun violence, focusing on the impact of gun violence on one's community, and encouraging collaboration, research, and comprehensive policies. Hemenway (2004) explains what would be necessary for a public health approach to gun control:

> Like the approach to reducing motor vehicle injuries, a public health approach to curtailing problems caused by firearms suggests pursuing a wide variety of policies while maintaining the ability of law-abiding Americans to use guns responsibly. This approach emphasizes the importance of obtaining accurate, detailed and comparable information each year on the extent and nature of the problem. For each motor vehicle death in the United States, the Fatality Analysis Reporting System collects data on more than one hundred variables. This information suggests interventions and permits evaluation of which policies are effective and which are not.
>
> A major problem is that the detailed national information about firearm injuries does not exist. For example, whether most unintentional firearm injuries occur at home or away from home, or with long guns or handguns, is unknown. Many groups have backed the creation of a national violent death reporting system to provide detailed information on all homicides, suicides, and unintentional firearm deaths.
>
> Although firearms are among the most lethal consumer products, killing tens of thousands of civilians each year, firearm manufacturing is one of the least-regulated industries in the United States. No federal regulatory body has specific authority over firearm manufacturing, which is exempt from regulation by the

Consumer Product Safety Commission. The industry has also escaped any comprehensive examination by Congress. Instead, Congress is considering giving the industry immunity from tort liability for negligence.

A public health approach would create incentives for firearm manufacturers to make products that reduce rather than increase the burden on law enforcement. Rather than producing and promoting firearms that appear primarily designed for criminal use, such as those who do not retain fingerprints, manufacturers could produce guns with unique, tamper resistant serial numbers. They could also make guns that "finger-print" each bullet to permit authorities to match bullet and firearm with a high degree of accuracy.

Policies common in other developed countries—registration of handguns, licensing of owners, and background checks for all gun transfers—could reduce the U.S. homicide rate substantially by making it harder for adolescents and criminals to obtain handguns.

The public health approach to reducing gun violence emphasizes the need for prevention as well as punishment, recognizes that alternations in the product and the environment are more likely to be effective than attempts to change individual behavior, and urges the pursuit of multiple strategies to tackle the problem. The public health community understands the importance of involving the entire community and sees roles for many groups, including educational institutions, religious organizations, medical associations and the media. (Hemenway 2004:91–93, 95)

Source: Hemenway 2004.

Voices in the Community

Max Kenner

The brainchild of Max Kenner, the Bard Prison Initiative (BPI), was created in 1999 to address the educational needs of prisoners and to provide them with the opportunity and the means to attain higher education while remaining within the correctional system.

To understand the logic behind such a program as BPI, one must revisit the 1970s, a time when the federal government looked favorably upon college in prison programs. Since then, numerous studies have shown that college in prison programs reduce the rate of recidivism, lower the number of violent incidents that occur within prisons, reestablish broken relationships between incarcerated parents and their children, and create a general sense of hope among inmates. Despite these beneficial consequences, in 1994, President Clinton signed the Violent Crime Control and Law Enforcement Act into law, essentially abrogating federal support and funding for existing programs. As a result, of the 350 programs that had arisen, only three remained.

"The prison system is so large," Kenner muses, "because it locks people up at a young age, and when they return home, they are less equipped to work, to attend school, and to function as social beings." These deficiencies result in an increased chance that released prisoners will commit another crime of a greater magnitude, thereby paving the road back to prison, but this time for a much longer sentence.

As an undergraduate of Bard College, Kenner immersed himself in the prevailing culture of social justice advocacy on campus. In 1999, he and a group of like-minded individuals made the unsettling discovery that of the 72,000 men and women in the New York State prison system, four out of every five inmates were from New York City. Armed with this finding, and an increasing frustration with governmental divestment from education in social services, the group set out to tackle the issue of educating prison inmates. "We felt that if we were really going to commit ourselves to some kind of effort to improve social justice it should be broad-based, and it should be based on public institutions," explains Kenner.

With that in mind, Kenner embarked on a mission to make Bard College an institutional home that would allow either faculty or students to gain access to prisons by lending its transcript services and by offering credit-bearing courses and degrees to prison inmates.

After the national collapse of the college in prison programs, however, there was an incredible distrust among people in corrections who wanted to see the colleges come back and people in higher education who wanted colleges in the prison. According to Kenner, colleges only wanted to offer courses if they could make a profit or if they could do so under ideal circumstances. Some colleges were simply not interested.

It took Kenner one and a half years to begin working with prisons. He was able to organize student volunteer programs that allowed students to conduct writing, GED, literacy, and theology workshops within the prison. "By the spring of my senior year, we had some 40 students volunteering at the prison on a weekly basis. Many of them said that it was the single most profound and influential thing that they had done at their time at Bard," says Kenner.

Upon graduation, Kenner made a proposal to Bard College President Leon Botstein, requesting that the college provide him with an office and grant him access to its transcripts so that they could begin offering college credit to prison inmates. The only stipulation was that Kenner would have to find a way to raise money to support the program.

Following graduation, Kenner was given a salaried position by Episcopal Social Services (EPS). "The Bard Prison Initiative officially started as a partnership between EPS and Bard College," says Kenner, "and five months later, in 2001, we began offering credit bearing courses to 17 students."

Currently, BPI offers two educational programs to inmates. Anyone with a GED can apply for the pre-college program and those with a higher level of education can apply for the associate's degree program. In the fall [of 2005], BPI will begin offering a bachelor's program that is consistent with the degree conferred to Bard College students. Those who have successfully completed the associate's degree program in two or three years can then reapply for admission into the bachelor's degree program.

Kenner hopes that the programs that have been implemented thus far will remain active and prove to be self-sustaining. He remains a passionate advocate for the return of college in prison programs and will continue to play an integral role in enhancing their opportunities.

Source: Excerpt from Malik 2005.

Since the publication of this original article, the program has expanded. BPI currently enrolls 250 incarcerated men and women in five prisons across New York state. The curriculum offerings include more than 50 courses each semester. By 2011, 157 degrees were awarded to BPI graduates (Bard Prison Initiative 2011).

Community Approaches to Law

Community Oriented Policing Services or COPS was created in response to the Violent Crime Control and Law Enforcement Act of 1994. The goal of the program is to shift from traditional law enforcement to community-oriented policing services, a change that includes putting law enforcement officers within a community and emphasizing crime prevention rather than law enforcement (COPS 2003). As stated on the COPS website, "By earning the trust of the members of their communities and making those individuals stakeholders in their own safety, community policing makes law enforcement easier and more efficient, and makes America safer" (COPS 2003). Researchers found that "police administrators have hailed community oriented policing as the preferred strategy for the delivery of services" (Novak, Alarid, and Lucas 2003:57).

Budget & Crime

One of the central premises of community policing is the relationships among the police, citizens, and other agencies. Since 1981, the National Night Out program has worked to strengthen police-community partnerships in anticrime efforts. Usually scheduled in August, National Night Out activities first involved just turning on the front porch lights of houses, but they now include block parties, cookouts, parades, and neighborhood walks involving community members and police officers (National Night Out 2003). The community plays an important role in ensuring its own safety. In community policing, "Problem solving requires that police and the community work together in identifying neighborhood problems, and that the community assumes greater 'guardianship' of the neighborhood" (Greene and Pelfrey 1997:395).

Prison Budgets

COPS sponsors grants and initiatives in selected communities, offering specialized training and programs to police professionals, such as technological innovations (mobile computing, computer-aided dispatch, automated fingerprint identification systems) or policing methods. In addition, the program supports innovative strategies linking police with their communities. COPS highlighted the Metropolitan Nashville Police Department's El Protector Program as one of the best strategies for working with communities whose members have limited English proficiencies. The program, established in 2004, includes two full-time officers who speak fluent Spanish. Assigned to precinct areas with the highest Latino populations, the officers work with community members and business leaders to reduce DUIs, traffic fatalities, and domestic violence.

It is difficult to assess the effectiveness of community policing methods because many of these community approaches have not been sufficiently implemented (MacDonald 2002). Jihong Zhao, Matthew Scheider, and Quint Thurman (2002) report that an additional problem is that much of the research designed to assess COPS programs is limited to the individual programs or cities. However, based on their analysis of COPS programs in 6,100 cities, the researchers discovered that COPS hiring and innovative programs resulted in significant reductions in local violent and nonviolent crime rates in cities with populations greater than 10,000. In addition, an increase of $1 in grant funding per resident for hiring contributed to a decline of 5.26 violent crimes and 21.63 property crimes per 100,000 residents. However, COPS grants had no significant impact on violent and property crime rates in cities with fewer than 10,000 residents. Data also indicate how the COPS program accelerated the establishment of new community policing programs and tactics, such as late-night recreation programs, victim assistance programs, and efficiencies in police work in funded cities (Roth and Ryan 2000).

Prison Advocacy and Death Penalty Reform

Several national, state, and local organizations are committed to reforming our prison system and advocating for prisoner rights. Most of their work comes in the form of advocacy, educational campaigns, and litigation.

Prison Reform

In the early 2000s, a network of student and community activists mobilized to end the use of prisons for profit. The group, Not With Our Money, successfully mobilized against Sodexho Marriott, a food service provider that owned more than 10% of Corrections Corporation of America (CCA), one of the largest owners and operators of U.S. private prisons. Efforts to pressure university administrators to end their food service contracts with Sodexho Marriott were successful at several colleges and universities. Since protests against Sodexho Marriott began, its parent company, Sodexho Alliance, divested all its interest in CCA (Bigda 2001).

State and local grassroots organizations, such as Coloradans Against the Death Penalty, Mississippians for Alternatives to the Death Penalty, and the Texas Coalition to Abolish the Death Penalty, support prisoners' rights and legislation to abolish the death penalty in their states. Citizens United for Alternatives to the Death Penalty (CUADP) attempts to "end the death penalty through aggressive campaigns of public education and the promotion of tactical grassroots activism" (CUADP 2003a). CUADP is using public education, funding, direct action, and professional media campaigns to send its message to the public. CUADP (2003b) believes that "we as a people, and the media in particular, have a responsibility to the public to expose wrongful convictions." On its website, the organization includes a list of cases that it believes may merit the attention of investigative reporters.

One organization that has accepted the mission of correcting wrongful convictions is the Innocence Project. Established in 1992 by attorneys Barry Scheck and Peter Neufeld, the Innocence Project is a nonprofit legal clinic at the Benjamin N. Cardozo School of Law at Yeshiva University in New York. The clinic is dedicated to "exonerating the innocent through postconviction DNA testing" (Innocence Project 2007a). By May 2012, the project had exonerated 290 individuals. These cases highlight the problems of misidentification, corrupt scientists and police, overzealous prosecutors, inept defense attorneys, and the influence of poverty and race in the criminal justice system. The Innocence Project is currently working to establish the Innocence Network, a group of law and journalism schools and public defender offices that assist inmates trying to prove their innocence, even if their cases do not involve biological or DNA evidence. Several states have established their own innocence or justice projects.

The Innocence Project and similar organizations consistently draw the public's attention when an innocent inmate is released. Byron Halsey was convicted in 1988 of the brutal sexual assault and murders of two of his girlfriend's children, Tyrone and Tina Urquhart. He was exonerated in 2007 after the Innocence Project showed that DNA evidence used to convict Halsey actually belonged to Cliff Hall, Halsey's next-door neighbor during the time of the children's murders. Already in prison for other sex crimes committed in the early 1990s, Hall has been charged with the Urquhart murders. In police custody and prison for 22 years, Halsey was released in May 2007 and returned home (Innocence Project 2007b).

Photo 13.5

Byron Halsey hugs a supporter as he leaves the Union County Courthouse in New Jersey following his hearing. Halsey served 22 years before being released in 2007 through efforts by the Innocence Project.

Main Points

- A crime is any behavior that violates criminal law and is punishable. Crime is divided into two legal categories: felonies (serious offenses) and misdemeanors (minor offenses).

- Biological and psychological theories of crime address how crime is determined by individual characteristics or predispositions but do not explain why crime rates vary in certain areas. Sociological theories attempt to address these reasons.

- Functionalists argue that society sets goals and expectations, but people feel strain when they do not have the access or resources to achieve these goals. They then experience anomie and create new norms or rules. Functionalists argue that solutions to crime should target strained groups, providing access to resources to attain goals.

- A second functionalist explanation links social control to criminal behavior. Social control theorists ask why someone *doesn't* commit crime. When societal elements are strong, criminal behavior is unlikely to occur.

- Conflict theorists believe that criminality is a way to define a person's social status according to how that person is perceived and treated by law enforcement. An act is not inherently criminal; society defines it that way. Theorists argue that criminal laws exist to preserve the interests and power of specific groups. Problems emerge when particular groups are disadvantaged by the criminal justice system, which conflict theorists argue is intentionally unequal.

- In feminist scholarship, gender inequality theories have been presented as explanations of female crime. In this view, patriarchal power relations shape gender differences in crime, pushing women into criminal behavior through role entrapment, economic marginalization, and victimization or as a survival response.

- Interactionists examine the process that defines certain individuals and acts as criminal. The theory is called labeling theory, highlighting that what's important isn't the criminal or act, but rather the audience that labels the person or act as criminal. Once a criminal label is attached, a criminal career is set in motion.

- There are different types of crime, including violent crime and property crime (three fourths of all crime in the United States). Juvenile crime refers to youths in trouble with the law. White-collar crime includes crimes committed by someone of high social status, for financial gain, or in a particular organization.

- Within the prison system, African American males are overrepresented. A number of studies confirm that regardless of the seriousness of the crime, racial and ethnic minorities are more likely to be arrested or incarcerated than their White counterparts. Studies also show that police in high-crime areas are more likely to be harsh on suspected criminals, to use coercive authority, and to make arrests than they are in lower-crime areas.

- No consistent pattern can be identified in sentencing practices in state and federal courts. The exception is that Blacks are more likely to receive a death sentence than Whites, especially in cases involving a White victim.

- Research indicates that some individuals are more prone than others to become victims. Victimization rates are substantially higher for the poor, the young, males, Blacks, single people, renters, and central city residents.

- American policing has gone through substantial changes during the past several decades. Traditional models emphasized high visibility and the use of force and arrests as deterrents. These models reinforce an "us" versus "them" division. Police departments are now incorporating new methods based on the community and problem-solving approaches.

- Despite the decline in crime rates, prison populations are increasing. Mandatory sentencing, especially for nonviolent drug offenders, and probation and parole revocations are key reasons why inmate populations have increased for 30 years.

- Some argue that the prison system is intended to rehabilitate offenders. But rates of recidivism, or repeat offenses, indicate how badly the system is working.

- The death penalty was instituted as a deterrent to serious crime. However, research indicates that capital punishment has no deterrent effect on committing murder. In fact, states with the death penalty have murder rates significantly higher than states without the death penalty.

- Several national, state, and local organizations are committed to reforming our prison system and advocating for prisoner rights. Most of their work comes in the form of advocacy, educational campaigns, and litigation.

On Your Own

Log on to the open-access Student Study Site at www.sagepub.com/leonguerrero4e for these additional learning tools:

- Interactive quizzes
- Video clips
- NPR audio links
- Handbook articles

- E-flashcards
- Journal articles
- End-of-chapter web exercises
- Additional web resources and current events

Internet and Community Exercises

1. Investigate the two official sources of U.S. crime data: the U.S. Department of Justice's Bureau of Justice Statistics and the FBI's Uniform Crime Reports. On both sites, search and compare information for one type of crime (e.g., homicide, property crime, rape). Log on to *Study Site Chapter 13* for the web links.

2. The debate about gun control has two vocal sides: those advocating for gun control and those supporting the right to own guns. Investigate local or national organizations on both sides of this issue. You can start by visiting the following sites: the Brady Campaign to Prevent Gun Violence and the National Rifle Association (log on to *Study Site Chapter 13* for links). How do these organizations define the problem of handgun violence? How does each side identify the pros and cons of gun control? What solutions does each side offer?

3. Do your local police support the National Night Out program? Contact the local police station to learn more about the program and other community policing efforts in your city. What community programs are implemented? What residents or social groups are police attempting to reach? To learn more about the program, visit the National Association of Town Watch, the sponsor of the program. The website includes links to selected city and state programs. Log on to *Study Site Chapter 13*.

4. The United Nations Office on Drugs and Crime (UNODC) annually collects data on crime and criminal justice from national government sources and international and regional agencies. Data are compiled for more than 100 countries and member states. For more information about the UNODC's crime and criminal justice statistics, go to *Study Site Chapter 13*.

Study Questions

1. Define the different types of crime considered by criminologists and sociologists.

2. Compare and contrast the explanations of crime offered by strain and social control theorists. According to these theories, is crime motivated by money or greed?

3. Examine how crime exists to preserve the interests and power of specific groups.

4. What is unique about the experiences of female offenders and prisoners? How has our criminal justice system responded? What else needs to be done?

5. Explain how crime is a learned behavior. Are there any crimes that do not fit this perspective?

6. Identify the three sources of crime data in the United States. How would you assess the reliability of these sources?

7. Is the function of our prisons to punish or rehabilitate? Review the evidence for each.

CHAPTER 14

Cities and Suburbs

Welcome to the urban millennium. During the past century, the percentage of the world's population living in urban areas grew from 13% in 1900 to 50% in 2008 (United Nations Population Fund 2007). The number and proportion of urban dwellers will continue to rise, growing to 4.9 billion by 2030. Most of the growth will be in developing countries—Africa and Asia (United Nations Population Fund 2007). China is experiencing the "greatest migration in human history" (French 2007); in 1978, 18% of the Chinese population lived in cities and urban areas, but by 2010, more than 50% likely did. The urban growth is inevitable; as sociologist Tang Jun observes, "To ask whether China wants urbanization is like asking whether a person needs to eat" (French 2007:A13).

Chinese Urbanization

Cities have always maintained an allure of better living and opportunities. But an examination of our cities and their surrounding areas reveals a "profound duality" (Stanback 1991). Although our urban areas are shining examples of economic and social progress, they also harbor significant social problems such as poverty, crime, crowding, pollution, and collapsing infrastructures. Moreover, opportunities and resources are unevenly distributed in cities: Some neighborhoods have safer streets and better services and may offer a better quality of life than others do (Massey 2001). "Cities in different countries with different socioeconomic and political systems often face quite similar problems, although their scales, trends, or causes differ from place to place" (Kim and Gottdiener 2004:172).

Before we begin our analysis of urban problems, we will first review two sociological fields of study. Both remind us that cities don't just happen overnight; rather, social and demographic factors help shape our urban areas and their problems. Our urban areas are produced by economic, political, and cultural forces operating at international, national, and local levels (Kim and Gottdiener 2004).

Urban Sociology and Demography

Industrial Revolution

In the 1920s, sociologists from the University of Chicago examined their city and the impact of city life and its problems on its residents. Their research provided the basis for urban study and for understanding the determinants of urbanization. **Urban sociology** examines the social, political, and economic structures and their impact within an urban setting. Rural sociology is the study of the same structures within a rural setting.

The first studies on urbanization or urban sociology adopted a functionalist approach, comparing a city to a biological organism. The growth of a city was likened to the development of a social organism, with each part of the city serving a specific and necessary function. A city's core, for example, served as its business or industrial center; and areas outside of a city were reserved for residential or commuting activity. Out of the Chicago School of Sociology came two dominant traditions in urban studies, one focusing on **human ecology** (the study of the relationship between individuals and their physical environment) and population dynamics and the second focusing on community studies and ethnographies (Feagin 1998a).

Although this chapter's primary focus is on urban problems, an essential part of urbanization is the number of residents in an area, its population. The second sociological field we will rely on is demography: the study of the size, composition, and distribution of human populations (see also Chapter 6). Demography isn't just about counting people. Demographers analyze the changes and trends in the population. Their work begins with two fundamental facts: We are born, and then we die. Recall how in Chapter 10, "Health and Medicine," we reviewed two demographic elements, fertility and mortality, identifying how each is determined by biological and social factors.

An additional demographic element is **migration**, the movement of individuals from one area to another. Migration is distinguished by the type of movement: **Immigration** is the movement of people into a geographic area; **emigration** is the movement of people out of a geographic area. **Domestic migration** (the movement of people within a country) plays a large role in the population redistribution in the United States (Perry 2006). In the United States, about 35 million people moved between 2010 and 2011, the majority to the same county in their state (U.S. Census Bureau 2012a). People migrate to pursue employment opportunities, to be closer to family, to find a more temperate climate, and to seek the opportunity of a better life. Most movers have housing-related reasons: They move to a new, better, or more affordable home or apartment (Schachter 2004).

The Processes of Urbanization and Suburbanization

Urbanization, the process by which a population shifts from rural to urban, took off in the latter half of the nineteenth century (Williams 2000). Urbanization in the United States, as in other developed countries, was closely linked with economic development and industrialization. The U.S. economy in the middle of the nineteenth century was divided: The northern economy was characterized by a mixture of family-based agriculture, commerce, finance, and an increasing industrial base, whereas the southern economy remained dependent on agriculture (Gordon 2001). But as the industrial economy began to grow in the North and extended into the Midwest, thousands of people were attracted to these emerging urban centers, drawn by the promise of work in factories and mills (Williams 2000). Also contributing to early urban growth was the immigration of Europeans and the migration of rural Blacks and Whites from the South to northern and midwestern urban areas (Dreier 1996).

The process of global urbanization is described in waves. The first wave occurred in North America and Europe from 1750 to 1950 (United Nations Population Fund 2007), closely linked with industrialization and economic development (Kim and Gottdiener 2004). This wave involved a few hundred million people and produced urban industrial societies that now dominate the world (United Nations Population Fund 2007).

The second wave of urbanization took place during the past half-century in developing countries. Some have referred to the shift as **overurbanization**, the process where an excess population is concentrated in an urban area that lacks the capacity to provide basic services and shelter. Overurbanization is characterized by a lack of employment, housing, and education or health infrastructures for an area's residents (Kim and Gottdiener 2004). This second urbanization wave is problematic because it involves large populations of poor people—instead of hundreds of millions as in the first wave, the second wave involves billions residing mostly in Africa and Asia (United Nations Population Fund 2007). Refer to Table 14.1 for a comparison of urban populations between developed and less developed regions.

After World War II, the United States experienced another significant population shift: suburbanization. Although **suburbanization** has come to represent the outward expansion of central cities into suburban areas (Smith 1986), it has also been linked with two additional population shifts: from the Snow Belt (industrial regions of the North and Midwest) to the Sun Belt (South and Southwest) and from rural to metropolitan areas (Dreier 1996). Though many factors contributed to suburbanization, the key players were government leaders and their policies. The U.S. Congress passed the Housing Act of 1949, which encouraged construction outside city boundaries and made home purchasing easier through the Federal Housing Administration (FHA) and Veterans Affairs home mortgage loan programs. The 1956 Federal Aid Highway Act, which established the modern interstate highway system, made rural areas more accessible. President Dwight Eisenhower, a chief proponent of the act, believed in the importance of the interstate highway system. Eisenhower (1963) declared,

Suburban Discrimination

> More than any single action by the government since the end of the war, this one would change the face of America. . . . Its impact on the American economy—the jobs it would produce in manufacturing and construction, the rural areas it would open up—was beyond calculation. (pp. 548–49)

Table 14.1

Urban Population Distribution of the World by Development Groups, 1975, 2000, 2010, and 2020 (Population in Millions)

	1975	2000	2010	2020
World (total)	1,538	2,859	3,559	4,290
More developed regions	718	881	957	1,018
Less developed regions	819	1,977	2,601	3,271

Source: United Nations, Department of Economic and Social Affairs 2011.

The U.S. Census Bureau defines an **urban population** as an area with 2,500 or more individuals. An **urbanized area** is a densely populated area with 50,000 or more residents, and a metropolitan statistical area is a densely populated area with 100,000 or more people. U.S. Census data indicate a rapid increase in the urban population, especially after World War II (Table 14.2). For 2010, the three largest metropolitan statistical areas were New York City, Los Angeles, and Chicago (U.S. Census Bureau 2012a). The largest area was New York City–northern New Jersey–Long Island with 1,889,700 people. A complete list of the 10 largest metropolitan statistical areas is presented in Table 14.3. The New York–Newark area remains one of the world's largest megacities (10 million residents or more). Refer to Table 14.4 for the complete list of megacities.

Table 14.2

U.S. Population, Percentage of Urban Residents, Selected Years

Year	Percentage Urban
1900	40.0
1910	45.8
1920	51.4
1930	56.2
1940	56.5
1950	64.0
1960	69.9
1970	73.5
1980	73.7
1990	75.2
2000	79.0

Source: U.S. Census Bureau 1995, 2010.

Table 14.3

10 Largest U.S. Metropolitan Statistical Areas, 2010

	Population in Millions
New York City–northern New Jersey–Long Island [NY-NJ]	18,897
Los Angeles–Long Beach–Santa Ana [CA]	12,829
Chicago–Naperville–Joliet [IL-IN-WI]	9,461
Dallas–Ft. Worth–Arlington [TX]	6,372
Philadelphia–Camden–Wilmington [PA-NJ-DE-MD]	5,965
Houston–Sugar Land–Baytown [TX]	5,947
Washington–Arlington–Alexandria [DC-VA-MD-WV]	5,582
Miami–Ft. Lauderdale–Pompano Beach [FL]	5,565
Atlanta–Sandy Springs–Marietta [GA]	5,269
Boston–Cambridge–Quincy [MA-NH]	4,552

Source: U.S. Census Bureau 2012c.

Table 14.4

Largest Megacities in the World—1950, 2000, 2005, and 2015 (Population in Millions)

1950	Pop.	2000	Pop.	2005	Pop.	2015 Predicted	Pop.
New York–Newark, USA	12.3	Tokyo, Japan	34.4	Tokyo, Japan	35.2	Tokyo, Japan	35.5
Tokyo, Japan	11.3	Ciudad de Mexico (Mexico City), Mexico	18.1	Ciudad de Mexico, Mexico	19.4	Mumbai, India	21.9
		New York–Newark, USA	17.8	New York–Newark, USA	18.7	Ciudad de Mexico, Mexico	21.6
		São Paulo, Brazil	17.1	São Paulo, Brazil	18.3	São Paulo, Brazil	20.5
		Mumbai, India	16.1	Mumbai, India	18.2	New York–Newark, USA	19.9
		Shanghai, China	13.2	Delhi, India	15.0	Delhi, India	18.6
		Calcutta, India	13.1	Shanghai, China	14.5	Shanghai, China	17.2
		Delhi, India	12.4	Calcutta, India	14.3	Calcutta, India	17.0
		Buenos Aires, Argentina	11.8	Jakarta, Indonesia	13.2	Dhaka, Bangladesh	16.8
		Los Angeles–Long Beach–Santa Ana, USA	11.8	Buenos Aires, Argentina	12.6	Jakarta, Indonesia	16.8

Note: In 1950, there were only two megacities in the world. By 2005, their number had increased to 20 (though only the top 10 are listed here). By 2015, there will be 22 megacities in the world, 17 located in developing countries.

Source: United Nations Population Division 2006.

Photo 14.1

The largest megacity in the world is Tokyo, Japan. Tokyo's population is predicted to increase to 35.5 million in 2015. Pictured here is Tokyo's Kanto region.

The Population Composition

Changes in the fertility, mortality, and migration rates of a population affect its composition, its biological and social characteristics. For example, **age distribution**, the distribution of individuals by age, is particularly important because it provides a community with some direction in its social and economic planning, assessing its education, health, housing, and employment needs. As discussed in Chapter 6, "Age and Aging," demographers have long predicted the graying of the U.S. population, warning of the growing number of elderly and the increasing demands they will make on health care and social security programs.

In addition, demographers have noted that the ethnic composition (the composition of **ethnic groups** within a population) affects social and human services. In 2007, the U.S. Census Bureau announced that 1 in 3 Americans were ethnic minorities, about 101 million. Roberto Suro and Audrey Singer (2002) explain how the Latino population has spread out further and faster across the nation than any previous wave of immigrants. In 2012(b), the U.S. Census Bureau announced that Hispanics were the largest and fastest-growing minority group in the United States, numbering 52 million in 2011.

 Demography

Housing, education, health, and public transportation demands are affected by the rate of Latino population growth. For example, cities and areas with large established Latino communities (e.g., New York, Chicago, Miami, Southern California) should prepare for a growing Latino population characterized by low-wage workers, large families, and significant numbers of adults with little English proficiency (Suro and Singer 2002). In California, researchers from the University of California–Los Angeles Medical School recommended shifting health care services because Hispanic Californians tend to live longer than non-Hispanics and are less likely to die from heart disease or cancer (Murphy 2003).

The increasing number of ethnic Americans and their age distribution has caught demographers' attention. When data for the 2007 U.S. Census were announced, researchers noted that younger Americans were more ethnically diverse than were older generations—the average age of non-Hispanic Whites was 40.5 years, whereas among Hispanics, the average age was 27.4 years. This age gap may lead to competing political and social agendas. Communities may be divided between older Americans advocating for social security, lower taxes, and better health care and younger ethnically diverse Americans demanding better education, jobs, and social services (Roberts 2007).

What Does It Mean to Me?

Link to the U.S. Census Bureau American Community Survey website to find out the age and ethnic composition of your state. Would you characterize your state as a "young" state or as ethnically diverse?

 STATE STATS

Sociological Perspectives on Urbanization

Functionalist Perspective

Early functionalists were critical about the transition from simple to complex social communities. Émile Durkheim described this transition as a movement from mechanical solidarity to organic solidarity. Under **mechanical solidarity**, individuals in small simple societies are united through a set of common values, beliefs, and customs and a simple division of labor. Most individuals are engaged in the same type of economic activity or labor. In contrast, Durkheim argued, **organic solidarity** is the result of increasing industrialization and the growth of large complex societies, where individuals are linked through a complex division of labor. Under organic solidarity, individuals begin to share the responsibility for the production of goods and services, each with a specific role in production. New relationships are created according to what people can do or provide for each other. For example, most of us do not raise the food for our meals. We depend on others to grow, harvest, deliver, and sell our food and groceries, and others depend on us for our specific labor activity. Durkheim believed that as a result of industrialization, the social bonds that unite us will eventually weaken, leading to social problems.

Taking a World View

Global Urbanization and Population Growth

In its 1996 *State of World Population* report, the United Nations Population Fund predicted that population growth in cities would be the single largest influence in the twenty-first century. More than a decade later, the organization believes its statement is proving more accurate by the day.

In its 2007 report, the United Nations Population Fund predicted that "at the global level, all future population growth will [thus] be in towns and cities" (p. 6). More than half of the world's population was living in urban areas by 2008, approximately 3.3 billion individuals. In contrast, the world's rural population will decline by about 28 million between 2005 and 2030. Urban population growth is expected to occur in developing nations such as Africa and Asia, with slower expansion expected in Latin America and in the Caribbean. Most of the growth is attributed to natural increases (more births than deaths) rather than migration. In the developed world, the urban population is expected to grow very little, from 870 million to 1 billion.

There are many negative consequences of urban population growth for individuals, nations, and the world: increased demand for social and human services; increased economic and political burdens, particularly for poorer developing countries; and global environmental degradation (Desai 2004). Some segments of the population are more vulnerable than others are. By 2030, 60% of all urban dwellers will be younger than age 18. Cities need to ensure that appropriate levels of basic services, education, housing, and medical care are available for these youth; if not, life on these urban streets will threaten the quality of youths' health, education, safety, and future (United Nations Population Fund 2007).

(Continued)

(Continued)

Despite its dire message, the United Nations Population Fund (2007) concludes, "Urban and national governments, together with civil society, and supported by international organizations, can take steps now that will make a huge difference for the social, economic and environmental living conditions of a majority of the world's population" (p. 3). Suggesting the need for more proactive and creative approaches, the organization recommends strategies to improve the social conditions of the poor, promote gender equality, and ensure environmental sustainability. A major component of the recommendations is to empower women and increase the level of reproductive health services available to families, believing that these interventions will influence individuals' fertility preferences (the number of children and the timing of births) and their ability to meet them. Such a strategy "empowers the exercise of human rights and gives people greater control over their lives" (United Nations Population Fund 2007:70).

Although industrialization and urbanization have been functional, creating a more efficient, interdependent, and productive society, they have also been problematic. Because of the weakening of social bonds and an absence of norms, society begins to lose its ability to function effectively. As our social bonds with each other have loosened, our sense of obligation or duty to one another has declined.

Urbanization can lead to social problems such as crime, poverty, violence, and deviant behavior. Functional solutions to these problems may encourage reinforcing or re-creating social bonds through such existing institutions as churches, families, and schools or instituting societal changes through political or economic initiatives. For example, under mechanical solidarity, the strong social bonds linking an individual to society (through one's family and friends) deter criminal behavior. A person would not think of committing a criminal act because it would be inherently wrong or would harm the individual's relationship with other members of society. Under organic solidarity, criminal laws, police, and prison systems serve as formal structures to deter criminal activity.

Conflict and Feminist Perspectives

Political Geography

Since the late 1960s, a new perspective on urban study has emerged. Referred to as the **critical political-economy perspective** or **socio-spatial perspective**, this approach uses a conflict perspective to focus on how cities are formed on the basis of racial, gender, or class inequalities. From this perspective, cities are shaped by powerful social and political actors from the private and public sectors, working within the modern capitalistic structure (Feagin 1998b). Social problems are natural to the system, rising from the unequal distribution of power between politicians and taxpayers, the rich and the poor, the homeowner and the renter, or Whites and Blacks.

March for Housing

Residential segregation is defined as the neighborhood clustering or separation of groups by racial, ethnic, or economic characteristics within a geographic area. Residential segregation is a form of social organization that enables differential access to resources and opportunities, such as public services, schools, and employment opportunities (Dickerson 2008), advantaging one group over another. From this perspective residential segregation is not accidental, but is the product of institutional discrimination, city governments, zoning laws, mortgage redlining policies, tax bases, and school systems that perpetuate racialized socioeconomic inequalities (Hanlon 2011; Judd and Swanstrom 2004). Martha Mahoney (1997) explains:

For whites, residential segregation is one of the forces giving race a "natural" appearance: "good" neighborhoods are equated with whiteness, and "black" neighborhoods are equated with joblessness. This equation allows whiteness to remain a dominant background norm, associated with positive qualities for white people, at the same time that it allows unemployment and underemployment to seem like natural features of black communities. (p. 330)

Within this tradition, scholars also examine the role of capitalism and capitalists in shaping cities (Feagin 1998b). Land-use decisions are made by politicians and businesspeople (Gottdiener 1977), real estate developers and financiers (Molotch 1976), or coalitions between public officials and private citizens (Rast 2001). Joe Feagin (1998b) presented a theory of urban ecology that accented the role of class structure and powerful land-oriented capitalist actors in shaping the location, development, and decline of U.S. cities. Land speculators shape the internal structure of cities by identifying and packaging particular parcels of land for business or residential use. As Feagin (1998b) describes it,

Powerful land-interested capitalists have contributed substantially to the internal physical structure and patterning of cities themselves. The central areas of cities such as San Francisco have been intentionally remade, in the name of private profit, by combinations of speculators and other capitalists, such as developers. (p. 154)

Although women play a pivotal role in urban life, theories about urbanization have taken a gender-blind approach (Women's International Network News 1999). Urban studies have not systematically considered cities as sites of institutionalized patriarchy (Garber and Turner 1995) and have not legitimately considered the role of women in urban development. Feminist urbanists have argued for the development of a comprehensive field of theory and research that acknowledges the role of women in urban structures (Masson 1984).

By incorporating feminist theory in patriarchy and urban studies, we can understand an additional dimension of urban life, namely the complex ways in which cities reproduce and challenge patriarchy (Appleton 1995) and the problems this creates. Cities are places where gender is experienced and constituted. As Judith Garber and Robyne Turner (1995) explain,

Urban environments are constructed around the delivery of public services and the development of policies. These shape women's ability to cope with complex urban locations, largely through the responsiveness of public and private organizations to the needs of diverse groups of women and children. (p. xxiii)

Turner (1995) argues that the living conditions of lower-income, inner-city women have been affected by the economic restructuring of cities and the patterns of downtown development. Woman-headed households increasingly make up the majority of inner-city households. Turner explains that although low-income women may find inner-city housing less costly and more accessible than housing in the suburbs is, urban living also presents a unique set of challenges in transportation, housing, employment, services, and safety. Inner-city women have less control over their living situations than suburban women do. City development decisions are made by those in power, often men, whereas the decisions affect women, the young, and the elderly. Turner (1995) concludes, "It is important to recognize the implications for women, as the heads of households, in the debate on economic restructuring, land based economies, and the portrayal of political power" (pp. 287–88).

Interactionist Perspective

Georg Simmel ([1903] 1997) was the first sociologist to explain how city life is also a state of mind. In his 1903 essay, "The Metropolis and Mental Life," Simmel described how life in a small town is self-contained; interactions with others are routine and rather ordinary. But a city's economic, personal, and intellectual relationships cannot be defined or confined by its physical space; rather, they are as extensive as the number of interactions between its residents. City dwellers must interact with a variety of people for goods and services and for personal and professional relationships. City living stimulates the intellect and individuality of its residents (Karp, Stone, and Yoels 1991). Within this complex web of city life, Simmel ([1903] 1997) argued, man would struggle to define his own individuality "in order to preserve his most personal core" (p. 184). A city represents an opportunity for individuals to find self-expression while being connected with fellow city dwellers.

But how well are city dwellers connected with their neighbors? The answer is that they may not be as connected as Simmel predicted. The way a city is constructed might actually interfere with social interaction. Our dependency on automobiles compartmentalizes neighborhood relations (we only know neighbors on our block or street) and interferes with street life (no space for ball games, block parties, bike riding, and joggers) (Gottdiener 1977). Home and residential designs limit our face-to-face contact with our neighbors. Without porches, there is no place to sit out front and visit with one's neighbors; without sidewalks or local parks, families find it less appealing to take walks around their neighborhood and less easy to meet with neighbors.

Tridib Banerjee and William Baer (1984) discovered that how we define our cities is linked to what we value or use within them. What goods and services do people use in their community? Is it the coffee shop, the local dry cleaner, or the neighborhood grocery store? Or is it the local park, the bicycle lanes, or the athletic center down the street? The researchers asked residents of several Southern California cities to draw maps of their residential areas and discovered that illustrations by middle- and upper-income individuals contained more details and area than illustrations by lower-income people did. Upper-income groups included amenities such as tree-lined streets, wooded areas, and golf courses, whereas middle- and low-income groups included commercial and retail locations, such as gas stations, discount stores, or drug stores. Corporate symbols were commonly used to define landmarks in middle- and low-income illustrations. Banerjee and Baer concluded that income was the single most

Photo 14.2

Does urban living (and the preoccupation with personal technology) unite or divide residents?

important variable in explaining the quality of residential experiences and residents' judgments about what constitutes a "good place" to live.

Based on his examination of the transformation of European cities from industrial centers to recreational destinations, Mathis Stock (2006) discovered that a city may be defined by conflicting constituent groups (residents vs. tourists) and the vastly different experiences of the city they share. The transformation of cities such as Paris, Venice, and Florence into tourist destinations is often intentional, with city leaders and businesses embracing the symbols of tourism—the language, images, practices, and customs—in their cities. To entice visitors to their city, they promote their city's annual festivals and package them along with well-known cultural and historical sites as part of a cultural heritage experience. This transformation has its detractors, who, though acknowledging the revenue benefit of tourism, question whether this process has stripped these historical European cities of their authentic identities and subordinated native residents as a result. In 2009, Venetians held a mock funeral as a sign of protest for their city, complete with a fake coffin floating down the Grand Canal. The number of historic center residents dropped from 74,000 in 1993 to 60,000 in 2009; the decline is blamed on rising rents and increasing numbers of tourists that pushed locals onto the mainland (Donadio 2009).

For a summary of the different sociological perspectives, see Table 14.5.

 Urban Renewal

Table 14.5

Summary of Sociological Perspectives: Cities and Suburbs

	Functional	Conflict/Feminist	Interactionist
Explanation of urbanization and its social problems	This perspective focuses on the weakening of social bonds and the functions and dysfunctions of urbanization.	Both perspectives focus on how cities are formed on the basis of racial, gender, or class inequalities.	City living is a state of mind. Urban living and its related social problems are socially defined.
Questions asked about urbanization and its social problems	How does urbanization enhance or destroy our social bonds? In what ways does urbanization affect existing institutions such as churches, families, and schools? How can we strengthen our social bonds?	Do one's race, gender, and social class determine the quality of urban living? How can we address the needs of all urban dwellers? How does one urban group gain power over the others?	How is urban living defined? How can we establish common ideas on urban life and its social problems?

Source: Adapted from Norris 2001.

What Does It Mean to Me?

Can't a person find some personal space? Symbolic interactionists have noted that urban dwellers are able to create a "public privacy" while living in a demanding urban world (Karp et al. 1991). Using props such as a newspaper or an iPod, individuals send messages that they aren't interested in talking with others. You may bump into people while walking on a busy street but never stop to say, "Excuse me." The proportion of unlisted phone numbers is greater in the city than in small towns or suburban areas (Karp et al. 1991). Your coffee barista may have memorized your morning coffee order, but does your barista know your name or any other personal information? How do you create and maintain your public privacy?

The Consequences of Urbanization and Suburbanization

Urban Sociology

Along with suburbanization came the decentralization, some may even say the demise, of U.S. cities. Inner cities became repositories for low-income individuals and families, as the suburbs enjoyed higher tax bases and fewer social programs (Massey and Eggers 1993). Researchers have suggested that the poor economic outcomes of racial minorities, particularly African Americans, are partly the result of patterns of housing prejudice and discrimination that have prevented minority groups from moving at the same pace as the suburbanization of employment (Massey 2001; Pastor 2001). According to Douglas Massey and Mitchell Eggers (1993),

> The simultaneous proliferation of poverty and affluence created a situation in which social problems among those at the bottom of the income hierarchy multiplied rapidly at a time when more and more people had the means to escape these maladies. (p. 313)

Many of the social problems we discuss in this text seem to be magnified in urban areas. In this next section, we will review specific social problems plaguing urban areas: affordable and quality housing, crowding, homelessness, gentrification, and urban sprawl and transportation.

Affordable and Quality Housing

In 2011, 66% of Americans owned their own homes. Not until the passage of the 1949 Housing Act did the majority of Americans become homeowners. In 1940, only 43.6% of Americans were homeowners, but by 1950, more than half, 55%, were (Bunce et al. 1996). Although most Americans still aspire to own a home, for many poor and working Americans, homeownership is just a dream (Freeman 2002). For 2011, Whites (non-Hispanic) had the highest homeownership rates (74%), followed by Asians/Pacific Islanders (58%) and Hispanics (46.9%) (U.S. Census Bureau 2012a). Blacks had the lowest ownership rate: 44.9%. Central city residents of all income levels are less likely to own a home than are suburban residents with the same income (U.S. Department of Housing and Urban Development [HUD] 1999). Refer to U.S. Data Map 14.1 for the rate of homeownership by state.

Despite the decline in home sales and values, housing affordability has declined (Savage 1999). The generally accepted definition of affordability is for a family to pay no more than 28% of its annual income on housing (30% for a rental unit). Nearly one in four working households (households where individuals work more than 20 hours per week and have a household income of no more than 120% of the median income in the area) spends more than half its income on housing costs (Williams 2012).

Housing Market Discrimination

Lance Freeman (2002) explains that because housing is the single largest expenditure for most households, "housing affordability has the potential to affect all domains of life that are subject to cost constraints, including health" (p. 710). Most families pay their rent first, buying basic needs such as food, clothing, and health care with what they have left. The lack of public assistance, increasing prices, slow wage growth, and a limited inventory of affordable apartments and houses make it nearly impossible for some to find adequate housing (Pugh 2007).

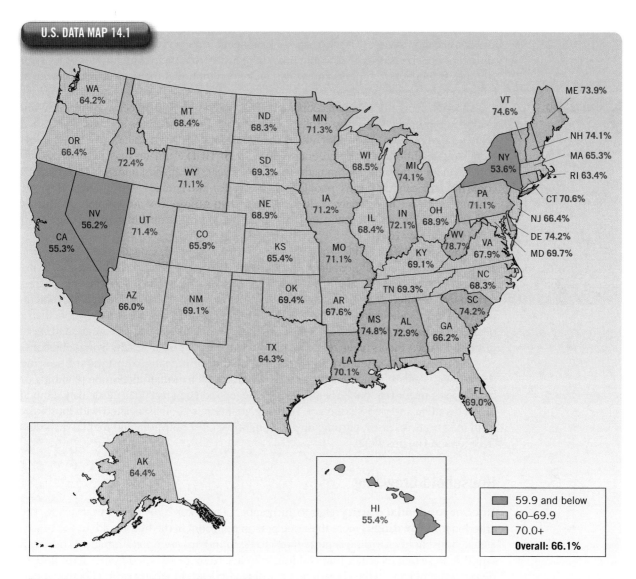

U.S. DATA MAP 14.1

Percentage Homeowner Rates by States, 2011

Source: U.S. Census Bureau 2012a.

Renters are limited by more than just the increasing cost of housing; there is also a shortage of rental properties. The gap between the demand and the supply of affordable housing continues to grow. Higher land prices have made it less profitable to build new low- and moderate-priced housing. The National Low Income Housing Coalition (2007) reports that the nation is 2.8 million apartments short of meeting the need among people with the lowest incomes. For every new affordable housing unit constructed, two are demolished, abandoned, or converted into condominiums (Pugh 2007).

Consider the housing situation of Alice Greenwood and her 6-year-old son, Makalii (Magin 2006). When the home she rented for 30 years for $300 a month was sold, she and her son joined some 1,000 people living in tents along the 13-mile stretch of beaches on the Waianae Coast of Oahu, Hawaii. In Waianae, homes that rented for $200 to $300 per month a couple of years ago now average more than $1,000 per month. For 2007, the median price of

Affordable Housing

a home on Oahu was $665,000. Most of Greenwood's tent neighbors are employed in service and construction sectors. The state's homeless shelter is not a viable option for Greenwood and other beach residents—it would take them away from their communities (it is about 10 miles from the beach park) and would make commuting difficult (it is located several miles from the nearest bus route).

Housing Crisis

Although economic factors account for much of the disparity in homeownership, discrimination and prejudice also play a role. African Americans and Latinos are more likely than Whites are to be turned down for a home loan, even if they have similar financial, employment, and neighborhood backgrounds (Oliver 2003). HUD estimates that more than 2 million instances of housing discrimination occur each year. The highest numbers of complaints come from African Americans, people with disabilities, and families with children. Hispanic renters experience higher rates of discrimination than African American renters do (Turner et al. 2002) and are discriminated against as much as 70% of the time in their housing search (Fair Housing Law 2004).

Many aspects of urban life—quality of air and drinking water, sanitation and fire services, and the availability and affordability of health care—have well-established connections to the health of urban dwellers (Cohen and Northridge 2000). For example, India's cities are characterized by "teeming hovels of dirt and garbage, overcrowded and noisy lanes, and proliferation of slums" (Siddiqui and Pandey 2003:590). India's urban centers are home to more than a quarter of India's total population. Deprived of the basic amenities of water, sewage, and waste disposal facilities, India's urban residents are subject to unsafe and unhealthy living conditions.

One area that is often overlooked is the quality of housing. Substandard housing (homes with severe or moderate structural problems such as malfunctioning plumbing or heating) is a major U.S. public health issue (Krieger and Higgins 2002), particularly among urban dwellers and people of color. Housing quality has been associated with morbidity from infectious diseases, chronic illnesses, injuries, poor nutrition, and mental disorders (Krieger and Higgins 2002).

Household Crowding

Interior residential density refers to the number of individuals per room in a dwelling. The criterion for **crowding** is more than one person per room in the household. In the United States, household crowding is more likely to be found among poor, immigrant, or urban families. Research indicates that children who live in more crowded homes have greater behavioral problems in the classroom. Crowding also leads to greater conflict between parents and children. In crowded homes, parents have been found to be more critical of and less responsive to their children (Evans, Saegert, and Harris 2001).

William Clark, Marinus Deurloo, and Frans Dieleman (2000) argue that household crowding is linked to inequalities in housing consumption. The researchers explain that the rising income of a large segment of U.S. society has led to increases in the overall quality of housing in the United States. But at the same time, growing income inequalities create affordability and crowding problems for very-low-income households. Affluent households demand better-quality and larger houses, increasing their consumption of livable space, pushing housing outside of inner-city boundaries. Clark et al. explain that as middle-class families move to the suburbs, they leave behind inner cities plagued with increased density and housing shortages.

Cities with large numbers of immigrants—such as those in such states as California, Texas, Arizona, and Florida—are especially subject to crowding. A study based in Southern California reveals that households of Hispanics who immigrated in the 1970s are 212 times more likely to be overcrowded than are those of earlier Hispanic immigrants or White immigrants (Myers and Lee 1996). Clark et al. (2000) also report that in metropolitan areas with high levels of recent immigration, overcrowding is higher than in nonimmigrant areas. Poor immigrant households experience the most crowding and have the most difficulty in transitioning to better, more affordable housing. Studies suggest that competition for housing in cities with many immigrants may increase the cost of housing and can lead to a housing squeeze. Cultural norms may also play a role in encouraging crowding among Hispanic immigrant homes.

Crowding is also a global issue, in countries experiencing rapid population growth. For example, the population of Lagos, Nigeria, has doubled over 15 years to 21 million (Rosenthal 2012). City residents typically live in apartments, 7- by 11-foot rooms described as "Face Me, Face You." Up to 50 people may share a kitchen, toilet, and sink (Rosenthal 2012).

Homelessness

By its very nature, homelessness is impossible to measure with 100% accuracy (National Coalition for the Homeless 2002). Most estimates are based on head counts in shelters, on the streets, or at soup kitchens. These estimates do not include those who live in temporary or unstable housing (e.g., those who move in with friends or relatives). There are several national estimates of homelessness. The U.S. Department of Housing and Urban Development (2011) estimates that in 2010 as many as 1.6 million people experienced homelessness and more than 649,879 people were homeless on any given night. Among those who sought emergency shelter or transitional housing in 2010, 78% were adults, 62% were male, 58% were members of a minority group, 63% were single adults, and 37% had a disability. Most public and private sources agree that the number of homeless people is at least in the hundreds of thousands, not counting those who live with relatives or friends (Choi and Snyder 1999).

Homelessness

Globally, the highest concentrations of homeless people tend to be located in urban settings and segregated in some of the traditionally poorest areas (Toro 2007). In contrast to the United States, European countries experience lower rates of homelessness because their social welfare system guarantees some level of income, health care, and housing for all citizens. Japan is facing a rapidly growing problem of homelessness because its welfare system is even more underdeveloped than that of the United States (Toro 2007).

Peter Rossi (1989) maintains that the homeless are likely to be more visible, female, members of ethnic minorities, somewhere in their 20s or 30s, and unemployed, with no or low monthly incomes. Other developed countries have also seen an increase in the numbers of homeless families and youth (Toro 2007). Before the mid-1970s, the majority of the homeless were older, single males with substance abuse or physical or mental problems (Choi and Snyder 1999). Their individual disabilities or personal pathologies were likely to have caused their homelessness. Since the mid-1970s, however, the increasing number of homeless men, women, and families indicates that more than individual disabilities or personal characteristics are causing homelessness (Choi and Snyder 1999). Studies indicate that family homelessness in the 1980s and 1990s was primarily attributable not to individual deficits but to the increased number of the poor, especially minority, single, female-headed households, and to the lack of affordable low-income housing units (Choi and Snyder 1999).

The U.S. Conference of Mayors (2011) identified several interrelated causes of homelessness for families and single adults: unemployment and lack of affordable housing. Unemployment was identified as the primary cause of homelessness for both groups. When asked what three things cities should do to address homelessness, the mayors identified more mainstream assisted housing, permanent supportive housing for people with disabilities, and more or better-paying employment opportunities.

Surplus Government Property

Gentrification

Gentrification

In their report, "Dealing With Neighborhood Change," Maureen Kennedy and Paul Leonard (2001) reveal that **gentrification**, "the process of neighborhood change which results in the replacement of lower-income residents with higher-income ones, has changed the character of hundreds of urban neighborhoods in America over the last 50 years" (p. 1). Gentrification has occurred in waves: the urban renewal efforts in the 1950s and 1960s and the "back-to-the-city" movement of the late 1970s and 1980s. Gentrification is a global experience, with renewal efforts documented in Tokyo, London, Mexico City, Cape Town, Paris, Shanghai, and Sydney, as well as in many other countries and cities (Smith 2002).

The researchers describe gentrification as a "double edged sword." Officials and developers point to the increasing real estate values, tax revenues, and commercial activity that take place in revitalized communities. But is there a price for these capital and economic improvements? The most contentious by-product of gentrification is the involuntary displacement of a neighborhood's low-income residents. Gentrification is most often associated with the disproportionate pressure it puts on marginalized poor, elderly, or minorities, particularly renters. No consistent data exist on the number of individuals who have been displaced through gentrification; yet the evidence suggests that where housing markets are tight (or limited), the amount of displacement is likely to be greater and the impacts on those displaced more serious (Kennedy and Leonard 2001).

Though overall U.S. home values dropped between 2008 and 2011, values of homes in close-in or mixed-use neighborhoods held or increased their value. Demand for walkable urban places, with amenities of mixed housing types, destinations within walking distance, and public transportation options, increased above homes in suburban areas with large home lots, ample parking, and driving as the primary means of transportation (Leinberger and Alfonzo 2012). In their analysis of sample neighborhoods in the Washington, DC, metropolitan area, Christopher Leinberger and Mariela Alfonzo (2012) documented how residents of more walkable places have lower transportation costs and higher transit access, but higher housing costs. Residents of walkable places are more affluent than residents of places with poor walkability. Leinberger (2012) reported how similar class and cost patterns are present in other urban areas, such as Seattle, Washington; Denver, Colorado; Columbus, Ohio; and Atlanta, Georgia.

Urban Sprawl and Transportation

Urban Sprawl

As urban areas spread out, they create a phenomenon referred to as **urban sprawl**. Urban sprawl began with land development after World War II. Sprawl is defined as the process in which the spread of development across the landscape outpaces population growth (Ewing, Pendall, and Chen 2002). Sprawl creates four conditions for an urban area: a population that is widely dispersed in low-density developments; rigidly separated homes, shops, and workplaces; a network of roads marked by huge blocks and poor access; and a lack of well-defined activity centers, such as downtowns or town centers (Ewing et al. 2002). Sprawl increases stress on urban livability as goods and services, along with economic and educational opportunities, become less accessible to inner-city residents (Johnson 2007; Powell 2007).

As sprawl increases, so do the number of miles traveled, the number of vehicles owned per household, traffic fatality rates, air pollution (Corvin 2001; Ewing et al. 2002), and, eventually, our risk of asthma, obesity, and poor health. On average, an American spends 443 hours per year behind the wheel (Crenson 2003). Public transportation usage is higher in metro areas. Inside a principal city in a metro area, only 10.6% of workers take public transportation to work, whereas in areas outside any metro area, only 1.2% of workers take public transportation. The New York–northern New Jersey–Long Island metro area had the highest percentage of workers who commuted to work via public transportation, 30.5% (McKenzie and Rapino 2011). New suburban residential developments don't include sidewalks, and automobiles are needed to get from place to place.

The Centers for Disease Control and Prevention report that urban sprawl increases our time on the road and decreases our time spent exercising, including walking, jogging, or riding a bike (Corvin 2001). Residents who live in spread-out areas spend fewer minutes each month walking and weigh about 6 pounds more on average than do those who live in densely populated areas (Stein 2003).

Americans spend more than 100 hours per year commuting to work (U.S. Census Bureau 2005). On average, an American worker's daily commute is about 25 minutes (one-way commute time), and 75% of workers drive alone to work (McKenzie and Rapino 2011). Residents from larger cities tend to have longer commutes: New York (38 minutes); Chicago (33 minutes); Newark, New Jersey (31 minutes); and Riverside, California (31 minutes) (U.S. Census Bureau 2005). Long commutes are also a global experience, particularly for poor disadvantaged workers. For example, commuting to Brazil's largest industrial city, São Paulo, can take as much as 4 hours each way. São Paulo commuters are mostly minimum-wage laborers, commuting daily from their working-class poor suburbs to the city's factories.

What Does It Mean to Me?

Examine the public transportation system for your college city. First, is one available? Second, assess its effectiveness. Does the system serve all areas of your community? How much does it cost to use the system? How does the system serve disadvantaged populations—elderly, poor, or disabled residents? Does the system provide discounted fares for students?

 STATE STATS

Photo 14.3

The average American spends 443 hours per year behind the wheel. In areas with high urban sprawl, only 2.3% of workers take public transportation to work (U.S. Census Bureau 2005).

In Focus

Living Car Free

North Americans are known for their love affair with, maybe even addiction to, their automobiles (Boddy 2000). Though the average number of persons per household has declined, 3.16 in 1969 to 2.66 in 2009, the number of vehicles has increased in the same time period from 1.16 to 1.92 (U.S. Department of Energy 2010). Despite rising fuel prices, U.S. housing and work patterns make it hard for suburban commuters to change their driving habits (Ohlemacher 2007). As of May 2012, the highest recorded average price for a gallon of regular gas was $4.14 in 2008.

However, many European countries and cities have found innovative and community-friendly ways to deal with gas prices consistently higher than $6.00 per gallon. For example, most of the 4,700 residents of Vauban, Germany, live car free. The rate of Vauban car ownership is 150 per 1,000 inhabitants compared with 640 per 1,000 residents in the United States. How does Vauban do it? Extensive city planning and innovative public policy. The city was built with an extensive system of bike paths and few parking spots. Parking spots for vehicles are available in a garage at the edge of the community for €17,500 (more than $20,000 per year). Vauban city planners also encouraged residents to use public transportation such as tramways and buses.

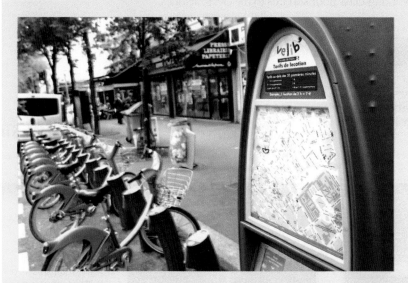

Many of the city's streets were designed to be too narrow for cars (de Pommereau 2006).

Car use is discouraged in many different ways throughout the world. In Germany, there is a yearly car tax based on the automobile engine size—the bigger the engine, the higher the tax. Several European cities maintain fleets of bikes for public use to encourage bike riding as a transportation alternative. European Union countries, such as France, Italy, and Germany, have closed off parts of their city centers to cars for a day or permanently. In 1983, Bogotá, Colombia, initiated a program called *ciclovía* (bike path). Designated streets are closed to cars every Sunday, encouraging residents to jog, walk, or ride their bikes on the streets and revitalizing their neighborhoods as a result. One and a half million people are said to turn out for the Sunday *ciclovía* (Wood 2007).

Car-free zones have also been embraced in several U.S. cities. New York, San Francisco, Kansas City, Atlanta, Philadelphia, Cleveland, Chicago, St. Louis, and El Paso have begun promoting car-free days in public parks, designated neighborhoods, and green spaces. Since 2010, the city of Los Angeles has sponsored CicLAvias, a car-free event spanning about 10 miles of city roads and streets. Advocates argue that these car-free practices promote family activities, active lifestyles, and closer communities (Wood 2007).

Photo 14.4

In 2007, the city of Paris introduced Vélib', a self-service bicycle transit system. From more than 700 locations throughout the city, individuals can rent bikes by the hour. There are 230 miles of cycling lanes in Paris.

What Does It Mean to Me?

Could you go car free? Why or why not? Explain your dependence (or lack of dependence) on an automobile.

Community, Policy, and Social Action

U.S. Department of Housing and Urban Development (HUD)

The federal agency responsible for addressing the nation's housing needs and improving and developing the nation's communities is HUD. Created in 1965 as part of President Lyndon Johnson's War on Poverty, HUD was given the authority to enforce fair housing laws and to administer a variety of federal programs to provide a decent, safe, and sanitary living environment for every American (HUD 2003b; Martinez 2000).

HUD's history extends back to the National Housing Act of 1934 and to the 1937 amendment that created the U.S. Housing Authority for low-rent housing. HUD's efforts to encourage homeownership are rooted in the Housing Act of 1949, a declaration that all Americans have the right to become homeowners. Despite its expressed goal of creating "well planned and integrated residential neighborhoods," the Housing Act did not improve housing conditions for nonminority households (Martinez 2000). The goals of the Housing Act of 1949 were reaffirmed in the Fair Housing Act of 1968, authorizing the Federal Housing Administration (FHA) to make sure that homeownership was affordable and accessible for every U.S. family, including minorities and the poor (Martinez 2000). HUD continues its housing mission, expanding services to elderly residents and overseeing health care facilities and lead hazard control.

In addition, HUD has been a major player in influencing land-use decisions in urban areas (Williams 2000), spurring economic growth and development in distressed communities (HUD 2003b). HUD's major urban initiatives have included the Housing and Urban Development Act of 1970, which established a national growth policy that emphasized new community and inner-city development; the Housing and Community Development Act of 1974, which established community development block grants; and the Omnibus Budget Reconciliation Act of 1993, which created the first enterprise zones to stimulate economic development in distressed areas. Enacted in 2000, the Community Renewal and New Markets Initiative reinforced HUD's focus on fostering economic opportunity, enhancing the quality of life, and building a stronger sense of community in impoverished inner-city neighborhoods (Williams 2000).

With oversight provided by HUD, the renewal communities, empowerment zones, and enterprise communities program took an innovative approach to revitalization that targets inner cities and rural areas. The program brought communities together through public and private partnerships to attract the social and economic investment necessary for sustainable economic and community development (HUD 2003c). Each program integrated four principles: a strategic vision for change, community-based partnerships, economic opportunity, and sustainable community development. The program began with the assumption that local communities can best identify and develop local solutions to the problems they face (HUD 2003c). The empowerment zones and renewal communities program ended in December 2011.

Voices in the Community

Magic Johnson

Magic Johnson Enterprises

Since his retirement from the Los Angeles Lakers, Earvin "Magic" Johnson has become a commercial developer opening state-of-the-art multiplex theaters including restaurants, retail, personal service, and Starbucks locations. Johnson's company, Magic Johnson Enterprises, specifically targets business opportunities in minority inner-city and suburban neighborhoods.

At the opening of a 12-screen multiplex, the Magic Johnson Theatres, in South Central Los Angeles, Johnson was confident that such a business would succeed in inner cities because African Americans make up about 13% of the moviegoing audience (Dretzka 1995). Johnson said,

> We're the No. 1 movie goers of any (minority) group but you can't find any theaters in your neighborhood. That's why our theaters are doing so much business. We have great numbers, and for everybody in the neighborhood, it means more to them than just a theater. It's a pride situation, bringing the community together. (quoted in Dretzka 1995:1)

The Magic Johnson Theatres cost an estimated $11 million and feature an art deco lobby with a large concession stand and a two-level parking garage. The Johnson Development Corporation has also opened theaters in Atlanta, Houston, Cleveland, and Harlem. The five theater complexes grossed $30 million in revenue in 2002 (Johnson 2003).

Johnson brought his understanding of the inner-city community to the business. In his movie concessions, knowing that inner-city children grew up drinking Kool-Aid, Johnson sells flavored sodas. "Used to be we couldn't afford to go to dinner and the movie afterward. I told Loew's [his theater partner], 'Black people are going to eat dinner at the movies,'" says Johnson (quoted in Wilborn 2002). As a result, in addition to hot dogs and popcorn, the concessions sell chicken wings and buffalo shrimp.

At his theaters, no gang colors or hanging out in large groups is allowed. Before each movie, a clip of Johnson is played, reminding his audiences: "So we got a few policies that apply to everyone. They are not meant to disrespect. They're there so we can all have a good time. So if you have a problem, leave it in the street" (Wilborn 2002).

Johnson has joined Howard Schultz, chief executive officer of Starbucks, in a franchise deal. Their partnership opened more than 100 stores. Their first location was in Ladera Center, a few miles away from the Los Angeles International Airport. The location is one of the biggest grossing in the Starbucks chain. Schultz explains that through the partnership, "We could create unique opportunities for the community—employment opportunities, opportunities for vendors—and also some hope and aspiration about a leading consumer brand doing business in underserved communities, and perhaps other companies would follow us in" (Johnson 2003:77).

Johnson's business philosophy is simple: "All of my businesses deal with people, customer service, and entertainment because that's what I'm good at. Everything flows together from that, and all the companies help each other" (quoted in Smith 1999:80).

In 2002, Johnson established a technology initiative program, currently operating in 11 states and the District of Columbia. Attempting to address the digital divide (refer to

Photo 14.5

Magic Johnson greets children at the Branch Brook School in Newark, New Jersey. Along with corporate sponsors Samsung and Microsoft, the Magic Johnson Foundation awarded the school $200,000 in software and technology products.

Chapter 11, "The Media") affecting poor and minority children, the program establishes Community Empowerment Centers providing youth and community members access to computer technology, training, and experience. As of 2011, the centers provided direct services to 250,000 students in 16 urban markets.

Urban Revitalization Demonstration Program: HOPE VI

The HOPE VI program was established by Congress in 1992. Originally called the Urban Revitalization Demonstration Program, from 1993 to 2006 HOPE VI spent nearly $6.2 billion to tear down public housing facilities and revitalize others into larger modern townhomes and detached homes with the goal of creating mixed-income communities in inner cities. Community and service programs are also established as part of the funding. In 2008, six housing authorities in four states (Illinois, Texas, Washington, and Wisconsin) were awarded a total of $97 million (HUD 2009).

The HOPE VI program was created based on recommendations from the National Commission on Severely Distressed Public Housing (HUD 2003a). The commission recommended revitalization in three areas: physical improvements, management improvements, and social and community services to address residents' needs. Program grants pay for demolition of distressed public housing and rehabilitation or new construction. The program has been criticized for worsening the local housing situation because not all demolished units are replaced and program data reveal that not all residents return to the redeveloped HOPE VI sites.

Although the program's primary focus is on the quality of housing units, HUD officials report that the HOPE VI program has made an impact on its residents through community and supportive programs for residents. When the program was honored in 2000 by the Institute for Government Innovation, HOPE VI officials reported that nearly 3,500 public housing residents left welfare and more than 6,500 residents found new jobs as a result of the program (Institute for Government Innovation 2000).

In 1995, the Seattle Housing Authority was one of the first public housing authorities to receive HOPE VI funding (Naparstek et al. 2000). With $48 million, the authority tore down and replaced Holly Park, one of the most distressed public housing projects in Seattle, Washington. Holly Park, with 893 units, has been replaced with NewHolly, a mixed-income community with 400 public housing units, 400 tax credit rental units for low-income households, and 400 affordable homeownership units. Of the original 893 residents, 393 moved into NewHolly. Most residents who did not return moved into other public housing or into Section 8 rental housing. The renovation of Holly Park also involved a collection of supportive service programs and educational initiatives called the Campus of Learners, each program promoting self-sufficiency. The Campus of Learners includes a career development center, the Atlantic Street Center, a branch campus of South Seattle Community College, child care resources, and an onsite public library, among other community partners. Through the program, "The housing authority moved to a new kind of partnership—a collaborative, community-resource, community building model" (Naparstek et al. 2000:16). The HOPE VI program continues, with funding provided to smaller communities to rejuvenate their older downtown business districts.

Creating Sustainable Communities

Sustainable Communities

Booming Africa

Sustainability

Tyler Norris (2001) chronicled the emergence and importance of the sustainable community movement. Since the early 1960s, thousands of public-private partnerships have been formed to work for economic development, educational improvement, environmental protection, health care, social issues, and other issues critical to communities. An array of private and public community groups form these partnerships. These alliances have been identified by several names and terms: *healthy communities, sustainable communities, livable communities, safe communities, whole communities,* and *smart growth.* Much of the improvement in public health, community revitalization, and quality of life can be attributed to these alliances. The best partnerships, according to Norris, bring together traditional leaders and community members often not included in the decision-making process. A summary of best practices from successful sustainable communities is presented in Table 14.6.

Examples of sustainable communities include the following:

- Highlander Research and Education Center, New Market, Tennessee. The center was established in 1932, working primarily on social change and education in the areas of labor, civil rights, and Appalachian issues. In the 2000s, the center defined its focus on four broad, interconnected issues—economic justice, racial justice, environmental justice, and democratic participation—that it believed were critical to making progress toward a more just and humane society. Current programs include an internship program, a children's camp, a capacity building–leadership program, and cultural programs. Each program serves as an invaluable resource to community groups in Appalachia and in the South.
- Greensburg GreenTown, Greensburg, Kansas. After an EF5 tornado leveled the town of Greensburg in 2007, residents, city officials, and businesses made a commitment to rebuild their city sustainably. GreenTown documents and coordinates the community's green building projects. The program offers green tours, allowing visitors to see examples of public, single-family residential, multifamily residential, and commercial construction. GreenTown also provides technical assistance to individuals, community groups, businesses, and local governments wishing to adopt similar green building strategies.

Table 14.6

Best Practices for Sustainable Communities

1. Define community broadly, using not only physical space but also community of interest (e.g., youth assets).
2. Make the community's vision reflect the core values of all its members.
3. Define health as the optimum state of well-being—physical, mental, emotional, and spiritual.
4. Address the quality of life as experienced by all residents.
5. Invite diverse participation and promote widespread community ownership.
6. Focus on system change to address how people live and work together.
7. Use local assets and resources to build capacity.
8. Measure and report your progress and outcomes to keep citizens informed and to keep partners accountable.

Source: Adapted from Norris 2001.

Housing and Homelessness Programs

The one community response to homelessness that most of us are familiar with is the homeless shelter. These shelters have been referred to as "Band-Aid" solutions, helping but not really fixing the problem. However, these emergency programs can provide immediate and necessary assistance and, in particular, security for families with children. If these shelters are to be truly effective, more humane and supportive shelter environments should be promoted to assist families and to better prepare them for independent living (Choi and Snyder 1999). For example, existing social and human services programs will be more effective if the homeless are able to obtain the benefits that they are already eligible for (Rossi 1989), such as social security, disability payments, and food stamps.

In 1987, Congress passed the Stewart B. McKinney Homeless Assistance Act, which established assistance programs for homeless individuals and families. Under this act, 20 programs were authorized to provide emergency food and shelter, transitional and permanent housing, education, mental health care, primary health care, and veterans' assistance services. In an effort to create more affordable housing, under Title II of the 1998 Cranston-Gonzalez National Affordable Housing Act, the HOME program provides grants to state and local governments to build, buy, or rehabilitate affordable housing for rent or homeownership. Working with community groups, the HOME program continues to serve low-income families.

Community efforts are important for the homeless and low-income families. The best-known community-based housing program is Habitat for Humanity International. Habitat serves primarily low- and very-low-income families with support from local volunteers, churches, and businesses, as well as from the sweat equity of future homeowners. Habitat families have incomes of about 30%–50% of the area's median income.

Project Homeless Connect

Project Homeless Connect began in San Francisco in 2004 when Mayor Gavin Newsom had the idea of bringing city hall staff and programs to the homeless community. The project, replicated in more than 260 U.S cities and in Canada and Australia, attempts to reach out to a city's homeless population by delivering an array of services—social, medical, mental health, housing—all under one roof at a local venue. Quality-of-life services are also offered for the day including haircuts, wheelchair repair, eyeglasses, and dental services. The project connects homeless men and women with program representatives and members of the community. It is staffed by more than 1,000 volunteers and is supported through donations from local businesses.

Although supportive services are necessary for the homeless, homelessness cannot be prevented or eliminated without enough housing for the poor. Homelessness cannot be prevented or eliminated without a livable wage, employment opportunities for inner-city residents, more efficient management of public housing projects, emergency rent assistance programs, and the expansion of low-income housing subsidies (Choi and Snyder 1999).

Main Points

- Although urban areas provide examples of economic and social progress, they also have many social problems, with opportunities and resources distributed unevenly. Urban sociology examines social, political, and economic structures and their impact within an urban setting.

- The first studies in urban sociology adopted a functionalist approach, comparing a city to a biological organism. The Chicago School developed two dominant traditions in urban study, one focusing on human ecology (the study of the relationship between individuals and their physical environment) and population dynamics and the second focusing on community studies and ethnographies.

- Demography, an essential part of urban studies, is the study of the size, composition, and distribution of human populations, as well as changes and trends in those areas. An additional demographic element is migration, the movement of individuals from one area to another.

- Urbanization, the process by which a population shifts from rural to urban locales, expanded in the latter half of the nineteenth century. Overurbanization, the process where an excess population is concentrated in an urban area that lacks the capacity to provide basic services and shelter, began during the late twentieth century in developing countries, for example those in Africa and Asia. After World War II, the United States experienced another significant population shift: suburbanization, or the outward expansion of central cities into suburban areas.

- Changes in fertility, mortality, and migration rates affect the population composition. Age distribution, or the distribution of individuals by age, is particularly important as it provides a community with some direction in its social and economic planning. Demographers have predicted the graying of the U.S. population and accompanying problems. Ethnic and age compositions will also affect community services and priorities.

- Functional solutions to urban social problems encourage reinforcing social bonds through existing institutions or instituting societal changes.

- Since the late 1960s, a new approach called the critical political-economy or socio-spatial perspective uses a conflict perspective to focus on how cities are formed on the basis of racial, gender, or class inequalities stemming from capitalism. In this view, social problems are natural to the system, arising from the unequal distribution of power among various groups.

- Feminist theorists have argued for the development of a comprehensive field of theory and research that acknowledges the role and experiences of women in urban environments.

- Urban communities continue to be segregated by income, race/ethnicity, or immigrant status. This contributes to isolation, not just physically but also through the meanings attached to different neighborhoods, a focus of the interactionist perspective. This social isolation leads us to believe that certain social problems are unique to someone else's neighborhood.

- Along with suburbanization came the decentralization of U.S. cities. Inner cities became repositories for low-income individuals and families.

- Substandard housing and crowding are major public health issues, particularly among urban dwellers. Housing quality has been associated with morbidity from infectious diseases, chronic illnesses, injuries, poor nutrition, and mental disorders. People of color and those with low income are disproportionately exposed to substandard housing.

- The increasing number of homeless people in the 1990s and 2000s was primarily attributable to the increased number of the poor, especially minority, single, female-headed households, and to the lack of affordable low-income housing units. Substance abuse, mental illness, domestic violence, poverty, and low-paying jobs also have contributed.

■ Another problem is gentrification, or the process of neighborhood change that results in the replacement of lower-income residents with higher-income ones, a process most often associated with the disproportionate pressure it puts on marginalized groups.

■ As urban areas spread out, they create urban sprawl, in which development across the landscape outpaces population growth. As sprawl increases, so do the number of miles traveled, the number of vehicles owned, traffic fatality rates, air pollution, and, eventually, the risk of poor health.

■ The federal agency responsible for addressing the nation's housing needs and improving and developing the nation's communities is HUD. With HUD oversight, renewal communities, empowerment zones, and enterprise communities have attempted to bring communities together through public and private partnerships to attract necessary social and economic investments.

■ Since the early 1960s, a sustainable community movement composed of thousands of public-private partnerships has worked for economic development, educational improvement, environmental protection, health care, social issues, and other issues critical to communities. Much of the improvements in public health, community revitalization, and quality of life can be attributed to these alliances.

On Your Own

Log on to the open-access Student Study Site at www.sagepub.com/leonguerrero4e for these additional learning tools:

■ Interactive quizzes
■ Video clips
■ NPR audio links
■ Handbook articles

■ E-flashcards
■ Journal articles
■ End-of-chapter web exercises
■ Additional web resources and current event

Internet and Community Exercises

1. Use U.S. Census (log on to *Study Site Chapter 14*) or local data to determine the population growth or decline for your community. What areas of your community are thriving? What areas are declining? Overall, how would you characterize the state of your community?

2. Investigate the Center for Neighborhood Technology and U.S. Conference of Mayors websites. These organizations attempt to address various urban living, quality-of-life, and urbanization issues. What solutions, policies, and programs are promoted by each? How does this affect your community? Log on to *Study Site Chapter 14*.

3. If you can't live without a car, perhaps you might consider sharing one. Car-sharing programs began in the 1980s in Switzerland and Germany, with Canadian and U.S. programs established in the 1990s and early 2000s. By 2011, there were 46 car-sharing programs in the United States and Canada. Zipcar, the largest national car-sharing service, provides access to a vehicle for a monthly user fee. Subscribers prepay for hours per month and are able to pick up and drop off a vehicle in a designated location. Zipcar also has a campus-based program. Investigate whether a car-sharing program exists serving your city, state, or campus.

What advantages and disadvantages can you identify with sharing a car?

4. Community interest developments are private subdivisions where residents own their homes and pay an annual or monthly home association fee. For their nominal or sometimes large fee, residents ensure that their "neighborhood" is strictly managed by a residential board backed by a series of covenants, codes, and restrictions dictating the color of one's home, how many cars can be parked in the driveway, or where fences or a garden shed can be built. These communities have also been referred to as "gated communities," reinforcing the notion that their residents are separating themselves physically and psychically from the general population in their city or town. Although the exact number of community interest developments is not known, industry estimates suggest that by 2000, some 48 million Americans were living under such agreements (Drew 1998). Determine if there are any community interest developments in your community. If available, interview a member or an officer of a development's board. What does the development's codes statement cover? How does the board member describe the quality of life in the development? Would you want to live in this development? Why or why not?

5. Log on the United Nations Human Development Report website and review data for the total population and the percentage (rate) of urban population. Identify the five countries with the highest rates and the five countries with the lowest rates for the most recent year. How would you characterize the five countries with the highest rates? What do these countries have in common? Log on to *Study Site Chapter 14* for more information.

6. What is the extent of homelessness in your community? Contact a housing agency or homeless shelter to determine the estimated number of homeless. How are the experiences of the homeless invisible to mainstream society? To students on your campus?

Study Questions

1. Define urbanization and suburbanization. What are some ways that urbanization and suburbanization contribute to social problems?

2. Explain the societal transition from mechanical to organic solidarity as identified by Émile Durkheim.

3. From an interactionist's perspective, how connected are you to your community? Do you define your community by what you value in it or what you use within it?

4. Access to affordable and/or quality housing is a problem facing urban and suburban dwellers. Identify the extent of each problem and identify solutions for each.

5. It is difficult to accurately measure the extent of the homeless problem in the United States. How does this disadvantage our understanding of homelessness? Of attempting to solve it?

6. How can sociology be used to encourage the expansion of car-free or pedestrian zones? Which sociological perspective(s) would best apply?

CHAPTER 15

The Environment

Mega. That's the word used to describe recent environmental disasters that have seriously threatened and damaged our physical and social worlds. A **megadisaster** is defined as a catastrophe that threatens or overwhelms an area's capacity to get people to safety, treat casualties, protect infrastructure, and control panic (Choi 2011). On April 2010, British Petroleum's Deepwater Horizon drilling platform exploded in the Gulf of Mexico. In addition to killing 11 workers and injuring 17 others, the explosion led to the release of an estimated 4.9 million barrels of oil until July 15, 2010, when the damaged wellhead was finally capped. Officials responded quickly to the disaster, addressing the threats to wildlife and to the fishing and tourism industries along the coasts of Alabama, Florida, Louisiana, Mississippi, and Texas. Years after the disaster, oil continues to wash up on shore.

In 2011, northeastern Japan was struck by a 9.0 earthquake. This megadisaster has been characterized as a natural catastrophe overlaid by a technical situation (Choi 2011). The earthquake was followed by a tsunami, damage to three nuclear reactors in Fukushima, and the displacement of hundreds of thousands of people. John Schwartz (2011) writes, "The sobering fact is that megadisasters like the Japanese earthquake can overcome the best efforts of our species to protect against them. No matter how high the levee or how flexible the foundation, disaster experts say, nature bats last" (p. 5).

Environmental Problems Are Human Problems

Pollution in Peru

Photo 15.1

This nickel refinery in Norilsk, Russia, releases 2.8 million metric tons of sulfur dioxide into the atmosphere, 6 times the emissions of the entire U.S. nonferrous metals industry. Norilsk has been named as one of the Blacksmith Institute's most polluted places in the world (refer to Table 15.1).

The field of **environmental sociology** considers the interactions between our physical and natural environment, on the one hand, and our social organization and behavior on the other (Dunlap and Catton 1994). Human beings are an integral part of the ecosystem (Irwin 2001). The state of the environment is also influenced by our cultural values and attitudes toward the environment, our social class, our technology, and our relationship with others (Cable and Cable 1995). When we use a sociological perspective to understand environmental problems, we acknowledge that "human activities are causing the deterioration in the quality of the environment and that environmental deterioration in turn has negative impacts on people" (Dunlap 1997:27).

Humans create environmental problems through intentional efforts to exploit or manage nature. Rivers that are dammed, straightened, or treated as sewers may create unintended downstream environmental problems (Caldwell 1997). The removal of rain forests to harvest wood or to create farmland decreases the number of plants and trees that absorb carbon dioxide, leading to higher amounts of greenhouse gases in the air. But environmental problems don't exist just because of our actions.

Our pursuit of economic development, growth, and jobs has also led to the degradation of the environment (Caldwell 1997). Azerbaijan, China, India, Peru, Russia, Ukraine, and Zambia are among the world's most polluted places. These countries (refer to Table 15.1) are

Table 15.1

Top 10 Most Polluted Places (Alphabetical by Country), 2007

Site Name and Location	Major Pollutants and Sources
Sumgayit, Azerbaijan	Organic chemicals and mercury, from petrochemical and industrial complexes
Linfen, China	Particulates and gases from industry and traffic
Tianying, China	Heavy metals and particulates from industry
Sukinda, India	Hexavalent chromium from chromium mines
Vapi, India	Wide variety of industry effluents from industrial estates
La Oroya, Peru	Lead and other heavy metals from mining and metal processing
Dzerzhinsk, Russia	Chemicals and toxic by-products, lead from chemical weapons and industrial manufacturing
Norilsk, Russia	Heavy metals, particulates from mining and smelting
Chernobyl, Ukraine	Radioactive materials from nuclear reactor explosion
Kabwe, Zambia	Lead from mining and smelting

Source: Blacksmith Institute 2007.

exposed to organic and industrial pollutants caused by mining, manufacturing, and transportation. Although much of this pollution can be attributed to the countries' substandard infrastructures or the absence of regulatory controls, even if both were brought up to industrial country standards, "the legacy of old contamination from the past would continue to poison the local population" (Blacksmith Institute 2007:3).

The Shanxi Province is at the center of China's coal mining industry. The country's industrial and urban growth has increased the demand for coal, one of the dirtiest sources of energy (Kahn and Yardley 2007). Coal provides China with two thirds of its energy supply. During recent years, Shanxi residents have witnessed the development of hundreds of unregulated coal mines, steel factories, and refineries. In Linfen, a Shanxi city referred to as the most polluted city in China, there has been an increase in the number of bronchitis, pneumonia, and lung cancer cases linked with air pollution. In addition, lead poisoning and arsenicosis (a disease caused by drinking water with high levels of arsenic) are found in higher levels among Linfen residents than among residents in other parts of China (Blacksmith Institute 2007).

But China's pollution problem is a world problem. Sulfur dioxide and nitrogen oxides from its coal-fired power plants turn into acid rain falling on Seoul, South Korea, and Tokyo, Japan (Casey 2007; Kahn and Yardley 2007). It takes 5 to 10 days for China's coal pollution to reach the United States. Scientists have identified China as the source of mercury (a by-product of coal mining) in fish living in Oregon's Willamette River (Casey 2007) and particulate pollution over Los Angeles, California (Kahn and Yardley 2007).

Environmentalist Paul Hawken (1997) refers to the Biosphere 2 experiment to demonstrate just how vital and fragile our ecosystem is. The Biosphere 2 was a 3-acre, glass-enclosed ecosystem intended to sustain eight people for a two-year experiment, from September 1991 through September 1993. The Biosphere 2's $200 million budget was not enough to create a viable ecosystem for eight people. By the time the experiment ended, the Biosphere's air and drinking water were polluted, crops and trees had been killed by other vegetation, and 19 of the 25 small animal species the participants brought with them had died. The scientists who lived in the biosphere showed signs of oxygen starvation from living at the equivalent of an altitude of 17,500 feet. Even with scientific knowledge and planning, there are no human-made substitutions for essential natural resources.[1] As Hawken (1997) explains,

> We have not come up with an economical way to manufacture watershed, gene pools, topsoil, wetlands, river systems, pollinators, or fisheries. Technological fixes can't solve problems with soil fertility or guarantee clean air, biological diversity, pure water, and climatic stability; nor can they increase the capacity of the environment to absorb 25 billion tons of waste created annually by America alone. (p. 41)

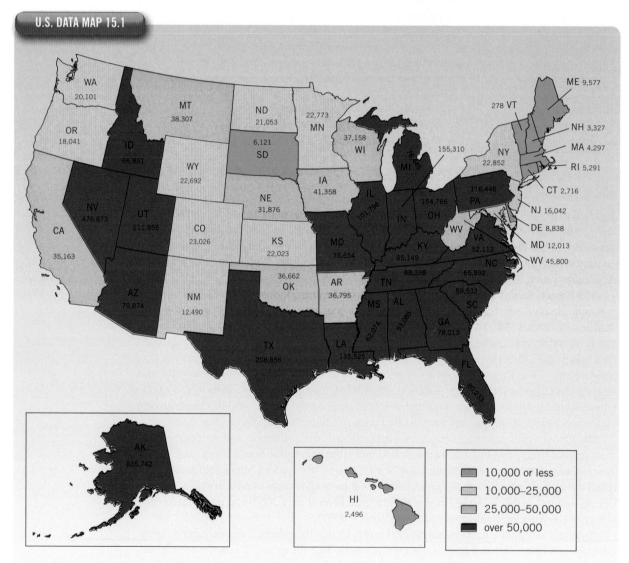

U.S. DATA MAP 15.1

Toxic Releases—On Site or Off Site Disposal or Other Releases, by State, 2010 (by Thousand Pounds)

Source: Environmental Protection Agency 2012a.

---

[1]After a second experiment from 1993 to 1994, no other human experiments were conducted. Columbia University took over the management of the Biosphere and was using the facility as a research and education center from 1995 to 2007. In 2007, the University of Arizona assumed the project.

What Does It Mean to Me?

Refer to U.S. State Map 15.1 for the total pollution released by state in 2010. Which state produces the highest level of pollution in the United States? Where does your state rank?

 STATE STATS

Sociological Perspectives on Environmental Problems

Functionalist Perspective

Whether they are looking at a social system or an ecosystem, functionalists examine the entire system and its components. Where are environmental problems likely to arise? Functionalists would answer that problems develop from the system itself. Agricultural and industrial modes of production are destabilizing forces in our ecosystem. Agriculture replaces complex natural systems with simpler artificial ones to sustain select highly productive crops. These crops require constant attention in the form of cultivation, fertilizers, and pesticides, all foreign elements to the natural environment (Ehrlich, Ehrlich, and Holdren 1973). When it first began, industrialization entered a society that had fewer people, less material well-being, and abundant natural resources. But modern industrialization uses "more resources to make few people more productive," and as a result, "more people are chasing fewer natural resources" (Hawken 1997:40). As much as agriculture, industrialization, and related technologies have improved the quality of our lives, we must deal with the negative consequences of waste, pollution, and the destruction of our natural resources. Human activities have become a dominant influence on the Earth's climate and ecosystems (Kanter 2007).

Biologists Paul Ehrlich and Anne Ehrlich (1990) contend that the impact of any human group on the environment is the product of three different factors. First is the population, second is the average person's consumption of resources or level of affluence, and third is the amount of damage caused by technology. They present a final formula: Environmental Damage = (People) × (Level of Affluence) × (Technological Damage). A high rate of population growth or consumption can lead to a "hasty application" of new technologies in an attempt to meet new and increasing demands. "The larger the absolute size of the population and its level of consumption, the larger the scale of the technology must be, and, hence, the more serious are the mistakes that are made" (Ehrlich et al. 1973:15). "What matters to the environment," writes Robert Engelman (2009), "are sums of human pulls and pushes, the extractions of resources and the injections of waste" (p. 24).

There is no simple way to stop the escalation of environmental problems. Halting population growth would be a good start but by itself could not solve the problem. The United Nations announced in 2011 that the world's population had reached 7 billion, with 10 billion predicted for 2100 (UN News Centre 2011). Reducing technology's impact on the environment might be useful, but not if our population and affluence were allowed to grow. According to Ehrlich et al. (1973), the only way to address environmental problems is to simultaneously attack all components.

Conflict Perspective

Public discourse on environmental problems is often framed in terms of costs and interests. Do you save the spotted owl habitat or hundreds of logging jobs? Should you close a factory or save the river where its waste is being dumped? From this sociological perspective, environmental problems are created by humans competing for power, income, and their own interests.

Our capitalist economic system has been identified as a primary source of the conflict over polluting (or conserving) our natural world. Competing political and economic interests ensure that this conflict will continue. J. Clarence Davies (1970) argues that the capitalist system encourages pollution, simply because air and water are treated as infinite and free resources. Polluters don't really consider who or what is being affected by environmental problems. If a paper mill is polluting the river, it doesn't affect the paper mill itself but, rather, affects the users of the water or the residents downstream. If a power plant is polluting the air, the plant doesn't pay for the cost of using the air, but pays only the cost of cleaning up a polluted area (Davies 1970).

Environmental problems occasionally make life unpleasant and inconvenient, but most Americans will tolerate this in exchange for the benefits and comforts associated with a developed industrial economy (Tobin 2000). A higher standard of living has been confused with consumption: More is better. As Henri Lefebvre ([1971] 2000) argues, the objective of a consumer capitalist society is to satisfy real or imagined material needs. Television and print media overwhelm us with products and services and tell us that we cannot live without them. Politicians encourage lower taxes so that we have more money to spend. But increased consumption requires increased production and energy, which in turn leads to environmental damage. As David Korten (1995) explains,

Photo 15.2

A woman stands atop a mountain of rubbish in a China landfill. China generates an estimated 150 million tons of rubbish per year, with as much as 400 million tons estimated by 2020.

About 70 percent of this productivity growth has been in . . . economic activity accounted for by the petroleum, petrochemical, and metal industries; chemical intensive agriculture; public utilities; road building; transportation; and mining . . . the industries that are most rapidly drawing down natural capital, generating the bulk of our toxic waste, and consuming a substantial portion of our renewable energy. (pp. 37–38)

What Does It Mean to Me?

Hawken (1993) contends that we should be able to put an economic value on our renewable (forests, fisheries) and nonrenewable (coal, oil) natural resources. He advocates for **natural capitalism**, the awareness of the value of nature as a system, no different than assessing the value of human or financial capital. We are able to attach a dollar amount to a tree once it is cut down for its timber, but what is its value as a living part of our ecosystem? What is the price tag on nature?

Polluters target those with the least amount of power. Robert Bullard (1994) defines **environmental racism** as "any environmental policy, practice or directive that differentially affects or disadvantages individuals, groups, or communities based on race or color" (p. 98). Research consistently indicates that low-income people and people of color are exposed to greater environmental risks than are those who live in White or affluent communities. Evidence also indicates that low-income people and people of color suffer higher levels of environmentally generated diseases and death as a result of their elevated risk (Ringquist 2000). Environmental racism has been expanded to include members of other disadvantaged communities, examining heightened environmental risk based on race, class, gender, education, and political power.

Environmental Sociology

What Does It Mean to Me?

Major U.S. corporations have joined the environmental movement. Walmart, for example, has implemented a no-package waste program, sells seafood from certified sustainable fisheries, and is transitioning its trucking fleet to vehicles that run on biofuels generated from the waste grease that is collected from stores' delis. According to Jared Diamond (2009), while Walmart and other corporations are motivated by money and efficiency, they are also interested in creating an earth-friendly, public-pleasing image. Should we be skeptical about these corporations' earth-friendly initiatives? Does this change the way you think about them?

Feminist Perspective

The feminist perspective argues that a masculine worldview is responsible for the domination of nature, the domination of women, and the domination of minorities (Scarce 1990). Ecofeminism may be the dominant feminist perspective for explaining the relationship between humans and the environment (Littig 2001). Ecofeminism was introduced in 1974 in an effort to bring attention to the power of women to bring about an ecological revolution. Ecofeminists argue that "men driven by rationalism, domination, competitiveness, individualism, and a need to control, are most often the culprits in the exploitation of animals and the environment" (Scarce 1990:40). According to ecofeminists, "Respect for nature generally

Environmental Justice

promotes human welfare, and genuine respect for all human beings tends to protect nature" (Wenz 2001:190). Other feminist approaches include the feminist critique of natural science, feminist analyses of specific environmental issues (work, garbage, consumption), and feminist contributions to sustainable development (Littig 2001).

Cynthia Hamilton (1994) argues that environmental conflicts mirror social injustice struggles in other areas—for women, for people of color, for the poor. In environmental movements, Hamilton explains, what motivates activist women is the need to protect home and children. As the home is defined as the woman's domain, her position places her closest to the dangers of hazardous waste, providing her with an opportunity to monitor illnesses and possible environmental causes within her family and among her neighbors. As Hamilton sees it, these women are responding not to "'nature' in the abstract but to their homes and the health of their children" (p. 210).

The modern **environmental justice** movement emerged out of citizen protests at Love Canal, near Niagara Falls, New York (Newman 2001). The movement is based on the principle that "all peoples and communities are entitled to equal protection of environmental and public health laws and regulations" (Bullard 1994). For many years, the movement has effectively brought racial and economic discrimination in waste disposal, polluting industries, access to services, and the impacts of transportation and city planning to the public's attention (Morland and Wing 2007).

At the center of Love Canal's citizens' protest movement was a group of local women who called themselves "housewives turned activists." Lois Gibbs and Debbie Cerillo formed the Love Canal Homeowners Association in 1978. Concerned about the number of miscarriages, birth defects, illnesses, and rare forms of cancer among their families and neighbors, the women worked with Beverly Paigen, a research scientist, to document the health problems in their community (Breton 1998). The information they collected became known as "housewife data" (Newman 2001). The women held demonstrations, wrote press releases, distributed petitions, and provided testimony before state and federal officials (Newman 2001). In 1978, Love Canal was declared a disaster area, some 800 residents were evacuated and relocated, and the site was cleaned up. Gibbs went on to form the Center for Health, Environment, and Justice and continues to work on behalf of communities fighting toxic waste problems. More information about Love Canal is presented in the section titled "Hazardous Waste Sites and Brownfields."

Interactionist Perspective

Climate and Politics

Theorists working within the interactionist perspective address how environmental problems are created and defined. Riley Dunlap and William Catton (1994) explain: "Environmental sociologists have a long tradition of highlighting the development of societal recognition and definition of environmental conditions as 'problems'" (p. 20). Environmental problems do not materialize by themselves (Irwin 2001). As John Hannigan (1995:55) describes, the successful construction of an environmental problem requires six factors: the scientific authority for and validation of claims; the existence of "popularisers" (activists, scientists) who can frame and package the "problem" to journalists, political leaders, and other opinion makers; media attention that frames the problem as novel and important (such as the problems of rain forest destruction or ozone depletion); the dramatization of the problem in symbolic or visual terms; visible economic incentives for taking positive action; and the emergence of an institutional sponsor who can ensure legitimacy and continuity of the problem.

The Natural World

Social constructionists do not deny that real environmental problems exist. Rather their interest is in "the process through which environmental claims-makers influence those who hold the reins of power to recognize definitions of environmental problems, to implement them and to accept responsibility for their solution" (Hannigan 1995:185). This perspective helps us understand how environmental concerns vary over time and how some problems are given higher priority than others. For a summary of sociological perspectives on the environment, see Table 15.2.

Table 15.2

Summary of Sociological Perspectives: The Environment

	Functional	Conflict/Feminist	Interactionist
Explanation of environmental problems	Environmental problems are dysfunctions of modern living, the result of agricultural and industrial modes of production.	Problems are created by humans competing for power, income, and their own interests. Our capitalist economic system has been identified as a primary source of the conflict over polluting (or conserving) our physical and natural worlds. According to the feminist perspective, a masculine worldview is responsible for the domination of nature, the domination of women, and the domination of other minorities.	Theorists from this perspective address how environmental problems are created and defined.
Questions asked about the environment and environmental problems	How are environmental problems related to our modes of production or to our patterns of consumption? Are environmental problems inevitable consequences of modern living?	How do environmental problems emerge from our capitalist economic system or from a patriarchal society? Which particular groups are at risk for experiencing environmental problems or their impacts?	How are environmental problems created? What factors are included in the process? How is a problem legitimized? What individuals or groups play a role in the process?

What Does It Mean to Me?

Which sociological perspective best explains the 2010 BP *Deepwater Horizon* disaster? In what has been called the biggest environmental disaster in the United States, an estimated 35,000 to 65,000 barrels of oil were spilled per day, surpassing the 1989 *Exxon Valdez* oil spill. How is this disaster or any other environmental disaster a social problem?

 STATE STATS

Social Problems and the Environment

Climate Change

To sustain life on Earth, a certain amount of surface heat is required. Heat becomes trapped through the buildup of greenhouse gases—water vapor, carbon dioxide, and other gases—making the Earth's average temperature a comfortable and sustainable 60 degrees Fahrenheit

(Environmental Protection Agency [EPA] 2003b). Also referred to as global warming, **climate change** refers, literally, to the warming of the Earth's surface. It refers to perceptible climate trends on a time scale of decades or more rather than weather conditions or atmospheric events in a specific area at a particular time. The Earth's surface temperature has risen by about 1.4 degrees Fahrenheit over the past century (EPA 2012b). The problem is the accumulation of specific greenhouse gases—carbon dioxide, methane, and nitrous oxide—primarily attributable to human activity during the past 50 years (EPA 2012b). The decade 2000–2009 was the warmest on record for the globe. The global combined land and ocean surface temperature was 0.96 degrees Fahrenheit above the twentieth-century average (56.9 degrees Fahrenheit, for the period 1901–2000). In comparison, for the 1990s decade, the combined land and ocean surface temperature was 0.65 degrees Fahrenheit above the twentieth-century average (National Oceanic and Atmospheric Administration [NOAA] 2010). The Intergovernmental Panel on Climate Change (IPCC) projects that climate change should increase by 2.2 to 11.5 degrees Fahrenheit over the next 100 years (EPA 2012b).

Since the **Industrial Revolution**, concentrations of carbon dioxide have increased nearly 30%, methane concentrations have increased by 145%, and nitrous oxide concentrations have increased 15% (Ehrlich and Ehrlich 1996). Fossil fuels used to run cars and trucks, heat homes and businesses, and power factories are responsible for about 98% of carbon dioxide emissions, 24% of methane emissions, and 18% of nitrous oxide emissions. Agriculture, deforestation, landfills, and mining also add to the amount of emissions. China and the United States have the highest fossil fuel carbon dioxide emissions worldwide (a list of the top 10 countries is provided in Table 15.3).

Although they are unable to predict specifically what will happen, where it will happen, and when it will happen, scientists have identified how our health, agriculture, resources, forests, and wildlife are vulnerable to the changes brought about by climate change. Soil moisture may decline in many regions; rainstorms may become more frequent. Changing regional climates could alter forests, crop yields, and water supplies. Sea levels could rise 2 feet along

Photo 15.3

Climate change is causing glaciers to melt or recede throughout the world. This photo offers an aerial view of a receding glacier in Los Glaciares National Park, Argentina. The loss of glaciers affects human populations and ecosystems.

Table 15.3

Total Fossil Fuel Carbon Dioxide Emissions, Per Capita Emissions in Metric Tons of Carbon, 2010

China	2,247,534
United States	1,497,865
India	564,473
Russian Federation	460,551
Japan	310,481
Germany	207,966
Iran	156,730
South Korea	153,579
Canada	141,402
Saudi Arabia	134,652

Source: Carbon Dioxide Information Analysis Center 2010.

most of the U.S. coast. In its 2007 report, IPCC (Kanter and Revkin 2007) predicted that the most severe effects would be felt in poor countries and areas facing existing dangers from climate and coastal hazards. Poor households are especially vulnerable to climate change because they lack resources or services to protect themselves and their communities against the threats from changing conditions or crises. Human activity was also identified as the main cause of warming since 1950 (Kanter and Revkin 2007).

The hottest year ever recorded in U.S. history was 2012. The country experienced the worst drought in nearly a half-century, affecting 88% of the corn crop, a key ingredient in processed foods and animal feed. The shortage in corn, soybeans, and other crops was expected to lead to increased food prices (Lowrey and Nixon 2012). Extreme weather minimums and maximums also threatened parts of the country's infrastructure. During the 2012 drought, the excessive heat and dryness caused sections of U.S. roads and highways to crack or pop up, overheated subway rails, and stressed local and regional power grids (Wald and Schwartz 2012).

Though the science confirming climate change has been attacked and questioned, most Americans believe that climate change is a real problem and that human activity is a contributing factor. A 2007 national poll revealed that, asked to choose between stimulating the economy and protecting the environment, 52% of Americans chose protecting the environment. There was strong agreement to several strategies to reduce climate change—more than 90% of those surveyed favored requiring car manufacturers to produce more energy-efficient cars, and 75% were willing to pay more for electricity generated by renewable energy resources such as wind or solar power. Americans indicated that the United States should be a global leader in addressing environmental problems and in the development of alternative energy resources (Broder and Connelly 2007). A 2012 poll revealed that rather than thinking that global warming was a problem in other countries or for other populations (like polar bears), about 69% of those surveyed believed that global warming was affecting the U.S. weather (Gillis 2012).

During his presidency, George W. Bush downplayed the problem of climate change, referring to the lack of scientific evidence confirming its causes and consequences. In March 2001, President Bush announced that the United States would not support the Kyoto Protocol, which was drawn up in 1997 to implement the United Nations Framework Convention on Climate Change. The treaty limits the emissions of greenhouse gases by an average of 5.2% below 1990 levels. According to Bush, the Kyoto regulations would have become too burdensome for U.S. industry at a time when businesses were struggling with a slowing economy. In addition, the president noted that leading world polluters, India and China, were exempted from the treaty.

In his second term, Bush began to reverse his position. In 2005, he agreed for the first time that human action was responsible for climate change, and in 2007, the president called for a long-term plan for cutting greenhouse gas emissions in the United States and throughout the world. Acknowledging how science has "deepened our understanding of climate change," the president called for other countries to set national targets to reduce greenhouse gas emissions in 10 and 20 years (Stolberg 2007).

Shortly after taking office, President Barack Obama observed that climate change, if left unchecked, would result in an irreversible catastrophe. While the United States has not yet ratified the Kyoto treaty, during the United Nations Climate Change Conference in 2009, the United States joined an international agreement to curtail greenhouse gas emissions. The nonbinding agreement, dubbed the Copenhagen Accord, brought together industrial and developing nations, such as the United States, China, India, Brazil, and South Africa. The accord calls for limiting the rise in global temperatures to no more than 3.6 degrees Fahrenheit and for economic support for emerging countries to develop low-carbon energy systems, to adapt to climate change, and to protect tropical forests (Broder 2010). The nations' leaders acknowledged that climate change is "one of the greatest challenges of our time. . . . We recognize the critical impacts of climate change and the potential impacts of response measures on countries particularly vulnerable to its adverse effects and stress the need to establish a comprehensive adaptation programme including international support" (United Nations 2009). In 2010, the Obama administration announced the formation of a National Climate Service agency to work with the NOAA's National Weather Service and National Ocean Service. Funding for the new agency was blocked by congressional lawmakers in 2011.

Air Quality

The quality of the air we breathe is subject to pollution from two sources: particulate matter and smog. Research has linked air pollution to acute and chronic illnesses (e.g., burning eyes and nose, asthma), as well as death. Air pollution also leads to environmental and property damage.

Particulate or particle pollution is caused by the combustion of fossil fuels—the burning of coal, diesel, gasoline, and wood. Particulate matter includes road dust, diesel soot, ash, wood smoke, and sulfate aerosols that are suspended in the air (Natural Resources Defense Council [NRDC] 1996). The EPA is concerned about small particulate matter, 10 micrometers in diameter or smaller, because these smaller particles are able to pass through the throat and nose and enter the lungs, causing respiratory problems (EPA 2007a).

Environmental Changes

Particulate pollution caused by traffic and diesel engines is a growing problem in many European Union cities. The World Health Organization (WHO) set the acceptable air quality standard at 10 micrograms of particles per cubic meter. However, nowhere in Europe is this standard being met—at the lower end of the spectrum are Paris and London (16 micrograms per cubic meter), and at the highest are cities such as Warsaw (34), Turin (41), and Milan (38) (Rosenthal 2007). The standard in the United States is 15 micrograms per cubic meter.

Smog or ground-level ozone has been referred to as a public health crisis, affecting people in nearly every U.S. state (Clean Air Network 2003). Smog is formed when nitrogen oxides emitted from electric power plants and automobiles react with organic compounds in the presence of sunlight and heat. Our reliance on automobiles has been blamed for much of the increase in smog levels.

The EPA monitors smog levels throughout the nation. The EPA sets federal eight-hour smog standards and collects data on the number of days that exceed the standard. A day is considered unhealthy if smog levels exceed the eight-hour standard. The EPA reported that 2002 was the worst recorded smog season; the eight-hour health standard was exceeded 8,818 times nationwide. The states with the highest number of unhealthy ozone days were California, Texas, and Tennessee (Clean Air Network 2003). In 2008, the EPA revised national air quality standards, the first time standards have been tightened since 1997. Nationally, ground-level ozone concentrations in 2008 were among the lowest since 2002 (EPA 2010).

Scientists report that one of every three people in the United States is at a higher risk of experiencing ozone-related health effects. Those most vulnerable to the health effects of smoggy air are children, people who work or exercise regularly outdoors, the elderly, and people with respiratory diseases. Short-term effects of smog mostly attack the lungs and lung functioning: irritating the lungs, reducing lung function, aggravating asthma, and inflaming and damaging the lining of the lungs (EPA 1999).

During the past two decades, the prevalence of asthma has increased globally, suggesting growing problems associated with indoor and outdoor air quality. Among children, who tend to be outdoors more than adults, asthma is the most common chronic disorder worldwide (WHO 2006), the leading cause of missing school, and the leading cause of hospitalization (Eisele 2003). In the same way that the ozone damages human health, it affects the health of other animals and vegetation and damages buildings (Palmer 1997).

Hazardous Waste Sites and Brownfields

The story of Love Canal awakened the world to chemical dumping hazards (Breton 1998). During the 1940s and 1950s, the Hooker Electrochemical Company dumped 20,000 tons of chemicals into the Love Canal in Niagara Falls, New York (Center for Health, Environment, and Justice 2001). In 1953, after filling the canal and covering it with dirt, the company sold the land to the Board of Education for a dollar. Homes and an elementary school were built next to the canal. By the late 1970s, dioxin and benzene chemicals began seeping through backyards and basements. Because of the efforts of the Love Canal Homeowners Association, state and federal agencies responded by cleaning the area and relocating many residents. In 1995, the Occidental Chemical Corporation (which bought out the Hooker Electrochemical Company) agreed to pay the government $129 million to cover the costs of the incident.

As a result of the Love Canal incident, the EPA created the Superfund program to clean hazardous waste sites. Hazardous materials may come from chemical manufacturers, electroplating companies, petroleum refineries, and common businesses such as dry cleaners, auto repair shops, hospitals, and photo processing centers (EPA 2003a). Sites may be placed on the national priority list (NPL) by their state if they meet specific hazard and cleanup criteria. To date, 1,723 NPL sites have been identified; of these, 360 sites have been removed from the list after cleanup efforts were completed (EPA 2012c).

Toxic sites continue to be identified today. The Childproofing Our Communities Campaign is a collaboration of groups concerned about children's environmental health. The campaign focuses on where children spend most of their time: in school. In its 2001 report, the campaign identified more than 1,100 public schools within a half-mile radius of known contaminated sites in California, Massachusetts, Michigan, New Jersey, and New York. The campaign estimates that more than 600,000 students attend classes in

 Brownfields

schools near contaminated land (Center for Health, Environment, and Justice 2001). In a state-by-state survey of laws and regulations regarding the siting of new school construction, the campaign found that only five states restrict siting schools on or near hazardous or toxic waste sites and nine additional states prohibit siting of schools on or near sources of pollution or other hazards (Center for Health, Environment, and Justice 2005).

In 2002, President Bush signed the Brownfields Revitalization Act, which authorized up to $250 million annually for the cleanup of brownfields. **Brownfields** are abandoned or underused industrial or commercial properties where expansion or redevelopment is complicated by the presence or potential presence of hazardous substances, pollutants, or contaminants. There are more than 450,000 sites throughout the United States. Redevelopment efforts have included restoring waterfront parks and converting landfills to golf courses, as well as commercial and business expansion (EPA 2003a).

Water Quality

With the passage of the Water Pollution Control Act or the Clean Water Act in 1972, the federal government declared its commitment to cleaning the nation's waterways, which had become badly polluted from industrial contaminants and untreated sewage (Ehrlich and Ehrlich 1996). Since the passage of the act, the overall quality of water in U.S. lakes and streams has improved or at least has not significantly deteriorated. Yet, a variety of harmful substances, including chemical compounds unknown in nature, have found their way into bodies of water. A recent study conducted by the Pew Oceans Commission revealed a "crisis" in U.S. waters caused by pollution and fishing practices (Weiss 2003). The commission expressed concern about runoff from agricultural fields, lawns, and roads. Oil from gas stations and nutrients from agricultural fields disrupt the balance of river and ocean ecosystems. A "dead zone" in the Gulf of Mexico near the mouth of the Mississippi River has been attributed to contaminated runoff (Revkin 2003).

Toxic substances are turning up with greater frequency in groundwater, the source of drinking water for one of every two Americans (Ehrlich and Ehrlich 1996). The EPA (2009a) reports, "While tap water that meets federal and state standards generally is safe to drink, threats to water quality and quantity are increasing." Groundwater contaminant problems are being reported throughout the country (Kraft and Vig 2000). Our drinking water is monitored in more than 55,000 community water systems for more than 80 known contaminants, including arsenic, nitrates, human and animal fecal waste, or legionella (the cause of Legionnaire's Disease). Nearly 1,000 deaths per year and at least 400,000 cases of waterborne illness may be attributed to contaminated water (Kraft and Vig 2000).

Photo 15.4

Cars travel on a Beijing highway under smog-covered skies. City officials reduced carbon monoxide levels by 47% and sulfur dioxide levels by 38% in time for the 2008 Summer Olympic Games (Tran 2009). The government pledged to continue to pursue energy efficiency and clean technology.

Toxic Water

Taking a World View

Home Sweet Landfill

China and the United States produce more waste than any other countries in the world. Traditional waste disposal includes incineration and landfills. Most U.S. waste, about 222 million tons per year, is sent to landfills. Each American creates 4.6 pounds of trash per day (Kaufman 2009). Landfills have been identified as one of the largest emitters of greenhouse gases, primarily methane (an odorless, colorless gas caused by the decomposition of animal and plant matter).

Yet, in many countries, many individuals and families call landfills their homes. In Mexico, landfill residents are called *pepenadores*. To make money, they scavenge through garbage piles, finding items (appliances, metals, or clothing) that can be reused or sold. Meals are harvested from discarded waste, and they build their homes using scrap material. Matthew Power (2006) explains: "Household and industrial trash has become for the world's poor a more viable source of sustenance than agriculture and husbandry" (p. 62).

In his article "The Magic Mountain," Power (2006) focuses on life on Payatas, a 50-acre landfill in Quezon City, the Philippines. Here the scavengers are called *mangangalahigs,* which translated means "chicken scratchers," describing the way they pick through piles of trash. Payatas has been called the "second Smoky Mountain." The first Smoky Mountain was a landfill site in Manila that supported about 30,000 men, women, and children who lived on the landfill. In 1995, the Philippine government closed the site, moving residents to temporary housing. However, over time, some Smoky Mountain residents moved to Payatas and resumed their lives as mangangalahigs.

Power (2006) claims that so much garbage is piled at the Payatas dump that it would take 3,000 trucks a day for 11 years to move it all to another landfill. He writes,

> As trucks dump each new load with a shriek of gears and a sickening glorp of wet garbage, the scavengers surge forward, tearing open plastic bags, spearing cans and plastic bottles with choreographed efficiency. . . . The ability to discern value at a glimpse, to sift the useful out of the rejected with as little expenditure of energy as possible, is the great talent of the scavenger. (p. 62)

Scavengers can make as much as 150 pesos a day, about $3 for their work on the dump.

Scientists have collected global evidence identifying the unhealthy consequences of landfills on human health. Increased risk in adverse health effects (e.g., low birth weight, respiratory illnesses, birth defects, and certain types of cancers) have been found near individual landfill sites and in several multisite and multicountry studies (Vrijheid 2000).

A zero waste movement is growing in the United States. Consumers and businesses are encouraged not to use polystyrene foam containers or any packaging that is not biodegradable. Several cities have initiated yard waste composting collection and expanded their collection of recyclable household items beyond the traditional paper, glass, and aluminum to include tires, batteries, and household appliances (Kaufman 2009).

What Does It Mean to Me?

Where does your drinking water come from? Is there a concern about limits to the water supply? Contact your local water company or public works department for information.

 STATE STATS

Frank and Earnestene Roberson from DeBerry, Texas, first complained about their water quality in 1996. Mrs. Roberson attributed her discolored bathtub and stomach problems to using the water from her well (Blumenthal 2006). According to the EPA (2007b), in 2003,

Texas officials determined that DeBerry's groundwater was contaminated with arsenic, benzene, lead, and mercury. Residents in this historically Black enclave were informed that they could not use their groundwater and began to rely on bottled water for drinking, cooking, and bathing. In 2005, the EPA began delivering bottled water to residents. The EPA determined that groundwater contamination was caused by oil and gas waste deposited by an oil-field services company. In 2007, cleanup of the area and construction of a new water line began (EPA 2007b).

According to the Organisation for Economic Co-operation and Development (OECD), approximately 880 million people do not have access to a decent source of drinking water and 2.5 billion do not have access to proper sanitation (EurActiv.com 2009). In 2009, representatives from 100 countries at the World Water Forum recognized water as a basic human need. Other countries and organizations, including the WHO, have recognized water as a basic human right.

Our Water Supply

Only 1% of the world's water can be used for drinking. Nearly 97% of the water is salty or undrinkable; the other 2% is in ice caps and glaciers (EPA 2003b). Freshwater comes from surface water sources (lakes, rivers, and streams) and groundwater sources (wells and underground aquifers). About 66% of people get their drinking water from surface water sources. Large metropolitan areas rely on surface water whereas small communities and rural areas depend on groundwater sources. In recent years, there has been growing concern about the availability of freshwater sources. Because of pollution, increasing urbanization, and sprawling development, we may be running out of freshwater.

Almost 30 million residents in seven western states (Colorado, Utah, Wyoming, New Mexico, Nevada, Arizona, and California) rely on the Colorado River for their drinking water. The river basin covers 240,000 square miles in the United States and a portion of northwestern Mexico. So much of the river is diverted for drinking and agricultural use that by the time it reaches the Sea of Cortez, it isn't much more than a trickle. A 2007 report by the National Academies on the Colorado River concluded that the combination of limited water supplies, increasing population demands, warmer temperatures, and the prospect of future droughts is likely to cause conflict among existing and future water users. The report predicted that this would "inevitably lead to increasingly costly, controversial, and unavoidable trade-offs among water managers, policy makers, and their constituents" (National Academies 2007).

Humans have attempted to harness water and its power through the construction of dams. About 75,000 dams in the United States provide water for irrigation, drinking, water control, and hydroelectricity. Once lauded as engineering miracles, dams have been blamed for serious environmental impacts affecting surrounding forests, watersheds, beaches, habitats, and lives. Former Secretary of Interior Bruce Babbitt (1998) explains,

> The public is now learning that we have paid a steadily accumulating price for these projects in the form of: fish spawning runs destroyed, downstream rivers altered by changes in temperature, unnatural nutrient load and seasonal flows, wedges of sediment piling up behind structures, and delta wetlands degraded by lack of fresh water and saltwater intrusion. Rivers are always on the move and their inhabitants know no boundaries; salmon and shad do not read maps, only streams.

More than 400 dams have been decommissioned nationwide (American Rivers 2002).

Drought and development exacerbate the pressure on water supply. An intense battle continues to be waged over Oregon's Klamath River. As described by Bruce Barcott (2003), the Klamath was born "a cripple." The river begins in Klamath Falls, Oregon, at the southern outlet of Klamath Lake, in "a body of water so shallow that a tall man could nearly cross it without wetting his hat" (Barcott 2003:46). First, water is diverted to irrigate more than 1,400 farms and ranches. Later, some of the water drains back into local lakes and refuges and is eventually pumped back into the Klamath River itself. The area used to be the picture of growth and prosperity, flourishing with housing development, farming, ranching, and expanding recreational activities.

But in recent years, as the area has suffered severe droughts and with the Klamath water supply dwindling, contentious battle lines have been drawn between the farmers, ranchers, fishermen, native tribes, recreational outfitters, and environmental groups over the benefits of removing the river's dams. Add to the list PacifiCorp, a regional power company. PacifiCorp owns four hydroelectric dams on the Klamath that provide power to about 70,000 homes in Oregon and California (Yardley 2007). Citing the need to preserve the river, in 2010 a historical agreement was signed by Oregon and California government officials, the chief executive of PacifiCorp, and three Native American tribes, planning the removal of four hydroelectric dams on the Klamath River. The first dam is scheduled for removal in 2020.

Land Conservation and Wilderness Protection

Efforts in land conservation and wilderness protection seem to be successful largely because of federal protection policies. Since adopting the 1964 Wilderness Act, Congress has designated more than 106 million acres as "wilderness areas" through the National Wilderness Preservation System (2004). Under the act, timber cutting, mechanized vehicles, mining, and grazing activities are restricted. Human activity is limited to primitive recreation activities. The wilderness lands are protected for their ecological, historical, scientific, and experiential resources. The areas range in size from the smallest, Pelican Island, Florida (5 acres), to the largest, Wrangell–St. Elias, Alaska (almost 10 million acres of land).

Energy Conservation

The Endangered Species Act of 1973 attempts to preserve species of fish, wildlife, and plants that are of "aesthetic, ecological, educational, historical, recreational and scientific value to the Nation and its people." The act has been controversial because it preserves the interests of the species above economic and human interests. For example, if endangered species are present, the act will restrict what landowners can do on their land (Palmer 1997). Currently, 2,000 U.S. and foreign animal and plant species have been listed as endangered or threatened, with recovery plans approved or implemented for 1,138 species (U.S. Fish and Wildlife Service 2012). Although federal funding for the Endangered Species Act expired in October 1992, Congress has appropriated funds in each fiscal year to support the program.

The National Park System includes 397 national parks covering more than 84 million acres. Unlike the National Wilderness Preservation System, the National Park System allows and supports recreational activities. However, human activity in the form of motorized access, road and highway developments, logging, and pollution threatens the health of several national parks. The Great Smoky Mountains National Park is the most visited national park, with about 10 million visitors each year (National Parks Conservation Association 2003). The park features an ecosystem of rare plants and wildlife along with historical structures representing southern Appalachian culture, all of which are endangered according to the National Parks Conservation Association. The park has been listed as "endangered" for several years primarily because of chronic air pollution problems. The pollution has been attributed to coal-fired power plants and other industrial sources. Local developers are allowed to build right up to the park's boundaries.

Community, Policy, and Social Action

Federal Responses

The government's first response to the environment was directed at cleaning the nation's polluted water, air, and land. In 1969, Congress adopted the National Environmental Policy Act (NEPA), a comprehensive policy statement on our environment. For the first time in our nation's history, the government was committed to maintaining and preserving the environment (Caldwell 1970). The EPA, established in 1970, is charged with providing leadership in the nation's environmental science, research, education, and assessment efforts (EPA 2004). As the chief environmental agency, the EPA sets national standards and delegates to states and tribes the responsibility for issuing permits and monitoring and enforcing compliance. Beginning in the 1980s, the agency shifted its policies from cleanup to pollution management or prevention through market-based and collaborative mechanisms with business and industry and environmental strategic planning (Mazmanian and Kraft 1999). Additional environmental legislation, some of which we have already reviewed, includes the following:

- The Land and Water Conservation Fund Act and the Wilderness Act of 1964. In our discussion on land conservation, we already reviewed the Wilderness Act. The Land and Water Conservation Fund Act provides the necessary funds and assistance to states in planning, acquiring, and developing recreational lands and natural areas. The act also regulates admission and special user fees at national recreational areas. These two acts have been referred to as the "initial building blocks of environmental action" (Caulfield 1989:31).
- The Clean Air Act of 1970 regulates air emissions from area, stationary, and mobile sources. The act helped establish maximum pollutant standards. In 1990, the Clean Air Act was amended to address acid rain, ground-level ozone, ozone depletion, and air toxins. In 2003, seven state attorneys general filed a lawsuit against the EPA, accusing the agency of neglecting to update air pollution standards. The suit seeks regulations on carbon dioxide emissions, which are not listed under the Clean Air Act (Lee 2003). In 2007, the U.S. Supreme Court found in favor of the seven states, ruling that greenhouse gases are air pollutants covered by the Clean Air Act (EPA 2009b).
- The Clean Water Act followed in 1972. This act established standards and regulations regarding the discharge of pollutants into the waters of the United States. The EPA was authorized to implement pollution control programs, setting wastewater standards and water-quality standards for all contaminants in surface waters.
- The Endangered Species Act of 1973 created a program for the conservation of threatened and endangered plants and animals and their habitats.
- Under the Toxic Substances Control Act of 1976, the EPA has the authority to track 75,000 industrial chemicals being produced or imported into the United States.
- The Food Quality Protection Act of 1996 modified earlier statutes and created a single, health-based standard for all pesticides in foods.

In its strategic plan for 2009–2014, the EPA identified five long-term goals: achieve clean air, ensure clean and safe water, preserve and restore the land, build healthy communities and ecosystems, and ensure compliance and environmental stewardship.

State and Local Responses

 Environmental Heresies

The EPA highlights work done by states in "developing and implementing a range of programs and strategies that are cost-effectively reducing greenhouse gases, improving air quality, enhancing economic development and increasing the nation's energy security" (EPA 2007c). Calling state action "a key component of the U.S. response to climate change," the agency notes that 35 states and Puerto Rico have completed or implemented action plans for reducing greenhouse gas emissions or enhancing greenhouse gas capture.

Recognizing that there are no real borders for carbon emissions and becoming increasingly frustrated with the slow progress of federal legislation on the matter (Broder 2007), many state leaders have formed regional coalitions to combat climate change. For example, the Regional Greenhouse Gas Initiative (RGGI) is a cooperative effort by northeastern and mid-Atlantic states to determine a regional strategy for controlling greenhouse gas emissions. In 2006, the Clean and Diversified Energy Initiative was signed by governors of 19 western states, along with those from American Samoa, Guam, and the Northern Mariana Islands. The goal of their initiative is to identify and produce affordable, sustainable, and environmentally responsible energy for the western states and islands.

Cities throughout the nation have embraced sustainability goals, along with environmentally responsible planning and consumption. In 2005, the U.S. Conference of Mayors endorsed the U.S. Mayors Climate Protection Agreement. Through the agreement, the mayors agreed to strive to meet or exceed Kyoto Protocol targets for reducing global warming pollution. More than 600 mayors have signed the agreement. The list of top 10 green cities is presented in Table 15.4.

Recently, two major U.S. cities made news for their environmental vision and leadership. Declaring New York City as the "first environmentally sustainable twenty-first-century city," Mayor Michael R. Bloomberg proposed a master plan to reduce energy consumption in six areas by 2030: land, transportation, water, energy, air quality, and climate change. Much of the plan would require state approval. One of the most contentious strategies involved the city's transportation burdens. Calling it "congestion pricing," Bloomberg proposed charging a fee for vehicles entering the city from 6 a.m. to 6 p.m. on weekdays—$8 for cars and $21 for trucks. The pricing plan would have reduced traffic congestion and improved air quality, as it

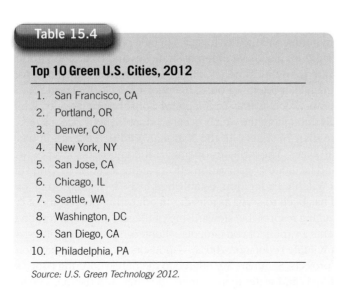

Table 15.4

Top 10 Green U.S. Cities, 2012

1. San Francisco, CA
2. Portland, OR
3. Denver, CO
4. New York, NY
5. San Jose, CA
6. Chicago, IL
7. Seattle, WA
8. Washington, DC
9. San Diego, CA
10. Philadelphia, PA

Source: U.S. Green Technology 2012.

has in parts of London and Singapore (Lueck 2007). Despite approval from the New York City Council, the state legislature failed to pass the pricing plan.

On the West Coast, San Francisco was the first city in the nation to ban the use of petroleum-based shopping bags. These plastic shopping bags take many years to degrade, meanwhile contaminating our land and water and endangering animal and marine life. Nearly 90% of all U.S. shopping bags are plastic. Beginning in 2007, plastic bags were to be replaced with biodegradable plastic bags or recyclable bags in San Francisco grocery and drug stores. Several countries, including Bhutan, Bangladesh, and China, have banned the use of nonbiodegradable plastic bags. Other countries, such as Germany and Ireland, charge a nominal fee for plastic shopping bags.

Environmental Interest Groups

Organizations concerned with the protection of the environment have played an important role in American politics since the foundation of the Sierra Club in 1892. The first wave of environmental interest groups included the National Audubon Society (1905), the National Parks Conservation Association (1919), and the National Wildlife Federation (1935). These groups were concerned with land conservation and the protection of specific sites and wild-life species. These first-wave groups depended on member support and involvement. These organizations remain among the most influential groups in the environmental movement (Ingram and Mann 1989).

As public attention shifted to the problems of environmental pollution, a second wave of environmental groups emerged during the 1960s and 1970s. These new organizations focused their efforts on fighting pollution. In general, the second wave of environmental groups adopted an ecological approach to our natural environment, recognizing the inter-relationship between all living things and using science as a tool for understanding and pro-tecting the environment. The Environmental Defense Fund (1967) and the Natural Resources Defense Council (1970) were started with funding support from the Ford Foundation. Both organizations relied on litigation as their instrument of reform. Other second-wave groups include Friends of the Earth, the Environmental Policy Institute, and Environmental Action. After the 1970s, environmental groups began to direct their appeals to policy makers rather than to the general public (Ingram and Mann 1989).

Voluntary Associations

Although each group is committed to the environment, each has adopted its own cause, from broad environmental themes to such specific problems as toxic pollution or land con-servation. The groups also have different strategies and tactics. Environmental groups may attempt to influence political policy, litigate environmental disputes, form coalitions with other environmental or interest groups, or endorse specific political candidates (Ingram and Mann 1989). Some, such as the Sea Shepherd Conservation Society, which rams and sinks whaling vessels throughout the word's oceans, adopt "in your face" tactics.

Now more than 70 years old, the National Wildlife Federation has nine field offices and 48 state affiliates. The affiliates operate at the grassroots level by working to educate, encourage, and facilitate conservation efforts at the state level. One such organization is the Arkansas Wildlife Federation, established in 1936 by a group of sportsmen. The fed-eration's goal has been to serve as a leader in educating people about conservation issues and in encouraging responsible stewardship of the state's natural resources. The federation, which represents a variety of constituents—hunters, sportsmen, hikers, anglers, and camp-ers (Arkansas Wildlife Federation 2003a)—sponsors a variety of educational and community activities and projects. Seminars are offered to the public covering issues such as forest man-agement, wetlands and water management, hunting, and fishing. The federation sponsors annual conservation achievement awards to honor citizens and organizations dedicated to natural resource endeavors. The organization also sponsors political candidate forums where citizens can ask candidates about their positions on various conservation and environmental issues (Arkansas Wildlife Federation 2003b).

A new environmental interest group is the Earth Island Institute, founded in 1982 by David Brower, who was the first executive director of the Sierra Club and cofounder of Friends of the Earth. The institute supports more than 100 projects worldwide, pledging to support campaigns "dedicated to conserving, preserving, and restoring the ecosystems on which our civilization depends" (Earth Island Institute 2010). The organization also honors youth for their environmental community work. Among those recognized in 2009 was Hai Vo, a 22-year-old student at the University of California–Irvine. Vo cofounded the Real Food Challenge (RFC) to encourage UC Irvine and other schools to purchase and eat real food—food that is ecologically sound, community based, humane, and fair. RFC worked with the University of California to develop a system-wide commitment to 20% real food procurement by the year 2020 (Earth Island Institute 2009).

In Focus

Local and Sustainable Food

After cars, our food system uses more fossil fuel than any other sector of the economy, about 19% (Pollan 2008). According to the Worldwatch Institute, food in the average American meal travels about 1,500 miles from farm to home. Food is brought into most communities via trucks, trains, or airplanes in refrigerated or storage containers. The 1,500-mile meal is said to consume as much as four times the energy and produce four times as much greenhouse gas emissions as a locally grown meal (Ketcham 2007). In addition to energy expended for transport, concern has been expressed over the amount of fossil fuel energy used in producing the food products brought to our table. In 2009, the Swedish National Food Administration began requiring the reporting of carbon dioxide emissions associated with the production of specific foods. For example, one serving per week of beef from dairy cows produces 120 kilograms of carbon dioxide emissions per year. The information will appear on some grocery items and restaurant menus throughout the country (Rosenthal 2009).

In response, environmentalists and foodies (people who have an avid interest in the latest food fads) throughout the United States and elsewhere in the world have adopted what is referred to as the 100-Mile Diet. For a week, a month, a year, or life, the rules of the diet are simple: You may only consume food grown and produced within a 100-mile radius of your home. Called locavores, these 100-mile eaters advocate the value in being able to know the source of your food, supporting the local economy, and eating fresh and healthy food in season. They argue, "The distance from which our food comes represents our separation from the knowledge of how and by whom what we consume is produced, processed and transported" (Locavores 2007). This is not a diet for fast-food junkies.

Canadians Alisa Smith and J. B. MacKinnon first coined the term *100-Mile Diet* when they began a yearlong local food experiment in Vancouver, British Columbia. The couple discovered several food items that they had to live without for most or part of the year, such as chocolate, coffee, and wheat. (Most locavores make exceptions for these items, including salt and spices.) Unable to purchase local bread and wheat for baking, for one lunch meal, MacKinnon, the family chef, fashioned bread out of turnip slices. But the couple found success (eventually finding a local supplier of wheat) and satisfaction in their diet. Their experience helped fuel broader interest in the benefits of a 100-mile diet.

One way to support local agriculture is through community-supported agriculture (CSA), a partnership between community members and an independent local farm. The CSA movement began in Japan almost

(Continued)

(Continued)

30 years ago with a group of women who were concerned about pesticides, the increase in processed foods, and their country's shrinking rural population. Community members purchase seasonal shares, for about $300 to $400, which entitles them to weekly food allowances throughout the growing season. There are an estimated 2,500 CSA groups in the United States. According to FoodRoutes.org, independent local farms encourage biodiversity by diversifying the local landscape and natural environment. The CSA arrangement is beneficial to the farmer and to his or her customers. Customers receive fresh produce and have the satisfaction of supporting a local business. Customers can help at the farm and provide input and suggestions to their farmer. Instead of spending time marketing produce, farmers can focus their efforts on growing quality produce and working with their community members.

Alongside first graders from Washington, DC's Bancroft Elementary School, Michelle Obama broke ground on an organic vegetable garden on the South Lawn of the White House. This is the first garden at the White House since Eleanor Roosevelt's World War II victory garden. The garden was planted with a variety of lettuces, greens, and herbs as well as a patch of berries. At the planting, Mrs. Obama expressed her interest in promoting healthy eating and local food, particularly from the more than 1 million community gardens throughout the country.

Grassroots Movements

Grassroot Organizations

Sherry and Charles Cable (1995) argue that the grassroots environmental movement has improved the lives of many individuals and has spread environmental awareness among the public. In contrast with national environmental organizations, grassroots organizations usually consist of working-class participants, people of color, and women. Although experienced organizers or community activists lead some groups, many grassroots groups are led by inexperienced but passionate leaders. In the fight against environmental racism, these grassroots environmental groups have given a voice to communities of color (Epstein 1995).

Cable and Cable (1995) suggest that the motivating factor for most grassroots organizations is a desire to protect the health and safety of families against some immediate environmental threat. Grassroots organizations emphasize environmental justice, acting in the belief that some injustice has been committed by a corporation, business, or industry and that appropriate action should be taken to correct, improve, or remove the injustice(s). These organizations have tackled toxic waste issues and have sought justice for housing, transportation, air quality, and economic development issues (Bullard 1994). In 2011, responding to the nuclear fallout from the Fukushima nuclear plant, citizen monitoring groups were formed across Japan. Men and women armed with dosimeters began taking radiation readings near their homes. The organized effort grew out of a perceived lack of government response and citizens' disbelief with the government's insistence that the nuclear fallout would not pose a threat or contaminate food sources (Tabuchi 2011).

Saving Indigenous Peoples

Sociologists Riley Dunlap and Angela Mertig (1992) note that the environmental movement is among the few movements that "significantly changed society" (p. xi). Nicolas Freudenberg and Carol Steinsapir (1992:33–35) identify seven achievements of grassroots organizations:

Nuclear Power

1. A number of environmentally hazardous facilities have been controlled by cleaning up contaminated sites, blocking the construction of new facilities, and upgrading corporate pollution control equipment.

2. Grassroots organizations have forced businesses to consider the environmental consequences of their actions.

3. These groups encourage preventative approaches to environmental problems such as reducing or limiting the use of environmental contamination.

4. The grassroots movement has expanded citizens' rights to participate in environmental decision making.

5. Grassroots organizations have served as psychological and social support networks for victims and their families.

6. The movement has brought environmental concerns and action to working-class and minority Americans.

7. The grassroots movement has influenced how the general public thinks about the environment and public health.

Radical Environmentalists

Rik Scarce (1990) explains that radical environmentalists want to preserve our biological diversity. This isn't just a question of preserving the living things in our ecosystem, such as plants and animals; nonliving entities such as mountains, rivers, and oceans must also be protected. Radical groups confront problems through direct action, such as picketing an office building, breaking

Photo 15.5

Local farmers' markets, like this one in Seattle, Washington, help support local farmers and encourage seasonal food consumption.

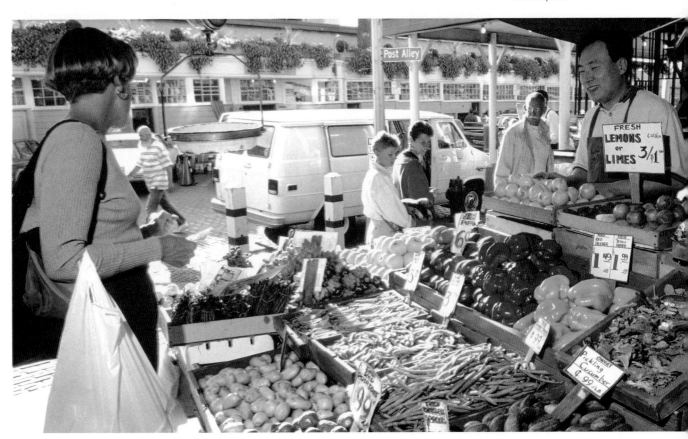

the law, or performing acts of civil disobedience. Other radical environmentalists may destroy machinery, property, or equipment used to build roads, kill animals, or harvest trees. Most "eco-warriors" act on their own and without the leadership of an organizational hierarchy.

Scarce (1990) says radical environmentalists adopt lifestyles that have minimal impact on the environment: They don't own cars, they adopt vegetarian diets, and they avoid occupations that involve the destruction of the environment. Although they are committed to their issues, radical environmentalists recognize that on their own, they will never be able to end the practices they protest. Their actions usually attract media attention, creating a groundswell of public support for their particular issues. Or their actions are done in concert with mainstream efforts; for example, radicals might stage tree sittings in Oregon to delay the cutting of timber until courts can hear a more mainstream group's request for injunction.

Tree sitting is a form of protest targeting timber companies at the point of production, slowing or even stopping tree cutting. Scarce (1990) explains how tree sitters make their protest in areas with active cutting, finding and choosing trees that will make the right statement. The trees they choose are the tallest, most impressive, and clearly visible from a road, or those that overlook a recently cut area. Although we may think of tree sitting as a lonely activity, tree sitters require a support group for assistance, food, and clothing, including the hauling of waste (including human) from the site. The group will carry about 250 pounds of gear and provisions—food, water, clothing, and platform materials—as far as 10 miles to their intended site. Suspended about 80 to 150 feet off the ground, the 2.5- by 6-foot wooden platform becomes the tree sitter's home for days, weeks, or months. Julia "Butterfly" Hill sat in a 600-year-old California redwood tree for 738 days, withstanding eviction threats and legal action from the Pacific Lumber Company, which owned the tree. Tree sitting has been effective in bringing public and media attention to the practices of timber and logging companies and in rallying support for the tree sitter's message. In several cases, agreements have been made with lumber companies to divert logging to other areas or to pursue viable logging programs.

Is Your School Green?

Green Schools

Several hundred green U.S. elementary and secondary schools have been established nationally, supported by state grants, legislation, and partners such as the Sierra Club and the National Wildlife Federation. Schools like the Environmental Charter High School in Los Angeles and the Growing Up Green Charter School in Long Island City, Queens, New York, offer students more than an environmental issues curriculum. These private, charter, and traditional public schools have adopted a focus that goes beyond the environment, addressing politics, social justice, environmental careers, social activism, and community involvement (Navarro and Bhanoo 2010).

"Universities are huge institutions with huge carbon footprints, but they are also laboratories for concepts of sustainability," says Michael Crow, president of Arizona State University (Deutsch 2007:A21). Colleges and universities are taking the environmental lead by constructing green buildings, purchasing alternative energy, incorporating local and sustainable food products, and investing in efforts to make campuses carbon neutral. Their efforts include the following (Deutsch 2007; Lipka 2006):

- Bowdoin and Evergreen State Colleges purchase 100% of their energy from renewable sources or pay for energy offsets from solar or wind power.
- Arizona State University distributes free bus passes to every student, employee, and faculty member.
- Dickinson College students operate an organic garden, using some of the produce in their campus dining hall.

- Students at Central Oregon Community College and the University of Kentucky voted to pay additional fees to cover their institutions' clean-energy purchases.
- University of California–Irvine, University of Massachusetts–Amherst, Montana State University, and Eastern Tennessee State University are just some of the schools that have established a local chapter of the Real Food Challenge, an organization that promotes just and sustainable food systems on college campuses and in their communities.

Crow was among the first university presidents who signed the American College and University Presidents' Climate Commitment. The presidents acknowledge their role in leading environmental responsibility in their campuses and broader communities. The commitment, signed by more than 600 college and university presidents, includes a pledge to develop and implement a plan to achieve carbon neutrality on their campuses. Ninety college dorms are certified in Leadership in Energy and Environmental Design (LEED), the national standard for green design (Wilson 2009).

Writer Sara Lipka (2006) portrays college students as the "watchdogs for sustainability." She explains,

Armed with Internet research, they are investigating institutional operations like energy use, food purchasing, investments, transportation, and waste disposal. They are pushing administrators to approve new projects and set higher goals for sustainability. National networks are helping students share strategies with one another and organize sophisticated, often successful proposals for campus innovations and reforms. (Lipka 2006:11)

Similar environmental programs have been established in elementary and secondary schools across the country. To learn more about what you can do to protect the environment, refer to Table 15.5.

Table 15.5

Living Green—Tips for College and University Students

1. Practice the three *R*s: Reduce, Reuse, and Recycle.
2. Use less ink and paper. If possible, print on both sides of the page. Think twice about whether you need a hard copy of a webpage or document. Could you bookmark a page or save a file on your computer?
3. Limit your use of disposable products. This includes cups, plates, and paper napkins. The next time you grab a handful of napkins at your dining hall or in a restaurant, ask yourself if you really need that many. One might be enough.
4. Use compact fluorescent light bulbs in your dorm room or apartment. They may cost more, but they will last longer and save you money.
5. Walk, bike, and limit the use of your car.
6. Carry a refillable water bottle. Stop using bottled water.
7. Buy recycled products; this includes paper for printing.
8. Use refillable binders instead of notebooks. Or go electronic and take all your notes on your laptop.
9. Buy used clothing and furniture. It is a great way to save money, and it is a great thing to do for the environment.
10. Share your message: Tell others how you are living green on your campus.

Source: Adapted from Rockler-Gladen 2007.

Voices in the Community

Chad Pregracke

Chad Pregracke

Chad Pregracke started his career as an environmental activist in his own backyard. A native of Hampton, Illinois, he spent most of his life on the shores of the Mississippi River as a resident, shell diver, and commercial fisherman. Pregracke often saw garbage floating on the river or caught within its banks.

> I woke up like that many times—loving the natural world and hating the despicable mess. I saw the garbage on the river, and it didn't look right. It may have been commonplace, but I didn't like it and I didn't accept it. And the more garbage sites I noticed, the more it made me want to do something about it. (Pregracke and Barrow 2007:12–13)

He admits that his attempts to organize and fund his first river cleanup were less than perfect. He recalls how he did everything wrong. He didn't have a clear message, didn't have a plan, and didn't talk to the right people at local agencies. But he persevered and received funding from his first corporate sponsor, the Alcoa Corporation. Pregracke started cleaning up the river in 1997, collecting 45,000 pounds of debris from its shores. In 1998, Pregracke established his nonprofit organization, Living Lands and Waters (LLW), dedicated to cleaning up the Mississippi River.

Since its establishment, LLW has removed 4 million pounds of trash from the Mississippi and its tributary rivers Missouri and Ohio. The cleanup efforts are staffed primarily by community volunteers. Their annual haul of trash includes items such as refrigerators, tires, bowling balls, baby dolls, and Styrofoam. In 2003, LLW established the Riverbottom Forest Restoration Project. Through the project, volunteers remove invasive plant species from the riverbanks, planting native trees in their place. In August 2005, Pregracke and his crew provided assistance with cleanup and rebuilding efforts in New Orleans after Hurricane Katrina struck the area. In 2007, the MillionTrees Project was established to encourage the planting and growth of 1 million native hardwood nut-bearing trees throughout the Midwest.

Hurricane Katrina

Pregracke is modest in describing his life's mission:

> I've been on a mission to clean up the rivers. It was a simple concept then and it's a simple concept now, but doing it has been far from simple or easy. I realize that we're not solving all the problems or necessarily saving America's rivers—we're simply doing our part, just as I hope you're doing yours. (Pregracke and Barrow 2007:282–83)

> We all make a difference, even if we don't intend to, and it's either negative or positive. My question to you is, how big a difference do you want to make? I can't say how big a difference I've made or will continue to make, but I know this—I will plant a lot of trees and leave a cleaner river. (Pregracke and Barrow 2007:288)

For more information about Living Lands and Waters, visit the organization's website at http://www.livinglandsandwaters.org.

Main Points

- Daily human activity, economic development, cultural values, social class, and technology all affect the health of the environment. Environmental sociology considers the interactions between our physical and natural environments and our social organization and behavior.

- Functionalists believe that environmental problems develop from the system itself. Thus, although agriculture, industrialization, and related technologies have improved quality of life, they have also led to waste, pollution, and the destruction of natural resources. Functionalists believe that the only way to address environmental problems is to simultaneously halt population growth and reduce technology's impact.

- Conflict theorists believe that environmental problems are created by humans competing for power, income, and their own interests in a capitalist system. Those with the least amount of power are targeted in environmental racism, in which marginalized groups are disadvantaged. Research indicates that low-income people and people of color are exposed to greater environmental risks than White or affluent people.

- Feminists argue that a masculine worldview is responsible for the domination of nature, women, and minorities. One strand of thought, ecofeminism, believes that men are the primary culprits in the exploitation of animals and the environment. Other feminist approaches include feminist critiques of natural science, analyses of specific environmental issues, and contributions to sustainable development.

- Interaction theorists believe that environmental problems do not materialize by themselves. Social constructionists focus on the political process affecting the environment rather than on the problems themselves.

- Environmental problems include climate change, air pollution, hazardous waste sites, brownfields (abandoned or underused commercial properties with hazardous substances), and polluted and toxic water.

- Because of pollution, increasing urbanization, and sprawling development, we may be running out of water. Human efforts to conserve water, such as building dams, are now recognized as causes of serious and negative environmental problems.

- Efforts in land conservation and wilderness protection seem to be successful largely because of federal protection policies and legislation. Examples, among many, are the Wilderness Act, the Endangered Species Act, and the formation of the Environmental Protection Agency (EPA).

- Established in 1970 as the chief environmental agency, the EPA provides leadership in the nation's environmental science, research, education, and assessment efforts. It sets national standards and delegates certain functions of enforcement to states. The EPA's five long-term goals through 2014 are to achieve clean air, ensure clean and safe water, preserve and restore the land, build healthy communities and ecosystems, and ensure compliance and environmental stewardship.

- Environmental organizations have played an important role in American politics since the foundation of the Sierra Club in 1892. Groups include the National Audubon Society and the National Wildlife Federation. These first-wave groups are concerned with land conservation and the protection of specific sites and species, and they rely on member support and involvement.

- A second wave of environmental groups, which emerged during the 1960s and 1970s, includes the Environmental Defense Fund and the Natural Resources Defense Council. They focus on fighting pollution, and they adopt an ecological approach, recognizing the interrelationship between all living things and using science as a tool for understanding and protecting the environment. After the 1970s, environmental groups began to direct their appeals to policy makers rather than the general public.

- Each environmental group has its own cause and strategies. Groups may attempt to influence political policy, litigate disputes, form coalitions with other environmental or interest groups, endorse specific political candidates, or even adopt more radical tactics.

- Grassroots organizations usually consist of inexperienced but passionate working-class participants, people of color, and women. These groups are motivated by a desire to protect the health and safety of families against some immediate environmental threat. Grassroots organizations emphasize environmental justice.

- Radical groups confront problems through direct action, such as breaking the law, destroying property or equipment, or performing acts of civil disobedience. Most "eco-warriors" act on their own and without the leadership of an organizational hierarchy. They recognize that they cannot effect change on their own, but their actions usually draw media attention and thus engender public support. They also work with mainstream groups.

- The environmental movement has had a significant impact in controlling hazardous facilities, urging businesses to consider environmental impact, encouraging preventative approaches to problems, expanding citizens' rights to participate in decision making, serving as psychological and social support networks for victims and their families, bringing concerns and action to working-class and minority Americans, and influencing how the general public thinks about the environment and public health.

- Colleges and universities are demonstrating environmental leadership by constructing green buildings, purchasing alternative energy, and investing in efforts to make campuses carbon neutral and sustainable.

On Your Own

Log on to the open-access Student Study Site at www.sagepub.com/leonguerrero4e for these additional learning tools:

- Interactive quizzes
- Video clips
- NPR audio links
- Handbook articles

- E-flashcards
- Journal articles
- End-of-chapter web exercises
- Additional web resources and current events

Internet and Community Exercises

1. Access "Envirofacts," a one-stop source for environmental information about your community sponsored by the EPA. Go to *Study Site Chapter 15*. You can retrieve information about your location by typing your area's zip code, city, county, water body, or park name. Or you can select a topic— air, land, water, waste, toxics, radiation, facility, compliance, or other—to find out if the EPA is monitoring any local emissions, sites, violations, or companies. Based on the information provided, how would you rate the environmental quality of your community or of your state?

2. The Edible Schoolyard Project, located at the Martin Luther King Middle School in Berkeley, California, was established in 1995. Founded by Chef Alice Waters, the nonprofit organization embraces a "Seed to Table" philosophy, allowing students to experience firsthand the cycle of food production from garden to table via gardening and cooking classes. The organization promotes the establishment of garden-kitchens in schools, with a listing of school gardens throughout the United States. Explore whether a school garden exists in your university or in an elementary or secondary school in your area.

3. Invite a faculty member from the biology, ecology, or natural sciences department to talk about the ecosystem of your college campus. How do your faculty and student populations affect the environmental habitat? How much waste is produced on campus? What environmentally friendly practices are supported on campus?

4. What sustainability programs does your university have in place for faculty, students, and the campus? Is your school part of the American College and University Presidents' Climate Commitment?

5. Whether we look at individuals, cities, or nations, everyone and everything has an impact on the Earth because we consume the finite products and services of nature. As a result, we each leave an **ecological footprint**, some environmental impact on the amount of natural resources we use and waste output we create. Footprints are calculated for countries by measuring the amount of resources (e.g., fossil fuel, acreage and land, housing, and transportation) consumed in a given year. Individual footprints can also be estimated. To estimate your personal footprint, visit *Study Site Chapter 15.*

Study Questions

1. Explain the association of human action and environmental problems.

2. From a functionalist perspective, how has human behavior and our way of life contributed to environmental problems?

3. Explain how women contributed to the environmental justice movement.

4. Identify the six factors related to the construction of an environmental problem. From this perspective, how has climate change been defined as a social problem? Or hasn't it?

5. How have interest groups and grassroots movements contributed to the success of the environmental movement?

6. What are the strategies of radical environmentalists?

CHAPTER 16

War and Terrorism

President Obama

Barack Obama was inaugurated as the first president to take office during the Age of Terrorism. Inheriting two wars and a nation debating whether we are safer as a country since September 2001, Obama rejected the phrase "war on terror," preferring instead to cast our wars as one of the many challenges this country is facing (Baker 2010). Within days of his inauguration, Obama set a deadline to close the prison in Guantánamo, halted military commission trials, and officially restricted prisoner interrogation to authorized methods. In 2010, Obama ordered the deployment of 30,000 additional troops to Afghanistan, with a goal of transitioning power to Afghanistan's Security Forces in 2011. Before a national television audience and 4,000 West Point cadets, Obama stated, "Let me be clear: none of this will be easy. The struggle against violent extremism will not be finished quickly, and it extends well beyond Afghanistan and Pakistan. It will be an enduring test of our free society, and our leadership in the world" (quoted in Stolberg and Cooper 2009). The war in Afghanistan is the longest U.S. war.

A decade after 9/11, a wave of revolutionary demonstrations and protests swept across the Arab world. It began in Tunisia on December 17, 2010, when a police officer took away Mohamed Bouazizi's vegetable cart because Bouazizi didn't have a license to sell his goods. After his confrontation with the police and after local officials refused to hear his complaint, Bouazizi set himself on fire in front of the provincial headquarters. Bouazizi's martyrdom spurred on a "people's revolution" (Abouzeid 2011). Tunisians took to the streets in protest ultimately leading to the end of President Zine El Abidine Ben Ali's authoritarian rule. The Arab Spring extended to other countries where citizens participated in public demonstrations, some relatively peaceful, to protest against the hardships and cruelties under ruling regimes. Ruling governments were overthrown in Egypt, Libya, and Yemen.

President Bush

The secure life that many Americans took for granted changed on the morning of September 11, 2001 (Hoge and Rose 2001); we now live in a subtly different country (Danner 2011). It is a country whose public and political discourse has been preoccupied with war, terrorism, suicide bombs, torture, patriotism, and human loss. There is an awareness of war and terrorism in other countries and ultimately concern over whether these conflicts will threaten U.S. national security. Sociologists acknowledge that "war is never an isolated act" (Clausweitz 1984:78) and that the consequences are felt and experienced beyond specific battlefields and borders. In this chapter, we will examine the consequences and responses to war and terrorism.

Defining Conflict

War

War is a violent political instrument (Walter 1964). It is a violent activity between armed combatants, one side hoping to impose its will on the other. Whether or not war has been declared by its leadership, war involves armed conflict between two or more states or military forces. The majority of today's wars are civil wars (fought within, not between, countries), and most often, they take place in the poorest countries.

The Ultimate Weapon

Myanmar

The United Kingdom, France, and Russia have fought the most international armed conflicts since the end of World War II (refer to Table 16.1). The most conflict-prone countries (including civil wars) have been Myanmar (previously known as Burma), India, and Ethiopia (refer to Table 16.2) (Human Security Report Project 2011).

Since 1945, there have been 140 civil wars throughout the world, killing approximately 20 million people and displacing about 67 million. Civil wars typically occur in developing

Table 16.1

Countries That Have Experienced the Highest Number of State-Based Armed Conflicts, 1946 to 2008

Country	Number of Wars
United Kingdom	25
France	22
Russia	19
United States	17
India	14
Ethiopia	10
Burma	10
China	9

Source: Human Security Report Project 2011.

Table 16.2	
The 10 Most Conflict-Prone Countries, 1946 to 2008	
Number of Conflict Years*	**Country**
246	Myanmar
180	India
113	Ethiopia
100	Philippines
91	United Kingdom
89	France
79	Israel
71	Vietnam

Source: Human Security Report Project 2011.

*A conflict year is a calendar year in which a country has been involved in a state-based armed conflict of any type. Because a country can experience several different armed conflicts at the same time, it can experience two or more conflict years within a single calendar year.

countries and are fought by small, poorly trained, poorly armed forces that avoid major military engagements, but frequently target civilians (Human Security Report Project 2005). **Genocide** (the systematic targeting of ethnic or religious groups) and **politicide** (targeting specific groups because of their political beliefs) have been part of many civil wars, for example, the wars in Rwanda (1994) and Cambodia (1977–1979) (Human Security Report Project 2005). In 1994, 800,000 Tutsis were massacred by the majority Hutu ethnic group in Rwanda.

U.S. Conflicts

"The United States was born of violence and revolution," writes Ken Cunningham (2004), "violence against the native population and among and against the various European imperial powers" (p. 556). Our nation's birth was marked by a war—the American Revolution of 1775 to 1783. In 1776, the Declaration of Independence was adopted, a public statement of a new nation's independence from Great Britain and its rights to "life, liberty, and the pursuit of happiness." The British were defeated in 1783. More than 4,000 lives were lost in the revolution against the British.

The American Revolution was followed by the War of 1812 (1812–1815) and the Mexican War (1846–1848), both part of the economic and continental expansion of the United States. The effort was justified under the principle of manifest destiny. U.S. leaders felt it was their mission to extend freedom and democracy to others. At the end of the Mexican War, the United States acquired the northern part of Mexico, later dividing the area into Arizona, California, Nevada, New Mexico, and Utah. A **revolution** constitutes an overthrow of the existing government or political structure. Revolutions do not always lead to violent conflict.

The Civil War (1861–1865) between northern and southern states has been referred to as the bloodiest battle on U.S. soil. Although we tend to think that the war was waged solely over the issue of slavery, it was also based on deep economic, political, and social differences between the two groups of states. During his second inaugural address in 1865, President Abraham Lincoln said, "One of them would make war rather than let the nation survive, and the other would accept war rather than let it perish, and the war came." More than 600,000 died.

Beginning with the Spanish–American War (1898), U.S. troops and soldiers began to wage war in other countries, mostly responding to tyranny, oppression, and communism. The Spanish–American War was fought to liberate Cuba from Spain and to protect U.S. interests in Cuban sugar, tobacco, and iron industries. U.S. participation during World War I (1917–1918) and World War II (1940–1945) helped establish its dominance as a worldwide military force. That accomplishment, however, came with great cost: The United States had heavy losses, 53,000 deaths in World War I and 400,000 deaths in World War II. In the latter war, the United States and its allies claimed victory against Germany, Japan, and Italy. After the North Korean People's Army invaded the Republic of Korea, the United States joined UN forces in the Korean War (1950–1953). No winner of the war has ever been declared. An armistice was agreed upon in 1953, forever separating North and South Korea. Fifty years after the invasion, Communist and UN soldiers still guard their sides of the demilitarized zone in Panmunjom. The United States fought against North Vietnamese Communists in the jungles of South Vietnam from 1964 to 1973. Although U.S. troops had begun withdrawing from Vietnam in 1969, the formal cease-fire was declared in January 1973.

U.S. engagement in Middle East wars began with the Persian Gulf War of 1990 to 1991. The United States was joined by UN forces to liberate Kuwait from Iraqi forces. Operations Desert Shield and Desert Storm were the first display of high-tech warfare: cruise missiles, stealth fighters, and precision-guided munitions. Iraq accepted the terms for the cease-fire in April 1991. After September 11, 2001, U.S. forces attacked Afghanistan in an effort to destroy al-Qaeda forces and to locate their leader, Osama bin Laden. The first war of the twenty-first century was the U.S. war against Iraq (2003–2011) and Afghanistan (2003–). As of August 24, 2012, the number of reported military casualties (killed in action or nonhostile deaths) was 4,422 for Operation Iraqi Freedom and 2,092 for Operation Enduring Freedom in Afghanistan. In May 2011, U.S. Navy SEALs killed Osama bin Laden in Pakistan. A listing of U.S. wars and casualties is presented in Table 16.3. The list does not include the numerous American Indian Wars, the conflicts between American settlers and the U.S. federal government with the indigenous populations of North America.

Terrorism

Terrorism is a specific form of conflict. According to the U.S. federal code, **terrorism** is "the unlawful use of force or violence against persons or property to intimidate or coerce a government, the civilian population, or any segment thereof, in furtherance of political or social objectives" (28 C.F.R. Section 0.85). Todd Sandler (2011) offers the following definition of terrorism: "the premeditated use or threat to use violence by individuals or subnational groups to obtain political or social objective through the intimidation of a large audience beyond that of the immediate victims" (p. 280).

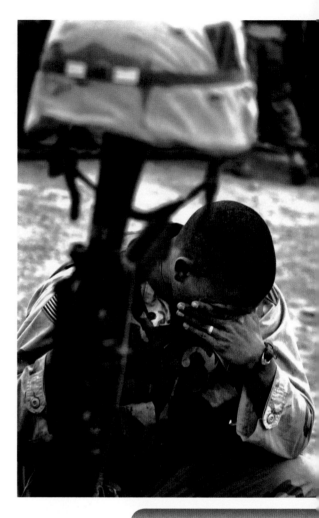

Photo 16.1

The official end of the U.S. war in Iraq was declared in 2011. By June 2012, 3,479 U.S. military personnel had been killed in hostile conflict.

 Operation Homecoming

 Terrorism Effects

Table 16.3

America's Wars and Casualties (Dates Indicate U.S. Troop Involvement)

War	Participants	Deaths in Service
American Revolution 1775–1783	Unknown	4,435
War of 1812 1812–1815	286,730	2,260
Mexican War 1846–1848	78,718	13,283
Civil War, Union Only 1861–1865	2,213,363	364,511
Spanish–American War 1898–1902	306,760	2,446
World War I 1917–1918	4,734,991	116,516
World War II 1941–1945	16,112,566	405,399
Korean War 1950–1953	5,720,000	36,576
Vietnam War 1964–1973	8,744,000	58,209
Persian Gulf War 1990–1991	2,322,000	382

Source: U.S. Department of Veterans Affairs 2007.

Political terrorism expert Grant Wardlaw (1988) states, "Terrorism is a phenomenon that is increasingly coming to dominate our lives." The effects of terrorism are widespread:

> It influences the way governments conduct their foreign policy and corporations transact their business. It causes changes to the structure and role of our security forces and necessitates huge expenditures on measures to protect public figures, vital installations, citizens and perhaps in the final analysis, our system of government. It affects the way we travel, the places we visit and the manner in which we live our daily lives. (Wardlaw 1988:206)

Domestic terrorism is defined as terrorism supported or coordinated by groups or individuals based in a country. The venue and targets are also in the same country. Domestic terrorist groups are likely to be found in large countries and are found more often in democracies than in authoritarian states (Human Security Report Project 2005). **International terrorism** is defined as terrorism supported or coordinated by foreign groups threatening the security of another nation or its citizens. For example, international terrorism can occur outside of the United States but may be directed at U.S. targets. Acts of terrorism have occurred on every continent, and perpetrators come from diverse religious and ethnic groups; however, Islamic governments and networks have committed the most extreme acts of terror (Booth and Dunne 2002). Though in terms of the number killed, international terrorism poses far less of a threat than do other forms of political violence or violent crime, it is an important human security issue (Human Security Report Project 2005). Al-Qaeda has come to symbolize terrorism in the twenty-first century.

Paul Pillar (2001) explains that there are five elements of terrorism: First, terrorism is a premeditated act. It requires intent and prior decision to commit an act of terrorism. Terrorism doesn't happen by accident; rather, it is the result of an individual's or a group's policy or decision. Second, terrorism is purposeful; it is political in its motive to change or challenge the status quo. Religiously oriented or national terrorists are driven by social forces or shaped by circumstances specific to their particular religious or nationalistic experiences (Reich 1998). According to Max Abrahms (2012), terrorist groups have process and outcome goals. **Process goals** are aimed to sustain the group and its activities by securing financial support, gaining media attention, and boosting group morale. **Outcome goals** are the group's stated political ends, which require the cooperation of the target authority or government. Third, terrorism is not like a war in which both sides can shoot at one another. Terrorism targets noncombatants, such as civilians who cannot defend themselves against the violence. The direct targets of terrorist activity are not the main targets. Fourth, terrorism is usually carried out by subnational groups or clandestine agents. If uniformed military soldiers attack a group, it is considered an act of war; an attack conducted by nongovernmental perpetrators is considered terrorism. Individuals acting alone may also commit terrorism. Finally, terrorism includes the threat of violence. It does not involve only terrorist acts that may have occurred; it also involves the potential for future attacks.

 Terrorism

Terrorist activity has changed little over the years. Six basic tactics account for 95% of all incidents: bombings, assassinations, armed assaults, kidnappings, hijackings, and other kinds of hostage seizures. As Brian Jenkins (1988) states, "Terrorists blow up things, kill people, or seize hostages. Every terrorist attack is merely a variation on these three activities" (p. 257).

What Does It Mean to Me?

Are you concerned about a terrorist attack on U.S. soil? Do you believe we are at risk of an attack from domestic or foreign terrorists? Explain the reason for your answer.

Sociological Perspectives on War and Terrorism

Functionalist Perspective

Functionalists examine how conflicts help maintain the social order, creating and reinforcing social, religious, or national boundaries. War creates social stability by letting everyone know what side they are on: the good guys versus the bad guys or us versus them. There are norms and boundaries in war: Individuals will know what their roles are, what they should believe in, how they should respond in case of an attack, and how they should interact with members of the other side. But unlike war, the social boundaries in terrorist activities are less certain. In some cases, the identity of terrorists and their goals may never be known.

War provides a "safety valve" function, giving marginalized or oppressed groups a means to express their discontent or anger. Acts of terrorism, according to Martha Crenshaw (1998), are selected as a course of action from a range of alternatives. Groups may choose terrorism because the other methods may be expected not to work or may be too time-consuming for the group. Radical groups choose terrorism when they want immediate action and when they want their message to be heard. As they act, they spread their group's message and recruit others for their cause.

The social structure contributes to conflict. For example, a country's education and age structure are demographic characteristics that help us understand the current situation in the Greater Middle East (Spindel 2011). Educational attainment in these countries is rising, and as a result, so are citizen demands and expectations for resolving the countries' social problems. The age structure of the population has been identified as a central component in the Arab Spring. Compared to western countries, the majority of residents are under 25 years of age—52% in Egypt, 55.2% in Syria, and 54.4% in Jordan. In Germany, 25% of the population is under 25 years of age.

Finally, warfare establishes power and domination. The victor is able to acquire the "spoils of war"—a country's land, people, and resources. Beyond those tangible fruits of victory, the winning side gets to make new rules or impose its rules about appropriate political, social, and economic structures.

Conflict Perspective

President Eisenhower's Warning

From this perspective war is not natural; it is a product of oppression and domination. Conflict may be based on disputes over resources or land. Modern conflict theorists have focused on how war is used to promote economic and political interests. In 1961, President Dwight D. Eisenhower cautioned the nation about the **military-industrial complex**, the growing collaboration of the government, the military, and the armament industry. Years earlier, Eisenhower (1953) warned,

> Every gun that is made, every warship launched, every rocket fired, signifies in the final sense a theft of those who hunger and are not fed, those who are cold and are not clothed. The world in arms is not spending money alone. It is spending the sweat of its laborers, the genius of its scientists, the hopes of its children.

Military Sociology

He explained that the complex had a corrupting influence—economic, political, and spiritual—in every city, state, and federal office of government. A decision to go to war could be motivated not by ideals to preserve or promote freedom, but to ensure the economic well-being of the defense contractor. For example, during the Iraq war, the role of oil services firm Halliburton and its subsidiary company, KBR, was closely scrutinized. Critics identify that Halliburton had an unfair advantage with no-bid military contracting because of its relationship with Vice President Dick Cheney. Cheney served as Halliburton's CEO from 1996 to 1998 and briefly in 2000. In 2007, federal investigators alleged that Halliburton was responsible for $2.7 billion in contractor waste and overcharging in Iraq.

Targeting Businesses

Social scientists have noted the far-reaching and devastating impact of U.S. militarism for Americans and the rest of the world. Cunningham (2004) identifies a "vast, entrenched, bureaucratic national security apparatus" that reaches into all areas of American life and politics, including businesses, universities, primary and secondary schools, the media, and popular culture. U.S. militarism also reaches into foreign countries, through its direct military intervention and war and covert operations (conducted by the Central Intelligence Agency [CIA], the National Security Agency [NSA], and other agencies).

Feminist Perspective

New Terrorism Recruits

From this perspective, war is considered a primarily male activity that enhances the position of males in society. "War is a patriarchal tool always used by men to create new structures of dominance and to subjugate a large mass of people" ("The Events" 2002:96). In our military system, decision making and economic power are held primarily by men;

as a result, international relations and politics are played out on women's bodies (Cuomo 1996). According to Cynthia Enloe (1990), local and global sexual politics shape and are shaped through the presence of national and international U.S. military bases—through the symbolism of the U.S. soldier, the reproduction of family structures on bases, and systems of prostitution that coexist alongside bases. As she explains, "Bases are artificial societies created out of unequal relations between men and women of different races and classes" (Enloe 1990:2).

Men reserve the right to make war themselves and claim that they fight wars to protect vulnerable people, such as women and children, who are viewed as not being able to protect themselves (Tickner 2002). During wars, women are charged with caring for their husbands, their sons, and the victims of war. The ideal of the "caretaking woman" helps exclude women from public and political institutions by reminding them that their first responsibility is to the family. According to Laura Kaplan (1994), this ideal "helps co-opt women's resistance to the war by convincing women that their immediate responsibility to ameliorate the effects of war takes precedence over organized public action against war" (p. 131).

The role of women in active combat continues to be redefined. In 2012, the U.S. Marine Corps, the most male-dominated of the armed services, announced that women would be allowed to attend its infantry officer course (Dao 2012). The new policy will allow the military to assess how women perform in formerly male-only units, as well as to evaluate the relative strength thresholds of male and female Marines. In 2013, the Pentagon removed its ban on women serving in combat. Implementation will take several years.

Feminist theorists focus on the gender rhetoric used in war. After September 11, Judith Lorber (2002) observed, "The gender rhetoric heard over and over portrayed our men as heroes and theirs as terrorists, our women as sad widows and theirs as equally sad oppressed wives" (p. 379). Most of the images represented men "acting" while women were "reacting" to the events of September 11. The one exception was First Lady Laura Bush, who after maintaining a low profile before September 11 became highly visible in the archetypal role of nurturer for the nation (Jansen 2002). Instead of focusing on the female soldiers deployed against Afghanistan, the media chose to focus on faceless, helpless Afghan women in blue burkas (Tickner 2002). As mostly men perpetuate the violence, respond with additional violence, and present media stories about it, world media portrayals of war are dominated by patriarchal images and logic (Lemish 2005).

As more women are serving as active duty personnel, however, their profile in military service has increased—negatively in some cases. Mary Ann Tétreault (2006) examined the portrayal of women involved in the torture of male prisoners at Abu Ghraib prison. In 2004, a *60 Minutes II* story and a series of articles in the *New Yorker* magazine first exposed the crimes being committed by U.S. military personnel. At the center of the story was a set of sensational photographs of naked and tortured prisoners taken by U.S. military men and women. Tétreault explains that although both male and female soldiers were involved in the torture, the popular face of the scandal and the official scapegoat were both women—Private Lynndie England and General Janis Karpinski. The focus on these women detracted public attention and ultimately deflected responsibility from the male soldiers responsible for the prison abuse. Tétreault (2006) writes,

Photo 16.2

U.S. Army Private First Class Lynndie England was convicted on charges stemming from her involvement in the Iraq Abu Ghraib prison scandal. England was sentenced to three years in prison. Six other soldiers were convicted and sentenced.

Military Women

Military Rape

Those who chose to focus on the sex of General Karpinski, like those who chose to focus on that of Lynndie England, could reframe the meaning of the torture and humiliation taking place at Abu Ghraib as nothing more than what might have been expected from putting a woman in charge of a group of impressionable young men. (p. 43)

Interactionist Perspective

Interactionists focus on the social messages and meaning of war and conflict. *Terrorism* is a word with intrinsically negative connotations. According to political scientist Crenshaw (1995), the word "projects images, communicates messages, and creates myths that transcend historical circumstances and motivate future generations" (p. 12). In addition, the concept serves as "an organizing concept that both describes the phenomenon as it exists and offers a moral judgment" (Crenshaw 1995:9). As Jenkins (1980) explains,

> What is called terrorism thus seems to be dependent on one's point of view. Use of the term implies a moral judgment; and if one party can successfully attach the label terrorist to its opponent, then it has indirectly persuaded others to adopt its moral viewpoint. (p. 10)

Crenshaw (1995) cautions that once political concepts such as terrorism are constructed, "They take on a certain autonomy, especially when they are adopted by news media, disseminated to the public, and integrated into a general context of norms and values" (p. 9). Use of the word *terrorism* promotes condemnation of the actors and may reflect an ideological or political bias (Gibbs 1989). Terrorism is a social construct.

Terrorism is particularly useful for agenda setting (Crenshaw 1998) by the terrorist group and its target. If the reasons behind the violence are articulated clearly, terrorists can put their issues on the public agenda. Instantly, the public is aware of the group and its cause. The act may make some sympathetic to the group or could elicit anger and calls for retaliation. But the target—such as the U.S. government—can also use terrorism to set its own agenda. According to Crenshaw (1998), "Conceptions of terrorism affect the ways in which governments define their interests, and also determine reliance on labels or their abandonment when politically convenient" (p. 10). When the problem is labeled *terrorism* or a group is labeled *terrorists*, a set of predetermined preferred solutions begins to emerge. When these terms depict the group as "fanatical and irrational," making attempts at diplomacy or compromise seem impossible, the inference is that the U.S. government has nothing left to do but retaliate with force. But the labeling doesn't stop: Such defensive actions are often "appropriate" and "legitimate" expressions of "self-defense," but not "terrorism."

David Altheide (2006) explains how decision makers and politicians promote and use the public's beliefs and assumptions about terrorism in order to achieve certain goals. He refers to this as the **politics of fear**. The politics of fear promotes attacking a target, limits civil liberties, and anticipates further victimization. Altheide warns how fear promotes fear, changing our behavior and perspective. Sarah Oates (2006), in her analysis of the role of terrorism coverage in the 2004 presidential/parliamentary election campaigns in Russia, Great Britain, and the United States, concluded that terrorism played an emotive role for American and Russian voters. American and Russian voters identified terrorism as the most important issue in the election, leading them to vote for the candidate they perceived as "stronger" against the threat of terrorism, regardless of the candidate's specific policies or political views. Oates reported that terrorism did not play a role in the Great Britain election as it was mentioned in only 10% of all British news segments in her sample, whereas it was mentioned in 25% of all U.S. election news segments. In Great Britain, the primary issues were the lack of public support for the country's involvement in the Iraq war and the state of Great Britain's economy.

For a summary of sociological perspectives, see Table 16.4.

Table 16.4

Summary of Sociological Perspectives: War and Conflict

	Functional	Conflict/Feminist	Interactionist
Explanation of war and conflict	Functionalists examine how war and terrorism help maintain the social order.	War and terrorism may be based on conflict over resources, territory, and power. From a feminist perspective, war is considered a primarily male activity that enhances the position of males in society.	An interactionist focuses on the social messages and meaning of war and terrorism.
Questions asked about war and conflict	What functions do war and terrorism serve? For terrorist groups? For the targets of terrorism? For groups in conflict? For revolutionaries?	What groups are in conflict and why?	How do our conceptions of war and conflict shape political and diplomatic responses? How do they shape our own behavior?

What Does It Mean to Me?

The rhetoric of September 11 also highlighted social differences based on social class and ethnicity/race. Media stories focused on the heroism of White firefighters and financial brokers, rather than on the victims and heroes who were busboys and maintenance or mailroom workers who were poor, non-White, working-class, immigrant men (Lorber 2002). Why do you think the public and media ignored their stories?

The Problems of War and Terrorism

The Impact of War and Terrorism

Psychological Impact

According to Crenshaw (1983), small incremental societal changes in trust, social cohesion, and integration occur as a result of terrorism. Terrorism has a particular impact in small or homogeneous societies. Research on the long-term impact of terrorism is limited, although some case studies have been conducted in Northern Ireland, where residents have lived with domestic terrorism since the late 1960s. (See this chapter's Taking a World View discussion for more about the Irish Republican Army [IRA].)

War takes a psychological toll, particularly for soldiers involved in battle. Mental health experts have identified posttraumatic stress disorder (PTSD) as a common aftereffect of battle. Those suffering from PTSD feel depressed and detached and have nightmares and flashbacks of their war experience. This anxiety disorder may occur with related issues, such as depression, substance abuse, cognition problems, and other problems of physical or

 Soldiers

mental health (National Center for PTSD 2003a). About 8% of the U.S. population will experience PTSD symptoms in their lifetimes.

Vietnam veterans were particularly hard-hit because of extensive war-related trauma: serving hazardous duty, witnessing death and harm to self or others, and being on frequent or prolonged combat missions. The estimated lifetime prevalence of PTSD among Vietnam veterans is 30.9% for men and 26.9% for women. An additional 22.5% of men and 21.2% of women have had partial PTSD sometime in their lives (National Center for PTSD 2003b). In a study of postservice mortality comparing more than 9,000 U.S. Army veterans who served in Vietnam with more than 8,000 veterans who served in Korea, Germany, or the United States during the same period, the total mortality of those who served in Vietnam was reported to be 17% higher than that of other veteran groups (National Center for PTSD 2003b). The excess mortality occurred primarily in the first five years after discharge, as a result of motor vehicle accidents, suicide, homicide, and accidental poisonings. Drug-related deaths among Vietnam vets were also higher than among other veteran groups (Centers for Disease Control and Prevention 2003).

For information on the Iraq war's impact on veterans, turn to this chapter's In Focus feature.

In Focus

The Hidden Costs of War

Of the 1.4 million U.S. forces deployed in Iraq and Afghanistan, almost 200,000 have sought care and assistance from the U.S. Department of Veterans Affairs. The number is predicted to increase to at least 700,000 by the end of the war (Donn and Hefling 2007). Government, health, and veterans service administrators have observed how different the needs of Iraq war veterans are from those of veterans of past wars and conflicts.

Because of the nature of the conflict itself, forces deployed in Iraq have had more contact with the enemy and more exposure to terrorist attacks than did troops in the earlier Iraq war (O'Connor 2004). The frequency and intensity of operations for active and reserve members increased during the height of the recent wars, with multiple deployments and overseas assignments for soldiers. Estimates range from one in six to one in three soldiers and Marines seeking help for mental health problems or PTSD as a result of their Iraq experiences. Between 80% and 85% of military personnel have witnessed or been part of traumatic events (Vedantam 2006).

About 240,000 female soldiers, Marines, and airmen have been deployed to Iraq or Afghanistan (Perry 2010), 11% of the overall force. As of July 2009, 5,103 female Iraq or Afghanistan veterans received PTSD disability benefits compared with more than 57,000 males. Doctors and therapists note how men traumatized by the war are able to share their experience with other male soldiers, while women are likely to suffer alone. Women are perceived as the nurturers, not the ones needing to be nurtured, thus limiting their access to diagnosis and treatment (Cave 2009).

More wounded soldiers are returning home alive from Iraq. In the past, many would not have survived traumatic brain injuries (TBIs) as a result of improvised explosive device (IED), bomb, or rocket attacks. This shockwave injury is caused when the brain is literally shaken in the soldier's skull, damaging brain tissue. Warfare and medical technology have increased survival rates, however, by making it possible to treat and mobilize wounded soldiers more quickly and closer to combat zones. TBI has been referred to as the signature injury of the Iraq war, much like Agent Orange poisoning was for the Vietnam War. Doctors at the U.S. Army's Walter Reed hospital screened all incoming patients between January 2003 and January 2005 and discovered that 60% of all wounded soldiers had some form of TBI (Zoroya 2005). TBI symptoms include severe headaches, impaired memory, and sensitivity to light and sound. These symptoms may be temporary or permanent.

Policy analysts blame the lack of planning by the U.S. Department of Veterans Affairs (VA), noting that the administration did not expect the conflict to last as long as it has and did not predict the nature and extent of mental and physical injuries for its active-duty and retired personnel (Donn and Hefling 2007). In 2002, the VA guaranteed two years of free care to returning combat veterans for any combat-related medical condition. The cost of these benefits, as well as that of providing long-term disability support for soldiers and veterans and their families, is straining the department's budget and government resources. Some predict that in the end, caring for returning veterans may cost as much as the war itself.

Economic Impact

President George W. Bush pledged that the United States would win the fight against terrorism, "whatever it takes, whatever it costs." Although the United States now has a smaller army and is using technologies that are less human intensive, military expenditures have been increasing, and with those increases comes the greater likelihood of waste, inefficiency, and "good old fashioned pork," according to opponents (Knickerbocker 2002).

The final cost of the Iraq war is estimated to be more than $2 trillion (and unlike past U.S. wars, the Iraq war is being paid almost entirely with debt). The expenditures have been justified as necessary to maintain a high state of military readiness and ground force strength, enhance the combat capabilities of U.S. armed forces, continue the development of capabilities to maintain U.S. superiority against potential threats, and continue the department's support of service members and their families. Though some believe that these additional defense expenses are necessary to win the global war on terrorism, others have criticized the escalation in military expenditures. A comparison of U.S. war expenditures with other countries is presented in Table 16.5.

Do you recall President Eisenhower's warning? Billions of dollars spent on the war means that other programs are not receiving any funding. The National Priorities Project, a nonprofit, nonpartisan organization, analyzes the impact of federal spending policies on city and state funding and budgets. Since the beginning of the Iraq war, the project has tracked the expanding war budget along with increasing budget cuts in nonsecurity (nonwar) discretionary spending. Based on its 2008 budget, the Bush administration proposed cutting $13 billion from social service and education programming—for example, a 35% budget cut in Community Development Block Grants, a 6% cut in the Head Start program, a 40% cut in the Low Income Home Energy Assistance Program, and 6% in special education programming. At the same time, the administration requested an additional $100 billion for war-related spending (National Priorities Project 2007).

The Budget Control Act of 2011 mandates reductions in federal spending, including defense spending. In 2012, President Obama and Defense Secretary Leon Panetta announced a new strategic military plan and the goal to reduce the budget by $259 billion over the next decade.

Environmental Impact

One of the most serious byproducts of war is the mass destruction of ecosystems, also referred to as **ecocide** (Adley and Grant 2003).

Photo 16.3

Marine Cpl. Larry Bailey II (pictured here with his father Larry) is recovering from injuries he received after tripping a rooftop bomb in Afghanistan. Iraq and Afghanistan war veterans are able to survive wounds that in past wars would have been fatal.

Cost of War

Table 16.5

Top 10 Military Spenders (2011)

Country	2011 Expenditures (in Billions)	Share of World Arms Expenditures (%)
United States	$711	41.0
China	[143]	[8.2]
Russia	[71.9]	[4.1]
U.K.	62.7	3.6
France	62.5	3.6
Japan	59.3	3.4
India	48.9	2.8
Saudi Arabia	48.5	2.8
Germany	[46.7]	2.7
Brazil	35.4	2.1

Source: Stockholm International Peace Research Institute 2012.

Note: Numbers in brackets refer to estimated figures.

Bioterrorism

During the Vietnam War, the United States used chemical and biological agents, such as the herbicide Agent Orange, to destroy food crops and defoliate forestlands. Herbicides were used from 1962 to 1969, covering 43% of South Vietnam's arable land and 44% of its forestland at least once, and in many cases two or more times (Falk 1973). The application rate was 13 times the dose recommended for domestic use by the U.S. Food and Drug Administration. More than 1.3 million individuals were poisoned or contaminated. The military justified this environmental destruction in order to deny the Vietnamese army protective cover and to cut off the food supply to peasants and soldiers. The contamination of soil and food crops due to Agent Orange continues to threaten the health of the Vietnamese (Adley and Grant 2003). Another method of clearing vegetation and forests in Vietnam was the use of the Rome plow. The plow is a heavily armored Caterpillar bulldozer used to clear several hundred yards on each side of the main roads. It was estimated that about 2,000 acres (3 square miles) were cleared per day until the end of the war. The croplands and forests of Vietnam were damaged, along with rare tree and animal species (Falk 1973).

Other examples of environmental degradation and destruction resulting from war include the burning of oil wells in Kuwait (1991), the health risks associated with the use of depleted uranium weapons in Iraq (since the first Gulf War in 1991), and the destruction of the mountain gorilla habitat in Rwanda (1994) (Adley and Grant 2003).

Efforts to prevent and redress wartime environmental degradation and destruction have not been successful. The primary issue has been accountability—how should a nation be punished for ecocide? The environmental destructiveness of war and conflict has been acknowledged by world leaders, and in 1992 the Rio Declaration on Environment and Development (signed by all member states of the United Nations) required states to "respect international law providing protection for the environment in times of armed conflict and cooperate in its further development, as necessary" (United Nations 1992).

Political Impact

Terrorism can effect change in two political areas: the overall distribution of political power and government policies (Crenshaw 1983). Terrorism may result in radical changes in the power relationships within a state, involving shifts in who governs and under what rules. As a target of terrorism, the U.S. government has also experienced a redistribution of power as federal and state agencies sought to improve intelligence gathering and security procedures. Institutional changes have occurred, with each major intelligence agency improving its anti-terrorism activities, culminating in the creation of the Department of Homeland Security. In extreme cases, terrorism may lead to the replacement of one government by another.

Government policies usually have two goals: to destroy the terrorist group and to protect potential targets from attack. Policies may include foreign policy efforts seeking the cooperation and support of international allies. After September 11, the U.S. government attempted to destroy terrorist groups and to ensure U.S. security through a series of executive orders, regulations, and laws. In 2001, Congress passed the PATRIOT Act, which established a separate counterterrorism fund, expanded government authority to gather and share evidence with wire and electronic communications, allowed agencies to detain suspected foreign terrorists, and provided for victims of terrorism.

Constitutional and civil rights attorneys have been critical of the PATRIOT Act, alarmed that it would erode individual liberties and increase law enforcement abuses. Often cited is the act's disregard for the principles of political freedom, due process, and the protections of privacy—all principles at the core of a democratic society (Cole and Dempsey 2002). More than 330 cities, towns, and counties, as well as four states, have passed resolutions critical of the federal antiterrorism law (Egan 2004). Two provisions of the act have caused particular concern among citizens. One is the provision that empowers authorities to search people's homes without notification. The provision may have been used by federal agents to search the home of Brandon Mayfield, a lawyer from Oregon who was suspected, but later cleared, in connection with the 2004 bombings in Madrid, Spain. A second clause allows government officials the right to review a person's library, business, and medical records.

What Does It Mean to Me?

President Obama proposed a 2013 budget that included $525 billion for the Department of Defense. The budget includes an additional $89 billion for military operations in Iraq and Afghanistan. What is your opinion of military spending? Are we spending too much or not enough? What do our military expenditures say about the values of our country? Of our role as a global leader?

STATE STATS

Taking a World View

Ireland and the Decommissioning of the IRA

The trouble with the Irish is the English.

—A line from a popular Irish song
(quoted in Whittaker 2002)

In August 2007, the British Army ended Operation Banner, a 38-year security operation in Northern Ireland. Violence and bloodshed first began in 1969, the result

of confrontations between Nationalist and Unionist (or Loyalist) forces. The Nationalist or Catholic groups were led by the IRA and its splinter groups. In 1970, the Provisional IRA was created (*provisional* to honor the provisional government declared by the leaders of the 1916 Easter Rising in Dublin). The Provisional IRA formed to defend the Catholic community and to throw

(Continued)

(Continued)

out the British army and police (Wilkinson 1993). The Unionist or Protestant forces represented the Ulster Defence Association and its splinter groups: the Ulster Volunteer Force, the Red Hand Commandos, and the Ulster Freedom Fighters. Ulster Protestants saw themselves as Britons, loyal to the Protestant crown. These groups represent "Orange Extremism," as described by Paul Wilkinson (1993). Orange extremism has also been blamed for provoking the open conflict in the late 1960s and for creating the conditions in which the Provisional IRA could grow. The division between the groups emphasized their polarization in religion, politics, and economics (Whittaker 2002).

Between them, both sides amassed an impressive armory of rifles, homemade machine guns, grenade throwers, antitank weapons, and explosives. Bombing seemed to be a favorite tactic of both sides. In more than 30 years of conflict, 3,500 civilians have been killed and some 30,000 have been injured, and there has been a loss of property amounting to millions of pounds (Whittaker 2002). IRA terrorists also have taken their own lives without attempting to harm others. There was a chain suicide of 11 IRA members who starved themselves to death in a Belfast prison in 1981. The IRA used the hunger strikes and deaths to its organizational advantage, "to reap emotive propaganda, to restore the flow of cash and weapons from the previously dwindling U.S. sources, and to regroup and rearm" (Wilkinson 1993). Many Irish Americans embraced members of the IRA as freedom fighters and supported their cause politically and financially.

In 1998, both sides accepted the Good Friday Agreement, a 65-page document that sought to define relationships within Northern Ireland, between Northern Ireland and the Republic, and between Ireland, England, Scotland, and Wales. The agreement acknowledges that the people of Northern and Southern Ireland are the only ones with the power to bring about a united Ireland. Through the agreement, new government institutions were set in place. A cabinet-style Executive of Ministers, with members in proportion to party support, allows the participation of all groups (Ahern 2003). The new government composed of unionists and nationalists was established with the first elections for the new Northern Ireland Assembly in June 1998.

A number of political obstacles slowed down the implementation of the agreement, including difficulties over the total disarmament of the Provisional IRA and the dismantling of British military installations in Nationalist areas (Ahern 2003). After experiencing sectarian squabbling, the assembly failed to hold a session for five years (2001–2006); however, elections were held in March 2007 to reestablish the Northern Ireland Assembly and determine how many members from unionist (Protestant) and nationalist (Catholic) parties would be represented (Lyall and Quinn 2007). Self-rule was restored in Belfast in May 2007.

In 2012, Queen Elizabeth was photographed shaking hands with Martin McGuinness, a former IRA commander, a historic moment in Anglo-Irish relations. McGuinness serves as deputy first minister in Northern Ireland's provincial government.

The Next Threat

Domestic Terrorism

Michael Leiter, then director of the National Counterterrorism Center, told the 2011 U.S. House Intelligence Committee that his number-one priority was identifying men and women intent on doing harm in the United States. This included concern with al-Qaeda's efforts to recruit Americans for their own efforts (Mulrine 2011).

On April 19, 1995, the worst domestic terrorism attack occurred around 9:00 a.m. in Oklahoma City, Oklahoma. A rental truck loaded with a mixture of fertilizer and fuel oil exploded in front of the Alfred P. Murrah Federal Building. The blast blew off the front side of the nine-story building, killing 169 and injuring hundreds more. The attack was conducted by Timothy McVeigh and Terry Nichols, motivated by antigovernment sentiment over the failed 1993 federal raid on the Branch Davidian compound in Texas. The bombing occurred on the second anniversary of the Branch Davidian incident. McVeigh was executed for his crime in 2001; Nichols is serving a life sentence.

Louis J. Freeh (2001), former director of the Federal Bureau of Investigation (FBI), identified three types of domestic groups operating in the United States: right-wing extremists, left-wing and Puerto Rican extremists, and special interest extremists. Right-wing groups, such as the World Church of the Creator, Aryan Nations, and the Southeastern States Alliance, advocate for the principles of racial supremacy and tend to embrace antigovernment or antiregulatory beliefs. They have also been characterized as hate groups. The Southern Poverty Law Center (2012) identified 1,018 active hate groups in the United States for 2011, noting an increase in the number of antigovernment patriot movements. (See U.S. Data Map 16.1 for the distribution of known hate groups by state.)

U.S. DATA MAP 16.1

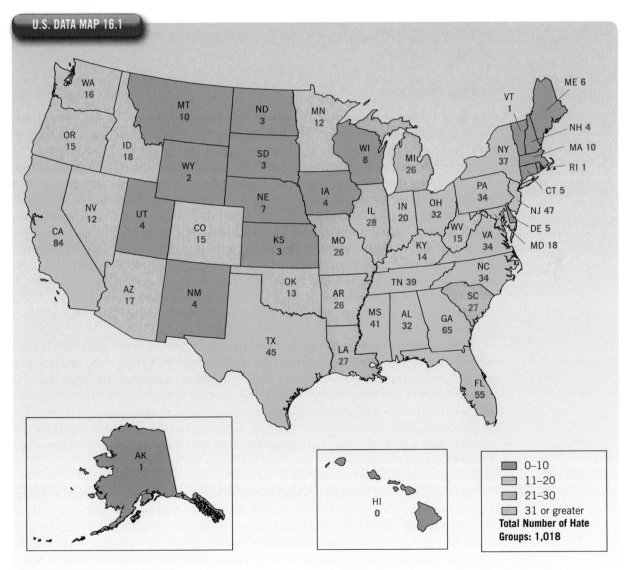

Number of Hate Groups, 2011

Source: Southern Poverty Law Center 2012.

Left-wing groups want to bring about revolutionary change, adopting a socialist doctrine, and see themselves as protectors of the people. Groups in this category include terrorist or separatist groups seeking Puerto Rico's independence from the United States and anarchists and extremist socialist groups such as the Workers World Party, Reclaim the Streets, and Carnival Against Capitalism. Many of these anarchist groups were blamed for the damage caused at the 1999 World Trade Organization meeting in Seattle, Washington.

Animal Activists

Special interest groups want to resolve specific issues, rather than effect political change. These groups are at the fringes of animal rights, pro-life, environmental, antinuclear, and other political and social movements. Animal rights and environmental groups, such as the Animal Liberation Front (ALF) and the Earth Liberation Front (ELF), have recently increased their activities. Activists from these groups usually use arson and incendiary devices equipped with timers to target government and company facilities. The FBI says that these groups are responsible for more than 1,800 criminal acts and more than $110 million in damages (FBI 2009).

Nuclear Weapons

The nuclear weapons age began on July 16, 1945, when the United States exploded the first nuclear bomb in Alamogordo, New Mexico. Three weeks later, an atomic bomb was used on the city of Hiroshima, Japan, killing 100,000 residents. Three days later, an atomic bomb was used on the city of Nagasaki, Japan, killing about 74,000 and injuring 75,000. During the 1950s and 1960s, the United States was engaged in a cold war with Russia and other nuclear countries, locked in a stalemate over who would be the first to launch a nuclear attack. In 1963, the countries agreed to sign a partial test ban treaty, banning nuclear tests in the atmosphere, under water, and in space, and a nonproliferation treaty was signed in 1968, prohibiting nonnuclear countries from possessing or developing nuclear weapons. In 1996, President Bill Clinton was the first world leader to sign the Comprehensive Nuclear Test Ban Treaty, which prohibits all nuclear test explosions in all environments. However, the treaty has yet to be ratified by the U.S. Senate. All North Atlantic Treaty Organization (NATO) members, except for the United States, have ratified the treaty.

Nuclear weapons are still held by more than eight nations in the world. Suspected weapons have been identified in China (250–320), France (350), India (50+), North Korea (5–12), Pakistan (40–70), Russia (about 7,200), the United Kingdom (180–200), and the United States (5,736) (Center for Defense Information 2009). In 2010, Iran's President Mahmoud Ahmadinejad announced that his country was a "nuclear state." Though his claims could not be independently verified, nuclear watchdog groups and experts say it would take several years for Iran to produce a nuclear weapon. The United States has called for United Nations–backed sanctions to discourage Iran from pursuing its weapons development program.

In 2010, Obama and Russian President Dmitry Medvedev signed a treaty to reduce American and Russian strategic nuclear arsenals by 30%, to the lowest levels since the early years of the cold war. The United States and Russia possess 95% of the world's nuclear weapons. The treaty is subject to ratification by lawmakers in both countries and according to Obama and Medvedev sets the stage for further nuclear weapons reduction. Obama has pledged not to develop any new nuclear weapons.

Community, Policy, and Social Action

The National Commission on Terrorist Attacks Upon the United States, also known as the 9-11 Commission, was an independent bipartisan commission created by congressional legislation. The 9-11 Commission was charged with documenting and preparing a full account of the September 11 terrorist attacks. Throughout 2003 and 2004, hearings were held investigating Osama bin Laden's network, the performance of the intelligence community, emergency preparedness and response, and national policy coordination. The commission concluded that U.S. intelligence gathering by the FBI and CIA was inadequate, fragmented, and poorly coordinated.

In 2002, Bush established the Department of Homeland Security. (Before September 11, the U.S. Commission on National Security in the 21st Century [2001] had recommended the creation of a National Homeland Security Agency, responsible for planning, coordinating, and integrating all U.S. agencies responsible for security.) The primary mission of the department is to prevent terrorist attacks and reduce the vulnerability of the United States to terrorism through coordination with component agencies: U.S. Secret Service, U.S. Coast Guard, U.S. Citizenship and Immigration Services, U.S. Immigration and Customs Enforcement, U.S. Customs and Border Protection, the Federal Emergency Management Agency, and the Transportation Security Administration. The Department of Homeland Security is also responsible for the Homeland Security Advisory System, which informs the public of the current level of terrorist threat.

As a nation, the United States has used several approaches to combat and to reduce the risk of war and conflict: diplomacy, economic sanctions, and military force. Usually, war is justified as being the last resort in circumstances where there are severe domestic rights violations or international aggression by an offending state (Garfield 2002).

Political Diplomacy

According to Christopher Harmon (2000), "Political will, more than new laws or new direction[s] in international politics, is the most important component of an enhanced effort against foreign supported terrorism" (p. 236). Political diplomacy includes articulating policy to foreign leaders, persuading them, and reaching agreements with them (Pillar 2001). Wars reshape diplomacy; victory becomes the goal of foreign policy, and diplomatic relationships are adjusted to achieve it (Mandelbaum 2003). Political scientist Stephen Van Evera (2006) argues the United States must develop and use its power to make peace.

Relationship building and persuasion are at the heart of U.S. diplomatic efforts. As the lead foreign affairs agency, the Department of State attempts to formulate, represent, and implement the president's foreign policy (U.S. Department of State 2003). The secretary of state is the president's principal adviser on foreign policy and represents the United States abroad in foreign affairs. Primarily, the department manages diplomatic relations with other countries and international institutions (such as the United Nations, NATO, the World Bank, and the International Monetary Fund [IMF]). The Department of State conducts negotiations and concludes agreements and treaties with other countries on issues ranging from trade to nuclear weapons. The United States maintains diplomatic relations with more than 180 countries (U.S. Department of State 2003). Diplomacy is conducted by the secretary of state and by foreign service officers, immigration officers, FBI special agents, intelligence officers, transportation specialists, defense attachés, and other officials (Pillar 2001).

Peacebuilding

In contrast with the hard-line diplomacy embraced by George W. Bush's administration, President Obama's diplomacy has been described as a **soft-power approach**, where a nation-state is perceived as having values, motives, and actions that should be emulated (Nye 2008). A nation-state with soft power leads with noncoercive persuasion through its attitudes toward international norms, embracing the rules of law and demonstrating respect for diversity and cultural history (Hayden 2011). The president serves as the chief diplomat, setting the tone and agenda for political diplomacy. Obama's 2009 speech at the Al-Azhar University in Cairo, Egypt, has been described as a significant diplomatic address, as the president openly acknowledged the plight of the Palestinians and Israel's relationship with the United States. Craig Hayden (2011) writes, "The speech was a signal that the United States would take a more balanced approach to acknowledge the particular perspectives of the Middle East crises. The speech was also important as a function of public diplomacy in the manner of its delivery, its location and the way it signaled the course of U.S. foreign policy in the region" (p. 791). Obama's soft-power approach has been praised for improving the U.S. status as the world's most admired country, yet has been criticized for not being effective or strong enough.

The Use of Economic Sanctions

For many years, the United States and the United Nations have used nonviolent approaches in the form of economic sanctions to punish or pressure countries that have violated U.S. laws or values. Sanctions are considered an alternative to diplomacy or military force. By July 1999, the United States had imposed sanctions on no fewer than 28 countries. From World War I to 1990, the United States imposed sanctions 77 times. The United Nations has imposed economic sanctions 13 times (Marks 1999).

Economic sanctions, in the form of trade embargoes and the termination of development assistance, are the most commonly applied form of sanctions, and they have the most significant public health consequences. U.S. sanctions were used against Iraq in 1990 to force its withdrawal from Kuwait and against Yugoslavia (1991–1996) and Serbia and Montenegro (1992–1996) during the Serbian war (Marks 1999). According to Richard Haas (1997), "Economic sanctions are popular because they offer what appears to be a proportional response to challenges in which the interests at stake are less than vital" (p. 75). Sanctions can also serve as a signal of official displeasure with a country's behavior or action.

Economic Sanctions

Many attempts have focused on cutting aid to countries sponsoring or supporting terrorism. The problem is that most terrorist states do not receive significant aid from the United States, and based on past experience, sanctions have only made target countries and nations more angry and impassioned against the United States (Flores 1981). Shaheen Ayubi et al. (1982) concluded that economic sanctions in U.S. foreign policy may not be effective in their objectives and have often failed to achieve their political purposes. For example, sanctions applied against Cuba since 1960 have failed to destabilize the Castro regime.

Sanctions may not hurt dictators and terrorists, but they may increase suffering and death among civilians (Garfield 2002), and research suggests that economic coercion may worsen public health, economic conditions, educational attainment, and the development of a civil society in the sanctioned country (Peksen 2009). A report issued in 1993 by the Harvard Center for Population and Development Studies maintained that sanctions exacerbated malnutrition in Haiti and increased child deaths caused by misgovernment (Neier 1993). One approach has been to freeze only economic assets while continuing to provide food and medical aid through private agencies (Neier 1993). However, although only economic sanctions were directed against Iraq in the early 1990s, the Harvard Study Team (1991) reported that essential goods—food, medicine, and infrastructure support—were not reaching those in need. All health facilities surveyed reported major drug shortages. Children were most vulnerable, dying of preventable diseases and starvation. The chance of dying before age 5 in Iraq more than doubled, from 54 per 1,000 between 1984 and 1989 to 131 per 1,000 between 1995 and 1999 (Ali and Shah 2000).

Military Response

Military action is based on the idea that the most effective way to defeat an enemy is by the destruction of the enemy's armies, equipment, transport systems, industrial centers, and cities.

Military intervention has also been defined as a form of **humanitarian intervention**. For example in 1999, NATO countries declared a humanitarian war in Kosovo, in response to claims that thousands of Kosovo Albanians were the victims of a systematic campaign of ethnic cleansing by Serbian forces. It was the first time that violence was used by outside forces to resolve an internal national dispute. NATO countries were criticized for engaging in an unlawful bloody war. Yet, the concept of humanitarian warfare continues to be deliberated from ethical, political, and legal perspectives (Zajadlo 2005). Canada's International Commission on Intervention and State Sovereignty (2001) suggested that humanitarian intervention should be defined as a responsibility to protect. According to the commission, there are three aspects of this responsibility: how to prevent humanitarian crises in the first place, under which conditions and in what way to intervene, and how to maintain peace after a military conflict and rebuild the country.

Retaliation has been the most important counterterrorist use of U.S. military force. The United States first used it against Libya in 1986, responding to the April 4 bombing of a nightclub in Berlin where two Americans were killed and seventy-one were wounded. One hundred military aircraft were used to attack military targets in and around Tripoli and Benghazi in Libya (Pillar 2001). After September 11, 2001, U.S. troops were deployed to destroy Taliban operations based in Afghanistan.

According to Pillar (2001), evidence suggests that military retaliation does not serve as an effective deterrent to terrorism. First, terrorists who threaten the United States present few suitable military targets. It is tough to attack an enemy that can't be located. Many terrorist groups lack any high-value targets, whose destruction would be costly to their organization. Second, a military attack against a terrorist group may serve political and organizational goals of the terrorist leaders. Such attacks may increase recruiting, sympathy, and resources for terrorist groups. And finally, there is no evidence that terrorists will respond peacefully after a retaliatory attack. Terrorists may also respond by fighting back.

Voices in the Community

Aung San Suu Kyi

Between 1989 and 2010, Daw Aung San Suu Kyi was a political prisoner in Myanmar (also known as Burma). For more than 15 years during this period, she was detained under house arrest as the Burma junta declared martial law. As reported by Amnesty International (2012),

Photo 16.4

Aung San Suu Kyi was a political prisoner for 15 years in her own country of Myanmar. After her release in 2010, she was elected in 2012 to serve as a representative in the Myanmar parliament, as a member of the National League for Democracy.

many of Myanmar's citizens live in poverty and suffer from human rights violations. Political and social dissent is controlled by arrests, torture, and imprisonment. The number of political prisoners in Myanmar is estimated at 1,995 (Amnesty International 2012).

Suu Kyi served as chairperson of the National League for Democracy (NLD), promoting democracy in the military-ruled country. The organization was banned during her arrest. The military authorities consented to her release in 2010. In 2012, Suu Kyi along with 44 other NLD candidates ran for seats in Myanmar's parliament. Suu Kyi won her seat. Eighty percent of the parliamentary seats are still held by members of the military-backed ruling party.

After the election, Suu Kyi traveled to Oslo, Norway, to collect her Nobel Peace Prize. She received the honor in 1991 but due to her imprisonment was not able to receive her award.

During the 2012 ceremony, Suu Kyi (2012) spoke of her goal for a free, secure and just society in Myanmar. She spoke of the effectiveness of reform in her country:

> We can say that reform is effective only if the lives of the people are improved and in this regard, the international community has a vital role to play. Development and humanitarian aid, bi-lateral agreements and investments should be coordinated and calibrated to ensure that these will promote social, political and economic growth that is balanced and sustainable. The potential of our country is enormous. This should be nurtured and developed to create not just a more prosperous but also a more harmonious, democratic society where our people can live in peace, security and freedom.

Antiwar and Peace Movements

Antiwar movements have been characterized as reactive, occurring only in response to specific wars or the threat of war. Every twentieth-century war conducted by the United States elicited organized protest and opposition (Chatfield 1992). The public's response to the Iraq and Afghanistan wars was described as apathetic. The lack of public outrage or protest over the wars was attributed to several factors: the social construction of a common enemy (terrorism), the pervasive rhetoric of patriotism and nationalism, and an overall decline in civic and political engagement. The Bush administration's policy banning media coverage of fallen soldiers' caskets was blamed for shielding the public from the personal toll of these wars. The ban was lifted in 2009.

Peace movements represent organized coalitions that are "fundamentally concerned with the problems of war, militarism, conscription, and mass violence, and the ideals of internationalism, globalism and non-violent relations between people" (Young 1999:228). According to Nigel Young (1999), there are different peace traditions: groups that provide ideas and initiatives for the entire peace movement. For example, the tradition of liberalism and internationalism attempts to prevent war through reformed behavior of states: peace plans, treaties, international law, and arbitration between all groups. Another tradition, anticonscriptionism, links the peace movement with individual civil rights.

Women as Peacemakers

Another peace tradition is feminist antimilitarism. Peace movements within this tradition are united by the ideal of a distinctive role for women on the issue of peace and female unity across national boundaries (Young 1999). Feminist antimilitary groups first began in the early 1900s. In 1914, Jane Addams, founder of Hull House, led a women's peace parade in New York to protest World War I. Addams, along with Carrie Chapman Catt, the main strategist and leader for the women's suffrage movement, and other women activists, formed the Women's Peace Party in 1915. Later that year, the party was renamed the Women's International League for Peace and Freedom. The organization exists today, with chapters in Africa, Asia, South Asia, the Middle East, Europe, and the Americas. Its current global mission includes building a "culture of peace" rather than a "culture of war."

College Activists

There is a tradition of student involvement in politics in the United States (Altbach and Peterson 1971). Paul Knott (1971) explains that college students before World War II were mainly upper-middle-class students who treated their education as a privilege. Except for a few campuses, most undergraduates showed little social consciousness and were unwilling to challenge or question the status quo. But increasing diversity on college campuses—in students' ages, gender, and ethnic backgrounds—helped increase social awareness and infused students with a greater sense of empowerment. Student activism was at its peak in the 1960s and 1970s, supporting the civil rights movement and later protesting the Vietnam War. During the late 1970s, campuses institutionalized many of the gains made in the previous decade: establishing women's centers, Black student unions, and gay and lesbian organizations and ensuring that student government had a greater role in university operations (Vellela 1988).

 Young Voters

The college student population is less politicized as a whole than it was 45 years ago. According to the University of California–Los Angeles (UCLA) annual survey of freshmen, 60% of students viewed "keeping up with politics" as "very important" or "essential" in 1966 compared with only 32.8% in 2011 (Pryor et al. 2011). Some argue, however, that progressive student activism didn't stop after the Vietnam War era (Vellela 1988). Student activism is on the rise, but it doesn't reproduce the civil rights and war protests of the 1960s and 1970s. Students are engaged in a broad range of issues: women's rights, discrimination, homophobia, immigration, the homeless, labor unions, and political action groups.

What Does It Mean to Me?

How important is keeping up with politics to you? How well informed are you about local and national political issues? Are you a registered voter? How have you been educated about your rights as a voter? About local and national issues?

STATE STATS

The new wave of peace activism builds on existing networks established by the student anticorporate movement, which focused on economic justice related to sweatshop labor and unionization on campuses (refer to Chapter 9, "Work and the Economy"). The current wave of peace activism includes a diverse set of schools: rural southern schools (Appalachian State University in North Carolina, University of Southern Mississippi), historically Black colleges (Morehouse College, University of Georgia), community

Photo 16.5

After her son Casey was killed in Iraq in 2004, Cindy Sheehan became an antiwar activist, taking her message to President Bush at his Crawford, Texas, ranch and at the White House. Sheehan and other protestors were arrested in front of the White House (pictured here). Sheehan stepped away from her activism in 2007, saying that she wanted to return home and be a mother to her surviving children.

colleges from Hawaii to Massachusetts, and urban public universities (City University of New York and University of Illinois–Chicago), as well as high schools and middle schools. Student groups have held teach-ins, vigils, and fasts to call attention to a variety of issues (Featherstone 2003).

Although most recent peace activism has protested against the war in Iraq, this sentiment has not been universal. Student peace groups have been sensitive to the message that they send (Featherstone 2003). Peace groups are linking their opposition to war to the campaign for social justice, dealing with racism, economic inequality, and sexism at home. Student protestors seem to have learned from the protests of the 1960s, wanting to prevent the kind of alienation experienced by Vietnam War veterans (Rhoads 1991).

Main Points

- War is a violent but legitimate political instrument between armed combatants. From the American Revolution to the twenty-first-century war in Iraq, U.S. history is replete with war.

- Terrorism is the unlawful use of force to intimidate or coerce compliance with a particular set of beliefs and can be either domestic (based in the United States) or foreign (supported by foreign groups threatening the security of U.S. nationals or U.S. national security).

- Terrorism is a premeditated, purposeful, political act targeting noncombatants to force the main target to change course, and it is usually carried out by subnational groups or clandestine agents.

- Terrorist activity has changed little over the years. Six basic tactics account for 95% of all incidents: bombings, assassinations, armed assaults, kidnappings, hijackings, and other hostage seizures.

- Functionalists examine how war and terrorism help maintain the social order, creating and reinforcing boundaries. War creates social stability by letting everyone know what side they are on; there are norms and boundaries in war. But unlike in war, the social boundaries in terrorist activities are less certain.

- War and conflict may be based on disputes over resources or land. Modern conflict theorists have focused on how war is used to promote economic and political interests, such as replacing social program funding with military expenditures.

- From the feminist perspective, war is considered a primarily male activity that enhances the position of males in society. Women are expected either to be caretakers or to take over certain jobs vacated by men, as occurred in World War II. More recently, women combatants have redefined notions of courage. Feminist theorists focus on the gender rhetoric used in war.

- Interactionists focus on the social messages and meaning of war and conflict. For example, *terrorism* is a word with intrinsically negative connotations. Use of the word promotes condemnation of the actors and may reflect an ideological or a political bias.

- Domestic terrorist groups continue to pose a threat. The worst domestic terrorist act was the 1995 Oklahoma City bombing.

- Three types of domestic groups operate in the United States. Right-wing ("hate") groups are antigovernment and advocate for the principles of racial supremacy. Left-wing groups want to bring about socialist revolutionary change. Special interest groups focus on resolving specific issues rather than bringing about political change.

- Terrorism can effect change in two political areas: the overall distribution of political power and government policies. In extreme cases, terrorism may lead to the replacement of one government by another.

- Government policies usually have two goals: to destroy the terrorist group and to protect potential targets from attack. One recent policy is the 2001 PATRIOT Act, which has brought criticism from constitutional and civil liberty groups.

- Modes of counterterrorism appear piecemeal and ineffective. The current counterterrorist policy includes several tenets: make no deals with terrorists, bring terrorists to justice, isolate and apply pressure to states sponsoring terrorism, and improve the counterterrorist capabilities of U.S. allies.

- Political diplomacy includes articulating policy to foreign leaders, persuading them, and reaching agreements with them. Wars reshape diplomacy; victory becomes the goal of foreign policy. As the lead foreign affairs agency, the Department of State attempts to formulate, represent, and implement the president's foreign policy.

- For many years, the United States and the United Nations have used nonviolent approaches, in the form of economic sanctions, to punish or pressure countries that have violated U.S. laws or values. Sanctions are considered an alternative to diplomacy or military force. Economic sanctions such as trade embargoes, which are the most commonly applied form, can significantly affect the health of the targeted country's citizens.

- Many counterterrorism attempts have focused on cutting off aid to countries sponsoring or supporting terrorism. However, most such states do not receive significant aid from the United States, and sanctions may have only made targets angrier with the United States.

- There are four types of military response to terrorism: preemptive operations, search and recovery operations, rescue operations, and retaliatory or punitive raids. Retaliation has been the most important counterterrorist use of U.S. military force, but evidence suggests that military retaliation does not serve as an effective deterrent to terrorism because terrorists present few suitable military targets, military attacks may actually help the goals of terrorist leaders, and terrorists may respond violently.

- Every twentieth-century war conducted by the United States has elicited organized antiwar movements. At the college level, student activism was at its peak in the 1960s and 1970s. Activism is on the rise, but not as much as in the 1960s and 1970s. Students now are engaged in a broad range of issues: women's rights, discrimination, homophobia, the homeless, labor unions, and political action groups.

On Your Own

Log on to the open-access Student Study Site at www.sagepub.com/leonguerrero4e for these additional learning tools:

- Interactive quizzes
- Video clips
- NPR audio links
- Handbook articles

- E-flashcards
- Journal articles
- End-of-chapter web exercises
- Additional web resources and current events

Internet and Community Exercises

1. Investigate the history of women's peace movements through the Swarthmore College Peace Collection, established in 1930 by Jane Addams of Hull House in Chicago. Current women's peace organizations include Women Waging Peace and the Women's International League for Peace and Freedom. The site for the Women's International League for Peace and Freedom also lists state branches. Log on to *Study Site Chapter 16* for more information.

2. Investigate a peace and social justice organization on your campus. (Student Peace Action Network [SPAN] is an example of a campus-based organization. SPAN has chapters throughout the country and in Europe.) What is the mission of the organization? How many students and faculty members belong to it? What activities does the organization sponsor? If your campus does not have such an organization, can you determine why this is the case?

3. Select a country (other than the United States) and research whether peace or social justice organizations exist on university campuses. Examine one organization's mission and activities. What similarities and differences can you identify between this organization and the one based on your own campus?

Study Questions

1. From a functionalist's perspective, how do war and terrorism serve a "safety valve" function?
2. How does the military industrial complex contribute to war and conflict?
3. From an interactionist perspective, how has the war on terrorism been socially constructed?

4. Identify the psychological, economic, and political impacts of war and conflict.
5. Explain warfare as a humanitarian intervention.
6. What role have college students and activists played in antiwar and peace movements?

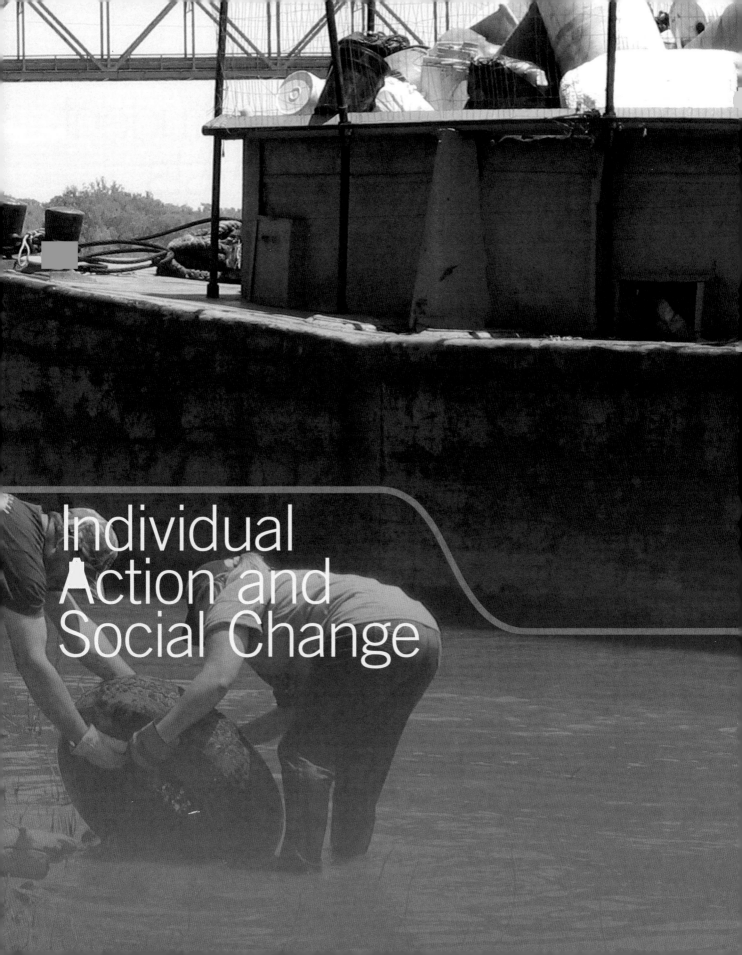

PART V

Individual
Action and
Social Change

Thanks to Student Activists . . .

Student activists have had considerable impact on social movements, past and present. Consider their role in some of the past century's expressive movements, which aim to change individuals and individual behavior in matters both small and large.

▲ Thanks to these 1946 high school students and many others like them, young women are no longer required to wear skirts and hosiery in school and other public places.

Largely because of the voices of students after the terrorist attacks of September 11, 2001, many Americans understand that most Muslims and people who look Middle Eastern are not to blame.

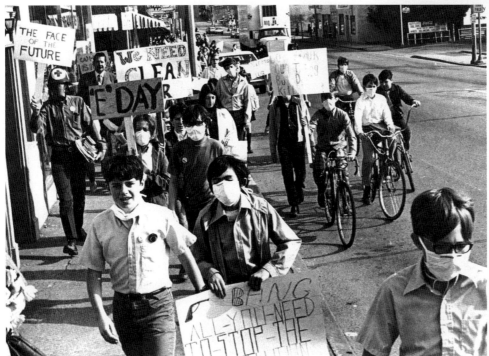

Thanks in part to the environmental concerns expressed by students in the 1970s, most Americans now support environmental causes and try to recycle and conserve the earth's resources.

Students have also been major players in instrumental movements meant to change the structure of society, institutions, and organizations. Although some of these movements have not yet achieved all their goals, they have made a noticeable difference in people's lives.

Thanks to the dedication of students like these NAACP members working on a 1942 campaign for the equal treatment of African American teachers in Norfolk, Virginia, the movement for civil rights gathered strength and stayed on the path that led to far-reaching legislation during Lyndon Johnson's presidency.

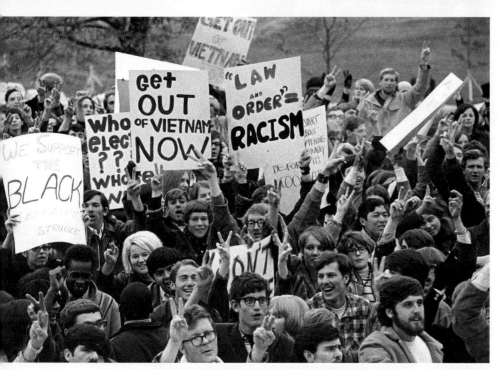

Amid massive antiwar protests in the late 1960s and early 1970s, students learned how powerful their voices could be, extended the civil rights movement, and helped to end the Vietnam War.

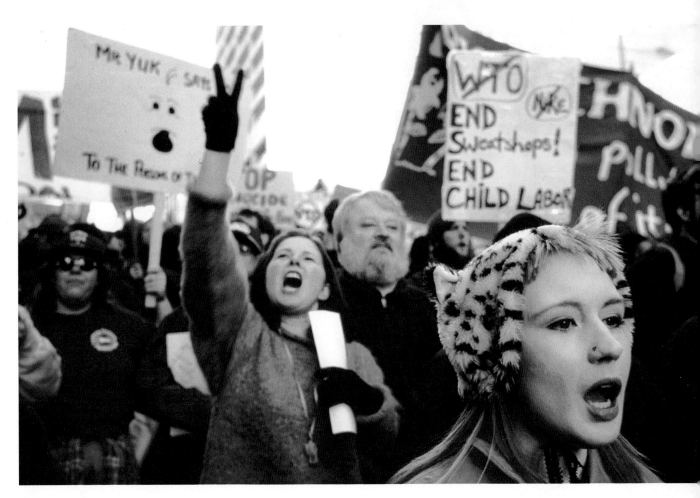

▲ Thanks to students joining protests against the 1999 World Trade Organization meetings in Seattle, Washington, we have all become more sensitive to the inequities of globalization.

What other student movements—local or global in scope—do you believe have made a difference? Have you participated in a social movement?

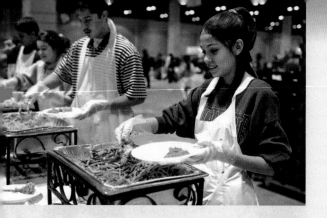

CHAPTER 17

Social Problems and Social Action

I n our first chapter, I introduced you to three connections that would be made throughout this text. The first was the connection between sociology and social problems. We began with two concepts offered by C. Wright Mills: personal troubles and public issues. Mills explained that personal troubles transform into public issues when we recognize that troubles exist not because of individual characteristics or traits but because of social forces. This book has not focused on "nuts, sluts, and perverts" (Liazos 1972) as the source of our social problems. Rather, using our sociological imagination, we've examined how social forces shape social problems in U.S. society. We have relied on four sociological perspectives—functionalist, conflict, feminist, and interactionist—to guide us through each chapter and each set of problems. These four perspectives provide a unique look at social problems and, as a consequence, offer insights about how we may solve them.

According to a functionalist, all society's needs are met by its **social institutions** (family, education, politics, religion, and economics). Working interdependently, these institutions ensure social order. When society experiences significant social change (e.g., the Industrial Revolution, war), the social order is particularly susceptible to social problems (e.g., crime, poverty, or violence). Social problems do not emerge from individuals; rather, problems emerge when the order is disrupted or tested. Functionalist solutions focus on restoring the social order, repairing the broken institutions, and avoiding dramatic social change.

Like the functionalists, conflict and feminist theorists examine social problems at the macro or societal level. For conflict theorists, social problems are the result of social, economic, or political inequalities inherent in our society. Feminist perspectives consider how gender inequalities lead to social problems. Whereas functionalists assume that order is normal for society, the conflict and feminist theorists believe that conflict over resources and power is the status quo. From this perspective, how does one eliminate social problems? The existing social order needs to be replaced with a more equitable society. Midrange solutions attempt to redefine opportunity and power structures to include the participation of marginalized individuals or groups.

 Radical Women

The interactionist perspective focuses on social problems at the micro or individual level. According to this perspective, we create our reality through social interaction. Social problems are created by the labels we attach to individuals and their situations (e.g., the "welfare mom" or a "crack addict"). In addition, problematic behavior is learned from others; for example, interactionists believe that criminal behavior is learned from other criminals. Social problems are not objective realities. Rather, they are subjectively constructed by religious, political, and social leaders who influence our opinions and conceptions of what is a social problem. This perspective leads us to many different solutions: changing the labeling process (being careful of who is being labeled and what the label is), resocialization for deviant or inappropriate behavior (if the behavior was learned, it can be unlearned), and recognizing the social construction of social problems (acknowledging that it is a subjective process).

What Does It Mean to Me?

Throughout this text, you have been introduced to four sociological perspectives. Which sociological perspective do you agree with most? Which perspective best explains the reasons and solutions for social problems?

Social Problems and Their Solutions

Since its inception, sociology has been considered a means to understand and improve what is wrong with the world. Early sociological thinking emerged from the late eighteenth and early nineteenth centuries during periods of dramatic social, economic, and political change, such as the Industrial Revolution, the French Revolution, and the Enlightenment period. The first sociological thinkers, Karl Marx, Émile Durkheim, and Max Weber, were preoccupied with these social changes and the problems they created for society. These thinkers spent their lives studying these problems and attempted to develop programs that would help solve them (Ritzer 2000).

Sociology provides us with the means to examine the social structure or "machinery" that runs our lives. In his book *Invitation to Sociology,* sociologist Peter Berger (1963) likens our human experience to that of puppets on a stage:

> We located ourselves in society and thus recognize our own position as we hang from subtle strings. For a moment we see ourselves as puppets. . . . Unlike the puppets, we have the possibility of stopping in our movements, looking up and perceiving the machinery by which we have been moved. In this act lies the first step towards freedom. (p. 176)

Freedom comes first in identifying the social "machinery" that controls us and second in recognizing that the way society controls us is fundamentally different from the way strings control puppets. We have the power to transform or alter that machinery; we have the power to create social change.

The past sixteen chapters have revealed how we continue to experience many social problems—and bear in mind that not every social problem could be addressed in the pages of this text. Yet, considering the past decade, strong evidence suggests that problems such as crime, drug abuse, and poverty have been minimized because of effective social policies and solutions. We tend to think of the government as the only effective agent of social change because the politicians pass new laws and policies. But the government is not the only agent of social change. In each chapter, I introduced you to individuals, groups, and communities that have attempted to address a particular social problem. All in their own way are making the second connection, the one between social problems and their solutions.

Our nation's history is filled with groups of people who attempted to promote change or prevent it from taking place (Harper and Leicht 2002). **Social movements** are defined as conscious, collective, organized attempts to bring about or resist large-scale change in the social order (Wilson 1973). In today's society, almost every critical public issue leads to a social movement supporting change (and an opposing countermovement to discourage it) (Meyer and Staggenbord 1996). Social movements are the most potent forces of social change in our society (Sztompka 1994). Social movements lead the way for social reform and policies by first identifying and calling attention to social problems.

Understanding Social Movements

Social Movements Today

Social movements are classified by two factors. First, how much change is intended by the social movement: Is it limited or radical change? And second, what is the scope of the intended change: Is it a group of people or an entire society? Sociologists Charles Harper and Kevin Leicht (2002) distinguish between two dimensions of social movements in their book, *Exploring Social Change: America and the World*. The first dimension identifies how much change is intended by the movement, distinguishing between reform and revolutionary movements. According to Harper and Leicht, **reform movements** try to bring about limited social change by working within the existing system, usually targeting social structures such as education or medicine and directly targeting policy makers. Examples of reform movements are proabortion or antiabortion groups. On the other hand, **revolutionary social movements** seek fundamental changes of the system itself. These types of social movements, such as the U.S. civil rights movement or the antiapartheid movement in South Africa, consider the political system the key to system change.

The second dimension of social movements identified by Harper and Leicht (2002) is instrumental versus expressive, addressing the scope of intended change. **Instrumental movements** seek to change the structure of society; examples are the civil rights movement and the environmental movement. **Expressive movements** attempt to change individuals and individual behavior. Based on these dimensions, John Wilson (1973) specified four types of social movements: reformative, transformative, alternative, and redemptive (see Table 17.1).

New social movements theory emphasizes the distinctive features of recent social movements. New social movements first appeared in cultural and radical feminist movements in the late 1960s, in some radical sections of the environmental movement in the 1970s, in parts of the peace movement of the late 1970s through the mid-1980s, and in radical sections of the gay rights movement since the 1980s (Plotke 1995).

John Hannigan (1991) and David Plotke (1995) distinguish between new social movements and early social movements. First, new movements have different ideologies than did earlier movements. Instead of fighting for human rights, such as voting or freedom of speech, new movements are framed around concerns about cultural and community rights, such as the right to be different, to choose one's lifestyle, and to be protected from particular risks like nuclear or environmental hazards (Hannigan 1991). Second, new social movements distrust formal organizations. Consequently, they tend to be small-scale, informal organizations. Finally, whereas previous movements were identified with the economic oppression of workers or minorities, new social movements are associated with a new middle class of "younger, social and cultural specialists" (Plotke 1995). Instead of acting on behalf of their own interests, this new middle class acts on behalf of groups who cannot act on their own.

Table 17.1

Types of Social Movements

	Instrumental	Expressive
Reform	*Reformative:* Partial change within the social structure via policy reform	*Alternative:* Partial change in individuals via individual reform
	Examples: Labor movement, NAACP, antiabortion	*Examples:* Christian evangelism, temperance movement
Revolutionary	*Transformative:* Total change of the social structure	*Redemptive:* Total change in the individuals
	Examples: Bolsheviks, Islamic fundamentalism	*Examples:* Millenarian movements, cults, the People's Temple

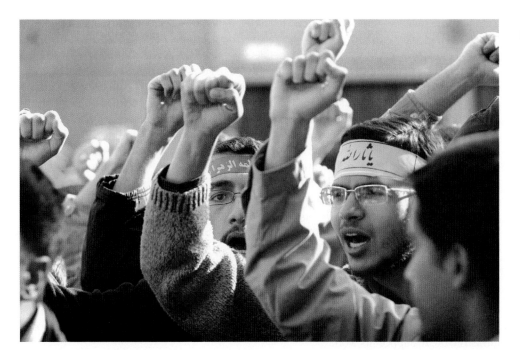

Photo 17.1

In 2009, hundreds of Iranian university students staged protests before the Saudi Arabian and Yemeni embassies in Tehran. Students were protesting against the Yemeni government's battle against Shiite rebels in northern Yemen and the alleged contribution of Saudi Arabia to the conflict.

How Do Social Movements Begin?

Social Movements

Social scientists offer several explanations of how social movements emerge. Individual explanations focus on the psychological dispositions or motivations of those drawn to social movements. Women and men are depicted as either frustrated or calculating actors in political or social movements. Empirical studies have not consistently supported these explanations, demonstrating that individual predispositions are insufficient to account for collective action in social movements. In addition, such theories tend to deflect attention from the real causes of discontent and injustice in our social and political structures (Wilson and Orum 1976).

Social movements do not generally arise from a stable social context; rather, they arise from a changing social order (Lauer 1976). Social movements arise from the structure itself, primarily the result of social and economic deprivation. People are not acting just because of their suffering. They are likely to act when they experience **relative deprivation**, a perceived gap between what they expect and what they actually get. James Davies (1974) argued that social movements were likely to occur when a long period of economic and social improvement is followed by a period of decline. Relative deprivation theory has been used to explain the development of urban protests among African Americans during the 1960s, which were initiated by middle-class African Americans who perceived social and economic gaps between Black and White Americans (Harper and Leicht 2002). But relative deprivation alone isn't enough to create a social movement.

Black Social Movements

Neil Smelser (1963) explains that six structural conditions are necessary for the development of collective behaviors and social movements. These conditions operate in an additive fashion. First, particular structures in society are more likely to generate certain kinds of social movements than others. For example, societies with racial divisions are more likely to develop racial movements. Second, people will become dissatisfied with the current structure only if the structure is perceived as oppressive or illegitimate. Third, there must be growth of a generalized belief system. People need to share an ideology, a set of ideas, that defines the sources of the structural problems or strains and the solutions necessary to alleviate them. The civil rights movement was based on the ideology that racism was the source of restricted opportunities for minorities (Harper and Leicht 2002). Fourth, dramatic events sharpen and concretize issues. These events may initiate or exaggerate people's dissatisfaction with the current structure or redefine their beliefs about the sources of the structural problems. Examples of dramatic or precipitating events include the 1968 Watts riots in relation to the Black Power phase of the civil rights movement and the 1979 Three Mile Island nuclear disaster in relation to the antinuclear power movement (Harper and Leicht 2002). Fifth, the movement gains momentum with the mobilization of leaders and members for the movement. At this time, the social movement also begins to take the shape of a formal organization. Finally, forces in society (the existing political structure or countermovements) respond to the social movement either by accepting or by suppressing it. One of the important features of Smelser's theory is his emphasis on the relationship between the social movement and society itself, a powerful force in shaping the development, the direction, and, ultimately, the success of the movement (Harper and Leicht 2002).

According to **resource mobilization theory**, no social movement can succeed without resources. John McCarthy and Mayer Zald (1977) argue that human and organizational resources must be mobilized to create a social movement. A social movement requires human skills in the form of leadership, talent, and knowledge, as well as an organizational infrastructure to support its work.

On the other hand, the **political process model** emphasizes the relationship between a mobilized social movement and a favorable structure of political opportunities. Social movements are seen as rational attempts by excluded groups to mobilize their political leverage to advance their interests. Social movements are political phenomena, attempting to change social policy and political coalitions, in this view. Political structures enhance the likelihood of a successful social movement by being receptive to change or by being more or less vulnerable at different points in time. For example, Doug McAdam (1982) noted that the efforts of the civil rights movement were enhanced by the expansion of the Black vote and the shift of Black voters to the Democratic Party. Without favorable support from the political structure, the civil rights movement might not have succeeded.

Social movements gain strength when they develop symbols and a sense of community, which generates strong feelings and helps direct this energy into organized action. People will form a social movement when they develop "a shared understanding of the world and of themselves that legitimate[s] and motivate[s] collective action" (McAdam, McCarthy, and Zald 1996:6). McAdam (1982) explains that resource mobilization must include cognitive liberation. Much like Karl Marx's concept of class consciousness, **cognitive liberation** begins when members of an aggrieved group begin to consider their situation as unjust. They must recognize their situation. The second part of cognitive liberation is the group's sense that its situation can be changed. Finally, those who considered themselves powerless begin to believe that they can make a difference (Piven and Cloward 1979). Individuals must move through all three stages to become cognitively liberated. They must organize, act on political opportunities, and instigate change: "In the absence of these necessary attributions, oppressive conditions are likely, even in the face of increased resources, to go unchallenged" (McAdam 1982:34).

Photo 17.2

More than 200,000 people participated in the March on Washington demonstrations in March 1963. This march, along with other nonviolent protests and marches, brought to the nation's attention the need for basic civil rights for all Americans, regardless of race. The U.S. Congress passed landmark legislation in the 1960s: the Civil Rights Act of 1964, the Voting Rights Act of 1965, and the Civil Rights Act of 1968 (also known as the Fair Housing Act).

 Watts Riots

Social Protest

The Occupy Wall Street movement has been described as the first worldwide post-modern uprising (Brucato 2012). What began with hundreds of protestors in Zuccotti Park, New York, spread to more than 900 cities globally (Adam 2011) and hundreds of college and university encampments across the United States. The movement has been described as a new model for organizing and protesting: a gathering of multiple groups with diverse issues and causes, developing politics through interaction and participatory structures and lacking a clear beginning and ending (Brucato 2012). Scholars debate the long-term viability and impact of the movement, citing the lack of central leadership, an organizational structure, and a single issue to unite protestors.

What Does It Mean to Me?

Barack Obama's presidential campaign has been characterized as a social movement, mobilizing a nation to envision a new society. His mantra of "Yes, we can!" energized community organizers, activists, and ordinary citizens to identify their role in creating social change. Is change possible? What is your role in creating social change?

How Have Reform Movements Made a Difference?

New Latin America

"The interest of many scholars in social movements stems from their belief that movements represent an important force for social change" (McAdam, McCarthy, and Zald 1988:727); yet, "the study of the consequences of social movements is one of the most neglected topics in literature" (Giugni 1999:xiv–xv). Early in human history, most social change was the result of chance or trial and error (Mannheim 1940), but in modern history, social movements have been the basic avenues by which social change takes place (Harper and Leicht 2002).

According to Harper and Leicht (2002), the most dramatic social, cultural, economic, and political transformations come from revolutions. Successful revolutions are rare and dramatic events, such as the early revolutions in France (1789), Russia (1917), and China (1949), and they include the political transformations in South America, Eastern Europe, and the former Soviet Union during the 1980s.

Most social movements that we're familiar with are reform movements that focus on either broad or narrow social reforms. They produce significant change, but in gradual or piecemeal ways (Harper and Leicht 2002). The most important U.S. reform movements in the first half of the twentieth century focused on grievances related to social class, such as the labor movements of the early 1900s, which helped ensure safer working conditions, eliminated child labor, and provided substantial increases in wages and benefits. After World War II, a new type of reform movement, which included the civil rights movement, the student movement, the feminist movement, the gay liberation movement, and ethnic/racial movements, addressed inequalities based on social status rather than social class (Harper and Leicht 2002). Successful reform movements generate change in three areas:

Arab Spring

1. *Culture.* Reform movements educate people and change beliefs and behaviors. Change can occur in our culture, identity, and everyday life (Taylor and Whittier 1995). By changing the ways individuals live, movements may effect long-term changes in society (Meyer 2000). The women's movement has established a clear

record of cultural change. The women's movement changed the way women viewed themselves and altered our language, our schools, the workplace, politics, the military, and the media.

2. *New organizations or institutions.* Movements lead to the creation of new organizations that continue to generate change. Through these new organizations, social movements may influence ongoing and future initiatives by altering the structure of political support, limiting resources to challengers, and changing the values and symbols used by supporters and challengers. David Meyer (2000) argues that by changing participants' lives, "movements alter the personnel available for subsequent challenges" (p. 51).

 NOW

From the women's movement, the National Organization for Women (NOW) was created in 1966, along with the Women's Equity Action League (1968), the National Women's Political Caucus (1971), the National Women's Law Center (1972), and the Feminist Majority Foundation (1987). NOW is the largest organization of feminist activists in the United States, with more than 500,000 members and 550 chapters in all 50 states. The organization continues its advocacy and legislative efforts in guaranteeing equal rights for women, ensuring abortion rights and reproductive freedom, opposing racism, and ending violence against women.

3. *Social policy and legislation.* Successful social policies have been nurtured by partnerships between the government and social movements (Skocpol 2000). Movements generally organize and mobilize themselves around specific policy demands (Meyer 2000), attempting to minimize or eliminate social problems. Public policy can do many things: New laws can be enacted or old ones may be struck down, social service programs can be created or ended, and taxes can be used to discourage bad behaviors (cigarette or alcohol taxes) or encourage other behaviors (tax breaks to build enterprise zones) (Loseke 2003).

 Political Sociology

For reform movements, the relationship between desired and actual change varies (Lauer 1976). So far, the women's movement has not achieved the passage of the Equal Rights Amendment (ERA), first proposed in 1923. As of 2012, 35 of the necessary 38 states had ratified the ERA. The women's movement has made progress in revising laws pertaining to violence against women, creating family-friendly business practices, and enhancing women's roles in the military, clergy, sports, and politics.

In Focus

Nongovernmental Organizations as a Source of Change

Nongovernmental organizations (NGOs) have been called a "positive force in domestic and international affairs, working to alleviate poverty, protect human rights, preserve the environment, and provide relief worldwide" (McGann and Johnstone 2006:65). The term refers to private, voluntary, civil society, and nonprofit organizations advocating on behalf of a range of issues: poverty, human rights, the environment, and social justice. NGOs also represent industry associations, religious organizations, and obscure causes (Paul 2000).

(Continued)

(Continued)

NGOs are known for their innovative campaigns and mobilization strategies, especially for their ability to work outside of traditional government structures and political networks. Notable NGO activity includes the collection of labor, antiglobalization, and environmental groups that converged on the 1999 World Trade Organization meeting. NGOs exerted their global influence on the United Nations Conference on Environment and Development (1992) and Fourth World Conference on Women (1995).

There is no definitive count of the number of domestic and international NGOs. In 2000, there were an estimated 25,000 international NGOs (with programs in multiple countries), an increase from 400 international NGOs in 1900 (Paul 2000). For example, Amnesty International, an activist group campaigning for human rights, has more than 2.2 million members and offices in 80 countries. The number of NGOs has grown, especially in Central and Eastern Europe, India, and developing countries in Africa and Latin America.

Making the Last Connection

Woolworth Sit-In

It was a Sunday evening, 31 January 1960, when four freshmen at North Carolina Agriculture and Technical College stayed up late talking about ending segregation in the South. They were extraordinarily poorly positioned to effect political or social change on campus, much less in the United States: young, Black, by no means affluent, and generally disconnected from the major centers of power in America. On Monday morning Ezell Blair, Jr., Franklin McCain, Joseph McNeill, and David Richmond dressed in their best clothes to visit the Woolworth's in downtown Greensboro. After buying some school supplies, they sat at the lunch counter and waited for service. They spent the rest of their day there.

The following day twenty-seven other Black students joined them and on Wednesday twice as many. By Thursday, a few sympathetic White students from nearby schools had enlisted and, with the lunch counter at Woolworth's filled, a few started a sit-in at another lunch counter down the street. By the end of the week, city officials offered to negotiate a settlement and, on Saturday night, 1,600 students rallied to celebrate this victory. News of the sit-in campaigns spread throughout the South and then elsewhere across the United States, spurring other activists to emulate their efforts. Sit-ins to desegregate lunch counters and restaurants, stores and libraries, and even buses swept the South. A new organization, the Student Non-Violent Coordinating Committee (SNCC) was formed in April 1960. SNCC would become a leading force in the civil rights movement, setting much of the agenda for liberal politics in the United States during the early 1960s, precipitating the passage of the Voting Rights Act of 1965 and politicizing student activists across the United States. (Meyer 2000:33)

Yes, solutions to social problems are complex and, as Mills advised, ultimately require attention to large social forces and structures, such as those targeted by social movements. But social movements don't appear overnight. Social movements begin with individual efforts such as those taken by college students Blair, McCain, McNeill, and Richmond. Grassroots organizations with strong community and local leadership, such as those on the front line of the modern environmental movement, have also proven effective in addressing social problems.

Some may believe that individual efforts don't amount to much, leading only to short-term solutions or effectively helping one person or one family at a time. But according to David Rayside (1998), the impact of any social movement should be measured over the long term. The isolated effort of thousands of individuals and groups "creates changes in social and political climates, which then enable particular groups to make more specific inroads into public policy and institutional practice" (p. 390).

College and university students have always played an important role in addressing social problems. According to longtime social activist Ralph Nader (1972), it is up to students "to prod and to provoke, to research and to act" (p. 23). What can a student accomplish? Nader thinks the answer is quite a lot:

 Student Activism

> Take the corporate polluter. Sit-ins and marches will not clean up rivers and the air that he fouls. He is too powerful and there are too many like him. Yet, the student has unique access to resources that can be effective in confronting the polluter. University and college campuses have the means for detecting the precise nature of the industrial effluent, through chemical and biological research. Through research such as they perform every day in the classroom, students can show the effect of the effluent on an entire watershed, and thus alert the community to real and demonstrable dangers to public health—a far more powerful way to arouse public support for a clean environment than a sit-in. Using the expertise of the campus, students can also demonstrate the technological means available for abating the discharge, and thus meet the polluter's argument that he can do nothing to control his pollution. By drawing on the knowledge of economists, students can counter arguments that an industry will go bankrupt or close down if forced to install pollution controls. Law and political science students can investigate the local, state, or federal regulations that may apply to the case, and publicly challenge the responsible agencies to fulfill their legal duties. (p. 21)

Student action may lead to significant social change. For example, voting drives led by 17- and 18-year-olds produced the Twenty-Sixth Amendment of the U.S. Constitution, granting voting rights to those 18 years of age and older (Nader 1972). The driving force behind the Twenty-Sixth Amendment came from youth who raised questions about the legitimacy of a representative government that asked 18- to 20-year-olds to fight in the Vietnam War but denied them the right to vote on war-related issues (Close Up Foundation 2004). Norvald Fimreite, a graduate student at the University of Western Ontario, was the first to report unusual levels of mercury residues in fish caught in the Great Lakes (Nader 1972). Fimreite's data led to a worldwide alert about the problems of mercury and other chemicals in the fish we eat. Globally, students have taken to the streets to express voices. For more on this, refer to the Voices in the Community section.

Voices in the Community

Camila Vallejo

In May 2011 Chilean high school and college students began participating in coordinated marches, sit-ins, and strikes. Their efforts have included thousands of individuals, in protests described as the largest since the days of the dictatorship of General Augusto Pinochet.

The students were mobilized by the Student Confederation of Chile (CONFECH, a group of all the student unions from public and some private universities), and the oldest union, the Student Federation of the University of Chile (FECH) (Goldman 2012). Camila Vallejo, a 23-year-old geography student from the University of Chile, emerged as the most prominent and charismatic leader of the student movement. When the protests began, Vallejo was FECH's elected president.

The young protestors had one primary issue: education reform. While Chile may have the highest income per capita in the region, it ranks as one of the most unequal countries in the world. According to Francisco Goldman (2012), a university education in Chile is proportionally the most expensive—$3,400 a year for tuition—while the average annual salary for a Chilean citizen is $8,500. Most college students take out bank loans and incur years of debt to pay for their education. While President Sebastián Piñera characterized education as a consumer good, Vallejo and her fellow protestors defined it as a fundamental right, advocating how "the university should be the motor of change in society" (Goldman 2012:23).

The student protests have been credited with the resignation of two education ministers, both ineffectual against the students (Goldman 2012). But what began as a student movement has expanded to other Chilean citizen and worker groups. Vallejo explains, "Something very powerful that has come out of the heart of this movement is that people are really questioning the economic policies of the country. People are not tolerating the way a small number of economic groups benefit from the system" (quoted in Moss Wilson 2012:5). The youth, according to Vallejo, have "revived and dignified politics" (quoted in Franklin 2011a). "It is always the youth that make the first move . . . we don't have family commitments, this allows us to be freer. We took the first step but we are no longer alone, the older generations are now joining this fight" (Vallejo quoted in Franklin 2011b).

Vallejo has been honored in other countries (Germany, the United Kingdom, and the United States) for her leadership and protest work. In 2012, Vallejo stated that she would be willing to run for a seat in the Chilean Congress as a Communist Party candidate.

Community Service

United We Serve

The last connection presented in this text is the connection between social problems and your community. Throughout the country, college students have affirmed their commitment to community service. In 2006, according to UCLA's annual survey of entering college freshmen, one in four freshmen surveyed believed that it was important to be involved in community programs. About 80% of freshmen had participated in community service during their senior year in high school, and 67% of them believed that they would continue volunteering in college (Engle 2006). High school students are also increasing their involvement in community service. School districts in every state except Wyoming, North Dakota, and South Dakota require community service.

President Obama and Michelle Obama have consistently highlighted the importance of volunteer service and its value for the nation. In 2009, President Obama launched the United We Serve initiative, calling for a "sustained, collaborative and focused effort to promote service as a way of life for all Americans" (Corporation for National and Community Service 2009). In the same year, Congress designated September 11 as the National Day of Service and Remembrance, and Obama signed the Edward M. Kennedy Serve America Act, which tripled the number of intensive service opportunities in the AmeriCorps program from 75,000 positions annually to 250,000 by 2017.

If you think there is nothing that you can do to effect change, you've not been paying attention. The first step is to recognize that you can make a difference. You do not have to believe in quick fixes, universal solutions, or change to the entire world to solve social problems. You do not have to join a national organization. To begin, you can join other

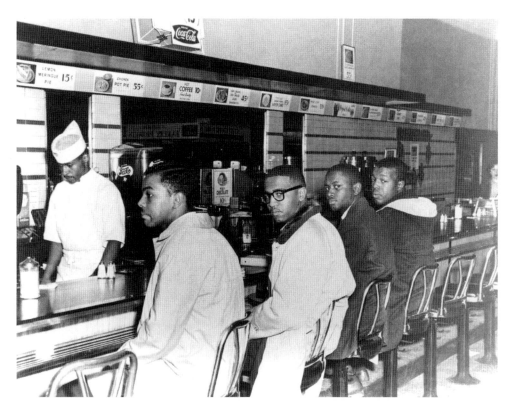

Photo 17.3

North Carolina Agriculture and Technical College students during the second day of protest at the Whites-only lunch counter at a Woolworth's in Greensboro, North Carolina.

college and university students who have chosen to become personally involved in their community. Most efforts are small and practical, but as one college student says, "I can't do anything about the theft of nuclear grade weapons materials in Azerbaijan, but I can clean up the local pond, help tutor a troubled kid, or work at a homeless shelter" (Levine and Cureton 1998:36).

What does it take to start making that connection with your community? The second step is to explore opportunities for service on your campus and in your community. Take the chapters in this text or the material presented by your instructor to consider what social problems you are passionate about. Determine what issues you'd like to address and determine what individuals or groups you'd like to serve. Even though you may be in your college community for only four or five years, act as if you're there for life: Take an interest in what happens in your community (Hollender and Catling 1996). Whatever your interests are, you can be sure that there are people and programs in your community who share them. And if they don't exist, what would it take to create such a program?

The third step is to do what you enjoy doing. When you know what you like, when you know what you can contribute, you will find the right connection. Whatever your talent, your community program will appreciate your contribution. It could be that you are an excellent writer; if so, you could help with a program's monthly newsletter, develop an informational brochure, or design the program's website. Do you enjoy working with others? Volunteer to work with clients, to answer phones, or to help at a rally. In addition to providing invaluable service to the program, recognize the experience and skills that you will gain from your efforts.

And what is the final step? Go out and do it. It doesn't have to last an entire semester or school year; you could just volunteer for a weekend or a day. Change doesn't happen

New Community Volunteers

Photo 17.4

First Lady Michelle Obama participates in a United We Serve service volunteer event at a Habitat for Humanity site. She is joined by Shakir Cannon-Moye, a senior at George Washington University, and Julie Bindelglass, a junior. The president and the first family are frequent volunteers in the Washington, DC, community.

automatically; it begins with individual action. As Paul Rogat Loeb (1994) explains, the hard questions must come from us:

> We need to ask what we want in this nation and why; how should we run our economy, meet human needs, protect the Earth, achieve greater justice? . . . The questions have to come from us, as we reach out to listen and learn, engage fellow citizens who aren't currently involved, and spur debate in environments that are habitually silent.

Sociologist Michael Burawoy (2004) advocates for **public sociology**,

> a sociology that seeks to bring sociology to the publics beyond the academy, promoting dialogue about issues that affect the fate of society, placing the values to which we adhere under a microscope. . . . The variety of publics stretches from our students to the readers of our books, from newspaper columns to interviews, from audiences in local civic groups such as churches or neighborhoods, to social movements we facilitate. The possibilities are endless. (p. 104)

Charles Lemert (1997) reminds us of the most valuable sociological lesson:

> Sociology . . . is different for all because each [must] find a way to live in a world that threatens even while it provides. Grace is never cheap. In the end, what remains is that we all have a stake in the world. Like it or not, life is always life together. Social living is the courage to accept what we cannot change in order to do what can be done about the rest. (p. 191)

Put your sociological imagination to work to see where change is possible. Do you have the courage?

What Does It Mean to Me?

Chapters 2 through 16 each included a Voices in the Community feature, highlighting an individual or individuals who saw a social problem and made a decision to do something about it. Several began their activism during college or in their youth—Max Kenner (Chapter 13, "Crime and Criminal Justice"), Wendy Kopp (Chapter 8, "Education"), and Chad Pregracke (Chapter 15, "Environment"). Here is your chance to be a voice in your community. What social problem do you see, and what can you do about it? Better yet, if you've already begun work in your community and you have a story to tell, let me know. Your story may be featured in the next edition!

Main Points

- In this book, we have reviewed several social problems, the theoretical perspectives that examine them, and the policies, organizations, and individuals that affect them.

- To functionalists, all of society's needs are met by its social institutions, which ensure social order. When there is significant social change, the social order is particularly susceptible to social problems. In this view, social problems stem from the disruption or testing of social order, and solutions focus on restoring the social order, repairing the broken institutions, and avoiding dramatic social change.

- For conflict theorists, social problems are the result of social, economic, or political inequalities inherent in our society. Feminist perspectives specifically consider how gender inequalities lead to social problems. In contrast to functionalists, conflict and feminist theorists argue that conflict over resources and power is the status quo and that the existing social order needs to be replaced with a more equitable society offering more opportunity to marginalized individuals or groups.

- Interactionists focus on social problems at the individual level, contending that we create our own reality through social interaction. Social problems are subjectively constructed by societal leaders who label people and influence our opinions of what is a social problem. Problematic behavior is also learned from others. This perspective leads us to many different solutions: changing the labeling process, resocializing people who exhibit deviant or inappropriate behavior, and recognizing the social construction of social problems.

- Sociology provides us with the means to examine the social structure or "machinery" that runs our lives. Evidence from the past decade suggests that some social problems have been minimized because of effective social policies and solutions. But the government is not the only source of change; individuals, groups, and communities also make a difference.

- Throughout American history, groups have acted to promote change. Social movements are conscious, collective, organized attempts to bring about or resist large-scale change in the social order. They are the most potent forces of social change in our society.

- Social movements are classified by two factors: the scope and the depth of change. Instrumental movements seek to change the structure of society itself, whereas expressive movements attempt to change individuals. And while reform movements try to bring about limited social change by working within the existing system, revolutionary social movements seek fundamental changes of the system itself.

- New social movements theory emphasizes the distinctive features of recent social movements. Instead of fighting for human rights, new movements focus on cultural and community rights. New social movements also distrust formal organizations and thus tend to be small-scale, informal organizations. Also, new social movements are associated with a new middle class that acts on behalf of groups that cannot act on their own.

- People are more likely to act when they experience relative deprivation, a perceived gap between what they expect and what they actually get. Relative deprivation, in conjunction with six necessary conditions surrounding social structure, works to produce social movements.

- In resource mobilization theory, no social movement can succeed without human and organizational resources. In contrast, the political process model presents social movements as political phenomena, attempting to change social policy and political coalitions.

- Social movements gain strength when they develop symbols and a sense of community, which helps direct energy into organized action. Resource mobilization must also include cognitive liberation, which begins only when members of an aggrieved group start to consider their situation unjust, to believe the situation can be changed, and to believe they can make a difference.

- Revolutions produce the most dramatic social, cultural, economic, and political transformations. However, most movements center on gradual but significant reforms. Successful reform movements generate change in three areas: culture, new organizations or institutions, and social policy and legislation.

- You also can make a difference by taking four steps. First, recognize that you can make a difference. Second, explore opportunities for service on your campus and in your community. Third, do what you enjoy doing. And finally, go out and do it. Change doesn't happen automatically; it begins with individual action. Put your sociological imagination to work to see where change is possible.

On Your Own

Log on to the open-access Student Study Site at www.sagepub.com/leonguerrero4e for these additional learning tools:

- Interactive quizzes
- Video clips
- NPR audio links
- Handbook articles

- E-flashcards
- Journal articles
- End-of-chapter web exercises
- Additional web resources and current events

Internet and Community Exercises

1. The Corporation for National and Community Service is part of the USA Freedom Corps, a White House initiative to "foster a culture of citizenship, service, and responsibility." The organization includes three programs: AmeriCorps, Senior Corps, and Learn and Serve America. The AmeriCorps program is a network of local, state, and national service programs. The Senior Corps includes volunteers older than age 55 serving local nonprofits and public agencies. Learn and Serve America supports service-learning programs for kindergarten through 12th-grade students, combining community service with student learning.

For more information on local initiatives and volunteer opportunities in your state, go to *Study Site Chapter 17.*

2. To learn more about the Woolworth's Greensboro sit-ins, go to *Study Site Chapter 17,* which includes recordings with sit-in participants, along with related stories and photos and links to other civil rights sites.

3. How can one person serve as an agent of social change? Eduardo Arias, a Kuna Indian from one of the San Blas Islands off Panama's Caribbean coast, did something in 2007 that affected business and trade on six continents and in 34 countries.

What did he do? He read the ingredient label on a 59-cent tube of toothpaste and saw two words, *diethylene glycol*, the same poisonous ingredient used in antifreeze. Arias purchased a tube and brought it as evidence to the Health Ministry office. His report set off a global recall of the product, along with increasing examination and scrutiny of Chinese manufacturers and their products (the source of the tainted toothpaste). On your own, find a story of one person who made a difference, who was part of some social change. The story could be based in the United States or elsewhere. Even if the person's actions didn't have worldwide influence, determine the impact of those actions.

4. If you do nothing else, make sure to show up on Election Day to support candidates who support your views (Hollender and Catling 1996). Tracking presidential election years, research indicates that electoral participation of Americans younger than 29 years of age has increased since 2004. In 2008, the youth voter turnout rate was 51%, a record high. African American youth posted the highest turnout rate ever observed for any racial or ethnic group of young Americans since 1972 (Kirby and Kawashima-Ginsberg 2009). Rock the Vote is a nonprofit, nonpartisan organization that attempts to mobilize youth to create positive social and political change in their lives and communities (Rock the Vote 2004). The organization works year-round, encouraging youth to become involved in a range of issues: education, economy, environment, violence, and national and personal debt. You may have seen a Rock the Vote Community Street Team register voters at a local concert or event. Go to *Study Site Chapter 17* for more information.

Study Questions

1. How does each sociological perspective identify the potential and sources for social change?
2. Identify and explain the four dimensions of social movements.
3. What is meant by the following statement: "Social movements arise from the structure itself, primarily the result of social and economic deprivation"?
4. Explain the relationship between cognitive liberation and social movements.
5. Successful reform movements generate change in three areas. Identify and explain these three areas of change.
6. Would you characterize the Occupy Movement as a social movement? Why or why not?

Glossary

Absolute poverty: Lack of basic necessities

Acculturative stress: Stress from adapting to a new country

Acute illnesses: Illnesses that strike suddenly and disappear quickly

Age distribution: The distribution of individuals by age

Ageism: Prejudice or discrimination based on someone's age

Alcoholism: Alcohol dependence, characterized by the symptoms of craving, loss of control, physical dependence, and tolerance

Alienation: Separation from one's true self; alienation occurs on multiple levels—from one's work, the product of one's work, other workers, and one's human potential

Anomie: State of normlessness

Applied research: Pursuit of knowledge for program application or policy evaluation

Assimilation: A process in which minority group members become part of the dominant group, losing their original group identity

Basic research: Exploration of the causes and consequences of a social problem

Bisexuality: Sexual orientation toward either sex

Boomerangers: Young adults who leave home for college, but return after graduation because of either economic constraints (they may be unemployed or underemployed) or personal choice

Bourgeoisie: Capitalist ruling class; owners of businesses

Brownfields: Abandoned or underused industrial or commercial properties where hazardous substances, pollutants, or contaminants are present or potentially present

Class consciousness: Awareness of one's social position

Climate change: The perceptible climate trends over time; also referred to as global warming

Cognitive liberation: The recognition of one's situation as unjust

Cohabiting: Sexual partners, not married to each other, but residing in the same household

Conflict perspective: A theoretical perspective that considers how society is held together by power and coercion for the benefit of those in power (based on social class, gender, race, or ethnicity)

Contingent workers: Full- or part-time temporary workers

Critical political-economy perspective: An approach using a conflict perspective to focus on city formation based on racial, gender, or class inequalities (also referred to as **socio-spatial perspective**)

Crowding: Defined as more than one person per room in the household

Cultural capital: Cultural skills and knowledge passed on to youth by their parents and through their social and economic position

Culture of poverty: A set of norms, values, and beliefs that encourage and perpetuate poverty

Cybercrime: A form of white-collar crime that involves Internet fraud and abuse

Decriminalization: Reduction of kinds of behavior included under the law

De facto segregation: A subtle process of segregation that is the result of other processes, such as housing segregation, rather than because of an official policy

Deindustrialization: Systematic disinvestment in manufacturing and production capacities

Demography: The study of the size, composition, and distribution of human populations

Dependent variable: The variable to be explained

Devaluation of women's work: When the higher societal value placed on men than on women is reproduced within the workplace

Differential association: The learning of behaviors and norms from the groups we have contact with

Digital divide: The gap separating individuals who have access to and understanding of new forms of technology from those who do not

Discrimination: Acts based on prejudiced beliefs against a specific individual or group

Disengagement theory: Theoretical perspective that defines aging as a natural process of withdrawal from active participation in social life

Distributive power: Power over other individuals or groups

Domestic migration: The movement of people within a country

Domestic terrorism: Terrorism supported or coordinated by groups or individuals based in a country

Double standard of aging: Separate standards of aging for men and women; men are judged in our culture according to what they can do (their competence, power, and control), but women are judged according to their appearance and beauty

Drug abuse: The use of any drug or medication for unintended purposes, which can lead to clinically significant impairment or distress

Drug addiction: Physical or psychological dependence on a drug or medication

Dysfunctions: Negative consequences of social structures

Ecocide: Mass destruction of ecosystems

Ecological footprint: A measure of our environmental impact based on the amount of natural resources we use and waste output we create

Emigration: Movement of people out of a geographic area

Environmental justice: Social justice movement based on the principle that all individuals and communities are entitled to equal protection of environmental and public health laws and regulations

Environmental racism: Environmental policy or practice that disadvantages people based on race or color

Environmental sociology: Study of the interactions between our physical and natural environment and our social organization and social behavior

Epidemiology: Study of patterns in the distribution and frequency of sickness, injury, and death and the social factors that shape them

Ethnic attrition: Individuals choosing not to self-identify as a member of a particular ethnic group

Ethnic groups: A group of people who are set off to some degree from other groups by displaying a unique set of cultural traits, such as their language, religion, or diet

Ethnocentrism: The belief that one's own group values and behaviors are right

Exclusion: The practice of prohibiting or restricting the entry or participation of groups in society

Expressive movements: An attempt to change individuals and individual behavior

Expulsion: The removal of a group by direct force or intimidation

Extended families: Two or more adult generations, related by blood, who live together in a single household

Family: Social unit based on kinship relations, a construct of meaning and relationships both emotional and economic

Fecundity: The maximum number of children that could be born, based on the number of women of childbearing age in a population

Felonies: Crimes that are serious offenses, punishable by more than one year's imprisonment or death

Femicide: The killing of women; the term is used in contrast to the literal meaning of *homicide* as the killing of men

Feminist perspective: A theoretical perspective that defines gender (and sometimes race or social class) as a source of social inequality, group conflict, and social problems

Fertility: The level of childbearing for an individual or a population

Food insecure: Lacking in access to sufficient food for all family members

Foreign born: Anyone who is not a U.S. citizen at birth

Functionalist perspective: A theoretical perspective that examines the functions or consequences of the structure of society; functionalists use a macro perspective, focusing on how society creates and maintains social order

Gender: Social construction of masculine and feminine attitudes and behaviors

Gender mainstreaming: The integration of the gender perspective into every stage of the policy process (design, implementation, monitoring, and evaluation)

Gendered division of labor: Assignment of different tasks to men and women

Genocide: The systematic targeting of members of an ethnic or a religious group

Gentrification: The process of neighborhood change from lower- to higher-income residents

Gerontology: The study of aging and the elderly

Globalization: A process of increasing transborder connectedness; the basis may be economic, political, environmental, or social

Heterosexism: The privileging of heterosexuality over homosexuality

Heterosexuality: Sexual orientation toward the opposite sex

Homophobia: An irrational fear or intolerance of homosexuals

Homosexuality: Sexual orientation toward the same sex

Horizontal segregation: The separation of men and women into different industries and occupations

Household: An economic and residential unit

Human agency: The active role of individuals in creating their social environment

Human capital: Job-related skills acquired through education and work experience

Human capital theory: Theory that attributes gender income differences to differences in the kind and amount of human capital men and women acquire

Human ecology: The study of the relationship between individuals and their physical environment

Humanitarian intervention: A responsibility to protect, including three aspects: how to prevent humanitarian crises in the first place, under which conditions and in what way to intervene, and how to maintain peace after a military conflict and rebuild the country

Hypothesis: Statement of a relationship between variables

Immigration: The movement of people, leaving their country of origin to move to another

Incidence rate: The number of new cases of disease within a population during a specific period

Income: Money earned for one's work

Independent variable: The variable expected to account for the cause of the dependent variable

Index crimes: Crimes including murder, rape, robbery, assault, burglary, motor vehicle theft, arson, and larceny

Individual discrimination: Prejudiced actions against minority members by individuals; may include avoiding contact or physical or verbal attacks

Industrial Revolution: Economic shift from family to market production

Infant mortality: Rate of infant deaths per 1,000 live births

Institutional discrimination: Discrimination practiced by political or social institutions

Instrumental movements: An attempt to change the structure of society

Interactionist perspective: A micro-level perspective that highlights what we take for granted: the expectations, rules, and norms that we learn and practice without even noticing; interactionists maintain that through our interaction, social problems are created and defined

Interior residential density: The number of individuals per room in a dwelling

International terrorism: Terrorism supported or coordinated by foreign groups threatening the security of U.S. nationals or the national security of the United States

Internet addiction: A variety of behaviors and impulse controls relating to Internet use

Juvenile crime: Criminal acts performed by juveniles

Juvenile delinquent: A youth who engages in criminal behavior

Juvenile status offender: A juvenile who has violated a law applying only to minors

Labeling theory: Theory stating that individuals and acts are defined or labeled as criminal

Labor migration: The movement of people from one country to another for employment

Latent functions: Unintended and often hidden consequences

Legalization: Removal from control of the law

LGBT: Term used to refer to lesbians, gays, bisexuals, and transgendered individuals as a group

Life chances: Access provided by social position to goods and services

Life course perspective: A theoretical perspective that considers the entire course of human life (from childhood, adolescence, and adulthood to old age) as social constructions that reflect the broader structural conditions of society

Macro level of analysis: Societal level of analysis

Manifest functions: Intended and recognized consequences

Master status: An identity that determines how others view individuals and how individuals view themselves

Mechanical solidarity: Union of individuals through a set of common values, beliefs, and customs and a simple division of labor

Media: Technological processes that facilitate communication

Media literacy: The ability to assess and analyze media messages

Medicalization: Process through which a condition or behavior becomes defined as a medical problem

Megadisaster: A catastrophe that threatens or overwhelms an area's capacity to get people to safety, treat casualties, protect infrastructure, and control panic

Micro level of analysis: Individual level of analysis

Migration: The movement of individuals from one area to another

Military-industrial complex: Collaboration of the government, military, and the armament industry

Minority stress: Stress minorities experience from discriminative treatment

Misdemeanors: Crimes that are minor offenses, punishable by a fine or less than one year's imprisonment

Modernization theory of aging: Theoretical perspective that links the role and status of the elderly with their labor contribution or their relationship to the means of production

Morbidity: Study of illnesses and disease

Mortality: Incidence of death in a population

Multiracial: Mixed or multiple race

Native: Anyone born in the United States or a U.S. island area or born abroad of a U.S. citizen parent

Natural capitalism: The awareness of the economic value of nature

Neglect: A failure to provide for a child's basic needs

New social movements theory: Theory emphasizing the distinctive features of recent social movements

Nuclear family: Family consisting of parents and their children

Objective reality: Actual existence of a particular condition

Occupational sex segregation: The degree to which men and women are concentrated in occupations that predominantly employ workers of one sex

Offshore outsourcing or offshoring: The hiring of international external contractors to complete work normally done by in-house employees

Organic solidarity: Union of individuals through a complex division of labor

Organizational child: A child prepared by education for a bureaucratic adult world

Outcome goals: Related to terrorism, the group's stated political ends, which require cooperation of the target authority or government

Outsourcing: Practice of hiring external contractors for jobs formerly performed by regular staff

Overurbanization: The process in which an excess population is concentrated in an urban area that lacks the capacity to provide basic services and shelter

Particulate or particle pollution: Air pollution caused by the combustion of fossil fuels—the burning of coal, diesel, gasoline, and wood; particulate matter includes road dust, diesel soot, ash, wood smoke, and sulfate aerosols that are suspended in the air

Patriarchy: Society in which the powerful (often men) dominate the powerless (often women)

Pluralism: Each ethnic or racial group maintains its own culture (cultural pluralism or multiculturalism) or a separate set of social structures and institutions (structural pluralism)

Political process model: Model of relationship between social movements and structures of political opportunities

Politics of fear: How decision makers and politicians promote and use the public's beliefs and assumptions about terrorism in order to achieve certain goals

Politicide: The systematic targeting of specific groups because of their political beliefs

Population aging: The increase in the number or proportion of older individuals in the population

Poverty guidelines: Used to determine family or individual eligibility for relevant federal programs

Poverty threshold: The original federal poverty measure, based on the economy food plan

Power: The ability to achieve one's goals despite resistance from others

Power elite: A select group possessing true power

Prejudice: A negative attitude based on the attributes of an individual

Prestige: Social respect or standing

Prevalence rate: Total number of cases involving a specific health problem during a specific period

Process goals: Related to terrorism, goals aimed to sustain the group and its activities by securing financial support, gaining media attention, and boosting group morale

Proletariat: The working class in a capitalist economy

Property crime: Criminal acts that involve the taking of money or property from another without force or the threat of force against the victims; burglary, larceny, theft, motor vehicle theft, and arson are examples of property crimes

Public sociology: Sociology that promotes a dialogue outside of the academy with a variety of public audiences

Race: Group or population sharing a set of genetic characteristics and physical features

Racism: The belief in the inferiority of certain racial or ethnic groups, often accompanied by discrimination

Reform movements: An attempt to bring about limited social change by working within the existing system

Refugees: Persons who are unable or unwilling to return to their country of origin due to persecution or fear of persecution on account of race, religion, nationality, membership in a particular social group, or political opinion

Relative deprivation: A perceived gap between what people expect and what they actually get

Relative poverty: Failure to achieve society's average income or lifestyle

Residential segregation: The neighborhood clustering or separation of groups by racial, ethnic, or economic characteristics within a geographic area

Resource mobilization theory: Theory about conditions for success of social movements

Revolution: An overthrow of the existing government or political structure

Revolutionary social movements: Attempts to create fundamental change in the system itself

Role strain: Strain experienced when the demands of one's role exceed one's ability and resources to fulfill that role

Scientific management: Analysis and implementation of the best way to complete a task

Segregation: Physical and social separation of ethnic or racial groups

Service revolution: Economic shift toward service and information occupations

Sex: Physiological distinctions between male and female

Sexism: Prejudice or discrimination based solely on someone's sex

Sexual orientation: The classification of individuals according to their preference for emotional-sexual relationships and lifestyle

Sick role: Set of behaviors regarding actions and treatment of ill persons

Smog or ground-level ozone: Air pollution formed when nitrogen oxides emitted from electric power plants and automobiles react with organic compounds in the presence of sunlight and heat

Social capital: Investments in social relationships and networks distributed unequally by social class

Social construction of reality: The world regarded as a social creation

Social constructionism: Subjective definition or perception of conditions

Social inequality: Unequal distribution of resources, services, and positions

Social innovation: Policy, program, or advocacy that features an untested or a unique approach

Social institutions: A stable set of statuses, roles, groups, and organizations that provides a foundation for addressing fundamental societal needs; an example of a social institution is the family

Social media: Media that are based on conversation and interaction with individuals online

Social movements: Conscious, collective, organized attempts to bring about or resist large-scale change in the social order

Social policy: Enactment of a course of action through a formal law or program

Social problem: A social condition that has negative consequences for individuals, our social world, or our physical world

Social stratification: The ranking of individuals into social strata or groups

Socioeconomic stress: Stress from social and economic inequalities

Sociological imagination: Link between our personal lives and experiences and our social world

Sociology: The systematic study of individuals and social structures

Socio-spatial perspective: An approach using a conflict perspective to focus on city formation based on race, gender, or class inequalities (also referred to as **critical political-economy perspective**)

Soft-power approach: Where a nation-state is perceived as having values, motives, and actions that should be emulated

Species being: A human being's true self

Stereotype threat: The risk of confirming in oneself a characteristic that is a negative stereotype

Stigma: A discrediting attribute

Strain theory: Robert K. Merton's theory that predicts that criminal behavior is likely to occur when individuals are unable to achieve social and material goals because of insufficient access or resources

Subjective reality: Attachment of meanings to our reality

Suburbanization: The process by which a population shifts to suburban areas

Sweatshop: A workplace that violates more than one federal or state labor law; the term has come to include exploitation of workers, for example, in workplaces with no livable wages or benefits, poor and hazardous working conditions, and possible verbal or physical abuse

Symbolic interactionism: Theoretical perspective that examines how we use language, words, and symbols to create and maintain our social reality

Terrorism: The unlawful use of force to intimidate or coerce compliance with a particular set of beliefs; can be either domestic (based in the United States) or foreign (supported by foreign groups threatening the security of U.S. nationals or U.S. national security)

Theory: A set of assumptions and propositions used for explanation, prediction, and understanding

Tracking: Designation of academic courses for students based on presumed aptitude

Transgendered: Individuals whose gender identity is different from that assigned to them at birth

Transnational: Immigrants who maintain social, economic, and cultural ties across international borders

Underemployment: Employment under less-than-optimal conditions regarding pay, skill, or working hours

Urbanization: The process by which a population shifts from rural to urban

Urbanized area: A densely populated area with 50,000 or more residents

Urban population: An area with 2,500 or more individuals

Urban sociology: Examination of social, political, and economic structures and their impact within an urban setting

Urban sprawl: The process in which the spread of development across the landscape outpaces population growth

Variables: A property of people or objects that can take on two or more values

Vertical segregation: The separation of men and women in workplace hierarchies; lower-ranking positions are dominated by women, while management ranks are dominated by men

Violent crime: Criminal acts that involve force or the threat of force against others and include aggravated assault, murder, rape, and robbery

Wealth: The value of one's personal assets

White-collar crime: Crimes committed by someone of high social status, for financial gain, or in a particular organization

References

Chapter 1

Adams, Bert and R. A. Sydie. 2001. *Sociological Theory*. Thousand Oaks, CA: Pine Forge.

Advisory Committee on Student Financial Assistance. 2002. "Empty Promises: The Myth of College Access in America." Retrieved May 7, 2010 (http://www.ed.gov/about/bdscomm/list/acsfa/emptypromises.pdf).

Akintola, Olagoke. 2010. "Perceptions of Rewards Among Volunteer Caregivers of People Living with AIDS Working in Faith-Based Organizations in South Africa: A Qualitative Study." *Journal of the International AIDS Society* 13:22.

Ballantine, Jeanne and Keith Roberts. 2012. *Our Social World, Condensed Version*. 2nd ed. Thousand Oaks, CA: Sage Publications.

Ballesteros, P., J. L. Estrada, G. Barriga, F. Molinar, M. C. Hernandez, L. Huerta, G. Cocho, and C. Villarreal. 2006. "Comparative Analysis of Gender Differences in HIV-1 Infection Dynamics." *AIP Conference Proceedings* 854(1):48–50.

Berger, Peter and Thomas Luckmann. 1966. *The Social Construction of Reality*. Garden City, NY: Anchor.

Bernard, Jessie. 1982. *The Future of Marriage*. 2nd ed. New Haven, CT: Yale University Press. (Original work published 1972)

Callan, Patrick and Joni Finney. 2002. "State Policies for Affordable Higher Education." Pp. 10–11, 13 in *Losing Ground: A National Status Report on the Affordability of American Higher Education*. San Jose, CA: National Center for Public Policy and Higher Education.

Centers for Disease Control and Prevention. 2007. "Basic Information." Retrieved May 7, 2010 (http://www.cdc.gov/hiv/topics/basic/index.htm).

Centers for Disease Control and Prevention. 2012. "HIV in the United States." Retrieved March 9, 2012 (http://www.cdc.gov/hiv/resources/factsheets/us.htm).

Chakrapani, Venkatesan, Peter Newman, Murali Shunmugam, Alan McLuckie, and Frederick Melwin. 2007. "Structural Violence Against Kothi-Identified Men Who Have Sex With Men in Chennai, India: A Qualitative Investigation." *AIDS Education and Prevention* 19(4):346–64.

Chodorow, Nancy. 1978. *The Reproduction of Mothering: Psychoanalysis and the Sociology of Gender*. Berkeley: University of California Press.

CNN. 1996. "Anti Gay Marriage Act Clears Congress." Retrieved September 27, 2003 (http://www.cnn.com/US9609/10/gay.marriage/).

College Board. 2011. *Trends in College Pricing 2011*. Retrieved January 23, 2012 (http://trends.collegeboard.org/downloads/College_Pricing_2011.pdf).

Collins, Patricia Hill. 1990. *Black Feminist Thought: Knowledge, Consciousness, and Empowerment*. Boston, MA: Unwin Hyman.

Coser, L. 1956. *The Functions of Social Conflict*. New York: Free Press.

Dahrendorf, Ralf. 1959. *Class and Class Conflict in Industrial Society*. Stanford, CA: Stanford University Press.

Dugger, Celia. 2009a. "Breaking With Past, South Africa Issues Broad AIDS Policy." *New York Times*, December 2, p. A6.

Dugger, Celia. 2009b. "As Donors Focus on AIDS, Child Illnesses Languish." *New York Times*, October 30, p. A8.

Durkheim, Émile. 1973. "The Dualism of Human Nature and Its Moral Condition." Pp. 149–63 in *Emile Durkheim on Morality and Society*, edited by R. Bellah. Chicago, IL: University of Chicago Press. (Original work published 1914)

Education Trust. 2009. *Priced Out: How the Wrong Financial-Aid Policies Hurt Low-Income Students*. Washington, DC: Education Trust.

Ellis, R. A. 2003. *Impacting Social Policy: A Practitioner's Guide to Analysis and Action*. Pacific Grove, CA: Thomson Brooks/Cole.

Feagin, Joel. 2002. "Social Justice and Sociology: Agendas for the Twenty-First Century: Presidential Address." *American Sociological Review* 66:1–20.

Fine, Gary Alan. 2006. "The Chaining of Social Problems: Solutions and Unintended Consequences in the Age of Betrayal." *Social Problems* 53(1):3–17.

Frankfort-Nachmias, Chava and Anna Leon-Guerrero. 2011. *Social Statistics for a Diverse Society*. Thousand Oaks, CA: Sage Publications.

Fumaz, C. R., J. A. Munoz-Moreno, A. L. Ballesteros, R. Paredes, M. J. Ferrer, A. Salas, D. Fuster, E. Masmitja, N. Perez-Alvarez, G. Gomez, C. Tural, and B. Clotet. 2007. "Influence of the Type of Pegylated Interferon on the Onset of Depressive and Neuropsychiatric Symptoms in HIV-HCV Coinfected Patients." *AIDS Care* 19(1):138–45.

Habitat for Humanity. 2004. "Millard Fuller." Retrieved May 7, 2010 (http://www.habitat.org/how/millard.html).

Heiner, Robert. 2002. *Social Problems: An Introduction to Critical Constructionism*. New York: Oxford University Press.

Herbert, Bob. 2011. "The Human Cost of Budget Cutting." *New York Times*, February 20, p. 11.

Hytrek, Gary and Kristine Zentgraf. 2007. *America Transformed: Globalization, Inequality and Power*. New York: Oxford University Press.

Institute for College Access & Success. 2012. "State by State Data." Retrieved January 28, 2012 (http://projectonstudentdebt.org/state_by_state-data.php).

Institute for College Access & Success. 2012. "Student Debt and the Class of 2011." Retrieved November 5, 2012 (http://projectonstudentdebt.org/files/pub/classof2011.pdf).

Irwin, Alan. 2001. *Sociology and the Environment.* Cambridge, England: Polity Press.

Kaplan, Laura Duhan. 1994. "Women as Caretaker: An Archetype That Supports Patriarchal Militarism." *Hypatia* 9(2):123–33.

Katzer, Jeffrey, Kenneth Cook, and Wayne Crouch. 1998. *Evaluating Information: A Guide for Users of Social Science Research.* 4th ed. Boston, MA: McGraw-Hill.

Lemert, Charles. 1997. *Social Things: An Introduction to the Sociological Life.* Lanham, MD: Rowman & Littlefield.

Lichtenstein, Bronwen. 2004. "AIDS as a Social Problem: The Creation of Social Pariahs in the Management of an Epidemic." Pp. 316–34 in *Handbook of Social Problems: A Comparative International Perspective,* edited by George Ritzer. Thousand Oaks, CA: Sage Publications.

Loseke, Denise. 2003. *Thinking About Social Problems.* New York: Aldine de Gruyter.

Loseke, Denise and Joel Best. 2003. *Social Problems: Constructionist Readings.* New York: Aldine De Gruyter.

Madoo Lengermann, Patricia and Jill Niebrugge-Brantley. 2004. "Contemporary Feminist Theory." Pp. 436–80 in *Sociological Theory,* edited by George Ritzer and Douglas Goodman. Boston, MA: McGraw-Hill.

Marx, Karl. 1972. "Theses on Feuerbach." In *The Marx-Engels Reader,* edited by Robert C. Tucker. New York: Norton.

Mead, George Herbert. 1962. *Mind, Self, and Society: From the Standpoint of a Social Behaviorist.* Chicago, IL: University of Chicago Press. (Original work published 1934)

Merton, Robert. 1957. *Social Theory and Social Structure.* Glencoe, IL: Free Press.

Mills, C. Wright. 2000. *The Sociological Imagination.* New York: Oxford University Press. (Original work published 1959)

National Center for Public Policy and Higher Education and Public Agenda. 2010. "Squeeze Play 2010: Continued Public Anxiety on Cost, Harsher Judgments on How Colleges Are Run." Retrieved May 7, 2010 (http://www.publicagenda.org/pages/squeeze-play-2010#CollidingChart).

Prior, Jon. 2011. "Foreclosures in 2011 to Break Last Year's Record." Retrieved January 23, 2012 (http://www.housingwire.com/2011/01/12/foreclosures-reach-record-high-in-2010-realtytrac).

Ritzer, George. 2000. *Sociological Theory.* New York: McGraw-Hill.

Sambisa, William, Sian Curtis, and Vinod Mishra. 2010. "AIDS Stigma as an Obstacle to Uptake of HIV Testing: Evidence from a Zimbabwean National Population-Based Survey." *AIDS Care* 22:170–86.

Schneider, Anne and Helen Ingram. 1993. "Social Construction of Target Populations: Implications for Politics and Policy." *American Political Science Review* 87(2):334–47.

Schroedel, Jean R. and Daniel R. Jordan. 1998. "Senate Voting and Social Construction of Target Populations: A Study of AIDS Policy Making,

1987–1992." *Journal of Health Politics, Policy and Law* 23(1):107–31.

Schutt, Russell. 2012. *Investigating the Social World: The Process and Practice of Research.* Thousand Oaks, CA: Sage Publications.

Simoni, Jane, Karina Walters, Kimberly Balsam, and Seth Meyers. 2006. "Victimization, Substance Abuse, and HIV Risk Behaviors Among Gay/Bisexual/Two-Spirit and Heterosexual American Indian Men in New York City." *American Journal of Public Health* 96(12):2240–45.

Smith, Dorothy. 1987. *The Everyday World as Problematic: A Feminist Sociology.* Boston, MA: Northeastern University Press.

Spector, Malcolm and John Kituse. 1987. *Constructing Social Problems.* New York: Aldine de Gruyter.

Steinberg, Jacques. 2009a. "Goal Is College. Hurdle Is Aid." *New York Times,* May 1, 2009, pp. A1, A15.

Steinberg, Jacques. 2009b. "Brennan's Quest Ends in Success." *New York Times,* May 11, 2009. Retrieved May 7, 2010 (http://thechoice.blogs.nytimes.com/tag/brennan-jackson/).

UNAIDS. 2006. *2006 Report on the Global AIDS Epidemic: Executive Summary.* Geneva, Switzerland: UNAIDS.

UNAIDS. 2011. *World AIDS Day Report 2011.* Geneva, Switzerland: UNAIDS.

Tabi, Marian and Robert Vogel. 2006. "Nutritional Counseling: An Intervention for HIV Positive Patients." *Journal of Advance Nursing* 54(6):676–82.

Tong, Rosemarie. 1989. *Feminist Thought: A Comprehensive Introduction.* Boulder, CO: Westview Press.

Turner, Jonathan. 1998. *The Structure of Sociological Theory.* 6th ed. Belmont, CA: Wadsworth.

Chapter 2

Abramovitz, Mimi. 1996. *Regulating the Lives of Women: Social Welfare Policy from the Colonial Times to the Present.* Boston, MA: South End Press.

Adams, Gina and Monica Rohacek. 2002. "Child Care and Welfare Reform." Pp. 121–42 in *Welfare Reform: The Next Act,* edited by A. Weil and K. Feingold. Washington, DC: Urban Institute.

Alder, J. 1994. "The Name of the Game Is Shame." *Newsweek* 124(24):41.

Alvarez, Lizette. 2012. "No Savings Are Found From Welfare Drug Tests." *New York Times,* April 18, p. A14.

Banfield, Edward. 1974. *The Unheavenly City Revisited.* Boston, MA: Little, Brown.

Besharov, D. 2002."The Past and Future of Welfare Reform." Retrieved May 9, 2010 (http://www.aei.org/article/14781).

Bhargava, D. and J. Kuriansky. 2002. "Defining Who's Poor: Families Suffer as the Government Continues to Rely on the Outdated Measure of the Poverty Line." Retrieved August 30, 2003

(http://www.wowonline.org/ourprograms/fess/state-resources/NY/MEDIA/9-22-02,%20Defining%20who's%20poor%20Families%20suffer%20as%20the%20governme.pdf).

Blank, Rebecca. 2011. "The Supplemental Poverty Measure: A New Tool for Understanding Poverty." *Pathways* (Fall):10–14.

Bornstein, David. 2011. "Out of Poverty, Family Style." Retrieved April 18, 2012 (http://opinionator.blogs.nytimes.com/2011/07/14/out-of-poverty-family-style/#).

Brady, David, Andrew Fullerton, and Jennifer Moren Cross. 2010. "More Than Just Nickels and Dimes: A Cross-National Analysis of Working Poverty in Affluent Democracies." *Social Problems* 57:559–85.

Bricker, Jesse, Arthur Kennickell, Kevin Moore, and John Sabelhaus. 2012. *Changes in U.S. Family Finances from 2007 to 2012: Evidence from the Survey of Consumer Finances.* Washington, DC: Federal Reserve System.

Briefel, R., Jonathan Jacobson, Nancy Clusen, Teresa Zavitsky, Miki Satake, Brittany Dawson, and Rhoda Cohen. 2003. *The Emergency Food Assistance System: Findings from the Client Survey: Executive Summary* (Food Assistance and Nutrition Research Report, No. 32). Washington, DC: U.S. Department of Agriculture, Economic Research Service.

Burak, Esra. 2011. "Spotlight on Family Independence Initiative." *Pathways* (Summer):27–28.

Cammisa, Ann Marie. 1998. *From Rhetoric to Reform? Welfare Policy in American Politics.* Boulder, CO: Westview Press.

Center on Budget and Policy Priorities. 2012. "Chartbook: SNAP Helps Struggling Families Put Food on the Table." Retrieved April 14, 2012 (http://www.cbpp.org/cms/index.cfm?fa=view&id=3744).

Center for Women Policy Studies. 2002. *From Poverty to Self Sufficiency: The Role of Postsecondary Education in Welfare Reform.*

Washington, DC: Center for Women Policy Studies.

Children's Defense Fund. 2011. *The State of America's Children*. Washington DC: Author.

Christopher, Karen. 2005. "The Poverty Line Forty Years Later: Alternative Poverty Measures and Women's Lives." *Race, Gender & Class* 12:34–52.

City of New Orleans Homeless Services Working Group. 2011. *Ten-Year Plan to End Homelessness*. Retrieved August 10, 2012 (http://unitygno .org/wp-content/uploads/2011/11/Homeless-Services-Working-Group_-Ten-Year-Plan-to-End-Homelessness.pdf).

Clemetson, Lynette. 2003. "Poor Workers Finding Modest Housing Unaffordable, Study Says." *New York Times,* September 9, p. A15.

Coalition on Human Needs. 2003. *Welfare: CHN Issue Brief.* Washington, DC: Author.

Coleman-Jensen, Alisha, Mark Nord, Margaret Andrews, and Steven Carlson. 2011. *Household Food Insecurity in the United States in 2010*. Washington DC: U.S. Department of Agriculture.

Confessore, Nicholas. 2012. "Super PAC for Gingrich to Get $5 Million Infusion." *New York Times,* January 24, pp. A1, A16.

Conley, Dalton. 1999. *Being Black, Living in the Red: Race, Wealth, and Social Policy in America*. Berkeley: University of California Press.

DeNavas-Walt, Carmen, Bernadette Proctor, and Jessica Smith. 2007. *Income, Poverty and Health Insurance Coverage in the United States: 2006* (Current Population Reports, P60-233). Washington, DC: U.S. Government Printing Office.

DeNavas-Walt, Carmen, Bernadette Proctor, and Jessica Smith. 2012. *Income, Poverty and Health Insurance Coverage in the United States: 2011* (Current Population Reports, P60–243). Washington, DC: U.S. Government Printing Office.

DeParle, Jason. 2012. "Welfare Limits Left Poor Adrift as Recession Hit." *New York Times,* April 8, pp. 1, 18.

DeParle, Jason and Sabrina Tavernise. 2011. "Poor Are Still Getting Poorer, but Downturn's Punch Varies, Census Data Show." *New York Times,* September 15, p. A24.

Domhoff, G. William. 2002. *Who Rules America? Power and Politics*. Boston, MA: McGraw-Hill.

Dowd, Tim and John Horowitz. 2011. "Income Mobility and the Earned Income Tax Credit: Short-Term Safety Net or Long-Term Income Support." *Public Finance Review* 39:619–52.

Dreier, Peter. 2006. "Katrina and Power in America." *Urban Affairs Review* 41(4):528–49.

European Commission. 1985. "85/8/EEC: Council Decision of 19 December 1984 on Specific Community Action to Combat Poverty" (No. 31985D0008). Retrieved June 4, 2010 (http:// eur-lex.europa.eu/smartapi/cgi/sga_doc?smarta pi!celexapi!prod!CELEXnumdoc&lg=EN&numd oc=31985D0008&model=guichett).

Family Economic Self-Sufficiency Project. 2001. "The Self Sufficiency Standard." Retrieved May 7, 2010 (http://www.selfsufficiencystandard.org/ docs/SSS%20General%20Handout_061909.pdf).

Farrell, Mary, Sarah Rich, Lesley Turner, David Seith, and Dan Bloom. 2008. *Welfare Time Limits: An Update on State Policies, Implementation and Effects on Families*. New York: Lewin Group and MDRC.

Federal Interagency Forum on Child and Family Statistics. 2002. *America's Children 2002*. Washington, DC: U.S. Government Printing Office.

Fessler, Pam. 2012. "Struggling Families Lift Themselves Out of Poverty." Retrieved July 31, 2012 (http://www.npr.org/2012/07/13/155103662/ struggling- families-lift-themselves-out-of-poverty).

Fraser, Nancy. 1989. *Unruly Practices: Power, Discourse, and Gender in Contemporary Social Theory*. Minneapolis: University of Minnesota Press.

Freidman, P. 2000. *The Earned Income Tax Credit* (Issue Notes, Vol. 4, No. 4, April). Washington, DC: Welfare Information Network.

Funiciello, Theresa. 1993. *Tyranny of Kindness: Dismantling the Welfare System to End Poverty in America*. New York: Atlantic Monthly Press.

Gans, Herbert. 1971. "The Uses of Poverty: The Poor Pay All." *Social Policy* 2:20–24.

Gennetian, Lisa, Aletha Huston, Danielle Crosby, Young EunChang, Edward Lowe, and Thomas Weisner. 2002. *Making Child Care Choices*. Washington, DC: Manpower Demonstration Research Corporation.

Gilbert, Dennis. 2003. *The American Class Structure in an Age of Growing Inequality*. Belmont, CA: Thomson Wadsworth.

Gilens, Martin. 1999. *Why Americans Hate Welfare: Race, Media, and the Politics of Antipoverty Policy*. Chicago, IL: University of Chicago Press.

Goffman, Erving. 1951. "Symbols of Class Status." *British Journal of Sociology* 2:294–304.

Gordon, Linda. 1994. *Pitied but Not Entitled*. New York: Free Press.

Gornick, Janet and Marcia Meyers. 2002. "Support for Working Families: What We Can Learn from Europe about Family Policies." Pp. 90–107 in *Making Welfare Work*, edited by R. Kuttner. New York: New Press.

Greater New Orleans Community Data Center. 2011. "Lower Ninth Ward Neighborhood." Retrieved April 22, 2012 (http://www.gnocdc.org/ NeighborhoodData/8/LowerNinthWard/index .html).

Guyer, Jocelyn. 2000. *Health Care After Welfare: An Update From the Findings From State-Level Leaver Studies*. Washington, DC: Center on Budget and Policy Priorities.

Hachen, David. 2001. *Sociology in Action*. Thousand Oaks, CA: Pine Forge.

Handler, Joel and Yeheskel Hasenfeld. 1991. *The Moral Construction of Poverty: Welfare Reform in America*. Newbury Park, CA: Sage Publications.

Harrington, Michael. 1963. *The Other America: Poverty in the United States*. Baltimore, MD: Penguin Books.

Harris, K. M. 1993. "Work and Welfare among Single Mothers in Poverty." *American Journal of Sociology* 99:317–52.

Henderson, Debra, Ann Tickamyer, and Barry Tadlock. 2005. "The Impact of Welfare Reform on the Parenting Role of Women in Rural Communities." *Journal of Children & Poverty* 11: 131–47.

Hennessy, Judith. 2005. "Welfare, Work, and Family Well-Being: A Comparative Analysis of Welfare and Employment Status for Single Female-Headed Families Post-TANF." *Sociological Perspectives* 48(1):77–104.

Holzer, Harry, Diane Whitmore Schanzenbach, Greg Duncan, and Jens Ludwig. 2008. "The Economic Costs of Childhood Poverty in the United States." *Journal of Children and Poverty* 14: 41–61.

Iceland, John. 2003. *Poverty in America*. Berkeley: University of California Press.

Johnson, Lyndon. 1965. *Public Papers of the Presidents of the United States: Lyndon B. Johnson, 1965* (Vol. 2, entry 301, pp. 635–40). Washington, DC: U.S. Government Printing Office.

Jones, Arthur and Daniel Weinberg. 2000. *The Changing Shape of the Nation's Income Distribution 1947–1998* (Current Population Reports, pp. 60–204). Washington, DC: Government Printing Office.

Kaufman, Phillip, James MacDonald, Steve Lutz, and David Smallwood. 1997. *Do the Poor Pay More for Food? Item Selection and Price Differences Affect Low-Income Household Food Costs* (Agricultural Economics Report, No. 759). Washington, DC: U.S. Department of Agriculture, Economic Research Service.

Keister, Lisa and Stephanie Moller. 2000. "Wealth Inequality in the United States." *Annual Review of Sociology* 26:63–81.

Kulongoski, Theodore. 2007. Press Release, April 24, 2007. Retrieved July 4, 2007 (http://governor. oregon.gov/Gov/P2007/press_042407.shtml).

Lafer, Gordon. 2002. *Let Them Eat Training: The False Promise of Federal Employment Policy since 1980*. Ithaca, NY: Cornell University Press.

Levernier, William, Mark Partridge, and Dan Rickman. 2000. "The Causes of Regional Variations in U.S. Poverty: A Cross-County Analysis." *Journal of Regional Science* 40: 473–97.

Lewis, Oscar. 1969. *On Understanding Poverty: Perspectives From the Social Sciences*. New York: Basic Books.

Lieberman, Robert C. 1998. *Shifting the Color Line: Race and the American Welfare State*. Cambridge, MA: Harvard University Press.

Llobrera, Joseph and Bob Zahradnik. 2004. *A Hand Up: How State Earned Income Tax Credits Help Working Families Escape Poverty in 2004*. Washington, DC: Center on Budget and Policy Priorities.

Loden, Marilyn and Judy Rosener. 1991. *Workforce America! Managing Employee Diversity as a Vital Resource*. New York: McGraw-Hill.

Logan, John. 2006. *The Impact of Katrina: Race and Class in Storm-Damaged Neighborhoods*.

Retrieved May 7, 2010 (http://www.s4.brown.edu/Katrina/report.pdf).

Luo, Michael and Megan Thee-Brenan. 2009. "Poll Reveals Depth and Trauma of Joblessness in the U.S." *New York Times,* December 15, pp. A1, A26.

Magnet, Myron. 2000. *The Dream and the Nightmare: Sixties' Legacy to the Underclass.* New York: Encounter Books. (Original work published in 1993)

Mann, Michael. 1986. *The Sources of Social Power: A History of Power From the Beginning to A.D. 1760,* Vol. 1. New York: Cambridge University Press.

Marable, Manning. 2000. *How Capitalism Underdeveloped Black America.* Cambridge, MA: South End Press.

Marger, Martin. 2002. *Social Inequality: Patterns and Processes.* Boston, MA: McGraw-Hill.

McCall, Leslie. 2002. *Complex Inequality: Gender, Class, and Race in the New Economy.* New York: Routledge.

Mills, C. Wright. 2000. *The Sociological Imagination.* New York: Oxford University Press. (Original work published 1959)

Morgen, Sandra, Joan Acker, and Jill Weigt. 2010. *Stretched Thin: Poor Families, Welfare Work, and Welfare Reform.* New York: Cornell University Press.

Morin, Rich. 2012. "Rising Share of Americans See Conflict Between Rich and Poor." Retrieved January 26, 2012 (http://www.pewsocialtrends.org/2012/01/11/rising-share-of-americans-see-conflict-between-rich-and-poor/?src=prc-headline).

National Campaign for Jobs and Income Support. 2001. *Leaving Welfare, Left Behind: Employment Status, Income, and Well-Being of Former TANF Recipients.* Washington, DC: Author.

National Center for Children in Poverty. 2001. "Child Poverty Fact Sheet: June 2001." Retrieved September 27, 2003 (http://cpmcent.columbia.edu/dept/nccp/ycpf).

Nelson, Kathryn, Mark Treskon, and Danilo Pelletiere. 2004. *Losing Ground in the Best of Times: Low Income Renters in the 1990s.* Washington, DC: National Low Income Housing Coalition.

Neubeck, Kenneth and Noel Cazenave. 2001. *Welfare Racism: Playing the Race Card Against America's Poor.* New York: Routledge.

Nicholas-Casebolt, Ann and Patricia McGrath Morris. 2001. "Making Ends Meet: Private Food Assistance and the Working Poor." (Discussion Paper, No. 1222-01). Madison, WI: Institute for Research on Poverty.

Nichols, Austin. 2011. "Poverty in the United States, September 13, 2011." Retrieved January 26, 2012 (http://www.urban.org/UploadedPDF/412399-Poverty-in-the-United-States.pdf).

Norris, Donald and Lyke Thompson. 1995. "Introduction." Pp. 1–18 in *The Politics of Welfare Reform,* edited by D. Norris and L. Thompson. Thousand Oaks, CA: Sage Publications.

Oliver, Melvin L. and Thomas M. Shapiro. 1995. *Black Wealth/White Wealth.* New York: Routledge.

Patterson, James T. 1981. *America's Struggle Against Poverty, 1900–1980.* Cambridge, MA: Harvard University Press.

Pew Research Center. 2008. "Inside the Middle Class: Bad Times Hit the Good Life." Retrieved May 7, 2010 (http://pewsocialtrends.org/assets/pdf/MC-Middle-class-report.pdf).

Piven, Frances Fox. 2002. "Globalization, American Politics, and Welfare Policy." Pp. 27–42 in *Lost Ground: Welfare Reform and Beyond,* edited by R. Albelda and A. Withorm. Cambridge, MA: South End Press.

Piven, Frances Fox and Richard A. Cloward. 1993. *Regulating the Poor: The Functions of Public Welfare.* New York: Vintage Books.

Polk, D. 1997. "Check Out the International Neighbors." Retrieved September 1, 2003 (http://www.4children.org/news/5-97intl.htm).

Quadagno, Jill. 1994. *The Color of Welfare Reform: How Racism Undermined the War on Poverty.* New York: Basic Books.

Rainwater, Lee and Timothy M. Smeeding. 2003. *Poor Kids in a Rich Country: America's Children in Comparative Perspective.* New York: Russell Sage Foundation.

Reardon, Sean and Kendra Bischoff. 2011. "Growth in the Residential Segregation of Families by Income 1970–2009." Retrieved June 13, 2012 (http://www.s4.brown.edu/us2010/Data/Report/report111111.pdf).

Rice, Douglas and Barbara Sard. 2007. *Cuts in Federal Housing Assistance Are Undermining Community Plans to End Homelessness.* Washington, DC: Center on Budget and Policy Priorities.

Ruggles, P. 1990. *Drawing the Line: Alternative Poverty Measures and Their Implications.* Washington, DC: Urban Institute Press.

Safran, Dana G., Patricia Neuman, Cathy Schoen, Michelle S. Kitchman, Ira B. Wilson, Barbara Cooper, Angela Li, Hong Chang, and William H. Rogers. 2005. "Prescription Drug Coverage and Seniors: Findings from a 2003 National Survey." *Health Affairs,* April 19, pp. 152–66.

Sard, Barbara and Margy Waller. 2002. *Housing Strategies to Strengthen Welfare Policy and Support Working Families.* Washington, DC: Brookings Institution and the Center on Budget and Policy Priorities.

Seccombe, Karen and C. Amey. 1995. "Playing by the Rules and Losing: Health Insurance and the Working Poor." *Journal of Health and Social Behavior* 36:168–81.

Sernau, Scott. 2001. *Worlds Apart: Social Inequalities in a New Century.* Thousand Oaks, CA: Pine Forge.

Short, Kathleen. 2001. *Experimental Poverty Measures: 1999* (Current Population Reports Consumer Income, P60-216). Washington, DC: U.S. Census Bureau.

Short, Katherine. 2011. *The Research Supplemental Poverty Measure: 2010, P60–241.* Washington DC: U.S. Census Bureau.

Skolverket/Swedish National Agency for Education. 2003. "Child Care in Sweden." Retrieved September 1, 2003 (http://www.skolverket.se/english/system/child.shtml).

Smeeding, Timothy, Katherine Ross, and Michael O'Conner. 1999. *The Economic Impact of the Earned Income Tax Credit (EITC): Consumption, Savings, and Debt.* Syracuse, NY: Syracuse University, Center for Policy Research.

Sulzberger, A. G. 2011. "States Adding Drug Test as Hurdle for Welfare." Retrieved January 28, 2012 (http://www.nytimes.com/2011/10/11/us/states-adding-drug-test-as-hurdle-for-welfare.html?pagewanted=all).

Tillmon, Johnnie. 2002. "Welfare Is a Women's Issue." *Ms. Magazine,* Spring. Retrieved May 7, 2010 (http://www.msmagazine.com/spring2002/tillmon.asp).

United Nations Children's Fund. 2012. *Measuring Child Poverty: New League Tables of Child Poverty in the World's Rich Countries.* Florence, Italy: Author.

U.S. Bureau of Labor Statistics. 2011. *A Profile of the Working Poor, 2009.* Report 1027. Washington, DC: U.S. Department of Labor.

U.S. Census Bureau. 2012. "Poverty Thresholds by Size of Family and Number of Children." Retrieved September 12, 2012 (http://www.census.gov/hhes/www/poverty/data/threshld/index.html).

U.S. Conference of Mayors. 2011. *A Status Report on Hunger and Homelessness in American Cities, 2011.* Washington, DC: Author.

U.S. Congressional Budget Office. 2011. *Trends in the Distribution of Household Income Between 1979 and 2007.* Washington, DC: Congressional Budget Office.

U.S. Department of Health and Human Services. 2006. "Welfare Reform: Deficit Reduction Act of 2005." Retrieved March 11, 2007 (http://www.acf.hhs.gov/programs/ofa/drafact.htm).

U.S. Department of Health and Human Services. 2012. "2012 HHS Poverty Guidelines." Retrieved March 10, 2012 (http://aspe.hhs.gov/poverty/12poverty.shtml#thresholds).

U.S. Department of Health and Human Services. 2012b. "Temporary Assistance for Needy Families Information Memorandum." Retrieved July 24, 2012 (http://www.acf.hhs.gov/programs/ofa/policy/im-ofa/2012/im201203/im201203.html).

U.S. Department of Labor. 2010. "Bureau of Labor Statistics." Retrieved June 4, 2010 (http://www.bls.gov/schedule/archives/empsit_nr.htm#2009).

U.S. Department of Labor. 2012. "Labor Force Statistics from the Current Population Survey." Retrieved March 10, 2012 (http://www.bls.gov/cps/).

Waldfogel, Jane. 2001. "International Policies Toward Parental Leave and Child Care." *The Future of Children* 11(1):99–111.

Weaver, R. Kent. 2000. *Ending Welfare as We Know It.* Washington, DC: Brookings Institution Press.

Weil, Alan and Kenneth Feingold. 2002. "Introduction." Pp. xi–xxxi in *Welfare Reform: The Next Act,* edited by A. Weil and K. Feingold. Washington, DC: Urban Institute.

White House. 2010. "President Obama Announces Members of the White House Council for Community Solutions." Retrieved April 18, 2012 (http://www.whitehouse.gov/the-press-office/2010/12/14/president-obama-announces-members-white-house-council-community-solution).

Wolff, Edward. 2006. "Changes in Household Wealth in the 1980s and 1990s in the US." Pp. 107–50 in *International Perspectives on Household Wealth,* edited by E. Wolff. Corwall, England: MPG Books.

Wood, Robert, Quinn Moore, and Anu Rangarajan. 2008. "Two Steps Forward, One Step Back: The Uneven Economic Progress of TANF Recipients." *Social Service Review* 82:3–28.

World Bank. 2009. "Overview: Understanding, Measuring and Overcoming Poverty." Retrieved May 7, 2010 (http://web.worldbank.org/WBSITE/EXTERNAL/TOPICS/EXTPOVERTY/0,,contentMDK:20153855~menuPK:373757~pagePK:148956~piPK:216618~theSitePK:336992,00.html).

World Bank. 2012. "New Estimates Reveal Real Drop in Extreme Poverty 2005–2010." Retrieved November 8, 2012 (http://econ.worldbank.org/WBSITE/EXTERNAL/EXTDEC/0,,contentMDK:23129612~pagePK:64165401~piPK:64165026~theSitePK:469372,00.html).

Yardley, William. 2007. "A Governor Truly Tightens His Belt." *New York Times,* May 1, p. A13.

Zedlewski, Shelia and Pamela Loprest. 2003. "Welfare Reform: One Size Doesn't Fit All." *Christian Science Monitor, Electronic Edition,* August 25. Retrieved May 7, 2010 (http://www.urban.org/url.cfm? ID=900648).

Zucchino, David. 1999. *Myth of the Welfare Queen.* New York: Touchstone/Simon & Schuster.

Chapter 3

Academy of Achievement. 2005. "Interview with Rosa Parks." Retrieved May 10, 2010 (http://www.achievement.org/autodoc/page/par0int-1).

Ackerman, Bruce. 2004. "The Emergency Constitution." *Yale Law Journal* 133(5):1029–91.

Acosta, Yesenia and G. Patricia de la Cruz. 2011. *The Foreign Born From Latin America and the Caribbean: 2010, ACSBR/10–15.* Washington, DC: U.S. Census Bureau.

Allport, Gordon. 1954. *The Nature of Prejudice.* Garden City, NY: Doubleday.

American Council on Education and American Association of University Professors. 2000. *Does Diversity Make a Difference? Three Research Studies on Diversity in College Classrooms, Executive Summary.* Washington, DC: Author.

Asahina, Robert. 2006. *Just Americans: How Japanese Americans Won the War at Home and Abroad.* New York: Gotham Books.

Association of American Colleges and Universities. 2000. "More Colleges and Universities Require Students to Take Diversity Classes." Retrieved May 13, 2007 (http://www.aacu-edu.org/news_room/2000archive/irvinesurveypr.cfm).

Bauman, Zygmunt. 2000. *Globalisation: The Human Consequences.* Cambridge, England: Polity Press.

Bendick, Mark, Jr., Mary Lou Egan, and Suzanne M. Lofhjelm. 1998. *The Documentation and Evaluation of Antidiscrimination Training in the United States.* Washington, DC: Bendick and Egan Economic Consultants.

Bernstein, Mary and Marcie de la Cruz. 2009. "'What Are You?' Explaining Identity as a Goal of the Multiracial Hapa Movement." *Social Problems* 56:722–45.

Bonacich, Edna. 1972. "A Theory of Ethnic Antagonism: The Split Labor Market." *American Sociological Review* 37:547–59.

Budrys, Grace. 2003. *Unequal Health: How Inequality Contributes to Health or Illness.* Lanham, MD: Rowman & Littlefield.

Byrd, W. Michael and Linda Clayton. 2002. *An American Health Dilemma: Race, Medicine, and Health Care in the United States, 1900–2000.* New York: Routledge.

Camarota, Steven. 2007. "Immigrants in the United States, 2007: A Profile of America's Foreign-Born Population." Retrieved May 10, 2010 (http://www.cis.org/articles/2007/back1007.html).

Camarota, Steven. 2009. "Immigration's Impact on U.S. Workers." Retrieved May 10, 2010 (http://www.cis.org/node/1582#20).

Camarota, Steven and Karen Jensenius. 2009. "Trends in Immigrant and Native Employment." Retrieved May 10, 2010 (http://www.cis.org/articles/2009/back509.pdf).

Camarota, Steven and Karen Zeigler. 2009. "Jobs Americans Won't Do? A Detailed Look at Immigrant Employment by Occupation." Retrieved May 26, 2012 (http://www.cis.org/illegalImmigration-employment).

Carby, Hazel. 1985. "White Woman Listen! Black Feminism and the Boundaries of Sisterhood." Pp. 389–403 in *The Empire Strikes Back: Race and Racism in Seventies Britain,* edited by Paul Gilroy. London, England: Hutchinson.

Castles, Stephen and Mark Miller. 1998. *The Age of Migration.* New York: Guilford Press.

Center for Immigration Studies. 2009. "Immigration History." Retrieved May 10, 2010 (http://www.cis.org/ImmigrationHistory).

Chaudry, Ajay, Randy Capps, Juan Manuel Pedroza, Rosa Maria Castaneda, Robert Santos, and Molly Scott. 2010. *Facing Our Future: Children in the Aftermath of Immigration Enforcement.* Washington DC: Urban Institute.

Collin, Jeff and Kelley Lee. 2003. *Globalization and Transborder Health Risk in the U.K.* London, England: Nuffield Trust.

Collins, Patricia Hill. 2000. *Black Feminist Thought: Knowledge, Consciousness, and the Politics of Empowerment.* New York: Routledge.

DaCosta, Kimberly. 2007. *Making Multiracials.* Stanford, CA: Stanford University Press.

DeNavas-Walt, Carmen, Bernadette Proctor, and Jessica Smith. 2012. *Income, Poverty and Health Insurance Coverage in the United States: 2011* (Current Population Reports, P60–243). Washington, DC: U.S. Government Printing Office.

DeParle, Jason. 2007. "In a World on the Move, a Tiny Land Strains to Cope." *New York Times,* June 24, pp. 1, 8.

Donadio, Rachel. 2010a. "Race Riots Grip an Italian Town, and a Mafia Role Is Investigated." *New York Times,* January 11, pp. A1, A7.

Donadio, Rachel. 2010b. "Looking Past the Façade of Italian City after Riots." *New York Times,* January 13, p. A6.

Du Bois, W. E. B. 1996. *Darkwater.* P. 532 in *The Oxford W. E. B. Du Bois Reader,* edited by Eric Sunquist. New York: Oxford University Press.

Duncan, Brian and Stephen Trejo. 2011. "Intermarriage and the Intergenerational Transmission of Ethnic Identity and Human Capital for Mexican Americans." *Journal of Labor Economics* 29(2):195–227.

Düvell, Franck. 2005. "Globalization of Migration Control." Pp. 23–46 in *Crossing Over: Comparing Recent Migration in the United States and Europe,* edited by Holger Henke. Oxford, England: Lexington Books.

Farley, John. 2005. *Majority-Minority Relations.* Upper Saddle River, NJ: Pearson-Prentice Hall.

Feagin, Joe. 1999. "Excluding Blacks and Others from Housing: The Foundation of White Racism." *Cityscape* 4(3):79–91.

Feagin, Joe and Pinar Batur. 2004. "Racism in Comparative Perspective." Pp. 316–34 in *Handbook of Social Problems: A Comparative International Perspective,* edited by George Ritzer. Thousand Oaks, CA: Sage Publications.

Foner, Nancy. 2000. *From Ellis Island to JFK: New York's Two Great Waves of Immigration.* New York: Russell Sage.

Fry, Richard. 2004. *Latino Youth Finishing College: The Role of Selective Pathways.* Washington, DC: Pew Hispanic Center.

Fry, Richard. 2005. *The High Schools Hispanics Attend: Size and Other Key Characteristics.* Washington, DC: Pew Hispanic Center.

Gabard, Donald and Terry Cooper. 1998. "Race: Constructs and Dilemmas." *Administration & Society* 30: 339–56.

Gagné, Patricia and Richard Tewksbury. 2003. *The Dynamics of Inequality: Race, Class, and Sexuality in the United States*. Upper Saddle River, NJ: Prentice Hall.

Galagan, Patricia. 1993. "Navigating the Differences." *Training and Development* 47(4): 28–33.

Global Commission on Immigration. 2005. *Migration in an Interconnected World: New Directions for Action*. Switzerland: SRO Kunding.

Godoy, Julio. 2002. "Rights-France: Anti-immigrant and Racist Views on the Rise." *Inter Press Service*. Retrieved April 22, 2007. Available: LEXIS-NEXIS.

Gordon, Milton. 1964. *Assimilation in American Life*. New York: Oxford University Press.

Greenberg, Cheryl. 1995. "Black and Jewish Responses to Japanese Internment." *Journal of American Ethnic History* 1(2): 3–38.

Greenhouse, Linda. 2003. "Justices Back Affirmative Action by 5 to 4, but Wider Vote Bans a Racial Point System." *New York Times*, June 24, pp. A1, A25.

Greenhouse, Linda. 2007. "Justices, 5–4, Limit Use of Race for School Integration Plans." *New York Times*, June 29, pp. A1, A20.

Grieco, Elizabeth. 2010. "Race and Hispanic Origin of the Foreign-Born Population in the United States: 2007." Retrieved May 10, 2010 (http://www.census.gov/prod/2010pubs/acs-11.pdf).

Grinde, D. A. 2001. "ALANA/Ethnic Studies Assessment." Retrieved May 13, 2007 (http://www.diversityweb.org/research_and_trends/research_evaluation_impact/curriculum_development/alana.cfm).

Gyory, Andrew. 1998. *Closing the Gate: Race, Politics and the Chinese Exclusion Act*. Chapel Hill: The University of North Carolina Press.

Harris, G. L. A. 2009. "Revising Affirmative Action in Leveling the Playing Field: Who Have Been the Beneficiaries Anyway?" *Review of Public Personnel Administration* 29: 354–372.

Heilman, Madeline E., Caryn J. Block, and Peter Stahatos. 1997. "The Affirmative Action Stigma of Incompetence: Effects of Performance Information Ambiguity." *Academy of Management Journal* 40:603–25.

Herring, Cedric and Sharon Collins. 1995. "Retreat from Equal Opportunity? The Case of Affirmative Action." Pp. 163–81 in *The Bubbling Cauldron: Race, Ethnicity, and the Urban Crisis*, edited by Michael Smith and Joe Feagin. Minneapolis: University of Minnesota Press.

Human Rights Watch. 2009. *Forced Apart (By the Numbers): Non-citizens Deported Mostly for Nonviolent Offenses*. New York: Author.

Humes, Karen, Nicholas Jones, and Roberto Ramirez. 2011. *Overview of Race and Hispanic Origin: 2010, C2010BR-02*. Washington DC: U.S. Census Bureau.

Hytrek, Gary and Kristine Zentgraf. 2007. *America Transformed: Globalization, Inequality and Power*. New York: Oxford University Press.

Idelson, Holly. 1995. "A 30-Year Experiment." *Congressional Quarterly Weekly Report* 53(22):1579.

International Organization for Migration. 2003. *World Migration Report*. Geneva, Switzerland: Author.

Jaspin, Eliot. 2006. *Buried in the Bitter Waters: The Hidden History of Racial Cleansing in America*. New York: Basic Books.

Johnson, Lyndon. 1965. *Public Papers of the Presidents of the United States: Lyndon B. Johnson, 1965* (Vol. 2, entry 301, pp. 635–40). Washington, DC: U.S. Government Printing Office.

Kalev, Alexandra, Frank Dobbin, and Erin Kelly. 2006. "Best Practices or Best Guesses? Assessing the Efficacy of Corporate Affirmative Action and Diversity Policies." *American Sociological Review* 71:589–617.

Kamiya, Gary. 2009. "Obama and Race: Silence is Golden." Retrieved May 10, 2010 (http://www.salon.com/opinion/kamiya/2009/04/29/race/).

Kaplan, W. and B. Lee. 1995. *The Law of Higher Education: A Comprehensive Guide to Legal Implications of Administrative Decision Making*. San Francisco, CA: Jossey-Bass.

Korgen, Kathleen, J. Mahon, and Gabe Wang. 2003. "Diversity of College Campuses Today: The Growing Need to Foster Campus Environments Capable of Countering a Possible Tipping Effect." *College Student Journal* 37:16–26.

Kotlowski, Dean. 1998. "Richard Nixon and the Origins of Affirmative Action." *Historian* 60(3): 523–42.

Lee, Erika. 2006. "A Nation of Immigrants and a Gatekeeping Nation: American Immigration Law and Policy." Pp. 5–35 in *A Companion to American Immigration*, edited by Reed Ueda. Cornwall, England: Blackwell.

Liptak, Adam. 2012a. "Court Splits Immigration Law Verdicts; Upholds Hotly Debated Centerpiece, 8–0." *New York Times*, June 26, pp. A1, A13.

Liptak, Adam. 2012b. "Justices Weigh Diversity Issue at Universities." *New York Times*, October 11, pp. A1, A23.

Marger, Martin. 2002. *Social Inequality: Patterns and Processes*. Boston, MA: McGraw-Hill.

Martin, Daniel. 2011. *Refugees and Asylees: 2010*. Washington DC: Office of Homeland Security.

McGary, Howard. 1999. *Race and Social Justice*. Oxford, England: Blackwell.

Migrant Clinicians Network. 2009. "Environmental and Occupational Health." Retrieved May 10, 2010 (http://www.migrantclinician.org/clinical_topics/environmental-and-occupational-health.html).

Myers, John P. 2005. *Minority Voices*. Boston, MA: Pearson Education.

National Conference of State Legislatures. 2011. "2011 Immigration-Related Laws and Resolutions in the States (Jan. 1–Dec. 7, 2011)." Retrieved February 5, 2012 (http://www.ncsl.org/issues-research/immigration/state-immigration-legislation-report-dec-2011.aspx).

Obama, Barack. 2008. "Barack Obama's Speech on Race." Retrieved May 10, 2010 (http://www.npr.org/templates/story/story.php?storyId=88478467).

Odell, Patricia, Kathleen Korgen, and Gabe Wang. 2005. "Cross-Racial Friendships and Social Distance Between Racial Groups on a College Campus." *Innovative Higher Education* 29(4):291–305.

Ohlemacher, Stephen. 2006. "Race Matters, and Minorities Still Suffer, Report Says." *News Tribune*, November 14, pp. A6–A7.

Oliver, Melvin and Thomas Shapiro. 1995. *Black Wealth/White Wealth*. New York: Routledge.

Omi, Michael and Howard Winant. 1994. *Racial Formation in the United States: From the 1960s to the 1990s*. New York: Routledge.

Ore, Tracy E., ed. 2003. *The Social Construction of Difference and Inequality: Race, Class, Gender, and Sexual Orientation*. Boston, MA: McGraw-Hill.

Passel, Jeffrey and D'Vera Cohn. 2012. *U.S. Foreign-Born Population: How Much Change from 2009 to 2010?* Washington, DC: Pew Hispanic Center.

Passel, Jeffrey, D'Vera Cohn, and Ana Gonzalez-Barrera. 2012. *Net Migration From Mexico Falls to Zero—and Perhaps Less*. Washington, DC: Pew Hispanic Center.

Pew Hispanic Center. 2011. *Statistical Portrait of Hispanics in the United States, 2009*. Retrieved February 5, 2012 (http://www.pewhispanic.org/files/2011/02/2009-Hispanic-Profile-Final.pdf).

Pincus, Fred. 2003. *Reverse Discrimination: Dismantling the Myth*. Boulder, CO: Lynne Rienner.

Preston, Julia. 2007. "Immigration Is at Center of New Laws Around U.S." *New York Times*, August 6, p. A12.

Preston, Julia 2009. "White House Plan on Immigration Includes Legal Status." *New York Times*, November 14, p. A10.

Preston, Julia. 2012a. "Immigration Ruling Leaves Issues Unresolved." *New York Times*, June 27, p A14.

Preston, Julia. 2012b. "Young Immigrants, in America Illegally, Line Up for Reprieve." *New York Times*, August 14, A8, A12.

Preston, Julia and John Cushman, Jr. 2012. "Obama to Permit Young Migrants to Remain in U.S." *New York Times*, June 16, pp. A1, A16.

Redfield, Robert. 1958. "Race as a Social Phenomenon." Pp. 66–71 in *Race: Individual and Collective Behavior*, edited by E. Thompson and E. C. Hughes. Glencoe, IL: Free Press.

Rosenbaum, Sara and Joel Teitelbaum. 2004. "Addressing Racial Inequality in Health Care." Pp. 135–50 in *Policy Challenges in Modern Health Care*, edited by D. Mechanic, L. Rogut, D. Colby, and J. Knickman. New Brunswick, NJ: Rutgers University Press.

Samers, Michael. 2003. "Invisible Capitalism: Political Economy and the Regulation of Undocumented Immigration in France." *Economy and Society* 32:555–83.

Sayare, Scott. 2009. "In Paris Without Papers, and Seeking Visibility: Camp for Immigrants Challenges the Law." *New York Times*, October 11, p. 12.

Schemo, Diana Jean. 2001. "U. of Georgia Won't Contest Ruling on Admissions Policy." *New York Times*, November 10, p. A8.

Schwartzman, Luis. 2007. "Does Money Whiten?" *American Sociological Review* 72(2):940–63.

Semple, Kirk. 2012. "In a Shift Biggest Wave of Migrants Now Asian." *New York Times,* June 19, pp. A11, A14.

Shook, Natalie and Russell Fazio. 2008. "Interracial Roommate Relationships: An Experimental Field Test of the Contact Hypothesis." *Psychological Science* 19:717–23.

Shuford, John. 2001. "Four DuBoisian Contributions to Critical Race Theory." *Transactions of the Charles S. Peirce Society* 37(3):301–37.

Silverman, Maxim. 1992. *Deconstructing the Country: Immigration, Racism, and Citizenship in Modern France.* London, England: Routledge.

Springer, Ann D. 2005. "Update on Affirmative Action in Higher Education: A Current Legal Overview, January 2005." Retrieved February 20, 2012 (http://www.aaup.org/issues/diversity-affirmative-action/update-2005).

Suárez-Orozco, Carola, Hirokazu Yoshikawa, Robert Teranish, and Marcelo Suárez-Orozco. 2011. "Growing Up in the Shadows: The Developmental Implications of Unauthorized Status." *Harvard Educational Review* 81(3): 438–72.

Swink, Dawn. 2003. "Back to Bakke: Affirmative Action Revisited in Educational Diversity." *BYU Education and Law Journal* 1:211–57.

Tavernise, Sabrina. 2012. "Whites Account for Under Half of Births in U.S." *New York Times,* May 17, pp. A1, A20.

Taylor, Paul. 2012. *The Rise of Asian Americans.* Washington, DC: Pew Social & Demographic Trends.

Tsang, Chiu-Wai Rita and Tracy Dietz. 2001. "The Unrelenting Significance of Minority Statuses: Gender, Ethnicity, and Economic Attainment Since Affirmative Action." *Sociological Spectrum* 21:61–80.

United Nations. 2009. *International Migration 2009.* Retrieved May 10, 2010 (http://www.un.org/esa/population/publications/2009Migration_Chart/ittmig_wallchart09.pdf).

United Nations. 2011. *The Age and Sex of Migrants 2011.* Retrieved February 5, 2012 (http://www.un.org/esa/population/publications/2011Migration_Chart/wallchart_2011.pdf).

U.S. Bureau of Labor Statistics. 2010. *Fatal Occupational Injuries 2009.* Retrieved February 5, 2012 (http://www.bls.gov/iif/oshwc/cfoi/cfch0008.pdf).

U.S. Census Bureau. 2005. "Directive No. 15, Race and Ethnic Standards for Federal Statistics and Administrative Reporting." Retrieved November 9, 2012 (http://wonder.cdc.gov/wonder/help/populations/bridged-race/Directive15.html).

U.S. Census Bureau. 2010. "Housing Vacancies and Homeownership Annual Statistics 2010." Retrieved February 5, 2012 (http://www.census.gov/housing/hvs/).

U.S. Census Bureau. 2012a. "Housing Vacancies and Homeownership: Annual Statistics 2011." Retrieved November 10, 2012 (http://www.census.gov/housing/hvs/data/ann11ind.html).

U.S. Census Bureau. 2012b. "Most Children Younger Than Age 1 Are Minorities, Census Bureau Reports." Retrieved May 22, 2012 (http://www.census.gov/newsroom/releases/archives/population/cb12-90.html).

U.S. Immigration and Customs Enforcement. 2011. "FY2011: ICE Announces Year-End Removal Numbers, Highlights Focus on Key Priorities Including Threats to Public Safety and National Security." Retrieved February 5, 2012 (http://www.ice.gov/news/releases/1110/111018washingtondc.htm).

Van Ausdale, Debra and Joe R. Feagin. 2001. *The First R: How Children Learn Race and Racism.* Lanham, MD: Rowman & Littlefield.

Walters, Nathan and Edward Trevelyan. 2011. *The Newly Arrived Foreign-Born Population of the United States: 2010 ACSBR/10–16.* Washington, DC: U.S. Census Bureau.

White House. 2012. "Remarks by the President on Immigration." Retrieved June 16, 2012 (http://www.whitehouse.gov/the-press-office/2012/06/15/remarks-president-immigration).

Wilgoren, J. 2000. "Affirmative Action Plan Is Upheld in Michigan." *New York Times,* December 14, p. A32.

Williams, Richard, Reynold Nesiba, and Eileen Diaz McConnell. 2005. "The Changing Face of Inequality in Home Mortgage Lending." *Social Problems* 52(2):181–208.

Wittig, Michele and Sheila Grant-Thompson. 1998. "The Utility of Allport's Conditions of Intergroup Contact for Predicting Perceptions of Improved Racial Attitudes and Beliefs." *Journal of Social Issues* 54(4):795–812.

Woodhouse, Shawn. 1999. "Faculty Perceptions of the Impact of Affirmative Action on Employment Practices in the University of Missouri System." PhD dissertation, University of Missouri, Columbia, MO.

Woodhouse, Shawn. 2002. "The Historical Development of Affirmative Action: An Aggregated Analysis." *Western Journal of Black Studies* 26(3):155–59.

Yardley, Jim. 2002. "The Ten Percent Solution." *New York Times Magazine,* April 14, pp. 28–31.

Yee, Shirley. 2001. "The Past, Present, and Future of Affirmative Action: AHA Roundtable, January 1998—Introduction." *NWSA Journal* 10(3):135–41.

Zhou, Min. 2004. "Assimilation, the Asian Way." Pp. 139–53 in *Reinventing the Melting Pot: The New Immigrants and What It Means to Be American,* edited by Tamar Jacoby. New York: Basic Books.

Chapter 4

Acosta, R. Vivian and Linda Jean Carpenter. 2009. "Thirty Seven Years Later, Title IX Hasn't Fixed It All." *Academe* July–August:22–4.

Bem, Sandra Lipsitz. 1993. *The Lenses of Gender: Transforming the Debate on Sexual Inequality.* New Haven, CT: Yale University Press.

Böhnisch, L. 2003. *The Delimitation of Masculinity: Confusions and Formations of Being a Man During Societal Transition.* Opladen, Germany: Leske + Budrich.

Bonvillian, Nancy. 2006. *Women and Men: Cultural Constructs of Gender.* New York: Prentice Hall.

Brady, Erik. 2003. "Poll: Most Adults Want Title IX Left Alone." Retrieved June 12, 2003 (http://www.usatoday.com/sports/college/other/2003-01-07-title-ix_x.htm).

Charles, Maria. 2003. "Deciphering Sex Segregation: Vertical and Horizontal Inequalities in Ten National Labor Markets." *Acta Sociologica* 46(4): 267–87.

Charles, Maria and David Grusky. 2004. "The Four Puzzles of Sex Segregation." Pp. 3–37 in *Occupational Ghettos: The Worldwide Segregation of Women and Men,* edited by Maria Charles and David Grusky. Stanford, CA: Stanford University Press.

Day, Jennifer Cheeseman and Jeffrey Rosenthal. 2009. "Detailed Occupations and Median Earnings: 2008." Retrieved May 11, 2010 (http://www.census.gov/hhes/www/ioindex/acs08_detailedoccupations.pdf).

Dey, Judy Goldberg and Catherine Hill. 2007. *Behind the Pay Gap.* Washington, DC: AAUW Educational Foundation.

Durkheim, Émile. 2007. "The Division of Labor and Marriage." Pp. 41–44 in *Before the Second Wave: Gender in the Sociological Tradition,* edited by Barbara Finlay. Upper Saddle River, NJ: Pearson Prentice Hall.

Elber, Lynn. 2012. "Doc McStuffins' TV Show Gives Black Girls, Aspiring Doctors Hope." Retrieved July 10, 2012 (http://www.huffingtonpost.com/2012/06/12/doc-mcstuffins-tv-show-give-black-doctors-hope_n_1590683.html).

Elliot, Jane. 2005. "Comparing Occupational Segregation in Great Britain and the United States: The Benefits of Using a Multi-group Measure of Segregation." *Work, Employment and Society* 19(1):153–74.

England, Paula. 2001. "Gender and Access to Money: What Do Trends in Earnings and Household

Poverty Tell Us?" Pp. 131–53 in *Reconfigurations of Class and Gender,* edited by Janine Baxter and Mark Western. Stanford, CA: Stanford University Press.

Ewert, Stephanie. 2012. *What It's Worth: Field of Training and Economic Status in 2009, P70–129.* Washington, DC: U.S. Census Bureau.

Farley, John. 2005. *Majority-Minority Relations.* Upper Saddle River, NJ: Pearson Prentice Hall.

Garber, Greg. 2002. "Landmark Law Faces New Challenges Even Now." Retrieved May 11, 2010 (http://espn.go.com/gen/womenandsports/020619title9.html).

Herbert, Bob. 2006. "Punished for Being Female." *New York Times,* November 2, p. A27.

Inter-Parliamentary Union. 2013. "Women in National Parliaments." Retrieved February 26, 2013 (http://www.ipu.org/wmn-e/classif.htm).

King, Jacqueline. 2006. *Gender Equity in Higher Education: 2006.* Washington, DC: American Council on Education Center for Policy Analysis.

Marger, Martin. 2008. *Social Inequality: Patterns and Processes.* Boston, MA: McGraw-Hill.

McFarland, Kay and Donna Rhoades. 1998. "Gender-Related Values and Medical Specialty Choice." *American Psychiatry* 22:236–39.

Mishel, Lawrence, Jared Bernstein, and Sylvia Allegretto. 2007. *The State of Working America: 2006/2007.* Ithaca, NY: ILR Press.

National Center for Education Statistics. 2010. "Table 296. Bachelor's Degrees Conferred by Degree-Granting Institutions, by Race/Ethnicity and Sex of Student: Selected Years, 1976–77 Through 2008–2009." Retrieved August 2, 2012 (http://nces.ed.gov/programs/digest/d10/tables/dt10_296.asp).

National Coalition for Women and Girls in Education. 2008. *Title IX at 35: Beyond the Headlines.* Retrieved May 11, 2010 (http://www.ncwge.org/PDF/TitleIXat35.pdf).

National Committee on Pay Equity. 2011. "The Wage Gap Over Time." Retrieved February 26, 2012 (http://www.pay-equity.org/info-time.html).

National Women's Law Center. 2002a. *The Battle for Gender Equity in Athletics: Title IX at Thirty.* Washington, DC: National Women's Law Center.

National Women's Law Center. 2002b. "Quick Facts on Women and Girls in Athletics." Retrieved May 11,

2010 (http://lobby.la.psu.edu/_107th/135_Title%20IX/Organizational_Statements/NWLC/NWLC_Quick_Facts_on_Women_and_Girls_in_Athletics_June_2002.pdf).

National Women's Law Center. 2010. "Wage Gap by State." Retrieved February 29, 2012 (http://www.nwlc.org/sites/default/files/pdfs/2010-wage-gap-by-state-table.pdf).

National Women's Law Center. 2012. "Debunking the Myths About Title IX and Athletics." Retrieved March 18, 2012 (http://www.nwlc.org/resource/debunking-myths-about-title-ix-and-athletics).

Pear, Robert. 2012. "Senate Rejects Steps Targeting Coverage of Contraception." Retrieved May 2, 2012 (http://www.nytimes.com/2012/03/02/us/politics/senate-kills-gop-bill-opposing-contraception-policy.html?pagewanted=all).

Pelosi, Nancy. 2007. "Pelosi Commemorates Women's History Month." Retrieved February 20, 2013 (http://www.democraticleader.gov/news/press/pelosi-commemorates-womens-history-month).

Ridgeway, Cecilia L. and Lynn Smith-Lovin. 1999. "The Gender System and Interaction." *Annual Review of Sociology* 25:191–216.

Rose, Stephen J. and Heidi I. Hartmann. 2004. *Still a Man's Labor Market: The Long-Term Earnings Gap.* Washington, DC: Institute for Women's Policy Research.

Roth, Louise Marie. 2006. *Selling Women Short: Gender and Money on Wall Street.* Princeton, NJ: Princeton University Press.

Sandler, Bernice. 1997. "'Too Strong for a Woman'—The Five Words That Created Title IX." Retrieved May 11, 2010 (http://bernicesandler.com/id44.htm).

Scambor, Christian and Elli Scambor. 2008. "Men and Gender Mainstreaming: Prospects and Pitfalls of a European Strategy." *Journal of Men's Studies* 16:301–15.

Simões, Solange and Marlise Matos. 2009. "Modern Ideas, Traditional Behaviors, and the Persistence of Gender Inequality in Brazil." *International Journal of Sociology* 38:94–100.

Stolberg, Sheryl Gay. 2003. "Working Mothers Swaying Senate Debate, as Senators." *New York Times,* June 7, pp. A1, A11.

Stolberg, Sheryl Gay. 2009. "Obama Signs Equal-Pay Legislation." Retrieved May 11, 2010 (http://www.nytimes.com/2009/01/30/us/politics/30ledbetter-web.html).

Tickner, J. Ann 2002. "Gendering World Politics: Issues and Approaches in the Post–Cold War Era." *Political Science Quarterly* 117(2):336–37.

United Nations. 2006a. "Executive Summary: Ending Violence against Women: From Words to Action. Study of the Secretary-General." Retrieved May 11, 2010 (http://www.un.org/womenwatch/daw/vaw/launch/english/v.a.w-exeE-use.pdf).

United Nations. 2006b. "Violence Against Women: Forms, Consequences and Costs: Ending Violence against Women: From Words to Action. Study of the Secretary-General." Retrieved May 11, 2010 (http://www.un.org/womenwatch/daw/vaw/launch/english/v.a.w-consequenceE-use.pdf).

U.S. Department of Education. 2011. *The Condition of Education 2011* (NCES 2011- 033). Washington, DC: Government Printing Office.

U.S. Department of Labor, Women's Bureau. 2009. "20 Leading Occupations of Employed Women, 2008." Retrieved May 11, 2010 (http://www.dol.gov/wb/factsheets/20lead2008.htm).

U.S. Department of Labor, Women's Bureau. 2010. "20 Leading Occupations of Employed Women: 2010 Annual Averages." Retrieved November 15, 2012 (http://www.dol.gov/wb/factsheets/20lead2010.htm#.UKKGF-Oe_cY).

U.S. Department of Labor, Bureau of Labor Statistics. 2011. "College Enrollment and Work Activity of 2011 High School Graduates." Retrieved March 18, 2012 (http://www.bls.gov/news.release/hsgec.nr0.htm).

Wharton, Amy. 2004. "Gender Inequality." Pp. 156–71 in *Handbook of Social Problems: A Comparative International Perspective,* edited by George Ritzer. Thousand Oaks, CA: Sage Publications.

Wildman, Stephanie and Adrienne Davis. 2000. "Language and Silence: Making Systems of Privilege Visible." Pp. 50–60 in *Readings for Diversity and Social Justice,* edited by Maurianne Adams, Warren Blumenfeld, Rosie Castañeda, Heather Hackman, Madeline Peters, and Ximena Zúñiga. New York: Routledge.

Chapter 5

Badgett, M. V. Lee. 1997. "Vulnerability in the Workplace: Evidence of Anti-gay Discrimination." *Angles* 2(1): 1–4.

Badgett, M. V. Lee and Mary King. 1997. "Lesbian and Gay Men Occupational Strategies." Pp. 73–86 in *HomoEconomics: Capitalism, Community and Lesbian and Gay Life,* edited by A. Gluckman and B. Reed. New York: Routledge.

Bailey, J. Michael and Alan Bell. 1993. "Familiality of Female and Male Homosexuality." *Behavior Genetics* 23: 313–22.

Bailey, J. Michael and Richard Pillard. 1991. "A Genetic Study of Male Sexual Orientation." *Archives of General Psychiatry* 48: 1089–96.

Barr, Bob. 2009. "It's Time to Do Away With Defense of Marriage Act." *The News Tribune,* January 7, p. B5.

Belkin, Aaron. 2003. "Don't Ask, Don't Tell: Is the Gay Ban Based on Military Necessity?" *Parameters* Summer:108–19.

Belkin, Aaron, Morten Ender, Nathaniel Frank, Stacie Furia, George Lucas, Gary Packard, Jr., Tammy Schultz, Steven Samuels, and David Segal. 2012. *One Year Out: An Assessment of DADT Repeal's Impact on Military Readiness.* Los

Angeles: Palm Center, University of California Los Angeles.

Bevacqua, Maria. 2004. "Feminist Theory and the Question of Lesbian and Gay Marriage." *Feminism and Psychology* 14(1):36–40.

Bronski, Michael. 1998. *The Pleasure Principle: Sex, Backlash, and the Struggle for Gay Freedom.* New York: Bedford/St. Martin's Press.

Bumiller, Elisabeth. 2002. "The Most Unlikely Story Behind a Gay Rights Victory." *New York Times,* June 27, p. A19.

Bumiller, Elisabeth. 2012. "Uneventful Year in Military After Key Change for Gays." *New York Times,* September 30, p. A17.

Card, Claudia. 1996. "Against Marriage and Motherhood." *Hypatia* 11:1–23.

Cass, V. C. 1979. "Homosexual Identity Formation: A Theoretical Model." *Journal of Homosexuality* 4: 219–35.

Chen, Jialu. 2012. "Dan Savage on 'It Gets Better' and Surging Santorum." Retrieved May 9, 2012 (http://www.motherjones.com/media/2012/02/dan-savage-interview-it-gets-better-rick-santorum).

Chou, W. S. 2001. "Homosexuality and the Cultural Practices of Tongzhi in Chinese Societies." *Journal of Homosexuality* 4:27–46.

D'Augelli, Anthony. 1998. "Developmental Implications of Victimization of Lesbian, Gay and Bisexual Youths." Pp. 187–210 in *Understanding Prejudice against Lesbians, Gay Men and Bisexuals,* edited by G. M. Herek. Thousand Oaks, CA: Sage Publications.

D'Augelli, Anthony, Scott Hershberger, and Neal Pilkington. 1998. "Lesbian, Gay, and Bisexual Youths and Their Families: Disclosure of Sexual Orientation and Its Consequences." *American Journal of Orthopsychiatry* 68:361–71.

Dubé, E. M. 2000. "The Role of Sexual Behavior in the Identification Process of Gay and Bisexual Men." *Journal of Sex Research* 48:139–62.

Feigenbaum, Erika Faith. 2007. "Heterosexual Privilege: The Political and the Personal." *Hypatia* 22(1): 1–9.

Feller, Ben. 2009. "Obama Inks Defense Bill With Hate Crimes Provision." Retrieved November 1, 2009 (http://abcnews.go.com/Business/wireStory?id=8938866).

Ferguson, Ann. 2007. "Gay Marriage: An American and Feminist Dilemma." *Hypatia* 22(2):39–57.

Gallup Organization. 2010. "Gay and Lesbian Rights." Retrieved May 13, 2012 (http://www.gallup.com/poll/1651/gay-lesbian-rights.aspx).

Gates, Gary and Frank Newport. 2012. "Special Report: 3.4% of U.S. Adults Identify as LGBT." Retrieved November 15, 2012 (http://www.gallup.com/poll/158066/special-report-adults-identify-lgbt.aspx).

Gettleman, Jeffrey. 2010. "After U.S. Evangelicals Visit, Uganda Considers Death for Gays." *New York Times,* January 4, pp. A1, A9.

Greenhouse, Linda. 2003. "Texas Sodomy Law Held Unconstitutional—Scathing Dissent." *New York Times,* June 27, pp. A1, A17.

Human Rights Campaign. 2011. "Marriage Equality & Other Relationship Recognition Laws." Retrieved March 10, 2012 (http://www.hrc.org/files/assets/resources/Relationship_Recognition_Laws_Map(1).pdf).

Human Rights Campaign. 2012. "Marriage Center." Retrieved November 15, 2012 (http://www.hrc.org/marriage-center#.UKTufl6xHEz).

Human Rights Campaign. 2013. "Employment Non-discrimination Act." Retrieved February 21, 2013 (http://www.hrc.org/laws-and-legislation/federal-legislation/employment-non-discrimination-act).

Hunter, Nan. 1995. "Marriage, Law and Gender: A Feminist Inquiry." Pp. 107–22 in *Sex Wars: Sexual Dissent and Political Culture,* edited by L. Duggan and N. D. Hunter. New York: Routledge.

Katz, Jonathan Ned. 2003. "The Invention of Heterosexuality." Pp. 136–48 in *The Social Construction of Difference and Inequality: Race, Class, Gender, and Sexuality,* edited by Tracy E. Ore. Boston, MA: McGraw-Hill.

Katz, Marsha and Helen LaVan. 2004. "Legal Protection From Discrimination Based on Sexual Orientation: Findings From Litigation." *Employee Responsibilities and Rights* 16(4):195–209.

Lambda Legal. 2003. "Landmark Victory." Retrieved July 8, 2003 (http://www.lambdalegal.org/news/pr/dc_20030626_landmark-ruling-for-gay-civil-rights-us-supreme-court.html).

Lambda Legal. 2004. "California Supreme Court Invalidates Marriages From San Francisco, Without Resolving Whether Same-Sex Couples Have the Right to Marry." Retrieved May 10, 2010 (http://www.lambdalegal.org/news/pr/california-supreme-court-marriage-license.html).

Leff, Lisa. 2004. "Bay City Licensed 4,037 Couples." Retrieved March 24, 2004 (http://www.dailynews.com).

Lehne, Gregory K. 1995. "Homophobia Among Men: Supporting and Defining the Male Role." Pp. 325–36 in *Men's Lives,* edited by M. Kimmel and M. Messner. Boston, MA: Allyn & Bacon.

Lind, Amy. 2004. "Legislating the Family: Heterosexist Bias in Social Welfare Policy Frameworks." *Journal of Sociology and Social Welfare* 31(4):21–35.

McLeod, Andrew and Isaiah Crawford. 1998. "The Postmodern Family: An Examination of the Psychosocial and Legal Perspectives of Gay and Lesbian Parenting." Pp. 211–23 in *Stigma and Sexual Orientation: Understanding Prejudice Against Lesbians, Gay Men, and Bisexuals,* edited by G. Herek. Thousand Oaks, CA: Sage Publications.

Michael, Robert, John Gagnon, Edward Laumann, and Gina Kolata. 1994. *Sex in America: A Definitive Survey.* Boston, MA: Little, Brown.

Movement Advancement Project, Family Equality Council, and Center for American Progress. 2012. "Securing Legal Ties for Children Living in LGBT Families." Retrieved July 21, 2012 (http://www.lgbtmap.org/file/securing-legal-ties.pdf).

Mustanski, Brian, Meredith Chivers, and J. Michael Bailey. 2002. "A Critical Review of Recent Biological Research on Human Sexuality." *Annual Review of Sex Research* 13:89–140.

Newport, Frank. 2011. "For the First Time, Majority of Americans Favor Legal Gay Marriage." Retrieved May 13, 2012 (http://www.gallup.com/poll/147662/first-time-majority-americans-favor-legal-gay-marriage.aspx).

O'Connell, Martin and Sarah Feliz. 2011. *Same-Sex Couple Household Statistics From the 2010 Census* (SEHSD Working Paper 2011–26). Washington, DC: U.S. Bureau of Census.

Patterson, Charlotte and Richard Redding. 1996. "Lesbian and Gay Families With Children: Implications of Social Science Research for Policy." *Journal of Social Issues* 52(3):29–50.

Quittner, Jeremy. 2004. "Newsom to Bush: 'Keep Your Hands Off the Constitution.'" Retrieved March 24, 2004 (http://www.advocate.com/html/stories/911/911_newsom.asp).

Radkowsky, M. and Lawrence J. Siegel. 1997. "The Gay Adolescent: Stressors, Adaptations, and Psychological Interventions." *Clinical Psychology Review* 17:191–216.

Rivers, Ian and Daniel Carragher. 2003. "Social-Developmental Factors Affecting Lesbian and Gay Youth: A Review of Cross-National Research Findings." *Children and Society* 17(5):374–85.

Robinson, Paul. 1976. *The Modernization of Sex: Havelock Ellis, Alfred Kinsey, William Masters and Virginia Johnson.* New York: Harper & Row.

Rosenbloom, Stephanie. 2006. "Is This Campus Gay-Friendly?" *New York Times,* September 14, pp. S1–S2.

Savage, Charles and Sheryl Gay Stolberg. 2011. "In Turnabout, U.S. Says Marriage Act Blocks Gay Rights." *New York Times,* February 24, pp. A1, A18.

Savage, Dan. 2010. "Give 'Em Hope." Retrieved March 9, 2012 (http://www.thestranger.com/seattle/SavageLove?oid=4940874).

Schneider, Beth. 1986. "Coming Out at Work: Bridging the Private/Public Gap." *Work and Occupations* 13(4):463–87.

Servicemembers Legal Defense Network. 2007. "Fact Sheet: Foreign Military Services Which Allow Open Service." Retrieved June 10, 2007 (http://sldn.3cdn.net/877fa9ce3ef2a2b2bc_wrm6bngt7.pdf).

Shalikashvili, John. 2007. "Second Thoughts on Gays in the Military." *New York Times,* January 2, p. A19.

Smith, David and Gary Gates. 2001. *Gay and Lesbian Families in the United States: Same-Sex Unmarried Partnership Households: Preliminary Analysis of 2000 U.S. Census Data.* Washington, DC: Human Rights Campaign.

Stacey, Judith and Timothy Biblarz. 2001. "(How) Does the Sexual Orientation of Parents Matter?" *American Sociological Review* 66:159–83.

Tavernise, Sabrina. 2011. "New Numbers, and Geography, for Gay Couples." *New York Times,* August 25, pp. A1, A4.

Vidal, Gore. 1988. "Someone to Laugh at the Squares With." In *At Home: Essays, 1982–1988,* edited by G. Vidal. New York: Random House.

Windmeyer, Shane. 2006. *The Advocate College Guide for LGBT Students.* New York: Allyson Books.

Berger, Joseph. 2012. "A Shift From Nursing Homes to Managed Care at Home." *New York Times,* February 24, p. A20.

Binstock, Robert. 2005. "Old-Age Policies, Politics and Ageism." *Generations* 29:73–78.

Binstock, Robert. 2006. "Older People and Political Engagement: From Avid Voters to 'Cooled-Out Marks.'" *Generations* 30:24–30.

Butler, Robert. 1969. "Ageism: Another Form of Bigotry." *Gerontologist* 9(3):243–46.

Byteway, William. 1995. *Ageism.* Buckingham, England: Open University Press.

Calasanti, Toni and Kathleen Slevin. 2001. *Gender, Social Inequalities, and Aging.* Walnut Creek, CA: AltaMira Press.

Calasanti, Toni, Kathleen Slevin, and Neal King. 2006. "Ageism and Feminism: From 'Et Cetera' to Center." *NWSA Journal* 18(1):13–30.

Campbell, A. 2003. *How Policies Make Citizens: Senior Political Activism and the American Welfare State.* Princeton, NJ: Princeton University Press.

Center for Information and Research on Civic Learning and Engagement. 2012. "Youth Turnout: At Least 49%, 22–23 Million Under-30 Voted." Retrieved November 16, 2012 (http://www.civicyouth.org/youth-turnout-at-least-49-22-23-million-under-30-voted/).

Centers for Medicare and Medicaid Services. 2012. "NHE Fact Sheet." Retrieved March 11, 2012 (https://www.cms.gov/NationalHealthExpendData/25_NHE_Fact_Sheet.asp).

Clark, Robert, Richard Burkhauser, Marilyn Moon, Joseph Quinn, and Timothy M. Smeeding. 2004. *Economics of an Aging Society.* Malden, MA: Blackwell.

Cowgill, Donald. 1974. "The Aging of Populations and Societies." *The Annals of the American Academy of Political and Social Science* 415:1–18.

Crary, David. 2008. "Advocates Address Challenges of Gay Seniors." Retrieved May 12, 2010 (http://articles.sfgate.com/2008-10-19/news/17138183_1_younger-gays-lesbian-task-force-gay-men).

Curl, Angela and M. C. Hokenstad. 2006. "Reshaping Retirement Policies in Post-industrial Nations: The Need for Flexibility." *Journal of Sociology and Social Welfare* 33(2):85–106.

DeNavas-Walt, Carmen, Bernadette Proctor, and Jessica Smith. 2012. *Income, Poverty and Health Insurance Coverage in the United States: 2011* (Current Population Reports, P60–243). Washington, DC: U.S. Government Printing Office.

Dennis, Helen and Kathryn Thomas. 2007. "Ageism in the Workplace." *Generations* 31:84–89.

Duncan, Colin and Wendy Loretto. 2004. "Never the Right Age? Gender and Age-Based Discrimination in Employment." *Gender, Work and Organizations* 11(1):95–115.

Feder, Judith and Robert Friedland. 2005. "The Value of Social Security and Medicare to Families." *Generations* 29:78–85.

Fisher, Anne. 2004. "Older, Wiser, Job-Hunting." *Fortune* 149(3):46.

Freedman, Rita. 1986. *Beauty Bound.* Lexington, MA: D. C. Heath.

Frey, William. 2007. *Mapping the Growth of Older America: Seniors and Boomers in the Early 21st Century.* Washington, DC: Brookings Institution.

Frey, William. 2011. "America Reaches Its Demographic Tipping Point." Retrieved March 11, 2012 (http://www.brookings.edu/opinions/2011/0826_census_race_frey.aspx).

Glionna, John. 2011a. "Retired Scientists Say It's Their Job." *Tacoma News Tribune,* July 17, p. AA1.

Glionna, John. 2011b. "Retired Scientists Still Say They Want to Help at Japan Nuclear Plant." Retrieved March 11, 2012 (http://latimesblogs.latimes.com/world_now/2011/12/japans-march-11-earthquake-and-tsunami-fukushima-daiichi-nuclar-power-plant-radioactive-fallout.html).

Goffman, Erving. 1986. *Stigma: Notes on the Management of Spoiled Identity.* New York: Touchstone. (Original work published in 1963)

Goodman, John C. 1998. "Why Your Grandchildren May Pay a 55 Percent Payroll Tax." *Wall Street Journal,* October 7, p. A22.

Hagestad, Gunhild and Peter Uhlenberg. 2005. "Should We Be Concerned About Age Segregation? Some Theoretical and Empirical Explorations." *Research on Aging* 28(6):638–53.

He, Wan, Manisha Sengupta, Victoria Velkoff, and Kimberly DeBarros. 2005. *65+ in the United States: 2005* (P23-209). Washington, DC: U.S. Census Bureau.

Himes, C. L. 2001. "Elderly Americans." *Population Bulletin* 56(4):4.

Howell, Karen. 2011. "Integrated Care Benefits Seniors and Government Budgets." *The Globe and Mail,* July 13, p. A7.

Hurd Clarke, Laura. 2000. "Older Women's Body Image and Embodied Experience: An Exploration." *Journal of Women and Aging* 12:77–97.

Issa, Philip and Sheila Zedlewski. 2011. "Poverty Among Older Americans, 2009." Retrieved May 2, 2012 (http://www.urban.org/uploadedpdf/412296-Poverty-Among-Older-Americans.pdf).

Keeter, Scott, Juliana Horowitz, and Alec Tyson. 2008. "Young Voters in the 2008 Election." Retrieved March 11, 2012 (http://pewresearch.org/pubs/1031/young-voters-in-the-2008-election).

Kessler, Eva-Marie, Katrin Rakoczy, and Ursula M. Staudinger. 2004. "The Portrayal of Older People in Prime Time Television Series: The Match With Gerontological Evidence." *Ageing & Society* 24:531–52.

Kincannon, Charles, Wan He, and Loraine West. 2005. "Demography of Aging in China and the United States and the Economic Well-Being of Their Older Populations." *Journal of Cross Cultural Gerontology* 20:243–55.

Kinsella, Kevin and Wan He. 2009. *An Aging World: 2008, International Population Reports P95/09-1.* Washington, DC: U.S. Department of Health and Human Services and U.S. Department of Commerce.

Landphair, Ted. 2007. "Aging Activist Still on Quest for Social Justice." Retrieved May 11, 2010 (http://www.commondreams.org/headlines07/0306-09.htm).

Levenson, A. J. 1981. "Ageism: A Major Deterrent to the Introduction of Curricula in Aging." *Gerontology and Geriatrics Education* 1:11–62.

Levin, Jack and William Levin. 1980. *Ageism: Prejudice and Discrimination against the Elderly.* Belmont, CA: Wadsworth.

Levy, B. and E. Langer. 1994. "Aging Free from Negative Stereotypes: Successful Memory in China and among the American Deaf." *Journal of Personality and Social Psychology* 66(6):989–97.

Luo, Ye, Jun Xu, Ellen Granberg, and William Wentworth. 2012. "A Longitudinal Study of Social Status, Perceived Discrimination, and Physical and Emotional Health Among Older Adults." *Research on Aging* 34(3):275–301.

Mabry, J. Beth and Vern Bengston. 2005. "Disengagement Theory." Pp. 113–17 in *Encyclopedia of Ageism,* edited by E. Palmore, L. Branch, and D. Harris. New York: Haworth Press.

McConatha, Jasim, Frauke Schnell, Karin Volkwein, Lori Riley, and Elizabeth Leach. 2003. "Attitudes Toward Aging: A Comparative Analysis of Young Adults from the United States and Germany." *International Journal of Aging and Human Development* 57(3):203–15.

Miller, Darryl, Teresita Leyell, and Julianna Mazachek. 2004. "Stereotypes of the Elderly in U.S. Television Commercials From the 1950s to the 1990s." *International Journal of Aging and Human Development* 58(4):315–40.

Moody, Harry. 2006. *Aging: Concepts and Controversies.* 5th ed. Thousand Oaks, CA: Pine Forge.

Moon, Marilyn. 1999. "Growth in Medicare Spending: What Will Beneficiaries Pay?" Retrieved March 16, 2003 (http://www.urban.org/publications/407788.html).

Murphy, Sherry, Jiaquan Xu, and Kenneth Kochanek. 2012. *Deaths: Preliminary Data for 2010.* Washington, DC: Centers for Disease Control and Prevention.

National Center for Health Statistics. 2009. *Health, United States, 2008 With Chartbook.* Hyattsville, MD: Author.

Nelson, Todd. 2002. *Ageism: Stereotyping and Prejudice against Older Adults.* Cambridge, MA: MIT Press.

Nelson, Todd. 2005. "Ageism: Prejudice Against Our Feared Future Self." *Journal of Social Issues* 61(2):207–21.

OASDI Trustees. 2007. *The 2007 Annual Report of the Board of Trustees of the Federal Old-Age and Survivors Insurance and Federal Disability Insurance Trust Funds.* Washington, DC: U.S. Government Printing Office.

Ohlemacher, Stephen. 2007. "The First Baby Boomer Applies for Social Security." *Seattle Times,* October 16, pp. A1, A11.

Packer, Dominic and Alison Chasteen. 2006. "Looking to the Future: How Possible Aged Selves Influence Prejudice Toward Older Adults." *Social Cognition,* 24:218–47.

Pampel, Fred C. 1998. *Aging, Social Inequality, and Public Policy.* Thousand Oaks, CA: Pine Forge.

Peterson, Robin T. and Douglas T. Ross. 1997. "A Content Analysis of the Portrayal of Mature Individuals in Television Commercials." *Journal of Business Ethics* 15:425–33.

Pope, Elizabeth. 2012. "Found: Older Volunteers to Fill Labor Shortage." *New York Times,* March 8, p. F9.

Rampell, Catherine and Matthew Saltmarsh. 2009. "A Reluctance to Retire Means Fewer Openings." Retrieved May 11, 2010 (http://www.nytimes.com/2009/09/03/business/03retire.html?pagewanted=all&_r=0).

Rhee, Nari. 2012. *Black and Latino Retirement (In)security.* Berkeley: University of California, Center of Labor Research and Education.

Robinson, Kristen. 2007. *Trends in Health Status and Health Care Use among Older Women, Aging Trends, No. 7.* Hyattsville, MD: National Center for Health Statistics.

Sanders, Marlene. 2002. "Older Women and the Media." *Women in Action* 3(September):56.

Saucier, Maggi. 2004. "Midlife and Beyond: Issue for Aging Women." *Journal of Counseling and Development* 82:420–25.

Slackman, Michael. 2011. "Bullets Stall Youthful Push for an Arab Spring." *New York Times,* March 18, pp. A1, A10.

Social Security and Medicare Boards of Trustees. 2007. "The Summary of the 2007 Annual Reports." Retrieved May 11, 2010 (http://www.ssa.gov/OACT/TRSUM/index.html).

Sontag, Susan. 1979. "The Double Standard of Aging." Retrieved February 11, 2007 (http://www.unz.org/Pub/SaturdayRev-1972sep23-00029?View=PDFPages).

Street, Debra and Jeralynn Sittig Crossman. 2006. "Greatest Generation or Greedy Geezers? Social Spending Preference and the Elderly." *Social Problems* 53(1):75–96.

Thornton, James. 2002. "Myths of Aging or Ageist Stereotypes." *Educational Gerontology* 28:301–12.

Turner, B. 1996. *The Body and Society: Explorations in Social Theory.* Thousand Oaks, CA: Sage Publications.

U.S. Census Bureau. 2011. "Household Data, Annual Averages, 3. Employment Status of the Civilian Noninstitutional Population by Age, Sex, and Race." Retrieved March 11, 2012 (http://www.bls.gov/cps/cpsaat03.pdf).

U.S. Census Bureau. 2012a. "State and County QuickFacts." Retrieved March 16, 2012 (http://quickfacts.census.gov/qfd/states/56000.html).

U.S. Census Bureau. 2012b. *The 2012 Statistical Abstract.* Retrieved March 11, 2012 (http://www.census.gov/compendia/statab/2012/tables/12s0007.pdf).

Wang, Wendy and Rich Morin. 2009. "Home for the Holidays . . . and Every Other Day." Retrieved May 11, 2010 (http://pewsocialtrends.org/pubs/748/recession-brings-many-young-adults-back-to-the-nest).

Wilson, Duff. 2007. "Aging: Disease or Business Opportunity?" *New York Times,* April 15, pp. BU1, 7–8.

Wood, Geoffrey, Mark Harcourt, and Sondra Harcourt. 2004. "The Effects of Age Discrimination Legislation on Workplace Practice: A New Zealand Case Study." *Industrial Relations* 35(4):359–71.

Yang, Frances and Sue Levkoff. 2005. "Ageism and Minority Populations: Strengths in the Face of Challenge." *Generations* 29:42–48.

Zaidi, Asghar. 2006. *Poverty of Elderly People in EU25.* Retrieved May 11, 2010 (http://www.euro.centre.org/data/1156245035_36346.pdf).

Chapter 7

AARP. 2002. "Facts About Grandparents Raising Children." Retrieved August 28, 2002 (http://www.aarp.org/congacts/grandparents/grandfacts).

Alvarez, Lizette. 2009. "Wartime Soldier, Conflicted Mom: Overseas and Back Home, Torn Between Service and Family." *New York Times,* September 27, pp. 1, 22.

Amato, Paul R. and Bruce Keith. 1991. "Parental Divorce and the Well-Being of Children: A Meta-Analysis." *Journal of Marriage and the Family* 53: 895–915.

Anderson, Kristin. 1997. "Gender, Status, and Domestic Violence: An Integration of Feminist and Family Violence Approaches." *Journal of Marriage and the Family* 59(3):655–79.

Annie E. Casey Foundation. 1998. *Kids Count Special Report: When Teens Have Sex: Issues and Trends.* Baltimore, MD: Author.

Armas, Genaro. 2002. "Census Shows More Grandparents Are Raising Their Grandchildren." *News Tribune,* July 8, pp. A1, A6.

Avellar, Sarah and Pamela Smock. 2005. "The Economic Consequences of the Dissolution of Cohabitating Unions." *Journal of Marriage and the Family* 67(2):315–27.

Bengston, Vern L. 2001. "Beyond the Nuclear Family: The Increasing Importance of Multigenerational Bonds." *Journal of Marriage and the Family* 63(1):1–17.

Bent-Goodley, Tricia. 2005. "Culture and Domestic Violence: Transforming Knowledge Development." *Journal of Interpersonal Violence* 20(2):195–203.

Bethea, Lesa. 1999. "Primary Prevention of Child Abuse." *American Family Physician* 59(6): 1577–86.

Bianchi, Suzanne, John Robinson, and Melissa Milkie. 2006. *Changing Rhythms of American Family Life.* New York: Russell Sage.

Breines, Winifred and Linda Gordon. 1983. "The New Scholarship on Family Violence." *Signs* 8: 490–531.

Brooks Conway, Morgan, Teresa Christensen, and Barbara Herlihy. 2003. "Adult Children of Divorce and Intimate Relationships: Implications for Counseling." *Family Journal* 11(4):364–73.

Brown, Allie. 2010. "From Sex Abuse Victim to Legal Advocate." Retrieved May 11, 2010 (http://www.cnn.com/2010/LIVING/01/07/cnnheroes.ward/).

Brownmiller, S. 1975. *Against Our Will: Men, Women, and Rape.* New York: Bantam Books.

Buckley, Cara. 2007. "Despite Alternatives, Many Newborns Are Abandoned." *New York Times,* January 13, p. A14.

Bumpass, Larry. 1998. "The Changing Significance of Marriage in the United States." Pp. 63–82 in *The Changing Family in Comparative Perspective: Asia and the United States,* edited by K. Oppenheim Mason, N. Tsuya, and M. Choe. Honolulu, HI: East-West Center.

Bumpass, Larry and Hsien-Hen Lu. 2000. "Trends in Cohabitation and Implications for Children's Family Contexts in the United States." *Population Studies* 54(1):29–41.

Bureau of Justice Statistics. 2012. "Intimate Partner Violence in the U.S." Retrieved March 16, 2012 (http://bjs.ojp.usdoj.gov/content/intimate/victims.cfm#age12).

Card, J. 1999. "Teen Pregnancy Prevention: Do Any Programs Work?" *Annual Review of Public Health* 20:257–85.

Casper, Lynne and Kenneth Bryson. 1998. "Co-resident Grandparents and Their Grandchildren: Grandparent Maintained Families" (Population Division Working Paper No. 26). Washington, DC: U.S. Census Bureau.

Centers for Disease Control and Prevention. 2002. *Births, Marriages, Divorces, and Deaths: Provisional Data for October 2001* (National Vital Statistics Reports Vol. 50, No. 11, June 26, 2002). Atlanta, GA: Author.

Centers for Disease Control and Prevention. 2010. *Births, Marriages, Divorces, and Deaths: Provisional Data for 2009.* Retrieved March 16, 2012 (http://www.cdc.gov/nchs/data/nvsr/nvsr58/nvsr58_25.pdf).

Chase Goodman, Catherine and Merril Silverstein. 2006. "Grandmothers Raising Grandchildren: Ethnic and Racial Differences in Well-Being Among Custodial and Coparenting Families." *Journal of Family Issues* 27(11):1605–26.

Cherlin, Andrew, Kathleen Kiernan, and P. Lindsay Chase-Lansdale. 1995. "Parental Divorce in Childhood and Demographic Outcomes in Young Adulthood." *Demography* 32:299–318.

Child Welfare Information Gateway. 2006. *Long-Term Consequences of Child Abuse and Neglect.* Washington, DC: U.S. Department of Health and Human Services, Administration for Children and Families.

Child Welfare Information Gateway. 2007. *Recognizing Child Abuse and Neglect: Signs and Symptoms.* Retrieved May 26, 2010 (http://www.childwelfare.gov/pubs/factsheets/signs.cfm).

Copeland, Anne P. and Kathleen. M. White. 1991. *Studying Families.* Newbury Park, CA: Sage Publications.

Dafoe Whitehead, Barbara and David Popenoe. 2005. *The State of Our Unions: The Social Health of Marriage in America, 2005.* Retrieved May 11, 2010 (http://www.stateofourunions.org/pdfs/SOOU2005.pdf).

Demo, David H. 1992. "Parent-Child Relations: Assessing Recent Changes." *Journal of Marriage and the Family* 54:104–17.

DeParle, Jason and Sabrina Tavernise. 2012. "Unwed Mothers Now a Majority in Births in 20's." *New York Times,* February 18, pp. A1, A14.

Dodson, Lisa, Tiffany Manuel, and Ellen Bravo. 2002. *Keeping Jobs and Raising Families in Low-Income America: It Just Doesn't Work.* Cambridge, MA: Radcliffe Public Policy Center and 9 to 5 National Association of Working Women.

Engels, Fredrich. 1902. *The Origin of Family, Private Property, and the State.* New York: International Publishers.

Eurostat. 2009. "Population, Eurostat Yearbook 2009." Retrieved December 29, 2009 (http://epp.eurostat.ec.europa.eu/cache/ITY_OFFPUB/KS-HA-09-001-01/EN/KS-HA-09-001-01-EN.PDF).

Fields, Jason. 2003. *America's Families and Living Arrangements: 2002* (Current Population Reports, P20-547). Washington, DC: U.S. Census Bureau.

Furstenberg, Frank F., Jeanne Brooks-Gunn, and S. Philip Morgan. 1987. *Adolescent Mothers in Later Life.* Cambridge, England: Cambridge University Press.

Garcia-Moreno, Claudia, Henrica Jansen, Mary Ellsberg, Lori Heise, and Charlotte Watts. 2006. "Prevalence of Intimate Partner Violence: Findings From the WHO Multi-country Study on Women's Health and Domestic Violence." *The Lancet* 368: 1260–69.

Gelles, Richard and Peter Maynard. 1987. "A Structural Family Systems Approach to Intervention in Cases of Family Violence." *Family Relations* 33(2): 270–76.

Goldman, Jill, Marsha Salus, Deborah Wolcott, and Kristie Kennedy. 2003. *A Coordinated Response to Child Abuse and Neglect: The Foundation for Practice.* Washington, DC: Office on Child Abuse and Neglect, Health and Human Services.

Goodwin, Paula Y., William D. Mosher, and Anjani Chandra. 2010. *Marriage and Cohabitation in the United States: A Statistical Portrait Based on Cycle 6 (2002) of the National Survey of Family Growth* (Vital Health Statistics, Series 23, Number 28). Washington, DC: National Center for Health Statistics.

Gubernskaya, Zoya. 2010. "Changing Attitudes Toward Marriage and Children in Six Countries." *Sociological Perspectives* 53(2): 179–200.

Hanson, Marci and Eleanor Lynch. 1992. "Family Diversity: Implications for Policy and Practice." *Topics in Early Childhood Special Education* 12(3): 283–305.

He, Wan, Manisha Sengupta, Victoria Velkoff, and Kimberly De Barros. 2005. *65+ in the United States, 2005* (P23-209). Washington, DC: U.S. Department of Commerce, Economics and Statistics Administration, U.S. Census Bureau.

Heymann, Jody, Alison Earle, and Jeffrey Hayes. 2007. *The Work, Family, and Equity Index: How Does the United States Measure Up?* Montreal, Quebec, Canada Project on Global Working Families.

Hiew, Chock C. 1992. "Separated by Their Work: Families with Fathers Living Apart." *Environment and Behavior* 24:206–25.

Hoffman, Saul. 1998. "Teenage Childbearing Is Not So Bad After All . . . Or Is It? A Review of the New Literature." *Family Planning Perspectives* 30(5):236–39, 243.

Hoffman, Saul. 2006. *By the Numbers: The Public Cost of Adolescent Childbearing.* Washington, DC: The National Campaign to Prevent Teen Pregnancy.

Jensen, Peter, David Martin, and Henry Watanabe. 1996. "Children's Response to Separation During Operation Desert Storm." *Journal of the American Academy of Child and Adolescent Psychiatry* 35:433–41.

Jetter, Alexis. 2000. "Uppity Women: Wynona Ward." Retrieved May 11, 2010 (http://www.msmagazine.com/feb00/uppitywomen.asp).

Johnson, Shannon, Michelle Sherman, Jeanne Hoffman, Larry James, Patti Johnson, and John Lochman. 2007. *The Psychological Needs of U.S. Military Service Members and Their Families: A Preliminary Report* (Presidential Task Force on Military Deployment Services for Youth, Families and Service Members). Washington, DC: American Psychological Association.

Kim, Eunjeong and King Davis. 2003. "Conceptualizing Unmarried Motherhood in South Korea: The Role of Patriarchy and Confucianism in the Lives of Women." *Journal of Social Work Research and Evaluation* 4:107–20.

Kirby, Douglas. 2007. "Abstinence, Sex and STD/HIV Education Programs for Teens: Their Impact on Sexual Behavior, Pregnancy and Sexually Transmitted Disease." *Annual Review of Sex Research* 18:143–77.

Kreider, Rose. 2005. *Number, Timing and Duration of Marriage and Divorces: 2001* (Current Population Reports, P70-97). Washington, DC: U.S. Census Bureau.

Kreider, Rose. 2010. "Increase in Opposite-sex Cohabiting Couples from 2009 to 2010 in the Annual and Economic Supplement (ASED) to the Current Population Survey (CPS)." Retrieved March 16, 2012 (http://www.census.gov/population/www/socdemo/Inc-Opp-sex-2009-to-2010.pdf).

Kreider, Rose and Diana Elliot. 2009. *America's Families and Living Arrangements: 2007* (Current Population Reports, P20-561). Washington, DC: U.S. Census Bureau.

Kreider, Rose and J. Fields. 2002. *Number, Timing, and Duration of Marriages and Divorces: Fall 1996* (Current Population Reports, P70-80). Washington, DC: U.S. Census Bureau.

Lang, Susan. 1993. "Findings Refute Traditional Views on Elder Abuse." *Human Ecology* 21(3):30.

Lenski, Gerhard and Jean Lenski. 1987. *Human Societies.* New York: McGraw-Hill.

Levai, Marion, Sheldon Kaplan, Karen Daly, and George McIntosh. 1994. "The Effect of the Persian Gulf Crisis on the Psychiatric Hospitalization of Navy Children and Adolescents." *Child Psychiatry and Human Development* 24:245–54.

Levendosky, Alytia and Sandra Graham-Bermann. 2000. "Behavioral Observations of Parenting in Battered Women." *Journal of Family Psychology* 14: 80–94.

Levendosky, Alytia, Shannon Lynch, and Sandra Graham-Bermann. 2000. "Mothers' Perceptions of the Impact of Woman Abuse on Their Parenting." *Violence against Women* 6(3):247–71.

Little, Kristin, Mary Malefyt, and Alexander Walker. 1998. "A Tool for Communities to Develop Coordinated Responses." In *Promising Practices Initiative of the STOP Violence Against Women Grants Technical Assistance Project.* Retrieved August 29, 2002 (http://www.vaw.umn.edu/Promise/PP3).

MacKinnon, Carol E., Zolinda Stoneman, and Gene H. Brody. 1984. "The Impact of Maternal Employment and Family Form on Children's Sex Role Stereotypes and Mothers' Traditional Attitudes." *Journal of Divorce* 8:51–60.

Manning, Wendy and Pamela Smock. 2002. "First Comes Cohabitation and Then Comes Marriage? A Research Note." *Journal of Family Issues* 23(8): 1065–87.

Martin, Joyce, Brady Hamilton, Paul Sutton, Stephanie Ventura, T. J. Matthews, and Michelle

Osterman. 2010. Births: Final Data for 2008. *National Vital Statistics Reports* 59(1):1–72.

Mays, Jennifer. 2006. "Feminist Disability Theory: Domestic Violence Against Women With a Disability." *Disability & Society* 21:147–58.

National Center on Elder Abuse. 2002a. "Frequently Asked Questions: What Is Elder Abuse?" Retrieved May 27, 2010 (http://www.ncea.aoa.gov/NCEAroot/Main_Site/FAQ/Questions.aspx).

National Center on Elder Abuse. 2002b. *Sentinels: Reaching Hidden Victims—Final Report, May 2002.* Washington, DC: Author.

National Center on Elder Abuse. 2006. *The 2004 Survey of State Protective Services: Abuse of Adults 60 Years of Age and Older.* Washington, DC: Author.

National Marriage Project. 2009. "State of Our Unions: The Marriage Report 2009." Retrieved January 7, 2010 (http://www.stateofourunions.org/2009/si-cohabitation.php).

National Marriage Project. 2011. *The State of Our Unions.* Charlottesville, VA: National Marriage Project.

National Partnership for Women and Families. 2009. "Paid Leave." Retrieved May 11, 2010 (http://www.nationalpartnership.org/site/PageServer?pagename=issues_work_paidleave).

Navaie-Waliser, Maryam, Penny Feldman, David Gould, Carol Levine, Alexis Kuebris, and Karen Donelan. 2002. "When the Caregiver Needs Care: The Plight of Vulnerable Caregivers." *American Journal of Public Health* 92(3):409–13.

New Jersey Safe Haven Protection Act. 2007. "FAQ's." Retrieved January 14, 2007 (http://www.njsafehaven.org/faq.html).

Newman, David. 2006. *Sociology: Exploring the Architecture of Everyday Life.* Thousand Oaks, CA: Pine Forge.

Organisation for Economic Co-operation and Development. 2010. Retrieved February 21, 2012 (http://www.oecd.org/els/soc/41920080.pdf).

Popenoe, David. 1993. "American Family Decline, 1960–1990: A Review and Appraisal." *Journal of Marriage and the Family* 55:527–55.

Popenoe, David. 2006. "Marriage and Family in the Scandinavian Experience." *Society* 43(4):68–72.

Povoledo, Elisabetta. 2007. "Updating an Old Way to Leave the Baby on the Doorstep." *New York Times,* February 28, p. A4.

Powell, Brian, Catherine Bolzendahl, Claudia Geist, and Lara Carr Steelman. 2010. *Counted Out: Same-Sex Relations and Americans' Definitions of Family.* New York: Russell Sage.

Radcliffe Public Policy Center. 2000. *Life's Work: Generational Attitudes Toward Work and Life Integration.* Cambridge, MA: Author.

Roberts, Sam. 2007. "51% of Women Are Now Living Without a Spouse." *New York Times,* January 16, pp. A1, A19.

Rubin, Lillian. 1995. *Families on the Fault Line: America's Working Class Speaks About the Family, the Economy and Ethnicity.* New York: Harper Perennial.

Rutter, Michael and Marta Tienda. 2005. "The Multiple Facets of Ethnicity." Pp. 50–59 in *Ethnicity and Causal Mechanisms,* edited by Michael Rutter and Marta Tienda. New York: Cambridge University Press.

Sang-Hun, Choe. 2009. "Group Resists Korean Stigma for Mothers on Their Own." *New York Times,* October 8, p. A6.

Simons, Ronald L. 1996. *Understanding Differences Between Divorced and Intact Families: Stress, Interaction, and Child Outcomes.* Thousand Oaks, CA: Sage Publications.

Smith, Dorothy. 1993. "The Standard North American Family: SNAF as an Ideological Code." *Journal of Family Issues* 14(1):50–65.

SmithBattle, Lee. 2007. "'I Wanna Have a Good Future': Teen Mothers' Rise in Educational Aspirations, Competing Demands, and Limited School Support." *Youth & Society* 38(3):348–71.

Smock, Pamela J. 1994. "Gender and Short Run Economic Consequences of Marital Disruption." *Social Forces* 73:243–62.

Somers, Cheryl and Mariane Fahlman. 2001. "Effectiveness of the 'Baby Think It Over' Teen Pregnancy Prevention Program." *Journal of School Health* 71(5):188–207.

Stacey, Judith. 1996. *In the Name of the Family: Rethinking Family Values in the Post-modern Age.* Boston, MA: Beacon Press.

Tjaden, Patricia and Nancy Thoennes. 2000. *Extent, Nature and Consequences of Intimate Partner Violence* (NCJ 18186). Washington, DC: National Institute of Justice, U.S. Department of Justice.

Trail Ross, Mary Ellen and Lu Ann Aday. 2006. "Stress and Coping Among African American Grandparents Who Are Raising Their Grandchildren." *Family Issues* 27: 912–932.

Truman, Jennifer. 2011. *Criminal Victimization, 2010* (NCJ 235508). Washington, DC: U.S. Department of Justice, Bureau of Justice Statistics.

U.S. Census Bureau. 1999. *Statistical Abstract of the United States: 1999* (Table No. 91). Washington, DC: Author.

U.S. Census Bureau. 2012a. *The 2012 Statistical Abstract.* Retrieved March 11, 2012 (http://www.census.gov/compendia/statab/2012/tables/12s0007.pdf).

U.S. Census Bureau. 2012b. "Grandchildren Characteristics: 2010 American Community Survey 1-Year Estimates." Retrieved March 16, 2012 (http://factfinder2.census.gov/faces/tableservices/jsf/pages/productview.xhtml?pid=ACS_10_1YR_S1001&prodType=table).

U.S. Department of Health and Human Services, Administration for Children and Families, Administration on Children, Youth and Families, Children's Bureau. 2011. *Child Maltreatment 2010.* Retrieved March 16, 2012 (http://www.acf.hhs.gov/programs/cb/stats_research/index.htm#can).

U.S. Department of Labor. 2007. "Federal vs. California Family and Medical Leave Laws." Retrieved January 13, 2007 (http://www.dol.gov/esa/programs/whd/state/fmla/ca.htm).

Uunk, Wilfred. 2004. "The Economic Consequences of Divorce for Women in the European Union: The Impact of Welfare State Arrangements." *European Journal of Population* 20(3):251–85.

Videon, Tami. 2002. "The Effects of Parent-Adolescent Relationships and Parental Separation on Adolescent Well-Being." *Journal of Marriage and Family* 64(2):489–504.

Ward, Wynona. 2002. "Transcript: Wynona Ward—Have Justice Will Travel." Retrieved May 11, 2010 (http://www.pbs.org/now/transcript/transcript_ward.html).

Weaver, Heather, Gary Smith, and Susan Kippax. 2005. "School-Based Sex Education Policies and Indicators of Sexual Health Among Young People: A Comparison of the Netherlands, France, Australia and the United States." *Sex Education* 5:171–88.

Chapter 8

Aber, J. L., Joshua Brown, and Christopher C. Henrich. 1999. *Teaching Conflict Resolution: An Effective School-Based Approach to Violence Prevention.* Washington, DC: National Center for Children in Poverty.

Adams, Mike S. and T. D. Evans. 1996. "Teacher Disapproval, Delinquent Peers, and Self-Reported Delinquency: A Longitudinal Test of Labeling Theory." *Urban Review* 28(3):199–211.

American Association of University Women. 1992. *How Schools Shortchange Girls: The AAUW Report.* New York: Author.

American Association of University Women. 2001. *Hostile Hallways: Bullying, Teasing, and Sexual Harassment in School.* Washington, DC: Author.

Anderson, Mark, Joanne Kaufman, Thomas R. Simon, Lisa Barrios, Len Paulozzi, George Ryan, Rodney Hammond, William Modzeleski, Thomas Feucht, Lloyd Potter, and the School-Associated Violent Deaths Study Group. 2001.

"School Associated Violent Deaths in the United States, 1994–1999." *Journal of the American Medical Association* 286(21):2695–702.

Ansalone, George. 2001. "Schooling, Tracking and Inequality." *Journal of Children and Poverty* 7(1):33–49.

Ansalone, George. 2004. "Educational Opportunity and Access to Knowledge: Tracking in the U.S. and Japan." *Race, Gender & Class* 11(3):140–52.

Ansell, Nicola. 2008. "Substituting for Families? Schools and Social Reproduction in AIDS-Affected Lesotho." *Antipode* 40:802–24.

Bauman, Kurt J. 2001. "Home Schooling in the United States: Trends and Characteristics" (Working Paper No. 530). Washington, DC: U.S. Census Bureau.

Berliner, David and Bruce Biddle. 1995. *The Manufactured Crisis: Myths, Frauds, and the Attack on America's Public Schools*. Reading, MA: Addison-Wesley.

Bjork, Christopher and Ryoko Tsuneyoshi. 2005. "Education Reform in Japan: Competing Visions for the Future." *Phi Delta Kappan* April:619–26.

Blume, Howard. 2009. "L.A. Unified Has Fewer Students; Charter School Enrolment Rises Sharply." *Los Angeles Times,* November 4. Retrieved May 14, 2010 (http://latimesblogs.latimes.com/lanow/2009/11/enrollment-in-traditional-los-angeles-area-schools-has-declined-this-fall-even-as-the-number-of-students-enrolled-in-charter.html).

Bohan, Janis and Glenda M. Russell. 1999. "Support Networks for Lesbian, Gay and Bisexual Students." Pp. 279–94 in *Coming into Her Own: Educational Successes in Girls and Women,* edited by S. N. Davis, M. Crawford, and J. Sebrechts. San Francisco, CA: Jossey-Bass.

Bourdieu, Pierre. 1977. "Cultural Reproduction and Social Reproduction." Pp. 71–84 in *Power and Ideology in Education,* edited by J. Karabel and A. H. Halsey. Oxford: Oxford University Press.

Bumiller, Elisabeth. 2002. "Bush Calls Ruling About Vouchers a 'Historic' Move.'" *New York Times,* July 2, pp. A1, A15.

Callan, Patrick. 2006. *Introduction: International Comparisons Highlight Educational Gaps Between Younger and Older Americans*. Washington, DC: National Center for Public Policy and Higher Education.

Callan, Patrick. 2008. *The 2008 National Report Card: Modest Improvements, Persistent Disparities, and Eroding Global Competitiveness*. Washington, DC: National Center for Public Policy and Higher Education.

Carnevale, Anthony and Stephen Rose. 2003. *Socioeconomic Status, Race/Ethnicity and Selective College Admission*. New York: Century Foundation.

Chapman, Chris, Jennifer Laird, Nicole Ifill, and Angelina KewalRamani. 2011. *Trends in High School Dropout and Completion Rates in the United States: 1972–2009*. Washington, DC: U.S. Department of Education.

College Board. 2009. *2009 College-Bound Seniors: Total Group Profile Report*. Retrieved March 14, 2012 (http://professionals.collegeboard.com/profdownload/cbs-2009-national-TOTAL-GROUP.pdf).

College Entrance Examination Board. 1999. *Reaching the Top: A Report of the National Task Force on Minority High Achievement*. New York: Author.

Dinkes, Rachel, Jana Kemp, Katrina Baum, and Thomas Snyder. 2009. *Indicators of School Crime and Safety: 2009* (NCES 2010-012/NCJ 228478). U.S. Departments of Education and Justice. Washington, DC: U.S. Government Printing Office.

Downey, Douglas, Paul von Hippel, and Beckett Broh. 2004. "Are Schools the Great Equalizer? Cognitive Inequality during the Summer Months and the School Year." *American Sociological Review* 69:613–35.

Eaton, Danice, Laura Kann, Steve Kinchen, Shair Shaklin, James Ross, Joseph Hawkins, William Harris, Richard Lowry, Tim McManus, David Chyen, Connie Lim, Lisa Whittle, Nancy Brener, and Howell Weschsler. 2010. "Youth Risk Behavior Surveillance—United States, 2009." Retrieved April 7, 2012 (http://www.cdc.gov/mmwr/pdf/ss/ss5905.pdf).

Equal Employment Opportunity Commission. 2001. "Facts about Sexual Harassment." Retrieved May 14, 2010 (http://www.eeoc.gov/facts/fs-sex.html).

Field, Kelly. 2012. "College Groups React to Obama's Higher-Education Budget with Praise and Caution." Retrieved May 24, 2012 (http://chronicle.com/article/College-Groups-React-With/130775/).

Fineran, Susan. 2002. "Sexual Harassment Between Same-Sex Peers: Intersection of Mental Health, Homophobia, and Sexual Violence in Schools." *Social Work* 47(1):65–74.

Finn, Chester. 1997. "The Politics of Change." Pp. 226–50 in *New Schools for a New Century: The Redesign of Urban Education,* edited by Diane Ravitch and Joseph Viteritti. New Haven, CT: Yale University Press.

Flannery, Daniel. 1997. *School Violence: Risk, Preventive Intervention, and Policy*. New York: ERIC Clearing House on Urban Education (ERIC Document Reproduction Services No. ED416272).

Freeman, Catherine. 2004. *Trends in Educational Equity of Girls & Women: 2004*. (NCES 2005-016). U.S. Department of Education, National Center for Education Statistics. Washington, DC: U.S. Government Printing Office.

Freeman, Kendralin and Dennis Condron. 2011. "Schmoozing in Elementary School: The Importance of Social Capital to First Graders." *Sociological Perspectives* 54:521–46.

Fry, Richard. 2011. *Hispanic College Enrollment Spikes, Narrowing Gaps with Other Groups*. Retrieved April 7, 2012 (http://www.pewhispanic.org/2011/08/25/hispanic-college-enrollment-spikes-narrowing-gaps-with-other-groups/).

Fry, Richard and Mark Hugo Lopez. 2012. *Hispanic Student Enrollments Reach New Highs in 2011*. Retrieved August 27, 2012 (http://www.pewhispanic.org/files/2012/08/Hispanic-Student-Enrollments-Reach-New-Highs-in-2011_FINAL.pdf).

Garcia, David. 2008. "The Impact of School Choice on Racial Segregation in Charter Schools." *Educational Policy* 22:805–29.

"Goals 2000: Reforming Education to Improve Student Achievement." 1998. Retrieved May 18, 2010 (http://www.ed.gov/pubs/G2KReforming/index.html).

Good, Thomas L. and Jennifer S. Braden. 2000. *The Great School Debate: Choice, Vouchers, and Charters*. Mahwah, NJ: Lawrence Erlbaum.

Hallinan, Maureen. 1994. "Tracking: From Theory to Practice." *Sociology of Education* 67(2):79–91.

Hill, Catherine and Holly Kearl. 2011. *Crossing the Line: Sexual Harassment at School*. Washington, DC: AAUW.

Hill, Paul T. 2005. "Assessing Achievement in Charter Schools." Pp. 21–32 in *Hopes, Fears and Reality: A Balanced Look at American Charter Schools in 2005,* edited by R. Lake and P. Hill. Seattle, WA: National Charter School Research Project, Center on Reinventing Public Education, University of Washington.

Holland, Dorothy C. and Margaret A. Eisenhart. 1990. *Educated in Romance: Women, Involvement, and College Culture*. Chicago, IL: University of Chicago Press.

Hu, Winnie. 2012. "10 States Are Given Waivers From Education Law." *New York Times,* February 10, p. A13.

Human Rights Watch. 2001. *Hatred in the Hallways: Violence and Discrimination Against Lesbian, Gay, Bisexual, and Transgender Students in U.S. Schools*. New York: Author.

Jacobs, Jerry A. 1996. "Gender Inequality and Higher Education." *Annual Review of Sociology* 22:153–85.

Johnson, Jean, Jon Rochkind, Amber Ott, and Samantha DuPont. 2009. *With Their Whole Lives Ahead of Them*. San Francisco, CA: Public Agenda.

Johnson, Robert C. and Debra Viadero. 2000. "Unmet Promise: Raising Minority Achievement." *Education Week* 17(43):1.

Kahlenberg, Richard. 2002. "Socioeconomic Integration." Presented at 20th Annual Magnet Schools of America Conference. Retrieved May 18, 2010 (http://www.tcf.org/list.asp?type=NC&pubid=906).

Kanter, Rosabeth Moss. 1972. "The Organization Child: Experience Management in a Nursery School." *Sociology of Education* 45:186–211.

Kennedy, Sheila. 2001. "Privatizing Education." *Phi Delta Kappan* 82(6):450–57.

Kingery, Paul M., B. E. Pruitt, G. Heuberger, and J. A. Brizzolara. 1993. "School Violence Reported by Adolescents in Rural Central Texas." Texas A&M University, College Station, TX. Unpublished manuscript.

Kirsch, Irwin, Ann Jungeblut, Lynn Jenkins, and Andrew Kolstad. 2002. *Adult Literacy in America: A First Look at the Results of the National Adult Literacy Survey*. Retrieved May 18, 2010 (http://nces.ed.gov/pubs93/93275.pdf).

Kopp, Wendy. 2001. *One Day, All Children: The Unlikely Triumph of Teach for America and What I Learned Along the Way.* New York: PublicAffairs.

Kosciw, Joseph, Emily Greytak, Mark Bartkiewicz, Madelyn Boesen, and Neal Palmer. 2012. *The 2011 National School Climate Survey: The Experiences of Lesbian, Gay, Bisexual and Transgender Youth in Our Nation's Schools.* New York: GLSEN.

Kozol, Jonathan. 1991. *Savage Inequalities: Children in America's Schools.* New York: Harper Perennial.

Kozol, Jonathan. 2005. *The Shame of the Nation: The Restoration of Apartheid Schooling in America.* New York: Crown.

Laird, J., S. Lew, M. DeBell, and C. Chapman. 2006. *Dropout Rates in the United States: 2002 and 2003* (NCES 2006-062). U.S. Department of Education. Washington, DC: National Center for Education Statistics.

Lareau, Annette. 2003. *Unequal Childhoods: Class, Race, and Family Life.* Berkeley: University of California Press.

Lin, Nan. 2011. *Social Capital: A Theory of Social Structure and Action.* Cambridge, England: Cambridge University Press.

Linn, Marcia and Cathy Kessel. 1996. "Success in Mathematics: Increasing Talent and Gender Diversity Among College Majors." Pp. 83–100 in *Issues in Mathematics Education, Conference of the Mathematical Sciences.* Vol. 6, *Research in Collegiate Mathematics Education II,* edited by J. Kaput, A. H. Schoenfeld, and E. Dubinsky. Providence, RI: American Mathematical Society.

Literacy Volunteers of America. 2002. "Facts on Literacy in America." Retrieved September 5, 2003 (http://www.literacyvolunteers.org/about/faqs/facts.html).

Marger, Martin. 2008. *Social Inequality: Patterns and Processes.* Boston, MA: McGraw-Hill.

Maruyama, G. 2003. "Disparities in Educational Opportunities and Outcomes: What Do You Know and What Can We Do?" *Journal of Social Issues* 59(3):653–76.

Meier, Deborah. 1995. *The Power of Their Ideas.* Boston, MA: Beacon Press.

Mori, Rie. 2002. "Entrance Examinations and Remedial Education in Japanese Higher Education." *Higher Education* 43:27–42.

National Advisory Council on Violence Against Women. 2001. *Toolkit to End Violence Against Women.* Retrieved November 5, 2012 (http://www.vaw.umn.edu/documents/toolkitendvaw/toolkitendvaw.pdf).

National Commission on Excellence in Education. 1983. *A Nation at Risk: The Imperatives for Educational Reform.* Washington, DC: U.S. Department of Education.

National Girls Collaborative Project. 2006. "Overview." Retrieved March 14, 2007 (http://www.psctlt.org/ngcp/about/index.cfm).

Ono, Hiroshi. 2001. "Who Goes to College? Features of Institutional Tracking in Japanese Higher Education." *American Journal of Education* 109(2):161–95.

Perkins-Gough, Deborah. 2006. "Do We Really Have a 'Boy Crisis'?" *Educational Leadership* 64(1):93–94.

Planty, Michael, William Hussar, Thomas Snyder, Grace Kena, Angelina Kewal Ramani, Jana Kemp, Kevin Bianco, and Rachel Dinkes. 2009. *The Condition of Education 2009* (NCES 2009-081). Washington, DC: National Center for Education Statistics, Institute of Education Sciences, U.S. Department of Education.

ProLiteracy Worldwide. 2006. *The State of Adult Literacy 2006.* New York: Author.

Ravitch, Diane. 1997. "Somebody's Children: Educational Opportunity for All American Children." Pp. 251–73 in *New Schools for a New Century: The Redesign of Urban Education,* edited by D. Ravitch and J. P. Viteritti. New Haven, CT: Yale University Press.

Ravitch, Diane and Joseph P. Viteritti. 1997. "Introduction." Pp. 1–16 in *New Schools for a New Century: The Redesign of Urban Education,* edited by D. Ravitch and J. P. Viteritti. New Haven, CT: Yale University Press.

Reardon, Sean. 2011. "The Widening Academic Achievement Gap Between the Rich and the Poor: New Evidence and Possible Explanations." Pp. 91–116 in *Whither Opportunity: Rising Inequality, Schools and Children's Life Chances,* edited by G. Duncan and R. Murnane. New York: Russell Sage.

Rohlen, Thomas. 1983. *Japan's High Schools.* Berkeley: University of California Press.

Ryan, Camille and Julie Siebens. 2012. *Educational Attainment in the United States: 2009,* P20–566. Washington DC: U.S. Printing Office.

Sacks, Peter. 2009. "Tearing Down the Gates: Confronting the Class Divide in American Education." *Liberal Education* 95:14–19.

Sadker, Myra and David Sadker. 1994. *Failing at Fairness: How Our Schools Cheat Girls.* New York: Simon & Schuster.

Sallie Mae and Ipsos. 2012. *How America Pays for College 2012.* Retrieved July 24, 2012 (https://www1.salliemae.com/NR/rdonlyres/75C6F178-9B25-48F5-8982-41F9B3F35BF6/0/HowAmericaPays2012.pdf).

Saporito, Salvatore and Annette Lareau. 1999. "School Selection as a Process: The Multiple Dimensions of Race in Framing Educational Choice." *Social Problems* 46:418–39.

Schemo, Diana Jean. 2002. "Few Exercise New Right to Leave Failing Schools." *New York Times,* August 28, pp. A1, A14.

Schemo, Diana Jean. 2006. "Study of Test Scores Finds Charter Schools Lagging." *New York Times,* August 23, p. A14.

Schmid, Randolph. 2010. "Teachers Give Girls Math Anxiety, Study Says." *News Tribune,* January 26, p. A6.

Scott, Janelle and Adriana Villavicencio. 2009. "School Context and Charter School Achievement: A Framework for Understanding the Performance 'Black Box.'" *Journal of Education* 84:227–43.

Shaw, Margaret. 2001. *Promoting Safety in Schools: International Experience and Action* (Bureau of Justice Assistance Monograph, NCJ 186937). Washington, DC: U.S. Department of Justice.

Silverman, Linda Kreger. 1986. "What Happens to the Gifted Girl?" Pp. 43–89 in *Critical Issues in Gifted Education.* Vol. 1, *Defensible Programs for the Gifted,* edited by C. J. Maker. Rockville, MD: Aspen.

Slaughter-Defoe, Diana and Henry Rubin. 2001. "A Longitudinal Case Study of Head Start Eligible Children: Implications for Urban Education." *Educational Psychologist* 36(1):31–44.

Smith, Dorothy E. 2000. "Schooling for Inequality." *Signs* 25(4):1147–51.

Smith, R. S. 1995. "Giving Credit Where Credit Is Due: Dorothy Swaine Thomas and the 'Thomas Theorem.'" *American Sociologist* 26(4):9–29.

Spencer, Steven J., Claude M. Steele, and Diane M. Quinn. 1999. "Stereotype Threat and Women's Math Performance." *Journal of Experimental Social Psychology* 35:4–28.

Stambach, Amy and Natalie Crow Becker. 2006. "Finding the Old in the New: On Race and Class in US Charter School Debates." *Race, Ethnicity and Education* 9:159–82.

Steele, Claude M. 1997. "A Threat in the Air: How Stereotypes Shape Intellectual Identity and Performance." *American Psychologist* 52:613–29.

Steele, Claude M. and Joshua Aronson. 1995. "Stereotype Threat and the Intellectual Test Performance of African Americans." *Journal of Personality and Social Psychology* 69(5):797–811.

Stombler, Mindy and Patricia Yancey Martin. 1994. "Bringing Women In, Keeping Women Down." *Journal of Contemporary Ethnography* 23(2):150–84.

Strand, K. and M. E. Mayfield. 2002. "Pedagogical Reform and College Women's Persistence in Mathematics." *Journal of Women and Minorities in Science and Engineering* 8:67–83.

Sum, Andrew, Irwin Kirsch, and Robert Taggart. 2002. *The Twin Challenges of Mediocrity and Inequality: Literacy in the U.S. from an International Perspective.* Princeton, NJ: Educational Testing Service.

Synder, Thomas and Sally Dillow. 2011. *Digest of Education Statistics 2010.* Washington, DC: U.S. Department of Education.

Taylor, Paul, Kim Parker, Richard Fry, D'Vera Cohn, Wendy Wang, Gabriel Velasco, and Daniel Dockterman. (2011). *Is College Worth It? College Presidents, Public Assess Value, Quality and Mission of Higher Education.* Washington, DC: Pew Social and Demographic Trends.

Thomas, William I. and Dorothy Swaine Thomas. 1928. *The Child in America: Behavior Problems and Programs.* New York: Knopf.

Traub, James. 2000. "What No School Can Do." *New York Times Magazine,* January 16, pp. 52–57, 68, 81, 90–91.

United Nations Educational, Scientific and Cultural Organization. 2009. *Overcoming Inequality: Why Governance Matters.* New York: Author.

U.S. Census Bureau. 2011. "Current Population Survey, 2011 Annual Social and Economic Supplement." Retrieved April 7, 2012 (http://www.census.gov/hhes/www/cpstables/032011/perinc/new03_001.htm)

U.S. Census Bureau. 2012. *U.S. Statistical Abstract.* Washington DC: U.S. Census Bureau.

U.S. Department of Education. 2010. *A Blueprint for Reform: The Reauthorization of the Elementary and Secondary Education Act.* Washington, DC: Author.

U.S. Department of Education, National Center for Education Statistics. 2009. *The Condition of Education 2009* (NCES 2009–081). Washington, DC: Author.

U.S. Department of Education, National Center for Education Statistics. 2011. *The Condition of Education 2011* (NCES 2011-033). Washington, DC: Author.

U.S. Department of Health and Human Services. 2005. *Head Start Impact Study: First Year Findings.* Washington, DC: Author.

Wall, Shavaun, Elizabeth Timberlake, Michaela Farber, Christine Sabatino, Harriett Liebow, Nancy Smith, and Nancy Taylor. 2000. "Needs and Aspirations of the Working Poor: Early Head Start Program Applicants." *Families in Society* 81(4):412–21.

Warren, David. 2012. "Statement by NAICU President David L. Warren on President Obama's Higher Education Proposals." Retrieved May 24, 2012 (http://www.naicu.edu/news_room/statement-by-naicu-president-david-1-warren-on-president-obamas-higher-education-proposals).

Washington, Valora and Ura J. Oyemade Bailey. 1995. *Project Head Start: Models and Strategies for the Twenty-first Century.* New York: Garland.

White House. 2012. "Fact Sheet: President Obama's Blueprint for Keeping College Affordable and Within Reach for All Americans." Retrieved May 24, 2012 (http://www.whitehouse.gov/the-press-office/2012/01/27/fact-sheet-president-obamas-blueprint-keeping-college-affordable-and-wi).

Wiland, Harry and Dale Bell. 2006. *Edens Lost & Found: How Ordinary Citizens Are Restoring Our Great American Cities.* White River Junction, VT: Chelsea Green.

Wilgoren, Jodi. 2001. "Schools Are Now Marketers Where Choice Is Taking Hold." *New York Times,* April 20, pp. A1, A12.

Zernike, K. 2010. "Annual Poll of Freshmen Shows Effect of Recession." *New York Times,* January 21, p. A23.

Zigler, Edward and Susan Muenchow. 1992. *Head Start: The Inside Story of America's Most Successful Educational Experiment.* New York: Basic Books.

Chapter 9

Abell, Hilary. 1999. "Endangering Women's Health for Profit: Health and Safety in Mexico's Maquiladoras." *Development in Practice* 9(5):595–601.

Armas, Genaro. 2004. "Outearning Men Women's Toughest Job." *News Tribune,* June 4, p. 7.

Bacon, David. 2011. "The Rebirth of Solidarity on the Border." Retrieved April 8, 2012 (http://www.cipamericas.org/archives/4697).

Bahnisch, Mark. 2000. "Embodied Work, Divided Labour: Subjectivity and the Scientific Management of the Body in Frederick W. Taylor's 1907 'Lecture on Management.'" *Body & Society* 6(1):51–68.

Bernanke, Ben. 2009. "Four Questions About the Financial Crisis." Retrieved May 13, 2010 (http://www.federalreserve.gov/newsevents/speech/bernanke20090414a.htm).

Bernstein, Jared. 1997. "Low-Wage Labor Market Indicators by City and State: The Constraints Facing Welfare Reform" (EPI Working Paper No. 118). Washington, DC: Economic Policy Institute.

Bernstein, Jared, Heidi Hartmann, and John Schmitt. 1999. *The Minimum Wage Increase: A Working Woman's Issue* (EPI Issue Brief No. 133). Washington, DC: Economic Policy Institute.

Bertrand, Marianne and Sendhil Mullainathan. 2003. "Are Emily and Greg More Employable Than Lakisha and Jamal? A Field Experiment in Market Discrimination" (NBER Working Paper No. 9873). Cambridge, MA: National Bureau of Economic Research.

Bluestone, Barry and Bennett Harrison. 1982. *The Deindustrialization of America.* New York: Basic Books.

Bosman, Julie. 2009. "Minus a Paycheck, Jobless Flock to Do Good." *New York Times,* March 16, pp. A1, A18.

Brady, David and Michael Wallace. 2001. "Deindustrialization and Poverty: Manufacturing Decline and AFDC Reciprocity in Lake County, Indiana 1964–93." *Sociological Forum* 16(2): 321–58.

Braverman, Harry. 1974. *Labor and Monopoly Capital: The Degradation of Work in the Twentieth Century.* New York: Monthly Review Press.

Brenner, Joanna. 1998. "On Gender and Class in U.S. Labor History." *Monthly Review: An Independent Socialist Magazine* 50(6):1–15.

Budig, Michelle. 2002. "Male Advantage and the Gender Composition of Jobs: Who Rides the Glass Escalator?" *Social Problems* 49(2):258–77.

Business Alliance for Local Living Economies. 2012. "About BALLE." Retrieved April 9, 2012 (http://www.livingeconomies.org/aboutus).

Byrne, Geraldine and Robert Heyman. 1997. "Understanding Nurses' Communication with Patients in Accident and Emergency Departments Using a Symbolic Interactionist Perspective." *Journal of Advanced Nursing* 26:93–100.

Carley, Michael. 2000. "Urban Partnerships, Governance and Regeneration of Britain's Cities." *International Planning Studies* 5(3): 273–97.

Carnevale, Anthony, Tamara Jayasundera, and Ban Cheah. 2012. *The College Advantage: Weathering the Economic Storm, Executive Summary.* Retrieved August 27, 2012 (http://www9.georgetown.edu/grad/gppi/hpi/cew/pdfs/CollegeAdvantage.ExecutiveSummary.081512.pdf).

Cave, Damien. 2010. "In Recession, Americans Doing More, Buying Less." *New York Times,* January 3, p. 12.

CNN Money. 2012. "Google: The King of Perks." Retrieved April 9, 2012 (http://money.cnn.com/galleries/2012/technology/1201/gallery.best-companies-google-perks.fortune/index.html).

Cook, Nancy. 2009. "What Mancession?" Retrieved May 13, 2010 (http://www.newsweek.com/id/206917).

Co-op America. 2003. "What Is a Sweatshop?" Retrieved April 26, 2003 (http://www.sweatshops.org/educated/issue.html).

Darity, William A. 2003. "Employment Discrimination, Segregation and Health." *American Journal of Public Health* 93(2):226–32.

Davidson, Linda. 1999. "Temp Workers Want a Better Deal." *Workforce* 78(10):44-49.

DeJong, Gordon F. and Anna Madamba. 2001. "A Double Disadvantage? Minority Group, Immigrant Status, and Underemployment in the United States." *Social Science Quarterly* 82(1):117–30.

DeNavas-Walt, Carmen, Bernadette Proctor, and Jessica Smith. 2012. *Income, Poverty and Health Insurance Coverage in the United States: 2011* (Current Population Reports, P60–243). Washington, DC: U.S. Government Printing Office.

Dobbs, Lou. 2004. "Coming Up Empty." *U.S. News & World Report,* January, 26:46.

Economic Policy Institute. 2012. "The Great Recession." Retrieved June 20, 2012 (http://stateofworkingamerica.org/great-recession/).

Economist. 2009. "Women and Work: We Did It!" Retrieved May 14, 2010 (http://www.economist.com/displayStory.cfm?story_id=E1_TVTSQQRJ&source=login_payBarrier).

Ehrenreich, Barbara. 2001. *Nickel and Dimed: On (Not) Getting By in America.* New York: Metropolitan Book/Henry Holt.

Eisenberg, Daniel. 1999. "Rise of Permatemp." *Time* 153(2):48.

Eitzen, D. Stanley and Maxine Baca Zinn. 2006. "Globalization: An Introduction." Pp. 1–11 in

Globalization: The Transformation of Social Worlds, edited by D. Stanley Eitzen and Maxine Baca Zinn. Belmont, CA: Wadsworth.

England, Paula and Irene Browne. 1992. "Trends in Women's Economic Status." *Sociological Perspectives* 35(1):17–51.

Enron Corporation. 2000. "Enron Milestones." Retrieved May 1, 2003 (http://www.enron.com/corp/pressroom/milestones).

Enron Corporation. 2001. "Enron Named Most Innovative for Sixth Year." Retrieved September 3, 2004 (http://www.enron.com/corp/pressroom/releases/2001/ene/15-MostInnovative-02-06-01-LTR.html).

Esbenshade, Jill. 2008. "Going Up Against the Global Economy: New Developments in the Anti-Sweatshops Movement." *Critical Sociology* 34:453–70.

Equal Employment Opportunity Commission. 2012. "Charge Statistics FY1997 though FY2011." Retrieved April 8, 2012 (http://www.eeoc.gov/eeoc/statistics/enforcement/charges.cfm).

Eurostat. 2012. "Unemployment Statistics, February 2012." Retrieved April 8, 2012 (http://epp.eurostat.ec.europa.eu/statistics_explained/index.php/Unemployment_statistics).

Fantasia, Rick and Kim Voss. 2004. *Hard Work: Remaking the American Labor Movement.* Berkeley: University of California Press.

Filion, Kai. 2009. "Fact Sheet for 2009 Minimum Wage Increase—Minimum Wage Issue Guide." Retrieved May 13, 2010 (http://www.epi.org/publications/entry/mwig_fact_sheet/).

Foo, Lora Jo. 1994. "The Vulnerable and Exploitable Immigrant Workforce and the Need for Strengthening Worker Protection Legislation." *Yale Law Review* 103(8):2179–212.

Fowler, Tom. 2001. "Formal Upgrade of Enron Investigation Gives Subpoena Power to SEC." Retrieved September 3, 2004 (http://www.chron.com/cs/CDA/ssistory.mpl/special/enron/oct01/1114532).

Fox, Mary Frank and Sharlene Hesse-Biber. 1984. *Women at Work.* Palo Alto, CA: Mayfield.

Frontline. 2002. "Accounting Lessons." Retrieved May 1, 2003 (http://www.pbs.org/wgbh/pages/frontline/shows/regulation/lessons/).

Fussell, Elizabeth. 2000. "Making Labor Flexible: The Recomposition of Tijuana's Maquiladora Female Labor Force." *Feminist Economics* 6(3):59–79.

General Accounting Office (GAO). 1994. "Garment Industry: Efforts to Address the Prevalence and Conditions of Sweatshops" (GAO/HEHS-95-29, November). Retrieved May 13, 2010 (http://www.gao.gov/archive/1995/he95029.pdf).

Gluck, Sherna Berger. 1987. *Rosie the Riveter Revisited: Women, the War, and Social Change.* Boston, MA: Twayne.

Gruben, William C. 2001. "Was NAFTA behind Mexico's High Maquiladora Growth?" *CATO Journal* 18(2):263–75.

Hall, Richard. 1994. *Sociology of Work: Perspectives, Analyses, and Issues.* Thousand Oaks, CA: Pine Forge.

Hard Hatted Women. 2006. "Adult Education." Retrieved May 13, 2010 (http://www.hardhattedwomen.org/adulted.asp).

Hirschhorn, Larry. 1984. *Beyond Mechanization: Work and Technology in a Post-industrial Age.* Cambridge, MA: MIT Press.

Human Rights Campaign. 2012. "Employment Non-Discrimination Act." Retrieved April 9, 2012 (http://www.hrc.org/laws-and-legislation/federal-legislation/employment-non-discrimination-act).

Information for Decision Making. 2000. "Minimum Wage Legislation and Living Wage Campaigns." Retrieved April 20, 2003 (http://www.financeprojectinfo.org/MWW/minimum.asp#effects).

International Labor Rights Forum. 2011. "Factory Profiles." Retrieved April 11, 2012 (http://www.laborrights.org/creating-a-sweatfree-world/fairness-in-flowers/factory-profiles).

International Labour Office. 2010. *Women in Labour Markets: Measuring Progress and Identifying Challenges.* Geneva, Switzerland: International Labour Office.

Kalleberg, Arne. 2011. *Good Jobs, Bad Jobs.* New York: Russell Sage Foundation.

King, Rachel. 2006. "Outsourcing: Beyond Bangalore." *Business Week Online.* December 11:6–6.

Labor Law Center. 2012. "State Minimum Wage Rates." Retrieved April 8, 2012 (http://www.laborlawcenter.com/t-State-Minimum-Wage-Rates.aspx).

Landler, Mark. 2008. "Global Fears of a Recession Grow Stronger." *New York Times,* October 6. Retrieved May 13, 2010 (http://www.nytimes.com/2008/10/07/business/worldbusiness/07global.html?pagewanted=all).

Lazes, Peter and Jane Savage. 2000. "Embracing the Future: Union Strategies for the 21st Century." *Journal for Quality and Participation* 23(4):18–24.

Lederer, Edith. 2012. "UN: 2.4 Million Human Trafficking Victims." Retrieved April 8, 2012 (http://abcnews.go.com/US/wireStory/24-million-human-trafficking-victims-16066837#.T4IZzWAz3hM).

Levering, Robert and Milton Moskowitz. 2007. "The 100 Best Companies to Work For." *Fortune* 155(1):94.

Lindquist, Diane. 2001. "Rules Change for Maquiladoras." *Industry Week* 250(1):23–26.

Maryland Department of Labor, Licensing and Regulation. 2011. "Maryland's Living Wage Frequently Asked Questions." Retrieved April 8, 2012 (http://www.dllr.state.md.us/labor/prev/livingwagefaqs.shtml#1).

McDonough, Sioban. 2003. "EEOC: Job Discrimination up since 9/11." Retrieved March 22, 2003 (http://www.softcom.net/webnews/wed/ch/Adiscrimination.RNTX_CD3).

McMahon, Brian, Richard Roessler, Phillip Rumrill, Jessica Hurley, Steven West, Fong Chan, and Linnea Carlson. 2008. "Hiring Discrimination Against People with Disabilities Under the ADA: Characteristics of Charging Parties." *Journal of Occupational Rehabilitation* 18:122–32.

Mishel, Lawrence, Jard Bernstein, and Heidi Shierholz. 2009. *State of Working America 2008/2009.* Washington, DC: Economic Policy Institute.

Moffatt, Allison. 2005. "Murder, Mystery and Mistreatment in Mexican Maquiladoras." *Women and Environments International Magazine* 66/67:19–21.

Mosisa, Abraham. 2002. "The Role of Foreign-Born Workers in the U.S. Economy." *Monthly Labor Review* 125(5):3–15.

National Association of Colleges and Employers. 2011. "The Unemployment Rate for College Graduates." Retrieved April 8, 2012 (http://www.naceweb.org/s11162011/unemployment_rate_college_grad/).

National Committee on Pay Equity. 2011. "The Wage Gap Over Time." Retrieved February 26, 2012 (http://www.pay-equity.org/info-time.html).

National Institute for Occupational Safety and Health (NIOSH). 2003. "Stress at Work." Retrieved May 13, 2010 (http://www.cdc.gov/niosh/docs/99-101/).

National Public Radio. 2003. "The Fall of Enron." Retrieved May 13, 2010 (http://www.npr.org/news/specials/enron/).

Newburger, Eric and Thomas Gryn. 2009. *The Foreign-Born Labor Force in the United States: 2007* (American Community Survey Reports, ACS-10). Washington, DC: U.S. Bureau of the Census.

Novak, Laura. 2007. "For Women, a Recipe to Create a Successful Business." *New York Times,* June 23, p. B4.

Parenti, Michael. 1988. *Democracy for the Few.* 5th ed. New York: St. Martin's.

Parker, Andrew. 2004. *Two-Speed Europe: Why 1 Million Jobs Will Move Offshore.* Cambridge, MA: Forester Research.

Pollina, Ronald. 2003. "Can We Maintain the American Dream?" *Economic Development Journal* 2(3):54–58.

Rampell, Catherine. 2010. "Women Now Majority in American Workplaces." *New York Times,* February 6, p. A10.

Reskin, Barbara and Irene Padavic. 1994. *Women and Men at Work.* Thousand Oaks, CA: Pine Forge Press.

Ritzer, George. 1989. "Sociology of Work: A Metatheoretical Analysis." *Social Forces* 67(3):593–604.

Ritzer, George. 2000. *Sociological Theory.* Boston, MA: McGraw-Hill.

Rix, Sarah. 2008. "Update on the Aged 55+ Worker: 2007." AARP Public Policy Institute. Retrieved April 8, 2012 (http://assets.aarp.org/rgcenter/econ/fs142_worker.pdf).

Rodriguez, Eunice. 2001. "Keeping the Unemployed Healthy." *American Journal of Public Health* 91(9):1403–12.

Rosser, Sue. 2005. "Through the Lenses of Feminist Theory." *Frontiers: A Journal of Women's Studies* 26(1):1–23.

Rubin, Stanford and Richard Roessler. 2008. *Foundations of the Vocational Rehabilitation Process.* Austin, TX: Pro-Ed.

Saftner, T. J. 1998. "Temps for Hire." *Career World* 27(3):18–22.

Schmidt, Diane and Gilbert Duenas. 2002. "Incentives to Encourage Worker-Friendly Organizations." *Public Personnel Management* 31(3):293–309.

Schur, Lisa, Douglas Kruse, and Peter Blanck. 2005. "Corporate Culture and the Employment of Persons with Disabilities." *Behavioral Sciences and the Law* 2:3–20.

Shevory, Kristina. 2010. "Architect, or Whatever." *New York Times,* January 21, pp. 1, 6.

Shin, Sang-Hyup. 2009. "A Study on the Economic Benefits of Globalization: Focusing on the Poverty and Inequality Between the Rich and the Poor." *International Area Studies Review* 12:191–214.

Student Labor Action Project. 2007. "About SLAP." Retrieved May 13, 2010 (http://www.jwj.org/projects/slap.html).

Sullivan, Teresa. 2004. "Work-Related Social Problems." Pp. 193–208 in *Handbook of Social Problems: A Comparative International Perspective,* edited by George Ritzer. Thousand Oaks, CA: Sage Publications.

Sweatshop Watch. 2000. "Student Organizing." Retrieved September 5, 2004 (http://swatch.igc.org/swatch/codes/).

Sweatshop Watch. 2003. "Frequently Asked Questions." Retrieved April 15, 2003 (http://www.sweatshopwatch.org/swatch/questions).

Taylor, Frederick W. 1911. *The Principles of Scientific Management.* New York: Harper.

Thottam, Jyoti. 2004. "Is Your Job Going Abroad?" *Time* 163(9):26–36.

Toossi, Mitra. 2005. "Labor Force Projections to 2014: Retiring Boomers." *Monthly Labor Review November 2005.* Washington, DC: Bureau of Labor Statistics.

Toossi, Mitra. 2009. "Labor Force Projections to 2018: Older Workers Staying More Active." *Monthly Labor Review.* Washington, DC: U.S. Department of Labor.

Uchitelle, Louis. 2006. "Raising the Floor on Pay: States Leap Ahead of Congress in Acting on Minimum Wage." *New York Times,* December 20, pp. C1, C15.

UNICEF. 2007. *The State of the World's Children: 2007.* New York: United Nations.

UNITE HERE. 2012. "Who We Are." Retrieved April 9, 2012 (http://www.unitehere.org/about/).

United Nations Office on Drugs and Crime—Anti-Human Trafficking Unit. 2006. *Trafficking in Persons: Global Patterns.* New York: United Nations Office on Drugs and Crime.

U.S. Bureau of Labor Statistics. 2005. "Contingent Workers." *Monthly Labor Review* 128(8):2.

U.S. Bureau of Labor Statistics. 2009a. Table 6. "The 30 Occupations With the Largest Employment Growth, 2008–18." Retrieved May 13, 2010 (http://data.bls.gov/cgi-bin/print.pl/news.release/ecopro.t06.htm).

U.S. Bureau of Labor Statistics. 2009b. "Census of Fatal Occupational Injuries—Current and Revised Data." Retrieved January 10, 2010 (http://www.bls.gov/iif/oshwc/cfoi/cfch0007.pdf).

U.S. Bureau of Labor Statistics. 2010. "Employment Situation Summary." Retrieved January 11, 2010 (http://www.bls.gov/news.release/empsit.nr0.htm).

U.S. Bureau of Labor Statistics. 2011. "Workplace Injuries and Illnesses—2010." Retrieved November 21, 2012 (http://www.bls.gov/news.release/archives/osh_10202011.pdf).

U.S. Bureau of Labor Statistics. 2012a. "The Employment Situation—March 2012." Retrieved April 8, 2012 (http://www.bls.gov/news.release/empsit.nr0.htm).

U.S. Bureau of Labor Statistics. 2012b. "Civilian Labor Force Participation Rates by Age, Sex, Race and Ethnicity." Retrieved April 8, 2012 (http://www.bls.gov/emp/ep_table_303.htm).

U.S. Bureau of Labor Statistics. 2012c. "Labor Force Characteristics of Foreign-Born Workers Summary." Retrieved November 21, 2012 (http://www.bls.gov/news.release/forbrn.nr0.htm).

U.S. Bureau of Labor Statistics. 2012d. "Union Members Summary." Retrieved April 8, 2012 (http://www.bls.gov/news.release/union2.nr0.htm).

U.S. Census Bureau. 1951. *Statistical Abstract of the United States* (Table 203). Washington, DC: Author.

U.S. Census Bureau. 1960. *Statistical Abstract of the United States* (Table 274). Washington, DC: Author.

U.S. Census Bureau. 1966. *Statistical Abstract of the United States* (Table 319). Washington, DC: Author.

U.S. Department of Labor. 2002. "Minimum Wage Laws in the States." Retrieved May 13, 2010 (http://www.dol.gov/esa/minwage/america.htm).

U.S. Department of Labor. 2003. "WANTO Grant Award 9-30-03." Retrieved May 13, 2010 (http://www.dol.gov/wb/03awards.htm).

U.S. Department of Labor, Women's Bureau. 2000. *Facts of Working Women: Hot Jobs for the 21st Century* (No. 00-03). Washington, DC: U.S. Department of Labor.

U.S. Department of Labor, Women's Bureau. 2011. "Quick Stats on Women Workers, 2010." Retrieved April 8, 2012 (http://www.dol.gov/wb/factsheets/QS-womenwork2010.htm).

Waldman, Amy. 2003. "More 'Can I Help You?' Jobs Migrate from U.S. to India." *New York Times,* May 11, p. 4.

Weber, Max. 1978. "Bureaucracy." Pp. 956–1005 in *Economy and Society,* Vols. 1 and 2, edited by Guenther Roth and Claus Wittich. Berkeley: University of California Press. (Original work published in 1925)

Weidenbaum, Murray. 2006. "Globalization: Wonder Land or Waste Land?" Pp. 53–60 in *Globalization: The Transformation of Social Worlds,* edited by D. Stanley Eitzen and Maxine Baca Zinn. Belmont, CA: Wadsworth.

Weller, Christian and Adam Hersh. 2006. "Free Markets and Poverty." Pp. 69–73 in *Globalization: The Transformation of Social Worlds,* edited by D. Stanley Eitzen and Maxine Baca Zinn. Belmont, CA: Wadsworth.

Yergin, Daniel. 2006. "Globalization Opens Door to New Dangers." Pp. 30–31 in *Globalization: The Transformation of Social Worlds,* edited by D. Stanley Eitzen and Maxine Baca Zinn. Belmont, CA: Wadsworth.

Zeitlin, Irving. 1997. *Ideology and the Development of Sociological Theory.* Englewood Cliffs, NJ: Prentice Hall.

Zhou, Min. 1993. "Underemployment and Economic Disparities Among Minority Groups." *Population Research and Policy Review* 12:139–57.

Chapter 10

Altman, Lawrence. 2006. "Children Slip through Cracks of AIDS Efforts, W.H.O. Says." *New York Times,* August 17, p. A8.

Altman, Stuart H. and Uwe E. Reinhardt. 1996. "Where Does Health Care Reform Go from Here? An Unchartered Odyssey." Pp. xxi–xxxii in *Strategic Choices for a Changing Health Care System,* edited by S. H. Altman and U. E. Reinhardt. Chicago, IL: Health Administration Press.

American Diabetes Association. 2003. "Type 2 Diabetes." Retrieved March 27, 2008 (http://www.diabetes.org/diabetes-basics/type-2/facts-about-type-2.html).

American Diabetes Association. 2012. "Diabetes Statistics." Retrieved April 11, 2012 (http://www.diabetes.org/diabetes-basics/diabetes-statistics/?loc=DropDownDB-stats).

American Medical Association. 2003. "AMA's 2003 Federal Legislative Agenda." Retrieved May 20, 2003 (http://www.ama-assn.org/ama/pub/category/7334.html).

Beatrice, Dennis. 1996. "States and Health Care Reform: The Importance of Program Implementation." Pp. 183–206 in *Strategic Choices for a Changing Health Care System,* edited by S. Altman and U. Reinhardt. Chicago, IL: Health Administration Press.

Becker, Gary S. and Casey B. Mulligan. 1994. *On the Endogenous Determination of Time Preference.* Discussion Paper No. 94-2, Economics Research Center/National Opinion Research Center, July.

Beckles, Gloria and Benedict Truman. 2011. "Education and Income—United States, 2005–2009." *CDC Health Disparities and Inequalities Report United States,* 2011: 13–15.

Belluck, Pam. 2012. "Medicaid Expansion May Lower Death Rates, Study Says." *New York Times,* July 26, p. A13.

Braveman, P. and E. Tarimo. 2002. "Social Inequalities in Health within Countries: Not Only an Issue for Affluent Countries." *Social Science and Medicine* 54:1621–35.

Broder, John M., Robert Pear, and Milt Freudenheim. 2002. "Problem of Lost Health Benefits Is Reaching into the Middle Class." *New York Times,* November 25, pp. A1, A17.

Brumberg, Joan J. 1988. *Fasting Girls: The History of Anorexia Nervosa.* Cambridge, MA: Harvard University Press.

Buse, Uwe. 2006. "A Woman's Fight to Save the Poor from Black Fever." *Spiegel Online,* December 21.

Calnan, Michael. 1987. *Health & Illness: The Lay Perspective.* London, England: Tavistock.

Centers for Medicare and Medicaid Services. 2012. "NHE Fact Sheet." Retrieved April 11, 2012 (http://www.cms.gov/Research-Statistics-Data-and-Systems/Statistics-Trends-and-Reports/NationalHealthExpendData/NHE-Fact-Sheet.html).

Citizens Council on Health Care. 2003. "Summary of Minnesota's 1992 Health Care Reform Law." Retrieved May 20, 2010 (http://www.cchconline.org/privacy/mncaresumm.php3).

Cockerman, William C. 2004. "Health as a Social Problem." Pp. 281–97 in *Handbook of Social Problems: A Comparative International Perspective,* edited by George Ritzer. Thousand Oaks, CA: Sage Publications.

Cockerman, William C. and Michael Glasser. 2001. "Epidemiology." Pp. 1–2 in *Readings in Medical Sociology,* edited by W. Cockerman and M. Glasser. Upper Saddle River, NJ: Prentice Hall.

Collins, Karen S., Dora L. Hughes, Michelle M. Doty, Brett L. Ives, Jennifer N. Edwards, and Katie Tenney. 2002. *Diverse Communities, Common Concerns: Assessing Health Care Quality for Minority Americans: Findings from the Commonwealth Fund 2001 Health Care Quality Survey.* New York: Commonwealth Fund.

Commonwealth Fund. 2003a. "Hispanics Face High Rates of Unstable Health Care Coverage, Low Rates of Preventative Care." Retrieved May 20, 2010 (http://www.commonwealthfund.org/newsroom/newsroom_show.htm?doc_id=223566).

Commonwealth Fund. 2003b. "Minority Americans Lag behind Whites on Nearly Every Measure of Health Care Quality." Retrieved May 20, 2010 (http://www.commonwealthfund.org/newsroom/newsroom_show.htm?doc_id=223608).

Congressional Budget Office. 2012a. *Updated Estimates for the Insurance Coverage Provisions of the Affordable Care Act.* Washington, DC: Congressional Budget Office.

Congressional Budget Office. 2012b. "Estimates for the Insurance Coverage Provision of the Affordable Care Act Updated for the Recent Supreme Court Decision." Retrieved February 21, 2013 (http://www.cbo.gov/publication/43472).

Conrad, Peter. 2001a. "General Introduction." Pp. 1–6 in *The Sociology of Health and Illness: Critical Perspectives,* edited by P. Conrad. New York: Worth.

Conrad, Peter. 2001b. "The Social and Cultural Meanings of Illness." Pp. 91–93 in *The Sociology of Health and Illness: Critical Perspectives,* edited by P. Conrad. New York: Worth.

Conrad, Peter and Valerie Leiter. 2003. "Introduction." Pp. 1–6 in *Health and Health Care as Social Problems,* edited by P. Conrad and V. Leiter. Lanham, MD: Rowman & Littlefield.

Cooper, Michael. 2012. "Many Governors Still Unsure about Medicaid Expansion." *New York Times,* July 15, p. 14.

Davis, Karen, Cathy Schoen, Stephen C. Schoenbaum, Michelle M. Doty, Alyssa L. Holmgren, Jennifer L. Kriss, and Katherine K. Shea. 2007. *Mirror, Mirror on the Wall: An International Update on the Comparative Performance of American Health Care.* Washington, DC: Commonwealth Fund.

DeNavas-Walt, Carmen, Bernadette Proctor, and Jessica Smith. 2012. *Income, Poverty and Health Insurance Coverage in the United States: 2011* (Current Population Reports, P60–243). Washington, DC: U.S. Government Printing Office.

Emanuel, Ezekiel. 2011. "How Much Does Health Care Cost?" *New York Times,* October 30, p. Review-5.

Federal Interagency Forum on Child and Family Statistics. 2007. *America's Children 2007.* Washington, DC: U.S. Government Printing Office.

Finkelstein, Amy, Sarah Taubman, Bill Wright, Mira Bernstein, Jonathan Gruber, Joseph Newhouse, Heidi Allen, Katherine Baicker, and the Oregon Health Study Group. 2011. *The Oregon Health Insurance Experiment: Evidence from the First Year.* Retrieved July 3, 2012 (http://www.oregonhealthstudy.org/en/researchers/Oregon_Health_Insura nce_Experiment.pdf).

Freudenheim, Milt. 2003. "States Organizing a Nonprofit Group to Cut Drug Costs." *New York Times,* January 14, pp. A1, A20.

Freudenheim, Milt. 2007. "Company Clinics Cut Health Costs." *New York Times,* January 14, pp. 1, 19.

Goffman, Erving. 1961. *Asylums: Essays on the Social Situation of Mental Health.* New York: Pantheon.

Goodnough, Abby. 2012. "Massachusetts Aims to Cut Growth of Its Health Costs." *New York Times,* August 1, p. A14.

Grossman, Michael and Robert Kaestner. 1997. "Effects of Education on Health." Pp. 69–123 in *The Social Benefits of Education,* edited by J. Behrman and N. Stacey. Ann Arbor: University of Michigan Press.

Hamilton, J. A. 1994. "Feminist Theory and Health Psychology: Tools for an Egalitarian, Women-Centered Approach to Women's Health." Pp. 56–66 in *Reframing Women's Health: Multidisciplinary Research and Practice,* edited by A. Dan. Thousand Oaks, CA: Sage Publications.

Haney, D. 2003. "Big Study Dispels More Myths about Estrogen." *News Tribune,* March 18, p. A3.

Hargreaves, Margaret, Carolyne Arnold, and William Blot. 2006. "Community Health Centers." Pp. 485–94 in *Multicultural Medicine and Health Disparities,* edited by D. Satcher and R. Pamies. New York: McGraw-Hill.

Heffernan, Tim. 2005. "Victoria Hale: Exec of the Year." Retrieved March 11, 2007 (http://www.keepmedia.com/pubs/Esquire/2005/12/01/1078555).

Kaiser Family Foundation. 2007. "Children's Coverage and SCHIP Reauthorization." Retrieved May 20, 2010 (http://www.kaiseredu.org/topics_im.asp?id=704&imID=1&parentID=65).

Kaiser Family Foundation. 2011. *Medicaid and the Uninsured.* Washington, DC: Author.

Kaiser Family Foundation. 2012. *Employer Health Benefits 2012 Annual Survey.* Menlo Park, CA: Author.

Kleinfield, N. R. 2006. "Modern Ways Open India's Doors to Diabetes." *New York Times,* September 13, pp. A1, A12.

Kolata, Gina. 2007. "A Surprising Secret to Long Life: Stay in School." *New York Times,* January 3, p. A1.

Krieger, Nancy, D. R. Williams, and N. Moss. 1997. "Measuring Social Class in U.S. Public Health Research: Concepts, Methodologies, and Guidelines." *Annual Review of Public Health* 18:341–78.

Lambert, Bruce L., Richard L. Street, Donald J. Cegala, David H. Smith, Suzanne Kurtz, and Theo Schofeld. 1997. "Provider-Patient Communication, Patient-Centered Care, and the Mangle of Practice." *Health Communication* 9(1):27–43.

Link, Bruce and Jo Phelan. 2001. "Social Conditions as Fundamental Causes of Disease." Pp. 3–17 in *Readings in Medical Sociology,* 2nd ed., edited by W. Cockerman and M. Glasser. Upper Saddle River, NJ: Prentice Hall.

Liptak, Adam. 2012. "Justices, by 5–4, Uphold Health Care Law; Roberts in Majority; Victory for Obama." *New York Times,* June 29, pp. A1, A12.

Lock, Margaret. 1993. *Encounters with Aging: Mythologies of Menopause in Japan and North America.* Berkeley: University of California Press.

Long, Sharon, Karen Stockley, and Heather Dahlen. 2012. *Health Reform in Massachusetts as of Fall 2010: Getting Ready for the Affordable Care Act & Addressing Affordability*. Washington, DC: Urban Institute.

Lowrey, Annie. 2012. "In Hopeful Sign, Health Spending Is Flattening Out." *New York Times,* April 29, pp. 1, 19.

Lurie, Nicole and Tamara Dubowitz. 2007. "Health Disparities and Access to Health." *Journal of the American Medical Association* 297(10):1118–21.

Magnus, Stephen and Stephen Mick. 2000. "Medical Schools, Affirmative Action and the Neglected Role of Social Class." *American Journal of Public Health* 90:1197–1201.

Markens, Susan. 1996. "The Problem of 'Experience': A Political and Cultural Critique of PMS." *Gender and Society* 10:42–58.

Marmot, Michael. 2004. *Status Syndrome: How Our Position on the Social Gradient Affects Longevity and Health*. London, England: Bloomsbury.

Marmot, Michael. 2005. "Social Determinants of Health Inequalities." *Lancet* 365:1099–104.

Martin, Joyce, Brady Hamilton, Stephanie Ventura, Michelle Osteman, Shannon Kimeyer, T. J. Matthews, and Elizabeth Wilson. 2012. "Births: Final Data for 2009." *National Vital Statistics Reports* 60:1.

Men's Health Network. 2002. "The Men's Disease Awareness and Prevention Project." Retrieved December 8, 2002 (http://www.menshealth network.org/Programareas/Prevention).

Murphy, Michael, Martin Bobak, Amanda Nicholson, Michael Marmot, and Richard Rose. 2006. "The Widening Gap in Mortality by Educational Level in the Russian Federation, 1980–2001." *American Journal of Public Health* 96(7):1293–99.

Murphy, Sherry, Jiaquan Xu, and Kenneth Kochanek. 2012. "Deaths: Preliminary Data for 2010." *National Vital Statistics Reports* 60:4.

National Center for Health Statistics. 2011. *Health, United States, 2010*. Hyattsville, MD: Author.

National Center for Health Statistics. 2012. *Health, United States, 2011*. Hyattsville, MD: Author.

National Institutes of Health. 2006. *Women of Color: Health Data Book*. Washington, DC: Office of Research on Women's Health, National Institutes of Health.

Obama, Barack. 2009. "Remarks by the President to a Joint Session of Congress on Health Care." Retrieved May 20, 2010 (http://www.whitehouse .gov/the_press_office/Remarks-by-the-President-to-a-Joint-Session-of-Congress-on-Health-Care).

Obama, Barack. 2010. "On Behalf of My Mother." Retrieved May 20, 2010 (http://www.whitehouse. gov/blog/2010/03/23/behalf-my-mother).

Oberlander, Jonathan. 2002. "The U.S. Health Care System: On a Road to Nowhere." *Canadian Medical Association Journal* 167(2):163–68.

Oregon Health Study. 2012. "About the Study." Retrieved July 3, 2012 (http://www.oregon healthstudy.org/en/about/index.php).

Organisation for Economic Co-operation and Development. 2011. "Health Expenditure Per Capita." In *Health at a Glance 2011: OECD Indicators*, OECD Publishing. Retrieved November 27, 2012 (http://dx.doi.org/10.1787/ health_glance-2011-60-en).

Parsons, Talcott. 1951. *The Social System*. New York: Free Press.

Pear, Robert. 2002. "Pennsylvania Struggles to Repair Model Prescription Aid Program." *New York Times,* July 13, pp. A1, A8.

Pear, Robert. 2007a. "Lacking Health Coverage, Good Life Turns Fragile." *New York Times,* March 5, pp. A1, A17.

Pear, Robert. 2007b. "Governors Worry Over Money for Child Health Program." *New York Times,* February 25, p. A15.

Pear, Robert. 2012. "Recession Holds Down Health Spending." *New York Times,* January 10, p. A16.

Peck, B. Mitchell and Sonya Conner. 2011. "Talking with Me or Talking at Me? The Impact of Status Characteristics on Doctor-Patient Interaction." *Sociological Perspectives* 54:547–67.

Peterson, Suni, Martin Heesacker, and Robert C. Schwartz. 2001. "Physical Illness: Social Construction or Biological Imperative?" *Journal of Community Health Nursing* 18(4):213–22.

Pew Hispanic Center. 2009. *Between Two Worlds: How Young Latinos Come of Age in America*. Retrieved May 20, 2010 (http://pewhispanic.org/ files/reports/117.pdf).

Phalen, K. 2000. "A Community of Men: Project Brotherhood, a Black Men's Clinic." Retrieved March 26, 2003 (http://www.ama-assn.org/ amednews/2000/10/02/hlsa1002.htm).

Project Brotherhood. 2006. "History." Retrieved February 8, 2007 (http://www.projectbrother hood.net).

Project Brotherhood. 2010. "About Us." Retrieved May 20, 2010 (http://www.projectbrotherhood .net).

Reid, T. R. 2009. *The Healing of America: A Global Quest for Better, Cheaper, and Fairer Health Care*. New York: Penguin Press.

Richman, Judith A. and Leonard A. Jason. 2001. "Gender Biases Underlying the Social Construction of Illness States: The Case of Chronic Fatigue Syndrome." *Current Sociology* 49(3):15–40.

Roberts, Sam. 2010. "Census Figures Challenge Views of Race and Ethnicity." *New York Times,* January 22, p. A13.

Roth, Kimberlee. 2006. "A Love of Science and a Vision to Save Millions of Lives Make Her Day." Retrieved March 11, 2007 (http://uk.ashoka.org/ node/920).

Sack, Kevin. 2009. "With Health Care for Nearly All, Massachusetts Now Faces Costs." *New York Times,* March 16, pp. A1, A13.

Sack, Kevin. 2010. "From the Hospital Room to Bankruptcy Court." *New York Times,* November 25, pp. A1, A21.

Sacks, Heather, Todd Kutyla, and Sharon Silow-Carroll. 2002. *Toward Comprehensive Health Coverage for All: Summaries of 20 State Planning Grants* (U.S. Health Resources and Services Administration, Report 577). Washington, DC: Commonwealth Fund.

Saul, Stephanie. 2008. "In Sour Economy, Some Scale Back on Medications." *New York Times,* October 22, pp. A1, A18.

Schondelmeyer, Stephen and Leigh Purvis. 2011. *Trends in Retail Prices of Specialty Prescription Drugs Widely Used by Medicare Beneficiaries 2005 to 2009*. Washington DC: AARP.

Seccombe, Karen and Cheryl Amey. 2001. "Playing by the Rules and Losing: Health Insurance and the Working Poor." Pp. 323–39 in *Readings in Medical Sociology,* edited by W. Cockerman and M. Glasser. Upper Saddle River, NJ: Prentice Hall.

Silverstein, Ken. 1999. "Millions for Viagra, Pennies for Diseases of the Poor." *The Nation,* July 19, pp. 13–19.

Singer, Natasha. 2007. "Is the 'Mom Job' Really Necessary?" *New York Times,* October 4, pp. E1, E3.

Smith, Barbara E. 1987. *Digging Our Own Grave: Coal Miners and the Struggle over Black Lung Disease*. Chicago, IL: University of Chicago Press.

Starr, Paul. 1982. *The Social Transformation of American Medicine*. New York: Basic Books.

Street, R. L. 1991. "Information-Giving in Medical Consultations: The Influence of Patients' Communicative Styles and Personal Characteristics." *Social Science and Medicine* 32:541–48.

Szasz, Thomas. 1960. "The Myth of Mental Illness." *American Psychologist* 15:113–18.

Tanner, Lindsey. 2003. "Barbershop/Clinic Serves Black Men in Familiar Setting." *News Tribune,* November 27, p. A12.

Testa, K. 2003. "More Drug Buyers Turn to Canada." *News Tribune,* December 10, p. A9.

UNICEF. 2012a. *The State of the World's Children 2012: Children in an Urban World*. New York: UNICEF.

UNICEF. 2012b. "Statistics: Uganda." Retrieved April 11, 2012 (http://www.unicef.org/infobycountry/ uganda_statistics.html#89).

U.S. Bureau of Labor Statistics. 2011. "Census of Fatal Occupational Injuries News Release." Retrieved April 8, 2012 (http://www.bls.gov/ news.release/cfoi.htm).

U.S. Census Bureau. 2002."Motherhood: The Fertility of American Women, 2000." *Population Profile of the United States: 2000* (Internet Release). Retrieved February 22, 2003 (http:// www.census.gov/population/pop-profile/2000/ chap04.pdf).

Waldron, Ingrid. 2001. "What Do We Know About Causes of Sex Differences in Mortality? A Review of the Literature." Pp. 37–49 in *The Sociology of Health and Illness: Critical Perspectives,* edited by A. Dan. New York: Worth.

Weitz, Rose. 2001. *The Sociology of Health, Illness, and Health Care: A Critical Approach*. Belmont, CA: Wadsworth/Thompson Learning.

Wells, Susan. 2006. "The Doctor Is In-House." *HR Magazine* April, pp. 48–54.

Wilkinson, Richard G. 1996. *Unhealthy Societies: The Afflictions of Inequality*. London, England: Routledge.

Chapter 11

Aboujaoude, Elias, Lorrin Koran, Nona Gamel, Michael Large, and Richard Serpe. 2006. "Potential Markers for Problematic Internet Use: A Telephone Survey of 2,513 Adults." *CNS Spectrums* 11:750–55.

Action Coalition for Media Education. 2004. *Questioning the Media: Ten Basic Principles of Media Literacy Education.* Albuquerque, NM: Author.

Alexander, Alison and Jarice Hanson. 1995. *Taking Sides: Clashing Views on Controversial Issues in Mass Media and Society.* Guilford, CT: Dushkin.

Altheide, David L. 1997. "The News Media, the Problem Frame, and the Production Fear." *Sociological Quarterly* 38(4):647–68.

American Academy of Pediatrics, Committee on Public Education. 2001a. "Children, Adolescents, and Television." *Pediatrics* 107(2):423–26.

American Academy of Pediatrics, Committee on Public Education. 2001b. "Media Violence." *Pediatrics* 108(5):1222–26.

Anderson, Craig, Leonard Berkowitz, Edward Donnerstein, Leonard Rowell Huesmann, James Johnson, Daniel Linz, Neil M. Malamuth, and Ellen Wartella. 2003. "The Influence of Media Violence on Youth." *Psychological Science in the Public Interest* 4(3):81–110.

Anderson, Craig and Brad Bushman. 2001. "Effects of Violent Video Games on Aggressive Behavior, Aggressive Cognition, Aggressive Affect, Physiological Arousal, and Prosocial Behavior." *Psychological Science* 12(5):353–59.

Bagdikian, Ben. 1997. *The Media Monopoly.* Boston, MA: Beacon Press.

Ball-Rokeach, Sandra and Muriel Cantor, eds. 1986. *Media, Audience, and Social Structure.* Beverly Hills, CA: Sage Publications.

Barner, Mark. 1999. "Sex-Role Stereotyping in FCC-Mandated Children's Educational Television." *Journal of Broadcasting and Electronic Media* 43:551–64.

Baron, David. 2006. "Persistent Media Bias." *Journal of Public Economics* 90:1–36.

Bauder, David. 2006. "Homes Have More TVs Than People." *News Tribune,* September 23, p. A11.

Blau, Ina. 2011. "Application Use, Online Relationship Types, Self-Disclosure, and Internet Abuse Among Children and Youth: Implications for Education and Internet Safety Programs." *Journal of Educational Computing Search* 45:95–116.

Blumberg, Stephen, Julian Luke, Nadarajasundaram Ganesh, Michael Davern, Michel Boudreaux, and Karen Soderberg. 2011. *Wireless Substitution: State-level Estimates From the National Health Interview Survey, January 2007–June 2010.* Washington, DC: U.S. Department of Health and Human Services.

Branton, Regina and Johanna Dunaway. 2008. "English- and Spanish-Language Media Coverage of Immigration: A Comparative Analysis." *Social Science Quarterly* 89:1006–22.

Case, Carl and Kimberly Young. 2002. "Employee Internet Management: Current Business Practices and Outcomes." *CyberPsychology and Behavior* 5(4):355–61.

Center for Media and Public Affairs. 2012. "About the Center for Media and Public Affairs." Retrieved April 21, 2012 (http://www.cmpa.com/about.htm).

Central Intelligence Agency. 2012. "Internet Users." Retrieved April 21, 2012 (https://www.cia.gov/library/publications/the-world-factbook/rankorder/2153rank.html).

Chomsky, Noam. 1989. *Necessary Illusions: Thought Control in Democratic Societies.* Boston, MA: South End Press.

CNN Money. 2011. "Industries." Retrieved April 20, 2012 (http://money.cnn.com/magazines/fortune/fortune500/2011/industries/145/index.html).

Committee to Protect Journalists. 2012. "46 Journalists Killed in 2011." Retrieved April 21, 2012 (http://www.cpj.org/killed/2011/).

Considine, David, Julie Horton, and Gary Moorman. 2009. "Teaching and Reading the Millennial Generation Through Media Literacy." *Journal of Adolescent and Adult Literacy* 52:472–81.

Croteau, David and William Hoynes. 2000. *Media Society: Industries, Images, and Audiences.* Thousand Oaks, CA: Pine Forge Press.

Croteau, David and William Hoynes. 2001. *The Business of Media: Corporate Media and the Public Interest.* Thousand Oaks, CA: Pine Forge Press.

Davis, Geena. 2006. "Where Are the Girls?" Retrieved July 25, 2007 (http://www.commonsenseblog.org/archives/2006/02/where_are_the_g.php).

Dietz, William and Steven Gortmaker. 1985. "Do We Fatten Our Children at the Television Set? Obesity and Television Viewing in Children and Adolescents." *Pediatrics* 75(5):807–12.

"Doctors Diagnose Extreme Internet Use." 2003. *Biotech Week,* August 27, pp. 512–15.

Drori, Gili. 2004. "The Internet as a Global Social Problem." Pp. 433–50 in *Handbook of Social Problems: A Comparative International Perspective,* edited by George Ritzer. Thousand Oaks, CA: Sage Publications.

Dunstan, D., E. Barr, G. Healy, J. Salmon, J. Shaw, B. Balkau, D. Magliano, A. Cameron, P. Zimmet, and N. Owen. 2010. "Television Viewing Time and Mortality: The Australian Diabetes, Obesity and Lifestyle Study." *Circulation* 121:384–91.

Epstein, Edward Jay. 1981. "The Selection of Reality." Pp. 119–32 in *What's News,* edited by E. Abel. San Francisco, CA: Institute for Contemporary Studies.

Eschholz, Sarah, Jana Bufkin, and Jenny Long. 2002. "Symbolic Reality Bites: Women and Racial/Ethnic Minorities in Modern Film." *Sociological Spectrum* 22:299–334.

Faith, Myles S., Nathaniel Berman, Moonseong Heo, Angelo Pietrobelli, Dympna Gallagher, Leonard H. Epstein, Mark T. Eiden, and David B. Allison. 2001. "Effects of Contingent Television on Physical Activity and Television Viewing on Obese Children." *Pediatrics* 107(5):1043–48.

Federal Communications Commission. 2004. "About the FCC." Retrieved May 13, 2010 (http://www.fcc.gov/aboutus.html).

Federal Trade Commission. 2011. "Facebook Settles FTC Charges That It Deceived Consumers by Failing to Keep Privacy Promises." Retrieved April 22, 2012 (http://ftc.gov/opa/2011/11/privacysettlement.shtm).

Galtung, Johan and Mari Ruge. 1973. "Structuring and Selecting News." Pp. 67–72 in *The Manufacture of News,* edited by S. Cohen and J. Young. London, England: Constable.

Gans, Herbert. 1979. *Deciding What's News: A Study of CBS Evening News, NBC Nightly News, Newsweek, and Time.* New York: Pantheon.

Gantz, Walter, Nancy Schwartz, James Angelini, and Victoria Rideout. 2007. *Food for Thought: Television Food Advertising for Children in the United States.* Menlo Park, CA: Henry J. Kaiser Family Foundation.

Gibson, Katie. 2009. "Undermining Katie Couric: The Discipline Function of the Press." *Women and Language* 32:51–59.

Glassner, Barry. 1997. *The Culture of Fear: Why Americans Are Afraid of the Wrong Things.* New York: Basic Books.

Greeson, Larry and Rose Williams. 1986. "Social Implications of Music Videos for Youth: An Analysis of the Content and Effects of MTV." *Youth and Society* 18(2):177–89.

Griffiths, Mark. 2002. "Occupational Health Issues Concerning Internet Use in the Workplace." *Work and Stress* 16(4):283–86.

Griffiths, Mark. 2003. "Internet Abuse in the Workplace: Issues and Concerns for Employers and Employment Counselors." *Journal of Employment Counseling* 40:87–96.

Guillén, Mauro and Sandra Suárez. 2005. "Explaining the Global Digital Divide: Economic, Political and Sociological Drivers of Cross-National Internet Use." *Social Forces* 84(2):681–708.

Gunkel, David J. 2003. "Second Thoughts: Towards a Critique of the Digital Divide." *New Media and Society* 5(4):499–522.

Gurevitch, Michael and Mark R. Levy. 1985. *Mass Communication Review Yearbook* (Vol. 5). Beverly Hills, CA: Sage Publications.

Huesmann, Leonard Rowell, Jessica Moise-Titus, Cheryl-Lynn Podolski, and Leonard D. Eron. 2003. "Longitudinal Relations Between Children's Exposure to TV Violence and Their Aggressive and Violent Behavior in Young Adulthood: 1977–1992." *Developmental Psychology* 39(2):201–22.

Kellner, Douglas M. 1995. *Media Culture: Cultural Studies, Identity, and Politics Between the Modern and the Postmodern.* New York: Routledge.

Kelly, Joe and Stacy Smith. 2006. *Where the Girls Aren't: Gender Disparity Saturates G-Rated Films.* Duluth, MN: Dads and Daughters Foundation.

Kelly, K., K. Clark, and L. Kulman. 2004. "Trash TV." *U.S. News and World Report* 136(6):48–51.

Klite, P., R. A. Bardwell, and J. Salzman. 1997. "Local TV News: Getting Away with Murder." *Harvard International Journal of Press/Politics* 2:102–12.

Lazarus, Wendy and Francisco Mora. 2000. *Online Content for Low-Income and Underserved Americans: The Digital Divide's New Frontier.* Santa Monica, CA: Children's Partnership.

Lin, Sunny and Chin-Chung Tsai. 2002. "Sensation Seeking and Internet Dependence of Taiwanese High School Adolescents." *Computers in Human Behavior* 18:411–26.

Martin, Andrew. 2007. "Kellogg to Phase Out Some Food Ads to Children." *New York Times,* June 14, pp. C1–C2.

McChesney, Robert and John Nichols. 2010. *The Death and Life of American Journalism: The Media Revolution That Will Begin the World Again.* Philadelphia, PA: First Nation Books.

McNair, B. 1998. *The Sociology of Journalism.* London, England: Oxford University Press.

Media Awareness Network. 2004. "What Is Media Literacy?" Retrieved May 13, 2010 (http://www.media-awareness.ca/english/teachers/media_literacy/what_is_media_literacy.cfm).

Miller, Claire Cain and Brad Stone. 2009. "News Without Newspapers." *New York Times,* April 13, pp. B1, B4.

Miller, Mark Crispin. 2002. "What's Wrong with This Picture?" *The Nation* 274(1):18–22.

Naoum, Chris. 2012. "The Future of Privacy in a Social Media and Networking World." Retrieved April 22, 2012 (http://broadbandbreakfast.com/2012/04/the-future-of-privacy-in-a-social-media-and-networking-world/).

Nathanson, Amy I. 1999. "Identifying and Explaining the Relationship Between Parental Mediation and Children's Aggression." *Communication Research* 26(2):124–43.

National Safety Council. 2012. *State of the Report on Cell Phone Distracted Driving.* Washington, DC: Author.

National Safety Council. 2010. "National Safety Council Estimates That at Least 1.6 Million Crashes Each Year Involve Drivers Using Cell Phones and Texting." Retrieved May 13, 2010 (http://www.nsc.org/Pages/NSCestimates16millioncrashescausedbydriversusingcellphonesandtexting.aspx).

Newspaper Association of America. 2010. "Newspaper Circulation Volume." Retrieved April 22, 2012 (http://www.naa.org/Trends-and-Numbers/Circulation/Newspaper-Circulation-Volume.aspx).

Nguyen, Jimmy. 2011. "Internet Privacy Class Actions: How to Manage Risks From Increasing Attacks Against Online and Social Media." *Computer & Internet Lawyer* 28(9):8–11.

Parekh, Angana. 2001. "Bringing Women's Stories to a Reluctant Mainstream Press." *Nieman Reports* 55(4):90–92.

Pérez-Peña, Richard. 2009. "As Cities Go From Two Newspapers to One, Some Talk of Zero." *New York Times,* March 12, pp. A1, A17.

Peterson, T. 1981. "Mass Media and Their Environments: A Journey into the Past." Pp. 13–32 in *What's News,* edited by E. Abel. San Francisco, CA: Institute for Contemporary Studies.

Pew Internet & American Life Project. 2012. *Digital Differences.* Retrieved April 22, 2012 (http://pewinternet.org/~/media//Files/Reports/2012/PIP_Digital_differences_041312.pdf).

Pew Research Center. 2010. "Americans Spending More Time Following the News." Retrieved April 22, 2012 (http://www.people-press.org/2010/09/12/americans-spending-more-time-following-the-news/).

Pew Research Center for the People and the Press. 2005. "People More Critical of Press, but Goodwill Persists." Retrieved May 13, 2010 (http://people-press.org/reports/display.php3?ReportID=248).

Pew Research Center for the People and the Press. 2009. *Press Accuracy Rating Hits Two Decade Low.* Retrieved May 13, 2010 (http://people-press.org/reports/pdf/543.pdf).

Porter, William E. 1981. "The Media Baronies: Bigger, Fewer, More Powerful." Pp. 97–118 in *What's News,* edited by E. Abel. San Francisco: Institute for Contemporary Studies.

Postman, N. 1989. *Amusing Ourselves to Death.* London, England: Methuen.

Powell, Kimberly and Lori Abels. 2002. "Sex Role Stereotypes in TV Programs Aimed at the Preschool Audience: An Analysis of Teletubbies and Barney and Friends." *Women and Language* 25(1):14–22.

Project for Excellence in Journalism. 2004. *The State of the News Media 2004.* Retrieved March 21, 2004 (http://www.stateofthemedia.org/2004/execsum.pdf).

Project for Excellence in Journalism. 2011. *The State of News Media 2011.* Retrieved November 30, 2012 (http://stateofthemedia.org/overview-2011/).

Project for Excellence in Journalism. 2012. *The State of News Media 2012.* Retrieved April 22, 2012 (http://stateofthemedia.org/).

Rideout, Victoria, Ulla Foehr, and Donald Roberts. 2010. *Generation M²: Media in the Lives of 8- to 18-Year-Olds.* Washington, DC: Kaiser Family Foundation.

Schorr, Daniel. 1998. "Mother Teresa and Diana." *Christian Science Monitor* 90(193):15.

Schudson, M. 1986. "The Menu of Media Research." Pp. 43–48 in *Media, Audience, and Social Structure,* edited by S. Ball-Rokeach and Muriel Cantor. Beverly Hills, CA: Sage Publications.

Servon, Lisa. 2002. *Bridging the Digital Divide: Technology, Community, and Public Policy.* Boston, MA: Blackwell.

Seymour-Ure, C. 1974. *The Political Impact of Mass Media.* Beverly Hills, CA: Sage Publications.

Shaw, Daniel L. and Maxwell E. McCombs. 1997. *The Emergence of American Political Issues: The Agenda Setting Function of the Press.* St. Paul, MN: West.

Snider, Michael. 2003. "Wired to Another World." *Maclean's* 116(9):23–24.

Tucker, Patrick. 2009. "Newspapers Face the Final Edition." *The Futurist.* September–October: 8–9.

TV Turnoff Network. 2004. "TV Facts and Figures." Retrieved March 1, 2004 (http://www.tvturnoff.org/facts.htm).

United Nations Development Programme. 2001. *Human Development Report 2001: Making New Technologies Work for Human Development.* New York: Author.

U.S. Census Bureau. 2009. "Computer and Internet Use in the United States: October 2009." Retrieved April 22, 2012 (http://www.census.gov/hhes/computer/publications/2009.html).

U.S. Census Bureau. 2010. *Statistical Abstract of the United States.* Washington, DC: Author.

U.S. Department of Commerce. 2011. *Digital Nation: Expanding Internet Usage.* Washington, DC: Author.

Van den Bulck, J. 2000. "Is Television Bad for Your Health? Behavior and Body Image of the Adolescent 'Couch Potato.'" *Journal of Youth and Adolescence* 29(3):273–88.

VandeBerg, Leah R. 1991. "Using Television to Teach Courses in Gender and Communication." *Communication Education* 40(1):105–11.

Vartanova, Elena. 2002. "Digital Divide and the Changing Political/Media Environment of Post-socialist Europe." *International Communication Gazette* 64:449–65.

Vessey, Judith and Joanne Lee. 2000. "Violent Video Games Affecting Our Children." *Pediatric Nursing* 26(6):607–10.

Wade, Marcia. 2008. "Business News: Media Monopolies." *Black Enterprise* 39:28.

Warschauer, M. 2003. *Technology and Social Inclusion.* Cambridge, MA: MIT Press.

Wasburn, Philo and Mara Wasburn 2011. "Media Coverage of Women in Politics: The Curious Case of Sarah Palin." *Media, Culture & Society* 33: 1027–1041.

Chapter 12

Abatemarco, Diane, Bernadette West, Vesna Zec, Andrea Russo, Persis Sosiak, and Vedran Mardesic. 2004. "Project Northland in Croatia: A Community Based Adolescent Alcohol Prevention Intervention." *Journal of Drug Education* 34(2):167–78.

Abramsky, Sasha. 2003. "The Drug War Goes Up in Smoke." *The Nation* 277(5):25–28.

Alaniz, Maria Luisa. 1998. "Alcohol Availability and Targeted Advertising in Racial/Ethnic Minorities Communities." *Alcohol Health and Research World* 22(4):286–89.

Alcohol Information Scotland. 2007. *Alcohol Information Scotland, 2007.* Edinburgh, Scotland: IDS Publications.

Alcohol Policies Project. 2001. "National Poll Shows 'Alcopop' Drinks Lure Teens." Retrieved May 21, 2010 (http://www.cspinet.org/booze/alcopops_press.htm).

Allen, Mike, William Donohue, Amy Griffin, Dan Ryan, and Monique Mitchell Turner. 2003. "Comparing the Influence of Parents and Peers on the Choice to Use Drugs: A Meta-Analysis of the Literature." *Criminal Justice and Behavior* 30:162–86.

Alleyne, Vanessa. 2007. "Locked Up Means Locked Out: Women, Addiction and Incarceration." *Women & Therapy* 29:181–94.

American Lung Association. 2006. "Smoking Fact Sheet." Retrieved February 21, 2007 (http://www.lungusa.org/site/pp.asp?c=dvLUK900E&b=39853).

American Medical Association. 2004. "Girlie Drinks . . . Women's Diseases." Retrieved April 27, 2007 (http://www.cslep.org/CSLEP/publications/girlie_drinks_survey.pdf).

Becker, Howard. 1963. *Outsiders: Studies in the Sociology of Deviance.* New York: Free Press.

Beckett, Katherine. 1995. "Fetal Rights and 'Crack Moms': Pregnant Women in the War on Drugs." *Contemporary Drug Problems* 22:587–612.

Benavie, Arthur. 2009. *Drugs: America's Holy War.* New York: Routledge Press.

Boyd, Carol, Sean E. McCabe, and Hannah d'Arcy. 2003. "Ecstasy Use Among College Undergraduates: Gender, Race, and Sexual Identity." *Journal of Substance Abuse Treatment* 24:209–15.

Brower, Aaron. 2002. "Are College Students Alcoholics?" *Journal of American College Health* 50:253–55.

Butler, Edward R. 1993. "Alcohol Use by College Students: A Rite of Passage Ritual." *NASPA Journal* 31(1):48–55.

Caetano, Raul, Catherine Clark, and Tammy Tam. 1998. "Alcohol Consumption Among Racial/Ethnic Minorities: Theory and Research." *Alcohol Health and Research World* 22(4):233–38.

Caetano, Raul and Lee Ann Kaskutas. 1995. "Changes in Drinking Patterns among Whites, Blacks, and Hispanics, 1984–1992." *Journal of Studies on Alcohol* 50:15–23.

Caetano, Raul, John Schafer, and Carol Cunradi. 2001. "Alcohol Related Intimate Partner Violence Among White, Black, and Hispanic Couples in the United States." *Alcohol Research and Health* 25(1):58–65.

Campbell-Grossman, Christie, Diane Hudson, and Margaret Fleck. 2003. "Chewing Tobacco Use: Perceptions and Knowledge in Rural Adolescent Youths." *Issues in Comprehensive Pediatric Nursing* 26:13–21.

Chen, Kevin and Denise B. Kandel. 1995. "The Natural History of Drug Use from Adolescence to the Mid-thirties in a General Population Sample." *American Journal of Public Health* 85:41–47.

Clapp, John, Audrey Shillington, and Lance Segars. 2000. "Deconstructing Contexts of Binge Drinking among College Students." *American Journal of Drug and Alcohol Abuse* 26(1):139–54.

Collins, R. Lorraine and Lily McNair. 2003. "Minority Women and Alcohol Use." Retrieved May 21, 2010 (http://pubs.niaaa.nih.gov/publications/arh26-4/251-256.htm).

Crispo, A., P. Brennan, K. H. Jockel, A. Schaffrath-Rosario, H. E. Wichmann, F. Nyberg, L. Simonato, F. Mereletti, F. Forastiere, P. Boffetta, and S. Darby. 2004. "The Cumulative Risk of Lung Cancer among Current, Ex- and Never-smokers in European Men." *British Journal of Cancer* 91:1280–86.

Crutchfield, Robert and Walter R. Gove. 1984. "Determinants of Drug Use: A Test of the Coping Hypothesis." *Social Science & Medicine* 18:503–509.

Cussen, Meaghan and Walter Block. 2000. "Legalize Drugs Now! An Analysis of the Benefits of Legalized Drugs." *American Journal of Economics and Sociology* 59(3):525–36.

Drug Policy Alliance. 2003a. "About the Alliance." Retrieved May 21, 2010 (http://www.drugpolicy.org/about).

Drug Policy Alliance. 2003b. "Women and the War on Drugs." Retrieved May 21, 2010 (http://www.drugpolicy.org/communities/women).

Durkin, Keith, Timothy Wolfe, and Gregory Clark. 2005. "College Students and Binge Drinking: An Evaluation of Social Learning Theory." *Sociological Spectrum* 25:255–72.

European Lung Association. 2006. "First Ever EU Figures on Passive Smoking Deaths." Retrieved May 21, 2010 (http://www.european-lung-foundation.org/uploads/Document/WEB_CHEMIN_285_1142589119.pdf).

Federal Bureau of Investigation. 2011. "Uniform Crime Reports: Crime in the United States 2011." Retrieved December 6, 2012 (http://www.fbi.gov/about-us/cjis/ucr/crime-in-the-u.s/2011/crime-in-the-u.s.-2011).

Fellner, Jamie. 2000. *Punishment and Prejudice: Racial Disparities in the War on Drugs* (Vol. 2, No. 2). New York: Human Rights Watch.

Filmore, K. M., J. M. Golding, E. V. Leino, M. Motoyoshi, C. Shoemaker, H. Terry, C. Ager, and H. Ferrer. 1997. "Patterns and Trends in Women's and Men's Drinking." Pp. 21–48 in *Gender and Alcohol,* edited by R. W. Wilsnack and S. C. Wilsnack. New Brunswick, NJ: Rutgers Center of Alcohol Studies.

Frone, Michael R. 2004. "Alcohol, Drugs and Workplace Safety Outcomes: A View from a General Model of Employee Substance Use and Productivity." Pp. 127–56 in *The Psychology of Workplace Safety,* edited by J. Barling and M. R. Frone. Washington, DC: American Psychological Association.

Glenn, B. 2000. "A Crusader Against Underage Drinking." Retrieved June 9, 2004 (http://www.madd.org/activism/0,1056,4028_print,00.html).

Goode, Erich. 2004. "Drug Use as a Global Social Problem." Pp. 494–520 in *Handbook of Social Problems: A Comparative International Perspective,* edited by G. Ritzer. Thousand Oaks, CA: Sage Publications.

Hawken, Paul. 1993. *The Ecology of Commerce: A Declaration of Sustainability.* New York: HarperCollins.

Herd, Denise and Joel Grube. 1996. "Black Identity and Drinking in the U.S.: A National Study." *Addiction* 91(6):845–57.

Hesselbrock, Michie N. and Victor M. Hesselbrock. 1997. "Gender, Alcoholism, and Psychiatric Comorbidity." Pp. 49–71 in *Gender and Alcohol,* edited by R. W. Wilsnack and S. C. Wilsnack. New Brunswick, NJ: Rutgers Center of Alcohol Studies.

Hoffman, John and Cindy Larison. 1999. "Worker Drug Use and Workplace Drug Testing Programs: Results from the 1994 National Household Survey on Drug Use." *Contemporary Drug Problems* 26:331–54.

Holmes, Malcolm and Judith Antell. 2001. "The Social Construction of American Indian Drinking: Perceptions of American Indian and White Officials." *Sociological Quarterly* 42(2):151–73.

Inciardi, James. 1999. "American Drug Policy: The Continuing Debate." Pp. 1–8 in *The Drug Legalization Debate,* edited by James Inciardi. Thousand Oaks, CA: Sage Publications.

Jacobs, Andrew. 2010. "China Turns Drug Rehab Into a Punishing Ordeal." *New York Times,* January 8, p. A4.

Johnston, Lloyd D., Patrick M. O'Malley, and Jerald G. Bachman. 2001. *Monitoring the Future: National Survey Results on Drug Use, 1975–2000* (Vol. 2, NIH Publication No. 01-4925). Bethesda, MD: National Institute on Drug Abuse.

Kaplan, Howard, Steven Martin, and Cynthia Robbins. 1984. "Pathways to Adolescent Drug Use: Self-derogation, Peer Influence, Weakening of Social Controls, and Early Substance Abuse." *Journal of Health and Social Behavior* 25: 270–289.

Karberg, Jennifer and Doris James. 2005. *Substance Dependence, Abuse, and Treatment of Jail Inmates, 2002* (NCJ 209588). Washington, DC: U.S. Department of Justice.

Klingner, Donald, Gary Roberts, and Valerie Patterson. 1998. "The Miami Coalition Surveys of Employee Drug Use and Attitudes: A Five-Year Retrospective." *Public Personnel Management* 27(2):201–22.

Larson, Sharon L., Joe Eyerman, Misty S. Foster, and Joseph C. Gfroerer. 2007. *Worker Substance Use and Workplace Policies and Programs* (DHHS Publication SMA 07-4273). Rockville, MD: Substance Abuse and Mental Health Services Administration, Office of Applied Studies.

Lederman, Linda, Lea Stewart, Fern Goodhart, and Lisa Laitman. 2003. "A Case Against 'Binge' as a Term of Choice: Convincing College Students to Personalize Messages About Dangerous Drinking." *Journal of Health Communications* 8:79–91.

Leon, Dean and Jim McCambridge. 2006. "Liver Cirrhosis Mortality Rates in Britain from 1950 to 2002: An Analysis of Routine Data." *Lancet* 367:52–56.

Leonard, K. E. and J. C. Rothbard. 1999. "Alcohol and the Marriage Effect." *Journal of Studies on Alcohol* (Suppl. 13):139–46.

Leventhal, Howard and Paul Cleary. 1980. "The Smoking Problem: A Review of the Research and Theory in Behavioral Risk Modification." *Psychological Bulletin* 88: 370–405.

Lewinsohn, Peter, Richard Brown, John Seeley, and Susan Ramsey. 2000. "Psychosocial Correlates of Cigarette Smoking Abstinence, Experimentation, Persistence and Frequency During Adolescence." *Nicotine and Tobacco Research* 2:121–31.

MacDonald, Scott, Samantha Wells, and T. Cameron Wild. 1999. "Occupational Risk Factors Associated With Alcohol and Drug Problems." *American Journal of Drug and Alcohol Abuse* 25(2):351–69.

MacDonald, Sharon. 1994. "Whisky, Women, and the Scottish Drink Problem: A View from the Highlands." Pp. 125–44 in *Gender, Drink, and Drugs,* edited by M. McDonald. Oxford, England: Berg.

Marshall, Carolyn. 2007. "Drinks With Youth Appeal Draw Growing Opposition." *New York Times,* April 13, p. A12.

McBride, Duane, Yvonne Terry, and James Inciardi. 1999. "Alternative Perspectives on the Drug Policy Debate." Pp. 9–54 in *The Drug Legalization Debate,* edited by James Inciardi. Thousand Oaks, CA: Sage Publications.

Muthén, Linda K. and Bengt Muthén. 2000. "The Development of Heavy Drinking and Alcohol-Related Problems from Ages 18 to 37 in a U.S. National Drinking Sample." *Journal of Studies on Alcohol* 61:290–300.

National Cancer Institute. 2003. "Smokeless Tobacco: Health and Other Effects." Retrieved May 21, 2010 (http://dccps.nci.nih.gov/tcrb/less_effects.html).

National Clearinghouse for Alcohol and Drug Information. 2003a. "Intensive Outpatient Treatment for Alcohol and Other Drug Abuse: The Treatment Needs of Special Groups." Retrieved May 21, 2010 (http://www.health.org/govpubs/bkd139/8g.aspx).

National Clearinghouse for Alcohol and Drug Information. 2003b. "Cigarettes and Other Nicotine Products." Retrieved August 2, 2003 (http://www.drugabuse.gov/infofacts/tobacco.html).

National Institute on Alcohol Abuse and Alcoholism. 2003a. "The Creation of the National Institute on Alcohol Abuse and Alcoholism." Retrieved March 21, 2008 (http://www.niaaa.nih.gov/AboutNIAAA/OrganizationalInformation/History.htm).

National Institute on Alcohol Abuse and Alcoholism. 2003b. "NIAAA's Purpose." Retrieved July 31, 2003 (http://pubs.niaaa.nih.gov/publications/HealthDisparities/Purpose&Vision.html).

National Institute on Alcohol Abuse and Alcoholism. 2004. "Alcoholism: Getting the Facts." Retrieved February 21, 2007 (http://www.healthieryou.com/alcohol.html).

National Institute on Alcohol Abuse and Alcoholism. 2005. "Alcoholism: Natural History and Background." Retrieved May 21, 2010 (http://pubs.niaaa.nih.gov/publications/HealthDisparities/Alcoholism1.htm).

National Institute on Drug Abuse. 1998. "Tobacco Addiction." Retrieved August 2, 2003 (http://www.nida.nih.gov/ResearchReports/Nicotine/addictive.html).

National Institute on Drug Abuse. 2002a. *Marijuana Abuse* (NIH Publication No. 02-3859, October). Rockville, MD: Author.

National Institute on Drug Abuse. 2002b. "What Are the Medical Complications of Cocaine Abuse?" Retrieved July 27, 2003 (http://www.drugabuse.gov/researchreports/cocaine/effects.html).

National Institute on Drug Abuse. 2002c. "What Is the Effect of Maternal Cocaine Use?" Retrieved July 27, 2003 (http://www.drugabuse.gov/ResearchReports/Cocaine/cocaine4.html#maternal).

National Institute on Drug Abuse. 2003a. "NIDA Info Facts: MDMA (Ecstasy)." Retrieved May 21, 2010 (http://www.drugabuse.gov/Infofax/ecstasy.html).

National Institute on Drug Abuse. 2003b. "Drug Addiction Treatment Methods." Retrieved August 2, 2003 (http://www.drugabuse.gov/infofacts/treatmeth.html).

National Institute on Drug Abuse. 2006. "Cigarettes and Other Tobacco Products." Retrieved May 21, 2010 (http://www.drugabuse.gov/infofacts/tobacco.html).

National Institute on Drug Abuse. 2007. "Cocaine." Retrieved May 21, 2010 (http://wwwnida.nih.gov/Infofacts/cocaine.html).

National Institute on Drug Abuse. 2010. "Info Facts: MDMA." Retrieved May 2, 2012 (http://www.drugabuse.gov/publications/infofacts/mdma-ecstasy).

Newman, Ian. 1999. *Adolescent Tobacco Use in Nebraska From Nebraska.* Lincoln, NE: Nebraska Prevention Center for Alcohol and Drug Abuse.

Office of National Drug Control Policy (ONDCP). 2003. "Enabling Legislation." Retrieved May 21, 2010 (http://www.whitehousedrugpolicy.gov/about/legislation.html).

Office of National Drug Control Policy. 2006a. "Marijuana Overview." Retrieved February 21, 2007 (http://www.whitehousedrugpolicy.gov/drugfact/marijuana/index.html#extentofuse).

Office of National Drug Control Policy. 2006b. "Methamphetamine." Retrieved May 21, 2010 (http://www.whitehousedrugpolicy.gov/drugfact/methamphetamine/index.html).

Office of National Drug Control Policy. 2006d. "MDMA Abuse." Retrieved May 21, 2010 (http://www.drugabuse.gov/ResearchReports/MDMA/default.html).

Office of National Drug Control Policy. 2012. "2012 National Drug Control Strategy." Retrieved May 2, 2012 (http://www.whitehouse.gov/ondcp/2012-national-drug-control-strategy).

O'Malley, Patrick, Lloyd Johnston, and Jerald Bachman. 1998. "Alcohol Use Among Adolescents." *Alcohol Health and Research World* 22(2):85–94.

PBS. 2000. "Frontline: Drug Wars." Retrieved August 2, 2003 (http://www.pbs.org/wgbh/pages/frontline/shows/drugs).

Pennell, Susan, Joe Ellett, Cynthia Rienick, and Jackie Grimes. 1999. *Meth Matters: Report on Methamphetamine Users in Five Western Cities.* Washington, DC: U.S. Department of Justice, Office of Justice Programs, National Institute of Justice.

Perry, Cheryl, Carolyn Williams, Kelli Komro, Sara Veblen-Mortenson, Melissa Stigler, Karen Munson, Kian Farbakhsh, Resa Jones, and Jean Forster. 2002. "Project Northland: Long-Term Outcomes of Community Action to Reduce Adolescent Alcohol Use." *Health Education Research* 17:117–32.

Pew Research Center. 2001. "Interdiction and Incarceration Still Top Remedies." Retrieved May 21, 2010 (http://people-press.org/reports/display.php3?ReportID=16).

Plant, M. A., P. Miller, and M. L. Plant. 2005. "Trends in Drinking, Smoking and Illicit Drug Use Among 15- and 16-Year Olds in the UK (1995–2003)." *Journal of Substance Use* 10(6):331–39.

Prinstein, Mitchell and Shirley Wang. 2005. False Consensus and Adolescent Peer Contagion: Examining Discrepancies Between Perceptions and Actual Reported Levels of Friends' Deviance and Health Risk Behaviors." *Journal of Abnormal Child Psychology* 33:293–306.

Reinarman, Craig and Harry G. Levine. 1997. *Crack in America: Demon Drugs and Social Justice.* Berkeley: University of California Press.

Ritson, Bruce. 2002. "Editorial: Scotland's National Plan on Alcohol Problems." *Drugs: Education, Prevention, and Policy* 9(3):217–20.

Roberts, Dorothy. 1991. "Punishing Drug Addicts Who Have Babies: Women of Color, Equality, and the Right of Privacy." *Harvard Law Review* 104(7):1419–82.

Roman, Paul and Terry Blum. 2002. "The Workplace and Alcohol Problem Prevention." *Alcohol Research and Health* 26(1):49–57.

Rose, Rebecca. 2009. *Combating Methamphetamine Abuse.* BJA Fact Sheet, FS000318. Washington, DC: U.S. Department of Justice.

Scalia, John. 2001. *Federal Drug Offenders, 1999, With Trends 1984–1999* (August 2001, NCJ 187285). Washington, DC: U.S. Department of Justice, Office of Justice Programs.

Scottish Government. 2009. *Changing Scotland's Relationship with Alcohol: A Framework for Action.* Edinburgh, Scotland: Scottish Government.

Silbering, Robert. 2001. "The 'War on Drugs': A View from the Trenches." *Social Research* 68(3):890–96.

Snell, Marilyn Berlin. 2001. "Welcome to Meth Country." Retrieved May 21, 2010 (http://www .sierraclub.org/sierra/200101/Meth.asp).

Social Issues Research Center. 1998. *Social and Cultural Aspects of Drinking.* Retrieved May 21, 2010 (http://www.sirc.org/publik/drinking3 .html#_VPID_5).

Substance Abuse and Mental Health Services Administration. 2003a. *Overview of Findings from the 2002 National Survey on Drug Use and Health* (Office of Applied Statistics, NHSDA Series H-21, DHHS Publication No. SMA 03-3774). Rockville, MD: U.S. Department of Health and Human Services.

Substance Abuse and Mental Health Services Administration. 2003b. "Drug Free Workplace Programs." Retrieved July 31, 2003 (http://www .gov/DrugFreeWP/Legal.html).

Substance Abuse and Mental Health Services Administration. 2003c. "Benefits and Costs." Retrieved July 31, 2003 (http://www.samhsa .gov/DrugFreeWP/Benefits.html).

Substance Abuse and Mental Health Services Administration. 2008. *Results from the 2007 National Survey on Drug Use and Health: National Findings.* Rockville, MD: Author.

Substance Abuse and Mental Health Services Administration. 2010. *Results from the 2009 National Survey on Drug Use and Health: Volume I. Summary of National Findings* (Office of Applied Studies, NSDUH Series H-38A, HHS Publication No. SMA 10–4856 Findings). Rockville, MD: Author.

Substance Abuse and Mental Health Services Administration. 2011. *Results from the 2010 National Survey on Drug Use and Health: Summary of National Findings* (Office of Applied Studies, NSDUH Series H-41, HHS Publication No. (SMA) 11–4658. Rockville, MD: Author.

Sutherland, Edwin. 1939. *Principles of Criminology.* 3rd ed. Philadelphia, PA: J. B. Lippincott.

Tanner, Lindsey. 2003. "Underage Drinkers Consume 20 Percent of Booze, Study Says." *News Tribune,* February 26, p. A7.

Task Force of the National Advisory Council on Alcohol Abuse and Alcoholism. 2010. "A Snapshot of High-Risk College Drinking Consequences." Retrieved May 2, 2012 (http:// www.collegedrinkingprevention.gov/Stats Summaries/snapshot.aspx).

Tonry, Michael. 2004. "Crime." Pp. 465–79 in *Handbook of Social Problems: A Comparative International Perspective,* edited by G. Ritzer. Thousand Oaks, CA: Sage Publications.

Trevino, Roberto and Alan Richard. 2002. "Attitudes Toward Drug Legalization Among Drug Users." *American Journal of Drug and Alcohol Abuse* 28(1):91–108.

United Nations Office on Drugs and Crime (UNODC). 2006. "Who Is Doing Drugs?" Retrieved June 27, 2007 (http://www.unodc.org/ unodc/drug_demand_who.html).

United Nations Office on Drugs and Crime. 2012. *World Drug Report 2011.* New York: Author.

Unterberger, Gail. 1989. "Twelve Steps for Women Alcoholics." *Christian Century* 106(37): 1150–52.

U.S. Department of Labor. 2003. "Working Partners: Small Business Workplace Kit: Facts and Figures." Retrieved May 21, 2010 (http://www.dol.gov/asp/ programs/drugs/workingpartners/Screen15 .htm).

U.S. Department of Labor. 2007. "Workplace Substance Abuse." Retrieved May 2, 2012 (http:// www.osha.gov/SLTC/substanceabuse/index .html).

Vaughn, Christy. 2002. "Ecstasy: More Deadly Than Many Young People Know." Retrieved August 2, 2003 (http://www.health.org/newsroom/ rep/182.aspx).

Wechsler, Henry. 1996. "Alcohol and the American College Campus." *Change* 28(4):20–25.

Wechsler, Henry, George W. Dowdall, Andrea Davenport, and Sonia Castillo. 1995. "Correlates of College Student Binge Drinking." *American Journal of Public Health* 85:921–26.

Weisheit, Ralph and Kathrine Johnson. 1992. "Exploring the Dimensions of Support for Decriminalizing Drugs." *Journal of Drug Issues* 92(22):53–75.

Weitzman, Elissa, Alison Folkman, Kerry Folkman, and Henry Wechsler. 2003. "The Relationship of Alcohol Outlet Density to Heavy and Frequent Drinking and Drinking-Related Problems among College Students at Eight Universities." *Health and Place* 9:1–6.

Wheaton, Blair. 1990. "Life Transitions, Role Histories, and Mental Health." *American Sociological Review* 55:209–23.

Widom, Cathy S. and Susanne Hiller-Sturmhofel. 2001. "Alcohol Abuse as a Risk Factor for and Consequence of Child Abuse." *Alcohol Research and Health* 25(1):52–57.

Williams, Carolyn and Cheryl Perry. 1998. "Lesson From Project Northland: Preventing Alcohol Problems During Adolescence." *Alcohol Health and Research World* 22(2):107–16.

Wilsnack, Richard W. and Sharon C. Wilsnack. 1992. "Women, Work, and Alcohol: Failures of Simple Theories." *Alcoholism: Clinical and Experimental Research* 16:172–79.

Wilsnack, Sharon C., Nancy D. Vogeltanz, Albert D. Klassen, and T. Robert Harris. 1997. "Childhood Sexual Abuse and Women's Substance Abuse: National Survey Findings." *Journal of Studies on Alcohol* 58:264–71.

Winter, Greg. 2003. "Study Finds No Sign That Testing Deters Student Drug Use." *New York Times,* May 17, pp. A1, A12.

World Health Organization. 2004. *Global Status Report on Alcohol 2004.* Singapore: World Health Organization.

World Health Organization. 2007a. "Why Tobacco Is a Public Health Priority." Retrieved May 21, 2010 (http://www.who.int/tobacco/health_priority/ en/index.html).

World Health Organization. 2007b. "Cocaine." Retrieved August 8, 2007 (http://www.who.int/ substance_abuse/facts/cocaine/en).

Yamaguchi, Ryoko, Lloyd Johnston, and Patrick O'Malley. 2003. "Relationship Between Student Illicit Drug Use and School Drug-Testing Policies." *Journal of School Health* 73(4):159–64.

Ziemelis, Andris, Ronald Buckman, and Abdulaziz Elfessi. 2002. "Prevention Efforts Underlying Decreases in Binge Drinking at Institutions of Higher Education." *Journal of American College Health* 50(5):238–52.

Chapter 13

Ackerman, William V. 1998. "Socioeconomic Correlates of Increasing Crime Rates in Smaller Communities." *Professional Geographer* 50(3):372–87.

Adler, Freda. 1975. *Sisters in Crime.* New York: McGraw-Hill.

Adler, Freda, Gerhard Mueller, and William Laufer. 1991. *Criminology.* New York: McGraw-Hill.

Agnew, Robert. 1992. "Foundation for a General Strain Theory of Crime and Delinquency." *Criminology* 30:47–88.

Akers, Ronald and Christine Sellers. 2009. *Criminological Theories: Introduction and Evaluation.* Los Angeles, CA: Roxbury.

Albrecht, Hans-Jorg. 2001. "Post-adjudication Dispositions in Comparative Perspective." Pp. 293–30 in *Sentencing and Sanctions in*

Western Countries, edited by Michael Tonry and Richard Frase. New York: Oxford University Press.

Alexander, Michelle. 2010. *The New Jim Crow: Mass Incarceration in the Age of Colorblindness.* New York: New Press.

American Civil Liberties Union (ACLU). 1999. "Prisoners' Rights" (ACLU Position Paper). New York: Author.

Amnesty International. 2000. "Pregnant and Imprisoned in the United States." *Birth* 27(4):266–71.

Amnesty International. 2011. "Appalling Prison Conditions in Liberia Must Be Improved." Retrieved December 7, 2012 (http://www.amnestyusa.org/research/reports/appalling-prison-conditions-in-liberia-must-be-improved).

Amnesty International. 2012. "Death Sentences and Executions, 2011." Retrieved May 13, 2012 (http://www.amnestyusa.org/research/reports/death-sentences-and-executions-2011).

Anderson, C. 2003."Prison Populations Challenge Already Cash-Strapped States." *News Tribune,* July 28, p. A7.

Bales, William, Laura Bedard, Susan Quinn, David Ensley, and Glen Holley. 2005. "Recidivism of Public and Private State Inmates in Florida." *Criminology and Public Policy* 4(1):57–82.

Bard Prison Initiative. 2011. "What We Do." Retrieved May 15, 2012 (http://bpi.bard.edu/what-we-do/).

Barnett, Cynthia. n.d. *The Measurement of White Collar Crime Using Uniform Crime Reporting (UCR) Data.* Washington, DC: U.S. Government Printing Office.

Becker, Sarah and Jill McCorkel. 2011. "The Gender of Criminal Opportunity: The Impact of Male Co-Defenders on Women's Crime." *Feminist Criminology* 6:79–110.

Beckett, Katherine, Kris Nyrop, Lori Pfingst, and Melissa Bowen. 2005. "Drug Use, Drug Possession Arrests, and the Question of Race: Lessons from Seattle." *Social Problems* 52: 419–41.

Beckett, Katherine and Theodore Sasson. 2000. *The Politics of Injustice.* Thousand Oaks, CA: Pine Forge Press.

Bigda, Carolyn. 2001. "College Students Oppose Private Prisons." Retrieved May 17, 2010 (http://www.dollarsandsense.org/archives/2001/0901bigda.html).

Blumstein, Alfred and Richard Rosenfeld. 1998. "Explaining Recent Trends in U.S. Homicide Rates." *The Journal of Criminal Law and Criminology* 88(4):1175–216.

Bonczar, Thomas. 2003. *Prevalence of Imprisonment in the U.S. Population, 1972–2001* (NCJ 197976). Washington, DC: Bureau of Justice Statistics.

Braithwaite, John. 1989. *Crime, Shame and Reintegration.* Cambridge, England: Cambridge University Press.

Brownstein, Henry. 2001. *The Social Reality of Violence and Violent Crime.* Boston, MA: Allyn & Bacon.

Bureau of Justice Statistics. 2003a. "Crime Characteristics." Retrieved July 8, 2003 (http://www.ojp.usdoj.gov/bjs/cvict_c.htm).

Bureau of Justice Statistics. 2003c. "State and Local Law Enforcement Statistics." Retrieved July 14, 2003 (http://www.ojp.usdoj.gov/bjs/sandlle.htm).

Caldeira, Teresa and James Holston. 1999. "Democracy and Violence in Brazil." *Society for Comparative Study of Society and History* 41(4):691–729.

Camp, Scott and Gerald Gaes. 2002. "Growth and Quality of U.S. Private Prisons: Evidence From a National Survey." *Criminology and Public Policy* 1(3):427–50.

Cao, Liqun, Anthony Troy Adams, and Vickie Jensen. 2000. "The Empirical Status of the Black-Subculture-of-Violence Thesis." Pp. 47–62 in *The System in Black and White,* edited by M. Markowitz and D. Jones-Brown. Westport, CT: Praeger.

Chambliss, William. 1988. *Exploring Criminology.* New York: Macmillan.

Chesney-Lind, Meda and Lisa Pasko. 2004. *The Female Offender: Girls, Women, and Crime.* Thousand Oaks, CA: Sage Publications.

Citizens United for Alternatives to the Death Penalty. 2003a. "About CUADP." Retrieved May 17, 2010 (http://www.cuadp.org/about.html).

Citizens United for Alternatives to the Death Penalty. 2003b. "Potential Cases for Wrongful Conviction." Retrieved August 2, 2003 (http://www.cuadp.org/pris/pot.html).

Community Oriented Policing Services. 2003. "A Guide to the COPS Office." Retrieved May 17, 2010 (http://www.cops.usdoj.gov/Default.asp?Item=35).

Cooper, Alexia and Erica Smith. 2011. *Homicide Trends in the United States, 1980- 2008* (NCJ 236018). Washington, DC: Bureau of Justice Statistics.

Davis, Robert, B. Taylor, and R. Titus. 1997. "Victims as Agents: Implications for Victim Services and Crime Prevention." Pp. 167–79 in *Victims of Crime,* edited by R. Davis, A. Lurigio, and W. Skogan. Thousand Oaks, CA: Sage Publications.

Death Penalty Information Center. 2012. "Facts About the Death Penalty." Retrieved May 13, 2012 (http://www.deathpenaltyinfo.org/documents/FactSheet.pdf).

Dixon, Travis and Daniel Linz. 2000. "Over-representation and Underrepresentation of African Americans and Latinos as Lawbreakers on Television News."*Journal of Communication* 50:131–54.

Eith, Christine and Matthew Durose. 2011. *Contacts Between Police and the Public, 2008* (NCJ 234599). Washington, DC: Bureau of Justice Statistics.

Elliot, Delbert S., Suzanne Ageton, and Rachelle Canter. 1979. "An Integrated Perspective on Delinquent Behavior." *Journal of Research in Crime and Delinquency* 16:3–27.

Erickson, Kai. 1964. "Notes on the Sociology of Deviance." Pp. 9–21 in *The Other Side: Perspectives of Deviance,* edited by Howard Becker. New York: Free Press.

Federal Bureau of Investigation. 1989. *White Collar Crime: A Report to the Public.* Washington, DC: Government Printing Office.

Federal Bureau of Investigation. 2009. "Financial Crimes Report to the Public Fiscal Year 2008." Retrieved May 17, 2010 (http://www.fbi.gov/publications/financial/fcs_report2008/financial_crime_2008.htm#health).

Federal Bureau of Investigation. 2010. *Law Enforcement Officers Killed and Assaulted 2010.* Washington, DC: U.S. Department of Justice, Federal Bureau of Investigation.

Flavin, Jeanne. 2001. "Feminism for the Mainstream Criminologist: An Invitation." *Journal of Criminal Justice* 29:271–85.

Gaes, Gerald, Timothy Flannagan, Laurence Motiuk, and Lynn Stewart. 1999. "Adult Correctional Treatment." Pp. 361–426 in *Crime and Criminal Justice: A Review of Research,* Vol. 26, *Prisons,* edited by Michael Tonry and Joan Petersilia. Chicago, IL: University of Chicago Press.

Galbraith, M. Susan. 2004. "So Tell Me, Why Do Women Need Something Different?" *Journal of Religion & Spirituality in Social Work* 23:197–212.

Glaze, Lauren and Thomas Bonczar. 2009. *Probation and Parole in the United States, 2007 Statistical Tables* (NCJ 224707). Washington, DC: Bureau of Justice Statistics.

Goldstein, Herman. 1990. *Problem-Oriented Policing.* Boston, MA: McGraw-Hill.

Greene, J. R. and W. V. Pelfrey. 1997. "Shifting the Balance of Power between Police and Community: Responsibility for Crime Control." Pp. 393–423 in *Critical Issues in Policing: Contemporary Readings,* edited by R. Dunham and G. Alpert. Prospect Heights, IL: Waveland Press.

Guerino, Paul, Paige Harrison, and William Sabol. 2011. *Prisoners in 2010* (NCJ 236096). Washington, DC: Bureau of Justice Statistics.

Haney, Craig and Philip Zimbardo. 1998. "The Past and Future of U.S. Prison Policy: Twenty-five Years After the Stanford Prison Experiment." *American Psychologist* 53:709–27.

Hannon, Lance and James Defronzo. 1998. "The Truly Disadvantaged, Public Assistance, and Crime." *Social Problems* 45(3):383–92.

Harlem Live. 1999. "The Blue Nile Rites of Passage." Retrieved August 7, 2003 (http://www.bluenilepassage.org/).

Harrell, Erika and Michael Rand. 2010. *Crime Against People with Disabilities, 2008* (NCJ 231328). Washington, DC: Bureau of Justice Statistics.

Hautzinger, Sarah. 1997. "'Calling a State a State': Feminist Politics and the Policing of Violence against Women in Brazil." *Feminist Issues* 15(1):3–30.

Hautzinger, Sarah. 2002. "Criminalizing Male Violence in Brazil's Women's Police Stations: From Flawed Essentialism to Imagined Communities." *Journal of Gender Studies* 11(3):243–51.

Hemenway, David. 2004. "A Public Health Approach to Firearms Policy." Pp. 85–98 in *Policy Challenges in Modern Health Care,* edited by David Mechanic, Lynn B. Rogut, David Colby, and James Knickman. New Brunswick, NJ: Rutgers University Press.

Hirschi, Travis. 1969. *Causes of Delinquency.* Berkeley: University of California Press.

Huggins, M. 1997. "From Bureaucratic Consolidation to Structural Devolution: Police Death Squads in Brazil." *Policing and Society* 7:207–34.

Human Rights Watch. 1995. "Global Report on Women's Human Rights 1990 to 1995." Retrieved July 30, 2003 (http://www.hrw.org/about/projects/womrep/General-187.htm#P2966_897325).

Human Rights Watch. 1997. *Police Brutality in Urban Brazil.* Retrieved May 18, 2010 (http://www.hrw.org/reports/1997/brazil/).

Human Rights Watch. 1997. *Punishment and Prejudice: Racial Disparities in the War on Drugs.* New York: Human Rights Watch.

Human Rights Watch. 2000. *The Impact of the War on Drugs on U.S. Incarceration.* New York: Human Rights Watch.

Human Rights Watch. 2009. "Lethal Force: Police Violence and Public Security in Rio de Janeiro and Sao Paulo." Retrieved February 16, 2010 (http://www.hrw.org/en/node/86987/section/1).

Human Rights Watch. 2012. *Old Behind Bars: The Aging Prison Population in the United States.* New York: Author.

Innocence Project. 2007a. "What Is the Innocence Project?" Retrieved May 18, 2010 (http://www.innocenceproject.org/Content/9.php).

Innocence Project. 2007b. "Byron Halsey Is Fully Exonerated in New Jersey After DNA Proves His Innocence in 1985 Child Rapes and Murders." Retrieved May 18, 2010 (http://www.innocenceproject.org/Content/689.php).

Irwin, Darrell. 2002. "Alternatives to Delinquency in Harlem: A Study of Faith-Based Community Mentoring." *Justice Professional* 15(2):29–36.

Jensen, Vickie. 2001. *Why Women Kill: Homicide and Gender Equality.* Boulder, CO: Lynne Rienner.

Joseph, J. 2000. "Overrepresentation of Minority Youth in the Juvenile Justice System: Discrimination or Disproportionality of Delinquent Acts? Status of the Black-Subculture-of-Violence Thesis." Pp. 227–40 in *The System in Black and White,* edited by M. Markowitz and D. Jones-Brown. Westport, CT: Praeger.

Justice Policy Institute. 2008. "Substance Abuse Treatment and Public Safety." Retrieved May 18, 2010 (http://www.justicepolicy.org/images/upload/08_01_REP_DrugTx_AC-PS.pdf).

Kappeler, Victor, Mark Blumberg, and Gary Potter. 2000. *The Mythologies of Crime and Criminal Justice.* Prospect Heights, IL: Waveland Press.

Kaufman, Joanne, Cesar Rebellon, Sherod Thaxton, and Robert Agnew. 2008. "A General Strain Theory of Racial Differences in Criminal Offending." *Australian and New Zealand Journal of Criminology* 41:421–37.

Klaus, Patsy A. 2004. *Crime and the Nation's Households, 2002* (Bureau of Justice Statistics Bulletin, NCJ 201797). Washington, DC: U.S. Department of Justice, Office of Justice Programs.

LaFree, Gary and Gwen Hunnicutt. 2006. "Female and Male Homicide Victimization Trends." Pp. 195–239 in *Gender and Crime: Patterns of Victimization and Offending,* edited by K. Heimer and C. Krusttschnitt. New York: New York University Press.

Langan, Patrick and David Levin. 2002. *Recidivism of Prisoners Released in 1994* (NCJ 193427). Washington, DC: U.S. Department of Justice, Office of Justice Programs.

Larason Schneider, A. 1999. "Public-Private Partnerships in the U.S. Prison System." *American Behavioral Scientist* 43(1):192–208.

Laub, John. 1983. "Urbanism, Race, and Crime." *Journal of Research of Crime and Delinquency* 20:183–98.

Laub, John. 1997. "Patterns of Criminal Victimization in the United States." Pp. 9–26 in *Victims of Crime,* edited by R. Davis, A. Lurigio, and W. Skogan. Thousand Oaks, CA: Sage Publications.

Lemert, Edwin M. 1967. *Human Deviance, Social Problems, and Social Control.* Englewood Cliffs, NJ: Prentice Hall.

Liska, Allen. 1992. *Social Threat and Social Control.* Albany: SUNY Press.

MacDonald, J. 2002. "The Effectiveness of Community Policing in Reducing Urban Violence." *Crime and Delinquency* 48(4):592–618.

Malik, Nazneen. 2005. "The Bard College Prison Initiative." *Education Update* 10(9):19.

Mitchell, Michael and Charles Wood. 1999. "Ironies of Citizenship: Skin Color, Police Brutality, and the Challenge of Democracy in Brazil." *Social Forces* 77(3):1001–20.

Moore, Mark. 1999. "Security and Community Development." Pp. 293–337 in *Urban Problems and Community Development,* edited by R. F. Ferguson and W. T. Dickens. Washington, DC: Brookings Institution.

Moore, Solomon. 2007. "States Export Their Inmates as Prisons Fill." *New York Times,* July 31, pp. A1, A14.

Moore, Solomon. 2009. "Hispanics Are Largest Ethnic Group in Federal Prisons, Study Shows." *New York Times,* February 19, p. A16.

Morash, Merry, Timothy Byrum, and Barbara Koons. 1998. *Women Offenders: Programming Needs and Promising Practices.* Washington, DC: National Institute of Justice.

Morenoff, Jeffrey. 2005. "Racial and Ethnic Disparities in Crime in the United States." Pp. 139–73 in *Ethnicity and Causal Mechanisms,* edited by M. Rutter and M. Tienda. New York: Cambridge University Press.

Naffine, Ngaire. 1996. *Feminism and Criminology.* Philadelphia, PA: Temple University Press.

National Night Out. 2003. "The History of NATW and National Night Out." Retrieved May 18, 2010 (http://www.nationaltownwatch.org/nno/history.html).

National White Collar Crime Center. 2010. *NW3C Annual Report 2009–2010.* Glen Allen, VA: Author.

Norris, Clive, Nigel Fielding, Clark Kemp, and Jane Fielding. 1992. "Black and Blue: An Analysis of the Influence on Being Stopped by the Police." *British Journal of Sociology* 43(2):207–24.

Novak, Kenneth, Leanne Alarid, and Wayne Lucas. 2003. "Exploring Officers' Acceptance of Community Policing: Implications for Policy Implementation." *Journal of Criminal Justice* 31:57–71.

Office on Violence Against Women. 2010. "About the Office." Retrieved May 18, 2010 (http://www.ovw.usdoj.gov/overview.htm).

Pew Center on the States. 2011. *State of Recidivism: The Revolving Door of America's Prisons.* Washington, DC: Pew Charitable Trusts.

Pratt, Travis and Jeff Maahs. 1999. "Are Private Prisons More Cost-Effective Than Public Prisons? A Meta-Analysis of Evaluation Research Studies." *Crime and Delinquency* 45(3):358–71.

Puzzanchera, Charles. 2009. *Juvenile Arrests 2008.* Retrieved May 18, 2010 (http://www.ncjrs.gov/pdffiles1/ojjdp/228479.pdf).

Radalet, Michael and Glenn Pierce. 2005. "The Impact of Legally Inappropriate Factors on Death Sentencing for California Homicides 1990–1999." *Santa Clara Law Review* 49:1–47.

Reaves, Brian. 2011. *Census of State and Local Law Enforcement Agencies, 2008* (NCJ 233982). Washington, DC: Bureau of Justice Statistics.

Reiman, Jeffrey. 1998. *The Rich Get Richer and the Poor Get Prison.* Boston, MA: Allyn & Bacon.

Rich, John and Marguerite Ro. 2002. *A Poor Man's Plight: Uncovering the Disparity in Men's Health.* Battle Creek, MI: W. K. Kellogg Foundation.

Rosen, Jeffrey. 2010. "Could Keeping Convicts From Violating Probation or Their Terms of Release Be the Answer to Prison Overcrowding?" *New York Times Magazine,* January 10, pp. 36–39.

Roth, Jeffrey and Joseph Ryan. 2000. "The COPS Program After 4 Years—National Evaluation." Retrieved May 18, 2010 (http://www.ncjrs.gov/pdffiles1/nij/183644.pdf).

Sabol, William, Heather West, and Matthew Cooper. 2009. *Prisoners in 2008* (NCJ 228417). Washington, DC: U.S. Department of Justice, Office of Justice Programs.

Sampson, Robert J. and William Julius Wilson. 1995. "Towards a Theory of Race, Crime, and Urban Inequality." Pp. 37–54 in *Crime and Inequality,* edited by John Hagen and Ruth Peterson. Palo Alto, CA: Stanford University Press.

Sanders, W. 1981. *Juvenile Delinquency: Causes, Patterns, and Reactions.* New York: Holt, Rinehart and Winston.

Savage, Charlie. 2012. "U.S. to Expand Its Definition of Rape in Statistics." *New York Times,* January 7, pp. A10, A15.

Simon, Thomas, James Mercy, and Craig Perkins. 2001. *Injuries from Violent Crime, 1992–1998* (NCJ 168633). Washington, DC: U.S. Department of Justice, Office of Justice Programs.

Snell, Tracy. 2011. *Capital Punishment, 2010* (NCJ 236510). Washington, DC: Bureau of Justice Statistics.

Stafford, Mark C. 2004. "Juvenile Delinquency." Pp. 480–93 in *Handbook of Social Problems: A Comparative International Perspective,* edited by George Ritzer. Thousand Oaks, CA: Sage Publications.

Steffensmeier, Darrell and Emilie Allan. 1996. "Gender and Crime: Toward a Gendered Theory of Female Offending." *Annual Review of Sociology* 22:459–87.

Stephan, James. 2004. *State Prison Expenditures, 2001* (NCJ 202949). Washington, DC: U.S.

Department of Justice, Bureau of Justice Statistics.

Stoutland, Sara. 2001. "The Multiple Dimensions of Trust in Resident/Police Relations in Boston." *Journal of Research in Crime and Delinquency* 38(3):226–56.

Subcommittee on Civil and Constitutional Rights, Committee on the Judiciary. 1994. "Racial Disparities in Federal Death Penalty Prosecutions 1988–1994." Retrieved May 18, 2010 (http://www.deathpenaltyinfo.org/article.php?scid=45&did=528).

Sutherland, Edwin H. 1949. *White Collar Crime.* New York: Dryden Press.

Tonry, Michael. 2004. "Crime." Pp. 465–79 in *Handbook of Social Problems: A Comparative International Perspective,* edited by George Ritzer. Thousand Oaks, CA: Sage Publications.

Tonry, Michael and David P. Farrington. 1995. "Strategic Approaches to Crime Prevention." Pp. 1–20 in *Crime and Justice: A Review of Research.* Vol. 19, *Building a Safer Society—Strategic Approaches to Crime Prevention,* edited by Michael Tonry and David P. Farrington. Chicago, IL: University of Chicago Press.

Travis, Jeremy and Sarah Lawrence. 2002. *California's Parole Experiment.* Washington, DC: The Urban Institute.

Truman, Jennifer. 2011. *Criminal Victimization, 2010* (NCJ 235505). Washington, DC: U.S. Department of Justice, Bureau of Justice Statistics.

Turk, Austin. 1969. *Criminality and Legal Order.* Chicago, IL: Rand McNally.

Turk, Austin. 1976. "Law as a Weapon in Social Conflict." *Social Problems* 23:276–91.

U.S. Congress. 2002. "Public Law 107-273, Title II Juvenile Justice." Retrieved May 18, 2010 (http://ojjdp.ncjrs.org/about/PL_107_273.html).

U.S. Department of Justice. 2002. "DOJ Seal—History and Motto." Retrieved May 18, 2010 (http://www.usdoj.gov/jmd/ls/dojseal.htm).

Walmsley, Roy. 2006. "World Female Imprisonment List." Retrieved February 25, 2007 (http://www.kcl.ac.uk/depsta/rel/icps/women-prison-list-2006.pdf).

Walmsley, Roy. 2011. "World Prison Population List." Retrieved May 10, 2012 (http://www.idcr.org.uk/wp-content/uploads/2010/09/WPPL-9–22.pdf).

Walsh, Anthony and Lee Ellis. 2007. *Criminology: An Interdisciplinary Approach.* Thousand Oaks, CA: Sage Publications.

Wilson, William Julius. 1996. *When Work Disappears: The World of the New Urban Poor.* New York: Knopf.

Wolf, J. 2000. "War Games Meets the Internet: Chasing 21st Century Cybercriminals with Old Laws and Little Money." *American Journal of Criminal Law* 28:95–117.

Wolfgang, Marvin and Franco Ferracuti. 1967. *The Subculture of Violence: Towards an Integrated Theory in Criminology.* New York: Tavistock.

World Health Organization. 2005. *WHO Multi-country Study on Women's Health and Domestic Partner Violence Against Women: Summary Report of Initial Results on Prevalence, Health Outcomes and Women's Responses.* Geneva, Switzerland: World Health Organization.

Zhao, Jihong, Matthew Scheider, and Quint Thurman. 2002. "Funding Community Policing to Reduce Crime: Have COPS Grants Made a Difference?" *Criminology and Public Policy* 2(1):7–32.

Chapter 14

Appleton, Lynn M. 1995. "The Gender Regimes in American Cities." Pp. 44–59 in *Gender in Urban Research,* edited by J. A. Garber and R. S. Turner. Thousand Oaks, CA: Sage Publications.

Banerjee, Tridib and William C. Baer. 1984. *Beyond the Neighborhood Unit: Residential Environments and Public Policy.* New York: Plenum Press.

Boddy, Sharon. 2000. "Car-Free and Carefree." *E Magazine* 11(2):14–18.

Bunce, Harold, Sue George Neal, William Reeder, and Ronald J. Sepanik. 1996. *New Trends in American Homeownership.* Washington, DC: U.S. Department of Housing and Urban Development.

Choi, Namkee G. and Lidia J. Snyder. 1999. *Homeless Families With Children: A Subjective Experience of Homelessness.* New York: Springer.

Clark, William A. V., Marinus C. Deurloo, and Frans M. Dieleman. 2000. "Housing Consumption and Residential Crowding in U.S. Housing Markets." *Journal of Urban Affairs* 22(1):49–64.

Cohen, Hillel W. and Mary E. Northridge. 2000. "Getting Political: Racism and Urban Health." *American Journal of Public Health* 90(6):841–43.

Corvin, A. 2001. "Urban Sprawl Creates Belly Sprawl, CDC Suggests." *News Tribune,* November 2, p. A11.

Crenson, Matt. 2003. "He Wants to Reclaim Towns for Pedestrians." *Christian Science Monitor,* October 15. Retrieved May 22, 2010 (http://www.csmonitor.com/2003/1015/p13s02-lihc.html).

de Pommereau, Isabelle. 2006. "New German Community Models for Car-Free Living." *Christian Science Monitor* 99(18):1, 11.

Desai, Sonalde. 2004. "Population Change." Pp. 69–86 in *Handbook of Social Problems: A Comparative International Perspective,* edited by G. Ritzer. Thousand Oaks, CA: Sage Publications.

Dickerson, Niki. 2008. "Occupational and Residential Segregation: The Confluence of Two Systems of Inequality." *Labor Studies Journal* 33:393–411.

Donadio, Rachel. 2009. "Mock Funeral for Venice Dramatizes Flight of Residents From City's Heart." *New York Times,* November 15, p. 10.

Dreier, Peter. 1996. "America's Urban Crisis: Symptoms, Causes, and Solutions." Pp. 79–141 in *Race, Poverty, and American Cities,* edited by J. C. Boger and J. W. Wegner. Chapel Hill: University of North Carolina Press.

Dretzka, G. 1995. "Filling Void, Real and Symbolic Ex-Laker 'Magic,' Sony Bring First-Run Movies, Hope to South-Central L.A." *Chicago Tribune,* July 21, Business section, p. 1.

Drew, Bettina. 1998. *Crossing the Expendable Landscape.* St. Paul, MN: Graywolf Press.

Eisenhower, Dwight. 1963. *Mandate for Change 1953–1956.* Garden City, NY: Doubleday.

Evans, Gary W., Susan Saegert, and Rebecca Harris. 2001. "Residential Density and Psychological Health among Children in Low-Income Families." *Environment and Behavior* 33(2):165–80.

Ewing, Reed, Rolf Pendall, and Don Chen. 2002. *Measuring Urban Sprawl and Its Impact.* Washington, DC: Smart Growth America.

Fair Housing Law. 2004. "About Fair Housing Campaign." Retrieved February 28, 2004 (http://www.civilrights.org/fairhousing/laws).

Feagin, Joe R. 1998a. "Introduction." Pp. 1–24 in *The New Urban Paradigm,* edited by J. R. Feagin. Lanham, MD: Rowman & Littlefield.

Feagin, Joe R. 1998b. "Urban Real Estate Speculation." Pp. 133–58 in *The New Urban Paradigm,* edited by J. R. Feagin. Lanham, MD: Rowman & Littlefield.

Freeman, Lance. 2002. "America's Affordable Housing Crisis: A Contract Unfulfilled." *American Journal of Public Health* 92(5):709–13.

French, Howard. 2007. "Big, Gritty Chongquing, City of 12 Million Is China's Model for Future." *New York Times,* June 1, p. A13.

Garber, Judith A. and Robyne S. Turner. 1995. "Introduction." Pp. x–xxvi in *Gender in Urban Research,* edited by J. A. Garber and R. S. Turner. Thousand Oaks, CA: Sage Publications.

Gordon, John S. 2001. "The Business of America." *American Heritage* 52(4):6–59.

Gottdiener, Mark. 1977. *Planned Sprawl: Private and Public Interests in Suburbia.* Beverly Hills, CA: Sage Publications.

Hanlon, James. 2011. "Unslightly Urban Menaces and the Rescaling of Residential Segregation in the United States." *Journal of Urban History* 37:732–56.

Institute for Government Innovation. 2000. "Awards Recipients: Hope VI Mixed Finance Public Housing." Retrieved May 22, 2010 (http://www.innovations.harvard.edu/awards.html?id=3853).

Johnson, Roy S. 2003. "It Must Be Magic." *Savoy,* February, pp. 70–71, 72–78, 80.

Johnson, William A. 2007. "Sprawl and Civil Rights: A Mayor's Reflections." Pp. 103–23 in *Growing Smarter: Achieving Livable Communities, Environmental Justice and Regional Equity,* edited by R. Bullard. Cambridge, MA: MIT Press.

Judd, Dennis and Todd Swanstrom. 2004. *City Politics: Private Power and Public Policy.* Lebanon, IN: Addison-Wesley.

Karp, David, Greg Stone, and William Yoels. 1991. *Being Urban: A Sociology of City Life.* London, England: Greenwood.

Kennedy, Maureen and Paul Leonard. 2001. "Dealing With Neighborhood Change: A Primer on Gentrification and Policy Choices" (Discussion paper). Washington, DC: Brookings Institution Center on Urban and Metropolitan Policy and Policy Link.

Kim, Chigon and Mark Gottdiener. 2004. "Urban Problems in Global Problems." Pp. 172–92 in *Handbook of Social Problems: A Comparative International Perspective,* edited by G. Ritzer. Thousand Oaks, CA: Sage Publications.

Krieger, James and Donna L. Higgins. 2002. "Housing and Health: Time Again for Public Health Action." *American Journal of Public Health* 92(5):758–68.

Leinberger, Christopher. 2012. "Now Coveted: A Walkable, Convenient Place." *New York Times,* May 27, pp. 6–7.

Leinberger, Christopher and Mariela Alfonzo. 2012. *Walk This Way: The Economic Promise of Walkable Places in Metropolitan Washington, D.C.* Washington, DC: Brookings Institution.

Magin, Janis. 2006. "For 1,000 or More Homeless in Hawaii, Beaches Are the Best Option." *New York Times,* December 5, p. A16.

Mahoney, Martha. 1997. "The Social Construction of Whiteness." Pp. 330–33 in *Critical White Studies: Looking Behind the Mirror,* edited by R. Delgado and J. Stefanic. Philadelphia, PA: Temple University Press.

Martinez, S. 2000. "The Housing Act of 1949: Its Place in the Realization of the American Dream of Homeownership." *Housing Policy Debate* 11(2):467–87.

Massey, Douglas. 2001. "Residential Segregation and Neighborhood Conditions on U.S. Metropolitan Areas." Pp. 391–434 in *America Becoming: Racial Trends and Their Consequences,* Vol. 1, edited by N. Smelser, W. J. Wilson, and F. Mitchell. Washington, DC: National Academy Press.

Massey, Douglas and Mitchell Eggers. 1993. "The Spatial Concentration of Affluence and Poverty during the 1970s." *Urban Affairs Quarterly* 29(2):299–315.

Masson, D. 1984. "Les Femmes dans les Structures Urbanies: Apercu d'un Nouveau Champ de Recherché." *Canadian Journal of Political Science* 17:753–82.

McKenzie, Brian and Melanie Rapino. 2011. *Commuting in the United States: 2009* (ACS-15). Washington, DC: U.S. Census Bureau.

Molotch, H. 1976. "The City as a Growth Machine." *American Journal of Sociology* 82:309–32.

Murphy, Dean E. 2003."New Californian Identity Predicted by Researchers." *New York Times,* February 17, p. A13.

Myers, Dowell and Seong Woo Lee. 1996. "Immigration Cohorts and Residential Overcrowding in Southern California." *Demography* 33:51–65.

Naparstek, Arthur, Susan Freis, G. Thomas Kingsley, Dennis Dooley, and Howard Lewis. 2000. *Hope VI: Community Building Makes a Difference.* Washington, DC: U.S. Department of Housing and Urban Development.

National Coalition for the Homeless. 2002. "How Many People Experience Homelessness?" Retrieved June 10, 2003 (http://www.nationalhomeless.org/factsheets/How_Many.html).

National Low Income Housing Coalition. 2007. *Why the National Housing Trust Fund Primarily Targets the Lowest Income Renters.* Washington, DC: Author.

Norris, Tyler. 2001. "Civic Gemstones: The Emergent Communities Movement." *National Civic Review* 90(4):307–18.

Ohlemacher, Stephen. 2007. "In Nation of Sprawl, We're All Just Single Dots in Our Cars." *News Tribune,* June 14, p. A3.

Oliver, Melvin. 2003. "American Dream? How Government Initiatives Made Blacks House Poor." *The New Crisis* 110(5):17–19.

Pastor, M. 2001. "Geography and Opportunity." Pp. 435–68 in *America Becoming: Racial Trends and Their Consequences,* Vol. 1, edited by N. J. Smelser, W. J. Wilson, and F. Mitchell. Washington, DC: National Academy Press.

Perry, Marc. 2006. *Domestic Net Migration in the United States: 2000 to 2004* (Current Population Reports, P25-1135). Washington, DC: U.S. Census Bureau.

Powell, John. 2007. "Race, Poverty and Urban Sprawl: Access to Opportunities through Regional Strategies." Pp. 51–71 in *Growing Smarter: Achieving Livable Communities, Environmental Justice and Regional Equity,* edited by R. Bullard. Cambridge, MA: MIT Press.

Pugh, Tony. 2007. "Housing Bleaker for Nation's Poor, Study Finds." *News Tribune,* July 15, p. A13.

Rast, J. 2001. "Manufacturing Industrial Decline: The Politics of Economic Change in Chicago, 1955–1998." *Journal of Urban Affairs* 23(2):175–90.

Roberts, Sam. 2007. "New Demographic Racial Gap Emerges." *New York Times,* May 17, p. A19.

Rosenthal, Elisabeth. 2012. "Nigeria's Population Is Soaring in Preview of a Global Problem." *New York Times,* April 15, pp. 1, 12.

Rossi, Peter. 1989. *Down and Out in America: The Origins of Homelessness.* Chicago, IL: University of Chicago Press.

Savage, Howard A. 1999. *Who Could Afford to Buy a House in 1995?* (U.S. Census Bureau Current Housing Reports, H121/99-1). Washington, DC: U.S. Census Bureau.

Schachter, J. 2004. *Geographical Mobility: 2002 to 2003* (Current Population Reports, P20-549). Washington, DC: U.S. Census Bureau.

Siddiqui, Roomana and Janak Pandey. 2003. "Coping with Environmental Stressors by Urban Slum Dwellers." *Environment and Behavior* 35: 589–604.

Simmel, Georg. 1997. "The Metropolis and Mental Life." Pp. 174–86 in *Simmel on Culture: Selected Writings,* edited by D. Frisby and M. Featherstone. London, England: Sage Publications. (Original work published 1903)

Smith, Eric L. 1999. "The Magic Touch." *Black Enterprise,* May, pp. 74–82.

Smith, Neil. 1986. "Gentrification, the Frontier, and the Restructuring of Urban Space." Pp. 15–34 in *Gentrification of the City,* edited by N. Smith and P. Williams. Boston, MA: Allen and Unwin.

Smith, Neil. 2002. "New Globalism, New Urbanism: Gentrification as Global Urban Strategy." *Antipode* 34(3):427–50.

Stanback, Thomas M., Jr. 1991. *The New Suburbanization: Challenge to the Central City.* Boulder, CO: Westview Press.

Stein, Rob. 2003. "Waistlines Sprawl With Suburbs, Study Finds." *News Tribune,* August 29, p. A3.

Stock, Mathis. 2006. "European Cities: Toward a Recreational Turn?" *Studies in Culture, Polity and Identities* 7(1):1–19.

Suro, Roberto and Audrey Singer. 2002. *Latino Growth in Metropolitan America: Changing Patterns, New Locations* (Brookings Institution Center on Urban and Metropolitan Policy and Pew Hispanic Center, Survey Series). Washington, DC: Brookings Institution.

Toro, Paul. 2007. "Toward an International Understanding of Homelessness." *Journal of Social Issues* 63(3):461–81.

Turner, Robyne S. 1995. "Concern for Gender in Central-City Development." Pp. 271–88 in *Gender in Urban Research,* edited by J. A. Garber and R. S. Turner. Thousand Oaks, CA: Sage Publications.

Turner, M. A., S. L. Ross, G. Galster, and J. Yinger. 2002. *Discrimination in Metropolitan Housing Markets: National Results from Phase 1 HDS 2000.* Washington, DC: Urban Institute and U.S. Department of Housing and Urban Development.

United Nations, Department of Economic and Social Affairs. 2011. "World Urbanization Prospects, the 2011 Revision." Retrieved May 18, 2012 (http://esa.un.org/unpd/wup/CD-ROM/Urban-Rural-Population.htm).

United Nations Population Division. 2006. "Fact Sheet 7: Mega-Cities." Retrieved June 6, 2010 (http://www.un.org/esa/population/publications/WUP2005/2005WUP_FS7.pdf).

United Nations Population Fund. 1996. *The State of World Population: Changing Places: Population, Development and the Urban Future.* New York: Author.

United Nations Population Fund. 2007. *The State of World Population: Unleashing the Potential of Urban Growth.* New York: Author.

U.S. Census Bureau. 1995. "Urban and Rural Populations 1900 to 1990." Retrieved May 21, 2010 (http://www.census.gov/population/censusdata/urpop0090.txt).

U.S. Census Bureau. 2005. "Americans Spend More Than 100 Hours Commuting to Work Each Year."

Retrieved October 12, 2007 (http://www.census .gov/Press-Release/www/releases/archives/ american_community_survey_acs/004489 .html).

U.S. Census Bureau. 2007. *Statistical Abstract of the United States*. Washington, DC: Author.

U.S. Census Bureau. 2010. *Statistical Abstract of the United States*. Washington, DC: Author.

U.S. Census Bureau. 2012a. "Housing Vacancies and Homeownership, Annual Statistics: 2011." Retrieved May 28, 2012 (http://www.census.gov/housing/ hvs/).

U.S. Census Bureau. 2012b. "Most Children Younger Than Age 1 Are Minorities, Census Bureau Reports." Retrieved December 10, 2012 (http:// www.census.gov/newsroom/releases/archives/ population/cb12-90.html).

U.S. Census Bureau. 2012c. *Statistical Abstract of the United States*. Washington, DC: Author.

U.S. Conference of Mayors. 2011. *Hunger and Homelessness Survey: A Status Report on Hunger and Homelessness in America's Cities, A 29 City Survey*. Washington, DC: Author.

U.S. Department of Energy. 2010. "Fact #618: April 12, 2010, Vehicles per Household and Other Demographic Statistics." Retrieved May 17, 2012 (http://www1.eere.energy.gov/vehiclesandfuels/ facts/2010_fotw618.html).

U.S. Department of Housing and Urban Development. 1999. "The State of Cities, 1999." Retrieved May 22, 2010 (http://www.huduser.org/ publications/polleg/tsoc99/summ-03.html).

U.S. Department of Housing and Urban Development. 2003a. "About HOPE VI." Retrieved May 22, 2010 (http://www.hud.gov:80/ offices/pih/programs/ph/hope6/about/index .cfm).

U.S. Department of Housing and Urban Development. 2003b."HUD's History." Retrieved March 11, 2003 (http://portal.hud.gov/portal/ page/portal/HUD/about/hud_history).

U.S. Department of Housing and Urban Development. 2003c. "Welcome to the Community Renewal Initiative." Retrieved June 24, 2004 (http://www.hud.gov/offices/cpd/economic development/programs/rc/index.cfm).

U.S. Department of Housing and Urban Development. 2009. "About HOPE VI." Retrieved May 22, 2010 (http://www.hud.gov/offices/pih/ programs/ph/hope6/about/index.cfm#4b).

U.S. Department of Housing and Urban Development. 2011. *The 2010 Annual Homeless Assessment Report to Congress*. Washington, DC: Author.

Wilborn, P. 2002. "Magic Johnson Now Winning at Business; Politics Could Be Next." *Cincinnati Enquirer On Line Edition*, May 26. Retrieved October 8, 2002 (http://enquirer.com/editions/ 2002/05/26/spt_Magic_ johnson_now .html).

Williams, Donald C. 2000. *Urban Sprawl: A Reference Handbook*. Santa Barbara, CA: ABC-CLIO.

Williams, Laura. 2012. *Housing Landscape 2012*. Washington, DC: Center for Housing Policy.

Women's International Network News. 1999. "Women and the Urban Environment." *Women's International Network News* 25(1):60–61.

Wood, Daniel. 2007. "On the Rise in American Cities: The Car-Free Zone." *Christian Science Monitor* 99(109):1, 12.

Chapter 15

American Rivers. 2002. "63 Dams in 16 States to Be Removed in 2002." Retrieved August 16, 2003 (http://www.amrivers.org/pressrelease/ damremova1071802.htm).

Arkansas Wildlife Federation. 2003a. "About the Arkansas Wildlife Federation." Retrieved May 18, 2010 (http://www.arkansaswildlifefederation .org/history.html).

Arkansas Wildlife Federation. 2003b. "Arkansas Wildlife Federation Education Projects." Retrieved May 18, 2010 (http://www.arkansaswildlife federation.org/programs/education.html).

Babbitt, Bruce. 1998. "Speech to the Ecological Society of America, August 4, 1998." Retrieved August 16, 2003 (http://www.hetchhetchy.org/ babbitt_on_dams_9_4-98.html).

Barcott, Bruce. 2003. "What's a River For?" *Mother Jones* 28(3):44–51.

Blacksmith Institute. 2007. *The World's Most Polluted Places*. New York: Author.

Blumenthal, Ralph. 2006. "Texas Lawsuit Includes a Mix of Race and Water." *New York Times*, July 9, p. 11.

Breton, Mary Joy. 1998. *Women Pioneers for the Environment*. Boston, MA: Northeastern University Press.

Broder, John. 2007. "Governors Join in Creating Regional Pacts on Climate Change." *New York Times*, November 15, p. A16.

Broder, John. 2010. "Climate Goal Is Supported by China and India." *New York Times*, March 10, p. A9.

Broder, John and Marjorie Connelly. 2007. "Public Says Warming Is a Problem, but Remains Split on Response." *New York Times*, April 27, p. A23.

Bullard, Robert. 1994. *Dumping in Dixie: Race, Class, and Environmental Quality*. Boulder, CO: Westview Press.

Cable, Sherry and Charles Cable. 1995. *Environmental Problems, Grassroots Solutions: The Politics of Grassroots Environmental Conflict*. New York: St. Martin's.

Caldwell, Lynton C. 1970. *Environment: Challenge to Modern Society*. Garden City, NY: Natural History Press.

Caldwell, Lynton C. 1997. "Environment as a Problem for Policy." P. 118 in *Environmental Policy: Transnational Issues and National Trends,* edited by L. Caldwell and R. Bartlett. Westport, CT: Quorum Books.

Carbon Dioxide Information Analysis Center. 2010. "Record High 2010 Global Carbon Dioxide Emissions from Fossil-Fuel Combustion and Cement Manufacture Posted on CDIAC Site." Retrieved June 14, 2012 (http://cdiac.ornl.gov/ trends/emis/prelim_2009_2010_estimates .html).

Casey, Michael. 2007. "World's Reliance on Coal Leaves Environmental Mess." *News Tribune*, November 5, p. A5.

Caulfield, Henry. 1989. "The Conservation and Environmental Movements: A Historical Analysis." Pp. 13–56 in *Environmental Politics and Policy,* edited by J. Lester. Durham, NC: Duke University Press.

Center for Health, Environment, and Justice. 2001. *Poisoned Schools: Invisible Threats, Visible Actions*. Falls Church, VA: Child Proofing Our Communities Campaign.

Center for Health, Environment, and Justice. 2005. *Building Safe Schools: Invisible Threats, Visible Actions*. Falls Church, VA: Child Proofing Our Communities Campaign.

Choi, Charles. 2011. "Mega-quakes and Mega-disasters: Will US Heed Wake-up Call in Japan?" Retrieved June 14, 2012 (http://www.csmonitor .com/Science/2011/0328/Mega-quakes-and-mega-disasters-Will-US-heed-wake-up-call-in-Japan).

Clean Air Network. 2003. *Danger in the Air: Unhealthy Levels of Smog in 2002*. Washington, DC: U.S. Public Interest Research Group Education Fund.

Davies, J. Clarence. 1970. *The Politics of Pollution*. New York: Pegasus.

Deutsch, Claudia. 2007. "College Leaders Push for Carbon Neutrality." *New York Times,* June 13, p. A21.

Diamond, Jared. 2009. "Will Big Business Save the Earth?" *New York Times,* December 6, p. I2.

Dunlap, Riley. 1997. "The Evolution of Environmental Sociology: A Brief History and Assessment of the American Experience." Pp. 21–39 in *The International Handbook of Environmental Sociology,* edited by M. R. Redclift and G. Woodgate. Cheltenham, England: Edward Elgar.

Dunlap, Riley and William Catton. 1994. "Struggling with Human Exemptionalism: The Rise, Decline, and Revitalization of Environmental Sociology." *American Sociologist* 25(1):5–30.

Dunlap, Riley and Angela Mertig. 1992. *American Environmentalism: The U.S. Environmental*

Movement, 1970–1990. Washington, DC: Taylor & Francis.

Earth Island Institute. 2009. "2009 Award Winners." Retrieved June 14, 2012 (http://www.broweryouthawards.org/userdata_display.php?modin=50&uid=7043).

Earth Island Institute. 2010. "About Us." May 18, 2010 (http://www.earthisland.org/index.php/aboutUs/).

Ehrlich, Paul and Anne Ehrlich. 1990. *The Population Explosion.* New York: Touchstone/Simon & Schuster.

Ehrlich, Paul and Anne Ehrlich. 1996. *Betrayal of Science and Reason: How Anti-environmental Rhetoric Threatens Our Future.* Washington, DC: Island Press.

Ehrlich, Paul, Anne Ehrlich, and John Holdren. 1973. *Human Ecology: Problems and Solutions.* San Francisco, CA: W. H. Freeman.

Eisele, K. 2003. "With Every Breath You Take." Retrieved May 18, 2010 (http://www.nrdc.org/onearth/03win/asthma1.asp).

Engelman, Robert. 2009. "Population Sustainability." *Scientific American Earth 3.0* 19:22–29.

Environmental Protection Agency. 1999. *Smog—Who Does It Hurt? What You Need to Know About Ozone and Your Health* (EPA-452/ K-99-001). Washington, DC: Author.

Environmental Protection Agency. 2003a. "EPA Announces $73.1 Million in National Brownfields Grants in 37 States and Seven Tribal Communities." Retrieved August 26, 2003 (http://www.epa.gov/brownfields/news/pr062003.htm).

Environmental Protection Agency. 2003b. *Water on Tap: What You Need to Know.* Washington, DC: Author.

Environmental Protection Agency. 2004. "About EPA." Retrieved May 18, 2010 (http://www.epa.gov/epahome/aboutepa.htm).

Environmental Protection Agency. 2007a. "Particulate Matter." Retrieved May 18, 2010 (http://www.epa.gov/air/particles/index.html).

Environmental Protection Agency. 2007b. *Complete Assessment Needed to Ensure Rural Texas Community Has Safe Drinking Water* (Report No. 2007-P-00034). Washington, DC: Author.

Environmental Protection Agency. 2007c. "State Actions." Retrieved October 24, 2007 (http://www.epa.gov/climatechange/wycd/statean dlocalgov/state.html).

Environmental Protection Agency. 2009a. "Water on Tap: A Consumer's Guide to the Nation's Drinking Water." Retrieved May 18, 2010 (http://www.epa.gov/safewater/wot/pdfs/book_waterontap_full.pdf).

Environmental Protection Agency. 2009b. "Endangerment and Cause or Contribute Findings for Greenhouse Gases under Section 202(a) of the Clean Air Act." Retrieved May 27, 2010 (http://www.epa.gov/climatechange/endangerment.html).

Environmental Protection Agency. 2010. *Our Nation's Air: Status and Trends Through 2008.* Washington, DC: Author.

Environmental Protection Agency. 2012a. *2010 TRI National Analysis.* Retrieved June 14, 2012 (http://www.epa.gov/tri/tridata/tri10/national analysis/index.htm).

Environmental Protection Agency. 2012b. "Climate Change Basics." Retrieved August 2, 2012 (http://www.epa.gov/climatechange/basics/).

Environmental Protection Agency. 2012c. "National Priorities List." Retrieved June 14, 2012 (http://www.epa.gov/superfund/sites/npl/index.htm).

Epstein, Barbara. 1995. "Grassroots Environmentalism and Strategies for Social Change." *New Political Science* 32(Summer):1–24.

EurActiv.com. 2009. "World Forum Backs Water as 'Basic Need.'" Retrieved May 18, 2010 (http://www.euractiv.com/en/sustainability/world-forum-backs-water-basic-need/article-180537).

Freudenberg, Nicolas and Carol Steinsapir. 1992. "Not in Our Backyard: The Grassroots Environmental Movement." Pp. 27–35 in *American Environmentalism: The U.S. Environmental Movement, 1970–1990,* edited by Riley Dunlap and Angela Mertig. Washington, DC: Taylor & Francis.

Gillis, Justin. 2012. "A Majority Believe Role of Warming in Weather." *New York Times,* April 18, p. A14.

Hamilton, Cynthia. 1994. "Concerned Citizens of South Central L.A." Pp. 207–19 in *Unequal Protection,* edited by Robert Bullard. San Francisco, CA: Sierra Club Books.

Hannigan, John. 1995. *Environmental Sociology: A Social Constructionist Perspective.* London, England: Routledge.

Hawken, Paul. 1993. *The Ecology of Commerce: A Declaration of Sustainability.* New York: HarperCollins.

Hawken, Paul. 1997. "Natural Capitalism." *Mother Jones* 22(2):40–58.

Ingram, Helen and David Mann. 1989. "Interest Groups and Environmental Policy." Pp. 135–57 in *Environmental Politics and Policy,* edited by J. Lester. Durham, NC: Duke University Press.

Irwin, Alan. 2001. *Sociology and the Environment.* Cambridge, England: Polity Press.

Kahn, Joseph and Jim Yardley. 2007. "As China Roars, Pollution Reaches Deadly Extremes." *New York Times,* August 26, pp. 1, 6–7.

Kanter, James. 2007. "U.N. Warns of Rapid Decay of Environment." *New York Times,* October 26, p. A8.

Kanter, James and Andrew Revkin. 2007. "Scientists Detail Climate Changes, Poles to Tropics." *New York Times,* April 7, pp. A1, A5.

Kaufman, Leslie. 2009. "Nudging Recycling From Less Waste to None." *New York Times,* October 20, pp. A1, A17.

Ketcham, Christopher. 2007. "The Hundred Mile Diet." Retrieved May 18, 2010 (http://www.thenation.com/article/hundred-mile-diet).

Korten, David. 1995. *When Corporations Rule the World.* West Hartford, CT: Kumarian Press.

Kraft, Michael and Norman Vig. 2000. "Environmental Policy From the 1970s to 2000: An Overview." Pp. 1–31 in *Environmental Policy,* edited by N. Vig and M. Kraft. Washington, DC: Congressional Quarterly Press.

Lee, J. 2003. "7 States to Sue EPA over Standards on Air Pollution." *New York Times,* February 21, p. A24.

Lefebvre, Henri. 2000. *Everyday Life in the Modern World.* London: Athlone Press. (Original work published in 1971)

Lipka, Sara. 2006. "Students Call for Action on Campuses." *Chronicle of Higher Education* 53(9):11.

Littig, Beate. 2001. *Feminist Perspectives on Environment and Society.* Harlow, England: Prentice Education.

Locavores. 2007. "Locavores." Retrieved May 18, 2010 (http://locavores.com/).

Lowrey, Annie and Ron Nixon. 2012. "Severe Drought Seen as Driving Cost of Food Up." *New York Times,* July 26, pp. A1, A4.

Lueck, Thomas J. 2007. "The Mayor Draws a Blueprint for a Greener City." *New York Times,* April 23, p. A18.

Mazmanian, Daniel and Michael Kraft. 1999. "The Three Epochs of the Environmental Movement." Pp. 3–42 in *Toward Sustainable Communities: Transition and Transformations in Environmental Policy,* edited by D. Mazmanian and M. Kraft. Cambridge, MA: MIT Press.

Morland, Kimberly and Steve Wing. 2007. "Food Justice and Health in Communities of Color." Pp. 171–88 in *Growing Smarter: Achieving Livable Communities, Environmental Justice and Regional Equity,* edited by Robert Bullard. Cambridge, MA: MIT Press.

National Academies. 2007. "Press Release February 21, 2007." Retrieved May 18, 2010 (http://www8.nationalacademies.org/onpinews/newsitem.aspx?RecordID=11857).

National Oceanic and Atmospheric Administration (NOAA). 2010. "State of the Climate Global Analysis: Annual 2009." Retrieved May 18, 2010 (http://www.ncdc.noaa.gov/sotc/?report=global&year=2009&month=13).

National Parks Conservation Association. 2003. "New List of America's Ten Most Endangered National Parks Highlights Widespread Problems." Retrieved May 18, 2010 (http://www.npca.org/media_center/press_releases/2003/page-27599890.html).

National Wilderness Preservation System. 2004. "Fast Facts at a Glance." Retrieved May 18, 2010 (http://www.wilderness.net/index.cfm?fuse=NWPS&sec=fastFacts).

Natural Resources Defense Council. 1996. "Particulate Pollution." Retrieved March 24, 2008 (http://www.nrdc.org/air/pollution/qbreath.asp).

Navarro, Mireya and Sindya Bhanoo. 2010. "Teaching Green, Beyond Recycling." *New York Times,* January 11, p. A12.

Newman, Rich. 2001. "Making Environmental Politics: Women and Love Canal Activism." *Women's Studies Quarterly* 1–2:65–84.

Palmer, Clare. 1997. *Environmental Ethics.* Santa Barbara, CA: ABC-CLIO.

Pollan, Michael. 2008. "Farmer in Chief." *New York Times Magazine,* October 12, pp. 63–71, 92.

Power, Matthew. 2006. "The Magic Mountain." *Harper's Magazine,* December, pp. 57–68.

Pregracke, Chad and Jeff Barrow. 2007. *From the Bottom Up: One's Man Crusade to Clean America's Rivers.* Washington, DC: National Geographic.

Revkin, Andrew. 2003. "U.S. Is Urged to Overhaul Its Approach to Protecting Oceans." *New York Times,* June 5, p. A32.

Ringquist, Evan J. 2000. "Environmental Justice: Normative Concerns and Empirical Evidence."

Pp. 232–56 in *Environmental Policy,* edited by N. Vig and M. Kraft. Washington, DC: Congressional Quarterly Press.

Rockler-Gladen, Naomi. 2007. "Green Tips for College Students." Retrieved May 18, 2010 (http://collegeuniversity.suite101.com/article.cfm/green_tips_for_college_students).

Rosenthal, Elisabeth. 2007. "Parents and Health Experts Try to Ease Italy's Pollution." *New York Times,* June 12, p. A3.

Rosenthal, Elisabeth. 2009. "Sweden Looks to Diet to Cut Global Warming." *New York Times,* October 23, pp. A1, A6.

Scarce, Rik. 1990. *Eco-warriors: Understanding the Radical Environmental Movement.* Chicago, IL: Noble Press.

Schwartz, John. 2011. "The Best-Laid Plans." *New York Times,* March 13, pp. 1, 5.

Stolberg, Sheryl Gay. 2007. "Bush Proposes Goal to Reduce Greenhouse Gas." *New York Times,* June 1, pp. A1, A12.

Tabuchi, Hiroko. 2011. "Citizens' Testing Finds 20 Radioactive Hot Spots Around Tokyo." *New York Times,* October 15, pp. A1, A3.

Tobin, Richard. 2000. "Environment, Population, and the Developing World." Pp. 326–49 in *Environmental Policy,* edited by N. Vig and M. Kraft. Washington, DC: Congressional Quarterly Press.

Tran, Trini. 2009. "Olympics, Economy Give China Cleanest Air in a Decade." Retrieved May 18, 2010 (http://www.huffingtonpost.com/2009/04/06/olympics-economy-give-chi_n_183414.html).

United Nations. 2009. "Draft Decision-/CP.15." Retrieved February 27, 2010 (http://unfccc.int/resource/docs/2009/cop15/eng/l07.pdf).

UN News Centre. 2011. "As World Passes 7 Billion Milestone, UN Urges Action to Meet Key Challenges." *UN News Service,* October 31. Retrieved December 12, 2012 (http://www.un.org/apps/news/story.asp?NewsID=40257#.UMZc3pPjncY).

U.S. Fish and Wildlife Service. 2012. "Summary of Listed Species Populations and Recovery Plans." Retrieved June 14, 2012 (http://ecos.fws.gov/tess_public/pub/Boxscore.do).

U.S. Green Technology. 2012. "Mayors of Top Ten American Green Cities Set Trends." Retrieved June 14, 2012 (http://usgreentechnology.com/stories/mayors-of-top-american-green-cities-set-trends/).

Vrijheid, Martine. 2000. "Health Effects of Residence Near Hazardous Waste Landfill Sites: A Review of Epidemiologic Literature." *Environmental Health Perspectives I* (108, Suppl. 1):101–12.

Wald, Matthew and John Schwartz. 2012. "Rise in Weather Extremes Threatens Infrastructure." *New York Times,* July 26, p. A4.

Weiss, Kenneth. 2003. "Life in U.S. Ocean Waters in Death Spiral, Study Says." *News Tribune,* June 5, p. A3.

Wenz, Peter. 2001. *Environmental Ethics Today.* New York: Oxford University Press.

Wilson, Charles. 2009. "When Your Dorm Goes Green and Local." Retrieved May 18, 2010 (http://www.nytimes.com/2009/09/27/magazine/27Ecodorm-t.html?_r=0).

World Health Organization. 2006. "Asthma." Retrieved May 18, 2010 (http://www.who.int/mediacentre/factsheets/fs307/en/index.html).

Yardley, William. 2007. "Climate Change Adds New Twist to Debate Over Dams." *New York Times,* April 23, p. A12.

Chapter 16

Abouzeid, Rania. 2011. "Bouazizi: The Man Who Set Himself and Tunisia on Fire." Retrieved August 1, 2012 (http://www.time.com/time/magazine/article/0,9171,2044723,00.html).

Abrahms, Max. 2012. "The Political Effectiveness of Terrorism Revisited." *Comparative Political Studies* 45:366–93.

Adley, Jessica and Andrea Grant. 2003. "The Environmental Consequences of War." Retrieved July 12, 2012 (http://www.sierraclub.ca/national/postings/war-and-environment.html).

Ahern, Bertie. 2003. "In Search of Peace: The Fate and Legacy of the Good Friday Agreement." *Harvard International Review* Winter:26–31.

Ali, Mohamed and Iqbal Shah. 2000. "Sanctions and Childhood Mortality in Iraq." *Lancet* 355(9218):1851–57.

Altbach, Philip and Patti Peterson. 1971. "Before Berkeley: Historical Perspectives on American Student Activism." *The ANNALS of the American Academy of Political and Social Science* 395:1–14.

Altheide, David. 2006. "Terrorism and the Politics of Fear." *Cultural Studies—Critical Methodologies* 6:415–39.

Amnesty International. 2012. "Myanmar (Burma) Human Rights." Retrieved June 25, 2012 (http://www.amnestyusa.org/our-work/countries/asia-and-the-pacific/Myanmar).

Ayubi, Shaheen, R. E. Bissell, N. Korsah, and L. Lerner. 1982. *Economic Sanctions in U.S. Foreign Policy.* Philadelphia, PA: Foreign Policy Research Institute.

Baker, Peter. 2010. "Obama's War Over Terror." *New York Times Magazine,* January 4.

Retrieved March 6, 2010 (http://www.nytimes.com/2010/01/17/magazine/17Terror-t.html?pagewanted=all).

Booth, Ken and Tim Dunne. 2002. *Worlds in Collision: Terror and the Future of Global Order.* New York: Palgrave Macmillan.

Cave, Damien. 2009. "A Combat Role, and Anguish, Too." *New York Times,* November 1, pp. 1, 32–33.

Center for Defense Information. 2009. "The World's Nuclear Arsenals." Retrieved May 22, 2010 (http://http://www.cdi.org/program/issue/document.cfm?DocumentID=2972&IssueID=46&StartRow=1&ListRows=10&appendURL=&Orderby=DateLastUpdated&ProgramID=32&issueID=460).

Centers for Disease Control and Prevention. 2003. *Veterans' Health Activities.* Retrieved August 15, 2003 (http://www.cdc.gov/nceh/veterans/vet_hlth_actvy.pdf).

Chatfield, Charles. 1992. *The American Peace Movement.* New York: Twayne.

Clausewitz, Karl. 1984. *On War* (translated by Michael Howard and Peter Paret). Princeton, NJ: Princeton University Press.

Cole, David and James X. Dempsey. 2002. *Terrorism and the Constitution.* New York: New Press.

Crenshaw, Martha. 1983. "Introduction: Reflections on the Effects of Terrorism." Pp. 1–37 in *Terrorism, Legitimacy, and Power,* edited by Martha Crenshaw. Middletown, CT: Wesleyan University Press.

Crenshaw, Martha. 1995. *Terrorism in Context.* University Park: Pennsylvania State University Press.

Crenshaw, Martha. 1998. "The Logic of Terrorism: Terrorist Behavior as a Product of Strategic Choice." Pp. 7–24 in *Origins of Terrorism: Psychologies, Ideologies, States of Mind,* edited by W. Reich. Washington, DC: Woodrow Wilson International Center for Scholars and Cambridge University Press.

Cunningham, Kenneth. 2004. "Permanent War? The Domestic Hegemony of the New American Militarism." *New Political Science* 26(4):551–67.

Cuomo, Chris. 1996. "War Is Not Just an Event: Reflections on the Significance of Everyday Violence." *Hypatia* 11(4):30–45.

Danner, Mark. 2011. "After September 11: Our State of Exception." Retrieved July 2, 2012 (http://www.nybooks.com/articles/archives/2011/oct/13/after-september-11-our-state-exception/?pagination=false).

Dao, James. 2012. "Marines Moving Women Toward the Front Lines." *New York Times,* April 25, p. A13.

Donn, Jeff and Kimberly Hefling. 2007. "Wounded Vets Return to Empty Pockets." *News Tribune,* September 30, pp. A6–A7.

Egan, Timothy. 2004. "Sensing the Eyes of Big Brother, and Pushing Back." *New York Times,* August 8, p. 16.

Eisenhower, Dwight. 1953. Speech to the American Society of Newspaper Editors, April 16, 1953, Washington, DC. Retrieved May 22, 2010 (http://www.eisenhower.archives.gov/all_about_ike/speeches/chance_for_peace.pdf).

Enloe, Cynthia. 1990. *Bananas, Beaches, and Bases: Making Feminist Sense of International Politics.* Berkeley: University of California Press.

"The Events of 11 September (2001) and Beyond." 2002. *International Feminist Journal of Politics* 4(1):95–113.

Falk, Richard. 1973. "Environmental Warfare and Ecocide—Facts, Appraisal, and Proposals." *Security Dialogue* 4:80–96.

Featherstone, Liza. 2003. "Students Wrestle With War." *The Nation* 273(20):18–20.

Federal Bureau of Investigation. 2009. "New Most Wanted Terrorist." Retrieved May 22, 2010 (http://www.fbi.gov/page2/april09/wanted 042109.html).

Flores, D. A. 1981. "Note: Export Controls and the US Effort to Combat International Terrorism." *Law and Policy in International Business* 13(2):521–90.

Freeh, Louis J. 2001. "Threat of Terrorism to the United States." Testimony before the U.S. Senate Committees on Appropriations, Armed Services, and Select Committee on Intelligence, May 10, 2001. Retrieved May 22, 2010 (http://www.fbi .gov/news/testimony/threat-of-terrorism-to-the-united-states).

Garfield, Richard. 2002. "Economic Sanctions, Humanitarianism, and Conflict after the Cold War." *Social Justice* 29(3):94–107.

Gibbs, Jack P. 1989. "Conceptualization of Terrorism." *American Sociological Review* 54:329–40.

Haas, Richard. 1997. "Sanctioning Madness." *Foreign Affairs* November/December:74–85.

Harvard Study Team. 1991. "The Effect of the Gulf Crisis on the Children of Iraq." *New England Journal of Medicine* 325(13):977–80.

Hayden, Craig. 2011. "Beyond the 'Obama Effect': Refining the Instruments of Engagement Through U.S. Public Diplomacy." *American Behavioral Scientist* 55:784–802.

Higher Education Research Institute at UCLA. 2010. *The American Freshman: National Norms Fall 2009.* Los Angeles: University of California, Los Angeles.

Hoge, James F., Jr., and Gideon Rose. 2001. "Introduction." Pp. ix–xiv in *How Did This Happen? Terrorism and the New War,* edited by J. F. Hoge, Jr., and G. Rose. New York: PublicAffairs.

Human Security Report Project. 2005. *Human Security Report 2005: War and Peace in the 21st Century.* New York: Oxford University Press.

Human Security Report Project. 2011. *Human Security Report 2009/2010: The Causes of Peace and the Shrinking Costs of War.* New York: Oxford University.

International Commission on Intervention and State Sovereignty. (2001). *The Responsibility to Protect.* Ottawa, Canada: International Development Research Center.

Jansen, Sue C. 2002. "Media in Crisis: Gender and Terror, September 2001." *Feminist Media Studies* 2(1):139–41.

Jenkins, Brian M. 1988. "Future Trends in International Terrorism." Pp. 246–66 in *Current Perspectives on International Terrorism,* edited by R. Slater and M. Stohl. New York: St. Martin's Press.

Kaplan, Laura D. 1994. "Woman as Caretaker: An Archetype That Supports Patriarchal Militarism." *Hypatia* 9(2):123–33.

Knickerbocker, Brad. 2002. "Return of the Military-Industrial Complex?" *Christian Science Monitor* 94(52):2.

Knott, Paul D. 1971. *Student Activism.* Dubuque, IA: William C. Brown.

Lemish, Dafna. 2005. "The Media Gendering of War and Conflict." *Feminist Media Studies* 5(3):367–70.

Lorber, Judith. 2002. "Heroes, Warriors, and Burquas: A Feminist Sociologist's Reflections on September 11." *Sociological Forum* 17(3):377–96.

Lyall, Sarah and Eamon Quinn. 2007. "At the Polls, Northern Ireland Tries to Resurrect Self-Rule." *New York Times,* March 8, p. A9.

Mandelbaum, Michael. 2003. "Diplomacy in War Time: New Priorities and Alignments." Pp. 255–68 in *How Did This Happen? Terrorism and the New War,* edited by J. F. Hoge, Jr., and G. Rose. New York: PublicAffairs.

Marks, Stephen. P. 1999. "Economic Sanctions as Human Rights Violations: Reconciling Political and Public Health Imperatives." *American Journal of Public Health* 89(10):1509–13.

Mulrine, Anna. 2011. "No. 1 Priority for U.S. Security: Domestic Terrorism, Threat Report Says." Retrieved June 20, 2012 (http://www .csmonitor.com/USA/2011/0210/No.-1-priority-for-US-security-domestic-terrorism-threat-report-says).

National Center for PTSD. 2003a. "What Is Posttraumatic Stress Disorder?" Retrieved August 15, 2003 (http://www.ncptsd.org/facts/general/ fs_what_is_ptsd.html).

National Center for PTSD. 2003b. "Epidemiological Facts About PTSD." Retrieved June 6, 2010 (http://www.ptsd.va.gov/professional/pages/ epidemiological-facts-ptsd.asp).

National Priorities Project. 2007. "Federal Budget Year in Review 2007." Retrieved May 22, 2010 (http://www.nationalpriorities.org/yearin review2007).

Neier, Aryeh. 1993. "Watching Rights." *The Nation* 257(19):683.

Nye, Joseph. 2008. "Public Diplomacy and Soft Power." *Annals of the American Academy of Political and Social Science* 616:94–109.

Oates, Sarah. 2006. "Comparing the Politics of Fear: The Role of Terrorism News in Election Campaigns in Russia, the United States and Britain." *International Relations* 4: 425–437.

O'Connor, Anahad. 2004. "The Reach of War: The Soldiers." *New York Times,* July 1. Retrieved June 6, 2010 (http://www.nytimes. com/2004/07/01/world/reach-war-soldiers-1-6-iraq-veterans-found-have-stress-related-disorder.html).

Peksen, Dursun. 2009. "Better or Worse? The Effect of Economic Sanctions on Human Rights." *Journal of Peace Research* 46: 59–77.

Perry, Tony. 2010. "Plight of Female Vets Put in the Spotlight." *News Tribune,* February 10, p. A10.

Pillar, Paul R. 2001. *Terrorism and U.S. Foreign Policy.* Washington, DC: Brookings Institution Press.

Pryor, John, Linda DeAngelo, Laura Palucki Blake, Sylvia Hurtado and Serge Tran. 2011. *The American Freshman: National Norms Fall 2011.* Los Angeles, CA: Higher Educational Research Institute.

Reich, Walter. 1998. "Understanding Terrorist Behavior: The Limits and Opportunities of Psychological Inquiry." Pp. 261–80 in *Origins of Terrorism: Psychologies, Ideologies, States*

of Mind, edited by W. Reich. Cambridge, MA: Woodrow Wilson International Center for Scholars and Cambridge University Press.

Rhoads, Heather. 1991. "Activism Revives on Campus." *The Progressive* 55(3):15–17.

Sandler, Todd. 2011. "New Frontiers of Terrorism Research: An Introduction." *Journal of Peace Research* 48:279–86.

Southern Poverty Law Center. 2012. "Hate Map 2011." Retrieved June 28, 2012 (http://www .splcenter.org/get-informed/hate-map).

Spindel, Chad. 2011. "The People Want to Topple the Regime: Exploring the Arab Spring in Egypt, Syria and Jordan." *Sage Open* October-December 2011 DOI:10.1177/2158244011428648.

Stockholm International Peace Research Institute. 2012. "Background Paper on SIPRI Military Expenditure Data, 2011." Retrieved June 25, 2012 (http://www.sipri.org/research/armaments/milex).

Stolberg, Sheryl Gay and Helene Cooper. 2009. "Obama Adds Troops, but Maps Exit Plan." *New York Times,* December 1. Retrieved May 22, 2010 (http://www.nytimes.com/2009/12/02/world/ asia/02prexy.html).

Suu Kyi, Aung Saa. 2012. "Nobel Lecture June 12, 2012." Retrieved June 25, 2012 (http://nobel peaceprize.org/en_GB/laureates/laureates-1991/ aung-san-2012/).

Tétreault, Mary Ann. 2006. "The Sexual Politics of Abu Ghraib: Hegemony, Spectacle, and the Global War on Terror." *NWSA Journal* 18(3):33–50.

Tickner, J. Ann. 2002. "Feminist Perspectives on 9/11." *International Studies Perspectives* 3:333–50.

United Nations. 1992. "The Rio Declaration on Environment and Development." Retrieved July 12, 2012 (http://www.unesco.org/education/ information/nfsunesco/pdf/RIO_E.PDF).

U.S. Commission on National Security in the 21st Century. 2001. "Road Map for National Security: Imperative for Change." Retrieved May 22, 2010 (http://govinfo.library.unt.edu/nssg/Reports/ reports.htm).

U.S. Department of State. 2003. "Diplomacy: The State Department at Work." Retrieved May 22, 2010 (http://www.state.gov/r/pa/ei/rls/dos/4078 .htm).

U.S. Department of Veterans Affairs. 2007. "Factsheet: America's Wars." Retrieved June 6, 2010 (http://www1.va.gov/opa/publications/ factsheets/fs_americas_wars.pdf).

Van Evera, Stephen. 2006. "Assessing U.S. Strategy Against the War on Terror." *Annuals of The American Academy of Political and Social Science* 607: 10–26.

Vedantam, Shankar. 2006. "Veterans Report Mental Illness." *Washington Post,* March 1, p. A01.

Vellela, Tony. 1988. *New Voices: Student Activism in the 80s and 90s.* Boston, MA: South End Press.

Walter, E. V. 1964. "Violence and the Process of Terror." *American Sociological Review* 29(2):248–57.

Wardlaw, Grant. 1988. "State Response to International Terrorism." Pp. 206–45 in *Current Perspectives on International Terrorism,* edited by R. Slater and M. Stohl. New York: St. Martin's Press.

Whittaker, David. 2002. *Terrorism: Understanding the Global Threat.* London, England: Longman.

Wilkinson, Paul. 1993. "The Orange and the Green: Extremism in Northern Ireland." Pp. 105–23 in *Terrorism, Legitimacy, and Power,* edited by M. Crenshaw. Middleton, CT: Wesleyan University Press.

Young, Nigel. 1999. "Peace Movements in History." Pp. 228–36 in *Approaches to Peace,* edited by D. P. Barash. New York: Oxford University Press.

Zajadlo, Jerzy. 2005. "Legality and Legitimization of Humanitarian Intervention: New Challenges in the Age of the War on Terrorism." *American Behavioral Scientist* 48: 653–670.

Zoroya, Greg. 2005. "Key Iraq Wound: Brain Trauma." Retrieved June 6, 2010 (http://www.usatoday.com/news/nation/2005-03-03-brain-trauma-lede_x.htm).

Chapter 17

Adam, Karla. 2011. "Occupy Wall Street Protests Go Global." Retrieved July 24, 2012 (http://www.washingtonpost.com/world/europe/occupy-wall-street-protests-continue-worldwide/2011/10/16/gIQAcJ1roL_story.html).

Berger, Peter. 1963. *Invitation to Sociology.* New York: Doubleday.

Brucato, Ben. 2012. "The Crisis and the Way Forward: What We Can Learn From Occupy Wall Street." *Humanity & Society* 36: 76–84.

Burawoy, Michael. 2004. "Public Sociologies: A Symposium from Boston College: Introduction." *Social Problems* 51:103–30.

Close Up Foundation. 2004. *The 26th Amendment: Pathway to Participation.* Alexandria, VA: Author.

Corporation for National and Community Service. 2009. "President Obama Joins President Bush in Call to Service." Retrieved May 21, 2010 (http://www.nationalservice.gov/about/newsroom/releases_detail.asp?tbl_pr_id=1555).

Davies, James. 1974. "The J-Curve and Power Struggle Theories of Collective Violence." *American Sociological Review* 87:363–87.

Engle, Shaena. 2006. "More College Freshmen Committed to Social and Civic Responsibility, UCLA Survey Reveals." Retrieved May 19, 2010 (http://newsroom.ucla.edu/portal/ucla/More-College-Freshmen-Committed-6754.aspx?RelNum=6754).

Franklin, Jonathan. 2011a. "Camila Vallejo—Latin America's 23 year–old New Revolutionary Folk Hero." Retrieved August 26, 2012 (http://www.guardian.co.uk/world/2011/oct/08/camila-vallejo-latin-america-revolutionary).

Franklin, Jonathan. 2011b. "Chile's Commander Camila, The Student Who Can Shut Down a City." Retrieved August 26, 2012 (http://www.guardian.co.uk/world/2011/aug/24/chile-student-leader-camila-vallejo).

Giugni, Marco. 1999. "Introduction." Pp. xiii–xxxiii in *How Social Movements Matter,* edited by M. Giugni, D. McAdam, and C. Tilly. Minneapolis: University of Minnesota Press.

Goldman, Francisco. 2012. "They Made Her an Icon, Which Is Impossible to Live Up To." *New York Times Magazine,* April 8, pp. 22–27, 46.

Hannigan, John. 1991. "Social Movement Theory and the Sociology of Religion: Toward a New Synthesis." *Sociological Analysis* 52(4):311–31.

Harper, Charles and Kevin Leicht. 2002. *Exploring Social Change: America and the World.* Upper Saddle River, NJ: Prentice Hall.

Hollender, Jeffrey and Linda Catling. 1996. *How to Make the World a Better Place.* New York: W. W. Norton.

Kirby, Emily Hoban and Kei Kawashima-Ginsberg. 2009. "The Youth Vote in 2008." Retrieved May 19, 2010 (http://www.civicyouth.org/PopUps/FactSheets/FS_youth_Voting_2008_updated_6.22.pdf).

Lauer, Robert H. 1976. "Introduction: Social Movements and Social Change: The Inter-relationships." Pp. xi–xxviii in *Social Movements and Social Change,* edited by R. Lauer. Carbondale: Southern Illinois University.

Lemert, Charles. 1997. *Social Things: An Introduction to the Sociological Life.* Lanham, MD: Rowman & Littlefield.

Levine, Arthur and Jeanette Cureton. 1998. *When Hope and Fear Collide: A Portrait of Today's College Student.* San Francisco, CA: Jossey-Bass.

Liazos, Alexander. 1972. "Nuts, Sluts, and Perverts: The Sociology of Deviance." *Social Problems* 20:103–20.

Loeb, Paul Rogat. 1994. *Generation at the Crossroads.* New Brunswick, NJ: Rutgers University Press.

Loseke, Denise. 2003. *Thinking About Social Problems.* New York: Aldine de Gruyter.

Mannheim, Karl. 1940. *Man and Society in an Age of Reconstruction.* New York: Harcourt Brace.

McAdam, Doug. 1982. *Political Process and the Development of Black Insurgency.* Chicago, IL: University of Chicago Press.

McAdam, Doug, John McCarthy, and Mayer Zald. 1988. "Social Movements." Pp. 695–737 in *Handbook of Sociology,* edited by N. Smelser. Newbury Park, CA: Sage Publications.

McAdam, Doug, John McCarthy, and Mayer Zald. 1996. *Comparative Perspectives on Social Movement: Political Opportunities, Mobilizing Structures, and Cultural Framings.* Thousand Oaks, CA: Sage Publications.

McCarthy, John and Mayer Zald. 1977. "Resource Mobilization and Social Movements: A Partial Theory." *American Journal of Sociology* 82: 1212–41.

Meyer, David. 2000. "Social Movements: Creating Communities of Change." Pp. 33–55 in *Feminist Approaches to Social Movements, Community, and Power,* Vol. 1, edited by R. Teske and M. A. Tetreault. Columbia: University of South Carolina Press.

Meyer, David and Suzanne Staggenbord. 1996. "Movements, Countermovements, and the Structure of Political Opportunity." *American Journal of Sociology* 101(6):1628–60.

Moss Wilson, William. 2012. "Just Don't Call Her Che." *New York Times,* January 29, p. 5.

Nader, Ralph. 1972. *Action for a Change.* New York: Grossman.

Paul, James A. 2000. "NGOs and Global Policy-Making." Retrieved May 19, 2010 (http://www.globalpolicy.org/component/content/article/177/31611.html).

Piven, Francis and Richard Cloward. 1979. *Poor People's Movements: Why They Succeed, How They Fail.* New York: Vintage Books.

Plotke, David. 1995. "What's So New About New Social Movements?" Pp. 113–36 in *Social Movements: Critique, Concepts, Case-Studies,* edited by S. Lyman. New York: New York University Press.

Rayside, David. 1998. *On the Fringe: Gays and Lesbians in Politics.* Ithaca, NY: Cornell University Press.

Ritzer, George. 2000. *Sociological Theory.* New York: McGraw-Hill.

Rock the Vote. 2004. "About Us." Retrieved May 19, 2010 (http://www.rockthevote/rtv_about.php).

Skocpol, Theda. 2000. *The Missing Middle.* New York: W. W. Norton.

Smelser, Neil. 1963. *Theory of Collective Behavior.* New York: Free Press.

Taylor, Verta and Nancy Whittier. 1995. "Analytical Approaches to Social Movement Culture: The Culture of the Women's Movement." Pp. 163–87 in *Social Movements and Culture,* edited by H. Johnson and B. Klandermans. Minneapolis: University of Minnesota Press.

Wilson, John. 1973. *Introduction to Social Movements.* New York: Basic Books.

Wilson, Kenneth and Anthony Orum. 1976. "Mobilizing People for Collective Political Action." *Journal of Political and Military Sociology* 4:187–202.

Photo Credits

Index